Rita Aero's

Walt Disney World®

The Essential Guide to Amazing Vacations

Odyssey Edition, Version 1.4

Great Web Site! Disney Updates

Universal Studios Guide

16 Find-It-Fast Disney Maps

Disney Discount Tips

Disney Cruise Reviews

D1514876

St. Martin's Griffin 🦁 New York

The Amazing Guide™ Team

Creative Director	David Villanueva
Editorial Director	Kathleen Clark
Executive Producer	Duchess Temescu
Reviews Editor	Todd Allen
Orlando Correspondent	Shannon Deganutti
Grammar Goddess	Erica Angle-Newman
Copy Editor	Bob Eissler
Technical Editor	Candice Getten
Cover Art	Catherine Venturini
Production Artist	Joe Gibson
Operations	Patsy Brown
Counsel	Amy Goldrich
Tech Wrangler	Jeff McCollough
Rock Band	The Rattlesnakes
Roadie	Joe Aucoin
Kid's Rating Team	Jordyn Rebeca
	Sage Alexander
	Xander Christian

Odyssey Edition v. 1.4 Update

Managing Editor	Paige Wright
Universal Editor	Bob Eissler

Special thanks to Deb Wills, Nanci Rossetti, Deb Conda, Sid Farsi, Maria Cole, Shabib Sheikh, Susan Trover, Steve Trover, Members of the Readers Clubhouse community online, and all the helpful Cast Members at Walt Disney World.

Acknowledgments

This, the Disney Odyssey Edition, has been a long time coming. We wanted to continue to evolve it into the best guidebook possible, and there were many new directions to explore. Thanks to the book's web site, we have grown closer to our Readers than ever before. Along with our own ideas about how to build a better "mousetrap," our Readers had many great suggestions. We are deeply indebted to those who participated in our Disney discussions on the web site, and those who returned the Reader's Surveys from the last edition. This book truly belongs to them.

The remarkable Elizabeth Beier, our editor at St. Martin's Press, helped us shape our vision of this project and inspired creative new ways to produce and publish it. Our agent, Robert Stricker, has been a steady supporter and good friend from beginning to end.

We are grateful to Mark Jaronski at Disney Cruise Lines and Rick Sylvain and Craig Dezern at Disney Media Relations. Our special thanks to Rhonda Murphy, Rick Gregory, and Jill Fennessy at Universal Studios.

We are indebted to the folks on our panel of Disney experts (E.A.R.S.) for their participation in this project. All of them publish works about Walt Disney World for the sheer passion of sharing this information with others. None are affiliated with the Disney Company, and the ratings they have provided for this book come from their considerable experience and thoughtful observations. We are very proud to share their insights with our Readers. Our very sincere thanks go to Rob Lindsey, E.A.R.S. Academy Chairman, for overseeing the ratings nominations and polling process.

Along the way, this project has gathered many good friends and helpers. We would like to thank Terry Temescu, Ray Champagne, Aaron Owens, Anne Marie and Eddie Diosomito, Attila Fisher, Robert Clark, Steve Clark, Bob and Linda Mann, Julie Johnson, Linda Briel, Anhalira Koan, and Jason Low.

Above all, we are deeply grateful to the Readers on our web site, who have built a wonderful community of sharing around the book and inspired us to be the best we could be.

ISBN 0-312-28159-5

10   9   8   7   6   5   4   3

Note: While every care has been taken to ensure the accuracy of the information in this guide, the passage of time will always bring changes, and consequently the publisher cannot accept responsibility for errors that may occur. All prices and operating schedules quoted herein are based on information available to us at press time. Operating hours, maps, resort policies, coming attractions, and admission fees and other costs may change, however, and the prudent will avoid inconvenience by calling ahead.

About the Guidebook:

I take trip planning seriously and own half a dozen current guides to Walt Disney World. Rita's book is the most accurate of the lot, and the only one with clear, easily read maps of every park in the World. It is also the only guide I am aware of to provide continuous updating through a web site and an incredibly friendly online community. For our next trip, because of the combination of advice from the book and tips received online, we are staying in better accommodations without a significant increase in costs, and we have learned touring strategies that save us hours a day.

Sid Farcy, Seattle, Washington

Rita Aero's guidebook is an incredible tool for anyone who wants more from their Disney vacation than what the park maps show. Inside information on tours, new rides, and exciting and romantic hideaway spots that no one else knows about keeps you on the insider's loop of the greatest vacation destination in the world. And with a terrific companion web site, that information never grows outdated! This book is perfect for those who need to watch their pennies. It has saved me many hundreds of dollars over the last few trips.

Paul Freiberger, Dayton, Ohio

Rita's book was one in a long line of Walt Disney World guidebooks that we bought … but the only one that we still have and refer to. It is so easy and enjoyable to read! There was so much information about hotels and restaurants — and just about everything else that you want to know before a first visit to the World. The book's web site is packed full of amazingly useful information. Everyone has a different Disney perspective and experience, so the wealth of knowledge is huge, and there is always something new to learn.

Samantha Goddard, Northamptonshire, England

Six months before going to Walt Disney World for our 25th Anniversary we bought Rita's book. It contained everything we needed to select the best place to stay, the most romantic places to eat, and how to do it all without breaking the bank. The phone numbers, the details, and the candid descriptions all helped us do the planning that made our trip as perfect as it could have been.

Alan Elliott, Cedar Hill, Texas

Rita Aero's guide is a must-read for anyone planning a trip to Walt Disney World. It doesn't matter if you are a Walt Disney World novice or an expert at touring. I have never seen another Disney guide that has a web site dedicated to it. In the "Great Hallway," you can find anything from the temperature in Florida to the latest money-saving tips. I read a tip (in the Turret) that saved me $50 per night at the Wilderness Lodge. The web site is fun, easy to navigate, and has priceless information in it.

Winona Payne, Dayton, Ohio

The book is terrific and the web site is absolutely THE best source of current Walt Disney World information and planning tips! I had been to Walt Disney World four times before I found this book, and I never knew anything about discounts and avoiding the crowds. After reading the book and visiting the web site, I was able to plan a great trip during peak summer months where we missed most of the crowds and paid less for two rooms at the Contemporary resort than we were originally going to pay for one!

Jan Paratore, Fishkill, New York

We have been to Walt Disney World over ten times in the last twenty years. We find the maps in Rita's guidebook easier to follow than the park maps given out at the gate. The multicolored design and the clear distinctions of the pathways never gave us a wrong turn! The book has a great section on getting around the Orlando airport and staying there on arrival and departure nights. It enabled us to cut a lot of confusion, save money, and have a comfortable night's stay before we got our vacation started.

Melinda Brickhouse, Hot Springs, Arkansas,

One difference between Rita Aero's book and the other Disney guides is that she addresses the emotional aspect of an adventure to Walt Disney World. It is a magical experience, especially for adults, who get to act like a kid again and fit right in! It's watching parades and fireworks through tear-filled eyes, posing with a favourite character, and eating breakfast in a castle. And the kids didn't even come with you this time!

Susan Pelletier, Camlachie, Ontario, Canada

About the Book's Web Site:

I have found the Readers Clubhouse web site to be a daily extension and update of one of the greatest books of information on Walt Disney World I have ever had the pleasure to pick up. I have yet to see a question go unanswered or a need ignored by fellow readers. In many instances they are aware of a promotion or a sale at Walt Disney World before the Cast Members who answer the phone at Disney. In most instances they give more accurate information and have yet to steer me wrong.

Lou-Ann Ploeser, Glendale, Arizona

This great book has a web site where all the information that is in the book is updated on a daily basis! There is always something new and exciting happening at Walt Disney World — it is constantly changing and the web site keeps you well informed of all the new adventures!

Michelle C. Hyatt, Greensboro, North Carolina

I used the tips and suggestions in the Readers Clubhouse to plan my FIRST trip with my family of four to Walt Disney World. The web site is so all-encompassing, and interactive — you get immediate feedback from wonderful, generous, helpful readers who add their own personal touch to the information they provide. I was able to find incredible bargains for airfare, hotels, and rental cars which made the trip affordable for my family, thanks to the help of many Clubhouse members.

Rhonda Barczynski, Pen Argyl, Pennsylvania

The Readers Clubhouse is pure magic! The friendships I have made here are amazing. One big Disney Family! I came at first for the great up-to-the-second info on Walt Disney World and stayed long after my trip for the great times at the message boards and in the chat rooms. Besides our love for Walt Disney World, we share laughs, and we share sorrows. We tease, comfort, and entertain each other. I don't know what magic Rita and her crew have worked, but I am so glad they have.

Peggy Hickey, Long Island, New York

The Readers Clubhouse is a wonderful place to get up-to-date information for upcoming trips to Walt Disney World. In "The Salon" you'll get current information about Walt Disney World. There are also areas to inquire about family-related questions (The Family Room), Disney's newest park, Animal Kingdom (The Safari Roundtable), and the Disney Cruise Line (The Marina). There is also a place for readers to post their trip reports. It's great to see how other people's trips went and discover great hints and ideas for yours.

I have visited many different types of web sites and have yet to find ANYTHING like the Readers Clubhouse. I'm not just talking about information, here. Rita intended to build a true cyber-community, and I think she has succeeded beyond anyone's wildest dreams.

Scott Humphreys, Summerville, South Carolina

The Readers Clubhouse is an incredible place. I've been online for four years and I have never come across a site like this: It's informative (forums, articles, trip reports), fun (chats and Member Magic forum), and even philosophical (the Tao of Disney). However, the most amazing feature of the Clubhouse is the high quality human interaction that it fosters: You are always sure to find information, support, and human kindness.

Alejandro Zarzalejos, Madrid, Spain

The Readers Clubhouse web site is the perfect companion to Rita's book. Both are indispensable for anyone looking for serious Disney fun at the best price possible. The web site provides current information on special rates and discounts, as well as package deals, and allows Disney fanatics to share their memories and get their questions answered. It's informative and a lot of fun!

Ashley Collins, San Antonio, Texas

Walt Disney World is continuously changing, and it is impossible for the guidebooks to be truly current. But, a visit to the Readers Clubhouse web site can get me information from as recently as last week, or yesterday, or sometimes within minutes of when I ask a question. The wonderful thing about the Clubhouse from a planning standpoint is that someone is always just getting back from their Disney vacation and sharing information.

Lori Ann Davis, Grand Rapids, Michigan

THE AMAZING GUIDE™

ESSENTIALS

Everything You Need to Know Before You Go:
The Bottom Line on Hotels, Restaurants, Crowds,
Schedules, and Saving Money!

ATTRACTIONS

Theme Parks, Recreation Areas, and
Entertainment Destinations: Creating Your Own
Amazing Tours and Magical Adventures

HOTELS

In and Around Walt Disney World:
Selecting the Best Hotel for Your Disney Vacation

RESTAURANTS

Memorable Meals and Entertaining Dining
at the Theme Parks and the Hotels

SPECIAL EVENTS

Extraordinary Adventures for Families and
Friends, Small Groups, and Solo Voyagers

RECREATION

Playful Adventures and Sporting Challenges:
Discoveries Outside the Theme Parks

RESOURCES

Important Travel Tips and Planning Logistics
for Smarter, Smoother, Carefree Vacations

UNIVERSAL STUDIOS ORLANDO

Orlando's Exciting Vacation Destination:
Theme Parks, Clubs, Restaurants, and Resorts

THE AMAZING GUIDE™

This is a travel guide to Walt Disney World, but it's not going to take you to the State of Florida. This travel guide is designed to take you to a special State of Mind — a place where you'll experience amazing things, in your own way, at your own pace.

Walt Disney World is a real-life adventure. It's also an odyssey of the heart and mind that lies as far as you can get from reality without adjusting your medication, and as close as you can get to what is truly amazing about the human spirit — our ability to create imaginary worlds and then to share them with one another.

More than 100 million people have visited Walt Disney World since we began writing this guidebook. Many of them have vacationed there dozens of times, and just about everyone who has gone has come back determined to return again sometime soon.

Walt Disney World has inspired a fierce love and longing among its millions of devotees and fans. It is the place where families come to reunite and be together year after year, it is where so many newlyweds begin their journey through life, and it's the first great odyssey they plan with their young children. It is truly the mecca of magic and it is the proving ground of many of the world's most creative and accomplished artists, performers, writers, musicians, and composers.

This guidebook you are holding is alive, like no other. It lives and breathes and celebrates the lives of its Readers and their own Disney odysseys. All of us who create this guidebook, and the thousands of Readers who use it, actively share information about planning amazing Disney vacations and saving hundreds upon hundreds of dollars while doing so. We hope you'll join us on the Internet in the Readers Clubhouse, where the book continues to expand and grow. In the Clubhouse, you can get up-to-the-minute Disney information, ask questions, and get fast, friendly answers from folks who really share your desire for the best possible Disney vacation. We'll be waiting inside to welcome you.

The Odyssey Edition, Version 1.4

What's New: As always, there have been many changes at Walt Disney World in the past year. Some significant trends and announcements have inspired us to update quite a few areas of this guidebook, which we call *Version 1.4.* This gave us a chance, too, to update our pricing guides, telephone numbers, and all those little things that mean so much to vacation planners.

Resort Trends: The Disney resorts continue to expand, especially the Disney Vacation Club's condo-style time-shares that are also available as hotel accommodations. In fact, some newer Vacation Club developments are attached to Disney's deluxe resorts and share their services, such as the Villas at Wilderness Lodge and the Villas at the Beach Club. Expect to see more of that. We see a vacation trend toward longer family stays and the popularity of multi-room units with kitchens and laundries shared by extended families and groups.

Attractions: Theme park development has slowed, although Disney-MGM Studios added a premier attraction and small, well-themed attractions have opened at the Magic Kingdom and at DisneyQuest. Animal Kingdom, however, continues to change as the park matures, and a delightful new mini-land has been added to appeal to the younger set. The slowdown gave us a chance to explore really worthwhile adventures beyond Walt Disney World, including SeaWorld's Discovery Cove and Kennedy Space Center.

Resort Update: Disney's unique African-themed resort, Animal Kingdom Lodge, has opened. It overlooks a rolling savanna filled with roaming herds of wild animals. The resort also brings fascinating new dining experiences to the Walt Disney World restaurant scene.

If for no other reason than to confuse guests and annoy guidebook writers, Disney merged its two most popular and unique moderate-priced resorts into one. The former Dixie Landings is now named Port Orleans – Riverside and the original Port Orleans is now named Port Orleans – French Quarter. Each resort still maintains separate check-ins, but the French Quarter lost its full-service restaurant, marina, and bike rentals. Inside this guide, you may run across a mention of Dixie Landings, which should be taken to refer to its new incarnation, Disney's Port Orleans – Riverside.

Meanwhile, the first phase of the largest budget hotel, Disney's Pop Century Resort, is scheduled to open in 2002. Over 5,700 rooms are clustered in twenty three-story buildings. The buildings feature brightly-designed exteriors inspired by American popular culture from each decade of the twentieth century. The look and feel is very similar to Disney's All-Star Resorts.

More Name Changes: After more than forty years, the Magic Kingdom Club, Disney's discount travel program, has been renamed the Disney Club. On page 20, in "Discount Strategies," we describe changes to the program and the types of travelers who can best take advantage of a paid membership in the Disney Club. If you see references to the Magic Kingdom Club, think Disney Club. On a similar note, it is likely that Disney-MGM Studios will become simply Disney Studios.

Hotel Reservations: Disney Central Reservations Office (CRO) is slowly being taken over by Disney Travel Company, which once handled mostly vacation packages. This agency has reservation policies similar to airlines or cruise ships. This will impact do-it-yourself vacation planners, who book hotel rooms only. Expect to pay up-front cash deposits to book a room and look for hefty cancellation or change fees. It is also likely that the entire stay must be paid in full well in advance.

Universal Studios Orlando: Universal Studios continues to develop into a vacation destination, and its on-property hotels are opening on schedule, Hard Rock Hotel being the latest. Universal has gone through yet another name change and is no longer Universal Studios Escape. It seems uncertain what to call its complex of theme parks and resorts to distinguish it from "Universal Studios," the theme park. We see a continuing trend where more Disney visitors are including several days at Universal and nearby hotels.

Coming Attractions

At Epcot's Future World, Mission: SPACE is scheduled to open in 2003. The premier attraction is designed to recreate the experience of NASA astronaut training.

Disney is committed to enhancing its resort-wide transportation system, which relies largely on buses. Within the next five years visitors can look forward to faster, more convenient methods of getting around, such as a light rail system and an extension of the monorail connecting the resorts to the major attractions.

To stay up-to-date on exciting new developments at the theme parks, restaurants, and resorts, be sure to visit the Readers Clubhouse (www.ReadersClubhouse.com) where our online community of Readers and experts discuss the myriad changes at Walt Disney World and nearby attractions — ranging from details like prices, phone numbers, and schedules to major events and changes that our Readers discover and share.

Guidebook Features

Essentials Checklists: The "Essentials" section at the beginning of this guide concentrates all the what-you-need-to-know information right up front. Here you'll find comparison charts of the hotels, selection guides for the restaurants, graphs showing crowds and weather patterns, and charts outlining theme park admissions, transportation options, year-round events, and more. The sophisticated comparison and selection guides replace old-fashioned and outmoded "opinion" ratings, which don't always help you find what *you* like. We wanted you to have more information, organized dynamically right up front.

Find it Fast! Tabbing System: You've probably already noticed the large side tabs on each page edge, indicating the "section" you are reading. Most section tabs also have a line of small, light gray print, showing the topics within that section. As you fan the book, just focus your eyes on the topic you want to read and flip the pages until the desired topic "lights up" (turns black).

Fun Factor Ratings: We rated each attraction with a twenty-level Fun Factor index using five animal icons to represent the emotional ages and temperaments of visitors. The Fun Factor key quickly and intuitively identifies how various emotional age groups (as a whole) react to each attraction. Just assign each person in your party a Fun-Factor icon and scan the attractions. In no time, you'll be able to instantly create the most appropriate tour for your group.

The E.A.R.S. Awards: From around the nation and across the Internet, we invited the most esteemed Walt Disney World experts in the world to help you identify the best of the best attractions, hotels, restaurants, and more! We call this the "Expert Advisor Rating System," or E.A.R.S., for short. Throughout the book, E.A.R.S. Awards are posted. They reveal the winners in such categories as "most romantic resorts," "best dining events," "best attractions for kids," "best nightclubs," and so forth.

Other Resources: Check page 10 for helpful web sites. The last page has a list of telephone numbers that will come in handy as you plan your vacation. ◆

MEET THE E.A.R.S. ACADEMY

From around the nation, the most noted Walt Disney World experts were nominated to our E.A.R.S. Academy. Our panel of experts submitted ballots naming their favorite attractions, restaurants, hotels, and vacation experiences. Throughout the book you'll find the E.A.R.S Awards lists, designed to help you select the best that Walt Disney World has to offer. Ratings don't get any better than this.

Dr. Rob Lindsey is the Chairman of the E.A.R.S. Academy. He assembled the panelists, managed the ballots, and submitted the tallies. He is a Disney vacation expert and an active host on several popular web sites, including www.ReadersClubhouse.com.

Margaret J. King, Ph. D., is the Director of Cultural Studies & Analysis, a think tank for the study of cultural values and theme parks. Her articles have appeared in over fifty publications, and include the Disney entries for the *Dictionary of Popular Culture*. She can be reached at cultureking@compuserve.com.

Deb Wills is the creator of one of the most celebrated and comprehensive resources for Disney vacation information on the web. Her *Walt Disney World Information Guide* can be found at www.wdwig.com.

Jeff Spencer, a NASA engineer in real life, is a specialist in Walt Disney World's theme parks and Fort Wilderness Resort and Campground. His web site, *The Spencer Family's Disney Page,* can be found at home.hiwaay.net/~jlspence.

Stephen M. Fjellman, Ph. D., is Chairperson of Anthropology and Sociology at Florida International University. He is the author of one of the foremost anthropological studies of Walt Disney World, *Vinyl Leaves: Walt Disney World and America*. He can be reached at fjellman@fiu.edu.

Jennifer Watson and **Dave Marx** are the authors of a popular guidebook, *PassPorter Walt Disney World,* a trip planner, organizer, and travel journal. They also host a companion Disney vacation web site at www.passporter.com.

Brian Bennett is the author of the *Walt Disney World Trip Planning Guide* and is also one of the leaders of the largest Disney discussion groups on the Internet, rec.arts.disney.parks. His Disney guide can be found at mouseplanet.com/dtp/wdwguide.

John Yaglenski is the creator of two well-known Disney information web sites: www.Intercot.com, *A Virtual Guide to Walt Disney World,* and www.WebDisney.com, the *Definitive Guide to Disney on the Net.*

Donnie and **Amy Sullivan** edit and publish *Mousetales, The Unofficial Newsletter of Walt Disney World,* a quarterly compendium of in-depth reviews and time and money saving tips for Disney vacation fans. They can be contacted at P.O. Box 383, Columbus, OH 43216.

Pete Werner is the creator of the *Unofficial Online Guide to Disney World,* one of the most popular Disney vacation planning web sites on the Internet. His web site, which is based in Orlando, can be found at www.wdwinfo.com.

Paul F. Anderson was the Disney Historian and Associate Producer on "Cartoon Mania!," an Emmy Award-winning PBS documentary. He is the editor and publisher of *Persistence of Vision,* a historical journal devoted to the creative legacy of Walt Disney. Information on his work can be found at www.disneypov.com.

Cathy McConnell is a travel specialist with Dreams Unlimited Travel, an online travel resource that specializes in booking vacations at Walt Disney World. She can be contacted at www.dreamsunlimitedtravel.com.

Brian Charles Kohn is an international quality specialist who applies his skills to the study of Disney as the preeminent example of a quality company. He is also a leader in the rec.arts.disney.parks discussion group on the Internet.

Andy Dannelley is the creator of *Anaheim to Orlando: A Bicoastal Comparison of Disney.* He is also a founding member of MousePlanet.com, an information and vacation planning resource for Disney parks worldwide. His web site is located at www.primenet.com/~dannell.

YOUR GUIDEBOOK ONLINE

Walt Disney World is in a constant state of change. These changes chip away at the accuracy of all printed guidebooks. A web site can offer fresher information but lacks the substance of a real guidebook. The perfect solution would be a guidebook with a warm and friendly web site community to keep it fresh with detailed reports and updates. That's exactly what you will find in our Readers Clubhouse!

Resources

These are some of our favorite Disney resources, including the publications of our E.A.R.S. Academy panelists.

Journals and Newsletters

Persistence of Vision

Edited and Published by Paul F. Anderson
www.disneypov.com

This print and online journal is the preeminent source of historical information about Walt Disney and his work.

Mousetales: The Unofficial Newsletter of Walt Disney World

Published by Donnie and Amy Sullivan
P.O. Box 383, Columbus, OH 43216.

Timely and fun reviews and tips are produced quarterly by a duo of Disney vacation experts.

More Disney Books

PassPorter Walt Disney World

By Jennifer Watson and Dave Marx
MediaMarx, Inc.; ISBN: 1587710005

This impressive guidebook has wonderful information and doubles as a vacation planning organizer!

**Vinyl Leaves:
Walt Disney World and America**

By Stephen M. Fjellman
Westview Press; ISBN: 0813314720

This book is a superb analysis of what makes the Disney company tick, written by an author with a passion for the Disney experience.

**Walt Disney World for Couples
With or Without Kids**

By Rick & Gayle Perlmutter
Prima Publishing; ISBN: 0760522190

This guidebook offers grand adventures with a personal point-of-view in exploring Disney's resorts, dining experiences, and more.

Internet Newsgroup

rec.arts.disney.parks

This spirited online discussion covers a huge variety of Walt Disney World topics. Hundreds of contributions posted throughout the day.

Join Us in the Readers Clubhouse!
www.ReadersClubhouse.com

Meet Chatsworth, the butler at the Readers Clubhouse, one of the most friendly, fun, and informative Disney vacation communities on the Internet. The Readers Clubhouse is the living extension of your guidebook. Here, you'll find find up-to-the minute vacation tips and great ways to save loads of money on your next Disney vacation. Chatsworth will be there to welcome you and show you around. You'll want to check out the latest ratings and reviews of the restaurants and hotels, visit the message boards where you can get instant answers to your specific vacation planning questions, and join our scheduled chats about exciting Disney topics. Drop by and say hello; you'll be glad you did.

Reader Recommended Web Sites

e Guides To Go

http://www.eguidestogo.com/

Download a Palm OS guide to Walt Disney World or Disneyland. Clever, accurate, and fast.

Go2Orlando

www.go2orlando.com

Vacation information for all Central Florida. Features a free Orlando discount newsletter.

Intercot: WDW Inside & Out

www.intercot.com

A virtual journey into the wonders of Disney, with message boards, resources, and links.

Mouseplanet: Family Vacation Planning

www.mouseplanet.com

Disney information to the extreme. Covers topics you wouldn't even think to ask about.

The Spencer Family's Disney Page

home.hiwaay.net/~jlspence

Fort Wilderness Resort and Campground family vacations. Great links to Disney resources.

Walt Disney World Entertainment

http://pages.prodigy.net/stevesoares/

The top website for current live entertainment schedules. Not even Disney does it so well.

Walt Disney World Information Guide

www.wdwig.com

A must-see! Extensive and detailed information on every aspect of WDW, including restaurant menus. Plus, a free top notch newsletter.

Unofficial Online Guide to Disney World

www.wdwinfo.com

Overviews of theme parks, hotels, and restaurants, plus message boards and chats. Lots of insight into the local Orlando scene.

Orlando Travel Services

The Official Walt Disney World Web Site

www.DisneyWorld.com

Information directly from the Disney Company!

All Star Vacation Homes

www.allstarvacationhomes.com

Vacation homes renting for a fraction of the equivalent lodging at WDW. Online previews and excellent management. (888 249-1779)

Atlantis Limousine

www.atlantislimo.com

Limousine and transportation service, including SUVs and Towncars. From the airport and around Orlando. Courteous and dependable.

Happy Limousine

www.happylimo.com

Friendly limousine and Towncar service. Airport transportation and local touring. Professional and dependable. Competitive rates.

Magical Journeys

www.yourmagicaljourneys.com

This travel agency offers expert knowledge of the Walt Disney World and Universal Studios vacation experience. Personal quality service at low cost.

ESSENTIALS

Everything You Need to Know Before You Go:
The Bottom Line on Hotels, Restaurants, Crowds, and Saving Money!

FIRST THINGS FIRST

We want you to have a great time planning your Disney vacation, so we're going to give you the answers to all the big questions right now and get them out of the way.

Where Should I Stay?

In selecting a hotel at Walt Disney World, you must first decide which is more important to you — cost or convenience. Convenience is synonymous with luxury on a Disney vacation. Disney does not build budget hotels on the monorail line or premium hotels out in the middle of nowhere. **The more expensive the hotel, the better the transportation and access to the attractions.** It is always desirable to stay on Disney property, but the nearby off-site hotels are less expensive (and a good value in terms of spaciousness). They are, however, less convenient; a rental car is a must. Nearby vacation home rentals offer excellent values for larger families. See:

 Hotel Features and Value, page 22;

 Hotel Amenities and Recreation, page 23;

 Hotel Locations, page 25.

Should I Rent a Car?

Disney's transportation is free, with one small catch: **The system is designed to transport guests directly to theme parks that charge admission.** This is how it pays for itself. It is not designed to take guests to other resorts where some of the best dining and entertainment can be had. So, it all depends on where you're staying, how much you want to see, and how you like to spend your vacation time. We created a chart to help you decide. See:

 Do You Need a Rental Car?, page 32.

How Do I Get Cheap Park Tickets?

The only legitimate discount to theme park tickets is the modest discount available only to members of the Disney Club or the American Automobile Association (AAA). You can save much more money by carefully planning and choosing the type of tickets that work best for you and your group. Avoid overbuying. Don't buy Length of Stay passes unless you are absolutely certain that you will be in the theme parks all day every day. Even then, they are not a good deal compared to Multiday Park Hoppers, which are good until used. Discover the joys of Walt Disney World outside the theme parks. Treat these days of "discovery" as "free days" and buy fewer ticket days. A single free day will save a family of four about $200. See:

 Admission Tickets, page 18;

 Discount Strategies, page 19.

When Should I Go?

The best time to go is when everyone else does not. To put it simply: **Go to Walt Disney World while most schools are in session. Avoid the summer months and Spring Break, if you can.**

During school vacations (generally summer and extended holiday periods, such as Spring Break), rooms are very much in demand, and the highest rates are charged. Not only is it most expensive during these times, but the parks are congested, the lines are longest, and the weather is often at its worst. From May through September, it is very hot and humid, with frequent thunder showers.

During the fall and winter, with the exception of holidays, crowds are lighter and room rates lower. The weather is mild, although December, January, and February can bring cold snaps. The Magic Kingdom closes early and there are fewer evening events. Some attractions may be closed for refurbishment. After Presidents' Day, the crowds pick up again, as do costs. See:

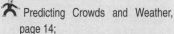 Predicting Crowds and Weather, page 14;

What to Expect Month by Month, page 16.

Essentials

Attractions • Hotels • Restaurants • Special Events • Recreation • Resources

Transportation • Restaurant Guides • Hotel Guides • Vacation Packages • Discounts • Admissions • Month by Month • Crowds & Weather • The World at a Glance • First Things First

THE "WORLD" AT A GLANCE

Walt Disney World lies south of Orlando on Interstate 4, about a 30-minute drive from the Orlando International Airport. This sprawling 47-square-mile playground contains thirteen distinct theme parks and recreation areas, nearly thirty resorts, more than 150 miles of road, a dozen lakes with miles of interconnected waterways, and five PGA golf courses — all surrounded by forests, wetlands, and wildlife preserves. It's a self-contained, self-sustaining world with its own communications network, power plant, waste management and recycling center, transportation system, and computer control center linked with Disney-owned space satellites that coordinate every aspect of this vacation paradise. There are five major resort clusters in Walt Disney World, each with themed resort hotels spanning a range of prices and amenities. (See "Hotel Comparison Guides" starting on page 22.)

Magic Kingdom Resorts Area: This area embodies the heart and spirit of Walt Disney World, and includes the Magic Kingdom, Fort Wilderness & River Country, Discovery Island, Magnolia Golf Course, and Palm Golf Course. Bay Lake, Seven Seas Lagoon, and the Fort Wilderness Waterways provide marinas and boating. A 14-mile monorail system connects several of the resorts in this area with the Magic Kingdom and Epcot. Disney's Polynesian Resort, Disney's Contemporary Resort, Disney's Grand Floridian Beach Resort, Disney's Fort Wilderness Resort and Campground, Disney's Wilderness Lodge, The Villas at Wilderness Lodge, and Shades of Green are located here.

Epcot Resorts Area: This diverse and eclectic area is conveniently located in the center of Walt Disney World. It incorporates Epcot, Disney-MGM Studios, Disney's BoardWalk, and Fantasia Gardens miniature golf. Water launches or Disney buses provide transportation between the resorts in this area and Epcot, Disney-MGM Studios, and Disney's BoardWalk. The

monorail provides transportation between Epcot and the Magic Kingdom. Disney's Beach Club Resort, Disney's Yacht Club Resort, Disney's Caribbean Beach Resort, Disney's Pop Century Resort, Walt Disney World Dolphin, Walt Disney World Swan, Disney's BoardWalk Inn, Disney's BoardWalk Villas, and Disney's Beach Club Villas are located here.

Downtown Disney Resorts Area: Downtown Disney, a shopping, dining, and evening entertainment district, is located here which includes Pleasure Island, The Marketplace, West Side, and DisneyQuest. Nearby is Typhoon Lagoon and the Disney Institute, which offers a full-service spa. Osprey Ridge, Eagle Pines, and Lake Buena Vista golf courses are located here. Water taxis provide transportation between Downtown Disney and the resorts in this area, which all offer marinas and boating. The hotels located here include Disney's Old Key West Resort, Disney's Port Orleans Resort – French Quarter, Disney's Port Orleans Resort – Riverside (formerly Dixie Landings), and The Villas at the Disney Institute.

Hotel Plaza at Downtown Disney: Hotel Plaza lies within walking distance to Downtown Disney. The Hotel Plaza resorts are on Walt Disney World property but are privately owned. Hotel buses provide transportation to the attractions. The Wyndham Palace Resort & Spa, The Hilton Resort, Grosvenor Resort, Hotel Royal Plaza, Courtyard by Marriott, DoubleTree Guest Suites Resort, and Buena Vista Hotel are located here.

Animal Kingdom Resorts Area: This area is at the southernmost point of Walt Disney World. Some of the newest Disney projects can be found here, including Winter Summerland miniature golf, Blizzard Beach, Disney's Wide World of Sports, and Disney's Animal Kingdom. Disney buses service the resorts located here, which include Disney's All-Star Resort complex, Disney's Animal Kingdom Lodge, and Disney's Coronado Springs Resort. ◆

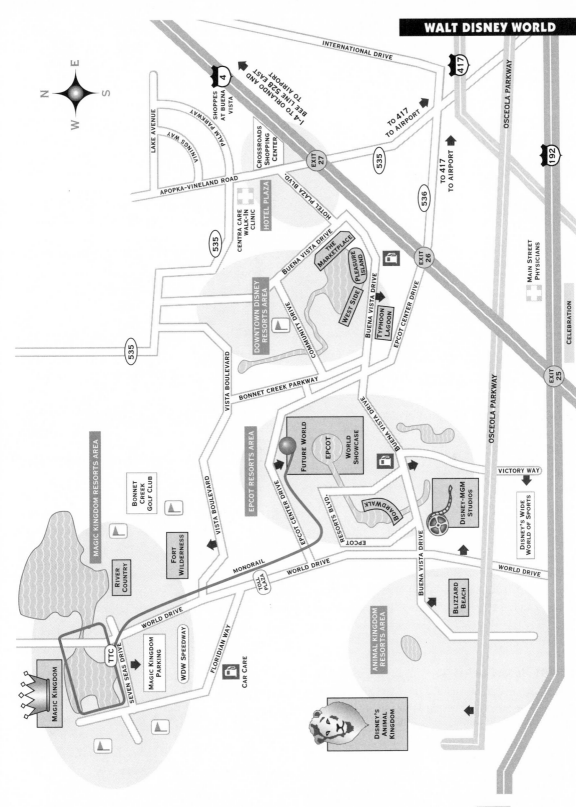

WALT DISNEY WORLD

Essentials

Attractions

Hotels

Restaurants

Special Events

Recreation

Resources

First Things First • **The World at a Glance** • Crowds & Weather • Month by Month • Admissions • Discounts • Vacation Packages • Hotel Guides • Restaurant Guides • Transportation

First Things First • The World at a Glance • Month by Month • **Crowds & Weather** • The World at a Glance • Month by Month • Discounts • Vacation Packages • Hotel Guides • Restaurant Guides • Transportation

CROWDS & WEATHER

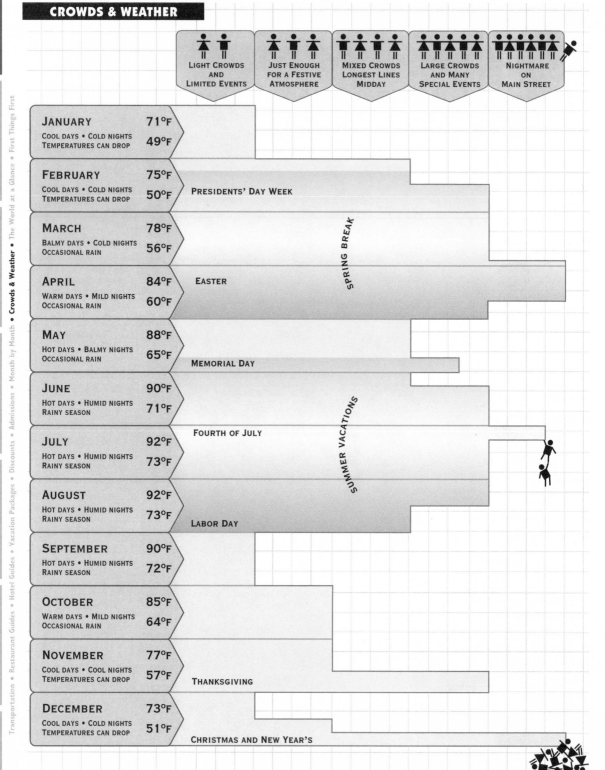

LIGHT CROWDS AND LIMITED EVENTS

JUST ENOUGH FOR A FESTIVE ATMOSPHERE

MIXED CROWDS LONGEST LINES MIDDAY

LARGE CROWDS AND MANY SPECIAL EVENTS

NIGHTMARE ON MAIN STREET

JANUARY 71°F / 49°F
COOL DAYS • COLD NIGHTS
TEMPERATURES CAN DROP

FEBRUARY 75°F / 50°F
COOL DAYS • COLD NIGHTS
TEMPERATURES CAN DROP
PRESIDENTS' DAY WEEK

MARCH 78°F / 56°F
BALMY DAYS • COLD NIGHTS
OCCASIONAL RAIN

APRIL 84°F / 60°F
WARM DAYS • MILD NIGHTS
OCCASIONAL RAIN
EASTER

SPRING BREAK

MAY 88°F / 65°F
HOT DAYS • BALMY NIGHTS
OCCASIONAL RAIN
MEMORIAL DAY

JUNE 90°F / 71°F
HOT DAYS • HUMID NIGHTS
RAINY SEASON

JULY 92°F / 73°F
HOT DAYS • HUMID NIGHTS
RAINY SEASON
FOURTH OF JULY

SUMMER VACATIONS

AUGUST 92°F / 73°F
HOT DAYS • HUMID NIGHTS
RAINY SEASON
LABOR DAY

SEPTEMBER 90°F / 72°F
HOT DAYS • HUMID NIGHTS
RAINY SEASON

OCTOBER 85°F / 64°F
WARM DAYS • MILD NIGHTS
OCCASIONAL RAIN

NOVEMBER 77°F / 57°F
COOL DAYS • COOL NIGHTS
TEMPERATURES CAN DROP
THANKSGIVING

DECEMBER 73°F / 51°F
COOL DAYS • COLD NIGHTS
TEMPERATURES CAN DROP
CHRISTMAS AND NEW YEAR'S

PREDICTING THE CROWDS & WEATHER

As you might expect, crowd size is directly linked to school vacations and national holidays. Although park hours are extended during peak attendance times, the parks can be extremely crowded with long lines. Try to avoid these busy times, especially during the summer, which is uncomfortably hot. Late fall and spring weather are ideal; winter can bring cold snaps. Check with Disney Weather (407 824-4104) before you leave. See also Resources → *"Packing."*

Winter: From Christmas week until New Year's Day, the crowds at Walt Disney World are overwhelming and the lines intimidating. The three weeks preceding Christmas, however, are an ideal time to visit. The holiday decor and festivities are underway and yet attendance is generally sparse, so you can experience many attractions without long lines. After New Year's Day, attendance drops again and remains low. The temperature may drop, too, and the weather can turn cold, although there is little precipitation. The theme parks close early in the winter, but the light crowds make attractions far more accessible. Attendance builds in February and peaks during Presidents' Day week.

Spring: From early March until Easter, the crowds become increasingly heavy, as schools across the country stagger their spring vacations. During Spring Break the parks are crowded, and during Easter week they are packed. Attendance dips slightly in late April as students return to school. During May, there are moderate crowds and the pleasant weather makes the lines tolerable. The days grow steadily warmer, although the nights remain balmy until June.

Summer: Summer attendance steadily builds, and by mid-June the parks are crowded and the lines are long. The weather can be brutally hot as well, climbing into the nineties with very high humidity. Almost-daily afternoon showers tend to clear out the parks a bit, so if you don't mind getting wet, it is a good time to tour. Although the lines can go on forever, the parks stay open late with many special entertainment events. The beginning of June and the end of August have slightly lower attendance, but while evenings can be balmy and delightful in June, it is just plain hot in August, day and night.

Fall: In September, the weather is still hot and wet and it remains so until mid-October. Attendance plummets and the parks close early, but lines are short and attractions are again accessible. In October, attendance swells with convention crowds, but from early November until the week before Christmas is some of the most pleasant vacation time at Walt Disney World. Thanksgiving is the best possible holiday for a visit, and although that week is busy, on Thanksgiving Day the crowd is almost always gathered around a dinner table. After Thanksgiving, the weather can turn cold, but the holiday decor, seasonal entertainment, and easy access to the theme park attractions are the right ingredients for an ideal vacation. ◆

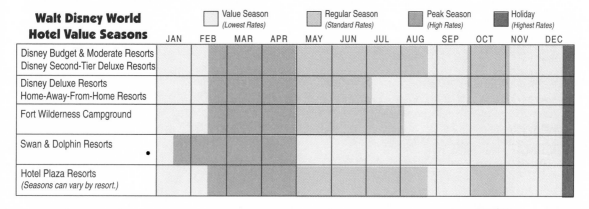

Walt Disney World Hotel Value Seasons

Legend: Value Season (Lowest Rates) · Regular Season (Standard Rates) · Peak Season (High Rates) · Holiday (Highest Rates)

	JAN	FEB	MAR	APR	MAY	JUN	JUL	AUG	SEP	OCT	NOV	DEC
Disney Budget & Moderate Resorts / Disney Second-Tier Deluxe Resorts												
Disney Deluxe Resorts / Home-Away-From-Home Resorts												
Fort Wilderness Campground												
Swan & Dolphin Resorts												
Hotel Plaza Resorts (Seasons can vary by resort.)												

First Things First • The World at a Glance • **Crowds & Weather** • Month by Month • Admissions • Discounts • Vacation Packages • Hotel Guides • Restaurant Guides • Transportation

Attractions · Hotels · Restaurants · Special Events · Recreation · Resources

WHAT TO EXPECT MONTH BY MONTH

Essentials

Attractions • The World at a Glance • First Things First

Hotels • Crowds & Weather

Restaurants • Month by Month

Special Events • Admissions • Discounts • Vacation Packages • Hotel Guides • Restaurant Guides • Transportation

Recreation

Resources

	Seasonal Events	Touring Conditions	Park Hours
JANUARY	For New Year's Eve there are fireworks extravaganzas at the major theme parks and special celebrations at Pleasure Island and Disney's BoardWalk. Sporting events include the Walt Disney World Marathon and Half Marathon, which runs throughout the theme parks and resorts. Traditionally, the Indy 200 at the Walt Disney World Speedway is held early in the year.	After New Year's, crowds are generally very light throughout the month. Disney's Sunshine Getaway vacation package begins in January at select Walt Disney World resorts.	The Magic Kingdom and Disney-MGM Studios close early throughout the month. The Magic Kingdom evening parade and fireworks are limited to weekends. Blizzard Beach and River Country are closed all month for refurbishment.
FEBRUARY	Black Heritage Month is celebrated throughout Walt Disney World with exhibits and shows celebrating African-American history. Events include Valentine's Day in the Magic Kingdom and Mardi Gras at Pleasure Island (Mardi Gras festivities are sometimes in March, depending on the year). Sporting events include Atlanta Braves Spring Training at Disney's Wide World of Sports and The UNCF/Bryant Gumbal Celebrity Golf Tournament.	Crowds are light at the beginning of the month and usually increase during Presidents' Day week and college Spring Break. Disney's Sunshine Getaway package is offered until mid-month at selected resorts.	Disney-MGM Studios and Magic Kingdom close early. Evening festivities at the Magic Kingdom are limited to weekends. Hours are extended during Presidents' Day week. Blizzard Beach is closed until mid-month. River Country is closed all month.
MARCH	Special celebrations include St. Patrick's Day and in some years, Mardi Gras at Pleasure Island. The annual celebration of Walt Disney art classics is held at Disney's Contemporary Resort. Atlanta Braves Spring Training continues at Disney's Wide World of Sports.	Crowds remain moderate to heavy as many school-age children and college students have Spring Break during the month.	The Magic Kingdom is usually open later and features fireworks and evening parades on the weekends. Waterparks have limited hours. Disney-MGM Studios closes early throughout the month.
APRIL	The Happy Easter Parade is held at the Magic Kingdom. In late April, Epcot hosts the Annual International Flower and Garden Festival. The annual U.S. Men's Clay Court Tennis Championships are held at Disney's Wide World of Sports.	Crowds remain heavy, peaking during the week before and after Easter.	During the week preceding and following Easter, the Magic Kingdom and Disney-MGM Studios are open late. Evening fireworks and parades are held at the Magic Kingdom on weekends throughout the month.
MAY	Festivities include Mother's Day events in the Magic Kingdom and in other locations around Walt Disney World. On Cinco de Mayo, celebrations are held at Pleasure Island and in the Mexico pavilion in the World Showcase at Epcot. The International Flower and Garden Festival continues throughout the month at Epcot. Disney-MGM Studios features Star Wars Weekends all month.	Crowds are manageable until the last week of the month, when attendance builds towards Memorial Day weekend.	Disney-MGM Studios and the Magic Kingdom are open late. On weekends, the Magic Kingdom features fireworks and evening parades. A full nightly schedule of parades and fireworks begins on Memorial Day weekend.
JUNE	Events include Father's Day celebrations at Disney-MGM Studios and other locations around Walt Disney World. At Pleasure Island, Black Music Month is commemorated with special concerts. The International Flower and Garden Festival continues throughout the month at Epcot.	Crowds are heavy most of the month, starting after the first week.	Disney-MGM Studios and the Magic Kingdom are open late. Animal Kingdom closes between 6 and 8 PM all summer. The evening parade and fireworks are staged nightly at the Magic Kingdom.

	Seasonal Events	Touring Conditions	Park Hours
JULY	For the Fourth of July, the theme parks host extended versions of fireworks shows. On July 14, Bastille Day is celebrated in the France pavilion in the World Showcase at Epcot. The Disney Cup International Youth Soccer Tournament is held at Disney's Wide World of Sports.	Crowds are heavy throughout the month.	The Magic Kingdom and Disney-MGM Studios are open late. Evening festivities at both parks are held nightly. Animal Kingdom closes between 6 PM and 8 PM in the summer.
AUGUST	Latin Rhythm begins at Epcot and Pleasure Island. Disney's Wide World of Sports hosts the Walt Disney World Soccer Classic.	Crowds are heavy throughout the month until the last week when attendance begins to drop. During the last week, select Walt Disney World resorts begin offering Disney's Fall Fantasy vacation package.	Disney-MGM Studios and the Magic Kingdom are open late. Animal Kingdom closes between 6 and 8 PM. The week before Labor Day, hours shorten at both parks, and Magic Kingdom fireworks and evening parades are held on weekends only.
SEPTEMBER	During the week of Labor Day, the Magic Kingdom hosts the annual Night of Joy Christian-music program. The Annual Disneyana Convention is held at Disney's Contemporary resort. At Disney-MGM Studios, ABC daytime drama stars and their fans converge for the Super Soap Weekend.	After the crowded Labor Day weekend, crowds fall off substantially. Disney's Fall Fantasy vacation Package is offered at selected resorts.	After Labor Day, the Magic Kingdom and Disney-MGM Studios close early. Evening festivities at the Magic Kingdom are held on weekends only. Some theme park attractions and River Country are closed for refurbishment.
OCTOBER	Disney's Contemporary Resort hosts the annual Teddy Bear and Doll Convention. The Annual Pleasure Island Jazz Festival features top jazz acts. Oktoberfest is celebrated at Pleasure Island and in the Germany pavilion in World Showcase at Epcot. The International Food and Wine Festival begins at Epcot. Halloween's big event is Mickey's Not-So-Scary Halloween Party at the Magic Kingdom.	October has a full slate of special events and heavy convention activity, and crowds can be heavy.	The Magic Kingdom and Disney-MGM Studios close early. Evening festivities at the Magic Kingdom are limited to weekends. Some theme park attractions are closed for refurbishment during the fall.
NOVEMBER	The International Food and Wine Festival at Epcot continues until the week before Thanksgiving. The Festival of the Masters art show begins at Downtown Disney mid-month. Many Walt Disney World restaurants and resorts offer Thanksgiving dinners and holiday festivities. After Thanksgiving, the resort begins an extensive program of Christmas celebrations.	Crowds are generally light except for Thanksgiving weekend. After Thanksgiving, select Walt Disney World resorts offer Disney's Magical Holidays vacation package.	Disney-MGM Studios and the Magic Kingdom close early. Evening events at the Magic Kingdom are limited to weekends. Typhoon Lagoon, River Country, and some theme park attractions are closed for refurbishment.
DECEMBER	Resort-wide Christmas decorations and holiday events are featured. Tree-lighting ceremonies occur at all major theme parks through Christmas Eve. Mickey's Very Merry Christmas Party is held on selected evenings at the Magic Kingdom. The Candlelight Processional and Holidays Around the World are held in the World Showcase at Epcot, and the Osborne Family Spectacle of Lights is on display at Disney-MGM Studios.	Crowds are very light until Christmas week, when they reach their yearly highs. Disney's Magical Holidays vacation package is offered at select resorts until the week before Christmas.	Disney-MGM Studios and the Magic Kingdom close early, except during Christmas week, when hours are extended and festivities are offered. Typhoon Lagoon is closed until Christmas week and River Country is closed all month.

ADMISSION TICKETS

Disney theme park admission tickets come in a range of prices to match different vacation styles. Once purchased, tickets are valid until used even if prices increase, which they tend to do each year. To lock in prices or avoid lines, tickets can be purchased in advance at Disney Stores, or by telephone with a credit card (407 934-7639). Disney Club and AAA members receive small discounts.

	How It Works	What It Costs (approximate adult / child with tax)	Who It's For
One-Day One-Park	Good for admission to any one Disney park that charges admission. This pass cannot be ordered over the phone.	Major Parks — about $54 / $43 Typhoon Lagoon — about $34 / $26 Blizzard Beach — about $34 / $26 River Country — about $18 / $14 Pleasure Island — about $20 DisneyQuest — about $28 / $22 Wide World of Sports — $10 / $8	A good choice for visitors on short stays or first-time visitors who will be staying in one park all day.
Park-Hopper	Good for four- or five-days' admission to the major theme parks. Visitors can visit more than one theme park each day. The pass does not have to be used on consecutive days and there is no expiration date. Visitors can spread the days out over multiple trips.	Four-Day Park-Hopper — about $214 / $170 Five-Day Park-Hopper — about $242 / $191	This pass offers flexibility for visitors who do not visit the parks every day or wish to visit more than one major park in one day.
Park-Hopper Plus	Good for five-, six-, or seven-days' admission to the major theme parks. These passes have the same flexibility as the Park-Hopper described above, plus they come with "options" for a day's admission to the water parks, Pleasure Island, or Disney's Wide World of Sports. The number of options depends on the length of the pass purchased.	Five-Day Park-Hopper Plus with two options — $275 / $220 Six-Day Park-Hopper Plus with three options — about $309 / $247 Seven-Day Park-Hopper Plus with four options — about $341 / $275	This pass offers flexibility for visitors who don't want to visit major theme parks every day but would like to see and do it all on their own schedule.
Ultimate Park-Hopper	This pass is offered exclusively for guests staying at Disney-owned resorts or the Swan and Dolphin. The pass includes unlimited admission to the parks, water parks, Pleasure Island, Disney's Wide World of Sports, and DisneyQuest. The pass must be purchased for the entire length of stay. The passes expire at the end of stay, regardless of the number of days actually used.	Prices vary according to the length of stay. For example, a two-night, three-day Ultimate Park-Hopper is about $171 / $137. A four-night, five-day pass is about $277 / $222.	The Ultimate Park-Hopper can be a fair deal when used to visit the parks each day of visitors' stay. It is also the only two- or three-day option available to visitors.
Annual Pass	The basic Annual Pass includes one year of unlimited admission to the major theme parks and free parking. Annual Passholders are also eligible for special discounts on Walt Disney World hotel accommodations. These discounts are only offered at certain seasons and vary from year to year.	Annual Pass — about $389 / $331	Visitors who are staying longer than eight days or those who are planning to return within the same year should consider buying an Annual Pass.
Premium Annual	The Premium Annual Pass includes the same amenities as the Annual Pass, plus unlimited admission to the Disney water parks, Pleasure Island, DisneyQuest, and Disney's Wide World of Sports. Annual Passholders are also eligible for special discounts on Walt Disney World hotel accommodations. These discounts are only offered at certain seasons and vary from year to year.	Premium Annual Pass — about $522 / $444	Visitors who are staying longer than ten days or those who are planning to return within the same year should consider buying a Premium Annual Pass.

DISCOUNT STRATEGIES

Travel clubs can help visitors stretch their vacation budgets. Most travel clubs offer discounts on accommodations, as well as Disney vacation packages. There are several discount strategies that are popular with experienced Disney visitors, including offers from local convention bureaus, commercial coupon books, and Disney's own discount outlets.

American Automobile Association: This national travel club provides members with a small discount on admission tickets; however, discounts may be more substantial if purchased through a local AAA office. At the AAA counter located in the Main Street Exposition Hall in the Magic Kingdom, members may book same-day reservations at Walt Disney World resorts at AAA discount rates when available. Members are also offered a 10 to 40 percent discount at the Swan and Dolphin resorts, most Hotel Plaza Resorts, and many off-site hotels. Members may also receive discounts on a range of Disney vacation packages (see page 21) and Disney Cruise Line vacations when they are booked through a local AAA office. Members who purchase their tickets or book vacations through a local AAA office also receive a Diamond Lot parking pass that allows parking near the entrances of the theme parks (parking charges still apply, however). Call your local AAA chapter for information.

American Express: American Express cardholders can use their Membership Rewards Program points to earn Walt Disney World vacation packages and theme park passes. American Express vacation packages to Walt Disney World include accommodations, park admissions, 250 Disney Dollars, and other amenities. Even when not booking vacations directly through American Express, card holders receive White Glove Treatment benefits when using their cards to book Walt Disney World resort accommodations for a minimum of two nights. Recent benefits include 10 to 20 percent off dining at selected Downtown Disney restaurants, 20 percent off selected seatings at Walt Disney World resort dinner shows, 10 percent off selected boating activities, 20 percent off selected tours, five dollars off admission at DisneyQuest, 15 percent off merchandise purchases of $50 or more at selected Downtown Disney shops, 15 percent off miniature golf at Fantasia Gardens and Disney's Winter Summerland, and other benefits. For information, or to book complete travel packages, call American Express Vacation Packages (407 939-7805).

Entertainment Publications: The Orlando version of this vacation coupon book offers 50 percent discounts at the Swan and Dolphin resorts, Hotel Royal Plaza, Lake Buena Vista Resort, Wyndham Palace Resort & Spa, Courtyard by Marriott Lake Buena Vista, Vistana Resort, Radisson Inn Lake Buena Vista, and Summerfield Suites Lake Buena Vista, as well as many other off-site hotels. Participating hotels change yearly. The book has local and national attraction, hotel, shopping, and dining discounts for most major U.S. cities. Discounts and coupons are valid for one year. Books cost between $20 and $50, depending on the city. The Orlando book costs about $40 with shipping. It is cheaper to order a book for areas other than your own. For more information, or to order a book, contact Entertainment Publications (800 374-4464).

Kissimmee-St. Cloud Vacation Discounts: Walt Disney World spans two counties, Orange County to the north and Osceola County to the south. Located mostly in Osceola County, the city of Kissimmee stretches along Highway 192, where the Main Gate to the Magic Kingdom is located. Moderately priced lodging, as well as numerous outlet malls and gift shops, are located here. The Kissimmee-St. Cloud Convention and Visitors Bureau offers a free vacation discount booklet that includes coupons for local attractions and dinner shows and special rates on area hotels and rental cars. The booklet has a toll-free number for reserving accommodations at discounted rates. For more information, contact the Kissimmee-St. Cloud Convention and Visitors Bureau (800 327-9159). ➤

Attractions • Hotels • Restaurants • Special Events • Recreation • Resources

First Things First • The World at a Glance • Crowds & Weather • Month by Month • Admissions • **Discounts** • Vacation Packages • Hotel Guides • Restaurant Guides • Transportation

The Disney Club: The Disney Club, run by the Disney Company, replaced the Magic Kingdom Club in 2001. Members are offered certain discounts at Walt Disney World in Orlando and Disneyland in California. Benefits include a 10 to 20 percent discount at some Disney-owned hotels during selected seasons; small discounts on theme park passes and on admission to Disney water parks, Pleasure Island, DisneyQuest, and Disney's Wide World of Sports; and a 10 percent discount at selected Downtown Disney shops. The card also entitles the holder to savings on Disney vacation packages (see page 21), seasonal discounts at Disney's Vero Beach and Disney's Hilton Head Resorts, and a 10 percent savings at most Disney Stores worldwide. The fee for a one-year family membership is about $40. The program best benefits people who purchase high-end vacation packages, travel between November and mid-February, make large purchases at the Disney Store, or buy several park admissions. On the downside, there are fees for changes, and cancellation policies are very restrictive with costly penalties. A substantial deposit is required at the time reservations are made and vacation packages must be paid in full well in advance. For more information, contact the Disney Club (888 347-6394).

Orlando Magicard: The Orlando Magicard is sponsored by the Orlando/Orange County Convention & Visitors Bureau, Inc. The card entitles visitors to discounts on accommodations, car rentals, restaurants, and some Orlando-area attractions. Discounts (ranging from 10 to 20 percent) are available on accommodations and vacation packages at the Caribe Royale Resort and Suites, Grosvenor Resort, Holiday Inn SunSpree Resort, Vistana Resort, and many other area hotels. Other benefits include discounts to Orlando-area attractions, including Sea World, Universal Studios, Wet 'N Wild, and Medieval Times Dinner and Tournament, as well as a 10 to 15 percent discount on Alamo, Budget, Dollar, and Thrifty rental cars. The Orlando Magicard is free and can be used for groups of up to six persons. Order early; it takes about six weeks for the card to arrive. For visitors driving into Florida, the card and brochure are available at the Florida Welcome Centers on the major Interstate highways. For more information, contact Orlando Magicard (800 643-9492 or 407 363-4871).

Annual Passholder Benefits: For frequent visitors to Walt Disney World, or for visitors who are planning single stays of longer than 8 days (or 11 days for the Premium Annual Pass), the Annual Pass can be an excellent choice for theme park tickets (see "Admissions," page 18). Annual passes come with a host of hotel and attraction discounts that make them a particularly good value. Benefits include a quarterly Passholder newsletter with the latest information on new attractions and events, Passholder offers, and park hours; reduced prices on special park events, such as Mickey's Very Merry Christmas Party; discounts of up to 20 percent at selected restaurants and dinner shows; 10 percent off purchases at selected shops at Downtown Disney; 15 percent off the regular price of DisneyQuest admission, plus a 10 percent discount on food and merchandise; discounts on selected backstage tours; and a 10 percent discount on sitting fees for a Disney Family Portrait. Discounts of up to 40 percent are periodically available at selected Walt Disney World resorts. These discounts are not usually announced until a few months before they go into effect. For information about policies regarding the Annual Pass, a complete list of discounts, or to inquire about ordering passes, call Walt Disney World Reservations (407 560-7277).

Disney Travel Center in Ocala: Located off State Road 200 at exit 68 of I-75 in Ocala, Florida, this information center is worth a stop for anyone driving this way to Walt Disney World. Walk-in visitors can make same-day reservations for Walt Disney World hotel rooms, often at a good discount when rooms are available; however, this can only be done in person and not by telephone. Discounts are generally greater at the more expensive hotels, and Walt Disney World budget hotels are not discounted at all. Visitors can also make dining reservations, purchase theme park tickets, and pick up Walt Disney World Guidemaps. The Center is open daily from 9 AM until 6 PM. ◆

Attractions • First Things First

Hotels • The World at a Glance • Crowds & Weather

Restaurants • Month by Month • Admissions

Special Events • Vacation Packages • Hotel Guides • Discounts

Recreation • Restaurant Guides

Resources • Transportation

VACATION PACKAGES

Visitors, especially first-timers, may find planning a trip to Walt Disney World easier with the purchase of a vacation package. The packages listed below are offered through Walt Disney World. Rates vary depending on the hotel and time of year. Reservations can be made by calling the Disney Travel Company, which can also offer transportation and other add-ons (800 828-0228).

Name	What's Included in the Vacation Package	Starting Cost	Available
Basic Plan	**Disney Budget or Better Resort Accommodations** **Plus Per Person:** Admission to Disney's Wide World of Sports.	About **$370** *(3 nights at Disney's All-Star Resort for two adults)*	Year Round
Resort Magic	**Disney Budget or Better Resort Accommodations** **Plus Per Person:** *Ultimate Park-Hopper, one Magic Wish (such as a Character Breakfast, or Mickey 'N You photo session).*	About **$890** *(4 days' admission and 3 nights at Disney's All-Star Resort for two adults)*	Year Round
Discovery Magic	**Disney Budget or Better Resort Accommodations** **Plus Per Person:** *Ultimate Park-Hopper, two Magic Wishes per day (such as meals, a round of golf, spa treatment, VIP fireworks viewing, or theme park tour).*	About **$1,300** *(4 days' admission and 3 nights at Disney's All-Star Resort for two adults)*	Year Round
Deluxe Magic	**Disney Moderate or Better Resort Accommodations** **Plus Per Person:** *Ultimate Park-Hopper, three meals daily, unlimited resort recreation, theme park tours, Cirque du Soleil admission, VIP fireworks viewing, and access to Disney Children's Activity Centers.*	About **$2,070** *(4 days' admission and 3 nights at Disney's Caribbean Beach Resort for two adults)*	Year Round
Grand Plan	**Disney Deluxe or Better Resort Accommodations** **Plus Per Person:** *Ultimate Park-Hopper, three meals and two snacks daily, unlimited resort recreation, theme park tours, Cirque du Soleil admission, fireworks cruise, spa treatment, VIP fireworks viewing, VIP seating at Fantasmic!, access to Disney Children's Activity Centers, and in-room child care.*	About **$3,400** *(4 days' admission and 3 nights at Disney's Beach Club Resort for two adults)*	Year Round
Sunshine Getaway	**Disney Budget or Better Resort Accommodations** **Plus Per Person:** *Ultimate Park-Hopper, daily breakfast, coupon book with modest discounts on merchandise, dining, and recreation.*	About **$810** *(3 nights at Disney's All-Star Resort for two adults)*	January through Mid-February
Fall Fantasy	**Disney Budget or Better Resort Accommodations** **Plus Per Person:** *Ultimate Park-Hopper, daily breakfast, coupon book with modest discounts on merchandise, dining, and recreation.*	About **$810** *(3 nights at Disney's All-Star Resort for two adults)*	Late August through September
Magical Holidays	**Disney Budget or Better Resort Accommodations** **Plus Per Person:** *Ultimate Park-Hopper, admission to Mickey's Very Merry Christmas Party, one dinner during stay, coupon book with modest discounts on merchandise, dining, and recreation.*	About **$760** *(3 nights at Disney's All-Star Resort for two adults)*	Late November until Christmas
Sand 'N Castle	**Disney Budget or Better Resort Accommodations** **Plus Per Person:** *Unlimited Magic Pass, two additional nights' accommodation at Disney's Vero Beach Resort.*	About **$1,150** *(3 nights at Disney's All-Star Resort and 2 nights at Disney's Vero Beach Resort for two adults)*	Year Round

Essentials

First Things First • The World at a Glance • Crowds & Weather • Month by Month • Admissions • Discounts • **Vacation Packages** • Hotel Guides • Restaurant Guides • Transportation

Attractions

Hotels

Restaurants

Special Events

Recreation

Resources

HOTEL COMPARISON GUIDES
Hotel Features and Value

	● A World of Choices	◐ Many Possibilities	◎ Limited Options	○ Restricted by Comparison

	Quick Convenient Location	Walking and Transportation Options	Hotel Services and Recreation	On Site and Nearby Dining Options	Standard Room Price Range
Disney Premier Resorts					
Disney's Beach Club Resort	●	●	●	●	$290 – 385
Disney's BoardWalk Inn	●	●	●	●	$290 – 385
Disney's Grand Floridian Resort & Spa	◎	◎	●	●	$320 – 430
Disney's Polynesian Resort	◎	◎	◎	◎	$290 – 390
Disney's Yacht Club Resort	●	●	●	●	$280 – 380
Disney Deluxe Resorts					
Disney's Animal Kingdom Lodge	○	○	◎	◎	$210 – 300
Disney's Contemporary Resort	◎	◎	●	●	$230 – 300
Disney's Wilderness Lodge	○	○	◎	◎	$190 – 280
Disney Home Away from Home Resorts					
Disney's BoardWalk Villas	●	●	●	●	$290 – 385
Disney's Fort Wilderness Homes	○	○	●	○	$190 – 240
Disney's Old Key West Resort	○	○	◎	○	$250 – 320
The Villas at the Disney Institute	○	◎	●	○	$220 – 280
The Villas at Wilderness Lodge	○	○	◎	◎	$270 – 360
Disney Moderate Resorts					
Disney's Caribbean Beach Resort	○	○	◎	◎	$130 – 185
Disney's Coronado Springs Resort	○	○	◎	◎	$130 – 185
Disney's Port Orleans Resort – French Quarter	○	○	○	○	$130 – 200
Disney's Port Orleans Resort – Riverside	○	○	◎	◎	$130 – 200
Disney Value Resorts					
Disney's All-Star Resorts	○	○	○	○	$80 – 115
Disney's Fort Wilderness Campsites	○	○	●	○	$45 – 75
Disney's Pop Century Resort (Open 2002)	○	○	○	○	$80 – 115
Independent Resorts					
Courtyard by Marriott	◎	◎	○	◎	$95 – 145
DoubleTree Guest Suites Resort	◎	◐	○	◎	$130 – 195
Grosvenor Resort	◎	◎	○	◎	$100 – 175
The Hilton Resort	◎	◎	○	◎	$160 – 230
Hotel Royal Plaza	◎	◎	○	◎	$130 – 150
Lake Buena Vista Resort	◎	◎	○	◎	$90 – 135
Shades of Green	○	◎	◎	○	$69 – 100
Walt Disney World Dolphin	●	●	◎	●	$220 – 260
Walt Disney World Swan	●	●	◎	●	$220 – 260
Wyndham Palace Resort & Spa	◎	◎	●	●	$150 – 260

Hotel Amenities and Recreation

	Hair Dryer	Coffee Maker	Mini Bar or Refrigerator	Room Service	Fitness Center	Tennis Courts	Boat Rental	Bicycle Rental
Disney Premier Resorts								
Disney's Beach Club Resort	■	■	fee	■	■	■	■	■
Disney's BoardWalk Inn	■		fee	■	■	■		■
Disney's Grand Floridian Resort & Spa	■		■	■	■	■	■	
Disney's Polynesian Resort	■		fee	limited			■	■
Disney's Yacht Club Resort	■	■	fee	■	■	■	■	■
Disney Deluxe Resorts								
Disney's Animal Kingdom Lodge	■	■	fee	■	■			
Disney's Contemporary Resort			fee	■	■	■	■	
Disney's Wilderness Lodge			fee	limited			■	■
Disney Home Away from Home Resorts								
Disney's BoardWalk Villas	■	■	■		■	■		■
Disney's Fort Wilderness Homes	■		■				■	■
Disney's Old Key West Resort		■	■		■	■	■	■
The Villas at the Disney Institute		■	■	limited	■	■	■	
The Villas at Wilderness Lodge	■	■	■	■			■	■
Disney Moderate Resorts								
Disney's Caribbean Beach Resort		■	■				■	■
Disney's Coronado Springs Resort	■	■	fee	limited	■			
Disney's Port Orleans Resort – French Quarter			fee				nearby	nearby
Disney's Port Orleans Resort – Riverside			fee				■	■
Disney Value Resorts								
Disney's All-Star Resorts			fee					
Disney's Fort Wilderness Campsites						■	■	■
Disney's Pop Century Resort *(Open 2002)*			fee					
Independent Resorts								
Courtyard by Marriott	■	■	fee	limited	■			
DoubleTree Guest Suites Resort	■	■	■	limited	■	■		
Grosvenor Resort	■	■	■	limited	■	■		
The Hilton Resort			■	■	■			
Hotel Royal Plaza	■	■	■	limited	■	■		
Lake Buena Vista Resort	■	■	■	limited				
Shades of Green			fee	limited	■	■		
Walt Disney World Dolphin	■		■	■	■	■	■	
Walt Disney World Swan	■	■	■	■	■	■	■	
Wyndham Palace Resort & Spa	■	■	■	■	■	■	■	

Essentials

Attractions | Hotels | Restaurants | Special Events | Recreation | Resources

Transportation • Restaurant Guides • **Hotel Guides** • Vacation Packages • Discounts • Admissions • Month by Month • Crowds & Weather • The World at a Glance • First Things First

HOTEL GUIDES

INTERNATIONAL DRIVE

417

OSCEOLA PARKWAY

192

I-4 TO ORLANDO AND
BEE LINE 528 EAST
TO AIRPORT

4

LAKE AVENUE

VININGS WAY

PALM PARKWAY

SHOPPES
AT BUENA
VISTA

CROSSROADS
SHOPPING CENTER

APOPKA-VINELAND ROAD

CENTRAL
CARE

HOTEL PLAZA

HOTEL PLAZA BLVD.

EXIT 27

TO 417
TO AIRPORT

535

536

TO 417
TO AIRPORT

535

CENTURION CT.

BUENA VISTA DRIVE

THE
MARKETPLACE

PLEASURE
ISLAND

WEST SIDE

BUENA VISTA DRIVE

TYPHOON
LAGOON

EPCOT CENTER DRIVE

MAIN STREET
PHYSICIANS

CELEBRATION

DOWNTOWN DISNEY
RESORTS AREA

COMMUNITY DRIVE

VISTA BOULEVARD

EXIT 26

BONNET CREEK PARKWAY

MAGIC KINGDOM RESORTS AREA

BONNET CREEK
GOLF CLUB

FORT
WILDERNESS

VISTA BOULEVARD

EPCOT RESORTS AREA

EPCOT CENTER DRIVE

FUTURE WORLD

EPCOT

WORLD SHOWCASE

BUENA VISTA DRIVE

VICTORY WAY

DISNEY'S WIDE
WORLD OF SPORTS

OSCEOLA PARKWAY

EXIT 25

MONORAIL

RIVER
COUNTRY

WORLD DRIVE

RESORTS BLVD.

BOARDWALK

EPCOT

DISNEY-MGM
STUDIOS

BUENA VISTA DRIVE

WORLD DRIVE

MAGIC
KINGDOM

TTC

MAGIC KINGDOM
PARKING

WDW SPEEDWAY

SEVEN SEAS DRIVE

WORLD DRIVE

TOLL
PLAZA

FLORIDIAN WAY

CAR CARE

ANIMAL KINGDOM
RESORTS AREA

BLIZZARD
BEACH

DISNEY'S ANIMAL
KINGDOM

24

Hotel Map Locations

Magic Kingdom Resorts Area

		Review Page
A	Disney's Contemporary Resort	145
B	Disney's Polynesian Resort	150
C	Disney's Grand Floridian Resort & Spa	148
D	Shades of Green	160
E	Disney's Wilderness Lodge	153
EE	The Villas at Wilderness Lodge	162
F	Disney's Fort Wilderness Resort and Campground	147

Epcot Resorts Area

		Review Page
G	Disney's BoardWalk Villas	143
H	Walt Disney World Swan	164
I	Walt Disney World Dolphin	163
J	Disney's Yacht Club Resort	154
K	Disney's Beach Club Resort	141
KK	Disney's Beach Club Villas (Open 2002)	
L	Disney's BoardWalk Inn	142
M	Disney's Caribbean Beach Resort	144
MM	Disney's Pop Century Resort (Open 2002)	

Downtown Disney Resorts Area

		Review Page
N	Disney's Old Key West Resort	149
O	The Villas at the Disney Institute	161
P	Disney's Port Orleans Resort – Riverside	152
Q	Disney's Port Orleans Resort – French Quarter	151

Hotel Plaza Resorts

		Review Page
R	Wyndham Palace Resort & Spa	165
S	Grosvenor Resort	156
T	Lake Buena Vista Resort	159
U	The Hilton Resort	157
V	Courtyard by Marriott (at Walt Disney World)	136

		Review Page
W	Hotel Royal Plaza	158
X	DoubleTree Guest Suites Resort	155

Animal Kingdom Resorts Area

		Review Page
Y	Disney's Coronado Springs Resort	146
Z	Disney's All-Star Resorts	137–139
ZZ	Disney's Animal Kingdom Lodge	140

Nearby Hotels

(See Hotels → "Off-Site Hotels")

		Review Page
1	Cypress Glen	169
2	Perri House, Bed & Breakfast Inn	171
3	Hyatt Regency Grand Cypress	170
4	Summerfield Suites Hotel	172
5	Sheraton Safari	172
6	Courtyard by Marriott (at Palm Parkway)	168
7	Clarion Suites	168
8	Radisson Inn, Lake Buena Vista	171
9	Homewood Suites	170
10	Hampton Inn, Lake Buena Vista	169
11	Sierra Suites, Lake Buena Vista	172
12	Embassy Suites Resort	169
13	Holiday Inn SunSpree Resort	170
14	Embassy Grand Beach	169
15	Buena Vista Suites	168
16	Caribe Royale Resort Suites	168
17	Premier Vacation Homes	171
18	Marriott's Orlando World Center	171
19	Holiday Inn Family Suites Resort	170
20	Vistana Resort	172
21	Celebration Hotel	172
22	Holiday Inn Nikki Bird	172
23	DoubleTree Orlando Resort and Conference Center	172

TOP 4 FAVORITE RESORTS FOR FAMILIES

Disney's Beach Club & Yacht Club Resorts

Disney's Moderate Resorts
(Port Orleans, Coronado Springs, Caribbean Beach)

Disney's Old Key West Resort

Disney's All Stars Resort

TOP 4 DELUXE RESORT EXPERIENCES

Disney's Grand Floridian Resort & Spa

Disney's Beach Club & Yacht Club Resorts

Disney's BoardWalk Villas

Disney's Polynesian Resort

TOP 4 FAVORITE OFF-SITE RESORTS

Homewood Suites

Holiday Inn SunSpree

Premier Vacation Homes

Marriott's Orlando World Center

Essentials • Attractions • Hotels • Restaurants • Special Events • Recreation • Resources

First Things First • The World at a Glance • Crowds & Weather • Month by Month • Admissions • Discounts • Vacation Packages • **Hotel Guides** • Restaurant Guides • Transportation

RESTAURANT SELECTION GUIDES
Restaurants by Location

Essentials

Attractions

Hotels

Restaurants

Special Events

Recreation

Resources

Transportation • Restaurant Guides • Hotel Guides • Vacation Packages • Discounts • Admissions • Month by Month • Crowds & Weather • The World at a Glance • First Things First

Restaurants by Cuisine

Restaurant	Breakfast, Lunch, Dinner
American	
Artist Point	B · D
Baskervilles	B L D
Beaches & Cream	B L D
Big River Grille & Brewing Works	· L D
California Grill	· · D
Chef Mickey's	B · D
Cinderella's Royal Table	B L D
Coral Cafe	B L D
The Crystal Palace	B L D
ESPN Club	· L D
50's Prime Time Cafe	· L D
The Garden Grill Restaurant	B L D
Garden Grove Cafe	B L ·
Grand Floridian Cafe	B L D
Gulliver's Grill	· · D
The Hollywood Brown Derby	· L D
Hollywood & Vine	B L D
Liberty Tree Tavern	· L D
Narcoossee's	· · D
1900 Park Fare	B · D
Official All Star Cafe	· L D
Olivia's Cafe	B L D
Planet Hollywood	· L D
The Plaza Restaurant	· L D
Rainforest Cafe, Animal Kingdom	B L D
Rainforest Cafe, Downtown Disney	· L D
Restaurantosaurus	B L D
Sci-Fi Dine-In Theater Restaurant	· L D
Whispering Canyon Cafe	B L D
Wildhorse Saloon	· L D
Wolfgang Puck Cafe	· L D
Yacht Club Galley	B L D
Continental	
Arthur's 27	· · D
Victoria & Albert's	· · D
Caribbean	
Bongos Cuban Cafe	· L D
Captain's Tavern	· · D

Restaurant	Breakfast, Lunch, Dinner
Seafood	
Cape May Cafe	B · D
Cap'n Jack's Restaurant	· L D
Coral Reef Restaurant	· L D
Finn's Grill	· · D
Flying Fish Café	· · D
Fulton's Crab House	· L D
Narcoossee's	· · D
Steak & Prime Rib	
Baskervilles	B L D
Concourse Steakhouse	B L D
Le Cellier Steakhouse	· L D
The Outback	· · D
Shula's Steakhouse	· · D
Yachtsman Steakhouse	· · D
French	
Bistro de Paris	· · D
Chefs de France	· L D
Italian	
L'Originale Alfredo di Roma Ristorante	· L D
Mama Melrose's Ristorante Italiano	· L D
Palio	· · D
Portobello Yacht Club	· L D
Tony's Town Square Restaurant	B L D
Asian & Polynesian	
Kona Cafe (Pacific Rim)	B L D
Nine Dragons Restaurant (Chinese)	· L D
'Ohana (Polynesian)	B · D
Tempura Kiku (Japanese)	· L D
Teppanyaki Dining Room (Japanese)	· L D
Mediterranean	
Spoodles	B L D
Citricos	· · D
Mexican	
Juan & Only's	· · D
Maya Grill	B · D
San Angel Inn Restaurante	· L D

Restaurant	Breakfast, Lunch, Dinner
Barbecue & Cajun	
Boatwright's Dining Hall	B · D
House of Blues	· L D
Wildhorse Saloon	· L D
International	
Biergarten (German)	· L D
Boma – Flavors of Africa (African)	B · D
Jiko – The Cooking Place (African)	· · D
Le Cellier Steakhouse (Canadian)	· L D
Restaurant Akershus (Norwegian)	· L D
Restaurant Marrakesh (Moroccan)	· L D
Rose & Crown Dining Room (British)	· L D
All-You-Care-to-Eat Meals	
Artist Point	B · D
Baskervilles	B L D
Biergarten	· L D
Boatwright's Dining Hall	B · D
Boma – Flavors of Africa	B · D
Cape May Cafe	B · D
Chef Mickey's	B · D
Cinderella's Royal Table	B L D
Coral Cafe	B L D
The Crystal Palace	B L D
Garden Grove Cafe	B L ·
The Garden Grill Restaurant	B L D
Hollywood & Vine	B L D
Liberty Tree Tavern	· L D
Maya Grill	B · D
1900 Park Fare	B · D
'Ohana	B · D
Olivia's Cafe	B L D
Restaurant Akershus	· L D
Restaurantosaurus	B L D
Spoodles	B L D
Whispering Canyon Cafe	B L D
Yacht Club Galley	B L D

Attractions · Hotels · Restaurants · Special Events · Recreation · Resources

First Things First • The World at a Glance • Crowds & Weather • Month by Month • Admissions • Discounts • Vacation Packages • Hotel Guides • Restaurant Guides • Transportation

Features: Restaurants at the Resorts

🎖 = E.A.R.S. Award	🍎 = Special Plate on Request
🍎🍎 = A Few Menu Selections	★ = Okay
🍎🍎🍎 = Many Menu Selections	★★ = Well Done
	★★★ = Extraordinary
♥ = Romantic Setting	B = Breakfast
	L = Lunch
	D = Dinner

Restaurant	Entertainment	Vegetarian Choices	Popular with Kids	Theming	All You Care to Eat Meals
Arthur's 27		🍎	★	★★★♥	
🎖 Artist Point	Character Breakfast	🍎🍎	★★★ B	★★★♥	B
Baskervilles	Dinner Show	🍎🍎	★	★	BD
Beaches & Cream		🍎🍎	★★★	★	
Boatwright's Dining Hall		🍎🍎	★★	★★	B
Boma — Flavors of Africa		🍎🍎	★★	★★	BD
🎖 California Grill		🍎🍎🍎	★	★★★♥	
Cape May Cafe	Character Breakfast	🍎🍎	★★★ B	★★	BD
Captain's Tavern		🍎🍎	★	★	
🎖 Chef Mickey's	Character Meals	🍎🍎🍎	★★★	★	BD
Citricos		🍎🍎	★	★★	
Concourse Steakhouse		🍎🍎	★	★	
Coral Cafe	Character Breakfast	🍎	★★★ B	★	BD
Finn's Grill		🍎🍎	★	★	
Garden Grove Cafe	Character Breakfast	🍎🍎	★★★ B	★	B
Grand Floridian Cafe		🍎	★	★	
Gulliver's Grill	Character Dinner	🍎	★★★	★★	
Jiko — The Cooking Place		🍎🍎🍎	★	★★★♥	
Juan & Only's		🍎🍎	★	★★	
🎖 Kona Cafe		🍎🍎	★	★★	
Maya Grill		🍎	★	★★	B
🎖 Narcoossee's		🍎🍎	★	★★★♥	
1900 Park Fare	Character Meals	🍎🍎🍎	★★★	★★	BD
🎖 'Ohana	Character Breakfast	🍎🍎🍎	★★★	★★★	BD
Olivia's Cafe	Character Breakfast	🍎🍎	★★★ B	★	B
The Outback		🍎	★	★★	
🎖 Palio	Strolling Musicians	🍎🍎🍎	★	★★★♥	
Shula's Steakhouse		🍎	★	★	
Victoria & Albert's	Harpist	🍎	★	★★★♥	
Whispering Canyon Cafe	Humor	🍎	★★★	★★	BLD
Yacht Club Galley		🍎🍎	★	★	B
🎖 Yachtsman Steakhouse		🍎	★	★★	

RESTAURANT GUIDES

Features: Restaurants at the Attractions

Restaurant	Entertainment	Vegetarian Choices	Popular with Kids	Theming	All You Care to Eat Meals
Biergarten	German Folk Show	🍎🍎	★	★★★	LD
Big River Grille & Brewing Works		🍎🍎	★	★	
Bistro de Paris		🍎	★	★★★♥	
🏅 Bongos Cuban Cafe	Live Mambo	🍎🍎	★★	★★★	
Cap'n Jack's Restaurant		🍎	★	★	
Chefs de France		🍎🍎	★	★★★	
Cinderella's Royal Table	Character Breakfast	🍎🍎	★★★	★★★	B
Coral Reef Restaurant	Aquarium	🍎🍎	★★	★★★	
The Crystal Palace	Character Meals	🍎🍎🍎	★★★	★★	BLD
ESPN Club	Sports Broadcasts	🍎🍎	★★	★	
🏅 50's Prime Time Cafe	Humor	🍎🍎	★★	★★★	
Flying Fish Café		🍎🍎🍎	★	★★★	
🏅 Fulton's Crab House		🍎	★	★★★	
The Garden Grill Restaurant	Character Meals	🍎🍎	★★★	★★★	BLD
🏅 Hollywood & Vine	Character Meals	🍎🍎🍎	★★★	★	BLD
🏅 The Hollywood Brown Derby	Pianist	🍎🍎	★	★★★♥	
🏅 House of Blues	Live Jazz	🍎🍎	★	★★★	
🏅 Le Cellier Steakhouse		🍎🍎	★	★★	
Liberty Tree Tavern	Character Dinner	🍎🍎🍎	★★★ D	★★	D
L'Originale Alfredo Ristorante	Singing Waiters	🍎🍎🍎	★	★★★	
🏅 Mama Melrose's		🍎🍎🍎	★	★★	
Nine Dragons		🍎🍎	★	★★★	
Official All Star Cafe	Sports Broadcasts	🍎🍎	★★	★★	
Planet Hollywood		🍎🍎🍎	★★	★★★	
The Plaza Restaurant		🍎🍎	★	★	
🏅 Portobello Yacht Club		🍎🍎	★	★★	
🏅 Rainforest Cafe	Interior Theming	🍎🍎🍎	★★★	★★★	
🏅 Restaurant Akershus		🍎🍎	★	★	LD
🏅 Restaurant Marrakesh	Belly Dancers	🍎🍎	★	★★★	
🏅 Restaurantosaurus	Character Breakfast	🍎🍎🍎	★★★	★	B
🏅 Rose & Crown Dining Room		🍎🍎	★	★★	
🏅 San Angel Inn Restaurante		🍎🍎	★	★★★♥	
🏅 Sci-Fi Dine-In Theater	Movie Watching	🍎🍎	★★★	★★★	
Spoodles		🍎🍎🍎	★	★	B
Tempura Kiku		🍎🍎	★	★	
Teppanyaki Dining Room	Tableside Chefs	🍎🍎	★	★★	
Tony's Town Square Restaurant		🍎	★★★	★★★	
Wildhorse Saloon	Country Western Dancing	🍎🍎	★	★★	
🏅 Wolfgang Puck Cafe		🍎🍎🍎	★	★★	

Restaurant Price Categories

VALUE

Many Entrees Priced Under $15

Page	Restaurants	Meals
214	Beaches & Cream	B L D
217	Coral Cafe 🔖	B L D
183	ESPN Club	· L D
217	Garden Grove Cafe	B L ·
196	Official All-Star Cafe	· L D
197	Planet Hollywood	· L D
198	The Plaza Restaurant	B L D
203	Restaurantosaurus	B L D

MODERATE

Most Dinner Entrees Priced Between $15 and $25

Page	Restaurants	Meals
214	Baskervilles 🔖	B L D
175	Big River Grille & Brewing Works	· L D
174	Biergarten 🔖	· L D
215	Boma – Flavors of Africa 🔖	B · D
216	Captain's Tavern	· · D
216	Concourse Steakhouse	B L D
184	50's Prime Time Cafe	· L D
217	Finn's Grill	· · D
187	The Garden Grill Restaurant 🔖	B L D
217	Grand Floridian Cafe	B L D
188	Hollywood & Vine 🔖	B L D
190	House of Blues	B L D
218	Kona Cafe	B L D
194	Mama Melrose's Ristorante Italiano	· L D
220	Olivia's Cafe	B L D
220	The Outback	· · D
200	Rainforest Cafe at Animal Kingdom	B L D
200	Rainforest Cafe at Downtown Disney	· L D
201	Restaurant Akershus 🔖	· L D
204	Rose & Crown Dining Room	· L D
205	San Angel Inn Restaurante	· L D
206	Sci-Fi Dine-In Theater Restaurant	· L D
208	Tempura Kiku	· L D
210	Tony's Town Square Restaurant	B L D
211	Wildhorse Saloon	· L D
212	Wolfgang Puck Cafe	· L D
221	Whispering Canyon Cafe 🔖	B L D

🔖 *Indicate buffets or all-you-care-to-eat plates at most meals.*

PRICEY

Most Dinner Entrees Priced Between $25 and $40

Page	Restaurants	Meals
214	Artist Point	B · D
176	Bistro de Paris	· · D
215	Boatwright's Dining Hall	B · D
177	Bongos Cuban Cafe	· L D
215	California Grill	· · D
215	Cape May Cafe 🔖	B · D
178	Cap'n Jack's Restaurant	· L D
179	Chefs de France	· L D
216	Chef Mickey's 🔖	B L D
216	Citricos	· · D
180	Cinderella's Royal Table	B L D
181	Coral Reef Restaurant	· L D
182	The Crystal Palace 🔖	B L D
185	Flying Fish Café	· · D
186	Fulton's Crab House	· · D
218	Gulliver's Grill	· · D
189	The Hollywood Brown Derby	· L D
218	Jiko – The Cooking Place	· · D
218	Juan & Only's	· · D
191	Le Cellier Steakhouse	· L D
192	Liberty Tree Tavern 🔖	· L D
193	L'Originale Alfredo di Roma	· L D
219	Maya Grill	B · D
219	Narcoossee's	· · D
195	Nine Dragons Restaurant	· L D
219	1900 Park Fare 🔖	B L D
219	'Ohana 🔖	· · D
220	Palio	· · D
199	Portobello Yacht Club	· L D
202	Restaurant Marrakesh	· L D
207	Spoodles	B L D
209	Teppanyaki Dining Room	· L D
221	Yacht Club Galley	B L D
221	Yachtsman Steakhouse	· · D

OVER-THE-TOP

Big Ticket Dining Experience

Page	Restaurants	Meals
214	Arthur's 27	· · D
220	Shula's Steakhouse	· · D
221	Victoria & Albert's	· · D

AIRPORT TRANSPORTATION

There are a quite a few transportation choices from the Orlando Airport to Walt Disney World. If you are not planning to rent a car, your options include taxis, shuttles, limousines, and towncars. The table below compares these services, their cost, and convenience. See page 32 for rental car information.

	SHUTTLE VAN	TAXI	TOWNCAR	LIMOUSINE
Service	These large vans can carry up to nine passengers. They shuttle between the airport and Walt Disney World. The ride is shared by others and there may be several stops along the way.	Sedan taxis can carry up to four passengers. Minivan cabs can carry up to six persons. They are available by baggage claim, curbside.	The term "towncar" refers to a Lincoln Towncar, a luxury sedan that can carry up to five passengers. Drivers meet passengers in the baggage claim area, or at the gate for a fee.	Limousines can carry from six to ten passengers. Drivers meet passengers at the gate by request or in the baggage claim area.
Cost	About $17 one-way per adult ($12 for children) from the airport to Walt Disney World. The driver is tipped if he handles your luggage (about a dollar per bag is customary).	About $50 one-way from the airport to Walt Disney World, plus Florida tolls (about $3). Gratuity is normally about 15 percent of the fare.	About $50 one-way, $90 round trip between the airport and the Disney resorts ($5 more to the Magic Kingdom resorts). Gratuity is normally about 15 percent; or 20 percent for meet and greet at your gate, or for a grocery stop.	Six passenger limos cost about $100 one-way from the airport to Walt Disney World; about $150 for a ten passenger limo. A 20 percent gratuity is normal, and often added to the bill. Some include grocery stops.
Notes	No reservation is necessary. A shuttle van may take well over an hour to arrive at your hotel The vans' route through other resorts to drop off passengers may appeal to those new to the area. Late-night shuttles are usually uncrowded. Shuttle vans service the airport and Orlando area attractions.	No reservation necessary. Vehicles may not be clean nor comfortable. Meter is time-based; a taxi may be more expensive than a Towncar during heavy traffic on I-4. Taxis are located outside baggage claim, making them very convenient. The minivan taxi represents the best value for five passengers.	Reservations are necessary. Some companies will include a short stop for groceries, some may tack on a small fee. Child car seats are available by request. Late model towncars are smaller than previous years. A family of five may find the long ride less comfortable than expected. This holds true for groups of four adults as well.	Reservations are necessary. Some companies will include a short stop for groceries, some will add a fee. Child car seats are available by request. Limos offer comfort, legroom, privacy, audio/visual consoles, luggage space, and of course, status. Some even offer video games and a laptop for checking e-mail.
Advice	Traveling alone? Low on cash? Not in a hurry? Shuttle vans may be a good option for you. May not be a good value for groups or 3 or more.	This is the best option for those who arrive without prior arrangements and would like to get to Walt Disney World quickly and efficiently.	Towncars are priced about the same as a taxi, but are usually cleaner, smoother, and slightly roomier. Good value for families of up to four passengers.	This is the most luxurious option and a good value for groups. For six passengers, it works out to about $20 per person.

Airport Transportation Providers

These Orlando transportation companies have been favorably reviewed by Readers at our Disney vacation planning online community:

www.Readers.Clubhouse.com

Limousine Services:
Happy Limousine	888 394-4277
Atlantis Limousine	407 592-7433
Advantage Limousine	800 438-4114

Towncar Services:
Atlantis Towncar	407 592-7433
Happy Towncar	888 394-4277
Tiffany Towncar	888 838-2161
Ann's Towncar Service	888 657-0936

Luxury SUV and Large Vans:
Atlantis Vans	407 592-7433

Taxis and Shuttle Vans:
Mears Transportation	407 423-5566

Driving Directions to Walt Disney World

There are two routes, both are toll roads. The northern route is more scenic with its many entertaining billboards. It passes near Universal Studios. The southern route is best suited for those heading to Epcot, Magic Kingdom, and Animal Kingdom resort areas. The southern route also avoids the heavy traffic on Interstate 4 during rush hours.

Airport North

To State Road 528 – West (Bee Line Expressway).
To Interstate 4 – West – to Walt Disney World.
(For Universal Studios, take Interstate 4 – East.)
Use the exit for your Disney destination.

Airport South

To State Route 417 – South (Central Florida Greeneway).
To State Road 536 – West.
Enter Walt Disney World.
Follow the signs to your Disney destination.

Interstate 4 Exits

Each Florida interstate exit has two numbers. The new exit numbers are based on the mile marker standard and replace the old arbitrary numbering system. Here are exits to Walt Disney World (listed from north-east to south-west on Interstate 4).

Old – **27** New – **68** (to SR 535)

Downtown Disney, Hotel Plaza, Disney Institute, Crossroads Shopping Center.

Old – **26B** New – **67B**

Epcot Resorts, Disney's BoardWalk, Port Orleans, and Old Key West Resorts.

Old – **25B** New – **64B** (to US 192 W)

Magic Kingdom Resorts, Animal Kingdom Resorts, Disney's Wide World of Sports.

Essentials

Attractions

Hotels

Restaurants

Special Events

Recreation

Resources

Transportation • Restaurant Guides • Hotel Guides • Vacation Packages • Discounts • Admissions • Month by Month • Crowds & Weather • The World at a Glance • Read Me First

DRIVING AROUND WALT DISNEY WORLD

Do You Need a Rental Car?
Will Disney Transportation Do?

Do you plan to visit other attractions located outside Walt Disney World ?

YES / **NO**

Will you be staying on Walt Disney World property?

NO

Rent a car.

YES

Will you be staying at an Epcot Resort or a resort on the Monorail?
(See *Hotel Locations,* page 24.)

NO / **YES**

Do you plan to visit primarily theme parks that charge admission?

NO

YES

Disney transportation was designed for you. There is no need to rent a car.

Which statement best describes you?

"Planning to visit many areas and eager to make every moment of my vacation count."

"Eager to stretch my vacation dollar and don't mind occasional long waits or bus transfers."

Consider renting a car or using taxis when convenient.

You can use Disney transportation as your primary option.

Car Rentals: In Orlando, the greatest convenience is offered by car rental agencies that have their vehicles located inside the airport. **Avis, Budget, Dollar, and National have cars inside the airport terminal**. The off-site agencies shuttle renters to a remote location but do not necessarily offer better rates, cars, or service. **Agencies with remotely located cars include Alamo, Hertz, and Thrifty**. All of the above agencies, except Hertz, also have car rentals at Walt Disney World: **National** (at the Walt Disney World Dolphin and at the Car Care Center near the Magic Kingdom), **Avis** (Hilton Resort), **Budget** (DoubleTree Guest Suites), **Dollar** (Courtyard by Marriott), **Alamo** (Wyndham Palace Resort & Spa), and **Thrifty** (Grosvenor Resort). Cars rented on Disney property may be returned to the agency's airport location (either remote or inside the terminal) at no additional charge. If your rental car requires service, call the agency for assistance. Except for Hertz, all agencies offer convenient on-property vehicle service or exchange.

Walt Disney World Resort Transportation: The Walt Disney World transportation system is impressive. Comprised of nearly 22 miles of monorail track and hundreds of buses and boats, the system is designed to minimize the need for cars. In some cases, it succeeds (see sidebar). Some Disney transportation options are attractions unto themselves. Riding the Monorail is considered by many to be an integral part of the Disney experience. The water taxi voyage to the Downtown Disney resorts is charming, and the ferries to the Magic Kingdom resorts are a magical way to end the day. Disney transportation is not always convenient or timely, but it is free and designed to shuttle resort guests to Disney's most popular attractions.

Taxis within Walt Disney World: For parties of four or less, taxis provide the flexibility of a car without the expense of renting or the inconvenience of parking. Taxis are readily available at all resorts and at the taxi stands outside all of the theme parks. A sample taxi fare from Port Orleans to the Hoop-Dee-Doo Revue is about $15 and will take about 10 minutes. The same trip on a Disney bus, although free, may take up to two hours. Other sample taxi fares include:

Disney's Caribbean Beach Resort to Downtown Disney — about $7
Disney's Wilderness Lodge to Disney's BoardWalk — about $12
Disney's Port Orleans Resort to Blizzard Beach — about $9.

Resort Parking: All resorts have free parking lots, but not always within convenient walking distance. The better resorts also offer valet parking services. At the Disney-owned resorts, valet parking is free. The independently operated resorts charge up to $10 for valet parking.

Tipping Tip: The customary gratuity is two dollars to the retrieving valet. Drivers requesting special care for their vehicle also tip the receiving valet in an amount commensurate with the expectation of service.

Theme Park Parking: It costs about $6 per day to park at the major theme parks. The parking lots are serviced by trams to the main entrance. One paid parking voucher is good all day at any theme park. Parking is free for guests who are staying at a Walt Disney World resort; just show your resort vehicle pass at the lot's main gate.

Automobile Fuel and Service: Walt Disney World has three refueling stations: the Car Care Center near the Magic Kingdom, a gas station across from Pleasure Island (with a 24 hour mini-mart), and service station near Disney's BoardWalk (with a mini-mart and car wash). The Car Care Center near the Magic Kingdom offers fuel, towing, and repairs (407 824-0976). Complimentary shuttles are provided to the resorts and theme parks while cars are being serviced. National Car Rental is also located here. ◆

Essentials

Magic Kingdom • Future World • World Showcase • Disney-MGM Studios • Animal Kingdom • Typhoon Lagoon • Blizzard Beach • Downtown Disney • Disney's BoardWalk • Fort Wilderness & River Country

Attractions

Hotels

Restaurants

Special Events

Recreation

Resources

ATTRACTIONS

**Theme Parks, Recreation Areas, and Entertainment Destinations:
Creating Your Own Amazing Tours and Magical Adventures**

The Attractions section explores all of the theme parks and entertainment areas inside Walt Disney World. It is filled with touring ideas and insider tips to help you plan tours and visit areas that meet your own special interests and vacation style. Combined with the Fun Factor Ratings and the E.A.R.S. Awards lists, you'll find everything you need to plan the best possible Disney vacation for you and your family and friends.

FUN FACTOR

Low ← POPULARITY → High

Tots
Kids
Teens
Adult
Mature

Fun Factor Ratings: On a typical vacation, you will have time to experience only a small part of what Walt Disney World has to offer. What's important is that you make your vacation as rewarding as possible by spending time in lines only for those attractions you will truly enjoy. The ratings below are designed to help you select attractions that match your interests and get the most enjoyment for the time and money you will spend.

FastPass: With the creation of Disney's FastPass system, forced-march tours that have you racing from attraction to attraction are a thing of the past. Now it is possible to tour themed areas at your leisure, then bypass the long lines at the most popular attractions and walk right on. Just go to the FastPass Machine for an appointment to ride and then explore, shop, sightsee, and take in other, less-crowded attractions nearby. Now you can experience more than ever before and no longer waste time in long lines. (Tip: FastPass works especially well during the busiest times of day.)

E.A.R.S. Tours: Throughout the attractions section, you will find sidebars with our E.A.R.S. Awards (see *"Expert Advisor Ratings System,"* page 9). Selected by a group of the nation's leading Disney experts, these are the best of the best attractions, dining, and entertainment events. If this is your first trip, or you only have a day in the park, plan the itinerary of your tour to include as many E.A.R.S. picks as possible. Incorporating these "must-sees" can really help you experience the theme parks fully. ◆

When Are There No Lines?

From Disney's point of view, no lines means that there are too many employees operating rides for too few visitors. Theme parks do not operate profitably when that happens, so adjustments are made throughout the year to ensure that the lines remain. Park hours are shortened, rides are operated with fewer vehicles, and some are closed for rehab.

There will almost always be lines, and that shouldn't concern you. Keep in mind, it's not the length of the lines, it's how much time you spend standing in them. Learn how to work with lines and minimize the waits. Here are some tips that can help you avoid waiting in long lines:

● Preplan your tour of the attractions. Don't waste time figuring it out after you arrive.

● Note parade and show times. The attractions near the show will have shorter lines during the performance.

● Take advantage of FastPass tickets for the attractions that offer it.

● Each day a different theme park offers "early entry" to Disney resort guests. Arrive at the park half hour before early entry time. Go directly to the most popular attraction on your list that does not have FastPass.

● If you are not using Early Entry privileges, avoid *that* park for that day. It will become very crowded.

● Eat when the restaurants are empty, ride when the restaurants are full.

● Discard the mentality that you *must* ride as many attractions as you can to get your money's worth. The best parts of each theme park are between the attractions.

● Consult the Fun Factor Ratings and be certain that any ride with a wait longer than 30 minutes is your type of ride. Consider riding any attraction you've never been on before, if there is no line at all. ◆

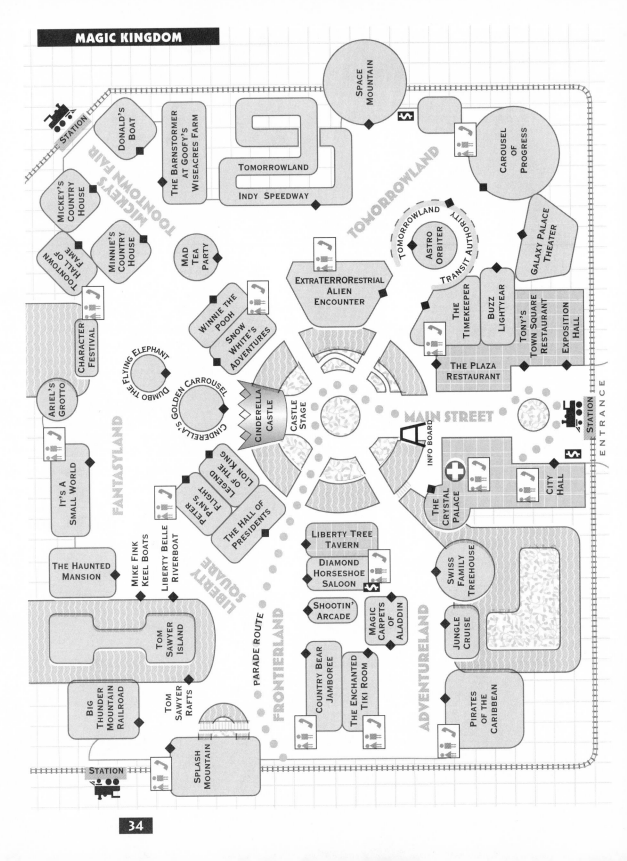

STATION

DONALD'S BOAT

THE BARNSTORMER AT GOOFY'S WISEACRES FARM

TOMORROWLAND INDY SPEEDWAY

SPACE MOUNTAIN

CAROUSEL OF PROGRESS

TOMORROWLAND

MICKEY'S COUNTRY HOUSE

MICKEY'S TOONTOWN FAIR

TOONTOWN HALL OF FAME

MINNIE'S COUNTRY HOUSE

MAD TEA PARTY

ExtraTERRORestrial ALIEN ENCOUNTER

TOMORROWLAND TRANSIT AUTHORITY

ASTRO ORBITER

GALAXY PALACE THEATER

THE TIMEKEEPER

BUZZ LIGHTYEAR

TONY'S TOWN SQUARE RESTAURANT

EXPOSITION HALL

CHARACTER FESTIVAL

WINNIE THE POOH

SNOW WHITE'S ADVENTURES

THE PLAZA RESTAURANT

ARIEL'S GROTTO

DUMBO THE FLYING ELEPHANT

CINDERELLA'S GOLDEN CARROUSEL

CINDERELLA CASTLE

CASTLE STAGE

MAIN STREET

STATION

ENTRANCE

IT'S A SMALL WORLD

FANTASYLAND

PETER PAN'S FLIGHT

LEGEND OF THE LION KING

THE HALL OF PRESIDENTS

INFO BOARD

THE CRYSTAL PALACE

CITY HALL

THE HAUNTED MANSION

MIKE FINK KEEL BOATS

LIBERTY BELLE RIVERBOAT

LIBERTY SQUARE

LIBERTY TREE TAVERN

DIAMOND HORSESHOE SALOON

SHOOTIN' ARCADE

MAGIC CARPETS OF ALADDIN

SWISS FAMILY TREEHOUSE

JUNGLE CRUISE

TOM SAWYER ISLAND

PARADE ROUTE

FRONTIERLAND

COUNTRY BEAR JAMBOREE

THE ENCHANTED TIKI ROOM

ADVENTURELAND

PIRATES OF THE CARIBBEAN

BIG THUNDER MOUNTAIN RAILROAD

TOM SAWYER RAFTS

SPLASH MOUNTAIN

STATION

Essentials

Magic Kingdom • Future World • World Showcase • Disney-MGM Studios • Animal Kingdom • Typhoon Lagoon • Blizzard Beach • Downtown Disney • Disney's BoardWalk • Fort Wilderness & River Country

Attractions

Hotels

Restaurants

Special Events

Recreation

Resources

THE MAGIC KINGDOM

*T*he Magic Kingdom was the first theme park built at Walt Disney World more than a quarter-century ago. It covers about one hundred acres (nearly twenty more than California's Disneyland, upon which it is based). The park opened with six themed areas: Main Street, U.S.A., Adventureland, Frontierland, Liberty Square, Fantasyland, and Tomorrowland. A seventh theme land, now called Mickey's Toontown Fair, was added to the park in 1988 and is the place where visitors can be certain to meet Disney Characters. The Magic Kingdom attractions are similar to Disneyland's, but each park has several that are unique. While Sleeping Beauty Castle is the centerpiece at Disneyland, Cinderella Castle stands at the heart of the Magic Kingdom. The Magic Kingdom holds a special enchantment for both children and adults.

ATTRACTIONS

Main Street, U.S.A.: *From the bustling Town Square at the entrance to the view of Cinderella Castle in the distance, Main Street, U.S.A., is the first environment visitors encounter in the Magic Kingdom. It is a picture-perfect turn-of-the-century town. Visitors can drop by City Hall for entertainment schedules and restaurant reservations or browse through a wide variety of specialty shops (including The Chapeau, featuring the monogrammed mouse ears made famous by the Mouseketeers, and the Main Street Athletic Shop, offering sports-themed merchandise and apparel). The Harmony Barber Shop offers haircuts for men, women, and children in an old-fashioned setting. At the center of it all is the Town Square, a pleasant plaza with benches, shade, and periodic live musical entertainment.*

City Hall Information Center: Maps, entertainment schedules, and other information are available at the podium in front of City Hall. A helpful staff inside operates a Message Center for visitors and makes reservations for resorts, guided tours, and restaurants. City Hall is also a good rendezvous point for visitors traveling in groups.

Town Square Exposition Hall: The Exposition Hall occupies a space behind the AAA Desk and the Kodak Camera Center, right next door to Tony's Town Square Restaurant. Here, visitors can mingle with Disney Characters throughout the day and tour a display of interesting artifacts from the history of Disney Animation. At the very back of the hall is an

When to Go: The least crowded times of year to visit the Magic Kingdom are while schools are in session, and not during the summer months or holidays. Even during off-peak seasons, it's a good idea to arrive early in the morning, at least one half hour before the official opening time. Crowds also thin out after 4 PM, when families with small children tend to leave.

Park Hours: During off-peak seasons (fall through spring) the Magic Kingdom closes early on weekdays (unlike Epcot), so if you're spending only one day at the Magic Kingdom, be sure to go on a weekend, especially Saturday, when the park has the longest hours, and the Nighttime Parade and Fantasy in the Sky fireworks are offered. Opening, closing, and event times vary throughout the year, so be sure to check ahead with Disney Information (407 824-4321).

FUN FACTOR			
Low ← POPULARITY → High			
Tots			
Kids			
Teens			
Adult			
Mature			

⭐ Premier Attractions

🧍 Height Requirement

Essentials · Attractions · Hotels · Restaurants · Special Events · Recreation · Resources

Fort Wilderness & River Country · Disney's BoardWalk · Downtown Disney · Blizzard Beach · Typhoon Lagoon · Animal Kingdom · Disney-MGM Studios · World Showcase · Future World · **Magic Kingdom**

MAGIC KINGDOM

See the "Essentials" section for ticket costs and attraction updates.

How to Get There: The vast Magic Kingdom parking lot is free to guests staying at any Walt Disney World resort (other visitors are charged about $6). The parking lot is serviced by trams that carry visitors to the Transportation and Ticket Center (TTC), a hub for much of Walt Disney World transportation. Water launches and monorails transport visitors from the TTC to the park entrance. Water launches also service the Magic Kingdom from the following resorts: Wilderness Lodge, Fort Wilderness, Polynesian, and Grand Floridian. Sleek monorails that glide overhead on nearly fourteen miles of track connect the Magic Kingdom to the following resorts: Contemporary, Polynesian, and Grand Floridian. Monorails also run between the TTC and Epcot. Buses travel between the Magic Kingdom and all Walt Disney World resorts and theme parks.

In-Park Transportation: Many unique transportation options are available in the Magic Kingdom. Visitors can travel down Main Street in horse-drawn trolleys, bell-clanging fire trucks, jitneys, and purring antique cars. The steam-powered trains of the Walt Disney World Railroad circle the park continuously picking up passengers at Main Street, U.S.A., Frontierland, and Mickey's Toontown Fair. ◆

air-conditioned movie theater with comfortable seats, showing continuous old-style Disney cartoons. It's an excellent place for visitors to simply sit down and cool off on a hot summer's day.

Walt Disney World Railroad   Four open-air rail-cars, pulled by whistle-blowing, steam-puffing engines, travel the Walt Disney World Railroad on a mile-and-a-half tour of the park. Absent here is the Grand-Canyon-and-dinosaur diorama, for which the trains at California's Disneyland are noted, but this leisurely trip through the lush foliage lining the track, coupled with views of most of the theme lands, is still well worth the ride. Visitors can board or disembark at Main Street, U.S.A., as well as at Frontierland and Mickey's Toontown Fair. The trains run every 4 to 7 minutes. Duration: Approximately 20 minutes for an entire circuit around the park.

Adventureland: *At the end of Main Street, off to the left, Adventureland welcomes visitors into a tropical fantasy that is a blend of Africa, the Caribbean, Asia, the South Seas, and a bit of New Orleans. The dense jungle foliage and the exotic rustles, squawks, and animal cries create a rich atmosphere for the attractions located here.*

The Enchanted Tiki Room   In the most recent version of this long-lived attraction, the familiar cast of singing birds is joined by the feathered stars of two more recent Disney animated features, namely, Iago from *Aladdin* and Zazu from *The Lion King*. The bird show gets hip to modern times with an updated roster of sing-along tunes. Die-hard fans of this attraction can still count on the presence of a satisfying selection of groan-eliciting puns. This was the first Disney attraction to use Audio-Animatronics figures, and the dimly lit lodge is always a pleasant place to relax and cool off on a hot day. Duration: 20 minutes.

The Magic Carpets of Aladdin: The enticing colors and exotic architecture of the Middle East are a wonderful addition to Adventureland. The Magic Carpets of Aladdin is based on the Disney animated feature and enhanced with music from the film. Not unlike Dumbo and Astro Orbiter, visitors riding in magic carpet vehicles circle a Genie lamp centerpiece. Whimsical camels occasionally spray, but the adroit can fly their carpets up and down and stay dry. While the ride is definitely for the young at heart, the surrounding shopping bazaar provides a truly atmospheric diversion.

Jungle Cruise   A lighthearted reminder of the Bogart-Hepburn classic film *The African Queen,* this boat ride attraction takes visitors on a steamy adventure cruise down some of the world's great rivers — the Amazon, Congo, Nile, and Mekong — with a detour through the cavernous interior of a mysterious Asian temple. Guides deliver witty, pun-laced narrations about the rivers and jungles, all the while "protecting" visitors from the local hostiles and wild animals. Exotic jungle plants, cascading waterfalls, Audio-Animatronics figures, and amusing special effects all add up to a truly comic adventure. Duration: 9 minutes.

⭐ **Pirates of the Caribbean** This popular attraction begins in the underground catacombs of a mysterious stone fortress, where visitors board boats for a ride through a coastal settlement under siege by a band of raucous, rum-sotted pirates. After floating through dimly lit passages with unexpected drops (some in complete darkness), visitors are treated to humorous vignettes of attacking ships with shots exploding overhead, buildings on fire, rooms heaped with treasure, and high-spirited drunken debauchery. The elaborate sets, rich costuming, and sophisticated Audio-Animatronics and special effects make this a must-see attraction. Duration: 9 minutes.

Swiss Family Treehouse This multilevel walk-through attraction invites visitors to tour the home of the storybook ship-wrecked family. Built into a giant replica of a banyan tree draped with Spanish moss, this is the ultimate fantasy treehouse, complete with cozy bedrooms perched in the limbs and an intricate plumbing system that provides running water in every room. There are many stairs to climb and almost always lots of kids enthusiastically exploring the novel rustic abode. Duration: Approximately 15 to 20 minutes.

Frontierland: *Just around the corner from Adventureland lies the rough-and-tumble American frontier of the nineteenth century, the world of Davy Crockett, Mark Twain, and the miners of the Gold Rush. Here, stone, clapboard, and split-log structures evoke the distinct frontier settings of the East, the Midwest, and the Southwest. Two of the Magic Kingdom's thrill rides are located in Frontierland.*

⭐ **Big Thunder Mountain Railroad** On this roller-coaster ride, visitors travel through a Gold Rush–era mining town on what quickly becomes a runaway train. The roller coaster relies on side-to-side, rather than up-and-down motion, but it is fast nonetheless. Creative special effects and scenery, including crashing rocks, rushing waterfalls, flapping bats, braying donkeys, and a flooded mining town make for a lively experience. The ride can be particularly enchanting at night. Duration: 4 minutes. Height requirement is 40 inches.

Country Bear Jamboree Nearly two dozen fun-loving, Audio-Animatronics bears participate in the lively antics at this performance in Grizzly Hall. Henry, the show's emcee, introduces the bears who tell tall tales, crack corny jokes, and perform musical numbers. The show and decor are changed throughout the year to reflect seasonal holidays. Duration: 15 minutes.

Full-Service Restaurants

Restaurant reservations may be made between 60 and 120 days in advance by all Walt Disney World visitors. Same-day reservations can be made at City Hall. No alcoholic beverages are served in the Magic Kingdom. See the "Restaurants" section for complete reviews and reservation information.

Main Street, U.S.A.

Tony's Town Square Restaurant — The menu of this spacious restaurant, with a sunny glassed-in patio and pleasant Victorian-style Lady and the Tramp decor, offers waffles, eggs, and pancakes in the morning, and pasta, pizza, and other Italian dishes throughout the day. Espresso and cappuccino are served. Open for breakfast, lunch, and dinner; reservations suggested.

The Plaza Restaurant — This light and airy restaurant with pleasant, fanciful, Art Nouveau decor is generally busy throughout the day. The menu features a selection of hot entrees, sandwiches, hamburgers, salads, and ice cream specialties. Espresso, cappuccino, and cafe mocha are served. Open for lunch and dinner; no reservations are accepted. ➤

Essentials · Attractions · Hotels · Restaurants · Special Events · Recreation · Resources

Fort Wilderness & River Country · Disney's BoardWalk · Blizzard Beach · Downtown Disney · Typhoon Lagoon · Animal Kingdom · Disney-MGM Studios · World Showcase · Future World · **Magic Kingdom**

MAGIC KINGDOM

See the "Essentials" section for ticket costs and attraction updates.

Main Street, U.S.A.

The Crystal Palace — This replica of a Victorian conservatory, with a circular atrium and skylights throughout, offers all-you-care-to-eat buffet-style Character Meals. At breakfast, egg dishes, French toast, and a breakfast lasagna are offered. Lunch includes soups, salads, pastas, and sandwiches. At dinner, chicken, beef, fish, and pasta dishes are offered. Open for breakfast, lunch, and dinner; reservations suggested.

Liberty Square

Liberty Tree Tavern — With its low lighting, plank floors, and giant fireplace, this friendly restaurant has a comfortable colonial ambience. At lunch, the menu features New England clam chowder, large salads, roast turkey, and sandwiches. Dinner is a Character Meal; entrees include traditionally prepared chicken, steak, and ham. Open for lunch and dinner; reservations required.

Fantasyland

Cinderella's Royal Table — High up in Cinderella Castle, this restaurant has a medieval elegance and fantasy decor. Cinderella herself drops in from time to time. Breakfast is a Character Meal, which includes egg dishes, banana French toast, fruit, and potato casserole. Well-prepared salads, sandwiches, roast beef, seafood, and chicken dishes are served at lunch and dinner. Open all day; reservations required. ◆

Frontierland Railroad Station With its open boarding platform and large wooden water tank, this rustic Old West railroad station artfully creates the ambience of nineteenth-century train travel. Of the three stops on the Walt Disney World Railroad, this one is the busiest. Duration: Approximately 20 minutes for the entire circuit.

Frontierland Shootin' Arcade This noisy arcade puts an electronic spin on the traditional carnival shooting gallery. Using replica buffalo rifles (fitted with infrared beams instead of bullets), visitors shoot at frontier-motif targets in a Tombstone Territory setting. Through the magic of special effects, "hit" targets twist, howl, or trigger a secondary humorous effect. Don't spend too long aiming; there are no prizes, and rifles are programmed to provide a specified number of either shots or minutes of service, whichever comes first. Kids flock to this arcade, which requires spending money in the form of small change. Duration: 25 shots for 50 cents.

⭐ 👫 **Splash Mountain**  The theme of this water-chute roller coaster comes from the Disney animated classic, *Song of the South*. Amid the antics of Brer Rabbit, Brer Fox, Brer Bear, and their friends, visitors are swept along in log boats on a half-mile journey through bayous, gardens, swamps, and caves. Sudden unexpected drops (some in complete darkness) and slow, lazy drifts alternately startle and lull visitors. However, when they confront Brer Fox, in a quandary about throwing Brer Rabbit into the briar patch, the ride goes downhill, literally, plunging almost five stories to splash into the giant briar patch below. The outstanding Audio-Animatronics and sets in this attraction, as well as the pacing and sound track, show Disney wizardry at its most creative. Expect to get fairly wet on the ride. As for visitors who have stopped to watch the action from the bridge above, every third ride vehicle splashes a cascade of water over the chute's edge to drench them. Souvenir photos of riders are snapped during the plunge. Duration: 12 minutes. Height requirement is 40 inches.

Tom Sawyer Island The island captures the mood of the Missouri frontier where Mark Twain's famed character, Tom Sawyer, was a boy. The woodsy setting inspires the imaginations of youngsters with plenty of energy to burn. Ferried back and forth to the island on rafts, visitors can spelunk in a spooky cave, wobble across a barrel bridge, trek the winding paths, inspect a working windmill and waterwheel, and explore the Fort Sam Clemens stockade. The island is often filled with free-wheeling children, but in the late afternoon, Aunt Polly's Dockside Inn is a pleasant place for light snacks and a relaxing interlude. The island closes at sundown. No time limit.

Liberty Square:

In Liberty Square, visitors discover a New England town at the time of the American Revolution. The buildings are accurate in architectural detail, right down to their leather-hinged shutters hanging slightly askew. A reproduction of the Liberty Bell, cast at the same foundry as the original, hangs in the square. A huge one-hundred-year-old live oak nearby is hung with thirteen metal lanterns representing the light of freedom in each of the original colonies.

The Hall of Presidents

The show opens with a 70mm film (narrated by author Maya Angelou) showcasing the U.S. Constitution and selected historical events that shaped its amendments. As the film ends, a curtain rises to reveal an Audio-Animatronics representation of all of the U.S. Presidents in a startlingly lifelike tableau. Rustles fill the air when a roll call begins, and each figure responds to his name as the others nod, turn to look, or shift restlessly. This attraction's tone is more serious than most at the Magic Kingdom, but its sophisticated Audio-Animatronics (plus the sit-down air-conditioned theater) make it worthwhile, especially for first-time visitors. Duration: 23 minutes.

⭐ The Haunted Mansion

By far the most popular attraction in Liberty Square can be found inside this eighteenth-century red-brick mansion, which creaks, groans, and moans with eerie sounds. Visitors pass by a town graveyard with wretchedly punned tombstone epitaphs, to be welcomed into the house by a creepy, supercilious butler and led into a waiting area decorated with some very unusual family portraits. Visitors then board ride vehicles that carry them off on a dark and spooky tour of the mansion. Ghosts dance while rattles, rustles, and screams fill the air. Quirky humor permeates the ongoing narration. The many clever sets and props and unusual visual effects make The Haunted Mansion a favorite attraction for many visitors. Duration: 9 minutes.

Liberty Belle Riverboat

The *Liberty Belle,* a replica steam-powered stern-wheeler, actually rides on an underwater rail as it ferries visitors on a pleasant, sedate journey around Tom Sawyer Island. The frontier scenes, circa 1850, include a burning cabin, Fort Sam Clemens, and pioneering tableaus along the shore. The boat leaves on the hour and the half hour. Occasionally, Disney Characters board the ship and mingle with visitors. Duration: 20 minutes.

Mike Fink Keelboats

The rustic squat boats on this water ride take visitors on a backwoods journey. Like the *Liberty Belle* riverboat, the keelboats circle Tom Sawyer Island, gliding past various riverbank sights that tell the legends of the pioneers who settled the frontier. This attraction operates when the weather is warm and closes at sundown. Duration: 20 minutes.

See the "Essentials" section for ticket costs and attraction updates.

Counter-Service Restaurants

In addition to the full-service restaurants, there is a large variety of surprisingly good and relatively inexpensive dining options in the Magic Kingdom. Many of these smaller eateries are also wonderful places to take a break, reunite your party for lunch or dinner, and enjoy different types of scenery and settings. Most of the lands in the Magic Kingdom have at least one good spot for a light meal or snack break.

Main Street, U.S.A.

Main Street Bake Shop — This old-fashioned cafe-style area is near the end of Main Street on the right, facing Cinderella Castle. It's excellent for a mid-morning stop, or a quick, light breakfast for those who jumped out of bed and ran to the park. The food choices are all delicious baked goods, which produce almost hypnotic aromas that waft all around the restaurant area — cakes, pies, croissants, cinnamon rolls, cookies, and tarts. Coffee, soft drinks, espresso, and cappuccino are also served. At particularly busy times, there is often a very short line to the right that leads to an express window with more limited (but still wonderful) choices. ➤

Essentials • Attractions • Hotels • Restaurants • Special Events • Recreation • Resources

Magic Kingdom • Future World • World Showcase • Disney-MGM Studios • Animal Kingdom • Typhoon Lagoon • Blizzard Beach • Downtown Disney • Disney's BoardWalk • Fort Wilderness & River Country

Essentials

Attractions

Hotels

Restaurants

Special Events

Recreation

Resources

Fort Wilderness & River Country • Downtown Disney • Disney's BoardWalk • Blizzard Beach • Typhoon Lagoon • Animal Kingdom • Disney-MGM Studios • Future World • World Showcase • Magic Kingdom

MAGIC KINGDOM

See the "Essentials" section for ticket costs and attraction updates.

Main Street, U.S.A.

Casey's Corner — Casey's serves the best hot dogs at Walt Disney World. Casey's is an old-fashioned, baseball-themed corner at the end of Main Street on the left, with a pleasant outdoor seating area perfect for people-watching. The menu offers hot dogs, skin-on French fries, soft drinks, and coffee. Guests can load their hot dog with toppings from a self-serve condiment bar.

Adventureland

El Pirata y el Perico — This stand serves sandwiches, snacks, and the only tacos in the Magic Kingdom, which visitors can enjoy at nearby umbrella-shaded tables. Visitors who want something different from other members of their party will find a cart serving eggrolls located directly across from the seating area.

Liberty Square

Columbia Harbour House — This American Colonial–styled restaurant with old-world thick glass windows is located between Fantasyland and Liberty Square, just across from the Haunted Mansion. Visitors descend into a cool and inviting interior with stone floors and sturdy wood furnishings. The menu is varied, with chicken and fish baskets, deli sandwiches, salads, and the restaurant's signature clam chowder. ➤

Fantasyland: *A potpourri of carousel horses, colorful banners, wacky rides, and fairy-tale encounters, Fantasyland is the theme land that best reflects the young-at-heart side of Walt Disney's imagination. The appealing Alpine-village setting with its half-timbered buildings and festive tentlike structures spreads out behind Cinderella Castle, the Magic Kingdom's beautiful centerpiece. Although most of the attractions in Fantasyland are designed with children in mind, visitors of all ages will enjoy taking in the sights.*

Ariel's Grotto   This small walkthrough pavilion portrays Ariel's underwater home from the Disney movie, *The Little Mermaid*. Colorful anemones and sea creatures perched on large rocks squirt visitors as they walk on the padded surface, and Ariel herself makes frequent appearances inside a rocky cave. No time limit.

Cinderella's Golden Carrousel   Sparkling with mirrors, gilded decorations, painted scenes from the movie *Cinderella,* and beautifully detailed horses, this elegant merry-go-round is a true classic. Riders are carried back in time in leisurely, pleasant circles. No two horses are alike, and the carrousel is especially pretty and evocative at twilight. Duration: 2 minutes.

Dumbo the Flying Elephant   Aboard this simple, charming, and colorful ride, visitors in sixteen big-eared Dumbo-shaped gondolas circle slowly with gentle lifts and drops around a golden crown. Adults can bypass this ride, but it is irresistible to the very young — and the young at heart. Duration: 2 minutes.

Fantasyland Character Festival   This is an opportunity for die-hard autograph hounds and those seeking photo opportunities to encounter Disney Characters. The characters who appear here vary, so ask the Cast Member attending the line which Characters are scheduled. There are also schedules in City Hall. Note: Small children may sometimes be frightened by the very large Characters. No time limit.

It's A Small World   Boats take visitors on a voyage through a whimsical fantasy world populated by dolls representing children of every nationality. The moving dolls, dressed in elaborate folk costumes, sing the verses to "It's A Small World" in the language of the culture they represent. Although the tune is difficult to shake off, visitors seem to come away happy (or perhaps mesmerized by the repetitive expressions of the designers' good intentions). Long lines move quickly here and during parades, you can often walk right on. On a hot day in Fantasyland, this ride can be a godsend — it's a long, relaxing air-conditioned respite. Duration: 11 minutes.

Legend of the Lion King 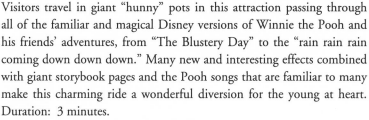 This stage show is based on the popular animated movie *The Lion King*. Visitors meet a sleepy Rafiki (the baboon, played by a live performer) and are shown the *Circle of Life* movie short before entering a sit-down theater where selected scenes from the film are re-created with Rafiki, large puppets, special effects, and animation clips. Don't sit too close — the elevated stage can partially block views. Duration: About 30 minutes.

Mad Tea Party Inspired by the book, *Alice in Wonderland,* this attraction features giant madly spinning pastel-painted teacups on a whirling ride that is not for the weak of stomach. The Mad Tea Party is a fairly simple ride that has been dressed up Disney style. Children and teens are its greatest fans. Duration: 2 minutes.

The Many Adventures of Winnie the Pooh Visitors travel in giant "hunny" pots in this attraction passing through all of the familiar and magical Disney versions of Winnie the Pooh and his friends' adventures, from "The Blustery Day" to the "rain rain rain coming down down down." Many new and interesting effects combined with giant storybook pages and the Pooh songs that are familiar to many make this charming ride a wonderful diversion for the young at heart. Duration: 3 minutes.

Peter Pan's Flight Set in Never-Never Land, this whimsical attraction takes visitors for a flight in miniature versions of Captain Hook's pirate ship. The ride starts high above the rooftops of London and dips down from time to time into settings that re-create scenes from Peter Pan. Although designed to amuse children, Peter Pan's Flight is surprisingly delightful and leaves visitors of all ages with a happy glow. Duration: 4 minutes.

Snow White's Scary Adventures Visitors ride in wooden mining cars past sets depicting scenes from the Disney animated classic. Originally designed to tell the story through Snow White's terrified eyes, the attraction was toned down to make the wicked witch less scary and include the heroine in some new, more colorful scenes. Some younger visitors find this ride through the dark a tad daunting and find little to enchant them. Duration: 2 minutes.

See the "Essentials" section for ticket costs and attraction updates.

Liberty Square

Sleepy Hollow — On the corner with views of the large Liberty Tree and the *Liberty Belle* Riverboat, this outdoor cafe features chili and sandwiches (including vegetarian fare) as well as lighter snacks. The restaurant offers a good view of the Afternoon Parade from the railside tables on the patio.

Frontierland

Pecos Bill Cafe — Tucked into the corner at the very end of Frontierland and continuing to near Pirates of the Caribbean in Adventureland, this sprawling restaurant more resembles half an Old West town than a single building. Hamburgers with fresh condiments and toppings are the specialty of the house; also served are hot dogs, wrap sandwiches, and chili cheese fries. Plenty of indoor and outdoor seating is available.

Fantasyland

Pinocchio Village Haus — Located in the center of Fantasyland, this large Bavarian–styled restaurant offers good hamburgers and cheeseburgers. Nicely appointed condiment bars are strategically placed to allow guests to create their own culinary masterpieces. For lighter meals, turkey sandwiches and pasta salads are also on the menu. A large picture window on the side overlooks the entrance to It's A Small World, where diners can watch as the ride boats are loaded. ➤

Essentials • Attractions • Hotels • Restaurants • Special Events • Recreation • Resources

Magic Kingdom • Future World • World Showcase • Disney–MGM Studios • Animal Kingdom • Typhoon Lagoon • Blizzard Beach • Downtown Disney • Disney's BoardWalk • Fort Wilderness & River Country

See the "Essentials" section for ticket costs and attraction updates.

Tomorrowland

Cosmic Ray's Starlight Cafe — This large restaurant sandwiched neatly between Tomorrowland and Fantasyland operates like a small food court. There are three large separate counter-service stations, with choices ranging from rotisserie chicken to hamburgers (including vegetarian hamburgers) to salads, soups, and wrap sandwiches. A generous condiment cart provides toppings for the hamburgers, including sautéed mushrooms and onions. Entertainment is provided in the form of the extraterrestrial lounge singer Sonny Eclipse on the AstroOrgan.

Plaza Pavilion — Showcasing what may well be one of the very best views of Cinderella Castle, this large open-air restaurant is located between Main Street and Tomorrowland. It offers simple fare, including chicken fingers, Mickey pizzas, salads, and deli-style sandwiches. Due to its location near the central hub of the Magic Kingdom, the Plaza Pavillion makes an excellent rendezvous point for groups of any size who would like to meet for a quick meal. ◆

Mickey's Toontown Fair:
Mickey's Toontown Fair is a visual feast of brightly colored buildings and tents that look as though they were cut out of a cartoon and set in a small country town. This is where Disney-Character devotees will find Mickey, Minnie, and their friends and neighbors.

Donald's Boat
Donald Duck's leaky, cartoon-like boat, the S.S. *Daisy,* is a popular play area in Mickey's Toontown. The boat spouts water from its smokestack and floats on a padded surface that spurts up fountains and squirts visitors when they step on certain spots. No time limit.

Goofy's Barnstormer
This big red barn filled with bric-a-brac, airplane parts, and amusing Audio-Animatronics chickens houses a kid-sized roller coaster with cars decorated as bright blue biplanes. This fairly mild ride is very popular with children but the wait in line can be ridiculously long for such a short-lived experience. Duration: Approximately 1 minute.

Mickey's Country House
Mickey's bright yellow house, with props and furnishings familiar to Disney cartoon lovers, is clearly the home of a sports enthusiast. Visitors exit at the rear and pass through Mickey's garden filled with whimsical and amusing plants. Just beyond is the large yellow-and-purple striped Judge's Tent, where Mickey Mouse fans have the chance to meet Mickey, take photographs, and collect autographs. No time limit.

Minnie's Country House
Hearts are everywhere at Minnie's pink-and-lavender house. The frilly furnishings and props inside the house attest to Minnie's romantic feminine nature. Visitors can hear a special message from her by pushing the button on her answering machine. When Minnie is home, visitors can meet her in the gazebo to take photographs and collect autographs. No time limit.

Toontown Hall of Fame
In this large, tentlike structure, Disney Characters appear in three classic categories: Disney Princesses, Disney Villains, and Mickey's Pals. Visitors can take photographs with the Characters and collect their autographs. Visitors can also shop for a variety of Disney collectables. No time limit.

Toontown Railroad Station
The festive circus-tent look and bright blue color of this Walt Disney World Railroad train station reflect the cartoon-fantasy setting of Mickey's Toontown Fair. Disney Characters can often be seen here greeting visitors or waving good-bye to them. Duration: Approximately 20 minutes for the entire circuit.

Essentials
Attractions
Hotels
Restaurants
Special Events
Recreation
Resources

Fort Wilderness & River Country • Disney's BoardWalk • Downtown Disney • Blizzard Beach • Typhoon Lagoon • Animal Kingdom • Disney-MGM Studios • World Showcase • Future World • **Magic Kingdom**

Tomorrowland:
The surroundings in Tomorrowland evoke an imaginary city-of-the-future as it might have been envisioned by Jules Verne and the machine-age dreamers of the past. Visitors who enter on the walkway from Main Street pass under an arch of rich-hued and jumbled metal rods, a "futuristic" element that is repeated in sculptures and building details. Sleek glass kiosks and oddly angular palm trees sprout out of the pavement. Tomorrowland's offbeat color scheme is accented by vividly colored graphics and neon lights.

Alien Encounter
During the preshow of ExtraTERRORestrial Alien Encounter, visitors are greeted with a sales pitch for XS Tech's new teletransporter. Forebodingly, a technical glitch in the demonstration slightly sizzles a cute fuzzy alien who is beamed from one cylinder to another. Visitors are then invited into the main chamber to observe a real interplanetary teletransport, where they are firmly harnessed in their seats. This demo, too, is botched, circuits blow, and an alien monster breaks loose in the darkness. Frightening sounds and scary effects attest to the monster's destructiveness. Visitors, stuck in their seats, can hear it move closer and closer, until it is so near they can feel its breath and sense it pulling at their harness. This attraction utilizes sophisticated psychological effects. It frequently terrifies young children and sensitive adolescents and delights thrill-seekers. Duration: Approximately 20 minutes. Height requirement is 44 inches.

Astro Orbiter
Gleaming color-splashed rockets spin, dip, and lift riders in circles as they rush past giant planets high above Tomorrowland. The riders are afforded a unique view of the Magic Kingdom. Though striking and imaginative, this ride is designed primarily to thrill youngsters. Duration: 2 minutes.

Buzz Lightyear's Space Ranger Spin
This extremely busy and colorful interactive attraction will delight and thrill kids of all ages. Visitors enter a world of giant toys and are instructed by none other than Buzz himself how to help defeat the Evil Emperor Zurg and his robot minions. Each space vehicle seats two, and is armed with two real laser weapons. Riders aim for the giant "Z" targets throughout the ride, and the vehicle keeps score for each occupant. Duration: 5 minutes.

Carousel of Progress
Visitors seated on a revolving turntable watch Audio-Animatronics figures depict lifestyles from the early 1900s through the not-too-distant future. In each humorous scene, the husband marvels at the age's technological advancements, while his family puts them to use with unexpected results. Carousel of Progress begins with vintage film footage of Walt Disney describing the attraction's development for the 1964 World's Fair in New York City. Duration: 22 minutes.

Services

Rest Rooms — Public rest rooms are numerous throughout the Magic Kingdom. On Main Street, the rest rooms to the right of City Hall, although crowded in the morning and evening, are relatively empty in the afternoon. Despite large crowds, there are rarely waits in the rest rooms located across from the Swiss Family Treehouse, in the breezeway between Adventureland and Frontierland. In Frontierland, the rest rooms located near the exit to Splash Mountain are generally uncrowded. In Fantasyland, the rest rooms behind the Enchanted Grove (near The Many Adventures of Winnie the Pooh) usually remain uncrowded. In Tomorrowland, the least-crowded rest rooms are those near Carousel of Progress. For quieter accommodations, Liberty Tree Tavern has rest rooms upstairs, although most restaurant rest rooms are crowded during meal-times.

Telephones — Public telephones are located near rest rooms throughout the Magic Kingdom. The least busy are those near The Crystal Palace restaurant at the end of Main Street; at the exit to Pirates of the Caribbean in Adventureland; behind the Enchanted Grove (near The Many Adventures of Winnie the Pooh) in Fantasyland; near Carousel of Progress in Tomorrowland; and at the Frontierland Railroad Station. To make quieter, air-conditioned calls, slip into a full-service restaurant (except Tony's Town Square Restaurant), where the telephones are located near the rest rooms.

Essentials · Attractions · Hotels · Restaurants · Special Events · Recreation · Resources

Magic Kingdom • Future World • World Showcase • Disney-MGM Studios • Animal Kingdom • Typhoon Lagoon • Blizzard Beach • Downtown Disney • Disney's BoardWalk • Fort Wilderness & River Country

Essentials

Attractions

Hotels

Restaurants

Special Events

Recreation

Resources

Fort Wilderness & River Country • Disney's BoardWalk • Downtown Disney • Blizzard Beach • Typhoon Lagoon • Animal Kingdom • Disney-MGM Studios • World Showcase • Future World • **Magic Kingdom**

MAGIC KINGDOM

See the "Essentials" section for ticket costs and attraction updates.

Message Center — The Message Center is located at Guest Relations in City Hall on Main Street. The Message Center is on a network also shared by Epcot, Animal Kingdom, and Disney-MGM Studios. Here, visitors can leave and retrieve messages for one another and exchange messages with companions visiting elsewhere. Anyone can phone in a message by calling 407 824-4321.

Lockers — Lockers are located on the lower level of the Main Street Railroad Station. Oversized packages may be left at Package Pickup, located outside City Hall on Main Street.

Banking — Although once provided on Main Street, there are no longer full banking services in the Magic Kingdom. Automated teller machines (ATMs) are located under the Main Street Railroad Station near the lockers, across from the Swiss Family Treehouse in Adventureland, near the Diamond Horseshoe Saloon, in the breezeway between Adventureland and Frontierland, and at the Tomorrowland Arcade.

Package Pickup — Visitors can forward their purchases free of charge to Package Pickup, located near City Hall on Main Street, and pick them up as they leave the park. Guests staying at a Walt Disney World resort can have packages delivered to their hotel.

 **Space Mountain**   This unique roller-coaster ride through the cosmos is enclosed in a huge spired and domed structure visible throughout the Magic Kingdom and beyond. The moment visitors enter the sleek spaceport's futuristic environment, they are caught up in the excitement. Once on board, they are hurtled through mostly dark space, illuminated occasionally by flashing comets, colorful bursts, and whirling galaxies. Space Mountain's distinctive special effects, the creative use of darkness, and two roller coasters running concurrently make it a must-try experience. The thrill can be taxing, however, and health restrictions and height requirements apply. Duration: 3 minutes. Height requirement is 44 inches.

The Timekeeper   In this very large theater, an intertemporal-tour planner named Timekeeper sends visitors on a wacky trip through time with his multiple-lensed assistant Nine-Eye. The results of Timekeeper's sloppy temporal technique are depicted in a Circle-Vision 360 film, which ricochets visitors through the centuries, brings them face to face with Jules Verne, and then swoops them off on a time-travel adventure. This attraction is adapted from Le Visionarium at Disneyland Paris, with the addition of Audio-Animatronics robots. The theater accommodates several hundred visitors, so waits are seldom long. Visitors must stand for the show. Duration: 18 minutes.

Tomorrowland Indy Speedway   One of the original Magic Kingdom attractions, the Speedway lets drivers get behind the wheel of miniature gasoline-powered cars that travel just about seven miles per hour along one of four parallel tracks. This noisy attraction provides thrills for young kids and a few grown men, as well. Duration: Less than 5 minutes, depending on crowd and driving speed. Height requirement is 48 inches.

Tomorrowland Transit Authority   This tram rides on an elevated track and takes visitors on an informative and relaxed narrated tour of Tomorrowland. The tram vehicles travel just about ten miles per hour above, alongside, and through several attractions, including Space Mountain. It's a terrific way for new visitors to get an overview of the Tomorrowland attractions. Duration: 10 minutes.

SPECIAL EVENTS & ENTERTAINMENT

Live entertainment events are scheduled throughout the day at the Magic Kingdom. As you enter the park, stop at City Hall and pick up a park Guidemap, which lists that day's scheduled events and times. When planning a trip, you can also call Walt Disney World Information a month or two ahead (407 824-4321).

⭐ **Afternoon Parade** This popular, large-scale extravaganza, which changes themes from time to time, is a festive Magic Kingdom treat every afternoon, usually at 3 PM. The parade features dancers and performers in beautiful and imaginative costumes. Disney Characters interact with visitors, providing mini performances along the way. The crowds are lighter along the parade route in Frontierland than on Main Street. Duration: Approximately 20 minutes.

Castle Forecourt Stage At this outdoor stage and gathering spot in front of Cinderella Castle (facing Main Street), visitors can enjoy a variety of musical and theatrical shows featuring Disney Characters from recent film releases, as well as guest artists. Pick up a park Guidemap for show times. Shows usually run about 15 minutes.

Diamond Horseshoe Saloon Songs and dances from the Gay Nineties performed by lively entertainers are the featured entertainment in this picturesque Old West saloon in Frontierland. Visitors can lounge at the long bar or sit themselves at tables scattered throughout. Shows run continuously from about 10:30 AM to 5 PM. Pick up a park Guidemap for scheduled times. Counter-service snacks, sandwiches, and beverages are available to enjoy during the show. Duration: Approximately 40 minutes.

⭐ **Fantasy in the Sky Fireworks** At selected times throughout the year, usually when Magic Kingdom hours are extended to 9 PM or later, fireworks burst above Cinderella Castle, preceded by Tinker Bell's dramatic flight across the sky from Cinderella Castle to Tomorrowland. The show is best watched from the walkway leading from Tomorrowland to Main Street, where crowds are thinner than on Main Street. Visitors interested in the fireworks only, and not Tinker Bell's flight, will find that Mickey's Toontown Fair offers an ideal, uncrowded vantage point. While the show is not an elaborate spectacle, its nostalgia value is priceless. Duration: Approximately 6 minutes.

Galaxy Palace Theater Live entertainment ranging from rock groups to brass bands to Disney Character skits is staged in this large open-air theater in Tomorrowland. These performances

See the "Essentials" section for ticket costs and attraction updates.

First Aid — The first-aid station is located just past The Crystal Palace, at the end of Main Street. Aspirin and other first-aid needs are dispensed free of charge. Over-the-counter medications are available at the Emporium on Main Street. They are not on display and must be requested at the counter.

Wheelchairs — Wheelchairs and a limited number of Electric Convenience Vehicles can be rented at the Stroller Shop, inside the Entrance Plaza. All rentals are on a first-come, first-served basis, so get there early. A guide for guests with disabilities is available at the Guest Relations window in the Entrance Plaza and at City Hall on Main Street.

Strollers — Strollers can be rented at the stroller shop, inside the entrance to the Magic Kingdom. Only single strollers are available.

Baby Care Center — This pleasant facility, located near the Crystal Palace next to First Aid, provides changing tables and rocking chairs. Diapers and other baby supplies are available for a fee.

Film Developing — Film is available at shops and kiosks throughout the Magic Kingdom. Drop-off points for express developing are at the Newsstand and the Kodak Camera Center on Main Street, at the Crow's Nest in Adventureland, at the Kodak Kiosk in Fantasyland, at Kodak's Funny Photos in Mickey's Toontown Fair, and at Geiger's Counter in Tomorrowland. Developed pictures can be picked up at the Kodak Camera Center on Main Street or be delivered to any Walt Disney World resort. ◆

Essentials

Attractions

Hotels

Restaurants

Special Events

Recreation

Resources

Fort Wilderness & River Country • Downtown Disney • Disney's BoardWalk • Blizzard Beach • Typhoon Lagoon • Animal Kingdom • Disney-MGM Studios • World Showcase • Future World • Magic Kingdom

MAGIC KINGDOM

See the "Essentials" section for ticket costs and attraction updates.

TOURING
Tips & Tricks

Early Entry: On three mornings per week (usually Monday, Thursday, and Saturday) the Magic Kingdom opens about 90 minutes early for guests staying at Walt Disney World resorts. This is a good touring strategy for early risers who want to focus their attention on attractions in Tomorrowland and Fantasyland without the long lines. In the busier months, the influx of regular visitors combined with folks taking advantage of Early Entry can make the park more crowded than usual. Late risers may want to avoid Early Entry days in the Magic Kingdom.

E-Ride Nights: On selected nights, guests staying at Walt Disney World resorts can opt to purchase a special ticket add-on (about $10), which allows them to remain in the Magic Kingdom for three hours after it closes to the general public. A maximum of five-thousand tickets is sold for an E-Ride Night (a slow day in the park draws around 25,000 visitors). This is an excellent way to enjoy the most popular rides without waiting in any lines at all. Fantasyland is closed during this time, and food service is limited.

FastPass: The FastPass system offers an alternative to waiting in long lines. At certain popular attractions, visitors can pick up FastPass tickets which allows them to return later and bypass the line. There is about a one hour delay and a one hour window when they can return to a special short line. FastPass time ranges are displayed above the attraction. While waiting, FastPass users have an opportunity to explore the area, shop, dine, or experience many of the nearby attractions with shorter lines. ◆

attract different age groups, depending on the type of show. Pick up a park Guidemap for show times. During the day, shows run about 20 minutes; evening performances, if scheduled, are usually longer.

⭐ *Nighttime Parade* On selected nights throughout the year, this magical parade of elaborate, brilliantly lit floats wends its way through the Magic Kingdom. Twinkling lights dance in perfect synchronicity to original music, while illusions and special effects combine to complete the dazzling show. The parade attracts huge crowds, especially along Main Street, where viewers gather as much as an hour before it begins. The parade is best watched from Frontierland or Liberty Square, where the crowds are thinner. On busy nights when the parade is held twice, the earlier one attracts the largest crowd, shortening many of the lines at the attractions. The later one attracts smaller crowds, and it's easier to find a good viewing spot. Duration: Approximately 18 minutes.

Tour: Keys to the Kingdom Departing daily from City Hall at about 10 AM, this walking tour is an informative and entertaining way for visitors to learn about the history of Walt Disney World and the Magic Kingdom, and catch a glimpse of some of the backstage areas and underground "utilidors." Attractions visited may vary with the season, but often include the Tomorrowland Transit Authority, It's A Small World, The Haunted Mansion, Country Bear Jamboree, and Pirates of the Caribbean. The tour is limited to fifteen people who must be age sixteen and over. The tour should be reserved well in advance through Walt Disney World Tours (407 939-8687). If space is available, visitors without reservations can sign up for the tour at City Hall. Cost: About $50, excluding food. Duration: 4 to 5 hours.

MAGICAL PLACES

Throughout Walt Disney World, there are hidden grottos, sheltered pathways, secret gardens, and private look-outs that exist to be discovered. They are wonderful places to stop and gather your thoughts or meet up with family and friends. Sometimes, just finding them is pleasurable and rejuvenating. We call these little discoveries Magical Places.

Cinderella Wishing Well: Tucked away behind Cinderella Castle, in the area between Tomorrowland and Fantasyland, is a pleasant self-enclosed stone alcove with benches and a wishing well. It is surrounded by a glade of trees and is easy to overlook. This area gets little traffic, as most visitors walking to Fantasyland from the central hub go through the center

Starlight Cafe in Tomorrowland, the Grotto is a great place to stop and catch your breath when between these two very crowded parts of the park.

Liberty Garden: Immediately behind the Ye Olde Christmas Shoppe in Liberty Square, accessible from the central hub bridge side or the side near the Liberty Tree Tavern, is a park which overlooks the Castle Moat and is sheltered by large shade trees. The park has several seating areas with benches and a scattering of small tables. It's probably one of the most overlooked places in the Magic Kingdom; great for rendezvousing or taking a moment to watch the crowds. There is a smoking area located here.

The Swan Dock: On a pathway that leads down to the castle moat from the Tomorrowland side of the central hub (in front of Cinderella Castle) is a charming wrought-iron shelter. In the early days of the Magic Kingdom this was the loading area for the Swan-shaped boats that plied the moat. Since the shelter is located off the path, it's a quiet spot in the midst of the excitement, and is an excellent place for taking photographs. It's also a good spot to reunite your party when touring separately.

Wilderness Getaway: Visitors who would like to escape the crowds without leaving the park need look no further than Tom Sawyer Island in Frontierland. It's a great place to get some breathing space, particularly in the afternoon hours when the park is packed. There are plenty of places on the island to sit and reflect or to walk among the large shade trees and small hills.

PLANNING YOUR TOUR

 There is a wide variety of daily live entertainment in the Magic Kingdom that can enhance your visit. Be sure to pick up a Guidemap as you enter, which lists all show times throughout the day. Take a few minutes to sit down with the entertainment schedule and note the times for shows and presentations that sound interesting. Plan your day around some of the live events, but don't panic if you find that you are going to miss one — it means that you're enjoying what you're already doing. The best touring itineraries leave plenty of room for change and serendipity. Another fun themed tour focuses on the early Disney attractions such as the Enchanted Tiki Room, Jungle Cruise, Peter Pan's Flight, Pirates of the Caribbean, and Haunted Mansion. Above all, take your time in the Magic Kingdom; the enchantment is in the details. You'll discover that your most memorable experiences occurred between the attractions, when you stopped, looked, and listened. ◆

Essentials · Attractions · Hotels · Restaurants · Special Events · Recreation · Resources

Magic Kingdom • Future World • World Showcase • Disney-MGM Studios • Animal Kingdom • Typhoon Lagoon • Blizzard Beach • Downtown Disney • Disney's BoardWalk • Fort Wilderness & River Country

MAGIC KINGDOM

See the "Essentials" section for ticket costs and attraction updates.

E.A.R.S.
Expert Advisor Rating System
AWARDS

TOP 10 FAVORITE ATTRACTIONS

Pirates of the Caribbean
The Haunted Mansion
Splash Mountain
Space Mountain
Big Thunder Mountain Railroad
Nighttime Parade
Peter Pan's Flight
Buzz Lightyear's Space Ranger Spin
Alien Encounter

TOP 8 FAVORITE ATTRACTIONS FOR KIDS

The Many Adventures of Winnie the Pooh
Buzz Lightyear's Space Ranger Spin
Dumbo the Flying Elephant
Peter Pan's Flight
It's A Small World
Cinderella's Golden Carrousel
Legend of the Lion King
Afternoon Parade

TOP 5 FAVORITE DINING EXPERIENCES

Cinderella's Royal Table for Breakfast
Tony's Town Square Restaurant for Lunch
The Crystal Palace Character Buffet
Cosmic Ray's Starlight Cafe
Liberty Tree Tavern for Dinner

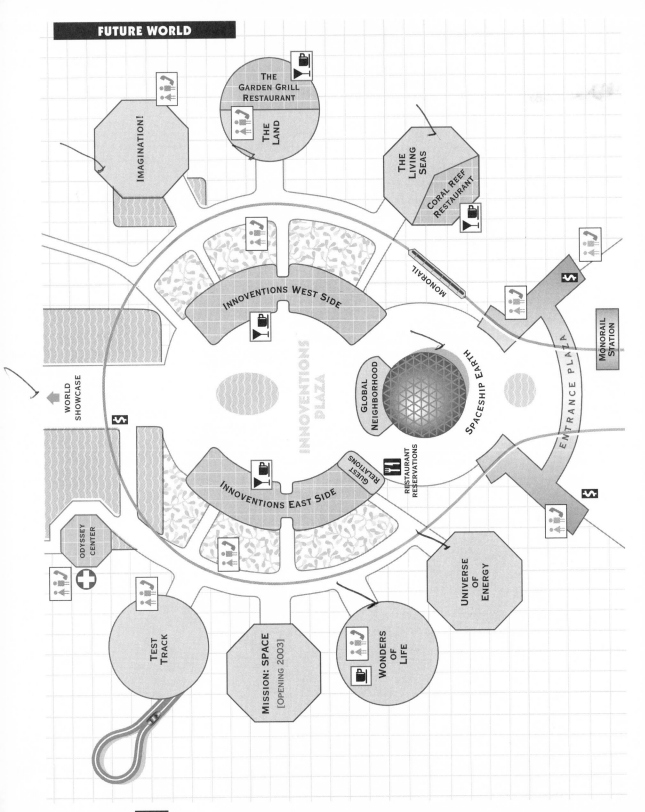

THE GARDEN GRILL RESTAURANT

THE LAND

IMAGINATION!

THE LIVING SEAS

CORAL REEF RESTAURANT

MONORAIL

INNOVENTIONS WEST SIDE

INNOVENTIONS PLAZA

GLOBAL NEIGHBORHOOD

SPACESHIP EARTH

ENTRANCE PLAZA

MONORAIL STATION

WORLD SHOWCASE

INNOVENTIONS EAST SIDE

GUEST RELATIONS

RESTAURANT RESERVATIONS

ODYSSEY CENTER

TEST TRACK

MISSION: SPACE [OPENING 2003]

WONDERS OF LIFE

UNIVERSE OF ENERGY

Essentials

Magic Kingdom • **Future World** • World Showcase • Disney-MGM Studios • Animal Kingdom • Typhoon Lagoon • Blizzard Beach • Downtown Disney • Disney's BoardWalk • Fort Wilderness & River Country

Attractions   Hotels   Restaurants   Special Events   Recreation   Resources

FUTURE WORLD AT EPCOT

Walt Disney's Experimental Prototype Community of Tomorrow, better known as Epcot, is distinguished by Spaceship Earth, the enormous silver geosphere at its entrance. The front half of Epcot is occupied by Future World, where eight themed pavilions present informative attractions on topics such as transportation, energy, communications, agriculture, and health. Some pavilions are actually ongoing experiments designed to test innovations in energy and resource management, food production, and life-style technologies.

ATTRACTIONS

Epcot's Entrance Plaza: Inside the Entrance Plaza, visitors first encounter the polished stone monoliths that display laser-etched "Leave a Legacy" photographs of visitors from Disney's Millennium celebration. Ahead is the huge multifaceted 180-foot-high silver geosphere that houses Spaceship Earth. The geosphere, clearly visible from any part of Epcot, serves as a point of orientation. The Entrance Plaza is the site of many of Epcot's services, including the Tour Window, Guest Relations, wheelchair and stroller rentals, lockers, camera center, ATM, and American Express.

 Spaceship Earth The Disney Imagineers collaborated with world-renowned science fiction writer Ray Bradbury to create the narration for this attraction. Visitors travel inside the Epcot geosphere on a journey that takes them through the history of communication, from the earliest cave paintings to the printing press, and from the age of radio to the future of satellite communications. The lifelike Audio-Animatronics figures, carefully researched dioramas, and a conceptual visualization of an interconnected earth make Spaceship Earth one of Future World's not-to-be-missed experiences. Spaceship Earth is routinely open about an hour before the rest of Future World. This is a real advantage for visitors who arrive early since lines can be very long during the day. Duration: 17 minutes.

The Global Neighborhood Spaceship Earth exits into this busy interactive exhibit hall where visitors can experiment with communication technologies of the future. Simulation devices allow

When to Go: For a morning visit, arrive at Epcot's Main Gate about one half hour before the scheduled opening time. This will allow ample time for touring the popular attractions before the park gets crowded. Spaceship Earth and Innoventions East and West generally open one half hour before the rest of the park officially opens. The crowds at Future World pavilions and attractions usually thin out after 4 PM.

Park Hours: Future World generally opens at 9 AM (the pavilions at the World Showcase open at 11 AM). The park generally closes at 9 PM, after the IllumiNations fireworks show over the World Showcase Lagoon. Opening, closing, and event times may vary during the year, so check ahead with Disney Information (407 824-4321).

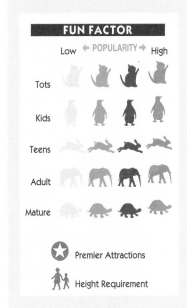

FUN FACTOR			
	Low ← POPULARITY → High		
Tots			
Kids			
Teens			
Adult			
Mature			

★ Premier Attractions

🚶 Height Requirement

Essentials • Attractions • Hotels • Restaurants • Special Events • Recreation • Resources

Fort Wilderness & River Country • Disney's BoardWalk • Downtown Disney • Blizzard Beach • Typhoon Lagoon • Animal Kingdom • Disney-MGM Studios • World Showcase • **Future World** • Magic Kingdom

FUTURE WORLD

See the "Essentials" section for ticket costs and attraction updates.

How to Get There: Future World is located at the main entrance to Epcot. The large Epcot parking lot is free to guests staying at a Walt Disney World resort (other visitors are charged about $6). The parking lot is serviced by trams. Buses travel between Epcot and most Walt Disney World resorts and theme parks. The monorail travels between Epcot and the Transportation and Ticket Center (TTC), the Magic Kingdom, and the following resorts: Contemporary, Polynesian, and Grand Floridian. Epcot can also be entered at the International Gateway, which is serviced by water launches that stop at the following resorts: Dolphin, Swan, Yacht Club, Beach Club, and BoardWalk. Both the Beach Club and BoardWalk are within walking distance.

In-Park Transportation: In the adjacent World Showcase, watercraft called FriendShips carry passengers back and forth across the World Showcase Lagoon. They leave from Showcase Plaza at the top of Future World and travel east to Germany pavilion or west to the Morocco pavilion. ◆

visitors to experience the sensation of traveling through the fiberoptic system of a worldwide information network. Visitors can also explore interactive television in one of several areas that resemble living rooms.

Innoventions East Located in one of a pair of large semicircular buildings facing the Innoventions Fountain at the center of Future World, Innoventions East houses exhibits that change frequently and focus on tomorrow's consumer goods. Here, manufacturers showcase new products and give visitors the chance to try them out. Recent exhibits include an interactive forest where visitors learn what the paper industry is doing to sustain forests, a family web page construction site, General Motors' new electric cars, and a tour of an electronically managed "smart home." MouseGear, a shop located inside, sells interesting clothing, books, and videos. Guest Relations is located in the first entryway to the building, and The Electric Umbrella restaurant is also located here.

Character Greeting Area: Behind Innoventions East is a sheltered Disney Character greeting area which is a great place to snap memorable photos. A red sign emblazoned with Mickey's white glove points the way. The cast of Disney Characters varies throughout the day.

Innoventions West Directly across the central plaza from Innoventions East, a matching structure houses Innoventions West. Here, the focus is on personal entertainment and communications systems of the future. Recent exhibits have included virtual reality experiences, interactive home theaters, and a variety of educational and entertainment software and high-tech toys. Sega of America, Inc., showcases its latest game systems here. Other software innovators have demonstrated voice recognition systems, new medical technologies, and instantaneous language translation. At the IBM Internet Postcards stations, visitors can have their picture taken with a special background and sent across the Internet to anyone in the world. Don't forget to bring along E-mail addresses of family and friends. For light meals, Pasta Piazza Ristorante and Fountain View Espresso and Bakery are also located here.

Ice Station Cool: On the back side of Innoventions West, adjacent to the Fountain View Espresso and Bakery, is a small tunnel marked by a Snow Cat and surrounded by a small mountain of ice. Inside, at the end of the Ice Station tunnel, is a unique attraction featuring multiple drink stations where visitors can sample unusual Coca-Cola flavors from around the world; among them watermelon flavor from China, beer flavor from Germany, and a bitter concoction from Italy. Ice Station Cool is a great place to cool off on a hot afternoon and enjoy a unique refreshment.

Universe of Energy: *Housed in a pyramidal building surfaced with mirrors, the Universe of Energy is a traveling theater that is part ride, part film, and total technical marvel. Although there is always a crowd, the attraction accommodates about six hundred people at a time, so lines disappear quickly. During peak touring hours, longer waits are the norm.*

⭐ ***The Energy Adventure*** This attraction takes visitors back in time to the dinosaur era to explore the origin of fossil fuels. In the preshow waiting area, a short film about energy is shown. The film introduces the tour guide who will narrate the journey, most recently, actress Ellen DeGeneres. Visitors are then seated in what appears to be a large theater, where another film describes the beginning of the universe. At this point, the "theater" breaks apart into six large traveling vehicles that journey through a primeval world populated with impressive Audio-Animatronics dinosaurs and you-are-there sensory effects achieved with lighting, sound, and smell. The vehicles pass through a fog into an adjacent theater where visitors are shown a final film (with a rather uncertain editorial message) that explores the many sources of energy that are available on earth, which fuels are being used currently, and how long the earth's remaining fossil fuels will last. At the exit of the attraction, Exxon sponsors the Save the Tiger exhibition and provides information on conservation efforts. Duration: 42 minutes, including preshow.

Wonders of Life: *Just beyond the Universe of Energy pavilion, where a steel double helical DNA sculpture looms near a gigantic golden dome, is the Wonders of Life pavilion. This pavilion houses the Fitness Fairgrounds exhibition center, the AnaComical Players theater, and three popular attractions: Body Wars, Cranium Command, and the film* The Making of Me.

⭐🚶 ***Body Wars*** In this thrill ride, visitors are "miniaturized" and injected into a human body to retrieve a technician investigating the effects of a splinter. Naturally, problems develop, and visitors find themselves hurtling along in the circulatory system in need of rescue as well. The theater is actually a flight simulator that moves, tilts, and rocks dramatically during the show. The seat belts serve a definite purpose on this ride, which is not for those prone to motion sickness. Some health restrictions apply. Expect long lines. Duration: 5 minutes. Height requirement is 40 inches.

Cranium Command One of the funnier shows in Future World, this attraction opens with a preshow cartoon introducing the Cranium Command, a specialized corps of Brain Pilots trained to run the systems that make up the human body. General Knowledge, the loudmouth trainer, continually reminds his cadets that those who fail get stuck running the bodies of mere chickens. Visitors then enter a multimedia

See the "Essentials" section for ticket costs and attraction updates. ▶

Full-Service Restaurants

Visitors can make dining reservations between 60 and 120 days in advance. Same-day reservations should be made as early as possible at the Disney Dining telephone kiosk near Guest Relations at Innoventions East or at the Disney Dining telephone kiosk in the Germany pavilion. See the "Restaurants" section for full reviews and reservation information.

The Land

The Garden Grill Restaurant — This pleasant restaurant is furnished with comfortable booths and revolves slowly through The Land's ecosystems: rainforest, desert, and prairie environments. Popular family-style Character Meals are hosted by Farmer Mickey, featuring all-you-care-to-eat traditional American cuisine including chicken, steak, and fish. Beer, wine, and spirits are served. Open for breakfast, lunch, and dinner; reservations necessary.

The Living Seas

Coral Reef Restaurant — The giant aquarium in The Living Seas pavilion forms one wall of this atmospheric, dimly lit restaurant. Tables are arranged in tiers so that all diners have a clear view. On arrival, visitors receive picture cards to help them identify the marine life they are watching. The menu features fresh seafood. Beer, wine, and spirits are served. Open for lunch and dinner; reservations necessary. ◆

Essentials • Attractions • Hotels • Restaurants • Special Events • Recreation • Resources

Magic Kingdom • Future World • World Showcase • Disney-MGM Studios • Animal Kingdom • Typhoon Lagoon • Blizzard Beach • Downtown Disney • Disney's BoardWalk • Fort Wilderness & River Country

Essentials

Attractions

Hotels

Restaurants

Special Events

Recreation

Resources

Fort Wilderness & River Country • Downtown Disney • Blizzard Beach • Typhoon Lagoon • Animal Kingdom • Disney-MGM Studios • World Showcase • **Future World** • Magic Kingdom

FUTURE WORLD

 See the "Essentials" section for ticket costs and attraction updates.

Counter-Service Restaurants

The eateries listed below are especially pleasant for light meals and make ideal rendezvous spots.

Innoventions East

Electric Umbrella Restaurant—This counter-service restaurant is open for lunch and dinner. The menu features chicken sandwiches, hamburgers, and salads. Visitors can find seating inside or outside on the terrace. Coffee, beer, and hot chocolate are available.

Innoventions West

Pasta Piazza Ristorante — This futuristic counter-service restaurant offers all-day dining, from an early-morning omelette or pastry to an evening meal of pasta, pizza, and salad. There are dining tables indoors and outside on the terrace. Coffee and beer are available.

Fountain View Espresso and Bakery This bakery opens earlier and stays open later than most restaurants in Future World. This is an ideal spot for that early-morning cappuccino and pastry or for a glass of wine or beer in the evening. The outdoor terrace provides a wonderful view of the occasional water and music performances that occur every 15 minutes at the Innoventions Fountain. ➤

theater, where they follow Buzzy, the youngest Cranium Command cadet, on his first venture into a truly frightful environment: the body and mind of a twelve-year-old boy on a typical school day. The clever humor strikes on an adult level. Cranium Command is hidden in the back of the pavilion, so lines are generally short. The animated preshow helps to make the rest of the show clear. Duration: 25 minutes, including preshow.

The Making of Me This light and humorous film tells visitors all about the facts of life. Created for a younger audience, *The Making of Me* is an open approach to the topic of reproduction, and once aroused some controversy. The film contains superb, though graphic footage of the stages of pregnancy from initial conception through birth. Lines are common at this attraction because of the theater's small size. Duration: 14 minutes.

AnaComical Players The actors and comedians in this small open theater in the Fitness Fairground put on an improvisational comedy performance, tagging a member of the audience to appear as a contestant in a game show about health. Duration: 15 minutes.

Fitness Fairgrounds This large, lively exhibition center presents both serious and lighthearted exhibits that focus on lifestyles and personal health. Visitors can try out the latest workout and fitness-monitoring equipment or use touch-screen computers to get personalized suggestions for improving their health and to learn about the latest medical and health breakthroughs. A gift shop features health-oriented books and products, and the Pure and Simple Cafe is a great place to grab a wholesome snack. Fitness Fairgrounds always attracts a crowd.

Mission: SPACE *(Opening 2003) — This attraction is set decades in the future and is designed to take visitors on a thrilling space adventure as they become astronauts-in-training. Advanced technologies will simulate the heart-stopping G-forces of a shuttle lift-off and visitors will experience the weightlessness of outer space as they face the challenges of space exploration.*

Test Track: *It's impossible to miss the high-pitched whine of vehicles zipping overhead on a track around this massive circular pavilion. The automobile is the focus at this pavilion, which houses Test Track, a wild ride through a new-vehicle testing facility. A huge exhibition area, patterned on an assembly plant, has a variety of interactive demonstrations, the latest General Motors models, and an emporium with car-motif collectibles and merchandise.*

Test Track Visitors enter a staging area filled with exhibits that explain the extensive procedures for testing the quality and safety of a new vehicle before it goes into full-scale production. After a briefing on the harrowing tests ahead, they then board the six-passenger test vehicles that speed up a steep incline, jounce over rough roads, brake and slide on slick surfaces, endure the rigors of extreme heat and cold in environmental chambers, and experience a head-on collision. "Crashing" through a wall, their vehicle shoots out of the pavilion onto a high-speed track, careens along straightaways and tight turns, and circles the pavilion's exterior at high speeds on a steeply banked track. This is one of the fastest — and at nearly one mile — the longest ride at Walt Disney World. The preshow lasts about 3 minutes. Duration: 5 minutes. Height requirement is 40 inches.

Test Track Exhibits

Visitors can enter this line-free exhibition area at any time through doors at the side of the pavilion. The area has a driving technology lab where they view innovative onboard navigation and hazard-warning systems as well as other new General Motors technologies in the making. The latest General Motors vehicles are on display here, and a retail boutique offers a selection of automotive collectibles and souvenir merchandise.

Imagination!:

This pavilion is housed in a pair of leaning glass pyramids fronted by unpredictable spurting and leaping fountains. It features the Journey Into Your Imagination attraction, a ride that explores the creative process; the Magic Eye Theater's special 3-D movie presentation; and The Image Works exhibition center, a hands-on electronic playground.

Journey Into Your Imagination

This attraction is hosted by Eric Idle (President of the fictional Imagination Institute and host of the *Honey I Shrunk the Audience* movie next door). In their ride vehicles, visitors are scanned for the amount of imagination power they have and then led through a series of clever illusory experiences designed to illustrate the power of imagination. Occasional comments are provided by Figment, animated star of the previous incarnation of this attraction. At the end of the experience, visitors are scanned a second time, and the imagination meter is off the scale. Duration: 5 minutes.

★ Magic Eye Theater

Honey, I Shrunk the Audience — This clever attraction is preceded with a short presentation about images and the imaginative process. Visitors are given 3-D glasses and enter a theater where they become the audience that the movie characters address directly. The "Imagination Institute" is presenting the Inventor of the Year Award to Wayne Szalinsky (the lead character from the popular movies *Honey, I Shrunk the Kids* and *Honey, I Blew Up the Kid)*. During the show, a variety of mishaps occur and the audience is accidentally reduced to the size of insects, followed by a rush of harrowing mayhem as attempts are made to rescue them. The 3-D effects are enhanced by exceptional sound, motion, visual, and sensory effects. This

See the "Essentials" section for ticket costs and attraction updates.

The Land

Sunshine Season Food Fair — Counter-service booths line one side of this large food court offering pasta dishes, barbecued chicken, soups, salads, and some of the best ice cream in Future World. Coffee, beer, wine, and frozen alcoholic beverages are also available. This food court is crowded at peak meal times; the best times to eat are before 11 AM or between 2 and 5 PM.

Wonders of Life

Pure and Simple Cafe — Located in the Wonders of Life pavilion, this health-inspired counter-service stop has a wide selection of choices for light meals and snacks. Entrees include vegetarian pizzas and soups, fresh salads, tuna pitas, and baked potatoes loaded with vegetable chili. Drinks include smoothies and root beer floats made with nonfat yogurt. Healthy dessert items are offered here as well, including low-fat muffins and sugar-free low-fat cheesecake. The Pure and Simple Cafe is a great place for the health conscious to grab a bite to eat. ◆

Essentials · Attractions · Hotels · Restaurants · Special Events · Recreation · Resources

Magic Kingdom • Future World • World Showcase • Disney-MGM Studios • Animal Kingdom • Typhoon Lagoon • Blizzard Beach • Downtown Disney • Disney's BoardWalk • Fort Wilderness & River Country

Essentials

Attractions

Hotels

Restaurants

Special Events

Recreation

Resources

Fort Wilderness & River Country • Disney's BoardWalk • Blizzard Beach • Typhoon Lagoon • Animal Kingdom • Downtown Disney • Disney-MGM Studios • World Showcase • **Future World** • Magic Kingdom

FUTURE WORLD

See the "Essentials" section for ticket costs and attraction updates.

Services

Rest Rooms — Public rest rooms are located outside Epcot's Main Gate; on either side of the Entrance Plaza, near Spaceship Earth; on the far side of Innoventions East; on the far side of Innoventions West; inside Innoventions West, near the Pasta Piazza Ristorante; and outside the Imagination! pavilion. There are fairly uncrowded rest rooms in The Land pavilion, next to The Garden Grill Restaurant, and in The Living Seas pavilion, in the entrance hall to the Coral Reef Restaurant.

Telephones — Public telephones are located on both sides of Epcot's Main Gate; on either side of the Entrance Plaza, near Spaceship Earth; on the far side of Innoventions East; on the far side of Innoventions West; in the breezeway through Innoventions West; and outside the Imagination! pavilion. For quieter, air-conditioned conversations, use the modern telephone booths at The Global Neighborhood or slip into either the Coral Reef Restaurant or The Garden Grill Restaurant, where phones are located in an alcove near the entrance.

Message Center — The Message Center is located at Guest Relations in Innoventions East. It is on a network also shared by the Magic Kingdom, Animal Kingdom, and Disney-MGM Studios. Here, visitors can leave and retrieve messages for one another and exchange messages with companions visiting elsewhere. Anyone can phone in a message by calling 407 824-4321. ➤

attraction is definitely worth seeing, even with a wait; however, arriving early in the day or late in the afternoon may alleviate waiting in long lines. Duration: 25 minutes.

The Image Works

This interactive environment is an electronic playground of music, color, video, and computer wizardry. Hand-on exhibits include an area where visitors can "conduct" a symphony by moving their arms through fields of light or create animal sounds by stepping on marked areas of the carpet. The most popular exhibit is a large array of computer kiosks featuring the latest in photo editing techniques. There is also a store featuring Kodak cameras, film, batteries, and souvenirs. Visitors here can also purchase pictures of themselves superimposed with Disney characters and famous Disney scenes. Those who have enjoyed Image Works in the past may be disappointed. The exhibits are limited compared to its predecessor.

The Land:

Food and farming — past, present, and future — are explored in The Land, the largest pavilion at Future World. The massive tri-level building, with its glass roof and greenhouses, is a combination science experiment and theme attraction. The Land pavilion houses the Harvest Theater film attraction, the Food Rocks stage show, the Living with The Land boat ride, and the Behind the Seeds Tour. Also in the pavilion are The Green Thumb Emporium (a gift shop selling gardeners' goodies), the Sunshine Season Food Fair food court, and The Garden Grill Restaurant, one of two full-service restaurants in Future World.

⭐ Living with The Land

Located on the lower level of The Land pavilion, this boat ride is a pleasant, relaxing, and informative journey through the history and future of agriculture. A Cast Member tour guide accompanies visitors explaining the ecological biomes they pass through, including a tropical rain forest; a hot, harsh desert; and a replica of the American prairie, depicting a small family farm at the turn of the century. As they cruise through The Land's impressive experimental greenhouses, visitors learn about emerging technologies in agriculture. The produce and fish grown in the greenhouses at The Land is served in some of the full-service restaurants at Walt Disney World. Duration: 13 minutes.

Harvest Theater

Circle of Life is a 70mm film presented at the Harvest Theater. Simba, Timon, and Pumbaa, characters from the Disney film *The Lion King*, examine the interrelationship between humans and the land. The movie portrays Timon and Pumbaa as land developers creating "Hakuna Matata Lakeside Village," with Simba stepping in to tell his father's tale of the human creatures who often forget that everything is connected in the great Circle of Life. Combined with the animated fable is a series of spectacular images, some beautiful and some nightmarish, depicting environmental scenes from around the world. The film provides good entertainment while presenting this serious topic. Duration: 20 minutes.

Food Rocks Host Füd Wrapper and a cast of singing and dancing Audio-Animatronics fruits, vegetables, and other foods — including stars such as Pita Gabriel, The Peach Boys, and Chubby Cheddar — present a musical revue based on the basic food groups and nutrition. Variations of familiar lyrics and tunes and the transformation of popular stars into vegetables is really quite humorous. Food Rocks turns a lesson in nutrition into a fun experience. Duration: 13 minutes.

The Living Seas: *The rippling façade of this massive pavilion suggests a natural shoreline, complete with crashing waves. In The Living Seas, visitors glimpse life under the oceans in one of the world's largest saltwater aquariums. A marine mammal research center is located here, as well as a living reef and several exhibits on marine topics. The Living Seas Gift Shop features marine-themed gifts, and the Coral Reef Restaurant offers diners a dramatic view of the aquarium as they eat.*

 Sea Base Alpha After a short dramatic film on the interrelationship between humans and the ocean, visitors descend in the Hydrolator (a simulated elevator ride) to the "ocean" floor, where they board sea cabs at the Caribbean Coral Reef Ride for a trip to Sea Base Alpha, an underwater research facility. Here, visitors can take some time to view the more than two hundred species of sea life in the huge, walk-through aquarium, watch the sleepy manatees and other residents of the Marine Mammal Research Center, and explore the exhibits on aquaculture and ocean ecosystems. A marine biologist is on hand to answer questions. Duration: 20 minutes; visitors may explore Sea Base Alpha as long as they wish.

SPECIAL EVENTS & ENTERTAINMENT

Live entertainment is scheduled throughout the day at various Future World sites. As you enter the park, pick up a Guidemap, which lists entertainment times. Schedules are also available at most Future World shops and at Guest Relations, located at Innoventions East.

IllumiNations This fireworks, laser, music, and water show occurs over the World Showcase Lagoon nightly either at 9 or 10 PM, depending on the time of year. The show is periodically re-created and redesigned and is a very impressive, must-see spectacle. Good viewing areas are scarce in Future World since the show is oriented to the World Showcase. For an unobstructed view of IllumiNations, visitors

Lockers — There are lockers located near the Kodak Camera Center at Epcot's Entrance Plaza. Lockers can also be found at the Bus Information Center in front of Epcot and at the International Gateway in the World Showcase.

Banking — There is an automated teller machine (ATM) just outside Epcot's Main Gate and another near Showcase Plaza at the World Showcase. There is an American Express cash machine just outside Epcot's Main Gate, near the Guest Services window.

First Aid — The first-aid office is adjacent to the Odyssey Center. Aspirin and other first-aid needs are dispensed free of charge. Over-the-counter medications are available at MouseGear in Innoventions East and at the Gift Stop in Epcot's Entrance Plaza. They are not on display and must be requested.

Package Pickup — Visitors can forward purchases free of charge to the Gift Stop at Epcot's Entrance Plaza, or to Showcase Gifts at the International Gateway in the World Showcase, and pick them up as they leave the park. Allow two to three hours between purchase and pickup. Visitors staying at a Walt Disney World resort may have packages delivered to their hotel.

Essentials

Attractions

Hotels

Restaurants

Special Events

Recreation

Resources

Magic Kingdom • **Future World** • World Showcase • Disney-MGM Studios • Animal Kingdom • Typhoon Lagoon • Blizzard Beach • Downtown Disney • Disney's BoardWalk • Fort Wilderness & River Country

Essentials

Attractions

Hotels

Restaurants

Special Events

Recreation

Resources

Fort Wilderness & River Country • Disney's BoardWalk • Downtown Disney • Blizzard Beach • Typhoon Lagoon • Animal Kingdom • Disney-MGM Studios • World Showcase • **Future World** • Magic Kingdom

FUTURE WORLD

*See the "Essentials" section for
ticket costs and attraction updates.*

Wheelchairs — Wheelchairs can be rented outside the Main Gate at Epcot, on the right in the Gift Stop, inside Epcot's Entrance Plaza; and at the International Gateway in the World Showcase. Electric Convenience Vehicles can be rented at Epcot's Entrance Plaza on a first-come, first-served basis. Replacement batteries, if needed, will be brought to your vehicle if you alert a Cast Member. A complimentary guidebook for visitors with disabilities is available at Guest Relations in Innoventions East.

Strollers — Strollers can be rented at the International Gateway and at Gateway Gifts inside of Epcot's Main Entrance Plaza underneath Spaceship Earth. Only single strollers are available; the cost is around $6, which includes a $1 refundable deposit.

Baby Care Center — This service is located in the Odyssey Center, adjacent to the bridge leading to the World Showcase near the Test Track pavilion. It is on the back side of the building next to the First Aid Center.

Film and Cameras — Film is available at most Future World shops. Drop-off points for two-hour express developing are at the Kodak Camera Center at Epcot's Entrance Plaza, and at the Cameras & Film shop in the Journey Into Imagination pavilion. Developed pictures can be picked up in the Kodak Camera Center at the Entrance Plaza. They can also be delivered to any Walt Disney World resort. ◆

need to arrive at the World Showcase at least one half hour before show time; during peak seasons, crowds begin gathering about an hour before show time. Some of the best viewing locations close to Future World are along the World Showcase Lagoon from Mexico to China and on the opposite side of the lagoon from the United Kingdom to the bridge promenade in front of France. Duration: About 15 minutes.

The Land — Behind the Seeds Tour This walking tour takes up where the Living with The Land boat cruise leaves off. Covering many of the same topics, the tour explores them in greater depth, with an emphasis on the experiments underway in the greenhouses. Visitors glimpse cutting-edge research laboratories, including the Biotechnology Lab; take an informative walk through several experimental greenhouses; and have a chance to ask questions and pick up horticultural tips from the tour guides, all of whom hold degrees in agricultural fields. The daily tours are limited to ten people and depart every half hour between 10 AM and 4:30 PM from the Behind the Seeds Tour podium, near The Green Thumb Emporium on the lower level of the pavilion. Reservations are required and should be made early in the day since the tour is popular and fills quickly. Only same-day reservations are taken, which must be made in person at the Behind the Seeds Tour podium. The price of the tour is about $6 for adults ($4 for children). Duration: About 1 hour.

The Living Seas — DiveQuest  This tour allows SCUBA-certified (open water) visitors to dive for 30 minutes in the coral reef environment of the aquarium at The Living Seas pavilion. The tour includes a pre-dive overview of The Living Seas pavilion and a presentation on the aquarium's marine life, the dive itself, and a post-dive question-and-answer period. All dive equipment is provided, along with lockers, showers, and changing rooms. DiveQuest is limited to eight people (two dives of four people) and departs daily at 4:30 PM and 5:30 PM from the Guest Relations window outside Epcot's Main Gate. Reservations must be made at least one day ahead and can be made up to one year in advance through Walt Disney World Tours (407 939-8687); the cost is about $150. Duration: 2 1/2 hours.

Cool Event — Innoventions Fountain On Epcot's opening day, as a gesture of international goodwill, representatives from more than twenty countries each poured a gallon of water from their nation to provide the substance and spirit of this energetic fountain. Located in the center of Innoventions Plaza, the fountain's jets shoot streams of sparkling water up to one hundred feet into the air, dancing in perfect synchronicity to sprightly Disney music in a mesmerizing water ballet. After nightfall, colored lights play on the spirited water ballet, creating a particularly dramatic effect. This delightful show can be viewed from the

patio at the Fountain View Espresso & Bakery, which is a good place to take a break from a day of touring in the hot sun. The music and water effects change with each show. Shows start about every 15 minutes.

TOURING TIPS & TRICKS

 Early Entry: Two mornings per week (usually Tuesday and Friday), Future World at Epcot opens about 90 minutes early for guests who are staying at a Walt Disney World resort. This is a good strategy for early risers who want to experience some of the most popular attractions without the long lines. In the busier months, the influx of regular visitors combined with folks taking advantage of Early Entry can make the park more crowded than usual. Visitors who are not taking advantage of Early Entry may want to tour elsewhere or visit in the late afternoon or evening.

FastPass: The FastPass system offers an alternative to waiting in long lines. At certain popular attractions, visitors can pick up FastPass return tickets with a one hour delay and a one hour window when they can return to a special short line, which whisks them to the front of the loading area. Current FastPass time ranges are displayed above the attraction. While waiting, FastPass users have an opportunity to explore the area, shop, dine, or experience many nearby attractions with shorter lines.

Evening Touring: There's a special magic to Epcot in the evening. The crowds thin out quite a bit after 4 PM, and the park seems quieter as darkness descends. There are many interesting dining choices in nearby World Showcase, and if you time it right, you can end the evening with a memorable bang by staying for IllumiNations. About twenty minutes before IllumiNations is scheduled to begin (usually at 9 PM), position yourself along the World Showcase promenade. During peak seasons, you may need to secure a viewing spot as much as an hour ahead; the best way to gauge whether this is necessary is to watch whether or not the crowds are taking up spots early on. The fireworks can produce a large amount of smoke, so it is best to view the show from a spot upwind of the center of the lagoon. Some better views of IllumiNations close to Future World can be found at the following locations:

- Behind the wheelchair viewing area at the World Showcase Plaza;
- Along the promenade near Mexico or Norway;
- Along the promenade near Canada or the United Kingdom.

After IllumiNations ends and as the crowds rush out, you may want to stroll through the World Showcase, past the uncrowded and quiet night-lit pavilions, and exit at the International Gateway. ◆

Essentials · Attractions · Hotels · Restaurants · Special Events · Recreation · Resources

Magic Kingdom • Future World • World Showcase • Disney-MGM Studios • Animal Kingdom • Typhoon Lagoon • Blizzard Beach • Downtown Disney • Disney's BoardWalk • Fort Wilderness & River Country

FUTURE WORLD

See the "Essentials" section for ticket costs and attraction updates.

E.A.R.S.
Expert Advisor Rating System
AWARDS

TOP 5 DO-NOT-MISS ATTRACTIONS

Test Track
Spaceship Earth
Magic Eye Theater
The Energy Adventure
Cranium Command

TOP 5 LEARNING EXPERIENCES

The Wonders of Life Pavilion
The Land Pavilion
The Living Seas Pavilion
Spaceship Earth
The Energy Adventure

TOP 5 FAVORITE SNACK STOPS

Fountain View Espresso and Bakery
Sunshine Season Food Fair
Pure and Simple Cafe
Mickey Ice Cream Bars
Pasta Piazza Ristorante

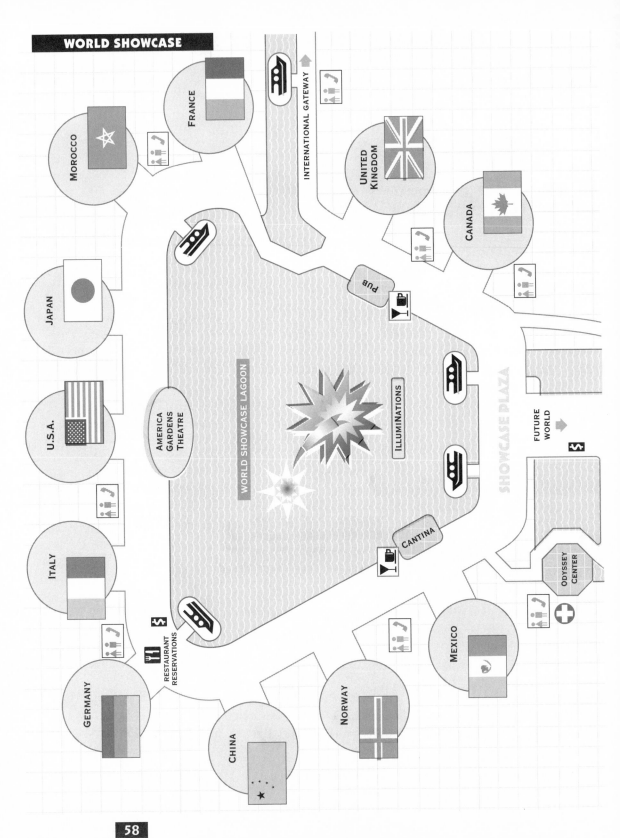

WORLD SHOWCASE

FRANCE

INTERNATIONAL GATEWAY

MOROCCO

UNITED KINGDOM

CANADA

JAPAN

PUB

U.S.A.

WORLD SHOWCASE LAGOON

ILLUMINATIONS

AMERICA GARDENS THEATRE

SHOWCASE PLAZA

FUTURE WORLD

ITALY

CANTINA

ODYSSEY CENTER

RESTAURANT RESERVATIONS

GERMANY

MEXICO

NORWAY

CHINA

Essentials

Attractions · Hotels · Restaurants · Special Events · Recreation · Resources

Magic Kingdom • Future World • **World Showcase** • Disney-MGM Studios • Animal Kingdom • Typhoon Lagoon • Blizzard Beach • Downtown Disney • Disney's BoardWalk • Fort Wilderness & River Country

WORLD SHOWCASE AT EPCOT

T*he World Showcase, which covers more than half of Epcot, was designed to be a permanent and ever-expanding world's fair. Currently, eleven international pavilions encircle the forty-acre World Showcase Lagoon. Each pavilion features restaurants and shops, and offers visitors a glimpse of its national culture through its architecture, horticulture, music, dance, cuisine, crafts, and fine arts. Throughout the day, live performances, engaging exhibitions, and atmospheric theatrics occur in each of the pavilions.*

INTERNATIONAL PAVILIONS

Mexico: *The Mexico pavilion has entertainment areas on both sides of the World Showcase promenade. On the lagoon side, Cantina de San Angel serves Mexican food and beverages. Across the promenade is a massive Mayan pyramid surrounded by tropical foliage. Just inside the entrance, past an exhibition of pre-Columbian art, the pyramid opens onto a night scene in a Mexican village square lined with colonial-style façades. Colorful shops are filled with handicrafts, jewelry, clothing, and souvenirs. At the rear of the pavilion, San Angel Inn Restaurante overlooks an indoor river and a distant view of a smoking volcano. Mariachi bands often perform inside the pavilion or outside on the promenade.*

El Rio del Tiempo This charming travelogue through Mexico by boat lacks the sophisticated special effects of many Disney attractions, but its simplicity is refreshing. The ride is a pleasant and relaxing interlude after lunch or dinner. Duration: 7 minutes.

Norway: *As visitors enter this serene Old World pavilion, a medieval church and fourteenth-century fortress give way to the cobblestone courtyards and steep gabled rooftops of a traditional Norwegian town square. Shops inside the fortress offer Norwegian hand-knit woolens, carved wood, and metal and glass handicrafts. At times, a brass band performs in the courtyard.*

Maelstrom Special effects and clever Audio-Animatronics enliven this short, dramatic boat ride that travels through the era of Viking sea exploration and into the present. Visitors in the front of the boat may get splashed. Afterward, a brief film showcases the spirit of the people of Norway. Duration: 15 minutes.

When to Go: Although large crowds arrive here between lunch and dinner, the World Showcase rarely feels overcrowded because it is spread out over a very large area. The best time to visit is at opening, usually about 11 AM, and at night when the pavilions are strikingly lit. In the early evening, the World Showcase restaurants fill with diners, and crowds linger on the promenade to wait for the IllumiNations fireworks show held at closing time (generally at 9 or 10 PM). Opening and closing times vary throughout the year, so check ahead with Walt Disney World Information (407 824-4321).

Park Hours: The pavilions at the World Showcase open at 11 AM (Future World opens at 9 AM). The park generally closes at 9 PM, after the IllumiNations fireworks show. Opening, closing, and event times may vary during the year, so check ahead with Disney Information (407 824-4321).

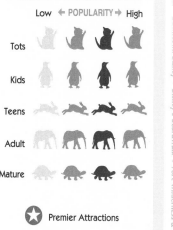

FUN FACTOR

Low ← POPULARITY → High

Tots

Kids

Teens

Adult

Mature

⭐ Premier Attractions

👨‍👦 Height Requirement

Essentials

Attractions

Hotels

Restaurants

Special Events

Recreation

Resources

Fort Wilderness & River Country • Disney's BoardWalk • Downtown Disney • Blizzard Beach • Typhoon Lagoon • Animal Kingdom • Disney-MGM Studios • **World Showcase** • Future World • Magic Kingdom

WORLD SHOWCASE

See the "Essentials" section for ticket costs and attraction updates.

How to Get There: Visitors can enter the World Showcase by walking through Epcot's Future World from the Main Gate toward the World Showcase Lagoon. The large Epcot parking lot is free to guests staying at a Walt Disney World resort (other visitors are charged about $6). The parking lot is serviced by trams. Buses travel between Epcot and most Walt Disney World resorts and theme parks. The monorail travels between Epcot and the Transportation and Ticket Center (TTC), the Magic Kingdom, and the following resorts: Contemporary, Polynesian, and Grand Floridian. The World Showcase can also be entered at the International Gateway, which is serviced by water launches that stop at the following resorts: Yacht Club, Beach Club, Dolphin, Swan, and BoardWalk. Both the Beach Club and BoardWalk resorts are within walking distance.

In-Park Transportation: The promenade around the World Showcase Lagoon is 1¼ miles long. Watercraft called FriendShips carry passengers back and forth across the lagoon, from Germany or Morocco to the Showcase Plaza near Future World. ◆

China: A colorful half-scale model of the Temple of Heaven is the spectacular centerpiece of this exotic pavilion. Traditional Chinese music accompanies visitors as they stroll through charming Oriental gardens accented with landscaped reflecting pools and filled with roses, mulberry trees, water oaks, and pomegranates. The large shopping gallery offers a multitude of Chinese gifts and goods, including furniture and fine art. The art exhibition at the House of the Whispering Willows gallery is particularly impressive. Chinese acrobatic troupes often perform in front of this pavilion.

Wonders of China This vivid, fast-paced Circle-Vision 360° film portrays the people and culture of China as narrated by Li Po, the treasured poet of ancient China. The lyrical movie, projected on a huge circular screen, surrounds viewers and transports them from the vast grasslands of Mongolia to modern-day Shanghai. There is no seating. Duration: 19 minutes.

Germany: Fairy-tale Bavarian architecture surrounds the charming town square of the Germany pavilion. A statue of St. George and the dragon dominates the center of the square, which is ringed by a festive Biergarten restaurant and entertainment hall, along with several colorfully stocked shops offering wines, toys, glassware, and timepieces. At the rear of the square, a chiming glockenspiel rings the hour, and a strolling musician plays waltzes and polkas on the accordion. Off to the side of this pavilion is a railroad garden with three model trains running through a miniature German village scene.

Italy: A scaled-down version of the Venetian Campanile and a faithful replica of the Doge's Palace dominate the piazza of the Italy pavilion. The fountain at the rear of the piazza is a true-to-life replica of the Fontana de Nettuno. Venetian bridges lead to a gondola landing at the edge of the World Showcase Lagoon. Live entertainment, ranging from operatic arias to street theater, is scheduled from time to time in the piazza. At Cucina Italiana, visitors can sample the foods and wines of Italy.

U.S.A.: The American Adventure pavilion is housed in a huge colonial-style red-brick mansion. The colorful gardens surrounding the pavilion are dotted with sycamore and magnolia trees, and a carefully tended rose garden at the side of the pavilion blooms with varieties named after U.S. presidents. The America Gardens Theatre, located at the edge of the World Showcase Lagoon, is a showcase for live entertainment throughout the day.

Voices of Liberty This a cappella singing group has been performing an appealing mix of patriotic and folk songs in the rotunda of the U.S.A. pavilion since it opened in 1982. There are several short performances throughout the day. The best acoustics are found underneath the dome, which greatly enhances the sound. Duration: Approximately 15 minutes.

The American Adventure In this dynamic and impressive multimedia tour of the history of the United States, hosts Benjamin Franklin and Mark Twain guide visitors through a stirring montage of historical vignettes. An incredible array of sounds, images in film, and Disney's finest examples of Audio-Animatronics create this extraordinary attraction. The detail is stunning, as in Will Rogers' lazily spinning lariat, Theodore Roosevelt's notoriously ruddy complexion, and even the careful movements of the quill on the parchment as Thomas Jefferson wonders if he will ever finish his work. Visitors who arrive early can linger over the historical paintings, portraits, and quotations in the waiting area. Duration: 29 minutes.

Japan: In the lovely gardens of the Japan pavilion, rocks, manicured trees, fish ponds, and wind chimes have been carefully blended to create a mood of serene reflection. A scarlet torii gate, a symbol of good luck, greets visitors arriving by way of the World Showcase Lagoon, and the pavilion's prominent pagoda is a replica of the eighth-century Horyuji Temple of Nara. Traditional dance and music is performed throughout the day, including a remarkable taiko drumming demonstration.

Morocco: This pavilion meticulously re-creates the architectural mystery of North Africa. A replica of the Koutoubia Minaret of Marrakesh greets visitors at the entrance to a flower-filled courtyard, complete with a splashing fountain. The Bab Boujouloud gate leads into the Medina, a bazaar where rugs, jewelry, clothing, leather goods, brassware, and pottery spill out of shops into narrow passageways. Belly dancers and troupes of acrobats appear throughout the day.

France: La Belle Epoque reigns once more in the France pavilion, where the Parisian streets are lined with mansard-roofed buildings, poster-covered kiosks, and sidewalk cafes. Quaint shops offer wine, perfumes, leather goods, jewelry, and crystal. Strolling street musicians sing familiar French ballads, mimes and comics perform on the street, and visitors are sketched by artists at their easels along the waterfront. The Eiffel Tower and the Galerie des Halles are reproduced here, and the French landscape is captured by the sweeping lawn and Lombardy poplars at the side of the pavilion.

Impressions de France This exquisite film, shown in panoramic, five-screen-wide format, sheds light on the pulse of the French country. Larger-than-life images of the architecture, landscape, and diverse culture of France are shown during the film. The soundtrack, a mix of classical and romantic music, showcases the distinctive contributions of French composers. Duration: 18 minutes.

Counter-Service Restaurants

Throughout the World Showcase, a wide variety of excellent, relatively inexpensive, and relaxed dining and sipping is at every corner. Many restaurants are wonderful places to rest, reunite friends or family for lunch or dinner, or simply enjoy a change of scenery. Wine tasting booths and other beverage stands are also located around the World Showcase.

Mexico

Cantina de San Angel — This outdoor cafe, a perennial favorite, has seating areas immediately adjacent to the World Showcase Lagoon. The cantina serves a selection of traditional Mexican cuisine, including tacos, nachos, churros, and Dos Equis beer. A separate booth on the side of the cantina serves an array of frozen Margaritas for a refreshing treat. In the evenings, the cantina can get very crowded because it is a prime viewing spot for IllumiNations. ▶

Essentials · Attractions · Hotels · Restaurants · Special Events · Recreation · Resources

Magic Kingdom • Future World • **World Showcase** • Disney-MGM Studios • Animal Kingdom • Typhoon Lagoon • Blizzard Beach • Downtown Disney • Disney's BoardWalk • Fort Wilderness & River Country

Essentials · Attractions · Hotels · Restaurants · Special Events · Recreation · Resources

Fort Wilderness & River Country • Disney's BoardWalk • Downtown Disney • Blizzard Beach • Typhoon Lagoon • Animal Kingdom • World Showcase • Disney-MGM Studios • Future World • Magic Kingdom

WORLD SHOWCASE

See the "Essentials" section for ticket costs and attraction updates.

Norway

Kringla Bakeri og Kafé — This cafe is located inside a traditional Norwegian wooden structure at the entrance to the pavilion. A large selection of open-faced sandwiches — including a favorite of many, the smoked salmon — is served along with mouth-watering desserts, beer, and soft drinks. The cafe has covered outdoor seating.

Wine tasting — On the lagoon side of the pathway along the front of the pavilion is an open-air booth offering Norwegian beer as well as a small selection of wines for tasting by the glass.

China

Lotus Blossom Café — This open-air counter-service restaurant, located at the front of the pavilion, offers a wide selection of American-style Chinese dishes. The menu includes stir-fried entrees, sesame noodles, eggrolls, fried rice, corn soup, ginger and red bean ice cream, and almond cookies, as well as a wide selection of Chinese beer, wine, and teas.

Germany

Sommerfest — This counter-service eatery is located at the rear of the pavilion adjacent to Biergarten restaurant. It features Bratwurst, Frankfurters, and soft pretzels, along with a selection of German beers and wines. There are cafe-style seating areas both indoors and out. ➤

United Kingdom: In this picturesque pavilion, visitors stroll from a British town square through English gardens and down a street filled with charming shops in small Tudor, Georgian, and Victorian buildings. London plane trees and box hedges line the sidewalks, and visitors can make calls from a classic red phone booth that was once a hallmark of the United Kingdom. Of special interest are a replica of Anne Hathaway's thatched-roof cottage and the hedged herb and perennial gardens behind the Tea Caddy shop. Periodically, musical performances are held in the gazebo at the rear of the pavilion and an acting troupe involves visitors in humorous street plays.

Canada: Magnificent towering totem poles frame the Northwest Mercantile trading post at the entrance to the Canada pavilion. The natural beauty of the Canadian Rockies is captured here, complete with a waterfall and a rushing stream. Northwest Mercantile sells Native American and Eskimo crafts and traditional trapper's clothing. The Caledonia Bagpipe Band can be heard by visitors walking under the birch, willow, maple, and plum trees in the pavilion's Victoria Gardens, where more than forty different flowering plants are always in bloom.

O Canada! From the rugged Pacific Coast to the majestic Rockies to the Arctic Ocean, this scenic film sweeps across the countryside of Canada. The Circle-Vision 360° screen surrounds visitors with Canada's natural wonders, along with scenes of its sporting events and urban and rural life. Visitors stand in the center of the theater during the show. Duration: 18 minutes.

SPECIAL EVENTS & ENTERTAINMENT

The World Showcase has a festival-oriented atmosphere, with lively, original entertainment events scheduled daily in each pavilion. The "street entertainment" is one of the most interesting and memorable experiences at the World Showcase. In addition, visiting artisans from the individual nations demonstrate their crafts, and the younger set can participate in "kid zones" at most pavilions. As you enter the park, be sure to pick up a Guidemap at the Main Entrance or at the International Gateway near the France pavilion. Schedules are also available at most World Showcase shops.

America Gardens Theatre This covered outdoor theater, located on the edge of the World Showcase Lagoon and in front of the U.S.A. pavilion, hosts concerts highlighting American music and other special performances. On summer weekends and during holidays, guest celebrities may make appearances. Ratings vary with the performers. Duration: About 30 minutes.

✪ **IllumiNations** This fireworks, laser, music, and water show bursts into action over the World Showcase Lagoon nightly at 9 or 10 PM, depending on the time of year. The show is redesigned periodically with new music and special effects. Arrive at the World Showcase early for a good viewing position along the promenade. Some of the best viewing locations are the Cantina de San Angel in Mexico; lagoonside at the Rose & Crown Dining Room in the United Kingdom; along the promenade between China, Germany, and Italy; and along the promenade between France, the United Kingdom, and Canada. There are somewhat limited but dramatic views at the gondola landing in front of Italy and on the upper deck in front of the Matsu No Ma Lounge in Japan. Since the fireworks from this show produce a large amount of smoke, try to get a spot that is upwind from the center of the lagoon. During busy times, expect to arrive as much as an hour ahead of time to secure a viewing spot; the best way to gauge whether this is necessary is to watch if the crowds are taking up spots early on. If traveling with a large party, it is a good idea to mark a spot (an inexpensive poncho makes a great marker) and take turns holding it down while some members explore the immediate area. Duration: 20 minutes.

Hidden Treasures of the World Showcase

This 2¹/₂ hour guided tour explores unique architecture and inventive construction techniques of the international pavilions. Half of the World Showcase (Mexico, Norway, China, Germany, Italy, and U.S.A.) is toured on Tuesdays at about 9:30 AM; the other half (Canada, United Kingdom, France, Morocco, Japan, and U.S.A.) is toured on Saturdays at 9:30 AM. All tours depart from the Tour Garden in Epcot's Entrance Plaza. A 5 hour tour is also offered, which visits all eleven pavilions and includes lunch (usually at Restaurant Marrakesh in Morocco). This longer tour departs at 9:30 AM on Wednesdays from the Guest Relations window outside Epcot's Main Gate. Advance reservations are required and can be made through Walt Disney World Tours (407 939-8687). The price for the 2¹/₂ hour tour is about $50. The price for the 5 hour comprehensive tour is about $90 (including lunch). Tour days may change, and prices do not include theme park admission.

Gardens of the World

This walking tour explores the unique landscaping found throughout the World Showcase. Many of the plants and care techniques were imported from the nations represented. The tour covers the entire World Showcase and departs at 9:30 AM from the Tour Garden in Epcot's Entrance Plaza. Tours usually run on Tuesdays and Thursdays. Advance reservations are recommended; call Walt Disney World Tours (407 939-8687). If space is available, visitors without reservations can sign up at the Tour Garden on the morning of the tour. The price is about $50 (excluding theme park admission). Tour days may change. Duration: 3 hours.

Essentials

Magic Kingdom • Future World • **World Showcase** • Disney-MGM Studios • Animal Kingdom • Typhoon Lagoon • Blizzard Beach • Downtown Disney • Disney's Boardwalk • Fort Wilderness & River Country

WORLD SHOWCASE

See the "Essentials" section for ticket costs and attraction updates.

Germany

Weinkeller — This wine shop has a small tasting bar in the rear of the store. The selection features mostly German white wines for tasting. It's a particularly pleasant place to cool off on a warm day.

Italy

La Cucina Italiana — This Italian shop features fine items for the kitchen as well as a wine tasting bar. The epicurean setting provides a cozy atmosphere.

U.S.A.

Liberty Inn — Hearty fast food represents America at the Liberty Inn. This cavernous brick restaurant, which has extensive indoor and outdoor seating areas, features hamburgers, cheeseburgers, hot dogs, chicken, and of course, apple pie.

Japan

Yakitori House — Located next to Japan's peaceful garden pathways, this pleasant counter-service restaurant offers Japanese-style chicken, beef, and shrimp dishes. Green tea, plum wine, and warm sake are available, in addition to soft drinks. Ginger and green tea ice cream are unique dessert offerings. There is a small indoor seating area; outdoor seating has umbrella-shaded tables which overlook the pavilion's lovely Japanese garden.

Japan

Matsu No Ma Lounge — This serene second-floor cocktail lounge has an excellent view of the World Showcase and is a great place to cool off on a hot day. The full bar serves hot sake, Japanese beer, cocktails, and green tea as well as sashimi and sushi.

Morocco

Tangierine Café — This unique counter-service restaurant located at the front of the pavilion offers tabbouleh salad as well as an assortment of Mediterranean sandwiches with fillings such as chicken, beef, and lamb. A side counter holds mouthwatering desserts, including freshly made baklava, and serves tea, cappuccino, and espresso.

France

Boulangerie Pâtisserie — As one of the favorite dessert stops anywhere at Walt Disney World, this pasty shop is often very crowded. Occupying one corner near the back of the pavilion, it features an astounding array of French pastry creations. A small seating area can be found next door in Galerie des Halles and there is also a scattering of sidewalk tables in front of the shop.

Crêpes des Chefs de France — This booth, directly across from the Chefs de France restaurant, features a delicious selection of crepes for snacking on the run; no seating is provided. ➤

INTERNATIONAL DINING

Visitors can make dining reservations between 60 and 120 days in advance. Same-day reservations should be made as early as possible at the Disney Dining telephone kiosk in the Germany pavilion or at the Disney Dining telephone kiosk near Guest Relations at Innoventions East at Future World. See the "Restaurants" section for full reviews and reservation information.

$ *Throughout the year, from 4 until 6 PM, a changing selection of restaurants in the World Showcase at Epcot offers Early Evening Value Meals that include an appetizer, menu entree, and beverage. You must ask which restaurants offer this when making reservations. You can also arrive at the restaurant after 4 PM without a reservation.*

Mexico — San Angel Inn Restaurante: This restaurant, located at the edge of an indoor river, serves Mexican specialties under a cleverly simulated evening sky. The atmosphere, complete with a pyramid and smoking volcano in the distance, is both romantic and entertaining. Beer (Dos Equis), wine, and spirits are served. Open for lunch and dinner; reservations necessary.

Norway — Restaurant Akershus: This all-you-care-to-eat smorgasbord features a hot and cold Norwegian–style buffet of fish, meats, and pasta and vegetable salads. The medieval decor sets the tone of Old Norway. Beer (Ringnes), wine, and spirits are available. Open for lunch and dinner; reservations recommended.

China — Nine Dragons Restaurant: Several traditional Chinese cooking styles are served in this formal Oriental dining room. Entrees are served as individual meals, not family-style dishes. Beer (Tsing Tao), wine, and spirits are available. Open for lunch and dinner; reservations recommended.

Germany — Biergarten: Diners seated at long communal tables select from a buffet of traditional German dishes in a huge Bavarian hall. German wines and beer (Beck's, in thirty-three-ounce steins) are served. Performances featuring musicians, yodelers, and folk dancers are scheduled throughout the day. Open for lunch and dinner; reservations necessary.

Italy — L'Originale Alfredo di Roma Ristorante: This popular restaurant features Italian dishes, including the house specialty, Fettuccine Alfredo. The pasta is made fresh, and chicken, beef, and veal dishes are also served. Musicians sing Italian ballads during dinner. Beer, wine, and spirits are served. Open for lunch and dinner; reservations necessary.

Essentials · Attractions · Hotels · Restaurants · Special Events · Recreation · Resources

Fort Wilderness & River Country · Disney's BoardWalk · Downtown Disney · Blizzard Beach · Typhoon Lagoon · Animal Kingdom · Disney-MGM Studios · World Showcase · Future World · Magic Kingdom

Japan — Teppanyaki Dining Room: This large second-floor restaurant features teppanyaki-style cooking. Guests are seated at large communal tables, each with its own grill, where a stir-fry chef prepares the meal — a show in itself. The menu includes beef, chicken, and seafood, with stir-fried vegetables. Beer, wine, and spirits are served. Open for lunch and dinner; reservations necessary.

Japan — Tempura Kiku: In this small restaurant adjacent to Teppanyaki Dining, guests are seated at a U-shaped counter surrounding a tempura bar and grill where they dine on batter-fried chicken, seafood, and vegetables. Beer, wine, and spirits are served. Open for lunch and dinner; no reservations are accepted.

Morocco — Restaurant Marrakesh: Traditional Moroccan cuisine is served in this exotic dining room. Beef, lamb, fish, and chicken are prepared with a variety of aromatic spices and served with couscous. Musicians and belly dancers entertain guests during meals. Beer, wine, and spirits are served. Open for lunch and dinner; reservations recommended.

France — Chefs de France: Traditional French cuisine created by three of France's celebrated chefs is served in this busy, pleasant restaurant with an atrium-style dining area overlooking the World Showcase Promenade. The classically French menu incorporates fresh seafood from Florida. The wine list is French, of course, and beer and spirits are also served. Open for lunch and dinner; reservations necessary.

France — Bistro de Paris: Located above Chefs de France, this restaurant serves French nouvelle cuisine in a romantic and intimate setting. French wines, beer, and spirits are served. Open for dinner only (lunch may be offered during peak-attendance times); reservations necessary.

United Kingdom — Rose & Crown Dining Room: This handsome lagoonside restaurant serves cottage pie, roast prime rib, and fish and chips. Guests may sit outside on the terrace overlooking the lagoon, an especially good location for viewing the IllumiNations performance. Spirits, wine, and a selection of ales on tap are available. Open for lunch and dinner; reservations necessary.

Canada — Le Cellier Steakhouse: In this large but cozy restaurant designed to resemble a wine cellar, the menu includes a selection of steaks, pastas, and some seafood dishes. A selection of Canadian wines and beers are featured as well. The restaurant is located on the underside of the Pavilion; its entrance is adjacent to the lovely Victoria Gardens. Open for lunch and dinner; reservations recommended.

France

Les Vins des Chefs de France — Across from Chefs de France restaurant is a small booth with a selection of fine French wines for tasting. No seating available; visitors can sit on a bench in front of the lagoon.

Canada

Beaver Tails — The Beaver Tails stand, located at the entrance to the Canada pavilion on the main pathway around the lagoon, offers this traditional Canadian confection. Dough is shaped like a beaver tail, fried, and then topped with a cinnamon sugar mixture or with chocolate and hazelnuts. A selection of cold Canadian beers and ales is sold nearby.

United Kingdom

Yorkshire County Fish Shop — This stand, located next to the Rose & Crown Pub, features the perennial English favorite, fish and chips. Baked potatoes are also available, along with soft drinks and Guinness and Bass Ale on tap. Limited seating is available around the pub on the lagoon side.

Rose & Crown Pub — Attached to the Rose & Crown Dining Room, yet distinctly separate from it, is this pleasant, dark-wood finished English pub. Libations, including beer, wine, and cocktails are available. The pub has limited seating, but many patrons sidle up to the bar and stand. The Rose & Crown Pub always has a comfortable, festive atmosphere. ◆

Future World • **World Showcase** • Disney-MGM Studios • Animal Kingdom • Typhoon Lagoon • Blizzard Beach • Downtown Disney • Disney's BoardWalk • Fort Wilderness & River Country

Attractions Hotels Restaurants Special Events Recreation Resources

Resources • Recreation • Special Events • Restaurants • Hotels • A

Fort Wilderness & River Country • Disney's BoardWalk • Downtown Disney • Blizzard Beach • Typhoon Lagoon • Animal Kingdom • Disney-MGM Studios • **World Showcase** •

... of truly ... World ... ospheric ... t impres- sive g... England, and Japan. Canada featur... small-scale reproduction of the sweeping lawns and vibrant flowers of the famous gardens in Victoria, British Columbia. The United Kingdom pavilion showcases a charming English garden and the Japanese pavilion presents a serene Japanese garden with meandering pathways and small bridges. Each pavilion offers a unique garden for visitors to enjoy.

Architecture

Architecture — The architectural detail of World Showcase is the true treasure of the park. There's a day's worth of discoveries to explore in each of the international pavilions surrounding the lagoon. Here, the world is on display, beginning with the imposing jungle-framed Mayan pyramid of Mexico with its twilight market square within, all the way around to Canada with its majestic totem poles and stone stairs leading to the reproduction of the Chateau Frontenac. Visitors will discover the simplicity of a traditional Norwegian town fronted by the Akershus fortress, the lacquered woodwork of Imperial China, the clean lines of Venice, the simple brick grandeur of Colonial America, the understated strength in the wood and stone towers of Japan, the intricate tiling and winding streets of Morocco, the cobblestone streets and mansard rooftops of Paris, and the charming shops and cozy pub of a very genteel England. Not bad at all for a day's travel. ◆

SERVICES

Rest Rooms: Public rest rooms are located in Norway, Germany, U.S.A., Morocco, the United Kingdom, at the International Gateway, and at the Odyssey Center, just past the Mexico pavilion on the walkway to Future World. There are quieter, fairly deserted rest rooms at the Rose & Crown Pub (United Kingdom), Matsu No Ma Lounge (Japan), and San Angel Inn Restaurante (Mexico).

Telephones: Public telephones are located at the International Gateway and near all the public rest rooms in the World Showcase. Telephones are also located near the rest rooms in the cooler, quieter restaurants in Mexico, Japan, and Morocco.

Message Center: The Message Center is located at Guest Relations in Innoventions East in Future World. The Message Center is on a network shared by the Magic Kingdom, Disney-MGM Studios, and Animal Kingdom. Here, visitors can leave and retrieve messages for one another and exchange messages with companions visiting elsewhere. Anyone can phone in a message by calling 407 824-4321.

Lockers: Lockers are available at the International Gateway; near the Kodak Camera Center at Epcot's Entrance Plaza; and at the Bus Information Center, just outside Epcot's Entrance Plaza.

Banking: There is an automated teller machine (ATM) outside Epcot's Main Gate, near Showcase Plaza. An American Express cash machine is located outside Epcot's Main Gate, near the Guest Relations window.

First Aid: The first-aid office is adjacent to the Odyssey Center, near the Mexico pavilion where Future World meets the World Showcase. Aspirin and other first-aid needs are dispensed free of charge. Over-the-counter medications are available at Disney Traders at Showcase Plaza. They are not on display and must be requested at the counter.

Baby Care Center: This service is located in the Odyssey Center, across the bridge from World Showcase near the Mexico Pavilion. It is on the back side of the building next to the First Aid Center.

Lost and Found: Items lost or found may be reported to the package pickup area, located just outside of the Epcot Entrance Plaza.

Package Pickup: Visitors can forward purchases free of charge to Showcase Gifts at the International Gateway or to the Gift Stop, outside of Epcot's Main Gate, and pick them up as they leave the park. Allow two to three hours between purchase and pickup. Guests staying at a Walt Disney World resort can have packages delivered to their hotel.

Wheelchairs: Wheelchairs can be rented at the International Gateway, outside of Epcot's Main Gate at the Gift Stop, and inside Epcot's Entrance Plaza in Future World. Electric Convenience Vehicles (ECVs) can be rented at Epcot's Entrance Plaza on a first-come, first-served basis. A complimentary guidebook for guests with disabilities is available at Guest Relations in Innoventions East in Future World.

Strollers: Strollers can be rented at the International Gateway and at Gateway Gifts inside of Epcot's main Entrance Plaza underneath Spaceship Earth. Only single strollers are available.

Film and Cameras: Film is available in at least one shop in every pavilion. Drop-off points for two-hour express developing are at Mexico (Artesanías Mexicanas), U.S.A. (Heritage Manor Gifts), Canada (Northwest Mercantile), and the International Gateway (World Traveler). Developed pictures can be picked up in the Kodak Camera Center at Epcot's Entrance Plaza or delivered to any Walt Disney World resort.

PLANNING YOUR TOUR

 Seasonal Events: The World Showcase has become the home for many annual festivals and events. Chinese New Year and Mardi Gras are celebrated with colorful parades. During April and May, the Flower and Garden Festival is held with displays, workshops, demonstrations, and garden tours. At the International Food and Wine Festival in October and November, numerous food and wine booths are set up along the World Showcase promenade where visitors can sample the tastes of the world. The Teddy Bear and Doll Convention comes in November, whereas December is devoted to seasonal celebrations, with storytellers from each country describing their nation's holiday traditions. The pavilions are traditionally decorated and there are festive holiday events and special performances every day leading up to Christmas and New Year's Eve.

Around the World with Kids: There are many ways for kids to get into the act in World Showcase. Passport kits (about $10) are available at most shops in Epcot. The passports come with stickers representing each country; Cast Members in the international pavilions will stamp them and write special messages. Passports become treasured souvenirs of friendly Cast Members kids met in the World. Additionally, each pavilion has a Kidcot station, where activities and crafts get underway at kid-sized tables and chairs. Little ones are encouraged to try new things and join in the fun as they make their way around the World Showcase. ◆

Future World ▪ **World Showcase** ▪ Disney-MGM Studios ▪ Animal Kingdom ▪ Typhoon Lagoon ▪ Blizzard Beach ▪ Downtown Disney ▪ Disney's BoardWalk ▪ Fort Wilderness & River Country

Actions ▪ Hotels ▪ Restaurants ▪ Special Events ▪ Recreation ▪ Resources

WOR...

See th...
ticket costs an...

E.A.R.
Expert Advisor Rating System
AWARDS

TOP 5 FAVORITE ATTRACTIONS

IllumiNations
The American Adventure
Impressions de France
Maelstrom
Wonders of China

TOP 5 FAVORITE SHOPPING SPOTS

Mitsokoshi in the Japan Pavilion
Mexico Plaza
United Kingdom Shops
Morocco Bazaar
Showcase Plaza Shops

TOP 5 FAVORITE DINING EXPERIENCES

Restaurant Marrakesh
at the Morocco pavilion

Le Cellier Steakhouse
at the Canada pavilion

Restaurant Akershus
at the Norway pavilion

San Angel Inn Restaurante
at the Mexico pavilion

Rose & Crown Pub
at the United Kingdom pavilion

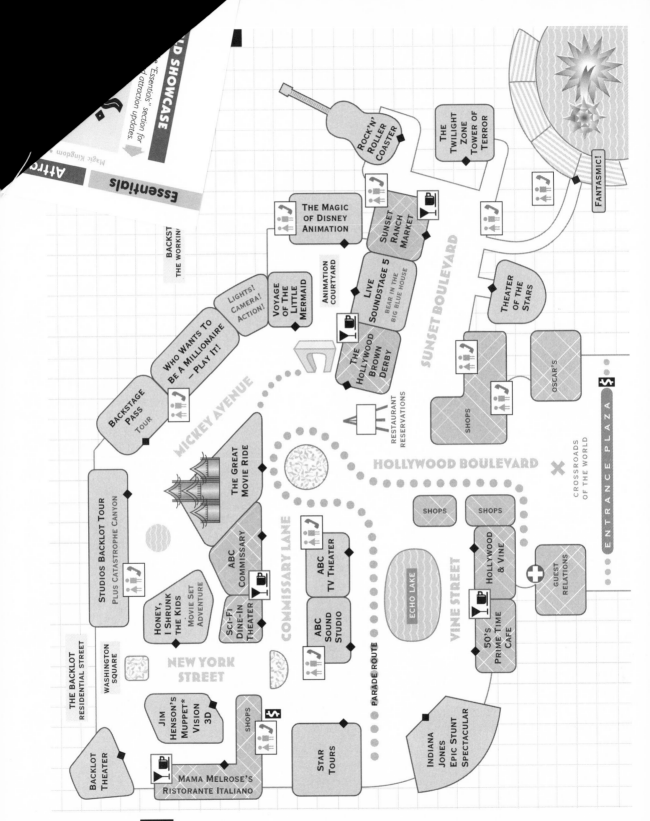

Essentials

LD SHOWCASE

e "Essentials" section for
d attraction updates.

Magic Kingdom

Att

BACKST
THE WORKIN

ROCK'N'
ROLLER
COASTER

THE
TWILIGHT
ZONE
TOWER OF
TERROR

FANTASMIC!

THE MAGIC
OF DISNEY
ANIMATION

SUNSET
RANCH
MARKET

LIGHTS!
CAMERA!
ACTION!

VOYAGE
OF THE LITTLE
MERMAID

ANIMATION
COURTYARD

LIVE
SOUNDSTAGE 5
BEAR IN THE
BIG BLUE HOUSE

WHO WANTS TO
BE A MILLIONAIRE
– PLAY IT!

THE
HOLLYWOOD
BROWN
DERBY

SUNSET BOULEVARD

THEATER
OF THE
STARS

BACKSTAGE
PASS
TOUR

MICKEY AVENUE

RESTAURANT
RESERVATIONS

SHOPS

OSCAR'S

THE GREAT
MOVIE RIDE

HOLLYWOOD BOULEVARD

CROSSROADS
OF THE WORLD

STUDIOS BACKLOT TOUR
PLUS CATASTROPHE CANYON

ABC
COMMISSARY

SHOPS

SHOPS

ENTRANCE PLAZA

HONEY,
I SHRUNK
THE KIDS
MOVIE SET
ADVENTURE

SCI-FI
DINE-IN
THEATER

COMMISSARY LANE

ABC
TV THEATER

ECHO LAKE

HOLLYWOOD
& VINE

GUEST
RELATIONS

THE BACKLOT
RESIDENTIAL STREET

ABC
SOUND
STUDIO

VINE STREET

50'S
PRIME TIME
CAFE

WASHINGTON
SQUARE

NEW YORK
STREET

PARADE ROUTE

JIM
HENSON'S
MUPPET*
VISION 3D

SHOPS

STAR
TOURS

INDIANA
JONES
EPIC STUNT
SPECTACULAR

BACKLOT
THEATER

MAMA MELROSE'S
RISTORANTE ITALIANO

DISNEY-MGM STUDIOS

Disney-MGM Studios offers visitors two distinct movie-making experiences: On one hand, it offers the aura and ambience of Hollywood's most glamorous era and entertains visitors with rides, tours, live performances, shops, and restaurants that reflect the exciting world of television and motion picture entertainment. On the other hand, it provides a glimpse into the nuts and bolts of film and television production and gives visitors access to Disney's working studios with tours that explore sound, animation, special effects, and editing. Disney-MGM Studios is the most dynamic of the major theme parks, and it continues to expand in many directions simultaneously. Because it is a working studio, it is also a creative center for film and new productions at Walt Disney World.

ATTRACTIONS

The Great Movie Ride Tucked into a replica of the Chinese Theater, this ride takes visitors on a multimedia journey through the history of the movies. Movie props and costumes are on display in the lobby, including a carousel horse from *Mary Poppins* and one of the three pairs of ruby slippers made for *The Wizard of Oz*. Visitors ride a large tram past spectacular sets featuring live talent, Audio-Animatronics figures, and convincing special effects that re-create detailed scenes from such popular films as *The Wizard of Oz, Public Enemy, Alien,* and *Raiders of the Lost Ark.* The ride ends with a grand finale of clips from Academy Award–winning films. Duration: 22 minutes.

⭐ **Jim Henson's Muppet*Vision 3D** This brilliantly conceived multimedia attraction is a favorite among Disney theme park fans. Visitors wear special glasses as they watch the escapades at Muppet Labs when Waldo, a new character symbolizing 3-D, is unleashed. Combining an amusing 3-D film with live Muppets, pyrotechnics, and a number of other special effects designed to evoke a you-are-there feeling, this attraction appeals to both the young and the young-at-heart. Duration: 25 minutes.

When to Go: The best time to visit is early in the morning when the park opens. Many live attractions close at dusk, although rides stay open late. On weekdays, television shows and movies are often in production on the soundstages. Visitors who would like to view a film production or join a television show audience (or even appear as guests) should check at Guest Relations, just inside the park entrance. Tickets are available on a first-come, first-served basis; for show times and information, call 407 560-4651. Opening, closing, and event times vary; call Disney Information (407 824-4321) for details. As you enter the park, be sure to pick up an entertainment schedule at the Crossroads of the World kiosk. Check the Guest Information Board, located at the junction of Hollywood and Sunset boulevards, which lists attraction wait times and special events. Restaurant reservations may also be made there.

FUN FACTOR			
Low ← POPULARITY → High			

⭐ Premier Attractions

🚶 Height Requirement

Essentials
Attractions
Hotels
Restaurants
Special Events
Recreation
Resources

Fort Wilderness & River Country • Disney's BoardWalk • Downtown Disney • Blizzard Beach • Typhoon Lagoon • Animal Kingdom • Disney-MGM Studios • World Showcase • Future World • Magic Kingdom

DISNEY-MGM STUDIOS

See the "Essentials" section for ticket costs and attraction updates.

How to Get There: The parking lot at Disney-MGM Studios is free to guests staying at a Walt Disney World resort (other visitors are charged about $6). The parking lot is serviced by trams. Buses travel between Disney-MGM Studios, Epcot, Downtown Disney, the Transportation and Ticket Center (TTC), and most Walt Disney World resorts. Water launches service the following resorts: Dolphin, Swan, BoardWalk, Yacht Club, and Beach Club. ◆

Honey, I Shrunk the Kids Movie Set Adventure

This elaborate playground, based on the film *Honey, I Shrunk the Kids,* resembles a gigantic backyard filled with huge blades of grass and monstrously large ants. While the oversized props are interesting because of their scale, this playground was really designed for the children who pack the place. No time limit; closes at dusk.

Lights! Camera! Action! Theater

This theater generally presents the behind-the-scenes view of the making of recent Disney movies. The films are filled with fascinating details and the air-conditioned theater is a nice break on a hot day. Shows change periodically with new Disney releases. Duration: Approximately 25 minutes.

Live Soundstage 5

This large soundstage forms one entire side of the Animation Courtyard and is generally home to live shows based on popular Disney productions. Recent productions have included the popular Disney Channel show, Jim Henson's "Bear in the Big Blue House." Instead of chairs or benches for the audience, there is a large open carpeted area where they can sit. Kids are invited to get into the action. Waiting times are rarely long here, as the sheer size of the floor area allows for a full line to enter all at once. Duration: Approximately 15 minutes.

Rock 'n' Roller Coaster

The stage is set for this thrilling "tour" of life in the fast lane with a Hollywood rock group. Visitors walk past an array of interesting music-related memorabilia, culminating with a recording studio, where Aerosmith is just wrapping up a session. Not wanting to disappoint fans, the band has their manager order a stretch limousine to meet visitors in the back alleyway. That limo is the ride vehicle, and what a ride it is. Visitors are launched on an incredibly fast journey through Los Angeles in the dark — looping upside down and sideways along the way. A high-energy soundtrack was provided by Aerosmith themselves. This thrilling attraction is definitely not for the faint-of-heart. The ride's harnesses surround the head, and it can get bumpy; earrings should be removed. Duration: 10 minutes, including preshow. Height requirement is 48 inches.

ABC Sound Studio

The focus here is sound effects — the work of film crew members known as Foley artists. The show changes from time to time; recent productions have showcased the sound effects in ABC Saturday morning cartoons and featured the ABC sitcom star Drew Carey in "Sounds Dangerous." During the show, visitors are caught up in special audio effects and 3-D sound. As the story unfolds, they discover how sound can impact their experiences. Duration: 12 minutes.

 **Star Tours** Motion simulation along with special effects and spectacular imagery enhance this attraction into a thrilling flight experience. The scenario begins with the beloved droids C3PO and R2D2 from *Star Wars,* who greet visitors at an intergalactic travel agency. Once inside the spacecraft, the pilot, a novice droid, takes unsuspecting passengers on a harried journey through space, climaxed by accidental involvement in a space battle. Additional storylines for the attraction are underway, based on recent episodes of the *Star Wars* movies. The realistic presentation of flight in this attraction may cause motion sickness. Duration: 10 minutes. Height requirement is 40 inches.

ABC TV Theater Television visual effects are explored in this audience-participation attraction. Toward the end of the 30 minute preshow, visitor volunteers are selected to act as participants in the production. They perform on the set in amusing skits based on popular television shows. Recent productions have included Disney's "Doug Live!" — a stage show based on the ABC Saturday morning cartoon. Duration: 25 minutes; closes at dusk.

 **The Twilight Zone Tower of Terror** Visitors pass through the lobby of the abandoned, lightning-seared Hollywood Tower Hotel and enter the hotel library, where Rod Serling tells the tale of guests who mysteriously vanished from the elevator during a storm long ago. Beyond the library, the next stop is … the boiler room. Here, visitors are loaded onto a battered freight elevator and travel upward into the abandoned hotel. At one stop, they catch a glimpse of the missing guests; at another, the whole car moves forward into an elevator shaft from "another dimension." The doors open briefly to a view high above the park before the elevator suddenly plunges, then reascends for another drop. The drop and ascent sequence is programmable, so the ride differs from time to time. Cutting-edge special effects and the programmable design make this a not-to-be-missed attraction. The thrill can be taxing, however, and health restrictions apply. Duration: 10 minutes. Height requirement is 40 inches.

Voyage of The Little Mermaid This charming attraction features scenes from the Disney movie *The Little Mermaid*. Special effects simulate rippling water overhead to evoke a sense of being under the sea. Visitors unfamiliar with the movie may wish to simply enjoy the familiar music and lively performances by colorful, cheerful denizens of the sea. On hot days, it's an ideal place to sit down and cool off — in fact, the audience is misted occasionally, in keeping with the watery theme. Shows are scheduled continuously. Duration: 17 minutes; closes at dusk.

Counter-Service Restaurants

Throughout Disney-MGM Studios, in addition to the full-service restaurants, there is a wide variety of surprisingly good and relatively inexpensive fast dining options. Several of these restaurants also make wonderful places to rest, reunite your party for lunch or dinner, and enjoy different types of scenery as well.

Backlot Express — Located between the Indiana Jones Stunt Show and the Star Tours attraction, this food stand features hamburgers, chicken sandwiches, hot dogs, and salads. Seating is fairly limited, but crowds are not too heavy in this area unless the Stunt Show has just let out.

The ABC Commissary — This large eatery, located almost adjacent to the Chinese Theater, is a good central location to regroup, have a sandwich, and relax. The menu includes hot and cold sandwiches and wraps, as well as kids' meals (grilled cheese or chicken strips) in special Character lunch boxes. There is extensive seating inside the air-conditioned building, as well as shaded tables outside. ➤

Essentials • Attractions • Hotels • Restaurants • Special Events • Recreation • Resources

Magic Kingdom • Future World • World Showcase • Disney-MGM Studios • Animal Kingdom • Typhoon Lagoon • Blizzard Beach • Downtown Disney • Disney's BoardWalk • Fort Wilderness & River Country

Essentials · Attractions · Hotels · Restaurants · Special Events · Recreation · Resources

Fort Wilderness & River Country · Downtown Disney · Disney's BoardWalk · Blizzard Beach · Typhoon Lagoon · Animal Kingdom · Disney-MGM Studios · World Showcase · Future World · Magic Kingdom

DISNEY-MGM STUDIOS

See the "Essentials" section for ticket costs and attraction updates.

Starring Rolls Bakery — Located

near the junction of Hollywood and Sunset boulevards, and just behind the Guest Information Board, this is an ideal breakfast stop and a good place for that tempting afternoon snack. The bakery is loaded with fresh baked delights, including a selection of sugar-free desserts. There is a small seating area inside, and an outdoor seating area with umbrellas in the shop's sunken patio.

Studio Catering Company — Near

the entrance to the Studios Backlot Tour and adjacent to the Honey I Shrunk the Audience Playground is a large covered counter-service eatery serving cold sandwiches, hot pretzels, and gourmet ice cream. The restaurant is surrounded by extra seats and shade trees. This is a welcoming place to sit and take a snack break.

Toy Story Pizza Planet — This res-

taurant, tucked in the back corner of the park near Mama Melrose's and the exit from the Muppet Theater, is a great kid-friendly place to stop for lunch. The menu consists of personal-sized pizzas, salads, and soft drinks. Most of the seating is upstairs; the lower level houses an extensive gaming arcade. A small seating area in front of the restaurant is sheltered by large shade umbrellas. ➤

LIVE SHOWS AND SPECIAL EVENTS

Live entertainment, celebrity appearances, and extemporaneous happenings occur daily throughout Disney-MGM Studios. Along the boulevards, visitors encounter zany Hollywood characters who involve them in Hollywood-related antics and altercations. Check the entertainment schedule for show times.

DON'T MISS: ***Who Wants To Be A Millionaire – Play It!*** Visitors compete for unique prizes in this live-studio version of the popular ABC-TV game show. Using keypads, audience members play along to earn enough points to occupy the "hot seat." Duration: Approximately 30 minutes.

Backlot Theater This large outdoor theater presents live shows based on recent Disney films. The productions feature singing and dancing performers, elaborate costumes, distinctive sets, and special effects, which enhance the story line and charm both adults and children. Recent productions have included *The Hunchback of Notre Dame.* In warm months, the early shows and those at the end of the day are the best ones to catch, since the Backlot Theater can become uncomfortably hot at midday. Duration: Approximately 30 minutes; closes at dusk.

⭐ ***Feature Parade*** The afternoon parades that appear at Disney-MGM Studios are unique extravaganzas employing ornately designed floats, giant figures, live performers, elaborate costumes, engaging music, and unexpected special effects. The parades change from time to time to reflect the theme of recently released Disney films, such as *Mulan.* They are held twice in the summer, at about 11:30 AM and 3:30 PM, and once daily, at about 3:30 PM, during the rest of the year. The parade route is less crowded near the Star Tours attraction. Duration: Approximately 15 minutes.

⭐ ***Fantasmic!*** Based upon the sensational nighttime attraction of the same name at California's Disneyland, this multimedia event takes place in its own seven-thousand-seat amphitheater every night. The Hollywood Hills amphitheater, which provides standing room for another three thousand visitors, is the largest at any Disney theme park. It hugs the shore of a man-made lagoon, which encircles a forty-foot mountain where much of the drama unfolds. The story is a monumental mythology of the eternal struggle between good and evil that takes place in the dreams and fantasies of a serious-minded mouse: Mickey Mouse, to be exact. The show mixes projected animations, live performers, enchanting music from Disney classics, and spectacular effects including fireworks, jet fountains, water screens, lasers, dense fog, soaring flames, and the largest Audio-Animatronics villain ever created. The show closes on a festive note as good prevails and the Steamboat Willie Riverboat emerges from behind the island, sailing past with all the Disney Characters onboard. Be prepared to be dazzled. There are generally two shows every evening. Duration: Approximately 25 minutes.

Indiana Jones Epic Stunt Spectacular

This live-action show dramatically demonstrates the work of stunt designers and performers. Several audience members are preselected to act as "extras." Then, professional stunt performers reenact familiar scenes from the Indiana Jones movies by falling from buildings and dodging threatening boulders, fiery explosions, and out-of-control trucks. The fascinating explanation of the secrets behind the stunts does not reduce their excitement or sense of realism. For the best view, arrive at least 20 minutes early and find a seat in the upper center. Shows are scheduled continuously throughout the day. Duration: 30 minutes; closes at dusk.

Theater of the Stars

This large, shaded outdoor theater on Sunset Boulevard is reminiscent of the famed Hollywood Bowl. Here, talented singers and dancers, top-flight choreography and stage direction, elaborate sets, and imaginative costumes combine to create memorable productions. The shows are generally based on popular Disney animated films, such as *Beauty and the Beast*, and they change periodically. Performances are scheduled throughout the day. Duration: Approximately 20 minutes; closes at dusk.

STUDIO TOURS

Studios Backlot Tour

This tour presents an overview of movie making and begins at a special-effects water tank for a demonstration of how sea battles and storm sequences are created. Visitors then board trams and head off for a truly informative behind-the-scenes look at motion picture production. The trams travel past costume and scenery shops, warehouses filled with props, and Residential Street sets that are used as backdrops in movies and television shows. The tour highlight has long been Catastrophe Canyon, where visitors feel the searing heat from an exploding tanker truck and, if sitting on the left side of the tram, are splashed by the waters of a flash flood. Tours are continuous. Duration: 35 minutes; closes at dusk.

Backstage Pass

This walking tour presents a more in-depth view of motion picture production than the Backlot Tour. The tour's theme is generally based on a recent Disney live-action production. For example, it may begin with a look at props and special effects, such as a visit to Jim Henson's Creature Shop where many of the animal

Sunset Market — At the end of Sunset Boulevard, near the entrances to the Rock 'n' Roller Coaster and the Twilight Zone Tower of Terror, visitors will find an open-air market with plenty of seating. This area includes four separate counters and is the perfect place for those times when members of the same party can't agree on what they want. It's a good location for early evening dining for those visitors waiting for Fantasmic! The counters are:

Anaheim Produce: Here, visitors will find a selection of chilled fresh fruits and fresh-cut seasonal vegetables.

Catalina Eddie's: This stand, located in the back corner of the Market area, serves up small pizzas and salads.

Hollywood Scoops: Visitors line up at this popular stand on hot days for hand-dipped ice cream cones.

Rosie's All-American Cafe: This is the largest and most varied stand in the Market area; it serves a good selection of hamburgers, including a vegetarian burger, as well as cold sandwiches, small salads, and soups.

Sunset Market Ranch: This counter serves up smoked turkey legs, baked potatoes, hot dogs, and hot pretzels. ◆

Essentials

Attractions

Hotels

Restaurants

Special Events

Recreation

Resources

Magic Kingdom • Future World • World Showcase • Disney-MGM Studios • Animal Kingdom • Typhoon Lagoon • Blizzard Beach • Downtown Disney • Disney's BoardWalk • Fort Wilderness & River Country

Essentials

Attractions

Hotels

Restaurants

Special Events

Recreation

Resources

Fort Wilderness & River Country • Disney's BoardWalk • Downtown Disney • Blizzard Beach • Typhoon Lagoon • Animal Kingdom • Disney-MGM Studios • World Showcase • Future World • Magic Kingdom

See the "Essentials" section for ticket costs and attraction updates.

Services

Rest Rooms — Public rest rooms are located throughout Disney-MGM Studios. The rest rooms at the beginning of Sunset Boulevard, between Theater of the Stars and The Twilight Zone Tower of Terror, are rarely crowded. Visitors can also find cool and quiet rest rooms at the ABC Commissary and the Tune In Lounge.

Telephones — Public telephones can be found near all rest rooms. The phones near the rest rooms at Mama Melrose's and near the ABC Commissary are not only quiet, but air-conditioned.

Message Center — This helpful service is located in Guest Relations at the Entrance Plaza. The Message Center is on a computer network also shared by Epcot, the Magic Kingdom, and Animal Kingdom. Here, visitors can leave and retrieve messages for one another and exchange messages with companions visiting elsewhere. Anyone can phone in a message by calling 407 824-4321.

Lockers — Lockers are located at Oscar's Classic Car Souvenirs at the Entrance Plaza. Larger luggage-sized lockers are located at the Bus Information Building, outside the turnstiles.

Banking — There is an automated teller machine (ATM) outside the main Entrance Plaza.

puppets from *101 Dalmatians* were created. On the soundstages, visitors may see an actual production if a film is being shot that day. One sound-stage may hold an entire set that was used for filming a recent Disney movie. The tour presents little opportunity to sit down and relies heavily on overhead videos for explanatory narration. It is much more interesting when there is a production underway, so before signing up, check at Guest Relations. Tours are continuous. Duration: Approximately 25 minutes; closes at dusk.

The Magic of Disney Animation

Beyond the preshow waiting area, which has displays of classic and current animation cels, visitors enter a theater for a highly entertaining and informative film about animation starring Robin Williams and Walter Cronkite. They then tour Disney's working animation studio, where artists create animated features. The various activities are explained on overhead monitors. Tours are continuous. Duration: Approximately 35 minutes.

Special Interest Tour — Inside Animation

This popular tour offers a more in-depth look inside the animation studios where Disney features are created. Visitors learn how to create animation cels and even paint a Mickey Mouse cel of their own. Tours depart at 9:30 AM from the Bus Information Building outside the studio's turnstiles, usually on Tuesdays and Thursdays. Reservations are required and should be made six weeks in advance through Walt Disney World Tours (407 939-8687). This tour is limited to visitors age sixteen and older; tour cost is about $55. Duration: 2½ hours.

STUDIO LOUNGES

The Writer's Stop: At the beginning of New York Street, around the corner from the Sci-Fi Dine-In Theater, is a small corner bookshop with comfortable overstuffed sofas and chairs. At the front counter there is a small but tempting array of oversized desserts and a full selection of specialty coffees. The Writer's Stop is the place to browse new books while enjoying a refreshing afternoon break.

Tune-In Lounge: Adjacent to the 50's Prime Time Cafe, this is the only full-service bar at Disney-MGM Studios. The decor is pure mid-twentieth century kitsch at its Disney best, including black-and-white televisions and Naugahyde sofas and chairs. In addition to drinks, the lounge serves up tasty appetizers. Visitors may also request some of the restaurant's specialty items, including their famous peanut butter and jelly milkshakes.

STUDIO DINING

Visitors can make full-service restaurant reservations between 60 and 120 days in advance. Same-day reservations can be made at Hollywood Junction, located at the intersection of Hollywood and Sunset boulevards. See the "Restaurants" section for full reviews and reservation information.

50's Prime Time Cafe: Decorated with 50s style kitchens and dinette tables, this entertaining restaurant airs sitcoms of the period on black-and-white televisions and serves up home cooked classics, such as Granny's Pot Roast. Servers take on the role of "Mom" and humorously treat diners as one of the kids. Soda fountain treats are also featured. Beer, wine, and spirits are available. Open for lunch and dinner; reservations necessary.

The Hollywood Brown Derby: Caricatures of famous personalities line the walls of this elegant, bustling restaurant. Steaks, seafood, pasta, and salads, including the house specialty, Cobb salad, are featured, along with a selection of specialty desserts. Beer, wine, and spirits are served, as are espresso and cappuccino. Open for lunch and dinner; reservations necessary.

Hollywood & Vine: This busy Art Deco–styled eatery, located on Vine Street, is home to the Studios' Character Meal. Minnie Mouse, Goofy, Pluto, and Chip and Dale are dressed in classic Hollywood black tie to host an extensive breakfast and lunch experience. The menu varies, but the buffet generally serves traditional fare and a few surprises, such as chocolate French toast at breakfast. Lunch features a selection of grilled meats and poultry, plus several pasta dishes and salads. The restaurant is open seasonally for dinner. Reservations necessary.

Mama Melrose's Ristorante Italiano: Loud good humor and basil-infused olive oil for dipping crusty Italian bread create a trattoria ambience in this restaurant, which features Italian cuisine and thin-crust pizzas baked in brick ovens. Beer, wine, and spirits are served, as are espresso and cappuccino. Open for lunch and dinner; reservations necessary.

Sci-Fi Dine-In Theater: Under a twinkling night sky, rows of booths shaped like vintage convertibles create a drive-in movie setting, complete with car-side speakers and a film screen showing classic science fiction and horror film clips. This is a popular restaurant for families. Hamburgers and specialty dishes such as The Towering Terror — half a smoked chicken with citrus barbecue sauce — are the order of the day. Beer and wine are served. Open for lunch and dinner; reservations necessary.

Package Pickup — Visitors can forward purchases free of charge to the Package Pickup window, located at the Entrance Plaza, and pick them up as they leave the park. Visitors staying at a Walt Disney World resort may have packages delivered to their hotel.

First Aid and Baby Care — The first-aid office is located at the Entrance Plaza, next to Guest Relations. Aspirin and other first aid is dispensed free of charge. Over-the-counter medications are available at Golden Age Souvenirs, near ABC Sound Studio. They must be requested at the counter.

Wheelchairs — Wheelchairs can be rented at Oscar's Classic Car Souvenirs, just inside the Entrance Plaza. A limited number of Electric Convenience Vehicles (ECVs) are also available on a first-come, first-served basis, so get there early. A guidebook for guests with disabilities is available at Guest Relations, located at the Entrance Plaza.

Strollers — Strollers can be rented at Oscar's, just inside the Entrance Plaza. Only single strollers are available. Supplies are limited, so arrive early.

Film and Cameras — Film is available at most Disney-MGM Studios shops. Film can be dropped off for express developing at the Darkroom on Hollywood Boulevard. Developed film can be picked up at the Darkroom or can be delivered to any Walt Disney World resort. ◆

Essentials · Attractions · Hotels · Restaurants · Special Events · Recreation · Resources

Fort Wilderness & River Country · Disney's BoardWalk · Downtown Disney · Blizzard Beach · Typhoon Lagoon · Animal Kingdom · **Disney-MGM Studios** · World Showcase · Future World · Magic Kingdom

DISNEY-MGM STUDIOS

See the "Essentials" section for ticket costs and attraction updates.

E.A.R.S.
Expert Advisor Rating System
AWARDS

TOP 8 FAVORITE EVENTS AND ATTRACTIONS

Rock 'n' Roller Coaster
Fantasmic!
The Twilight Zone Tower of Terror
The Great Movie Ride
Jim Henson's Muppet*Vision 3D
Star Tours
Backlot Theater
The Magic of Disney Animation

TOP 5 FAVORITE ATTRACTIONS FOR KIDS

Jim Henson's Muppet*Vision 3D
Voyage of the Little Mermaid
Honey, I Shrunk the Kid Movie Set
Theater of the Stars
Live Soundstage 5
(Bear in the Big Blue House)

TOP 5 FAVORITE DINING EXPERIENCES

The Hollywood Brown Derby
(especially the Cobb Salad)

50's Prime Time Cafe
(try the Peanut Butter and Jelly Shake)

Mama Melrose's Ristorante Italiano

Sci-Fi Dine-In Theater
(popular with the kids)

Hollywood & Vine
(Character Meal)

PLANNING YOUR TOUR

There are many touring tips and tricks that can help visitors customize their plans to match their touring style and maximize personal satisfaction. The best touring and most memorable experiences come from focusing on attractions you know you'll enjoy and employing the smart strategies that insiders use. These include:

Early Entry: This is a good strategy for those guests who are staying in the Walt Disney World resorts. On Early Entry days, usually Sunday and Wednesday, the gates to Disney-MGM Studios open to resort guests about 90 minutes before the posted opening time for the general public. Of course, one downside, particularly in the busier months, is that when the gates do officially open, the influx of visitors combined with those taking advantage of Early Entry can make the park more crowded than usual. Visitors who are not arriving early may want to visit a different park on Early Entry days at Disney-MGM Studios.

FastPass: This take-a-number concept in touring the attractions practically eliminates the need to stand in long lines on busy days. Disney's FastPass system is simple. Visitors run their park ticket through a machine at the entrance to the ride and out pops a special pass stamped with a one hour time range when visitors can return to a special short line which whisks them to the front of the loading area. The time range usually begins about an hour or longer after the FastPass is issued, which gives visitors an opportunity to shop, dine, or experience other nearby attractions with shorter lines. Current FastPass time ranges, as well as the waiting time for the regular line, are displayed above the line.

Fantasmic! Seating: There is no bad seating for this show. Cast Members will advise you to get to the theater at least an hour before show time; this will indeed get you a seat in or near the center, but it really doesn't matter. If you wait until 15 to 20 minutes before the show, there's a good chance that you will have a spot for standing. This is advantageous for exiting the theater ahead of the enormous crowd. If you are seated for the show, take your time exiting. You'll make it out in plenty of time to get to the parking lot or to resort transportation, and you won't feel trampled. If there are two shows, the later show is less crowded.

Late Evenings: If you are not seeing Fantasmic! in the evening, you will find that on nights when there are two showings, the rest of the park is nearly deserted. This is a great time to see attractions that you might otherwise have missed due to long lines. Keep in mind, however, that many Disney-MGM Studios attractions close at dusk. ◆

Essentials

Magic Kingdom • Future World • World Showcase • Disney-MGM Studios • **Animal Kingdom** • Typhoon Lagoon • Blizzard Beach • Downtown Disney • Disney's BoardWalk • Fort Wilderness & River Country

Attractions

Hotels

Restaurants

Special Events

Recreation

Resources

DISNEY'S ANIMAL KINGDOM

Animal Kingdom is Disney's most ambitious theme park creation to date, and it is a fitting tribute to Walt Disney's original inspiration for much of his greatest work: "I have learned from the animal world," he said, "and what anyone will learn who studies it is a renewed sense of kinship with the earth and all its inhabitants."

Disney's Animal Kingdom celebrates the animals of the past and the present in an innovative mix of attractions and open-habitat zoo areas. Many of the concepts at work in the design of the park are meant to engage visitors as participants as well as spectators, bringing a new dimension of reality to the Disney experience. At 500 acres, Animal Kingdom is almost five times the size of the Magic Kingdom. It is also the largest physical zoo anywhere in the world. Like the Magic Kingdom, the attractions are clustered into environments, or "lands," that branch off from a central hub. The monumental Tree of Life, with its intricate carvings of all types of animal life, is Animal Kingdom's signature icon, visible from many parts of the park.

Animal Kingdom will continue to expand over the years, as new animal habitats and visitor areas are added. It is interesting to note that this land is already home to many thriving species, including otters, frogs, egrets, heron, ducks, and deer. What appears to be taking place here is a controlled zoological experiment exploring the delicate balance among humankind, animals, and the forces of nature, as each finds a place together in this new Garden of Eden.

Animal Kingdom is designed with walking in mind, yet visitors are afforded many opportunities to stop along the way and immerse themselves in the exquisite beauty of the natural setting. The park does not follow the typical pacing of theme parks, and running from attraction to attraction will not deliver a magical experience. While it does provide a couple of "thrill" moments, this is a park with wondrous opportunities for exploration and peaceful reflection. The official park maps for Animal Kingdom are called "Adventurer's Guides," which sets the stage for the magic found within Animal Kingdom.

When to Go: In the wild, the day begins when the sun rises and ends when it sets, and the park hours at Animal Kingdom largely follow suit. This should be your first clue that this is not an ordinary theme park. Animal Kingdom tends to be at its busiest in the middle of the day. Morning and late afternoon are ideal times to tour. Both the Rainforest Cafe, which can be entered from outside the park gates, and Donald's Prehistoric Breakfastosaurus open an hour or so before the official park opening. Since Restaurantosaurus (where Donald's Prehistoric Breakfastosaurus is held) is located well within the park, visitors with a reservation that occurs before the park opens will be escorted to the restaurant by a Cast Member. Opening and closing times vary with the season. You can check ahead 30 days prior to arrival by calling Disney Information (407 824-4321).

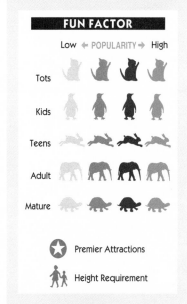

FUN FACTOR

Low ← POPULARITY → High

Tots

Kids

Teens

Adult

Mature

⭐ Premier Attractions

🚶 Height Requirement

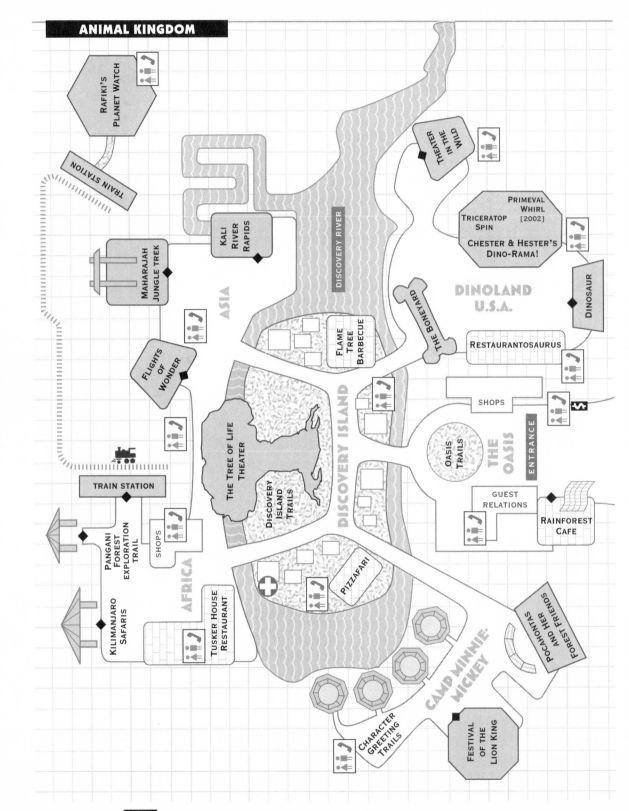

ANIMAL KINGDOM

RAFIKI'S PLANET WATCH

TRAIN STATION

KALI RIVER RAPIDS

MAHARAJAH JUNGLE TREK

ASIA

DISCOVERY RIVER

FLIGHTS OF WONDER

THE TREE OF LIFE THEATER

TRAIN STATION

SHOPS

PANGANI FOREST EXPLORATION TRAIL

KILIMANJARO SAFARIS

AFRICA

TUSKER HOUSE RESTAURANT

DISCOVERY ISLAND TRAILS

DISCOVERY ISLAND

FLAME TREE BARBECUE

THE BONEYARD

THEATER IN THE WILD

PRIMEVAL WHIRL [2002]
TRICERATOP SPIN
CHESTER & HESTER'S DINO-RAMA!

DINOLAND U.S.A.

DINOSAUR

RESTAURANTOSAURUS

SHOPS

OASIS TRAILS

THE OASIS

ENTRANCE

GUEST RELATIONS

RAINFOREST CAFE

PIZZAFARI

POCAHONTAS AND HER FOREST FRIENDS

CAMP MINNIE-MICKEY

CHARACTER GREETING TRAILS

FESTIVAL OF THE LION KING

ATTRACTIONS

The Oasis: *Visitors enter Animal Kingdom through The Oasis, a lush garden designed to set the Animal Kingdom "story" in motion quickly. Once inside, visitors are immersed in a natural paradise of grottos, glades, waterfalls, and animal viewing areas. As they make their way toward the bridge that spans the Discovery River, helpful and knowledgeable Disney Cast Members explain and discuss the various habitats and animals that visitors will encounter along the way. When emerging from the heavily foliated environment of The Oasis, visitors are treated to their first full view of the breathtaking Tree of Life, the park's signature icon.*

Discovery Island: *Encircled by the Discovery River and surrounding The Tree of Life, Discovery Island is the hub of Animal Kingdom and the departure point for all further journeys. Entering from The Oasis, visitors encounter the first of many brightly colored buildings covered with marvelous and fanciful animal carvings. Respectively, these are Disney Outfitters to the right and Island Mercantile to the left, the largest shops in Animal Kingdom. A collection of shops, eateries, and services in the same brightly colored theming lines the pathway around in each direction. Notice the lampposts and rooftops and see how many animals you can identify.*

Discovery River: The Discovery River circles Discovery Island and flows past all areas of Animal Kingdom. The far side of The Tree of Life and the Asian temple ruins are especially picturesque when viewed from the bridges that cross the Discovery River.

Discovery Island Trails: Surrounding The Tree of Life are a number of twisting pathways leading to small gardens and secluded grottos. Here, visitors will find many delightful small animal habitats, offering encounters with ring-tailed lemurs, exotic birds, red kangaroos, and many more. The foliage and flora of this area are arguably among the most beautiful in all of Animal Kingdom.

The Tree of Life This majestic tree towers over fourteen stories above Discovery Island. It looks convincingly real from a distance, but upon closer inspection visitors will see hundreds of hand-carved animals that seem to be growing out of its trunk, branches, and massive roots. There are more than 325 animals represented. It is surrounded by gardens, pathways, and small animal habitats.

⭐ **Tree of Life Theater** Located inside The Tree of Life, this multimedia theater delivers superior 3-D and sensory effects. The performance in the theater of *It's Tough to be a Bug* is a computer-animated look at life from the point of view of the insect world,

How to Get There: Disney's Animal Kingdom is tucked into a previously undeveloped area in the southwest quadrant of Walt Disney World. Buses travel between Animal Kingdom and all of the Walt Disney World resorts. Direct bus transportation is also provided between this park and Epcot, Disney-MGM Studios, Blizzard Beach, Downtown Disney, and the Transportation and Ticket Center (TTC). The large Animal Kingdom parking lot is free to guests staying at any Walt Disney World Resort (others are charged about $6). The parking lot is serviced by trams.

In-Park Transportation: There is limited transportation to take visitors around this vast park. Animal Kingdom is designed as a walking park, and the pathways are vast and varied. In the past, passenger boats cruised the Discovery River, which circles Discovery Island, the main hub of the park. Visitors can board a steam train to take them across the savanna to Rafiki's Planet Watch and back again. ◆

Essentials • Attractions • Hotels • Restaurants • Special Events • Recreation • Resources

Magic Kingdom • Future World • World Showcase • Disney-MGM Studios • Animal Kingdom • Typhoon Lagoon • Blizzard Beach • Downtown Disney • Disney's BoardWalk • Fort Wilderness & River Country

Essentials Attractions Hotels Restaurants Special Events Recreation Resources

Fort Wilderness & River Country • Disney's BoardWalk • Downtown Disney • Blizzard Beach • Typhoon Lagoon • **Animal Kingdom** • Disney-MGM Studios • World Showcase • Future World • Magic Kingdom

ANIMAL KINGDOM

See the "Essentials" section for ticket costs and attraction updates.

Eating in the Wild

The Animal Kingdom dining experience is somewhat different from the dining choices in the other Walt Disney World theme parks. It is the most ecologically sensitive of the parks, and for reasons of safety for the animal life, lids and straws are not provided with soft drinks. Nothing is served in Styrofoam or foil, and even the napkins are unbleached paper. Rainforest Cafe, located at the main entrance, is the only full-service restaurant in the park; however, all of the counter-service restaurants at Animal Kingdom offer a greatly enhanced quality and selection of dishes.

Main Entrance

Rainforest Cafe — This colorful and fun tropical jungle-themed restaurant has a signature waterfall at its entrance (just as its sister restaurant at Downtown Disney has an erupting volcano above it). The restaurant is filled with the sights and sounds of the rain forest, including a thunderstorm every 20 minutes or so. Guests select from steaks, chicken, seafood, pastas, flatbread pizzas, and a variety of vegetarian alternatives, all with unique flavor combinations. Fruit juices and smoothies, beer, wine, and spirits are served, as are espresso and cappuccino. The restaurant serves breakfast from 7:30 until 9:30 AM, and lunch and dinner from 10:30 AM until park closing; reservations recommended. ➤

hosted by Flik of *A Bug's Life* fame. The line for the show winds around and under the roots of the tree and provides visitors with up-close views of its magnificent carvings. Duration: 8 minutes.

Camp Minnie-Mickey: *This is the Disney Character section of the park, but it maintains a natural setting in keeping with the feel of Animal Kingdom. Themed as an old-fashioned summer camp, the emphasis here is on Character greetings and featured stage shows.*

Character Greeting Trails   Similar in nature to the Disney Character greeting areas in the Magic Kingdom, here guests will find four trails, each leading to a sheltered greeting pavilion in the forest. Autograph and photo opportunities abound as visitors choose from Mickey and Minnie, Friends from the Hundred Acre Wood, Jungle Friends, Goofy and Pluto, and other special Characters. No time limit.

⭐ *Festival of the Lion King*   This is one of the best crafted stage shows to ever appear in the Disney theme parks. The production combines the music of the popular animated feature *The Lion King* with Audio-Animatronics figures, brilliant costuming, acrobatics, dance, and audience participation to form a truly memorable experience. Duration: 25 minutes.

Pocahontas and Her Forest Friends   This environmental message stage show, utilizing music and themes from Disney's *Pocahontas,* is a live-action production with real animals. The front section of the small theater is strictly kids-only, so that the little ones can see the animals up close. Duration: 12 minutes.

Africa: *Across the bridge from Discovery Island, visitors enter into the East-African themed village of Harambe, which means "coming together" in Swahili. Here visitors can explore the exotic architecture as they roam the shops and eateries. Or they can join an exciting safari, walk among the gorillas, or ride an old, creaky train out of the themed area and into the backstage where the animals are cared for.*

⭐ *Kilimanjaro Safaris*   This attraction has been a favorite of visitors since the opening of Animal Kingdom. Long lines, particularly in the morning hours, bear this out. Visitors are taken on a ride narrated by the driver in large, open canopied, bus-like safari vehicles. They travel through the African savanna where they are likely to see a variety of animals, including herds of zebras, giraffes, hippos, antelopes, lions, cheetahs, and even warthogs. An encounter with "poachers" creates excitement along the way. Since this is an open-range attraction among live animals in a natural setting, no two rides are exactly the same; there's always something new to see. If it is rainy season, wait until the afternoon shower ends, then join the safari; the rains tend to bring out the animals in force. Duration: Approximately 20 minutes.

Pangani Forest Exploration Trail

In this walk-through attraction, visitors traipse through a lush tropical jungle containing several different habitats, which provide the opportunity to see wild animals up close. Pangani means "place of enchantment" in Swahili, and that's exactly what is found here. Areas include a large aviary with rare African birds, a naked mole rat underground "village," glassed-in rooms with views of crocodiles and hippos, as well as meerkats (that's *The Lion King*'s Timon to the little ones) on their lookout mounds. The final section of the trails, however, is often the most memorable; this is the lowland gorilla habitat. Visitors are treated to views of a large family of gorillas in their natural surroundings. No time limit.

Rafiki's Planet Watch

Here, visitors leave the theme park environment altogether and travel by train backstage. This ride is interesting if only for the detailed theming of the old African-style train itself. Rafiki's Planet Watch is an interactive area designed to illustrate the need for conservation and protection of our natural world. At Conservation Station, visitors get a chance to see veterinarians, animal researchers, and keepers working with park animals. In Habitat Habit, visitors can find out how to make their own backyards and communities animal friendly. Outside is Affection Section, a small fenced-in petting zoo with domestic animals sure to engage the young at heart. No time limit.

Asia:

This exotic area of Animal Kingdom takes visitors into the ancient Kingdom of Anandapur, Sanskrit for "place of all delights," a fitting name. Here, amid colorful and beautifully forested pathways, visitors can interact with all manner of Asian animal life, experience the unexpected delights and thrills of the mysterious Kali river, and enjoy the unique and amusing antics of birds from all over the world.

Flights of Wonder

This open-air amphitheater is located on the pathway between Asia and Africa that runs along the Discovery River. It is home to an entertaining and educational presentation showcasing many exotic birds and birds of prey. The trainers and actors demonstrate all manner of bird life and even provide a few surprises. A special kids-only seating area is provided in front so they can see the birds up close. Duration: 20 minutes.

Kali River Rapids

There are signs at the beginning, at the middle, and at the end of the line leading to this ride that warn visitors: "You *will* get wet." Take them seriously. Visitors wind their way through an amazingly realistic rain forest through a mysterious

See the "Essentials" section for ticket costs and attraction updates.

Discovery Island

Pizzafari — Here, guests will find a very large and brightly colored environment in which to enjoy freshly made, hand-tossed pizzas, Italian sandwiches, and salads. There is also a small outdoor seating area in front of the restaurant that is right beside the most heavily traveled pathway in the park; excellent for people watching. Amber Safari beer is served, along with soft drinks.

Flame Tree Barbecue — At first glance, Flame Tree appears to be a small outdoor stand selling freshly smoked beef, pork, chicken, and ribs (all of which produce a inviting aroma). But further exploration behind the stand reveals a massive outdoor seating area with pavilions, ponds, waterfalls, and excellent river views. On many afternoons, live musical entertainment is provided.

Africa

Tusker House Restaurant — This sprawling indoor restaurant complex serves up a great combination of fresh rotisserie or fried chicken with steamed green beans and garlic mashed potatoes, beef stew in a bread bowl, salads, and beef or vegetable sandwiches. Just inside the restaurant and apart from the main food lines is the Kusafiri Coffee Shop and Bakery, serving up a tempting array of desserts and fresh bakery items (a great morning stop). In a sheltered area just outside the restaurant is the Dawa Bar, featuring cocktails, Tusker beer from Kenya, and contemporary African music.

Essentials • Magic Kingdom • Future World • World Showcase • Disney-MGM Studios • Animal Kingdom • Typhoon Lagoon • Blizzard Beach • Downtown Disney • Disney's BoardWalk • Fort Wilderness & River Country

Attractions • Hotels • Restaurants • Special Events • Recreation • Resources

Essentials

Attractions

Hotels

Restaurants

Special Events

Recreation

Resources

Fort Wilderness & River Country • Disney's BoardWalk • Downtown Disney • Blizzard Beach • Typhoon Lagoon • **Animal Kingdom** • Disney-MGM Studios • Future World • World Showcase • Magic Kingdom

ANIMAL KINGDOM

See the "Essentials" section for ticket costs and attraction updates.

Asia

Mr. Kamal's Burger Grill — This small food booth, on the pathway between Asia and Africa, is the closest thing that this corner of the park has to a restaurant. Mr. Kamal's serves up large broiled burgers and soft drinks; there are pleasant small seating areas overlooking the Discovery River behind the booth, or up and across the main path on the branch path to the right. Open seasonally.

Dinoland U.S.A.

Restaurantosaurus — This restaurant pulls double duty. In the morning, it hosts Donald's Prehistoric Breakfastosaurus, an all-you-care-to-eat Character buffet breakfast. It features Donald Duck, Mickey, Goofy, and Pluto. For Breakfastosaurus, reservations are recommended. At noon, Restaurantosaurus converts to counter-service dining, serving hamburgers, hot dogs, and salads, along with McDonald's French fries, Chicken McNuggets, and Happy Meals. Safari Amber beer is available, along with soft drinks. ◆

Asian temple filled with exquisite and exotic artifacts. Beyond the temple, they are loaded into large, round raft vehicles and whisked off, disappearing into the mists. Throughout the journey, there are wonderful sights and watery adventures, including one last pachyderm surprise that is actually controlled by those faint-hearted folks in your party who remained behind. Duration: 5 minutes. Height requirement is 42 inches.

Maharajah Jungle Trek One of the park's walk-through animal attractions, this area is even more extensive than its African sister, Pangani. Visitors walk through Anandapur Royal Forest and the ruins of a great south Asian palace with intricate architectural detail and artwork. A remarkable variety of Asian animals are encountered along the way, including giant fruit bats, komodo dragons, and an array of birds in a cleverly enclosed aviary. The really big draw of the attraction is the majestic tigers, close enough to make the pulse race. No time limit.

Dinoland U.S.A.: *The look and feel of Dinoland could be described as a whimsical roadside attraction from another era. As visitors cross the bridge, they emerge into a world where Route 66 meets Jurassic Park. This is where kids and kids at heart can indulge their dinosaur obsessions in every size, shape, and flavor. Dinoland attractions are designed to allow visitors to envision life on earth as it existed millions of years ago.*

The Boneyard This imaginative playground for children has plenty of space to crawl, slide, climb, and dig about. And how about an extra twist? It's an archeological dig site, too, where kids can participate in unearthing the skeletal remains of a woolly mammoth. No time limit.

Chester & Hester's Dino-Rama! Once a fun-filled shop overflowing with dinosaur trinkets, Chester & Hester's has expanded into a dinosaur-themed fun fair for younger kids and the whole family. A 50-foot-tall "concreteasaurus" overlooks the brightly colored carnival-style midway with zany arcade games. The area features two tame but imaginative rides for the young-at-heart:

> ***Triceratop Spin:*** Designed to delight the imaginations of children and transport them to a world of charming dinosaur toys, this ride features fanciful four-person dinocabs on spokes that spin and fly up and down around a colorful central hub. At the end of the ride, a dinosaur is revealed as the center hub opens. Duration: 3 minutes.

> ***Primeval Whirl:*** Chester and Hester have created a wacky time machine, a ride with rider-controlled spinning cars. Youngsters are thrilled as the cars spin through curves and down short drops, and finally into the jaws of a dinosaur. Open in 2002.

Dinosaur Through state-of-the-art Audio-Animatronics and visual effects, visitors in time machine vehicles are whisked back sixty-five million years to moments before the asteroid collision that ultimately wiped out the dinosaurs. The thrilling ride actually takes place in a moving vehicle that rolls, pitches, climbs, and rocks through a Jurassic nightscape with many surprises along the way. The amusing preshow, starring Phylicia Rashad of "Cosby" fame and Wallace Langham of "Veronica's Closet," sets up the story line for the ride; Langham narrates the ride throughout. The motion effects of this attraction toss visitors around pretty forcefully. The attraction is dark and fairly noisy and small children may be frightened. Duration: 4 minutes. Height requirement is 46 inches.

Theater in the Wild Live stage shows based on recent Disney films are shown daily in this large, fifteen-hundred seat amphitheater. Fabulous sets and excellent musical productions combine to make for a thoroughly entertaining experience. Past productions have included *Journey into Jungle Book* and *Tarzan Rocks,* both of which also showcased talented acrobatic performances. Duration: 30 minutes.

MAGICAL PLACES

Here and there throughout the Walt Disney World resort there are hidden grottos, sheltered pathways, secret gardens, and private look-outs. They wait only to be discovered and enjoyed by those who venture off the beaten paths. They are great places to stop and gather your thoughts or meet up with family and friends. Sometimes, just finding them can be rewarding and rejuvenating. We call these little discoveries Magical Places.

Discovery Lookout: Arguably, this is the most picturesque hidden treasure in Animal Kingdom. The entrance is located off the direct path between Asia to Africa, facing the river. Blink, and you'll miss it. Most people do. The path leads to a small cul-de-sac with two long wooden benches that face the Discovery River and look across at The Tree of Life, which is not visible from the main path. It's a great place to take in this rare view of The Tree of Life — and it's a super photo opportunity. For visitors who would like to enjoy a few minutes of quiet and solitude, this hideaway can't be beat.

Flametree Shelter: On Discovery Island, the seating area for the Flame Tree Barbecue is a wonderful place for removing yourself from the bustling crowd. Sit down, relax, regroup, and decide what adventure to explore next. This is especially true in the morning hours before the

Services

Rest Rooms — Public rest rooms are located strategically throughout the park. The least crowded rest rooms are those on Discovery Island, near the bridge to Dinoland U.S.A. and those adjacent to Chester & Hester's Dino-Rama! at the back of Dinoland. There is a small and less busy set of rest rooms on the path between Asia and Africa, though it is rather busy when the Flights of Wonder show is just letting out. Also, the rest rooms at Camp Minnie-Mickey, near the Character Greeting Trails, remain relatively uncrowded throughout the day. The rest rooms in Africa and Asia both attract the larger crowds.

Telephones — Visitors will find public telephones throughout the park, near rest rooms in every single case. The quietest ones can be found at Camp Minnie-Mickey.

Message Center — The Message Center is located at Guest Relations at the park's entrance, and is accessible from either inside or outside of the gates. The Message Center is on a network also shared by the Magic Kingdom, Epcot, and Disney-MGM Studios. Here, visitors can leave and retrieve messages for one another and exchange messages with companions visiting elsewhere. Anyone can phone in a message by calling the Message Center (407 824-4321). ➤

Essentials

Magic Kingdom • Future World • World Showcase • Disney-MGM Studios • **Animal Kingdom** • Typhoon Lagoon • Blizzard Beach • Downtown Disney • Disney's BoardWalk • Fort Wilderness & River Country

Attractions

Hotels

Restaurants

Special Events

Recreation

Resources

Essentials

Attractions

Hotels

Restaurants

Special Events

Recreation

Resources

Fort Wilderness & River Country • Disney's BoardWalk • Downtown Disney • Blizzard Beach • Typhoon Lagoon • **Animal Kingdom** • Future World • World Showcase • Disney-MGM Studios • Magic Kingdom

ANIMAL KINGDOM

See the "Essentials" section for ticket costs and attraction updates.

Lockers — There are lockers at the Entrance Plaza to Animal Kingdom, both inside and outside the gates. Outside, visitors will find a small room next to the ATM with lockers available for rent. Inside, just beyond Guest Relations, is a much larger locker area called Expedition Storage.

Banking — There is an automated teller machine (ATM) just outside the Entrance Plaza.

First Aid, Baby Care, Lost and Found — In the back of Safari Village, behind the Creature Comforts shop near the bridge to Africa, is a cluster of services, including First Aid, the Baby Care Center, Lost Children, and the park's Lost and Found. Look for the large ladybug lightpost as an identifying marker. Over-the-counter medications are available at Island Mercantile on Discovery Island.

Package Pickup — Purchases sent for package pickup will be found at Garden Gate Gifts, which is located inside the Entrance Plaza, near the beginning of the Oasis trails.

Strollers and Wheelchairs — Single and double strollers can be rented in the area immediately adjacent to Garden Gate Gifts at the Entrance Plaza. This is also the place for renting wheelchairs and electric conveyance vehicles (ECVs). Come early, as selection is limited.

Film and Cameras — Film and cameras can be purchased at Garden Gate Gifts near the Entrance Plaza. This is also the place for dropping off and picking up express photos. ◆

restaurant opens for lunch; at this time, the multileveled, open-air seating areas are quiet and almost completely undisturbed. It's located behind the restaurant's façade and is not immediately visible from the main pathways that carry visitors to Dinoland or Asia. There are many tables grouped in small courtyards surrounded by lovely stone ponds, small waterfalls, and the shoreline of the Discovery River. Some are canopied by brightly colored shelters, and the entire area is framed with large shade trees.

Forest Glen Trail: While this area can be found on park maps, it's generally unnoticed by the crowds hurrying to and fro on the direct path between Asia and Africa. Midway along the main path is Mr. Kamal's Burger Grill, and across the path are seating areas, beyond which the trail begins. It crosses two bridges that pass over babbling brooks, each fed by a waterfall. The thick, jungle-like foliage is dotted with many colorful tropical flowers. Look closely and you'll see an almost hidden side trail leading off into the forest. Follow it and you'll find a charming stepping-stone pathway across two forest streams. The trail makes a great after-lunch stroll and rejoins the main path near Africa.

The Forgotten Animal Trails of Discovery Island: Behind The Tree of Life, just before the bridge to Africa, a small trail meanders off toward the tree itself. This trail is actually part of the Discovery Island Trails, but most visitors overlook it. The path parallels the Discovery River as it winds beneath the roots of the tree and wanders past several small animal habitats. Midway through the trail is the exit from The Tree of Life Theater. When the production lets out, the trail becomes instantly crowded, but only in one direction. If you see those doors opening, you can duck over the river and relax under a tree root until the crowds pass. Continue on and you'll see several more forgotten trails that most visitors seem to miss.

Temple of Reflections: After crossing the bridge from Discovery Island to Asia, a small path leads off to the right, following the shoreline of Discovery River. The path to the temple begins behind Mandala Gifts. This statue-lined area has a small enclave with stone benches that overlooks an old temple ruin populated by a tribe of monkeys. Stop for a moment at the end of the path and enjoy the view at the edge of Discovery River. Down the river, you can see three of Animal Kingdom's bridges. Other than the benches, there is no seating, but the area is a refreshing oasis off the crowded main path. There is a smoking area located here.

Essentials

Magic Kingdom • Future World • World Showcase • Disney-MGM Studios • Animal Kingdom • Typhoon Lagoon • Blizzard Beach • Downtown Disney • Disney's BoardWalk • Fort Wilderness & River Country

Attractions

Hotels

Restaurants

Special Events

Recreation

Resources

PLANNING YOUR TOUR

Stop and Smell the Exotic Plants: Animal Kingdom, above all others, is a true theme park; it is *not* merely an amusement park. Visitors who approach Animal Kingdom with an open heart and filled with the spirit of exploration are more likely to have an enriching and memorable experience. Beyond the attractions, there are nooks and crannies with wondrous flora and fauna from all over the globe. You'll find many opportunities to stop and talk with informed Animal Experts or just quietly stroll the trails and immerse yourself in the theme.

Manage the Morning Crowds: First thing in the morning, the crowds entering the park move quickly through Discovery Island and head off to Africa. There is a persistent rumor that the wild animals are out and about mostly in the morning, so visitors hurry to the lines at the Kilimanjaro Safari as quickly as their feet will carry them. It is simply not true. What this means, however, is that other areas of Animal Kingdom, for the first hour or so, are practically all yours. Head toward Dinoland U.S.A. or Asia, or explore the many pathways of Discovery Island instead. During this time, you can enjoy Dinosaur or Kali River Rapids with little wait and then explore their respective surroundings at your own pace. Later, you can go to the Kilimanjaro Safari, get your FastPass to skip the line, and explore Africa the same way.

See the Shows: Animal Kingdom is huge. At times, shade can feel scarce and the walking can be daunting. But it has also been blessed with spectacular live shows. If you are not planning to leave the park for a rest in the mid-afternoon, take advantage of the shows to give yourself a refreshing and enjoyable break. Be sure, as in the other parks, to take a few minutes upon arriving at the park to check your Adventurer's Guidemap to confirm show times.

Late Afternoon Touring: If you have the advantage of park-hopping privileges, then the late afternoon crowd patterns at Animal Kingdom are ideal for you. After about 2 or 3 PM, the crowds begin shifting out of the park and attraction wait times decrease. The pathways are clearer, and in some areas of the park, you may feel that it belongs to you and you alone. Unlike other Walt Disney World parks, there is no major parade or evening show for folks to wait for after a tiring day of touring.

Take Advantage of FastPass: At certain popular attractions, visitors can pick up FastPass return tickets. They usually have a one hour delay and a one hour return time to a special short line leading to the front of the attraction loading area. Current FastPass time ranges are displayed above the attraction. ◆

ANIMAL KINGDOM

See the "Essentials" section for ticket costs and attraction updates.

E.A.R.S.
Expert Advisor Rating System
AWARDS

TOP 5
DO-NOT-MISS
ATTRACTIONS

Kilimanjaro Safaris
Festival of the Lion King
Dinosaur
Maharaja Jungle Trek
It's Tough to be a Bug

TOP 6
FAVORITE
ATTRACTIONS FOR KIDS

Kilimanjaro Safaris
The Boneyard
Festival of the Lion King
Camp Minnie-Mickey
Rafiki's Planet Watch
Chester & Hester's Dino-Rama!

TOP 5
FAVORITE
DINING EXPERIENCES

Tusker House Restaurant for Lunch
Restaurantosaurus Character Breakfast
Rainforest Cafe for Breakfast
Pizzafari for Lunch
Flame Tree Barbecue for All-Day Dining

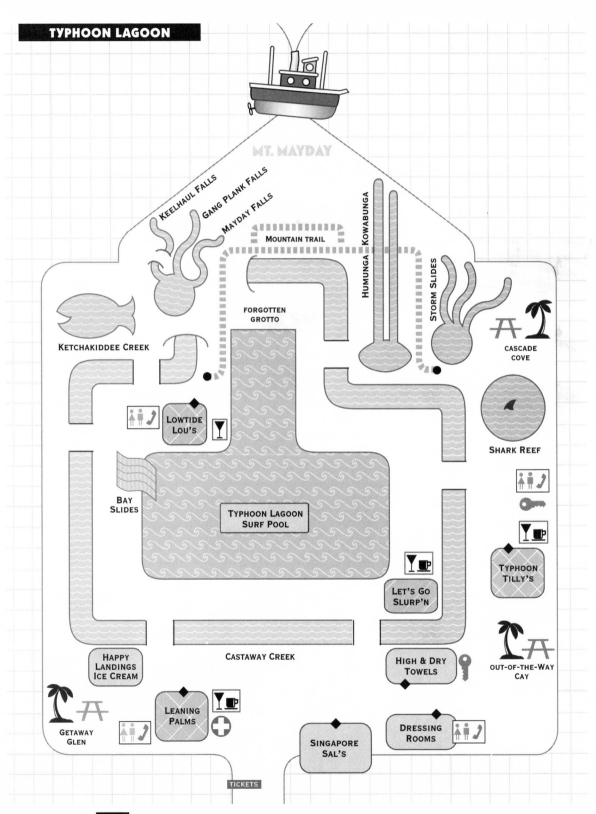

MT. MAYDAY

KEELHAUL FALLS

GANG PLANK FALLS

MAYDAY FALLS

HUMUNGA KOWABUNGA

STORM SLIDES

Mountain trail

FORGOTTEN GROTTO

KETCHAKIDDEE CREEK

CASCADE COVE

LOWTIDE LOU'S

SHARK REEF

BAY SLIDES

TYPHOON LAGOON SURF POOL

TYPHOON TILLY'S

LET'S GO SLURP'N

HAPPY LANDINGS ICE CREAM

CASTAWAY CREEK

HIGH & DRY TOWELS

OUT-OF-THE-WAY CAY

GETAWAY GLEN

LEANING PALMS

SINGAPORE SAL'S

DRESSING ROOMS

TICKETS

Essentials | Attractions | Hotels | Restaurants | Special Events | Recreation | Resources

Magic Kingdom • Future World • World Showcase • Disney-MGM Studios • Animal Kingdom • Typhoon Lagoon • Blizzard Beach • Downtown Disney • Disney's BoardWalk • Fort Wilderness & River Country

TYPHOON LAGOON

Typhoon Lagoon is an imaginatively designed fifty-six-acre theme park devoted to water play, with white-water rafting, snorkeling, waterslides, body surfing atop the largest machine-made waves in the world, and a long, lazy float down the meandering creek encircling the park. Depending on where their adventures take them, visitors can enjoy white sand beaches, shady coves, waterfalls, and misty rain forests. According to Disney legend, the lagoon was once the site of a peaceful fishing village, Safen Sound, Florida, that was devastated by a raging typhoon. When it was over, the Miss Tilly shrimp boat was neatly deposited on top of Mt. Mayday, the Placid Palms restaurant became the Leaning Palms, and a steamship moored at Shark Reef was permanently overturned. Part of the fun of Typhoon Lagoon is finding other telltale signs of the storm.

ATTRACTIONS

Typhoon Lagoon Surf Pool: The centerpiece of the park is the $2^{1}/_{2}$-acre lagoon and its famous wave maker, which creates impressive six-foot surfing waves. The machine also produces gentle bobbing waves that are perfect for floating on inner tubes, which are available for rent. The two types of waves alternate for an hour at a time all day long; surfing waves usually start on the even hours. Near the lagoon, a blackboard with the surf report gives information on the water temperature, weather, and alternating surf conditions. *Miss Tilly,* the former shrimp boat atop Mt. Mayday, gives a hoot and sprays a fifty-foot plume of water in the air every half hour, so visitors who are waiting for that first big curl can keep track of the time while experiencing other attractions.

Castaway Creek: Giant turquoise inner tubes draped with swimmers are swept along in the currents of Castaway Creek for a lazy 30 minute float around the perimeter of the park. At the five entrances (found at different points along the fifteen-foot-wide creek), visitors can wait for an empty tube to float by or grab one of the tubes stacked nearby for the taking. Visitors may also simply swim or drift along with the currents of the three-foot-deep creek if they wish. The currents are strong enough to keep floaters moving, and lifeguards stationed along the creek keep an eye on things. Rafters struggling to dodge flotsam and jetsam create laughing

When to Go: Typhoon Lagoon is open year round, except from mid-November through December when it is closed for refurbishing. The hours of operation vary throughout the year, so call Typhoon Lagoon Information (407 560-4141) to find out about opening and closing times.

During peak-attendance times (April through September) and weekends year round, it is essential to arrive before opening time (about 9 AM) since the park fills to capacity by about 10:30 AM and is closed to new arrivals until mid-afternoon. During low-attendance times (October through March), mornings can be cool, so plan to visit in the afternoon when Typhoon Lagoon provides a welcome respite from the frenzy of the theme parks. The park closes about 6 PM in cool months and at 8 PM during the summer.

Brief tropical rain showers are common in the summer months, usually in the late afternoon. During a storm, swimmers are chased from the water to wait it out, and many simply leave for the day. Once the storm passes, the park empties significantly, making a post-storm visit worthwhile. If the weather looks uncertain, call Disney Weather (824-4104) for details.

Essentials · Attractions · Hotels · Restaurants · Special Events · Recreation · Resources

Fort Wilderness & River Country • Disney's BoardWalk • Downtown Disney • Blizzard Beach • **Typhoon Lagoon** • Animal Kingdom • Disney-MGM Studios • World Showcase • Future World • Magic Kingdom

TYPHOON LAGOON

See the "Essentials" section for ticket costs and park updates.

How to Get There: Typhoon Lagoon is in the Downtown Disney Resorts Area, not far from Downtown Disney. Free parking is available in the Typhoon Lagoon parking lot. Buses service Typhoon Lagoon from the Walt Disney World resorts, the major theme parks, Downtown Disney, and the Transportation and Ticket Center.

Admission: Typhoon Lagoon admission is included with Length of Stay Passes and some Multiday Passes. At times during the summer months and Spring Break, when the park is open late, twilight admission prices may be offered. If you are arriving after about 3 PM, you can save as much as 30 to 50 percent on admission costs! These special savings are not announced, so always be sure to ask. See *Essentials* → "Admission Tickets" for entry costs. ◆

and bumping logjams. Where Castaway Creek passes through a misty rain forest, the going is slow enough to permit floaters-by to read the labels on the tropical trees and shrubs. A waterfall soaks all who pass under Mt. Mayday, so leave hats and cameras behind.

Shark Reef: Before entering the reef, be sure to visit the underwater viewing station. Fashioned as the boiler room of a half-sunken, overturned steamship, its windows reveal snorkelers swimming among the fish in the water above. The water in Shark Reef is salty and unheated to accommodate the Caribbean sea life. Those who wish to swim with the fish get life vests, snorkels and masks, and a 5 minute lesson in using them. Then it's off for a shower and a brief swim across the lagoon, which has two islands, loads of interesting fish, and several small sharks. Since Shark Reef is kept cooler than the rest of Typhoon Lagoon, it's a great place to really chill out on hot days.

Humunga Kowabunga: Thrill-seeking waterslide fans will be thoroughly satisfied by the terrifyingly steep and fast descent on these two slides: about a fifty-foot drop in less than 30 seconds. Clothing with rivets or buckles is not allowed, and one-piece bathing suits are advised for women. Sliding in thong-style suits may result in friction burns. Riders hit the water hard at the bottom, so nose plugs are also a good idea. The steepness of the slide is hidden from those in line by cleverly planted bushes. There are viewing bleachers at the bottom. You must be physically fit to ride this daring attraction. Height requirement is 48 inches.

Storm Slides: These three body slides are tamer than those at Humunga Kowabunga but still pretty exciting. Riders can choose from the Stern Burner, Jib Jammer, and Rudder Buster, all of which deliver more or less the same ride. Instead of a straight downward descent, these slides take riders on a circuitous corkscrew route through caves and waterfalls. The pool at the bottom is just deep enough to cushion landings (although they can be abrupt enough to wrench off the top of a two-piece bathing suit). There are viewing bleachers at the bottom.

Mayday Falls: Mayday Falls offers a twisty, speedy, bumps-and-ridges tube ride. The tubes are for single riders only, and riders are timed at the top and urged out at the bottom by lifeguards. Mayday Falls is slightly faster than Keelhaul Falls (see facing page).

Gang Plank Falls: Extra-large tubes that hold up to four people zip along speedily down the chute. Although this is the tamest of the three raft rides, in the process of shoving visitors off, the lifeguards duck every raft under a nearby waterfall, thoroughly soaking the occupants.

Keelhaul Falls: The tube ride down Keelhaul Falls is slower than the one down Mayday Falls, but it plunges into a pitch-black tunnel about half-way down. This is a real thrill and completely unexpected, since riders are hurtling along with no clue as to what's coming next. Riders end up safely at the common landing pool, where they quickly exit.

Bay Slides: These body slides for children, feeding directly into the quiet side of the Surf Pool and adjacent to the beach, are a great way for the kids to have some grown-up fun.

Ketchakiddee Creek: This little-kids-only area is specially designed for children and their parents. An assortment of scaled-down water rides similar to those found throughout the park is offered here, along with floating toys and a small waterfall. It's a happy, noisy area.

Surfing Lessons: Craig Carroll's Cocoa Beach Surfing School is offered on Tuesday mornings before park opening. Two instructors guide students through a half hour lesson on land and two hours in the water. Cost: About $125, including equipment. Reservations are required and can be made up to ninety days in advance through the Walt Disney World Recreation Line (407 939-7529).

SERVICES

Rest Rooms: Public rest rooms are located near Typhoon Tilly's snack bar, the Leaning Palms snack bar, and at the base of Gang Plank Falls, close to Lowtide Lou's snack bar. All the rest rooms can get quite crowded in the afternoons. The rest rooms at the Dressing Rooms are the largest.

Telephones: Public telephones are located outside the Dressing Rooms near Singapore Sal's and adjacent to all rest rooms. The phones inside the Dressing Rooms offer a shady spot for making calls. Those at Typhoon Tilly's are generally available.

Towels: Towels can be rented at High & Dry Towels, located to the right of the entrance walkway.

Changing Rooms & Showers: The Dressing Rooms, located next to Singapore Sal's, have many shower/changing rooms. Since all rest rooms in the park have shower cubicles, visitors can also use them to change, and most are less crowded than those at the Dressing Rooms.

See the "Essentials" section for ticket costs and park updates.

Refreshment Stands and Picnic Areas

The food stands at Typhoon Lagoon serve snacks and light meals all day, although the lines can be quite long. Snack and beverage carts throughout the park sell beer and soft drinks, and guests may bring food and beverages into the park, but no glass containers or alcoholic beverages. There are no cooking facilities.

Leaning Palms — The largest refreshment stand, Leaning Palms, is to the left of the main entrance. Pizza, hamburgers, hot dogs, salads, and turkey, tuna, and chicken sandwiches are sold here, along with soft drinks, milk shakes, beer, and coffee. Eating areas with shaded tables are nearby.

Typhoon Tilly's Galley & Grog — Located on the far right side of the lagoon, this large refreshment stand has two separate walk-up counters. Both sides offer snacks, beverages, and ice cream, but the left counter, which opens earlier in the day, serves hot dogs and sandwiches, as well as beer and coffee. There are shaded tables nearby, or diners can picnic on the sand at Cascade Cove. Typhoon Tilly's may be closed during slow seasons.

Let's Go Slurp'n — This thatch-roofed beach shack serves a limited supply of snacks, as well as beer, wine coolers, and spirits, including frozen fruit drinks. Nearby, facing the outer pathway around the beach, is another stand selling a variety of coffee creations. ➤

Essentials • Attractions • Hotels • Restaurants • Special Events • Recreation • Resources

Magic Kingdom • Future World • World Showcase • Disney-MGM Studios • Animal Kingdom • Typhoon Lagoon • Blizzard Beach • Downtown Disney • Disney's BoardWalk • Fort Wilderness & River Country

Essentials · Attractions · Hotels · Restaurants · Special Events · Recreation · Resources

Fort Wilderness & River Country · Disney's BoardWalk · Downtown Disney · Blizzard Beach · Typhoon Lagoon · Animal Kingdom · Disney MGM Studios · Future World · World Showcase · Magic Kingdom

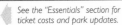

TYPHOON LAGOON

See the "Essentials" section for ticket costs and park updates.

Lowtide Lou's — This small beach shack near the entrance to Gang Plank Falls sells foot-long hot dogs and grilled cheese sandwiches as well as soft drinks, draft beer, wine coolers, and frozen rum punch, all of which can be enjoyed in the quaint shelter nearby. Lowtide Lou's is near Ketchakiddee Creek, so the noise level can be fairly high.

Happy Landings Ice Cream — This stand features ice cream treats that hit the spot on a hot day.

Getaway Glen Picnic Area — This picnic area on the left side of the lagoon near Leaning Palms offers several tables and a play area. A volleyball net is permanently installed, but there is plenty of room for eating as well as playing. Overhanging shelters provide a shady break from the sun, and mist from the rain forest keeps things cool on windy days.

Cascade Cove Picnic Area — This pleasant area is located between Shark Reef and Castaway Creek on the right side of the lagoon. Lounge chairs, wooden tables, and shady overhangs create a welcome picnic spot. Cascade Cove is larger than Getaway Glen but fills up rapidly because of its proximity to Typhoon Tilly's.

Out of the Way Cay Picnic Area — For a more secluded sunning experience away from the crowds of the park, this stretch of sand is a quiet alternative to the more frenetic beach area surrounding the Surf Pool. It is accessible from pathways leading around the Dressing Rooms or from behind Typhoon Tilly's. ◆

Lockers: Keys to lockers near the Dressing Rooms or near Typhoon Tilly's can be rented at High & Dry Towels. Visitors may specify the location that they prefer.

Watertoys: Life vests are available free of charge at High & Dry Towels. Tubes for the bobbing waves in Typhoon Lagoon can be rented at Castaway Creek Raft Rentals. During busy times, tubes are also rented on the beach. Visitors are not permitted to bring their own equipment into the park.

First Aid: The first-aid station is located to the left of the main entrance, near the Leaning Palms snack bar. Aspirin and other first-aid needs are dispensed free of charge.

Visitors with Disabilities: Wheelchairs may be rented just inside the entrance gate to Typhoon Lagoon, although only a limited number are available. All pathways are wheelchair accessible, and there is a ramp to the viewing station in Shark Reef. Most of the thrill rides may be inappropriate for people with serious disabilities, but Castaway Creek and the gentler bobbing waves in Typhoon Lagoon can be ideal.

PLANNING YOUR TOUR

This tour is designed for first-time visitors who would like to experience the best of Typhoon Lagoon in 3 to 4 hours. During peak seasons, this tour works best either in the early morning or late in the afternoon (3 or 4 PM), since the parks stay open later. In cooler seasons, the tour works best in the early afternoon (1 PM).

Visitors on the Peak Season Morning Tour can buy a snack-bar lunch inside the park, bring a box lunch from their hotel coffee shop, or plan to lunch back at their hotel or at nearby Downtown Disney. Visitors on the Peak Season Late Afternoon Tour may want to eat at the park and stay until closing (8 PM). Visitors on the Cool Season Early Afternoon Tour should eat lunch before they arrive.

Peak Season Late Afternoon Tour
April through September — Begin your tour after 3 PM.

Cool Season Early Afternoon Tour
October through March — Begin your tour at 1 PM.

Essentials

Magic Kingdom • Future World • World Showcase • Disney-MGM Studios • Animal Kingdom • Typhoon Lagoon • Blizzard Beach • Downtown Disney • Disney's BoardWalk • Fort Wilderness & River Country

Attractions

Hotels

Restaurants

Special Events

Recreation

Resources

Peak Season Morning Tour

April through September — Begin at 9 AM
(To avoid long lines, reverse the order of the numbered attractions.)

On the Peak Season Morning Tour, pack a tote bag with sun block and a hat or visor. Wear your bathing suit under your clothes. If you have a towel, bring it rather than waste time in the towel line. Arrive at the entrance to Typhoon Lagoon about twenty minutes before the park officially opens. Call Typhoon Lagoon Information (560-4141) or check with Guest Services in your resort for opening times.

● As soon as you enter the park, get in the line to rent towels and a locker (if you need them) at High & Dry Towels. Request a locker near Typhoon Tilly's.

● Set up camp in one of the sheltered coves near Typhoon Tilly's. On the Afternoon Tours you may need to wait and watch for the perfect site to appear as visitors begin to leave.

● Proceed to ❶ **Castaway Creek**. There is an entrance close to Typhoon Tilly's. Grab one of the extra tubes stacked here or look for an empty one floating by. Use the Water Tower as your exit landmark and take off down the creek for a revolution or two around the park.

● After you leave Castaway Creek, walk over to the ❷ **Shark Reef** viewing station for an underwater view. Then go topside to gear up and join the snorkeling tour of Shark Reef.

● When you're done at Shark Reef, return your diving gear and climb the stairs to Humunga Kowabunga, and turn off halfway up on Mayday Trail. Follow the trail across Mt. Mayday and behind Forgotten Grotto for a bird's-eye view of Typhoon Lagoon. Mountain Trail ends near ❸ **Keelhaul Falls**, where you can catch a white-water raft ride (or grab a beverage at Lowtide Lou's).

● If Keelhaul Falls whets your appetite for thrills, backtrack to ❹ **Storm Slides** and ride the spiraling water chutes. Daredevils can take the terrifying plunge at ❺ **Humunga Kowabunga**.

● Relax and ride the bobbing waves or body surf in Typhoon Lagoon (check the wave schedule in front of the Lagoon). The eruption of Mt. Mayday (every half hour) will tell you when surf's up. ◆

TYPHOON LAGOON

See the "Essentials" section for ticket costs and park updates. ▶

TOURING
Tips & Tricks

🚶 At peak-attendance times, there is always a long line for rental towels and locker keys. Bring your own towel if you can and leave valuables behind. If you must have a locker, get in this line when the park first opens and ask for a key to the lockers near Typhoon Tilly's.

🚶 Establish a "camp" by claiming a picnic table or lounge chair and leaving your towels, shoes, and belongings on top. At Typhoon Lagoon, this signals to all that it is occupied. Try to choose a site in the shade or under a shelter, which will keep your belongings dry in a sudden downpour and protect you against overexposure to the sun. If you want to work on your tan, you can always find a place in the sun.

🚶 In the summer months, Typhoon Lagoon is a tempting destination, but the crowds can make it difficult. A good time to visit is after 4 PM, when parents are taking their tired kids back to their hotels and others are leaving to pursue dinner plans. Late afternoon is an enchanting time at Typhoon Lagoon, which often stays open until 8 PM. The park takes on a tropical remoteness, and lines to the attractions are short or nonexistent, so you can frolic to your heart's content or simply plop down in a lounge chair with a cold drink under the swaying palms.

🚶 Many resort coffee shops will fix a box lunch, so you can eat well and avoid the long lines at refreshment stands. Purchase drinks at one of the Typhoon Lagoon beverage carts. ◆

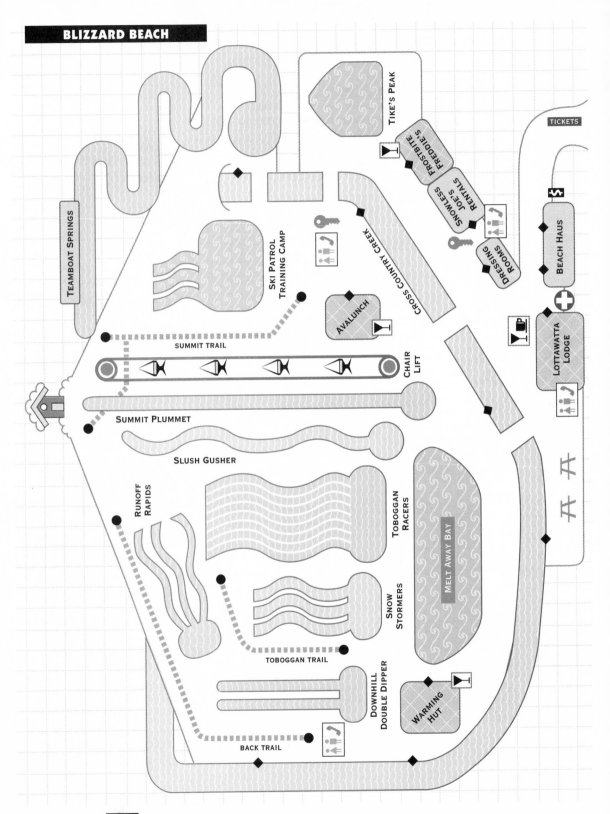

BLIZZARD BEACH

TIKE'S PEAK

TICKETS

FROSTBITE FREDDIE'S

SNOWLESS JOE'S RENTALS

DRESSING ROOMS

BEACH HAUS

TEAMBOAT SPRINGS

SKI PATROL TRAINING CAMP

CROSS COUNTRY CREEK

AVALUNCH

LOTTAWATTA LODGE

SUMMIT TRAIL

CHAIR LIFT

SUMMIT PLUMMET

SLUSH GUSHER

RUNOFF RAPIDS

TOBOGGAN RACERS

MELT AWAY BAY

SNOW STORMERS

TOBOGGAN TRAIL

DOWNHILL DOUBLE DIPPER

WARMING HUT

BACK TRAIL

Essentials

Magic Kingdom • Future World • World Showcase • Disney-MGM Studios • Animal Kingdom • Typhoon Lagoon • **Blizzard Beach** • Downtown Disney • Disney's BoardWalk • Fort Wilderness & River Country

Attractions Hotels Restaurants Special Events Recreation Resources

BLIZZARD BEACH

Blizzard Beach blends the wintery elements of a snowy landscape with the pleasures of splashing about under a warm tropical sun. Adventurous visitors can enjoy plunging waterslides and exciting tube and raft rides, while the more sedate can relax with around-the-park floats, beach picnics, and a stroll to Mt. Gushmore's summit for a bird's-eye view of the park. The Disney yarn about Blizzard Beach is that a capricious Mother Nature set a freak snowstorm raging on Florida's Mt. Gushmore, inspiring short-sighted developers to create an alpine snow park. When the climate returned to normal and the ice and snow began melting, so did the developers' dreams. As they surveyed their dismal situation, they noticed an alligator having fun sliding down the mountain slopes in the slush. The 'gator's good time gave the developers a brilliant idea: Instead of wintery activities like skiing and sledding, why not use the snow-park equipment to take advantage of the melting ice and provide challenging water sports instead? Blizzard Beach was the result.

ATTRACTIONS

Cross Country Creek: Relaxed riders on giant inner tubes drift along in the currents of Cross Country Creek for a pleasant 30 minute float around the perimeter of Blizzard Beach. Cross Country Creek may seem like a dull ride on first glance, but the alpine landscaping, occasional swift stretches, and a trip through a spooky cave of melting "ice" lend a bit of spice to the excursion. There are several entrances at different points along the creek where visitors can wait for an empty tube to float by or grab one of the tubes that stack up early or late in the day. Swimmers may also enter without tubes; the currents are strong enough to keep things moving.

Chair Lift: Visitors can walk to the top of Mt. Gushmore or board the zany, colorful Chair Lift to reach the following attractions: Summit Plummet, Slush Gusher, and Teamboat Springs. Riders on cable cars with mock skis attached beneath enjoy a sweeping view on their ascent. The trip is very slow, and riders must exit quickly at the top. The Chair Lift is a one-way ride — the only way back down from the top of Mt. Gushmore is on the Summit Trail or the Toboggan Trail.

When to Go: Blizzard Beach is open year-round, except from January to mid-February when it may be closed for maintenance. Operating hours vary throughout the year. To find out about opening and closing times, call Blizzard Beach Information (407 560-3400).

During peak-attendance times (April through September), it is essential to arrive before opening time (about 9 AM) since the park restricts new arrivals when its parking lot fills, usually by 11 AM. During low-attendance times (October through March), mornings can be cool, so plan your visit to Blizzard Beach in the early afternoon as a relaxing break from the theme parks. The park closes about 5 PM during the cooler months and at about 8 PM during the summer.

In the summer months, Florida has brief tropical rain showers, usually in the late afternoon. During a storm, swimmers are chased from the water to wait it out, and many leave for the day. After the storm passes, the park empties significantly, making a post-storm visit highly desirable. If the weather looks uncertain the day you want to go, call Disney Weather (824-4104) for details.

Essentials · Attractions · Hotels · Restaurants · Special Events · Recreation · Resources

Fort Wilderness & River Country • Disney's BoardWalk • Downtown Disney • **Blizzard Beach** • Typhoon Lagoon • Animal Kingdom • Disney-MGM Studios • World Showcase • Future World • Magic Kingdom

BLIZZARD BEACH

See the "Essentials" section for ticket costs and park updates.

How to Get There: Blizzard Beach is in the Animal Kingdom Resorts Area, not far from Disney-MGM Studios. Parking is free in the Blizzard Beach lot. Buses service Blizzard Beach from the Walt Disney World resorts, the major theme parks, Downtown Disney, and the Transportation and Ticket Center.

Admission: Blizzard Beach admission is included with Length of Stay Passes and some Multiday Passes. At times during the summer months and Spring Break, when the park is open late, twilight admission prices may be offered. If you are arriving after about 3 PM, you can save as much as 30 to 50 percent on admission costs! These special savings are not announced, so be sure to ask before you go. See *Essentials* → "Admission Tickets" for entry costs. ◆

Summit Plummet: Billed as the fastest waterslide on earth, Summit Plummet will delight thrill-seekers. The one-tenth-mile course starts at the "ski jump" perched on Mt. Gushmore's summit. At speeds over fifty miles per hour, riders free fall more than one hundred feet into a pool at the foot of the mountain. Viewers at the bottom will also get a thrill as they watch riders "vanish" from the slopes into a cloud of mist. Only physically fit people are allowed on the ride, which is over in less than a minute. One-piece suits are recommended for women and all swimmers should be "wedgie-aware." Height requirement is 48 inches.

Slush Gusher: At ninety feet, Slush Gusher is touted as the world's tallest waterslide. Although not quite as daunting an experience as Summit Plummet, Slush Gusher takes riders on a roller-coaster-like descent through a "wintery" canyon landscape. Riders are positioned feet first, on their backs, with arms and legs crossed, and actually become airborne on parts of this ride. The ride should be avoided by those with back problems. Height requirement is 48 inches.

Snow Stormers: Visitors ride rafts on one of three side-by-side slalom courses that zigzag down the mountainside. The challenge for rafters is to try to avoid bumping into the flags and "ski gates" as they speed down.

Toboggan Racers: Riders lie face down on toboggan-shaped rafts with front handles for a thrilling head-first plunge down Mt. Gushmore on one of eight side-by-side waterslides. Lifting the handles speeds the descent; to maintain control, push down when approaching the bottom.

Downhill Double Dipper: These wild slides drop riders on inner tubes down a fifty-foot slope as they race against each other side-by-side, reaching speeds of up to twenty-five miles per hour. The tubes are for single riders only. Height requirement is 48 inches.

Runoff Rapids: Three separate waterslides at Runoff Rapids, on Mt. Gushmore's back face, offer bumps-and-ridges inner tube rides for singles, doubles, and threesomes. One of the waterslides plunges riders into a twisty, pitch-black pipe slide.

Teamboat Springs: Extra-large inner tubes that hold up to five people zip over cascades as they race down a twisting one-quarter-mile-long flume, the longest of its kind anywhere.

Melt Away Bay: Nearly the size of a football field, Melt Away Bay with its white sand beach is located at the bottom of Mt. Gushmore. "Snow" from the mountain, "liquefied" by the warm Florida climate, cascades into the bay. The bay's wave-making machine, not nearly as dynamic as Typhoon

Lagoon's, creates gentle Caribbean-style swells for swimmers, floaters, and splashers. The beach is packed with lounge chairs for basking in the sun, but the shade value of the covered picnic tables makes them the most coveted and convenient hangouts.

Ski Patrol Training Camp: Designed primarily for pre-teens, the Training Camp offers three separate activities:

Mogul Mania: Mogul Mania offers a bumpy inner tube descent over a knobby, snow-lined water slide. The tubes are for single riders only.

Thin Ice Training Course: The challenge here is to walk across a swimming pool on floating, bobbing chunks of ersatz "ice" while holding onto an overhead cargo net.

Ski Patrol Shelter: Riders hang on to a suspended T-bar at Fahrenheit Drop and glide out before dropping into an "icy" pool. The fast slide at Frozen Pipe Springs exits into the same pool.

Tike's Peak: Specially designed for small children and their parents, this enchanting kids-only area offers a miniaturized Mt. Gushmore with selected scaled-down water rides similar to those found on the mountain. Squirting fountains add to the fun at this gleefully noisy area. Visitors seeking quiet relaxation should be sure to camp elsewhere.

SERVICES

Rest Rooms: Public rest rooms are located at the Dressing Rooms near the park's entrance and near Lottawatta Lodge, Avalunch, and the Warming Hut. Rest rooms can get quite crowded. The rest rooms at the Dressing Rooms are the largest; those at the Warming Hut are the least crowded.

Telephones: Public telephones are located just outside the park's entrance, outside the Dressing Rooms near the park's entrance, and near all the rest rooms. The telephones at Lottawatta Lodge are generally uncrowded. Those at the Warming Hut offer a quiet location for making calls.

Banking: There is an automated teller machine (ATM) just outside the park's entrance on the left.

Towels: Towels can be rented at Snowless Joe's Rentals near the park's entrance.

Shower & Changing Area: The Dressing Rooms near the park's entrance have the only indoor showers at Blizzard Beach.

Refreshment Stands and Picnic Areas

The refreshment stands at Blizzard Beach serve snacks and fast-food meals. Beverage carts near Melt Away Bay and across from Snowless Joe's Rentals sell ice cream, soft drinks, and beer. You may bring food and beverages into the park, but no glass containers or alcoholic beverages are permitted. There are no cooking facilities.

Lottawatta Lodge — The largest refreshment stand in Blizzard Beach, Lottawatta Lodge, resembles a ski lodge. Located near the park's entrance, the walk-up counter offers salads, hamburgers, hot dogs, pizza, and sandwiches, along with soft drinks, frozen fruit drinks, beer, wine coolers, and coffee. Tables on the partially shaded terrace provide great views of the action at Blizzard Beach.

Frostbite Freddie's — Tucked around the corner from Snowless Joe's Rentals, this refreshment stand sells soft drinks, frozen fruit drinks, wine coolers, and spirits. There are shaded tables in front of the stand.

Avalunch — Located near Tike's Peak, this food stand offers hot dogs, nachos, snacks, and ice cream, as well as soft drinks, beer, and wine coolers. There are shaded tables nearby.

Essentials

Magic Kingdom • Future World • World Showcase • Disney-MGM Studios • Animal Kingdom • Typhoon Lagoon • **Blizzard Beach** • Downtown Disney • Disney's BoardWalk • Fort Wilderness & River Country

Attractions

Hotels

Restaurants

Special Events

Recreation

Resources

Essentials • Attractions • Hotels • Restaurants • Special Events • Recreation • Resources

Fort Wilderness & River Country • Disney's BoardWalk • Downtown Disney • **Blizzard Beach** • Typhoon Lagoon • Animal Kingdom • Disney-MGM Studios • World Showcase • Future World • Magic Kingdom

BLIZZARD BEACH

See the "Essentials" section for ticket costs and park updates.

The Warming Hut — At this snow-covered snack shack, located on the far side of Melt Away Bay, visitors will find hot dogs, turkey legs, snacks, and ice cream, along with soft drinks, frozen fruit drinks, beer, and wine coolers. There are shaded tables nearby.

Polar Pub & Iced Cappuccino and Coffee — These two refreshment stands, one serving frozen alcoholic concoctions and the other serving iced cappuccino and coffee, are conveniently located just across the path that surrounds Melt Away Bay, near the picnic areas.

Picnic Spots — Shaded tables are not as abundant here as they are at Typhoon Lagoon. Your best bet is to arrive before opening time and rush to stake a claim at one of the covered picnic tables surrounding Melt Away Bay. If you want a picnic table, do this first. ◆

Lockers: Keys to the day lockers near the Dressing Rooms or near the rest rooms at Avalunch can be rented at Snowless Joe's Rentals.

Watertoys: Life vests are available free of charge (with a deposit) at Snowless Joe's Rentals. Visitors may bring flotation aids, such as water wings and flotation belts, but no masks or fins.

First Aid: The first-aid station is located near Lottawatta Lodge. Aspirin and other first-aid needs are dispensed free of charge.

Visitors with Disabilities: A limited number of wheelchairs are available just inside the entrance gate to Blizzard Beach. Most ground-level pathways are wheelchair accessible. The Chair Lift has a wheelchair car, and wheelchairs (but not visitors) are placed in it to return to the bottom. Most of the waterslides are off-limits to people with serious physical disabilities, but Teamboat Springs, Cross Country Creek, and the bobbing waves of Melt Away Bay are ideal for just about everyone.

PLANNING YOUR TOUR

This tour is designed for first-time visitors who would like to experience the best of Blizzard Beach in three to four hours. This tour works best in the early morning during warm months and in the afternoon year-round. Visitors on the Peak Season Morning Tour can buy lunch inside the park, bring a box lunch from their hotel coffee shop, or plan to lunch back at their hotel. Visitors on the Peak Season Late Afternoon Tour may want to eat at the park and stay until closing (8 PM) or plan a late dinner elsewhere. Visitors on the Cool Season Early Afternoon Tour should eat lunch before they arrive.

Peak Season Late Afternoon Tour
April through September — Begin your tour after 3 PM.

Cool Season Early Afternoon Tour
October through March — Begin your tour at 1 PM.

Peak Season Morning Tour
April through September — Begin at 9 AM
(To avoid long lines, reverse the order of the numbered attractions.)

On the Peak Season Morning Tour, pack a tote bag with sun block and a hat or visor. Wear your bathing suit under your clothes. If you have a towel, bring it along rather than waste time in the towel line. Arrive at the entrance to Blizzard Beach about 30 minutes before the park officially opens (between 9 and 10 AM). Call Blizzard Beach

Information (560-3400) for opening and closing times, which vary with the season.

● As you enter the park, you can rent towels and lockers (if you need them) at Snowless Joe's Rentals.

● Find a shady spot on the far side of Melt Away Bay, beyond the Warming Hut, and set up camp.

● Proceed to ❶ **Cross Country Creek**. There is an entrance close to the Warming Hut. Grab one of the extra tubes stacked here or look for an empty one floating by and take off down the creek for a float or two around the park. When you're ready for action, exit where you entered.

● Grab an inner tube at the Tube Pick-Up Station and head up the Back Trail to ❷ **Downhill Double Dipper** for a steep drop down this thrilling waterslide at speeds up to twenty-five miles per hour.

● Pick up another inner tube at the Tube Pick-Up Station and climb the winding Back Trail to ❸ **Runoff Rapids** for a white-knuckle tube ride down the back side of Mt. Gushmore.

a Grab a raft at the Mat Pick-Up Station and climb the Toboggan Trail to ❹ Snow Stormers to test your raft slalom skills, then grab another raft and ascend Toboggan Trail again for the downhill challenge at ❺ Toboggan Racers.

● Ride the Chair Lift to the summit of Mt. Gushmore — on busy days it may be faster to climb the steps of Summit Trail to the top — and take a wild tube ride down ❻ **Teamboat Springs**.

● Return to the top of Mt. Gushmore on the Chair Lift or climb the Summit Trail to the top, where thrill seekers can head for ❼ **Slush Gusher** to experience this very steep waterslide.

● If you are now ready for your big-time water adventure, head back to the top of Mt. Gushmore for the terrifying airborne plunge at ❽ **Summit Plummet**.

● Take a well-deserved rest and float on the waves in Melt Away Bay or relax on the beach to work on your tan and watch all the goings-on. ◆

BLIZZARD BEACH

See the "Essentials" section for ticket costs and park updates.

TOURING
TIPS & TRICKS

During high-attendance times in the warm months, long lines for rental towels and locker keys will greet you. If you are planning to visit on a crowded day, wear your bathing suit under your clothes. Bring your own towel, do not bring valuables or anything else you would want to store, and focus first on locating a place to "camp." Good shady spots are limited. If you do need a locker, get to the park well before opening time and get into the locker line first thing. There can be very long lines at the refreshment stands as well. Most resort coffee shops will prepare a box lunch for you to take into Blizzard Beach so you can avoid the lines. Many visitors also bring along beverages in small coolers.

The Florida sun is very hot and can give you a nasty sunburn, but its effects are especially powerful at Blizzard Beach, with its abundance of white reflective "snow." To protect your skin, bring along a tee-shirt to wear with your bathing suit; you can wear the shirt on the slides and when swimming. Protective footwear is also recommended; the walkways can become blisteringly hot.

During the busy summer months, Blizzard Beach is a tempting destination, but crowds can make it difficult to fully enjoy. A smart time to visit is after 3 PM on days when the park stays open until 7 PM or later. The crowds that arrived at opening time are starting to leave. Summer afternoon downpours, which last only a half hour or so, also drive crowds away. ◆

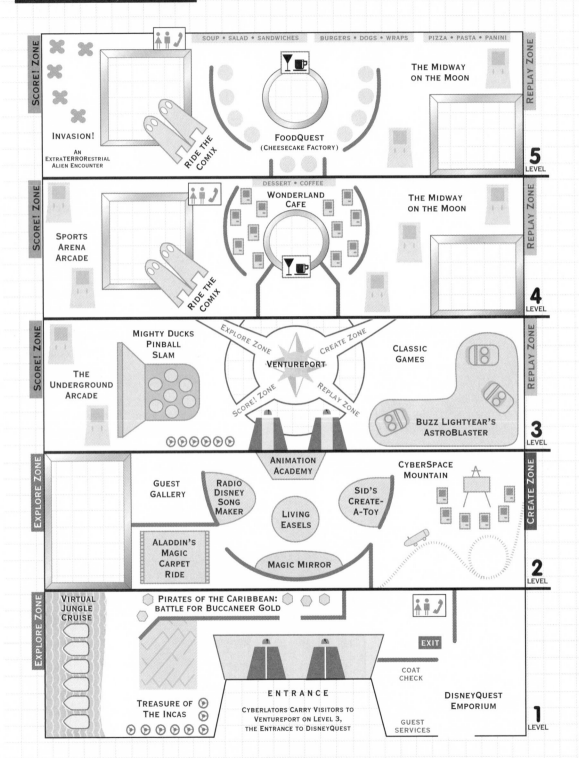

SCORE! ZONE

SOUP • SALAD • SANDWICHES   BURGERS • DOGS • WRAPS   PIZZA • PASTA • PANINI

REPLAY ZONE

THE MIDWAY ON THE MOON

INVASION!
AN EXTRATERRORESTRIAL ALIEN ENCOUNTER

RIDE THE COMIX

FOODQUEST
(CHEESECAKE FACTORY)

5 LEVEL

SCORE! ZONE

DESSERT • COFFEE

WONDERLAND CAFE

THE MIDWAY ON THE MOON

REPLAY ZONE

SPORTS ARENA ARCADE

RIDE THE COMIX

4 LEVEL

SCORE! ZONE

MIGHTY DUCKS PINBALL SLAM

EXPLORE ZONE   CREATE ZONE

VENTUREPORT

CLASSIC GAMES

REPLAY ZONE

THE UNDERGROUND ARCADE

SCORE! ZONE   REPLAY ZONE

BUZZ LIGHTYEAR'S ASTROBLASTER

3 LEVEL

EXPLORE ZONE

ANIMATION ACADEMY

CYBERSPACE MOUNTAIN

GUEST GALLERY

RADIO DISNEY SONG MAKER

LIVING EASELS

SID'S CREATE-A-TOY

CREATE ZONE

ALADDIN'S MAGIC CARPET RIDE

MAGIC MIRROR

2 LEVEL

EXPLORE ZONE

VIRTUAL JUNGLE CRUISE

PIRATES OF THE CARIBBEAN: BATTLE FOR BUCCANEER GOLD

EXIT

COAT CHECK

TREASURE OF THE INCAS

ENTRANCE
CYBERLATORS CARRY VISITORS TO VENTUREPORT ON LEVEL 3, THE ENTRANCE TO DISNEYQUEST

DISNEYQUEST EMPORIUM

GUEST SERVICES

1 LEVEL

DISNEYQUEST

The question most commonly overheard while waiting in line outside of the windowless, five-story teal-colored structure housing DisneyQuest is, "What exactly is this?" It's a question that has many answers. DisneyQuest is a world of interactive adventure; it can be likened to a futuristic, family-oriented arcade. The attraction combines traditional video games, old-fashioned prize redemption games (many with clever Disney themes), creative activities, and art projects. More significantly, however, Disney has created an entirely new breed of attractions and exciting virtual reality experiences that resemble a self-contained indoor theme park as much as it does an arcade.

Visitors purchase their admission tickets and enter the building through a small foyer with two elevators. These are no ordinary elevators — they are DisneyQuest's Cyberlators (hosted by Aladdin's Genie) that take visitors to Ventureport on the third floor, the heart of DisneyQuest and the jumping off point to the four entertainment zones that make the DisneyQuest adventure. Similar to themed "lands" that are found in a traditional theme park, the five floors of DisneyQuest are divided into four zones: Replay Zone, Create Zone, Score! Zone, and Explore Zone. And of course, when visitors have worked up an appetite with all of this strenuous adventure play, there is the two-story FoodQuest and Wonderland Cafe for refueling.

INTERACTIVE ADVENTURES

Upon emerging from the Cyberlators on the third floor, visitors find themselves at Ventureport, the crossroads of DisneyQuest. This area is the center of the third floor of the building and where visitors choose which of the four zones to visit first. There are staircases and elevators throughout the building, and the zones tend to meld into one another. The DisneyQuest building has five floors in all. What follows is a description of the interactive attractions by entertainment zone.

When to Go: DisneyQuest is open from 10:30 AM until midnight during the week; on weekends it stays open until 1 AM. Weekday mornings at opening seem to be the least crowded time to visit DisneyQuest. Crowds build quickly in the evenings after the theme parks begin to empty, and there is a sizable amount of local Orlando attendance on weekends and holidays.

How to Get There: DisneyQuest is located at Downtown Disney's West Side, next to the theater housing Cirque du Soleil and directly across from House of Blues. Direct bus service to the West Side is provided from the Transportation and Ticket Center and most Walt Disney World resorts. There is also a water taxi in the evenings that travels across Buena Vista Lagoon between West Side and The Marketplace.

This symbol next to an attraction designates a height requirement.

Magic Kingdom • Future World • World Showcase • Disney-MGM Studios • Animal Kingdom • Typhoon Lagoon • Blizzard Beach • **Downtown Disney** • Disney's BoardWalk • Fort Wilderness & River Country

Hotels   Restaurants   Special Events   Recreation   Resources

Essentials · Attractions · Hotels · Restaurants · Special Events · Recreation · Resources

Fort Wilderness & River Country · Disney's BoardWalk · **Downtown Disney** · Blizzard Beach · Typhoon Lagoon · Animal Kingdom · Disney-MGM Studios · World Showcase · Future World · Magic Kingdom

DISNEYQUEST

See the "Essentials" section for planning checklists and updates.

Admission: Admission to DisneyQuest generally includes unlimited play on all games and interactive attractions. There are additional fees for ticket vending prize redemption games, Sticker Shots vending machines, and for the tangible results of visitors' artistic creations. At various times, admission discounts are offered to Disney Annual Passholders, Disney Club Members, AAA Members, and American Express Cardholders. Discounts vary; be sure and ask which is best when you go. DisneyQuest admission may also be included in some Disney vacation packages. See *Essentials* → "Admission Tickets" for entry costs. ◆

Explore Zone: *This area, located on parts of the first and second floor, takes visitors on compelling adventures into the past. Visitors are transported to the primordial era of the dinosaurs, through an underground Incan kingdom, into the ancient Greek realm of Hades, and on a magic carpet ride.*

Aladdin's Magic Carpet Ride: On this virtual reality "ride," up to four visitors at a time race together on their magic carpets to rescue Genie, who has been imprisoned in the cave of wonders by the evil Jafar. Visitors mount contraptions that resemble motor scooters and place virtual reality helmets on their heads. Participants fly through Aladdin's palace on their magic carpet, which they pilot to collect sparkling gems. These treasures can be used on the quest to save Genie; however, Jafar serves up some nasty surprises along the way. Duration: 4 minutes.

Pirates of the Caribbean: Battle for Buccaneer Gold: This is a challenging and exciting virtual adventure for small groups. Visitors enter the bow of a pirate ship mounted on a motion platform. The ship has several firing cannons on both sides and a wrap-around video screen that creates a realistic 3-D view of a pirate's world. One of the group becomes captain and navigates, while the others man the cannons. The ship sets off across the high seas to terrorize and plunder other pirate ships and steal their treasures. When a ship is sunk, the treasure appears on the bow and the score is tallied. The adventure is filled with harrowing obstacles, including a fierce final battle to protect everything won during the action-packed voyage. Duration: 5 minutes. Height requirement is 35 inches.

Treasure of the Incas: Hear all that yelling? Visitors are trying to get through the maze of Treasure of the Incas to claim the prize at the middle. This attraction combines a wall of video driving stations manned by participants, who remotely control miniature utility vehicles mounted with cameras. The vehicles navigate a complex Incan maze underneath a see-through glass floor. Family, friends, and onlookers, acting as co-pilots, run along walkways over the glass floor, directing their favorite driver to the center of the maze, which holds the kingdom's treasure. This is a prize redemption game.

Virtual Jungle Cruise: In this attraction, visitors board rubber rafts that must be paddled to move. The rafts are whisked "back in time" sixty-five million years ago and dropped into a whitewater river that runs through caves, canyons, and dinosaur habitats. Visitors who are prone to motion sickness may want to avoid this ride; the simulation of water movement is very realistic. Duration: 4 minutes.

Essentials

Magic Kingdom • Future World • World Showcase • Disney-MGM Studios • Animal Kingdom • Typhoon Lagoon • Blizzard Beach • **Downtown Disney** • Disney's BoardWalk • Fort Wilderness & River Country

Create Zone: *This busy, colorful area, which is housed on the second floor of the building, is home to a variety of design stations, all devised to bring out the artist in everyone. Visitors may purchase souvenir copies of their creations to take home with them. Create Zone is also home to the most popular attraction at DisneyQuest, CyberSpace Mountain.*

Animation Academy: Visitors are seated at video design stations and are taught how to draw a Disney Character by a Disney animator. When finished, the designs and a "diploma" may be purchased for a small fee at the Guest Gallery at the back corner of the zone.

CyberSpace Mountain: This hair raising attraction is the most thrilling of the simulations at DisneyQuest. Visitors can create their own virtual roller coaster; the design process is hosted and explained by Bill Nye from the popular television show "Bill Nye The Science Guy." The design phase takes about 4 minutes to complete. The designs are rated on a "fear factor" of one through five, with one being very tame and five requiring a strong stomach. Once the design stage is completed, visitors proceed to the loading area where they are secured into a flight simulator that realistically reproduces the coaster design — including barrel rolls, hills, sharp drops, loops, and out-of-control skids. Up to two persons may ride a single coaster design simulation. Duration: 2 minutes. Height requirement is 51 inches.

Living Easels: At these design stations in the center of the zone, visitors create their own animated scene using an array of backgrounds, settings, accessories, and Disney Characters. Finished scenes may be purchased at the Guest Gallery.

Magic Mirror: At these design stations, the visitor's own facial image is captured in the "mirror." The image can then be manipulated, twisted, and changed in ways that resemble a high-tech funhouse mirror. Facial parts can be added, subtracted, distorted, and enhanced. Once finished, the copy of the picture may be purchased at the Guest Gallery.

Radio Disney Song Maker: This engaging attraction really brings out creative inspiration — especially in the musically-minded. Up to four visitors can enter a sound booth and become music producers and song arrangers. From a huge array of choices on a touch-screen computer, they select the style of music, the song lyrics, a male or female singer to perform it, and even the song title and album cover design. If visitors want a keepsake, the one-of-a-kind finished recording can be purchased in its own personalized CD jewel case.

DISNEYQUEST

See the "Essentials" section for planning checklists and updates.

Dining Quest

Only the dining options are grounded in reality at DisneyQuest. On floors four and five, respectively, are the Wonderland Cafe and FoodQuest, both operated by The Cheesecake Factory.

FoodQuest — This three-station food court offers a wide selection of salads, wrap sandwiches, hamburgers, hot dogs, French fries, pizzas, pastas, and panini. There's plenty of seating in the adjacent restaurant area.

The Wonderland Cafe — This small, comfortable dessert cafe entices visitors with incredibly decadent creations. Also available are fruit smoothies, espresso, and cappuccino, which can be enjoyed while relaxing in the cafe's whimsical over-stuffed chairs. Seating alcoves along the outer edge of the cafe feature Internet activities hosted by *Alice in Wonderland's* Cheshire Cat. ◆

Essentials

Attractions

Hotels

Restaurants

Special Events

Recreation

Resources

Fort Wilderness & River Country • Disney's BoardWalk • Blizzard Beach • Typhoon Lagoon • Animal Kingdom • Disney-MGM Studios • Future World • World Showcase • Magic Kingdom

DISNEYQUEST

See the "Essentials" section for planning checklists and updates.

Services

Rest Rooms: Rest rooms can be found on the fourth and fifth floors near the Wonderland Cafe and FoodQuest. These tend to be crowded, particularly at or near mealtimes. Additional rest rooms are located on the first floor, near the exit gates. These are almost always quieter. While there is no Baby Care Center at DisneyQuest, changing stations are provided in all of the rest rooms.

Telephones: Visitors will find telephones located near the rest rooms on the first and fifth floors. The first floor phones are more apt to be quiet, though the fifth floor bank is in an alcove somewhat away from the food service noises of FoodQuest.

Guest Services: A Downtown Disney information window is located outside the front of the building, near the exit from the DisneyQuest Emporium.

Lost and Found, Coat Check, and Storage: While there are no lockers at DisneyQuest, visitors may check their coats and packages at the window adjacent to the exit gates leading into the DisneyQuest Emporium. This window pulls double duty as the Lost and Found for the building. ◆

Sid's Create-A-Toy: The sadistic next-door neighbor boy in Disney's *Toy Story* and his horrifying hybrid toy creations are the inspiration for this attraction. Visitors choose from a medley of toy "parts" and come up with their own combination of weird and frightening creatures. Kits containing the actual parts may be purchased at the Guest Gallery.

Replay Zone: *This area of DisneyQuest, spanning parts of the third, fourth, and fifth floors of the building, is the DisneyQuest version of an old-fashioned gaming midway. Here, visitors will find Disney-themed prize redemption games, a slew of nostalgic video games, and a truly inventive take on old-fashioned bumper cars.*

Buzz Lightyear's AstroBlaster: Visitors board two-person vehicles which are an adaptation of the bumper cars of the past. The driver pilots the car, vacuuming up large plastic balls from the floor. The gunner then takes the balls from the compartment where they are deposited and fires them at other vehicles. A direct hit temporarily disables the targeted vehicle. Duration: 3 minutes. Height requirement is 51 inches.

Classic Games: The walls that surround Buzz Lightyear's AstroBlaster is surrounded by a comprehensive collection of fully-functioning games from the earliest days of video game play, such as Space Invaders, Asteroids, and Tron. Other video games include Burgertime, Marble Madness, Centipede, Millipede, DigDug, Battlezone, Donkey Kong, Pacman, Ms. Pacman, Mario Brothers, Berzerk, Zaxxon, Galaga, and more. No time limit; visitors may play as long as they wish.

The Midway on the Moon: These old-fashioned prize redemption games, many updated with Disney themes, are played using special point-value cards. Cards are purchased at a station located on the fourth floor.

Score! Zone: *This area, encompassing one side of floors three, four, and five, is a futuristic and state-of-the art gaming center. It is also the loudest area of DisneyQuest by far. Here, visitors can play live action sports-themed games, become human pinballs, travel into the comic book world, and even use some of that famous XS Technology of the Magic Kingdom's Tomorrowland.*

Invasion! An ExtraTERRORestrial Alien Encounter: In this exciting attraction inspired by The ExtraTERRORestrial Alien Encounter, two to four visitors — a driver and gunners — are escorted into rescue vehicles provided by XS Technology. The object of the mission is to rescue colonists on a hostile planet which is under attack by some pretty mean aliens —

and the crew only has 3 minutes to successfully rescue as many as they can. Gunners should try not to shoot the colonists as they hold off the invading aliens. Duration: 4 minutes.

Mighty Ducks Pinball Slam: On this attraction, visitors take their places at a console which resembles the Mighty Ducks team mascot. Players become a numbered ball that they can see moving on a two-story screen before them. In order to move their pinball up and down the field, players must rock the console back and forth and from side to side, which causes the ball to hit anything that's lit up and score points. The highest scores are announced to the crowd at the end of the game. Duration: 3 minutes. Height requirement is 48 inches.

Ride the Comix: This virtual reality attraction has two separate, exactly duplicated lines and entrances on the fourth and fifth floors. It pits human visitors in a vigorous fight against comic-book super villains. Visitors are escorted to simulators in which they wield lightsabers. Inside the virtual reality helmet, visitors can actually see the blade move exactly as their hands do. Several henchmen are thrown into the fray until the final battle showdown with the super villains. Winning battles — or even just trying to win battles — can make this attraction quite an aerobic workout. Up to six visitors may battle at once on each floor. Duration: 4 minutes.

Sports Arena Arcade: Another of DisneyQuests' arcade gaming areas, the Sports Arena, provides visitors with the latest in sports-oriented video game simulator technology. It encompasses much of the fourth floor. No time limit.

The Underground: All throughout the third floor, visitors will find the very latest in cutting-edge video games. Game room standards are here too, including race driving games, air hockey tables, and pinball machines. Although there are a few mildly violent martial arts games, there are none in which "gun fire" is aimed at on-screen characters. ◆

DISNEY QUESTIONS

When does DisneyQuest get really crowded?

DisneyQuest becomes uncomfortably crowded on weekend evenings. The best times to visit DisneyQuest are on Sundays and weekday mornings. DisneyQuest also receives an influx of visitors when the weather outside turns inclement or rainy.

Can I go in free of charge just to watch my kids play?

No, DisneyQuest is treated like any other paid attraction. However, it does have a handstamp and re-entry policy, so visitors who want to leave and meet with other members of their party may do so and then return.

What age groups enjoy DisneyQuest most?

Nearly every age group can have a great experience here. However, the very young — age five and below — will have limited choices due to height restrictions. Many adults assume that the DisneyQuest experience is geared towards older kids and teenagers, but once adults go inside, they quickly find that there are plenty of attractions to keep them entertained. The premier attractions, such as CyberSpace Mountain and Ride the Comix, are quite unique, and all are user-friendly. Cast Members are on hand to explain games and answer questions. Some visitors may find DisneyQuest to be quite noisy; most of the attractions generate some sound. ◆

BUENA VISTA LAGOON

HOUSE OF BLUES

CIRQUE DU SOLEIL

WOLFGANG PUCK CAFE

BONGOS CUBAN CAFE

FORTY THIRST STREET

VALET PARKING

DISNEYQUEST

VIRGIN MEGASTORE

SHOPS

AMC THEATRES

SHOPS

WEST SIDE

CLOSE UP

DISNEY INSTITUTE

HOTEL PLAZA BLVD.

BUENA VISTA LAGOON

PLEASURE ISLAND

MARKETPLACE

BUENA VISTA DRIVE

WEST SIDE

SERVICE STATION

DOWNTOWN DISNEY

DISNEY'S WEST SIDE

Magic Kingdom • Future World • World Showcase • Disney-MGM Studios • Animal Kingdom • Typhoon Lagoon • Blizzard Beach • Downtown Disney • Disney's BoardWalk • Fort Wilderness & River Country

Attractions
Hotels
Restaurants
Special Events
Recreation
Resources

T*he West Side is part of the waterfront dining, shopping, and entertainment complex at Downtown Disney, which also includes Pleasure Island and The Marketplace. A hip, eclectic place with trendy restaurants, live performances, and cutting-edge attractions at DisneyQuest, The West Side is Walt Disney World's pop-cultural crossroads, an entertainment venue for visiting artists and top-name performers, and an enclave, as well, for celebrity-owned restaurants and nightclubs. Wolfgang Puck displays his culinary genius in a casual cafe setting overlooking Buena Vista Lagoon. Bongos Cuban Cafe, a smart supper club created by pop star Gloria Estefan, features Latin music and Cuban cuisine in a colorful Caribbean setting. House of Blues, the famous concert club of musical worship created by Isaac Tigrett and Dan Aykroyd, offers regional Louisiana Delta cuisine and top musical talent in concert every night. The internationally acclaimed Cirque du Soleil perform their circus magic five days a week in a sensational performance hall designed just for the show.*

WEST SIDE SHOPS

Along the sides of the AMC Theatres complex is a fascinating selection of quirky and fun shops, each offering something unique. The view down the strip is a visual treat, with the brilliant colors and visually intriguing designs of the storefronts.

Disney's Candy Cauldron: This shop's official mascot is the wicked queen from *Snow White* in her witch guise; most appropriately, a specialty of the shop is wickedly delicious fresh-dipped caramel apples. A large variety of other hand-made and prepackaged candy treats is available, including fudge and chocolate favorites, and visitors can watch the treats being made through the shop's front window.

Celebrity Eyeworks Studio: From sporty to funky, the eye-popping assortment of designer eyeglass frames at this store will please even the most finicky fashion shopper. Frames can be bought as is, filled with prescription lenses, or made into sunglasses. Large movie canisters and director's chairs add to the celebrity atmosphere.

When to Go: Most West Side restaurants are open all day. The AMC Theatres show films from 10 AM until 1 AM (2 AM on the weekends). The shops are open from 10:30 AM until midnight. The most crowded nights are Friday and Saturday, when local residents come out to join the fun. Concert tickets can be reserved directly from the clubs, or in some cases, purchased from Ticketmaster. For a listing of entertainment events and reservation information, call Walt Disney World Information (407 824-4321). For a listing of films and show times or to order tickets, call the AMC Theatres (407 827-1308).

How to Get There: The West Side is located at Downtown Disney along the shore of Buena Vista Lagoon, next to Pleasure Island. The large Downtown Disney parking lot is free. Buses travel between the resorts and theme parks and Downtown Disney. Water taxis service the following resorts: Port Orleans and Old Key West. Starting at 5 PM, valet parking is available for about $6. Taxi service is available.

Admissions: Admission to Disney's West Side is free, and there are no age restrictions. Each nightclub or show has its own age policies and ticket price or cover charge. ◆

Essentials · Attractions · Hotels · Restaurants · Special Events · Recreation · Resources

Fort Wilderness & River Country • Disney's BoardWalk • Downtown Disney • Blizzard Beach • Typhoon Lagoon • Animal Kingdom • Disney-MGM Studios • World Showcase • Future World • Magic Kingdom

WEST SIDE

See the "Essentials" section for seasonal events and updates.

Live Performances!

Cirque du Soleil: Inside the enormous tent-like structure at the far end of Disney's West Side is one of a growing series of resident shows by the renowned circus group, Cirque du Soleil. This production, *La Nouba,* is exclusive to Downtown Disney. Here, visitors are treated to a seamless, dreamlike 90-minute production combining original music, surrealistic art, fanciful costuming, physical humor, unbelievable gravity-defying acrobatics, and pure grace. The show is likely to exceed visitors' every expectation. The unique structure of the theater, along with stadium seating and plenty of legroom, provides a comfortable and easy view from every seat. Shows are generally performed twice daily, five days per week. Tickets may be purchased at the box office or through will-call at 407 939-7600.

House of Blues: Performances by top musicians are a regular event at the House of Blues concert hall. The club's television studio and radio broadcast facilities make this the West Side's hot spot of sensational musical happenings. On Sundays, House of Blues hosts a Gospel Brunch with live entertainment. Advance reservations are a must. For performance schedules or to purchase tickets for concerts or brunch, contact House of Blues box office (407 934-2583) or a Ticketmaster outlet. ◆

Forty Thirst Street: Situated at the entrance to the West Side, across from the shops along the back of the AMC Theatres complex, this counter-service cafe serves up a great selection of coffee drinks (for the true caffeine addict, try the Red Eye), smoothies, and dessert creations. Interior seating is limited; however, quite a few tables and chairs can be found to the side and behind the building. This is a perfect morning spot overlooking Buena Vista Lagoon, and in the evenings, it's a prime place for people watching.

Guitar Gallery: Around the side of the AMC Theatres, facing the Virgin Megastore, is this small shop featuring an array of rare celebrity guitars. A display of vintage guitars changes frequently, and there's always something notable to be found.

Hoypoloi: This decorative art shop offers original and distinctive creations for the home. The eclectic selection includes windchimes, mobiles, glass sculptures, gift books, and delicate treasures.

Magnetron: All around the steel walls of this shop is a staggering selection of refrigerator magnets in every possible collectible category. Themes range from America's favorite television shows, Florida tourist spots, space aliens, pets, and life-size faux food items. Magnets that beep, play a tune, and glow in the dark can also be found here.

Mickey's Groove: A neat little shop with really unique Mickey Mouse merchandise and trendy treasures you won't find anywhere else.

Planet Hollywood on Location: This is an outlet for proprietary merchandise for Planet Hollywood restaurant, which is located nearby, adjacent to Pleasure Island. Visitors can choose from tee-shirts, athletic wear, jackets, and other Planet Hollywood logo merchandise.

Sosa Family Cigars: In addition to being one of the few places on Disney property to sell a variety of cigarettes and tobacco products, this shop also has an extensive selection of fine domestic and imported cigars. Humidors and the art of hand rolling cigars are showcased here.

Starabilias: Here, visitors will find an amazing array of movie-themed collectibles, one-of-a-kind artifacts and antiques, historical items, and autographed celebrity merchandise. Fans of classic movies and much-loved television shows, such as "I Love Lucy," will find plenty to choose from.

Wildhorse Store: This shop is the merchandise outlet and gift shop for the Wildhorse Saloon (located at nearby Pleasure Island). It features a wide variety of country-western clothing and accessories, including leather jackets, hats, western shirts, and work and dress boots. Wildhorse Saloon souvenirs, such as tee-shirts, can be purchased here.

MEDIA & ELECTRONIC ENTERTAINMENT

AMC Theatres: AMC Theatres is frequented by visitors to both the West Side and Pleasure Island. Twenty-four screens (including sixteen with Continental stadium seating) show first-run movies all day. Two of the larger theaters, used for new releases and first-run premieres, recall the splendor and luxury of the movie palaces from an earlier era, with three-story-tall screens and balcony seating. The lowest-priced movie tickets are available to all visitors for shows between 4 and 6 PM. Guests staying at a Walt Disney World resort may also receive a 30 percent discount on movie tickets throughout the evening (after 6 PM) with their resort ID. Be sure to ask! Visitors can get current movie listings and show times, as well as charge tickets up to 3 days before the show by calling the theater (407 827-1308).

DisneyQuest: This cutting-edge indoor theme park, amusement center, and multilevel arcade boasts the latest in gaming technology, including interactive play areas, virtual reality adventures, and the latest grand-scale arcade games. It's the best of the new breed of indoor attractions for the whole family, and a great air-conditioned or rainy-day alternative to the theme parks. Admission is charged. See *Attractions* → "DisneyQuest."

Virgin Megastore: This cavernous two-story structure, situated between the AMC Theatres complex and DisneyQuest, is much more than a music store. A retail spin-off of the London-based recording label, the store features thousands of music and video titles (including many hard-to-find imports), along with an impressive array of books and computer software. For shoppers, there are more than three hundred listening stations, video viewing stands, and computer terminals for trying out software. Jazz, Classical, and World Music enthusiasts will find entire rooms dedicated to their favorites; the Classical Music room's listening stations are particularly inviting, with large overstuffed chairs where visitors can relax while they listen. The book department, located on the second floor, features magazines from around the globe in addition to a full selection of book titles. Also upstairs is a robust array of software and children's video and music titles with kid-sized listening and viewing stations. In the Disney music department, the prices are often significantly lower than at Disney-owned outlets elsewhere at Walt Disney World. The cafe at Virgin Megastore serves up fresh-brewed gourmet coffees as well as teas and rich desserts, and shoppers can sit and pore over their book selections while sipping a drink. A small outdoor terrace that overhangs the main entrance provides extra seating for the cafe. The terrace is actually a hydraulic stage

Services

Rest Rooms — At the West Side, public rest rooms can be found inside all of the full-service restaurants and the attractions. Other rest rooms are on the back side of the Forty Thirst Street building (the ladies' room is on the back side facing the lagoon), upstairs in Virgin Megastore's book section (the quietest ones by far), and under the stairs outside of the Cirque du Soleil performance hall.

Telephones — Public telephones are fairly scarce in this area; a large bank of phones is located on the back side of the Forty Thirst Street building, and there are a few beneath the exterior staircase at Cirque du Soleil. Neither location is particularly quiet.

Guest Services — Walt Disney World Guest Services can be found on the entrance side of the DisneyQuest building; a larger desk is located inside the AMC Theatres complex.

Banking — An automated teller machine (ATM) is located near the box office at House of Blues, across from the main entrance to DisneyQuest. ◆

Essentials

Magic Kingdom • Future World • World Showcase • Disney-MGM Studios • Animal Kingdom • Typhoon Lagoon • Blizzard Beach • **Downtown Disney** • Disney's BoardWalk • Fort Wilderness & River Country

Attractions

Hotels

Restaurants

Special Events

Recreation

Resources

Essentials

Attractions

Hotels

Restaurants

Special Events

Recreation

Resources

Fort Wilderness & River Country • Disney's BoardWalk • **Downtown Disney** • Blizzard Beach • Typhoon Lagoon • Animal Kingdom • Disney-MGM Studios • World Showcase • Future World • Magic Kingdom

WEST SIDE

See the "Essentials" section for seasonal events and updates.

E.A.R.S.

Expert Advisor Rating System
AWARDS

TOP 6 FAVORITE DOWNTOWN DISNEY DINING EXPERIENCES

Wolfgang Puck
(sushi at the bar)

Rainforest Cafe
(coconut shrimp in the gorilla room)

Bongos Cuban Cafe
(steak on the terrace)

House of Blues

Portobello Yacht Club
(great martinis)

Wolfgang Puck Express

On Magical Moments...

"Riding the Monorail (in front, of course) as it circles around Future World at Epcot."

Pete Werner, E.A.R.S. Panelist

"A pontoon boat rental to watch IllumiNations."

Andy Dannelley, E.A.R.S. Panelist

"Seeing the sun set over The Tree of Life."

Deb Wills, E.A.R.S. Panelist

"Entering the turnstiles, walking under the train station, and viewing the castle for the first time every trip."

Brian Bennett, E.A.R.S. Panelist

"The common thread through these magical experiences — family — is more important than the specifics."

Brian Charles Kohn, E.A.R.S. Panelist

that can be lowered to eight feet above the ground for special events and featured musical artists. Virgin Megastore opens about half an hour before the rest of the West Side shops.

ENTERTAINING DINING

Dining is part of the entertainment on the West Side waterfront. See the "Restaurants" section for full reviews and reservation information.

Bongos Cuban Cafe: Cuban-style cuisine and live entertainment energize this festive dinner club created by pop star Gloria Estefan and her husband Emilio. A three-story pineapple growing up through the multilevel building sets the Caribbean mood, and as guests dine, a Latin guitar trio performs. On weekends, a Cuban band puts on a lively, upbeat performance with dancing, followed by a late-night cabaret during which guests can drop in and sample appetizers while they take in the show. Beer, wine, and spirits are served. Open for lunch and dinner from 11 AM until 2 AM; no reservations are accepted.

House of Blues: The House of Blues restaurant, adjacent to the music hall, offers authentic Southern favorites including jambalaya, étouffée, po'boys, and their award-winning bread pudding. The decor is a medley of bold colors and textures, African-American folk art, and musical artifacts. Video and audio monitors situated throughout the restaurant play tribute to blues greats. A jazz trio entertains while guests dine. Beer, wine, and spirits are served. Open for lunch and dinner from 11 AM until 2 AM; no reservations are accepted. House of Blues regularly hosts well-known performers in concert at their Music Hall next door; to purchase tickets contact Ticketmaster or call House of Blues directly at 407 934-2583.

Planet Hollywood: This restaurant serves up trendy music and the razzle dazzle of Hollywood movies along with tasty dishes served in jumbo portions, ranging from hamburgers and pizza to creative seasonal entrees. Beer, wine, and spirits are served, along with excellent cappuccino and espresso. Open from 11 AM until 2 AM; no reservations are accepted.

Wolfgang Puck Cafe: Internationally renowned chef Wolfgang Puck brings his unique cuisine to Downtown Disney. This relaxed two-story cafe, with soft lighting and snazzy decor, is a showcase of imaginative California cuisine and specialty pizzas that guests can enjoy while seated inside or outdoors overlooking the lagoon. Beer, wine, and spirits are served, as are cappuccino and espresso. In a separate area, Wolfgang Puck Express offers take-out delicacies. The restaurant is open all day from 11 AM until 2 AM; no reservations are accepted. ◆

Essentials

Magic Kingdom • Future World & World Showcase • Disney-MGM Studios • Animal Kingdom • Typhoon Lagoon • Blizzard Beach • **Downtown Disney** • Disney's BoardWalk • Fort Wilderness & River Country

Attractions   Hotels   Restaurants   Special Events   Recreation   Resources

PLEASURE ISLAND

Pleasure Island is a six-acre enclave of sophisticated evening entertainment. It is located in the center of Downtown Disney, between the shops at The Marketplace and the nightclubs and performance halls at Disney's West Side. By day, you can shop at the island's trendy stores, have lunch at one of several good restaurants, or catch a matinee at the 24 screen movie theater complex. At night, however, Pleasure Island is transformed: Limousines line up at the entrances, the streets fill with party-goers, and the nightclubs open their doors. At midnight, there's a splashy New Year's Eve celebration and fireworks show, and the partying continues into the wee hours. Every night on Pleasure Island is a street party, often with special entertainment events, visiting performers, or seasonal celebrations.

NIGHTCLUBS

Adventurers Club: Entered from above on a memorabilia-filled balcony that overlooks the main room, this take-off on a 1930s British explorers club revolves around a group of regular "club members." The members are actually delightfully eccentric performers who mingle with visitors and embroil them in zany interactive comedy skits. The downstairs features a parlor furnished with Victorian-style sofas and love seats, and a bar whose barstools rise and lower subtly and unexpectedly. The club appeals to anyone who likes to sit back and watch the goings-on, and it draws a core of regulars who like to participate in the wacky performances. Beer, wine, and spirits are served, including such specialty drinks as the Kungaloosh, a frozen blend of fruit juices laced with rum and blackberry brandy. A limited selection of snacks is also available. The Adventurers Club opens at 7 PM, and every hour or so, visitors are ushered into the Club's library for a delightful show. Check the club's entertainment schedule for show times. Smoking is not permitted in this club.

BET SoundStage Club: Jazz, rhythm and blues, soul, hip-hop, and hardcore rap share the stage at this waterfront club, owned by Black Entertainment Television. Video screens show a continuous stream of music videos and concerts by popular performers. The sophisticated lighting, state-of-the-art acoustics, and chrome-and-wood decor create the ideal atmosphere for visitors who love to dance and those who simply

When to Go: Pleasure Island's clubs are open from between 7 and 8 PM until 2 AM. Shops are open from 10 AM until 1 AM, and the AMC Theatres screen films from 10:30 AM until 1 AM (until 2 AM on weekends). The most crowded nights are Thursday (when Walt Disney World Cast Members receive a discount on admissions) and Friday and Saturday, when local residents join the ranks of Walt Disney World visitors.

To sample all of the island's legendary nightlife, you'll need to get an early start; some clubs get rolling as early as 7:30 PM. Club entertainment changes frequently. For special entertainment events, contact Disney Theme Park Information (407 824-4321). As you enter Pleasure Island, pick up an entertainment schedule, which lists performance times at the clubs. For information on the evening's feature films and show times or to order tickets, call the AMC Theatres (298-4488).

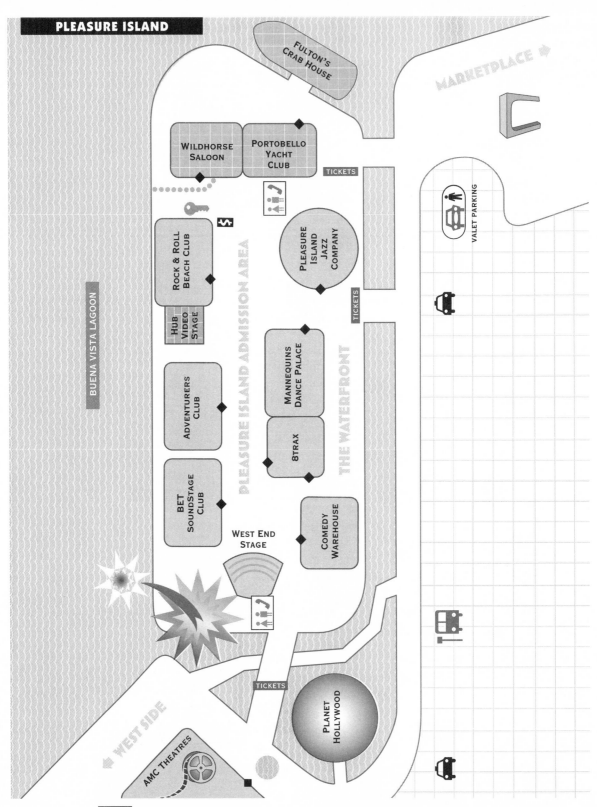

PLEASURE ISLAND

FULTON'S CRAB HOUSE

MARKETPLACE

WILDHORSE SALOON

PORTOBELLO YACHT CLUB

TICKETS

VALET PARKING

ROCK & ROLL BEACH CLUB

PLEASURE ISLAND JAZZ COMPANY

TICKETS

HUB VIDEO STAGE

BUENA VISTA LAGOON

PLEASURE ISLAND ADMISSION AREA

ADVENTURERS CLUB

MANNEQUINS DANCE PALACE

8TRAX

THE WATERFRONT

BET SOUNDSTAGE CLUB

WEST END STAGE

COMEDY WAREHOUSE

TICKETS

WEST SIDE

PLANET HOLLYWOOD

AMC THEATRES

want to listen. Downstairs near the dance floor there are a number of small alcoves with comfortable furnishings for socializing. The back window of the club, which is entirely glass, provides a spectacular nighttime view of Buena Vista Lagoon and the water taxis that ferry passengers to Downtown Disney. Beer, wine, and spirits are available. BET SoundStage Club opens at 8 PM. No one under the age of twenty-one may enter.

Comedy Warehouse: Every night, Pleasure Island visitors crowd into this large multilevel room and settle onto stools for non-stop comedy entertainment. Talented house comedians with a musician sidekick expertly improvise hilarious skits and routines that play heavily off the audience — and the audience loves every minute of it. Even though the routines are set, the improvisation keeps the regulars coming back. Well-known comedians also put in occasional appearances. Beer, wine, and spirits are served as well as specialty drinks and a limited selection of snacks and appetizers. On busy nights lines form at the door up to an hour before the 35 minute shows, which begin around 7 PM. The first show is the easiest to get into, and the fourth show is timed to get guests back out on the street for the New Year's Eve show. Check the entertainment schedule for show times. Smoking is not permitted in this club.

8trax: This continually reinvented club has an urban-industrial ambience and is very popular among visitors in their twenties. The superior (and very loud) sound system pumps out disco hits from the 70s at the volume they were meant to be enjoyed. Thursday nights feature favorite hits from the 80s. Inside the multileveled club, visitors can sit on catwalks overlooking the pipe-railed dance floor below. Other seating areas are tucked into alcoves created by black chain-link panels. 8trax opens at 8 PM. Beer, wine, and spirits are served.

Mannequins Dance Palace: Featuring dazzling light-and-sound shows and onstage dance performances, this three-story club is the most popular gathering spot on Pleasure Island. It draws twenty- to thirty-something locals and also is a favorite among Disney Cast Members. Mannequins features the world's largest revolving dance floor, which fills quickly as DJs spin contemporary music. Beer, wine, and spirits are served, as are specialty drinks. Mannequins opens at 8 PM; on weekends lines form at the club door. No one under the age of twenty-one may enter, except during dance shows, when minors escorted by Cast Members may visit. Professional dance performances with special sound and light effects are scheduled several times each night, and it's well worth the effort to catch one. Check the entertainment schedule for show times.

PLEASURE ISLAND

See the "Essentials" section for ticket costs and attraction updates.

How to Get There: Pleasure Island is located at Downtown Disney. There's free parking in the lots at Pleasure Island and at the nearby Marketplace and West Side. Starting at 5:30 PM, valet parking is available for about $6. Disney buses travel at night between all Walt Disney World resorts and theme parks and Pleasure Island. There are water taxis to Downtown Disney from the following resorts: Old Key West, Dixie Landings, and Port Orleans. Taxi service is available. Friday and Saturday nights draw huge crowds, and it can be very difficult to park at Pleasure Island.

Essentials

Attractions

Hotels

Restaurants

Special Events

Recreation

Resources

Fort Wilderness & River Country • Blizzard Beach • Typhoon Lagoon • Animal Kingdom • Disney-MGM Studios • World Showcase • Future World • Magic Kingdom

• Downtown Disney • Disney's BoardWalk

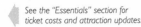

PLEASURE ISLAND

*See the "Essentials" section for
ticket costs and attraction updates.*

Admission: From 10 AM until 7 PM daily, Pleasure Island is free and only the shops and eateries are open. After 7 PM, admission is charged (about $20) and visitors wear wrist bands that allow them into the clubs. Pleasure Island admission is included with Length of Stay Passes and some Multiday Passes. Movie-Island combo tickets are also available. At various times throughout the year, Pleasure Island offers promotional discounts. Be sure to inquire at Guest Services in your resort. See *Essentials* → "Admission Tickets" for entry costs. ◆

Restrictions: After 7 PM, no one under eighteen is permitted on Pleasure Island or inside the clubs without an accompanying adult, except in Mannequins Dance Palace and BET SoundStage Club, which prohibit anyone under the age of twenty-one. Visitors over eighteen need a picture ID (valid passport, U.S. driver's license, or foreign driver's license with a backup ID). Florida law prohibits serving alcohol to anyone under twenty-one. Alcoholic beverages may be consumed anywhere on Pleasure Island as long as they are carried in plastic cups, which are conveniently placed at club exits. Smoking is not permitted inside some clubs. ◆

Pleasure Island Jazz Company: In a casual circular room decorated with steamer trunks and the paraphernalia of traveling musicians, visitors can enjoy live jazz, blues, and classic jam sessions featuring local, national, and international performers. The club appeals to jazz lovers of all ages, and many local residents show up when a favorite group is appearing. Beer, wine, and spirits are served, with a special focus on wines and champagnes by the glass. This is a nice spot to make an impromptu light meal of the appetizer-sized dishes featured here, such as Teriyaki Beef Tenderloin on a Rosemary Skewer with Lo Mein Salad or Portobello Mushroom with Crab Meat Stuffing. The club also features an assortment of desserts and specialty coffee drinks. The Pleasure Island Jazz Company opens at 8 PM, and live sets start at about 8:30 PM. Check the entertainment schedule for show times.

Rock & Roll Beach Club: Visitors climb an outside stairway lined with surfboards to enter this dance club on the third floor. Below are two levels of bars, pool tables, and video games; the stage and dance floor are on the ground floor. Live bands perform contemporary and classic rock and DJs spin a mean mix between sets. The atmosphere is relaxed and casual, and the music is full-volume. The crowd is split between late teens and twenty-somethings who come to dance and older visitors who like to listen to good rock-and-roll music. Beer, wine, and spirits are served, and pizza is sold whole or by the slice. The Rock & Roll Beach Club opens at 7 PM, and the 45 minute live sets start at about 8:30 PM. Check the club's entertainment schedule for show times.

Wildhorse Saloon: This high-energy entertainment club and restaurant is the hot spot for country-western music fans. Live performances from up-and-coming bands, as well as nationally known country artists, are regularly scheduled and pack the house with a friendly, boisterous crowd. Between sets, jockeys play the best in music and video for two- or ten-stepping on the large dance floor. Free hour-long dance classes, taught by professional country dancers, are offered on select nights each week. The action starts at about 7 PM. Check the entertainment schedule for dance class and show times.

Upstairs and overlooking the dance floor is the Wildhorse Saloon restaurant, which is open for dinner from about 5 PM until midnight. (See *Restaurants* → "Wildhorse Saloon" for a full description and review.) The restaurant is accessible to visitors without paying admission to the rest of Pleasure Island. The entrance can be reached by walking around to the lagoon side of the restaurant. To enter Pleasure Island from the restaurant, however, you must show proof of admission.

EVENTS & ENTERTAINMENT

AMC Theatres: The AMC Theatres are located at Disney's West Side, just outside the entrance to Pleasure Island behind the West End Stage. Twenty-four screens (including sixteen with stadium seating) show first-run movies, including the latest Disney releases, and all have Sony Digital Surround Sound. Recalling the glamor of the film industry's heyday, two theaters feature balcony seating and three-story-high viewing screens. Movies are shown after-hours, making it a popular late-night attraction for club-goers. The lowest priced movie tickets are available to all visitors for shows between 4 and 6 PM. Guests staying at a Walt Disney World resort also receive a 30 percent discount on movie tickets throughout the evening (after 6 PM) with their resort ID. Visitors can get current movie listings and show times, as well as charge tickets up to 3 days before the show by calling the theater (407 298-4488).

West End Stage: Framed by shiny high-tech lighting trusses and massive speakers, this huge outdoor performance platform presents live music that gets guests moving and keeps them jumping all night long, culminating with a flashy New Year's Eve countdown. Talented local bands and guest artists appear in concert nightly, beginning around 8 PM. Visitors who wish to avoid the dense crowd near the stage can watch the performances on the Hub Video Stage, an outdoor wall of twenty-five large video monitors. The Hub Video Stage also features live performances from time to time. Check the entertainment schedule for show times and events.

New Year's Eve Street Party: Every night, a loud and lively New Year's Eve party materializes at Pleasure Island. At about 11:30 PM visitors step out of the clubs and fill the streets for this Pleasure Island laser-and-light show tradition that takes place on the West End Stage. Professional dancers in sexy costumes power through a slick, complex routine to hard-driving music and motivate the crowd for the countdown to midnight. New Year's erupts with fireworks and confetti, and sometimes the street party continues with a live band.

The Waterfront: This area stretches along the shore between Mannequins and 8trax near the main gate to Pleasure Island. On weekends, entertainment events often appear here along with food booths that serve a variety of cuisines. The Waterfront is also used for seasonal festivals and special celebrations. Check the entertainment schedule for current events.

Cafes and Lounges

A number of refreshment stands and shops scattered around Pleasure Island serve fast-food meals and snacks. The lounges listed below are the most pleasant for a sit-down respite from the clubs. They stay open late and also make good rendezvous spots for visitors who want to club-hop separately and meet up later.

D'Zertz — Next to the Pleasure Island Jazz Company, this small coffee and dessert shop serves up great espresso and cappuccino and very tempting dessert choices. Tables scattered in front offer wonderful people watching. During the afternoon hours, this shop remains largely deserted. If The Marketplace is crowded with shoppers and snackers, it is a quiet spot for coffee and a snack.

Fulton's Stone Crab Lounge — The curved window wall of this lounge offers a marvelous view of Buena Vista Lagoon. The dark wood trim and the subdued lighting at night gives this spacious room an intimate atmosphere. During the day, light entrees and appetizers are available here, including many kinds of shellfish and salads. The full bar has an extensive assortment of liquors and wines.

Portobello Yacht Club Bar — Warm, dark mahogany paneling and polished brass fixtures create a pleasant, clubby atmosphere. The full bar features an extensive array of grappas and good Italian wines. Italian appetizers including pizza are available at the bar. Some of Walt Disney World's most potent espresso and cappuccino can be found here. ◆

Essentials • Attractions • Hotels • Restaurants • Special Events • Recreation • Resources

Magic Kingdom • Future World • World Showcase • Disney-MGM Studios • Animal Kingdom • Typhoon Lagoon • Blizzard Beach • **Downtown Disney** • Disney's BoardWalk • Fort Wilderness & River Country

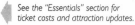

Essentials

Attractions

Hotels

Restaurants

Special Events

Recreation

Resources

Fort Wilderness & River Country • Disney's BoardWalk • Blizzard Beach • Typhoon Lagoon • Animal Kingdom • Disney-MGM Studios • World Showcase • Future World • Magic Kingdom

Downtown Disney

PLEASURE ISLAND

See the "Essentials" section for ticket costs and attraction updates.

E.A.R.S.
Expert Advisor Rating System
AWARDS

TOP 5 FAVORITE NIGHTCLUB EXPERIENCES AT PLEASURE ISLAND

Adventurers Club
(Mask Room, Main Salon, and the Library)

Comedy Warehouse

Pleasure Island Jazz Company

8trax

Mannequins Dance Palace

On the Adventurers Club...

"Face it, there's only one experience on Pleasure Island that can be truly called a "Disney" experience, and that's the Adventurers Club. Beside this ultimate 1930s themed nightclub experience, all others pale in comparison. Wait for the Library Show to begin (after you've seen it at least once), then take your pick of elephant-foot barstools. The bartenders are a wealth of information of dining and attractions, and they even remembered our drink preferences after one visit! The wry humor and antiquarian feel of the place, down to the smallest details, is priceless, and a good case study of themeing arts."

Margaret King, Ph.D., E.A.R.S. Panelist

FULL-SERVICE RESTAURANTS

The restaurants listed below can be entered from outside Pleasure Island and do not require an admission ticket to enjoy. See the "Restaurants" section for complete reviews and reservation information.

Fulton's Crab House: Fresh seafood, including crab and lobster, is the specialty at this restaurant located aboard a replica nineteenth-century riverboat. Diners are seated on one of the riverboat's three decks, and many tables have pleasant views of Buena Vista Lagoon. Beer, wine, and spirits are served. Open for dinner from 5 PM until midnight; lunch from 11:30 AM. Dinner reservations recommended.

Portobello Yacht Club: Guests can enjoy Italian specialties, fresh seafood, and a variety of oven-fired thin-crust pizzas in one of several spacious dining areas featuring yachting trophies and other maritime mementos. Beer, wine, and spirits are served, as are excellent espresso and cappuccino. Open all day from 11:30 AM until midnight; reservations recommended.

Wildhorse Saloon: This country western music and dance club has a separate restaurant featuring an "unbridled barbecue" of mesquite smoked ribs, chicken, and beef, along with large salads and hamburgers. Beer, wine, and spirits are served. Open for lunch on Friday and Saturday from 11:30 AM; open for dinner from 5 PM until 2 AM; no reservations are accepted.

Planet Hollywood: This striking restaurant is filled with motion-picture and movie-star memorabilia. Guests can enjoy classic American dishes including hamburgers, pizza, pasta, and salads, as well as memorable desserts. Beer, wine, and spirits are served, as are espresso and cappuccino. Open from 11 AM until 2 AM; no reservations are accepted.

SERVICES

Rest Rooms: All restaurants and clubs have rest rooms. An uncrowded public rest room can be found between the Wildhorse Saloon and the Portobello Yacht Club.

Telephones: Outdoor public telephones are located near the rest rooms between the Portobello Yacht Club and the Wildhorse Saloon, and also near the rest rooms behind the West End Stage. There are telephones near the rest rooms in all restaurants and clubs, but the quietest phones are those at the Adventurers Club.

Banking: An automatic teller machine (ATM) and a change machine are located in front of the Rock & Roll Beach Club.

Lockers: Lockers can be found under the stairs that lead up to the Rock & Roll Beach Club entrance, across from the Wildhorse Saloon. ◆

THE MARKETPLACE

The Marketplace at Downtown Disney is a shopping and dining complex with the atmosphere of a picturesque waterfront town. It's perched on the shoreline of Buena Vista Lagoon along with the rest of Downtown Disney, which includes Pleasure Island and Disney's West Side. At The Marketplace visitors can stroll along the pleasant waterfront promenade, studded with fanciful topiaries and fountains; relax in one of several restaurants or lounges; or explore the many shops and boutiques offering name-brand clothing, gourmet foods, special-interest gifts, and Disney collectibles. The Marketplace is also the site of several special events, holiday celebrations, and ongoing crafts demonstrations, and has a recreational marina for boating and fishing as well as outdoor play areas, attractions, and fountains for young children.

SHOPPING

The Art of Disney: This gallery's selection of upscale Disney collectibles and original works of art based on Disney themes will thrill die-hard Disney fans. The selections include sculptures, animation cels, mosaics, paintings, blown glass, and furniture. Prices above $10,000 are not unusual.

Captain's Tower: This octagonal shop is open on all sides and is sometimes the showcase store for special events and seasonal activities at Downtown Disney. Generally, the store's selection is dedicated exclusively to toys.

Disney at Home: For a selection of whimsical Disney Character-themed decorating items for every room in the house, including an especially large collection for the bath, this shop has no equal.

Disney's Days of Christmas: Year round, this Christmas shop is one of the most popular stores at The Marketplace. One-of-a-kind Christmas ornaments, collectibles, Nativity scenes, recordings of Christmas music, cards, garlands, wreaths, clothing, animated figures, Christmas ornaments and lights featuring Disney Characters, and almost anything else required for the Christmas season can be found here. Personalized ornaments are also available.

When to Go: The Marketplace shops are open every day from 9:30 AM until about 11 PM. Shops and restaurants are generally open later on weekends. It is always busy and the parking lots are full, but parking is much easier in the morning. For information about shops or scheduled special events, call Downtown Disney Guest Services (407 828-3058).

How to Get There: The Marketplace is located at Downtown Disney, a central transportation hub for all of Walt Disney World. Parking is free. The Marketplace is within walking distance of the Disney Institute and some of the Hotel Plaza resorts. Walt Disney World buses travel between all resorts and theme parks and Downtown Disney. There are water taxis to Downtown Disney from the following resorts: Port Orleans and Old Key West. Starting at 5 PM, valet parking is available near Pleasure Island for about $6.

Attractions · Hotels · Restaurants · Special Events · Recreation · Resources

Magic Kingdom • Future World • World Showcase • Disney-MGM Studios • Animal Kingdom • Typhoon Lagoon • Blizzard Beach • **Downtown Disney** • Disney's BoardWalk • Fort Wilderness & River Country

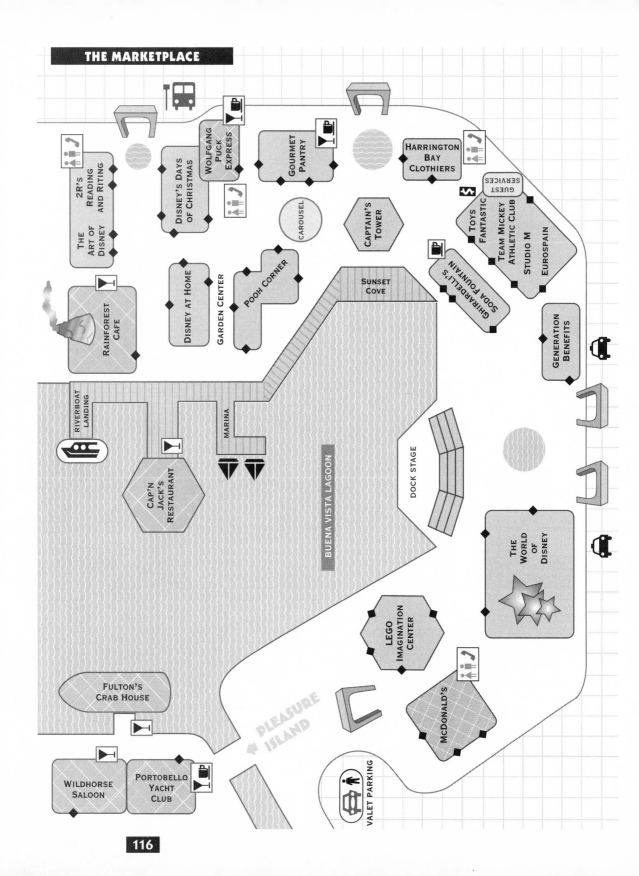

Eurospain: Eurospain offers a vast array of collectibles from around the world, all displayed in uniquely designed showcases. The shop stocks a selection of Austrian and Italian crystal, Goebels miniatures, ceramic masks, music boxes, porcelain figurines, and a variety of crystal and enameled jewelry. Crafts demonstrations include glass blowing and engraving.

Garden Center: Living topiary and bonsai, rocks and crystals, and nature-oriented books and gifts fill this pleasant outdoor shop occupying the breezeway between Disney at Home and Pooh's Corner. Garden-lovers will find seeds and bulbs, birdhouses, gardening books and tools, sun hats, and an array of tee-shirts and tote bags featuring nature-themed designs. The shop also offers herbal bath products and cosmetics and a small collection of exotic stuffed toys and beanies, such as giraffes, gorillas, lion cubs, and frogs.

Generation Benefits: In the summer months this is the place to find trendy brand-name casual wear for men and women, sun hats, sandals, sunglasses, and swimwear. During the winter months, jackets, slacks, and sweaters are also featured. The shop also carries costume jewelry and accessories. Brands include the trendier styles of Calvin Klein, Tommy Hilfiger, Tommy Girl, Roxy, and many others.

Ghirardelli's Soda Fountain & Chocolate Shop: This haven for ice cream–lovers and chocolate connoisseurs, reminiscent of a turn-of-the-century soda "shoppe," features San Francisco's well-known Ghirardelli chocolates. The sweet and soothing treats here include old-fashioned malts, milk shakes, floats, huge ice cream sundaes, and, of course, chocolate in almost every imaginable form. Ghirardelli's is a favorite meeting spot for those shopping or touring separately.

Gourmet Pantry: One side of this store is a culinary collectors' paradise, with a dizzying variety of gourmet cookware, utensils, and cookbooks. The other side houses a deli counter stocked with cheese, cold meats, salads, and Italian sandwiches sold by the inch. Gourmet Pantry also has a liquor and wine department; a tobacco shop featuring premium cigars, pipe tobacco, and smoking accessories; a candy shop; and a bakery that offers muffins, pastries, cookies, and gourmet coffees brewed strong enough to get shoppers back on their feet. Shaded tables are scattered about outside.

Harrington Bay Clothiers: With its pleasant masculine decor, this store provides a peaceful oasis for the shopping weary. Men's brand-name casual and dress fashions are featured, and accessories, tote bags, windbreakers, ties, and golf wear are also available.

THE MARKETPLACE

See the "Essentials" section for seasonal events and updates.

Full-Service Restaurants

All visitors to Walt Disney World can make advance reservations for any restaurant at The Marketplace that accepts them. See the "Restaurants" section for full reviews and reservation information.

Rainforest Cafe: An "active" volcano above the roof distinguishes this unique jungle-themed restaurant. Inside, there are cascading waterfalls, aquariums, and sound effects that include thunder, rain, and animal cries. Guests can enjoy steaks, chicken, seafood, pasta, pizza, and salads with unique flavor combinations. Fruit juices and smoothies, beer, wine, and spirits are served, as are espresso and cappuccino. Open all day from 10 AM until 11 PM; until midnight on the weekends. Reservations recommended.

Cap'n Jack's Restaurant: Occupying a pier out in the Buena Vista Lagoon, this restaurant offers diners a great water view from any table. The restaurant attracts a lively crowd for clams and oysters on the half shell, shrimp cocktails, crab cakes, lobster, and pasta. Beer, wine, and spirits are served. Open all day from 11:30 AM until 10:30 PM. Visitors who just want to snack or enjoy a cocktail can simply walk in and seat themselves at the bar. No reservations are accepted.

Essentials · Attractions · Hotels · Restaurants · Special Events · Recreation · Resources

Fort Wilderness & River Country · Disney's BoardWalk · **Downtown Disney** · Blizzard Beach · Typhoon Lagoon · Animal Kingdom · Disney-MGM Studios · Future World · World Showcase · Magic Kingdom

See the "Essentials" section for seasonal events and updates.

THE MARKETPLACE

Fulton's Crab House: Crab, lobster, and other fresh seafood are the specialties at this huge restaurant aboard a replica nineteenth-century riverboat. Diners are seated at tables on the riverboat's three decks, many with pleasant views of Buena Vista Lagoon. Beer, wine, and spirits are served. Open for lunch from 11:30 AM; dinner from 5 PM until midnight. Reservations recommended.

Portobello Yacht Club: Guests enjoy Italian entrees, fresh seafood, and oven-fired thin-crust pizzas in spacious dining areas featuring yachting trophies and other maritime mementos. Beer, wine, and spirits are served, as are excellent espresso and cappuccino. Open for lunch from 11:30 AM; dinner from 4 PM until midnight. Reservations recommended.

Wildhorse Saloon: The full menu of "unbridled barbecue" at this Pleasure Island restaurant and country-western club features mesquite-smoked chicken, ribs, and beef, along with meal-sized salads and hamburgers. Guests can hear country-western tunes from the Wildhorse Saloon's stage and dance floor downstairs. Pleasure Island admission is not required to enter the restaurant. Beer, wine, and spirits are served. Open for lunch Friday and Saturday from 11:30 AM, dinner from 5 PM until 2 AM. ◆

LEGO Imagination Center: A sea serpent rising from Buena Vista Lagoon and a number of other giant fanciful sculptures built with LEGO's interlocking blocks mark the site of this new superstore with a focus on creativity. The very latest LEGO products are featured here, along with hundreds of other items from LEGO's international product line. The store features hands-on play stations with LEGO products that visitors of all ages can try before they buy. Children can burn off energy at a whimsical outdoor LEGO playground.

Pooh Corner: This large shop features an extensive collection of Disney Character merchandise and clothing, featuring Pooh, Tigger, and all of the friends from the Hundred Acre Wood.

Studio M: In addition to being a fully stocked camera shop, this is also a digital photo studio. Visitors can pose for unique family portraits and also have them placed on their choice of dozens of Walt Disney World or Disney Character backgrounds. Personalized tee-shirts and coffee mugs are also available here.

Team Mickey Athletic Club: This popular store features a huge selection of sports accessories and apparel (most festooned with the Disney insignia), such as golfing sweaters and bags, baseball jerseys and jackets, bowling shirts and bags, rugby and polo shirts, bicycling gear, aerobics outfits, and warm-up suits. In the athletic shoe department, video monitors show sports events all day long.

Toys Fantastic: This Disney-Mattel collaboration stocks what is possibly the most complete selection of Barbie dolls and Barbie-doll paraphernalia anywhere. Mattel's Hot Wheels and truckloads of accessories are also featured here.

2R's Reading and Riting: The Art of Disney opens into this pleasant, busy bookstore, which features current best-sellers among its range of titles for children and adults. Stationery, videos, magazines, audiotapes and compact discs, and Disney software and CD-ROMs are also available here. A walk-up coffee bar in the store serves espresso and cappuccino.

The World of Disney: With ten themed shopping areas, The World of Disney is the largest Disney store in the world. The Great Hall and Rotunda form the core of this huge flow-through market filled with more Disney merchandise than has ever been amassed under one roof before. From luggage to sleepwear to jewelry to videos to toys, nothing has been left out in an effort to attract even the most judicious consumer. The largest selection ever of Disney-Character apparel for any age can be found here, as well as costumes, sportswear, and high fashion. This store is always busy, but it is least crowded during the first hour it is open.

CAFES AND LOUNGES

Several counter-service restaurants and lounges at The Marketplace serve light meals and tasty snacks. Those listed below are especially pleasant and make good rendezvous spots for visitors who would like to shop separately and meet up later.

Ghirardelli's Soda Fountain & Chocolate Shop: At this famous chocolate shop from San Francisco, ice cream lovers and chocoholics can take a break and indulge their sweet tooth with sundaes, floats, milk shakes, and candies. Coffee and espresso are also served.

Gourmet Pantry: Step up to the bakery and check out the selection of freshly brewed specialty coffees lined up along the back wall. A long deli counter offers take-out sandwiches and snacks. There are pleasant, shaded tables scattered outside the shop.

Wolfgang Puck Express: This counter-service restaurant features California cuisine such as rotisserie chicken, pizzas, specialty pastas, grilled seasonal vegetables, and distinctive desserts. Mineral water, beer, and wine are served, as are espresso and cappuccino.

McDonald's: The expanded menu at The Marketplace McDonald's restaurant also features personal pizzas and refill-your-own soft drinks, along with the traditional fast-food fare.

Cap'n Jack's Restaurant: The hexagonal copper bar in this lively restaurant is known for its tasty frozen strawberry Margaritas. This convivial bar is a great place to meet fellow visitors while enjoying a quick pick-me-up or to sit back for a long, relaxing view of the sunset over Buena Vista Lagoon. Coffee and espresso are served as well.

Rainforest Cafe's Magic Mushroom Juice & Coffee Bar: Guests at this lively, tropical-themed bar can enjoy appetizers with a multicultural influence as they sit beneath a giant mushroom on fanciful barstools representing jungle animals. The full-service bar serves fresh fruit and vegetable juices (which can be ordered with or without spirits), cappuccino, espresso, and a variety of specialty coffee beverages.

Fulton's Stone Crab Lounge: This lounge's curved and windowed wall gives guests a marvelous view of Lake Buena Vista. The dark wood trim and the subdued lighting at night lend a casual yet intimate atmosphere to

Activities & Entertainment

Live entertainment and seasonal events are scheduled throughout the year at The Marketplace. These include the classic car show in June, the boat show in October, the Festival of the Masters art show in November, and tree-lighting ceremonies and carolers during the Christmas season. Other activities include:

Dock Stage: The Dock Stage is located in an open plaza at the edge of Buena Vista Lagoon. Throughout the year, it is the site of jazz concerts, special holiday celebrations, high school band competitions, and other live entertainment.

Boating and Fishing: Cap'n Jack's Marina rents canopy boats, pontoon boats, and zippy Water Mice to visitors who would like to take a spin on Buena Vista Lagoon or explore the waterways and tour the themed resorts in the Downtown Disney Resorts Area (see *Recreation* → "Boating & Marinas").

Visitors who wish to test their fishing skills from the dock can rent old-fashioned cane poles at the Marina. Bait is provided. Guided fishing tours depart from here daily in search of largemouth bass. Reservations for these catch-and-release excursions should be made in advance (see *Recreation* → "Fishing Excursions"). Cap'n Jack's Marina is open daily from 10 AM until sundown. ◆

Essentials • Attractions • Hotels • Restaurants • Special Events • Recreation • Resources

Magic Kingdom • Future World • World Showcase • Disney-MGM Studios • Animal Kingdom • Typhoon Lagoon • Blizzard Beach • **Downtown Disney** • Disney's BoardWalk • Fort Wilderness & River Country

Essentials · Attractions · Hotels · Restaurants · Special Events · Recreation · Resources

Magic Kingdom · Future World · World Showcase · Disney-MGM Studios · Animal Kingdom · Typhoon Lagoon · Blizzard Beach · Downtown Disney · Disney's BoardWalk · Fort Wilderness & River Country

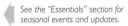
THE MARKETPLACE

See the "Essentials" section for seasonal events and updates.

E.A.R.S.
Expert Advisor Rating System
AWARDS

TOP 4 FAVORITE DOWNTOWN DISNEY SHOPPING SPOTS

The World of Disney
(largest Disney store in the world)

The Art of Disney
(upscale collectibles and original works of art)

LEGO Imagination Center
(great fun for the kids)

Disney at Home
(items for home and bath)

On The World of Disney...

"Look up if you can tear your eyes away from all the Disneyana; the ceilings and architectural details are beautifully themed."

Margaret King, Ph.D., E.A.R.S. Panelist

TOP 5 FAVORITE DOWNTOWN DISNEY SNACK STOPS

Ghirardelli's Soda Fountain
(hot fudge sundaes and ice cream sodas)

Gourmet Pantry
(chocolates and gooey rice crispy treats)

Forty Thirst Street
(for the smoothies)

The Cheesecake Factory
(at DisneyQuest)

Wolfgang Puck Express
(pizza and salads)

the spacious area. During the day, several kinds of shellfish, seafood, and salads are served in appetizer size portions and as light meals. The full bar features an extensive assortment of liquors and wines.

Portobello Yacht Club Bar: Dark mahogany paneling and polished brass fixtures create a pleasant, clubby atmosphere here. The full bar features an array of good Italian wines. Appetizers include Quattro Formaggi Pizza, Antipasto Assortito, and Calamaretti Fritti. Some of Walt Disney World's most potent espresso and cappuccino can be found here.

HOT TIPS

Disney Shopping Tips: Unique Disney merchandise is spread throughout the theme parks and resorts. If you see something you like, you will probably not run into it again. It's smarter to buy when you can, and return it if you must. If you have the receipt, you can return your purchase at any store in Walt Disney World. How do you know when Disney merchandise has been marked down? Look for prices ending in "99." If you see that shirt you want marked $12.99, grab it, because it's probably discontinued. For authentic Disney merchandise at rock-bottom prices, head over to Character Warehouse in Belz Outlet Mall, located on International Drive, about 20 minutes north of Walt Disney World, not far from Universal Studios. Most Guest Services desks at the attractions and resorts have printed directions to Belz Outlet Mall and other popular tourist spots. (See *Resources* → "Shopping & Services.")

The Marketplace Guest Services: The Guest Services desk (407 828-3058) at The Marketplace is one of the most helpful at Walt Disney World. Resort guests can drop their purchases at Guest Services for gift wrapping or for free delivery to their hotel. After 8 PM, Guest Services is the only location at Walt Disney World where late-arriving visitors can buy theme park tickets for the next day and avoid those long morning lines.

Rest Rooms: Public rest rooms are scattered liberally throughout The Marketplace. Oddly, the quietest rest rooms (and among the largest) are located in one of the busiest shopping venues — tucked in the back corner of the toy room at The World of Disney megastore. ◆

DISNEY'S BOARDWALK

*C*apturing the bustling turn-of-the-century ambience of Atlantic City's Boardwalk, Disney's BoardWalk is a very charming and festive waterfront complex with restaurants, nightclubs, and specialty shops fronting a quarter-mile stretch of Crescent Lake. It is a favorite destination for a casual evening out among both local visitors and vacationers.

On the wood-slatted BoardWalk Promenade, performers entertain passersby, artists sketch caricatures of visitors and create wax sculptures of their hands, and colorful carts offer unique souvenirs, snacks, and beverages. Surrey bikes, holding as many as eight, tour up and down the wide Promenade. When the sun goes down, the midway lights come up, transforming the BoardWalk into a re-creation of the early amusement parks designed for the pleasure of casual family outings by day and adults by night. In the evenings, aromas waft from the restaurants and music spills from the clubs.

Disney's BoardWalk is located near the International Gateway entrance to the World Showcase at Epcot. After the park closes, it is a great place to extend the evening's fun with a late dinner or dancing. With two deluxe hotels perched above the shops and restaurants — the informal yet elegant BoardWalk Inn and the homey and spacious BoardWalk Villas — Disney's BoardWalk is both an atmospheric recreation area and an ideally located vacation destination resort.

When to Go: The most crowded and festive times at the clubs are Friday and Saturday nights when local residents join the ranks of visitors. Most BoardWalk shops are open from 8 AM until midnight, and most restaurants are open throughout the day. The sports-oriented ESPN Club is open from 11:30 AM until 1 AM (until 2 AM on weekends). For information on scheduled events at ESPN Club, call the club's podium (407 939-1177). Jellyrolls (open from about 7 PM until 2 AM) and Atlantic Dance (open from about 9 PM until 2 AM) are the nightclubs at Disney's BoardWalk. Hours vary with the season. For entertainment information, call the Atlantic Dance hotline (407 939-2444).

ENTERTAINMENT

Atlantic Dance: With the giant "DANCE HALL" sign glowing from its rooftop and terraces looking out over the waters of Crescent Lake, Atlantic Dance captures the sleek elegance of the high-class casino dance clubs popular in the 1920s and 30s. Just past a foyer adorned with stylish supergraphics is the club's main area, where a ten-piece band on a raised stage performs dance hits from the 1940s to the 90s, with an emphasis on swing. Lights sparkle across the wooden dance floor, reflected from double mirrored balls overhead; the mood is sophisticated and romantic. A sweeping staircase leads to a second-floor balcony overlooking the dance

Attractions • Hotels • Restaurants • Special Events • Recreation • Resources

Magic Kingdom • Future World • World Showcase • Disney-MGM Studios • Animal Kingdom • Typhoon Lagoon • Blizzard Beach • Downtown Disney • Disney's BoardWalk • Fort Wilderness & River Country

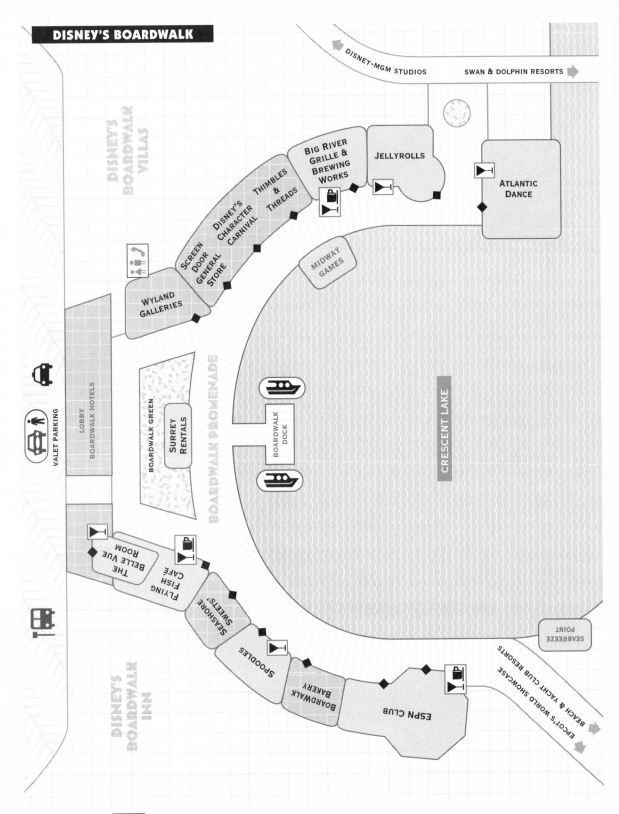

DISNEY'S BOARDWALK

DISNEY-MGM STUDIOS

SWAN & DOLPHIN RESORTS

DISNEY'S BOARDWALK VILLAS

BIG RIVER GRILLE & BREWING WORKS

JELLYROLLS

ATLANTIC DANCE

THIMBLES & THREADS

DISNEY'S CHARACTER CARNIVAL

SCREEN DOOR GENERAL STORE

MIDWAY GAMES

WYLAND GALLERIES

CRESCENT LAKE

VALET PARKING

LOBBY BOARDWALK HOTELS

BOARDWALK GREEN

SURREY RENTALS

BOARDWALK PROMENADE

BOARDWALK DOCK

THE BELLE VUE ROOM

FLYING FISH CAFE

SEASHORE SWEETS'

SPOODLES

BOARDWALK BAKERY

ESPN CLUB

DISNEY'S BOARDWALK INN

SEABREEZE POINT

EPCOT'S WORLD SHOWCASE

BEACH & YACHT CLUB RESORTS

area, which is furnished with small tables, carved-back chairs, and a few comfortable loveseats. Terraces overlooking Crescent Lake offer views of IllumiNations fireworks. Large bars with marble tops and dramatically lit mirrors can be found on both floors. Beer, wine, and spirits are served, including specialty martinis. Snacks such as Iced Jumbo Shrimp, Flat Bread Pizza, and a sampler of mini desserts are available. A selection of imported cigars, mostly Honduran, is also offered. Atlantic Dance opens at about 9 PM and has a modest cover charge (about $5). A one year club pass, good for two people, costs about $32. No one under the age of twenty-one may enter.

ESPN Club: Above the door, a giant arm holding a barbell and a basketball hoop for pick-up games are the tell-tale signs that this complex is the BoardWalk's entertainment spot for sports enthusiasts. More than seventy video monitors scattered throughout the club (including the rest rooms) broadcast an array of live sports events. In the evenings and any time that popular events are telecast, fans can be heard cheering for their favorites. The friendly exuberance is contagious, and even if you have little interest in sports, you can have a good time. ESPN Club has three main areas:

The Sidelines: In this large sports bar, video monitors overhead and inset into wood-paneled walls show a constant stream of televised events. Plaques, pictures, awards, and large murals add to the sports theme, as do the servers costumed in referee uniforms. Guests can seat themselves at the Penalty Box Bar or sit at tables where they can switch on an audio feed for their favorite sports events on the monitors. Four computer terminals near the entrance allow guests to explore ESPNNet on the World Wide Web. Appetizers, hot dogs, hamburgers, and sandwiches are served, as are sports-themed specialty drinks. Smoking is permitted.

Sports Central: Located to the left of the main entrance, this small stadium–style room resembling a basketball court is ESPN Club's main dining area and also a fully equipped television and radio broadcast studio. Tables are arranged in tiers and face a video wall and small sound stage. Smaller video monitors are also hung throughout the room, and a huge overhead scoreboard displays the latest scores. Live ESPN and ESPN2 sports wrap-ups, sports-oriented talk shows, and programs such as "SportsCenter" are beamed from Sports Central by satellite to worldwide feeds. Guests can dine as they watch the broadcasts in progress or live-action sports events on the monitors.

Essentials

Magic Kingdom • Future World • World Showcase • Disney-MGM Studios • Animal Kingdom • Typhoon Lagoon • Blizzard Beach • Downtown Disney • **Disney's BoardWalk** • Fort Wilderness & River Country

Attractions

Hotels

Restaurants

Special Events

Recreation

Resources

DISNEY'S BOARDWALK

See the "Essentials" section for seasonal events and updates.

How to Get There: Disney's BoardWalk is located in the Epcot Resorts Area. Parking is available at the BoardWalk's Guest Parking Lot on Epcot Resorts Boulevard. Valet parking and taxi service are also available. Water launches travel between Disney's BoardWalk, Disney-MGM Studios, and the World Showcase at Epcot, as well as the following resorts: Swan, Dolphin, Yacht Club, and Beach Club. Buses travel between Disney's BoardWalk and most theme parks; there are also direct buses from Disney's Coronado Springs Resort. Disney's BoardWalk is within walking distance of the International Gateway to the World Showcase at Epcot, and Disney-MGM Studios. It is also within walking distance of the following resorts: Swan, Dolphin, Yacht Club, and Beach Club.

Admission: Anyone may enter Disney's BoardWalk for free, although the nightclubs sometimes levy a modest cover charge (about $5). Florida law prohibits serving alcohol to anyone under twenty-one, and to enter Jellyrolls and Atlantic Dance, visitors must also be twenty-one. Unless otherwise noted, smoking is not permitted at the restaurants. ◆

Essentials · Attractions · Hotels · Restaurants · Special Events · Recreation · Resources

Magic Kingdom · Future World · World Showcase · Disney-MGM Studios · Animal Kingdom · Typhoon Lagoon · Blizzard Beach · Downtown Disney · Disney's BoardWalk · Fort Wilderness & River Country

DISNEY'S BOARDWALK

See the "Essentials" section for seasonal events and updates.

Full-Service Restaurants

Visitors can make restaurant reservations between 60 and 120 days in advance. See the "Restaurants" section for full reviews and reservation information.

Big River Grille & Brewing Works

The rich smell of malt greets guests as they enter this microbrewery/restaurant. A glassed-in area behind the bar houses the microbrewery's huge stainless steel vats. As they watch the brewmasters at work, guests can choose from five brews produced on the premises or order a special tasting sampler of all of them. The restaurant serves steak, chicken, and seafood, and also features homemade sausages. Both indoor and outdoor seating is available. Wine and spirits are also served. Open from 11 AM until 2 AM; no reservations are accepted.

ESPN Club Sports Central — ESPN

Club serves food in two areas: The Sidelines sports bar, filled with dozens of monitors playing a variety of sports events, and Sports Central, a broadcast studio where occasional live interviews with sports figures are beamed to ESPN's worldwide feeds. Tables are arranged in tiers with views of the video wall's televised sports events and other goings-on. The menu features sandwiches and hearty entrees. Beer, wine, and spirits are served, as are espresso and cappuccino. Open all day from 11:30 AM until 1 AM (2 AM on weekends); no reservations are accepted. ➤

The Yard: Chipped-brick walls, black chain-link fence, and aluminum siding create a clean, well-lit version of a gritty urban environment at this large arcade, which features interactive and virtual-reality sports and adventure games. The Yard is popular with visitors bent on challenging themselves and each other.

Jellyrolls: At this rambunctious club, a rounded storefront welcomes guests into a room with the look of an old warehouse. Beer-company banners hang from wooden beams above a large sunken seating area with tables and chairs, and a higher level with bar-stool seating runs around three sides of the club. On a raised stage, musicians at a pair of pianos play and sing classic rock tunes and attempt to outdo each other with their dancing digits and improvisational comedy routines. The club's enthusiastic guests need little encouragement to participate in the banter, suggesting tunes and sometimes singing along. The keyboard antics of the gifted performers are reflected on large mirrors at the back of the stage. Beer, wine, and spirits are served, including a rotating list of thirty-two-ounce specialty drinks. Popcorn is also available. Jellyrolls opens about 7 PM and has a modest cover charge (about $5). No one under twenty-one may enter.

Surrey Rentals: Visitors can enjoy the BoardWalk Promenade's sights as they pedal along in large wicker vehicles modeled on the rolling chairs of Atlantic City's Boardwalk. Visitors who would like to combine sightseeing with a little exercise can rent four-wheeled surreys with striped-canvas tops to pedal along the BoardWalk Promenade and over to the nearby Yacht and Beach Club resorts. Surreys seating four adults and two children cost about $18 for one half hour; those seating six adults and two children cost about $20 per half hour. Also available are surreys seating eight adults, which cost about $22 per half hour. Surreys are available on a first-come, first-served basis; no reservations are taken. Surrey Rentals is open from 11 AM until 10 PM, and is the only place at Walt Disney World where bicycles are rented at night.

SHOPS & STOPS

The Belle Vue Room: This 30s-era lounge is just off the upstairs lobby of the BoardWalk Inn. Period tables and comfortable couches are tucked among bookcases filled with curios and antique radios playing broadcasts of the era, making The Belle Vue Room a romantic spot for quiet talks and beautiful sunsets. It is also a cosy haven where visitors can play a game of chess or backgammon on a rainy afternoon. Beer, wine, and spirits are served, as are coffee, tea, espresso, and cappuccino. A Continental breakfast is served from 7 until 11 AM; open until midnight.

BoardWalk Bakery: Muffins, croissants, cakes, and a variety of other fresh-baked goods and snacks are available here, along with soft drinks, coffee, espresso, and cappuccino. Guests can enjoy their purchases sidewalk cafe–style at the bakery's outdoor tables. It's a great place to grab an early breakfast on the way to Epcot. Open from 7 AM until 11 PM.

Disney's Character Carnival: Distinguished by its multicolored striped awnings, this store offers Disney-themed merchandise such as hats, plush toys, accessories, resort wear, collectibles, and a wide variety of tee-shirts and children's apparel.

Screen Door General Store: Designed as an old-fashioned general store, the Screen Door carries Disney-themed dishes and cooking utensils, gifts, sundries, snacks, and a limited selection of groceries and frozen foods. The store also stocks several types of beer, wine, and spirits, as well as mixers, bar accessories, and cigarettes.

Seashore Sweets': "Miss America" is the theme at this brightly lit haven for guests with a sweet tooth. Numerous portraits of the pageant's winners decorate the shop, which offers ice cream, saltwater taffy, and a variety of candies, along with lemonade, coffee, espresso, and cappuccino. Open from 10 AM until midnight.

Thimbles & Threads: This small shop stocks a selection of seasonal resort wear (swimsuits in summer, sweaters and sweatshirts in winter) and accessories for men and women. Golf clothing with Disney motifs from Nike Golf and Titleist by Corbin is also available, along with golf balls, tees, and other golf accessories.

Wyland Galleries: Wood veneer surfaces, tall pillars, and curved walls create a sleek showcase for unique, often dramatic sculptures, paintings, books, and furnishings that feature a marine-mammal environmental theme. Wyland is considered to be the leading marine-life artist in America. His creations are featured here, along with selected pieces from other environmental artists. All gallery items are limited editions. Open daily from 10 AM until 11 PM. ◆

Flying Fish Café — Blue flying fish, rendered in glowing neon, welcome guests to this unique, sophisticated restaurant on the BoardWalk Green. Whimsical flying fish and large murals pay tribute to the midway rides of an earlier era at Atlantic City's Boardwalk. Guests can dine at individual tables or, if they prefer, at the copper-tiled counter facing the kitchen's open grill. Fresh seafood, steaks, and chicken are on the menu, along with grilled and sautéed vegetables. Beer, wine, and spirits are served, as are espresso and cappuccino. Open for dinner from 5:30 until 10:30 PM; reservations are recommended.

Spoodles — A hodgepodge of mismatched furniture and tableware create a casual setting for this noisy family-style restaurant. The open kitchen serves up pizza and tapas, appetizer-sized dishes served in the order they emerge from the kitchen. The restaurant's patio seating has views of Crescent Lake and the BoardWalk Promenade. Beer, wine, and spirits are served as are coffee, espresso, and cappuccino. Pizza, served whole or by the slice, can be ordered from a take-out window; there is outdoor seating nearby. Spoodles is open for breakfast and for all-day dining from 7:30 AM until 10 PM; reservations are recommended. ◆

Essentials • Magic Kingdom • Future World • World Showcase • Disney-MGM Studios • Animal Kingdom • Typhoon Lagoon • Blizzard Beach • Downtown Disney • **Disney's BoardWalk** • Fort Wilderness & River Country

Attractions Hotels Restaurants Special Events Recreation Resources

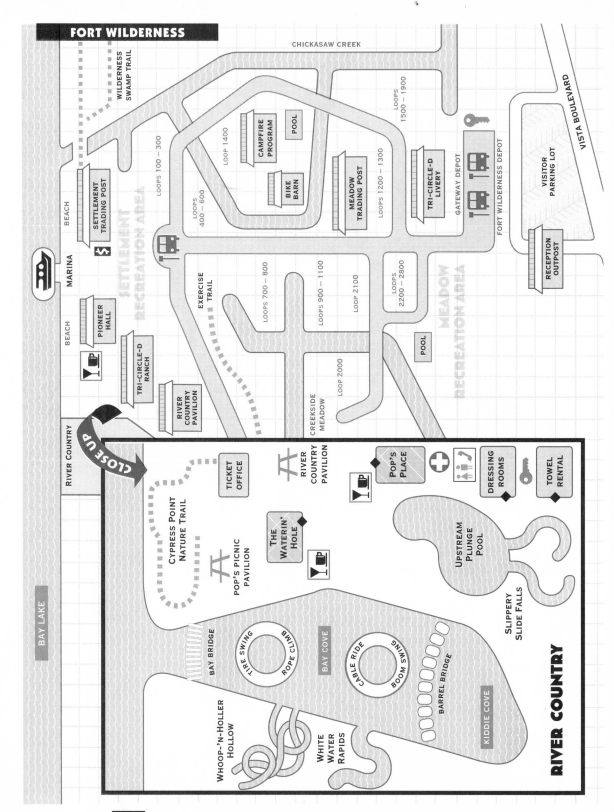

FORT WILDERNESS

CHICKASAW CREEK

WILDERNESS SWAMP TRAIL

BAY LAKE

SETTLEMENT RECREATION AREA

MARINA

BEACH

BEACH

SETTLEMENT TRADING POST

PIONEER HALL

TRI-CIRCLE-D RANCH

RIVER COUNTRY PAVILION

LOOPS 100 – 300

LOOP 1400

CAMPFIRE PROGRAM

POOL

BIKE BARN

LOOPS 400 – 600

MEADOW TRADING POST

LOOPS 1200 – 1300

LOOPS 1500 – 1900

TRI-CIRCLE-D LIVERY

GATEWAY DEPOT

FORT WILDERNESS DEPOT

VISITOR PARKING LOT

VISTA BOULEVARD

RECEPTION OUTPOST

EXERCISE TRAIL

LOOPS 700 – 800

LOOPS 900 – 1100

LOOP 2100

LOOPS 2200 – 2800

POOL

LOOP 2000

CREEKSIDE MEADOW

MEADOW RECREATION AREA

RIVER COUNTRY

CLOSE UP

RIVER COUNTRY

CYPRESS POINT NATURE TRAIL

TICKET OFFICE

RIVER COUNTRY PAVILION

POP'S PLACE

THE WATERIN' HOLE

POP'S PICNIC PAVILION

DRESSING ROOMS

TOWEL RENTAL

UPSTREAM PLUNGE POOL

SLIPPERY SLIDE FALLS

BAY BRIDGE

TIRE SWING

ROPE CLIMB

BAY COVE

CABLE RIDE

BOOM SWING

BARREL BRIDGE

KIDDIE COVE

WHOOP-'N-HOLLER HOLLOW

WHITE WATER RAPIDS

126

FORT WILDERNESS & RIVER COUNTRY

*F*ort Wilderness offers visitors an old-fashioned country get-away: swimming, boating, picnicking, hiking, horseback riding, fishing, and just kicking back in a seven-hundred-acre cypress- and pine-wooded recreation area and campground. This carefully maintained wilderness area is also a Walt Disney World resort where guests can camp in tents, hook up RVs, or stay in one of the resort's log cabin homes. It is not unusual to spot native white-tailed deer, raccoons, opossums, and armadillos; the wetlands are also home to indigenous waterfowl, including egrets, heron, and pelicans. (See Hotels → "Disney's Fort Wilderness Campground.")

Fort Wilderness has three main recreation complexes: Meadow Recreation Area in the center of the park, where meandering waterways attract both canoeists and anglers and where bike paths lead off in every direction; Settlement Recreation Area at the edge of Bay Lake, with a busy marina and white sand beach, a nature trail, a small ranch, and a restaurant; and River Country at Bay Lake, a Disney-designed version of an old-fashioned swimming hole, complete with waterslides and beaches. Throughout Fort Wilderness, visitors will find swimming pools, bicycle trails, volleyball nets, tennis courts, shuffleboard, fishing, waterskiing, horseback-riding, and live entertainment in the evenings.

Settlement Recreation Area:
This rustic area borders Bay Lake and encompasses the Fort Wilderness Marina and beach; Pioneer Hall, where the nightly Hoop-Dee-Doo Musical Revue dinner show is held; and the Tri-Circle-D Ranch. At the Settlement Trading Post, visitors can buy gifts, sundries, groceries, sandwiches, and beverages including beer, wine, and a limited selection of spirits. River Country is a short walk away.

Fort Wilderness Marina: The marina is situated on Bay Lake, in the center of the long, lovely white sand beach at Fort Wilderness. At the marina, visitors can rent motorboats and sailboats or join waterskiing or fishing excursions. (See *Recreation* → "Boating & Marinas.") At the beach, visitors can swim or simply relax in lounge chairs under umbrellas or in the shade

When to Go: Fort Wilderness is open year-round, and there are activities, attractions, and entertainment suitable for every type of weather. At the Fort Wilderness Marina, boats may be rented from 10 AM until dusk. At the Bike Barn, recreational equipment may be rented or borrowed from 8 AM until dusk. Closing times vary with the season.

River Country is a seasonal water park and closes during the winter, November through February. During peak-attendance months (April through August) and holidays, the water park is packed, but during times of low-attendance (September, October, and March), it can be a welcome break from the hectic theme parks. Opening and closing times at River Country vary throughout the year, so check ahead by calling River Country Information (407 824-2760). River Country may close during lightning storms. If the weather looks uncertain, call Disney Weather (824-4104) for details.

Admission: Fort Wilderness is free to all visitors at Walt Disney World. Admission to River Country water park is included with Length of Stay Passes and some Multiday Passes. See *Essentials* → "Admission Tickets" for current pricing.

Essentials   Attractions   Hotels   Restaurants   Special Events   Recreation   Resources

Fort Wilderness & River Country • Disney's BoardWalk • Downtown Disney • Blizzard Beach • Typhoon Lagoon • Animal Kingdom • Disney MGM Studios • Future World • World Showcase • Magic Kingdom

FORT WILDERNESS

See the "Essentials" section for ticket costs and recreation updates.

How to Get There: Fort Wilderness is in the Magic Kingdom Resorts Area, adjacent to Bonnet Creek Golf Club, and extends from Vista Boulevard to the shores of Bay Lake. The Fort Wilderness Marina is serviced by ferry from the Magic Kingdom and the Contemporary resort. Walt Disney World buses service Fort Wilderness from the Wilderness Lodge and the Transportation and Ticket Center. Visitors who are driving can reach Fort Wilderness by following the signs to the Magic Kingdom Resorts Area and then to Fort Wilderness — or they can take a shortcut and enter by way of Vista Boulevard. The Fort Wilderness Day Visitor Parking Lot is free to guests staying at a Walt Disney World resort (other visitors are charged about $6 to enter the Magic Kingdom Resorts Area). ➤

of the nearby trees. Lockers are available at the marina to store belongings, and the nearby Beach Shack provides refreshments and cold beer. The Fort Wilderness Marina is open every day from 10 AM until sundown.

Wilderness Swamp Trail: The Wilderness Swamp Trail is about two miles long and offers a gentle nature hike among the local flora and fauna. Only the sounds of nature break the silence along the trail, which begins behind the Settlement Trading Post. The trail meanders through the forest, crosses the sun-drenched grassy banks of the Fort Wilderness waterways, and skirts the wetlands — populated by egrets, herons, and other native waterfowl — before plunging back into the deep shade of the overgrown forest canopy. The array of swamp ferns, saw palmetto, ancient cypress hung with Spanish moss, and colorful berries and flowers creates a semitropical paradise for nature-lovers.

Wilderness Exercise Trail: This one-mile (round trip) path begins across from the Tri-Circle-D Ranch and links Fort Wilderness to Disney's Wilderness Lodge. Exercise stations along the way cue fitness enthusiasts through stretches, lunges, chin-ups, and other activities that add up to a serious workout. The trail winds through a deeply shaded pine forest, lush with ferns and palmettos. Twittering birds, shy marsh rabbits, deep shadows, and silence inspire a soothing sense of isolation and privacy. The trail turns back at Disney's Wilderness Lodge.

Tri-Circle-D Ranch: This stable and corral houses the horses used in the Magic Kingdom parades and the Blacksmith Shop where their hooves are tended. A small museum inside the Horse Barn displays photographs of Walt Disney and his beloved horses. Outside, the horses are bathed and groomed, much to their pleasure. Horse enthusiasts will enjoy close-up views of the beautiful Percherons that pull the trolleys along Main Street and the elegant steeds with elaborately braided manes that are featured in some parades and special events. At the Blacksmith Shop, visitors can watch the horses being shod and their hooves being dressed.

Petting Farm: This corral at the Tri-Circle-D Ranch is filled with chickens, turkeys, rabbits, goats, ducks, and some very beautiful and well-cared-for ponies. It is also home to Minnie Moo, Walt Disney World's famous heifer. This Holstein cow was born in Minnesota, and has a rare tri-circle marking on her flank resembling Mickey Mouse. The Disney company purchased her and brought her to Fort Wilderness, where she has become a star. Interestingly, the Petting Farm, with its hands-on opportunities, attracts as many adults as it does children.

Meadow Recreation Area:
The Meadow Recreation Area lies in the center of Fort Wilderness and offers access to the Fort Wilderness waterways and bicycle trails. This area encompasses the Bike Barn, where visitors can rent bicycles, boats, electric carts, fishing gear, and tennis equipment, and the Meadow Recreation Complex, which offers swimming, tennis, volleyball, and shuffleboard. The Meadow Trading Post sells gifts, sundries, groceries, sandwiches, soups, and beverages, including beer and wine. On hot afternoons, visitors can come inside to cool off and play a game of checkers, or they can picnic by the creek at the tree-shaded tables out back.

Bicycling: The nine miles of roads and trails in Fort Wilderness are ideal for bicycle expeditions. Bikers must contend with occasional traffic on the paved roads, but the extensive trail system was designed with bicycles in mind. The trails meander along waterways, past beaches and wetlands, through shady forests, and across bridges and boardwalks. The Bike Barn rents bicycles and tandem bikes from 8 AM until sundown. Bikers are provided with a map of the bike trails and roads of Fort Wilderness. (See *Recreation* → "Bicycling and Bike Paths.")

Canal Fishing: Fishing in the waterways at Fort Wilderness is one of the hidden pleasures at Walt Disney World. Anglers can walk along the shores or rent canoes, pedal boats, or kayaks and paddle to any fishing spot that appeals to them. The Meadow Trading Post sells lures and bait, and visitors who do not have their own gear can rent cane poles at the Bike Barn. The fishing rule at Fort Wilderness is catch and release. (See *Recreation* → "Fishing Excursions.")

Canoeing, Kayaking, and Pedal Boating: The grassy banks and waterways of Fort Wilderness are home to a variety of native waterfowl and fish. Visitors may tour the tree-canopied waterways by canoe, pedal boat, or kayak and are welcome to fish for bass and bream. The Bike Barn rents boats from 8 AM until sundown. Boaters are given a map of the waterway system and can take a picnic lunch along on their adventure. (See *Recreation* → "Boating & Marinas.")

Horseback Riding: On the Fort Wilderness Trail Ride, cowboy guides lead visitors on horses along a packed-sand trail wending through the shady forests and sunny glades. Novices will feel comfortable on this walk-paced ride astride well-behaved horses that are sometimes used in the Magic Kingdom parades. Participants must be at least nine years of age, shoes (not sandals or high heels) are required, and long pants are recommended. Fees are about $25 per person for a 45 minute ride. Rides leave daily at 8:30, 10, and 11:30 AM and at 1, 2:30, and 4 PM from the Trail Blaze Corral at Tri-Circle-D Livery, adjacent to the Fort Wilderness Guest Parking Lot. Times vary with the season, and rides may

See the "Essentials" section for ticket costs and recreation updates.

In-Park Transportation: The roads inside Fort Wilderness are reserved for its own buses, which operate daily from 7 AM until 2 AM. (Passenger cars and recreational vehicles are allowed on the roads only to reach campsites, and there is no parking at the Fort Wilderness attractions.) Visitors arriving by car can park in the Fort Wilderness Day Visitor Parking Lot and proceed to one of the two bus stops there, depending on their destination. The bus stop marked "Gateway Depot" is for the express bus to River Country; the smaller bus stop marked "Fort Wilderness Depot" makes local stops at the campsite loops and the Meadow and Settlement Recreation Areas, as well as River Country.

Electric Cart Rentals: Any visitor can rent an electric cart by the day or overnight for use in Fort Wilderness. Electric carts carry up to four passengers; the cost starts at about $25 for day use, and about $40 for overnight use. They can run up to an hour (depending on the number of passengers) before needing a recharge at one of the plug-in recharging posts located throughout Fort Wilderness and in front of all attractions there. Electric carts are stabled at the Bike Barn in the Meadow Recreation Area, which is open from 8 AM until sundown. Guests must be at least age eighteen to rent, and age sixteen to drive. Reservations are required and can be made up to a year in advance through the Bike Barn (407 824-2742).

Bicycle Rentals: Guests who want to get around Fort Wilderness under their own steam can rent bicycles by the day or week at the Bike Barn, located in the Meadow Recreation Area. ◆

Essentials · **Attractions** · **Hotels** · **Restaurants** · **Special Events** · **Recreation** · **Resources**

Magic Kingdom • Future World • World Showcase • Disney-MGM Studios • Animal Kingdom • Typhoon Lagoon • Blizzard Beach • Downtown Disney • Disney's BoardWalk • **Fort Wilderness & River Country**

Essentials

Attractions

Hotels

Restaurants

Special Events

Recreation

Resources

Fort Wilderness & River Country • Disney's BoardWalk • Downtown Disney • Blizzard Beach • Typhoon Lagoon • Animal Kingdom • Disney-MGM Studios • World Showcase • Future World • Magic Kingdom

FORT WILDERNESS

See the "Essentials" section for ticket costs and recreation updates.

Water Excursions

Waterskiing — Waterskiers enjoy ideal conditions on the smooth surface of Bay Lake. Skiers can bring their own equipment or use the skis, Scurfers, or Hydraslides provided. Excursion boats carry up to five skiers and leave from the Fort Wilderness Marina throughout the day. Guides will also pick up skiers from other Magic Kingdom resorts. Waterskiing excursions must be booked in advance and cost about $125 per hour. (See *Recreation* → "Watersports.")

Fishing — Anglers can try their luck reeling in largemouth bass, bluegill, and other fish from Bay Lake, the largest natural lake at Walt Disney World. The Fort Wilderness Marina offers two-hour fishing excursions several times daily, although the catch tends to be better early in the morning. Anglers can use their own equipment or the tackle provided on the boat; the fishing rule is catch and release. No fishing license is required. Fishing excursions must be booked in advance. (See *Recreation* → "Fishing.") ◆

be canceled in poor weather. Spring and fall are the best seasons for trail rides. Reservations are recommended and can be made up to two weeks ahead by calling Fort Wilderness Trail Rides (407 824-2832).

RIVER COUNTRY

River Country, a water park located just a short walk from the Settlement Recreation Area, is modeled on the imaginary "swimming hole" that Huck Finn might have enjoyed. Visitors pay admission at the gate, and once inside, they can rent lockers and towels and settle into lounge chairs around the pool or on the sandy beach. There are a number of waterslides and water activities here, but River Country has a gentler, more nature-oriented atmosphere than either Typhoon Lagoon or Blizzard Beach. It is one of the most relaxing spots at Fort Wilderness, and it's a great place to do absolutely nothing. Two snack bars, Pop's Place and the smaller Waterin' Hole, offer hamburgers, hot dogs, sandwiches, salads, ice cream, beer, wine, and coffee.

Bay Cove: Bay Cove, an inlet of Bay Lake, is bordered on one side by a large beach and on the other by a hill with waterslides. It features good old-fashioned water play at River Country, complete with the Boom Swing, Rope Climb, Tire Swing, and Cable Ride. Two rickety bridges, Barrel Bridge and Bay Bridge, span the cove and lead swimmers to the water-play equipment in the center and to the tube rides and body slides at Raft Rider Ridge on the far shore.

Cypress Point Nature Trail: This short but tranquil wooden boardwalk meanders through the wetlands at the edge of Bay Lake. Old-growth bald cypress trees provide shade, and egrets fish among the water reeds. Aviaries tucked into the moss-hung bayous house hawks and other rehabilitated birds that are no longer able to survive in the wild. Few visitors ever find the trail, which is set apart from River Country. Refer to the River Country map on page 126 for the location.

Upstream Plunge Pool and Slippery Slides: This huge 330,000-gallon swimming pool is heated in winter and is surrounded by lounge chairs, where most of the adults at River Country are busy relaxing. Slippery Slide Falls, at the back of the pool, offers two steeply angled waterslides for the adventurous youngsters who flock to them. The slides end with a thrilling free-fall splash landing.

White Water Rapids: Despite its name, this is actually a leisurely inner-tube ride among gentle currents and calm pools. Riders cross Barrel Bridge and plop onto inner tubes atop Raft Rider Ridge. They meander down a 330-foot-long contoured chute, sometimes revolving in a slow whirlpool, before being gently washed into Bay Cove.

Whoop-'n-Holler Hollow: Across Bay Cove from the beach is Whoop-'n-Holler Hollow, where swimmers climb to two thrilling corkscrewing waterslides. One is longer than the other, but both are fast. The slides twist and turn and wind around each other, finally depositing riders, with a splash, into Bay Cove. This attraction is big with the kids, and the lines move quickly.

EVENTS AND LIVE ENTERTAINMENT

Many of the activities at Fort Wilderness, such as hayrides, Disney movies, and campfire entertainment, are presented with younger guests in mind, but they are enjoyed by adults as well.

All-American Backyard Barbecue: Staged seasonally between March and October, this all-you-care-to-eat buffet dinner and country dance features live musical entertainment and visits from Disney Characters at the Cookout Pavilion between River Country and Fort Wilderness. Barbecued chicken and pork ribs, hot dogs, corn on the cob, baked beans, corn bread, and dessert (usually a fruit cobbler or strawberry shortcake) are served along with soft drinks, beer, and wine. This is a unique setting for family birthdays. (See *Special Events* → "Dinner Shows.")

Campfire Program: Visitors can join Chip 'N Dale to toast marshmallows and sing favorite and familiar tunes at this campfire show. Disney cartoons and feature films are shown after dark. Hot dogs, snacks, popcorn, soft drinks, beer, and canned frozen daiquiris may be purchased at the campfire's Chuck Wagon. Visitors who would enjoy a memorable night of free, laid-back entertainment, off the beaten path but undeniably Disney, should head on over. During the summer months, two Disney features are sometimes shown under the stars. The campfire happens nightly at the amphitheater in the forest near the Bike Barn in the Meadow Recreation Area. Show times vary with the season. Call the Bike Barn for details (407 824-2742). During rainy evenings, activities usually become a "Porch Jam" at the Meadow Trading Post.

Electrical Water Pageant: This shimmering light show appears on Seven Seas Lagoon and Bay Lake every night. A thousand-foot-long string of barges transports an intricate and dynamic light and music show past the Polynesian, Grand Floridian, Contemporary, Wilderness Lodge, and Fort Wilderness resorts. King Neptune presides over the dancing images of sea life that come alive in animated lights and are reflected across the black waters of Bay Lake. The show is brief, approximately 7 minutes,

FORT WILDERNESS

See the "Essentials" section for ticket costs and recreation updates.

Dining Hall & Saloon

Sandwiches, snacks, and picnic supplies are available at the Settlement Trading Post and the Meadow Trading Post. There are several snack bars in River Country that serve hamburgers and sandwiches as well. The restaurant below is located at Pioneer Hall in the Settlement Recreation Area, which is the heart of Fort Wilderness. The Hoop-Dee-Doo Musical Revue dinner show is presented here nightly.

Trail's End Buffeteria — Fried chicken, spaghetti, hamburgers, hot dogs, pizza, casseroles, soups, and a salad and fruit bar are offered in this casual cafeteria filled with tables and rustic props. The restaurant's late-night pizza buffet and take-out pizza services are popular with campers. Open for breakfast, lunch, and dinner; no reservations are accepted. ◆

Attractions · Hotels · Restaurants · Special Events · Recreation · Resources

Magic Kingdom • Future World • World Showcase • Disney-MGM Studios • Animal Kingdom • Typhoon Lagoon • Blizzard Beach • Downtown Disney • Disney's BoardWalk • **Fort Wilderness & River Country**

Essentials · Attractions · Hotels · Restaurants · Special Events · Recreation · Resources

Fort Wilderness & River Country · Disney's BoardWalk · Downtown Disney · Blizzard Beach · Typhoon Lagoon · Animal Kingdom · Disney-MGM Studios · World Showcase · Future World · Magic Kingdom

See the "Essentials" section for ticket costs and recreation updates.

Pets at Walt Disney World — Pets are allowed to stay with their owners in Fort Wilderness for about $3 per night. Pets must be kept on a leash and should be kennelled during the day if owners leave their campsite.

There is a kennel located near the entrance of Fort Wilderness, as well as at each major theme park. All kennels are members of the American Boarding Kennel Association and have facilities for cats and dogs. Among other frequent visitors at the Disney kennels are rodents, ferrets, birds, and nonvenomous snakes, who are all welcome when in their own carrier.

Kennels charge about $6 per day or about $10 for 24 hours. Be sure to bring a copy of your pet's vaccination records, or you will not be allowed to board them. Dogs require rabies, parvovirus (including corona), 4-in-1 (DHLP) and bordatella shots; cats require rabies and 4-in-1 (FPRC) shots. Call the Disney Kennels for more information. Kennel locations throughout Walt Disney World include:

Animal Kingdom (407 938-2100)
Disney-MGM Studios (407 560-4282)
Epcot (407 560-6229)
Fort Wilderness (407 824-2735)
Magic Kingdom (407 824-4407).

but enchanting nonetheless. The Electrical Water Pageant reaches Fort Wilderness at about 9:45 PM. The best viewing location is at the Fort Wilderness Marina and beach.

Hayrides: Visitors can enjoy a casual, old-fashioned hayride on a horse-drawn wagon twice each night, all year round. The hayride departs from Pioneer Hall and travels through the pine forest and along the beach. No reservations are taken and riders are welcome aboard on a first-come, first-served basis. Hayrides are scheduled at 7 and 9:30 PM, and riders should plan to arrive at Pioneer Hall at least fifteen minutes before departure time. The ride lasts about 45 minutes and costs about $6 for adults and about $4 for children.

Hoop-Dee-Doo Musical Revue: This popular dinner show is held three times nightly in rustic Pioneer Hall. Colorfully dressed entertainers rely heavily on audience participation for a song-and-dance performance laced with puns, broad humor, and groan-inducing punch lines. Reservations are difficult to get, so book well in advance. Walk-up seating and same-day reservations are occasionally available through Pioneer Hall (824-2858). (See *Special Events* → "Dinner Shows.")

CAMPING AT FORT WILDERNESS

Camping at Fort Wilderness, whether in a travel trailer, recreational vehicle, or tent, is by far the most economical way to visit Walt Disney World and still enjoy the privileges of staying at a Disney resort. Moreover, it's a great way to enjoy the pleasures of the great outdoors as only Disney can do it. Trailer Life, *a noted camping magazine, has rated Fort Wilderness campground the best in the United States.*

Campsites: Fort Wilderness is divided up into loops, or camping areas (see the "Fort Wilderness Map," page 126, for locations). Campsite categories include Partial Hookups (water and electricity), Full Hookups (water, electricity, sanitary disposal), and Preferred Campsites, which include cable television (bring your own cable). All sites have asphalt pads large enough for RVs, although guests bringing a Class A recreational vehicle should request a wider campsite. Campsites are surrounded by shrubbery and trees that provide relative privacy and have a grill and picnic table for cookouts and outdoor dining.

Costs: Camping at Fort Wilderness is one of the better values for a Walt Disney World vacation. During value seasons, hookups start between $40 and $55 per day, depending on the location and facilities. During peak seasons, prices can range from $65 to $80 per day.

Facilities: Each loop has its own air-conditioned comfort station with showers, laundry, ice, and telephones. Campers should bring along a flashlight, insect repellent, charcoal, matches, extension cord, television cable, clothesline cord, rolls of quarters for laundry, laundry detergent, and a drinking-water hose.

Loops: The most popular campsites are the Preferred Campsites close to the marina, beach, Trail's End Buffeteria, River Country, and Settlement Trading Post (loops 100 through 500 and 700). Also popular are the Full Hookup campsites near the Meadow Trading Post, campfire program, swimming pool, tennis courts, and Bike Barn, where electric golf carts, bikes, boats, and fishing equipment can be rented (loops 600 and 800 through 1600). Campsite loops 1700 through 2000 are near the Meadow Trading Post but are more secluded. They border on the loops for the Wilderness Homes permanent trailers. (See *Hotels* → "Disney's Fort Wilderness Campground.") Partial Hookup campsites are in loops 1500 and 2000. Pets are allowed to stay with their owners on loops 1600 through 1900.

Special Campsites: Groups of twenty or more visitors can camp at Creekside Meadow, a secluded tree-lined meadow reserved exclusively for large parties. Guests settling here can also rent camping gear such as tents and cots. For reservations, call Fort Wilderness Group Camping Reservations (407 939-7807).

Transportation: Except for getting to and from campsites, no cars are allowed inside Fort Wilderness. There is internal bus transportation that transports campers to various parts of Fort Wilderness, although many guests also rent bicycles or electric golf carts to get around. ◆

Essentials • Attractions • Hotels • Restaurants • Special Events • Recreation • Resources

Magic Kingdom • Future World • World Showcase • Disney-MGM Studios • Animal Kingdom • Typhoon Lagoon • Blizzard Beach • Downtown Disney • Disney's BoardWalk • **Fort Wilderness & River Country**

FORT WILDERNESS

See the "Essentials" section for ticket costs and recreation updates.

Services

Banking — An automated teller machine (ATM) can be found near the rest rooms at Pioneer Hall.

Rest Rooms — Rest rooms are located at the Meadow Trading Post, Settlement Trading Post, Pioneer Hall, Reception Outpost in the Fort Wilderness Day Visitor Parking Lot, and by the first-aid office in River Country. Air-conditioned comfort stations, complete with rest rooms, laundromats, showers, ice dispensers, and telephones, are located near all bus stops and campsite loops throughout Fort Wilderness.

Telephones — Telephones can be found at the Gateway Depot bus stop in the Fort Wilderness Guest Parking Lot, at the comfort stations throughout the Fort Wilderness campsite locations, at Pioneer Hall and the Settlement Trading Post in the Settlement Recreation Area, and at the Meadow Trading Post in the Meadow Recreation Area.

Lockers — Lockers are located at the Fort Wilderness Marina, River Country, and Meadow Recreation Area, and at the Gateway Depot bus stop in the Fort Wilderness Guest Parking Lot.

Visitors with Disabilities — Guests who would like to use a wheelchair must reserve it in advance through Guest Services (407 824-2900), located at the Reception Outpost in the Fort Wilderness Guest Parking Lot. Guests can also rent electric carts for use in Fort Wilderness by making same-day reservations at the Bike Barn (824-2742). ◆

HOTELS

The Resorts Located on Walt Disney World Property: Selecting the Best Hotel for Your Disney Vacation.

The hotel you choose for your Disney vacation will be a big part of the vacation memories you'll return home with. Sometimes, visitors select out-of-the-way, low-cost hotels with few services or dining and transportation options. They imagine themselves in the theme parks all day, returning to the hotel only to sleep at night, which can be an exhausting and stressful strategy. The ideal hotel is conveniently located: One that is simple to return to for a midday swim or snooze, continuing your tour later, refreshed and ready for fun. This section is filled with great hotels and tips on how to make them fit your budget. There are three categories of hotels to choose from:

Disney-Owned Resorts: The Disney resorts have fully-realized themed environments, and a warm embrace of Disney magic that continues 24 hours a day. Guests at Disney-owned resorts are afforded certain privileges: early admission to a different theme park each day, occasional after-hours admission options to the Magic Kingdom, free parking or transportation to the theme parks, and versatile resort ID charge cards. Accommodations range from campsites to luxury vacation homes and everything in between.

Partner Hotels at Walt Disney World: There are ten independently operated resorts inside Walt Disney World: seven near Downtown Disney, two in the Epcot Resorts Area, and one near the Magic Kingdom. They offer great locations, good transportation, and other Walt Disney World privileges, including discounts and advance reservations for golf, plus free taxis to the golf courses. Most are moderately priced and all are reviewed in the pages that follow.

Off-Site Hotels: Numerous hotels surround Walt Disney World, ranging from luxury resorts to shabby motels. Many provide shuttle service to the major attractions, but if you want to see and do a lot, you'll need a car. Among the best values are the suites hotels close to the Downtown Disney area. They are very spacious and priced reasonably. Most include breakfast. See *Hotels* → "Off-Site Hotels" for descriptions. ◆

Guide to Room Rates

The Walt Disney World hotels span a wide range of costs, depending on the hotel's amenities, services, and location. Hotel reviews show the starting price of a typical (non-view) room, averaged across peak and value seasons, excluding taxes (which are about 11 percent), as follows:

$ – $60 to $100

$$ – $80 to $150

$$$ – $130 to $200

♕ – $170 to $280

♕ ♕ – $260 to $380

♕ ♕ ♕ – $350 to $550

♚ – over $500

Saving Money — Hotel accommodations are the single greatest expense of a Walt Disney World vacation, and this is where the most money can be saved. Always ask about promotional rates when making reservations. See the "Essentials" section for discussions of other money-saving strategies.

Reservations Alert — All Disney hotel reservations services are moving to Disney Travel Company management, which once handled vacation packages only. Stringent advance payment requirements, and cancellation and change penalties may be imposed, even for booking hotel rooms only. Be sure to ask about these policies. ◆

Essentials

Attractions

Hotels

Restaurants

Special Events

Recreation

Resources

Hotels Inside Walt Disney World • Hotels Outside Walt Disney World

Essentials

Attractions

Hotels

Restaurants

Special Events

Recreation

Resources

Hotels Outside Walt Disney World • Hotels Inside Walt Disney World

COURTYARD BY MARRIOTT

See the "Essentials" section for Hotel Selection Guides and updates.

Rates — Standard rooms **$$** to **$$$**. Rates vary with the season.

Amenities — Room service (limited), in-room safe, hair dryer, coffeemaker, pay-per-view movies, daily newspaper, in-room Nintendo, refrigerator available on request for a fee.

Recreation — Two pools, jogging path, fitness center, whirlpool.

HOTEL TIPS

● Higher floors offer sweeping views. Request a room that faces Pleasure Island for a view of its nightly fireworks display.

● Courtyard by Marriott offers discounts to many organizations, including the American Association of Retired Persons (AARP). AAA members receive a 10 percent discount on rooms.

● Courtyard by Marriott offers a number of vacation packages that include accommodations, theme park admission, some meals, and other travel amenities. To receive a brochure, call the hotel's toll-free number (800 223-9930).

● A rental car can save considerable commuting time from this location.

A Marriott Hotel
1805 Hotel Plaza Boulevard, Lake Buena Vista, Florida 32830
Telephone (407) 828-8888 • Fax (407) 827-4623

A Hotel Plaza Resort: Courtyard by Marriott is one of seven independently owned Hotel Plaza Resorts located near Downtown Disney on Walt Disney World property. The hotel provides shuttle bus service to the major Walt Disney World attractions.

Ambience: This recently renovated high-rise hotel with a six-story garden wing has a modern white-stuccoed exterior, roofed with traditional terra-cotta mission tile. Inside, the fourteen-story atrium lobby has glass elevators that transport guests to the upper floors. A thatch-roofed bar at the back of the lobby, umbrella-shaded tables, and a small fountain to one side evoke a cool Caribbean mood. The turquoise, coral, and sand colored guest rooms have standard but comfortable hotel-style furnishings with tropical accents. All rooms have balconies, many with views of Walt Disney World.

Restaurants: *Courtyard Cafe & Grille* — American-style buffet and a la carte breakfast, lunch, and dinner.

Village Deli — New York–style deli sandwiches, pizza, frozen yogurt, and take-out menu for lunch, dinner, and late-night snacks.

Features: Courtyard Club members can earn points, have free local phone calls, and receive room discounts.

Courtyard guests receive a "Preferred Guest" shopping and dining discount card that can be used at many Downtown Disney shops and restaurants.

Hotel Transportation: Walk or bus to Downtown Disney. Bus to the Magic Kingdom, Disney-MGM Studios, Epcot, Animal Kingdom, Typhoon Lagoon, Blizzard Beach, and Disney's BoardWalk. For transportation to other theme parks or distant resorts, connect to destination buses at Downtown Disney. Taxi service is available.

Making Reservations: Check rates at Courtyard Central Reservations first (800 321-2211), then call the hotel's toll-free number and compare room rates (800 223-9930). Reservations can also be made through the Disney Central Reservations Office (407 934-7639). Be sure to ask about special promotional rates, which could cut room costs up to 40 percent depending on the day of arrival.

DISNEY'S ALL-STAR MOVIES RESORT

*See the "Essentials" section for
Hotel Selection Guides and updates.*

A Disney-Owned Hotel
1701 West Buena Vista Drive, Lake Buena Vista, Florida 32830
Telephone (407) 939-7000 • Fax (407) 939-7111

An Animal Kingdom Resort: Disney's budget All-Star Movies Resort is located in the Animal Kingdom Resorts Area. Nearby attractions include Blizzard Beach water park, Disney's Wide World of Sports, Disney Studios, and Animal Kingdom.

Ambience: This large resort is made up of ten buildings, each three stories high with exterior corridors. The otherwise plain block structures are distinguished by massive icons from beloved Disney films. Larger-than-life images from *101 Dalmatians, Toy Story, Fantasia, The Mighty Ducks,* and *The Love Bug* provide the scenery for the courtyards and adorn the buildings. The interior of the guest rooms features bedspreads adorned with the aforementioned characters. Movie posters decorate the walls of the brightly colored, albeit tiny rooms. This hotel provides many of the advantages of staying in a Disney resort to visitors on limited budgets.

Restaurants: *World Premiere Food Court* — Counter service for breakfast, lunch, and dinner; open all day.

Features: The hotel's *Toy Story*–themed area has an outside courtyard cleverly designed to look like Andy's room. It is fashioned out of shrubbery — complete with a doorway entrance and an "area rug" created entirely out of garden flowers.

Cinema Hall, the main building, is where check-in and Guest Services are located. The food court, gift shop, and arcade are located here as well. Out in front of the building is the bus stop. Directly behind Cinema Hall is the main pool, Fantasia, which features Sorcerer Mickey. The kiddie pool is beside it. Duck Pond pool, which is modeled after a hockey rink, is located in the Mighty Ducks section of the resort.

Hotel Transportation: Bus to all theme parks, including the Magic Kingdom, Animal Kingdom, Epcot, Disney-MGM Studios, Blizzard Beach, Typhoon Lagoon, and Downtown Disney. To reach other resorts or destinations, bus to Downtown Disney and connect to destination buses. Taxi service is available.

Making Reservations: Contact the Disney Central Reservations Office (407 934-7639). Ask about special rates and seasonal vacation packages.

Rates — Standard rooms **$$**. Rates vary with the season.

Amenities — In-room safe, pizza delivery, voice mail, refrigerator on request for a fee.

Recreation — Jogging path, two pools, kiddie pool, playground, video arcade.

HOTEL TIPS

● Guests who want to be in the heart of the action will enjoy the Fantasia section; those looking for something more quiet should request The Love Bug area.

● The All-Star Movies resort overall is well laid out; guests generally won't encounter long hikes from their room to the main areas.

● A rental car will save on commuting time, especially for guests who want to see all that Walt Disney World has to offer and for those who want to dine in full service restaurants at other resorts.

● Walt Disney World resorts offer discounts to members of Magic Kingdom Club and AAA, as well as to Annual Passholders and Florida residents. Be sure to inquire.

Attractions
Hotels
Restaurants
Special Events
Recreation
Resources
Hotels Inside Walt Disney World • Hotels Outside Walt Disney World

Essentials

Attractions

Hotels

Restaurants

Special Events

Recreation

Resources

Hotels Outside Walt Disney World • Hotels Inside Walt Disney World

DISNEY'S ALL-STAR MUSIC RESORT

See the "Essentials" section for Hotel Selection Guides and updates.

Rates — Standard rooms **$$**. Rates vary with the season.

Amenities — In-room safe, voice mail, pizza delivery, refrigerator on request for a fee.

Recreation — Jogging path, two pools, kiddie pool, playground, video arcade.

HOTEL TIPS

● For locations near the bus stop and food court, request a room in the Calypso section. For a quiet, secluded room, the best bet is County Fair; however, guests here have a long walk to Melody Hall.

● In the off season, the All-Star resorts sometimes share buses, adding a little time to the commute.

● A rental car will save on commuting time, especially for guests who want to see all that Walt Disney World has to offer and for those who want to dine in full service restaurants at other resorts.

● Walt Disney World resorts offer discounts to members of Magic Kingdom Club and AAA, as well as to Annual Passholders and Florida residents. Be sure to inquire.

A Disney-Owned Hotel
1701 West Buena Vista Drive, Lake Buena Vista, Florida 32830
Telephone (407) 939-6000 • Fax (407) 939-7222

An Animal Kingdom Resort: Disney's budget All-Star Music Resort is located in the Animal Kingdom Resorts Area. Nearby attractions include Blizzard Beach water park, Disney's Wide World of Sports, Disney-MGM Studios, and Animal Kingdom.

Ambience: This huge resort complex is made up of ten buildings, each three stories high with exterior corridors. The otherwise plain block structures are distinguished by massive musical decorations in a variety of instruments, as well as country western boots. The theme is carried over into the small guest rooms, which feature star covered light fixtures and bedspreads patterned with musical instruments.

Restaurants: *The Intermission Food Court* — Counter service for breakfast, lunch, and dinner; open all day.

Features: The main building, Melody Hall, is where check-in and Guest Services are located. The food court, gift shop, and arcade are located here as well. Out in front of the building is the bus stop.

The main pool, Calypso, themed with the Three Caballeros, and the kiddie pool are located directly behind Melody Hall. The second pool, shaped like a piano, is located toward the back of this long, spread-out resort.

In the morning, a breakfast cart is conveniently located by the piano pool for guests who don't want to make the long trek to the main building for their morning coffee.

This hotel provides many of the advantages of staying in a Disney resort to visitors on limited budgets.

Hotel Transportation: Bus to all theme parks, including the Magic Kingdom, Animal Kingdom, Epcot, Disney-MGM Studios, Blizzard Beach, Typhoon Lagoon, and Downtown Disney. To reach other resorts or destinations, bus to Downtown Disney and connect to destination buses. Taxi service is available.

Making Reservations: Contact the Disney Central Reservations Office (407 934-7639). Ask about special rates and seasonal vacation packages.

DISNEY'S ALL-STAR SPORTS RESORT

See the "Essentials" section for Hotel Selection Guides and updates.

A Disney-Owned Hotel
1701 West Buena Vista Drive, Lake Buena Vista, Florida 32830
Telephone (407) 939-5000 • Fax (407) 939-7333

An Animal Kingdom Resort: Disney's budget All-Star Sports Resort is located in the Animal Kingdom Resorts Area. Nearby attractions include Blizzard Beach water park, Disney's Wide World of Sports, Disney-MGM Studios, and Animal Kingdom.

Ambience: This resort complex is made up of ten buildings, each three stories high with exterior corridors. The otherwise plain structures are distinguished by massive sporting gear, such as huge football helmets, tennis ball cans, and even red paper Coca-Cola cups. The theme extends into the small guest rooms, which feature star fixtures over the lights and sporty bedspreads and wall paper borders.

Restaurants: *End Zone Food Court* — Counter service for breakfast, lunch, and dinner; open all day.

Features: The main building, Stadium Hall, houses the check-in and Guest Services desk, as well as the gift shop, arcade, and food court. Guests board buses to the theme parks in front of this building.

Just behind Stadium Hall is where the main pool and kiddie pool are located. In keeping with the sports theme, the main pool is called Surfboard Bay and the second pool, Grand Slam, is shaped like a baseball diamond with none other than Goofy as pitcher; it is in the infield of the Home Run buildings.

This hotel provides many of the advantages of staying in a Disney Resort to visitors on limited budgets.

Hotel Transportation: Bus to all theme parks, including the Magic Kingdom, Animal Kingdom, Epcot, Disney-MGM Studios, Blizzard Beach, Typhoon Lagoon, and Downtown Disney. To reach other resorts or destinations, bus to Downtown Disney and connect to destination buses. Taxi service is available.

Making Reservations: Contact the Disney Central Reservations Office (407 934-7639). Ask about special rates and seasonal vacation packages.

Rates — Standard Rooms **$$**. Rates vary with the season.

Amenities — In-room safe, voice mail, pizza delivery, refrigerator on request for a fee.

Recreation — Jogging path, two pools, kiddie pool, playground, video arcade.

HOTEL TIPS

● For locations near the bus stops and food courts, request a room in the Surf's Up! section. A more quiet location would be either the Hoops section or Center Court area, but these make for a longer walk to the main building.

● During the off season, the All-Star resorts occasionally share buses, making for a longer commute.

● A rental car will save on travel time and would be ideal for visitors who want to see all that Walt Disney World has to offer, such as dining in full service restaurants at other resorts.

● Walt Disney World resorts offer discounts to members of Magic Kingdom Club and AAA, as well as to Annual Passholders and Florida residents. Be sure to inquire.

Essentials

Attractions

Hotels

Hotels Inside Walt Disney World • Hotels Outside Walt Disney World

Restaurants

Special Events

Recreation

Resources

Essentials

Attractions

Hotels

Restaurants

Special Events

Recreation

Resources

Hotels Outside Walt Disney World • Hotels Inside Walt Disney World

DISNEY'S ANIMAL KINGDOM LODGE

*See the "Essentials" section for
Hotel Selection Guides and updates.*

Rates — Standard rooms 👑.
Concierge-service rooms 👑 👑 👑
(including Continental breakfast, afternoon snacks, evening wine, cordials, appetizers, and special room amenities). Rates vary with the season.

Amenities — Room service, valet parking, hair dryer, coffeemaker, refrigerator on request for a fee, in-room safe, voice mail.

Recreation — Themed pool, animal viewing, nature trails, fitness center, whirlpool, guest tours, kid's club, jogging path, video arcade.

HOTEL TIPS

● Rental cars and taxis will greatly assist those seeking to experience as much of Walt Disney World as possible during their stay, especially those planning to visit other resorts.

● Walt Disney World resorts offer discounts to members of Disney Club and may also extend discounts to AAA members, Annual Passholders, and Florida residents. Inquire when making reservations.

● The price of the room generally reflects the view of the savanna and the size of the room. The more expensive rooms are larger and have a better view. The lowest priced rooms face the parking lot.

● Animals will approach from the savanna to within ten feet of the Arusha Kopje lookout near the lobby.

A Disney-Owned Hotel
2901 Osceola Parkway, Bay Lake, Florida 32830
Telephone (407) 938-3000 • Fax (407) 938-7102

An Animal Kingdom Resort: Disney's newest deluxe hotel is located adjacent to Disney's Animal Kingdom theme park. Other nearby attractions include Blizzard Beach and Disney's Wide World of Sports.

Ambience: Understated by design, the front of this magnificent resort is visually foreshortened to resemble an African village with its rondoval thatched roofs. Guests enter the hotel on what is actually the third floor into a majestic open air lodge. The theming of a Serengeti preserve is quite evident. The lodge's immense picture window showcases the spectacular savanna that is exclusive to the resort and not shared with the nearby theme park. Giraffes, zebras, antelope, and other exotic wildlife wander the rolling savannas and may approach the hotel to the delight of guests watching from their balconies. The Arusha Kopje, named after a game preserve in Tanzania, is a lookout point in the lobby where guests can take in the panoramic splendor of 200 species living in harmony. Resort rooms are designed to accentuate the vibrant colors of the embroidered decor and the majestic view of the savanna beyond.

Restaurants: *Boma: Flavors of Africa* — Buffet style family restaurant open for breakfast and dinner, offers a large variety of dishes influenced by South African cuisine.

Jiko: The Cooking Place — Open for dinner only, this colorful full service restaurant serves flavorful creative entrees combining African, French, and English influences.

Mara — Counter-service restaurant; open from 6 AM until midnight.

Features: The stately savanna is partitioned into three zones; animals remain on at least two of these zones 24 hours every day. The hotel conducts interactive presentations of African habitat animals.

The 9,000 square foot pool has detailed safari theme complete with a water slide. Small children may use the kiddie pool. Simba's Clubhouse is a play center for children and a kid's club offering child care.

Hotel Transportation: Bus to the Magic Kingdom, Epcot, Disney-MGM Studios, Animal Kingdom, Downtown Disney, Typhoon Lagoon, and Blizzard Beach. To reach other destinations, bus to Downtown Disney and connect to destination buses. Taxi service is available.

Making Reservations: Contact the Disney Central Reservations Office (407 934-7639). Ask about special rates and seasonal vacation packages.

Essentials

Attractions

Hotels

Restaurants

Special Events

Recreation

Resources

DISNEY'S BEACH CLUB RESORT

See the "Essentials" section for
Hotel Selection Guides and updates.

A Disney-Owned Hotel
1800 Epcot Resorts Boulevard, Lake Buena Vista, Florida 32830
Telephone (407) 934-8000 • Fax (407) 934-3850

An Epcot Resort: Disney's Beach Club Resort is one of seven hotels in the Epcot Resorts Area. It is located within walking distance of the International Gateway to the World Showcase at Epcot. It faces Crescent Lake and shares a white sand beach and harbor waterfront with Disney's Yacht Club Resort.

Ambience: This sky blue multilevel resort was designed by architect Robert Stern and patterned after the fashionable New England seacoast-style resorts of the nineteenth century. It shares resort amenities with the more formal Yacht Club located next door. It has a sporty, casual decor, from the 1927 Chevrolet taxi parked in front to the striped wicker furnishings and caged finches in the lobby. Guest rooms are cheerful and light, furnished in beach-style pink and white cabana stripes and gauzy curtains. Many rooms have verandas or small balconies that overlook the hotel's white sand beach on Crescent Lake.

Restaurants: *Cape May Cafe* — Character Breakfast buffet and clambake dinner buffet. Lobster is available on a separate menu.

Beaches and Cream — Breakfast, hamburgers, and soda fountain specialties; served all day.

Hurricane Hanna's Grill — Located next to Stormalong Bay; it offers a full bar, hotdogs, and hamburgers.

Features: In terms of location, the Beach Club has it all. It is conveniently located for guests primarily interested in Epcot and Disney-MGM Studios, and is a short, scenic walk to Disney's BoardWalk for shopping, fine restaurants, and evening entertainment.

Hotel Transportation: Walk or water launch to the World Showcase at Epcot and Disney's BoardWalk. Water launch to Disney-MGM Studios. Bus to Typhoon Lagoon, the Magic Kingdom, Animal Kingdom, Blizzard Beach, and Downtown Disney. To reach other destinations or distant resorts, bus to Downtown Disney and connect to destination buses. Taxi service is available.

Making Reservations: Contact the Disney Central Reservations Office (407 934-7639). Ask about special rates and seasonal vacation packages.

Rates — Standard rooms ♛ ♛. Rates vary with the season.

Amenities — Room service (24 hour), coffeemaker, refrigerator (stocked), in-room safe, turndown service, hair dryer, voice mail, valet parking, beauty/barber shop, small refrigerator available upon request.

Recreation — White sand beach, tennis, boating, volleyball, lawn bowling, croquet, fitness center, beauty salon, sauna, whirlpool, massage, fitness training, bicycling, jogging path, mini water park, quiet pool, video arcade.

HOTEL TIPS

● At times, the rooms on the fifth floor are transformed into concierge rooms, so they are a bit more spacious and generous in comforts. Most upper-floor rooms have balconies. If the weather is pleasant, guests may want to request a "full balcony" room, which has outdoor seating.

● Standard rooms that face the front, but are not directly over the parking portico, are a good value. Rooms located at the far end of the hotel (with numbers ending in 11 to 30), although a bit of a trek from the lobby, offer pleasant views of the forest or the quiet pool and have fast access by foot to the International Gateway to the World Showcase at Epcot. Most rooms sleep five.

Essentials

Attractions

Hotels

Hotels Inside Walt Disney World • Hotels Outside Walt Disney World

Restaurants

Special Events

Recreation

Resources

DISNEY'S BOARDWALK INN

See the "Essentials" section for
Hotel Selection Guides and updates.

Rates — Standard rooms 👑 👑.
Concierge service rooms 👑 (including
Continental breakfast, private lounge,
afternoon snacks, evening cordials and
desserts, bathrobes, and other room
amenities). Honeymoon Cottages 👑.
Rates vary with the season.

Amenities — Room service (24 hour),
bathrobes, hair dryer, daily newspaper,
turndown service, voice mail, valet parking, in-room safe, iron and ironing board,
make up mirror, refrigerator on request for
a fee.

Recreation — Quiet pool, mini water
park, bicycling, tennis, jogging path, croquet, fishing, fitness center, sauna, steam
room, whirlpool, massage, boating.

HOTEL TIPS

● The rooms overlooking Crescent Lake
and the BoardWalk Promenade offer a
bustling, brightly lit view. If that's not what
you are looking for, request a room overlooking the gardens or the quiet-pool
area.

● The resort stretches over half the
BoardWalk. Request a close-in room if
you wish to be near the lobby and valet
parking areas.

● Daybeds here are somewhat small; they
are comfortably sized for a child.

● Walt Disney World resorts offer discounts to members of Magic Kingdom
Club and AAA, as well as to Annual
Passholders and Florida residents. Be
sure to inquire.

A Disney-Owned Hotel
2101 Epcot Resorts Boulevard, Lake Buena Vista, Florida 32830
Telephone (407) 939-5100 • Fax (407) 939-5150

An Epcot Resort: Disney's BoardWalk Inn is one of seven hotels in
the Epcot Resorts Area. It is located at Disney's BoardWalk, a short
distance from Disney-MGM Studios and within walking distance of the
International Gateway to the World Showcase at Epcot. The hotel sits
above Disney's BoardWalk Promenade overlooking Crescent Lake, and
shares a lobby and large outdoor terrace with Disney's BoardWalk Villas,
a Disney Vacation Club resort.

Ambience: Disney's BoardWalk Inn is built on several levels that rise
above and extend behind Disney's BoardWalk, a bustling promenade
reminiscent of the Atlantic City Boardwalk of the 1930s. The hotel's design
recalls the cheerful, casual luxury of turn-of-the-century Eastern Seaboard
summer resorts. The moderate-sized guest rooms have balconies with
French doors and are decorated with rosebud-patterned rugs, comfortable
beach house–style furnishings, and curtains printed with soft images of
vintage postcards. The hotel also has a number of charming two-story
"honeymoon cottages" with small gardens and private entrances.

Restaurants: The hotel is served by several restaurants along Disney's
BoardWalk, including *Spoodles, ESPN Club, Flying Fish Café,* and *Big
River Grille & Brewing Works.*

Belle Vue Room — Comfortable and popular lobby bar lounge, which
serves a Continental breakfast each morning.

Features: This full-amenity resort is especially ideal for guests primarily
interested in Epcot, Disney-MGM Studios, and the nightlife and clubs on
the BoardWalk Promenade.

The Belle Vue Room off the lobby is a pleasant place to watch a sunset
or play a quiet game of checkers or backgammon on a rainy afternoon.

Hotel Transportation: Walk or water launch to the World Showcase at
Epcot. Water launch to Disney-MGM Studios. Bus to the Magic Kingdom,
Animal Kingdom, Blizzard Beach, Typhoon Lagoon, and Downtown
Disney. To reach other destinations or resorts, bus to Downtown Disney
and connect to destination buses. Taxi service is available.

Making Reservations: Contact the Disney Central Reservations Office
(407 934-7639). Ask about special rates and seasonal vacation packages.

DISNEY'S BOARDWALK VILLAS

See the "Essentials" section for Hotel Selection Guides and updates.

Essentials
Attractions
Hotels
Restaurants
Special Events
Recreation
Resources

Hotels Inside Walt Disney World • Hotels Outside Walt Disney World

A Disney Vacation Club Timeshare
2101 Epcot Resorts Boulevard, Lake Buena Vista, Florida 32830
Telephone (407) 939-5100 • Fax (407) 939-5150

An Epcot Resort: Disney's BoardWalk Villas is one of seven hotels in the Epcot Resorts Area. It is located at Disney's BoardWalk, a short distance from Disney-MGM Studios and within walking distance of the International Gateway to the World Showcase at Epcot. The hotel sits above Disney's BoardWalk Promenade, overlooks Crescent Lake, and shares a lobby and a large outdoor terrace with Disney's BoardWalk Inn.

Ambience: Painted in shades of cream and terra-cotta and sporting festive striped awnings, Disney's BoardWalk Villas extends above and behind Disney's BoardWalk, an entertainment complex of restaurants, clubs, and shops that curves around Crescent Lake. Accommodations are designed to be "vacation homes." Studios have wet bars, and one-, two-, and three-bedroom suites have full kitchens. All units have comfortable beach house–style furnishings and French doors that open onto small balconies.

Restaurants: The hotel is served by several restaurants along Disney's BoardWalk, including *Spoodles, ESPN Club, Flying Fish Café,* and *Big River Grille & Brewing Works.*

Belle Vue Room — Comfortable lobby bar lounge, which serves a Continental breakfast each morning.

Features: The resort is conveniently located for guests primarily interested in Disney-MGM Studios and Epcot, as well as the nightlife and clubs on the BoardWalk Promenade.

For young-at-heart guests, the resort's carnival-themed pool area, Luna Park, has a roller-coaster waterslide and a whimsical poolside bar.

Hotel Transportation: Walk or water launch to the World Showcase at Epcot. Water launch to Disney-MGM Studios. Bus to the Magic Kingdom, Animal Kingdom, Blizzard Beach, Typhoon Lagoon, and Downtown Disney. To reach other destinations or resorts, bus to Downtown Disney and connect to destination buses. Taxi service is available.

Making Reservations: Contact the Disney Central Reservations Office (407 934-7639). Ask about special rates and seasonal vacation packages.

Rates — Studios 👑👑 (including a wet bar, refrigerator, microwave, and coffee maker). One-bedroom vacation homes 👑👑👑. Two-bedroom vacation homes 👑👑👑. Three-bedroom vacation homes 👑. All vacation homes except studios have fully equipped kitchens, laundry facilities, wide-screen televisions, and VCRs. Rates vary with the season.

Amenities — Room service (24 hour), coffeemaker, daily newspaper, in-room safe, hair dryer, valet parking, voice mail, microwave, refrigerator (unstocked), turn-down service, VCR, iron and ironing board.

Recreation — Quiet pool, mini water park, bicycling, tennis, jogging path, croquet, fishing, fitness center, sauna, steam room, whirlpool, massage, boating, video arcade.

HOTEL TIPS

● Some rooms overlooking the BoardWalk Promenade offer a partial view of the fireworks at Epcot.

● Disney's BoardWalk Villas is also a Disney Vacation Club timeshare resort. Units not used by timeshare owners are available to guests as full-service hotel accommodations.

● The resort stretches over half the BoardWalk. Request a close-in room if you wish to be near the lobby and valet parking areas. The studios seem a little cramped; the suites, while more expensive, offer a better value.

DISNEY'S CARIBBEAN BEACH RESORT

See the "Essentials" section for Hotel Selection Guides and updates.

Rates — Standard rooms **$$$**. Rates vary with the season.

Amenities — Coffeemaker, voice mail, pizza delivery, iron and ironing board available upon request.

Recreation — Seven pools, white sand beach, boating, bicycling, jogging path, nature walk, volleyball, whirlpool.

HOTEL TIPS

● To select a room close to Old Port Royale when making reservations, request Trinidad North, next door, or Jamaica, just across the bridge. For isolation, request Trinidad South, which has a quiet pool and secluded beach. The rooms on the second floor afford the most privacy. Some of the remote building locations can provide a romantic tropical setting.

● If you would like to be near Parrot Cay island, request a room in Jamaica or Aruba.

● A rental car can speed commuting time to the theme parks from this location and is essential if frequently visiting other resorts.

● The resort is especially popular among families with young children, making it an all-day noisy experience at the main pool.

● Because the resort sprawls over two hundred acres, it can be a long trek from guest rooms to the food court located at Old Port Royale.

A Disney-Owned Hotel
900 Cayman Way, Lake Buena Vista, Florida 32830
Telephone (407) 934-3400 • Fax (407) 934-3288

An Epcot Resort: Disney's Caribbean Beach Resort is one of seven hotels in the Epcot Resorts Area. The buildings of the resort encircle forty-acre Barefoot Bay, a series of three lakes created for the resort's exclusive use. From Disney's Caribbean Beach Resort it is a short drive to Epcot, Disney-MGM Studios, Typhoon Lagoon, and Downtown Disney.

Ambience: Built as Walt Disney World's first budget resort, the sprawling Caribbean Beach Resort consists of clusters of pitched-roof two-story buildings painted in very bright colors. Each area has a pool and is surrounded with expertly designed tropical landscaping. Instead of a formal lobby, the resort welcomes guests at its modest freestanding Customs House, where overhead fans and wicker settees set a tropical note. The limited-amenity guest rooms, with soft toned wood furnishings, are functional and cozy. Most resort activities are centered at Old Port Royale, a common area on one side of Barefoot Bay.

Restaurants: *Captain's Tavern* — Dinner featuring steaks and American cuisine.

Old Port Royale Food Court — Counter service for breakfast, lunch, and dinner; open all day.

Features: Parrot Cay, a small island in the middle of Barefoot Bay, has a fantasy Spanish-fort playground, a tropical nature walk, and an aviary stocked with colorful birds.

Many guests find that the hammocks that are scattered liberally around Barefoot Bay are a great way to relax and unwind.

Hotel Transportation: Bus to all theme parks and attractions, including the Magic Kingdom, Disney-MGM Studios, Epcot, Animal Kingdom, Blizzard Beach, Typhoon Lagoon, and Downtown Disney. To reach other destinations or distant resorts, bus to Downtown Disney and connect to destination buses. Taxi service is available.

Making Reservations: Contact the Disney Central Reservations Office (407 934-7639). Ask about special rates and seasonal vacation packages.

DISNEY'S CONTEMPORARY RESORT

See the "Essentials" section for
Hotel Selection Guides and updates.

A Disney-Owned Hotel
4600 North World Drive, Lake Buena Vista, Florida 32830
Telephone (407) 824-1000 • Fax (407) 824-3539

A Magic Kingdom Resort: Disney's Contemporary Resort is one of seven hotels in the Magic Kingdom Resorts Area. It is conveniently located on the monorail line that serves the Magic Kingdom and Epcot. It has a long white sand beach and sweeping views of Bay Lake.

Ambience: The elongated pyramidal structure of this resort has a futuristic look. The minimalist-style first-floor lobby is strictly functional, with angular furniture in stylish colors and sleek modern art. The main lobby is actually located on the Concourse level, where the monorail glides through the hotel's glass-and-steel atrium. The resort's outdoor pool area was recently enlarged and a waterslide added. The tower rooms and suites are decorated in sophisticated neutral colors with bright bold accents and streamlined furniture. The three-story garden wing rooms are spacious, but set at some distance from the lobby. Ground floor rooms have a small patio.

Restaurants: *California Grill* — The dinner menu changes daily in this trendy rooftop restaurant with an open kitchen. The food preparation is part of the show.

Chef Mickey's — Character buffet for breakfast and dinner.

Concourse Steakhouse — Breakfast, lunch, and dinner featuring steak and prime rib.

Features: In this most tennis-oriented of the Walt Disney World resorts, the Racquet Club offers practice courts and personal instruction.

The outdoor viewing platform on the fifteenth floor, adjacent to the California Grill, is ideal for watching the Magic Kingdom fireworks.

This hotel has many unique transportation options, including direct ferry service from its marina to Fort Wilderness.

Hotel Transportation: Walk to the Magic Kingdom. Monorail to the Magic Kingdom, the Transportation and Ticket Center (TTC), and Epcot (guests must change monorails at the TTC to reach Epcot). Water launch to Fort Wilderness and River Country. Bus to Animal Kingdom, Blizzard beach, and Disney-MGM Studios. Monorail to the TTC and transfer to destination buses for all other attractions and distant resorts. Taxi service is available.

Making Reservations: Contact the Disney Central Reservations Office (407 934-7639). Ask about special rates and seasonal vacation packages.

Rates — Garden wing standard rooms 👑. Tower rooms 👑 👑 👑. Tower concierge suites 👑 👑 👑 (including Continental breakfast, evening wine and cheese, and special room amenities). Rates vary with the season.

Amenities — Room service (24 hour), in-room safe, daily newspaper, voice mail, valet parking, refrigerator on request for a fee.

Recreation — Three pools, white sand beach, boating, waterskiing, parasailing, tennis, volleyball, shuffleboard, jogging path, fitness center, beauty salon, sauna, whirlpool, fitness training, massage.

HOTEL TIPS

● Tower rooms are the most popular, convenient, and expensive. Higher-floor rooms facing the Magic Kingdom have a view of the fireworks show. Most rooms sleep five.

● Garden wing rooms, although less expensive, are a distance from the lobby; request a location close in.

● The rooms on the first floor facing Bay Lake are popular because they have sliding glass doors that open onto private patios. The bathrooms are large and have a door separating the commode from the shower/vanity area, shortening the time it takes for a family to get ready in the morning.

Essentials

Attractions

Hotels

Hotels Inside Walt Disney World • Hotels Outside Walt Disney World

Restaurants

Special Events

Recreation

Resources

DISNEY'S CORONADO SPRINGS RESORT

See the "Essentials" section for
Hotel Selection Guides and updates.

Essentials
Attractions
Hotels
Restaurants
Special Events
Recreation
Resources

Hotels Inside Walt Disney World • Hotels Outside Walt Disney World

Rates — Standard rooms **$$$**. Rates vary with the season.

Amenities — Room service (limited), coffeemaker, hair dryer, in-room safe, valet parking, voice mail, iron and ironing board, refrigerator on request for a fee.

Recreation — Three pools, mini water park, white sand beach, boating, volleyball, bicycling, jogging path, nature walk, fitness center, whirlpool, massage, video arcade.

HOTEL TIPS

● The Cabanas are oriented to their own beach-lined section of Lago Dorado and have very picturesque views. Great views of sunrises may be had from the Casitas on top floors, facing the lake.

● For locations nearest the food court and restaurant, request a room in Casitas 1 or Cabanas 9B. Ranchos 7A and Cabanas 8B are nearest the Dig Site. Upper-floor rooms throughout the resort offer the most privacy.

● Guests relying on buses to reach minor attractions or other resorts for dining events may find them inconvenient from here.

● Walt Disney World resorts offer discounts to members of Magic Kingdom Club and AAA, as well as to Annual Passholders and Florida residents. Be sure to inquire.

A Disney-Owned Hotel
1000 West Buena Vista Drive, Lake Buena Vista, Florida 32830
Telephone (407) 939-1000 • Fax (407) 939-1003

An Animal Kingdom Resort: Disney's Coronado Springs Resort is located in the Animal Kingdom Resorts Area. Nearby attractions include Blizzard Beach, Disney's Wide World of Sports, and Disney's Animal Kingdom.

Ambience: This handsomely designed resort blends the stately architectural styles of Colonial Mexico with the rustic simplicity of the American Southwest. The landscaping varies from desert oasis to tropical beach. Three distinct clusters of hotel buildings with pools encircle Lago Dorado, the resort's private lake: the Cabanas, two-story Mexican-style beach front bungalows; the Ranchos, secluded rustic stucco buildings roofed in Spanish terra-cotta; and the Casitas, a bright festive village of three- and four-story buildings with pleasant courtyards and fountains. Guest rooms have whitewashed walls, ceiling fans, and colorful Southwestern-themed furnishings. The hotel's large lobby and common areas have open-beam ceilings with elaborate detailing. Coronado Springs was designed to be a moderately priced convention hotel, as well as a family vacation resort.

Restaurants: *Maya Grill* — Daily American breakfast buffet. A la carte dinner featuring Latin American specialties.

Pepper Market — Open all day, this upscale food court has the look of a festive Mexican market and offers traditional American and Mexican dishes.

Siesta's — Poolside bar and grill.

Features: Due the hotel's focus on convention travelers, services are a bit above average for a moderately-priced resort.

The resort's themed pool, the Dig Site, resembles an archaeological dig; it is dominated by a Mayan pyramid waterfall which is flanked by jaguars and contains a stylistic waterslide. This area also has an impressively large whirlpool spa, as well as a volleyball court.

Hotel Transportation: Bus to the Magic Kingdom, Epcot, Disney-MGM Studios, Animal Kingdom, Downtown Disney, Blizzard Beach, and Typhoon Lagoon, and after 4 PM to Disney's BoardWalk. To reach other destinations, bus to Downtown Disney and connect to destination buses. Taxi service is available.

Making Reservations: Contact the Disney Central Reservations Office (407 934-7639). Ask about special rates and seasonal vacation packages.

DISNEY'S FORT WILDERNESS CAMPGROUND

See the "Essentials" section for Hotel Selection Guides and updates.

A Disney-Owned Hotel and Campground
3520 N. Fort Wilderness Trail, Lake Buena Vista, Florida 32830
Telephone (407) 824-2900 • Fax (407) 824-3508

A Magic Kingdom Resort: Disney's rustic Fort Wilderness Resort and Campground is one of seven hotels in the Magic Kingdom Resorts Area. It stretches from Vista Boulevard to the shores of Bay Lake.

Ambience: This lush seven-hundred-acre pine forested campground is an ideal place for visitors who enjoy the outdoors. There are about 780 campsites that can be used for tents or for recreational vehicles, and about four-hundred fully appointed one-bedroom Wilderness Homes. These log cabins carry the woodsy theme throughout the interior of the trailers, and feature furniture made of branches. Fort Wilderness offers a peaceful, natural setting to return to after a hectic day at the theme parks and is itself a Walt Disney World attraction (see *Attractions* → "Fort Wilderness & River Country").

Restaurants: *Trail's End Buffeteria* — Cafeteria service for breakfast, lunch, and dinner, and late-night pizza to eat in or take out.

Features: Fort Wilderness offers daily entertainment events, including the Hoop-Dee-Doo Musical Revue dinner show, hayrides, and a nightly campfire program with movies. The "Chuck Wagon" is on hand for hot dogs, pizza, popcorn, and marshmallows for roasting.

Two on-site convenience stores, Settlement Trading Post and Meadow Trading Post, carry a limited supply of groceries and prepared foods.

The Wilderness Homes can be a very good value for families who have more than two children or for those who would like some privacy and extra space.

Hotel Transportation: Bus stops can be found throughout Fort Wilderness, which has its own internal bus system to all campsites and local attractions. (There is no public parking inside Fort Wilderness or at River Country.) Bikes and electric carts can also be rented for use within the resort. Walk or bus to River Country. Water launch to the Magic Kingdom and the Contemporary resort. Bus to Animal Kingdom and Blizzard Beach. To reach all other attractions and destinations, bus or water launch to the Transportation and Ticket Center (TTC) and transfer to destination buses or monorails.

Making Reservations: Contact the Disney Central Reservations Office (407 934-7639). Ask about special rates and seasonal vacation packages.

Rates — Wilderness Homes and cabins (fully equipped one-bedroom trailers) 👑. Campsites with full hookups 💲. Campsites with partial hookups 💲. Rates vary with the season.

Wilderness Home Amenities — Full kitchen, microwave, cable TV, VCR, voice mail, in-room safe, iron and ironing board, hair dryer, daily newspaper, deck, outdoor grill, and housekeeping services.

Campsite Amenities — Full-hookup campsites include sanitary disposal, water, cable TV outlet, electricity, and outdoor grill. Partial-hookup campsites include water, electricity, and outdoor grill. All campsite loops have air-conditioned rest rooms, showers, ice makers, laundry facilities, and telephones.

Recreation — Pool, lap pool, marina, white sand beach, volleyball, basketball, tetherball, shuffleboard, jogging path, nature trail, tennis, bicycling, horseback riding, waterskiing, fishing, canoeing, hayrides, petting farm, parasailing, and evening campfire and movies.

HOTEL TIPS

● A car is essential at this location, especially during the hot rainy season.

● The most requested Wilderness Home locations are on loops 2500 and 2700 near the pool. The most desirable campsites are on loops 100 through 500, near the marina and River Country. Pets are allowed to stay with their owners in loops 1600 through 1900.

Essentials

Attractions

Hotels

Restaurants

Special Events

Recreation

Resources

Hotels Outside Walt Disney World • Hotels Inside Walt Disney World

DISNEY'S GRAND FLORIDIAN RESORT & SPA

See the "Essentials" section for Hotel Selection Guides and updates.

Rates — Standard rooms ♔ ♔. Concierge service rooms ♔ (including Continental breakfast, afternoon snacks, evening cordials and appetizers, and special room amenities). Rates vary with the season.

Amenities — Daily newspaper, 24 hour room service, refrigerator (stocked), in-room safe, hair dryer, bathrobes, valet parking, voice mail, coffeemaker available upon request.

Recreation — One pool, white sand beach, boating, waterskiing, tennis, jogging path, volleyball, fitness center, fitness training, sauna, steam room, whirlpool, massage, parasailing, video arcade.

HOTEL TIPS

● While all the rooms are graciously appointed, the rooms on the upper floors are more private. Most rooms sleep five.

● The lagoon-view rooms are the most popular, but the rooms overlooking the central courtyard convey the enchantment of the Victorian-themed architecture, especially at night.

● Guests who would like to visit distant attractions or resorts for dining events will find a rental car very useful.

● Walt Disney World resorts offer discounts to members of the Disney Club and AAA, as well as to Annual Passholders and Florida residents. Be sure to inquire.

A Disney-Owned Hotel
4401 Floridian Way, Lake Buena Vista, Florida 32830
Telephone (407) 824-3000 • Fax (407) 824-3186

A Magic Kingdom Resort: Disney's Grand Floridian Resort & Spa is one of seven hotels in the Magic Kingdom Resorts Area. It is conveniently located on the monorail line that serves the Magic Kingdom and Epcot. It faces Seven Seas Lagoon and is adjacent to Disney's Wedding Pavilion.

Ambience: The most elegant and expensive of the Walt Disney World resorts, this rambling, romantic Victorian-style hotel is fashioned after the grand seaside resorts of the 1890s. With its white banisters and railings, paned–glass windows, peaked red-shingled roofs, and formal flower and shrub gardens, this resort is a favorite with honeymooners. Its spacious and luxurious stained-glass domed lobby has ornate wrought-iron elevators, potted trees, and clusters of intimately placed settees where guests can sit and enjoy the ongoing live music in the common areas. The guest rooms are handsomely decorated, and each has a patio or balcony.

Restaurants: *Narcoossee's* — Dinner featuring New Floridian cuisine on the waterfront.

Victoria & Albert's — Very elegant, award-winning candlelight dinner; prix-fixe menu with wine pairings.

1900 Park Fare — Buffet-style Character Breakfast and Dinner.

Grand Floridian Cafe — Breakfast, lunch, and dinner with an emphasis on Florida-style cuisine.

Citricos — Italian dinners in an elegant, contemporary dining room.

Features: A wonderful afternoon tea is served from 3 until 6 PM in the Garden View Lounge. A special children's tea is hosted by characters from Disney's animated *Alice in Wonderland*.

Guests can select from a range of pampering treatments at the Grand Floridian's full-service spa.

Hotel Transportation: Monorail or water launch to the Magic Kingdom. Monorail to the Transportation and Ticket Center (TTC) and Epcot. Monorail or water launch to the Magic Kingdom to transfer to water launch to Fort Wilderness and River Country. Bus to Animal Kingdom, Blizzard Beach, and Disney-MGM Studios. Monorail to the TTC and transfer to destination buses for all other attractions and distant resorts. Taxi service is available.

Making Reservations: Contact the Disney Central Reservations Office (407 934-7639). Ask about special rates and seasonal vacation packages.

DISNEY'S OLD KEY WEST RESORT

See the "Essentials" section for
Hotel Selection Guides and updates.

A Disney Vacation Club Timeshare
1510 North Cove Road, Lake Buena Vista, Florida 32830
Telephone (407) 827-7700 • Fax (407) 827-7710

A Downtown Disney Resort: Disney's Old Key West Resort is one of four hotels in the Downtown Disney Resorts Area. The resort is connected by waterway to Downtown Disney on Buena Vista Lagoon.

Ambience: The casual village atmosphere of Key West with a dash of Caribbean flair is the theme here, complete with a landmark lighthouse at the edge of the resort's private lagoon. Charming tin-roofed two- and three-story buildings, in pastel-colored clapboard with ornate white trim and picket fences, line the winding streets of the village. The accommodations feel like spacious vacation homes and are furnished in shades of apricot, aqua, and celadon, colors used throughout the resort exteriors. All rooms have balconies that overlook waterways, golf greens, or woodlands. Clustered around the lagoon at the center of the resort is a small lobby, an inviting library, and recreational facilities and services.

Restaurants: *Olivia's Cafe* — Breakfast, lunch, and dinner featuring Floridian cuisine.

Features: These accommodations are true vacation homes with fully equipped kitchens and laundry rooms. The studios have mini kitchens. The are very spacious, with outdoor patios, and are ideal for families.

The resort is conveniently located for guests interested in golfing at Walt Disney World. The resort offers golfing vacation packages.

Guests may rent their own boats and commute by water to Downtown Disney, as well as other nearby Disney resorts.

Hotel Transportation: Bus or water taxi to Downtown Disney. Bus to all theme parks, including the Magic Kingdom, Epcot, Disney-MGM Studios, Animal Kingdom, Typhoon Lagoon, and Blizzard Beach. To reach other destinations or resorts, bus to Downtown Disney and connect to destination buses. Taxi service is available.

Making Reservations: Contact the Disney Central Reservations Office (407 934-7639). Ask about special rates and seasonal vacation packages.

Rates — Studios ♔ (including a wet bar, refrigerator, microwave, and coffee maker). One-bedroom vacation homes ♔ ♔. Two-bedroom vacation homes ♔ . Three-bedroom vacation homes ♔ . All units except studios have fully equipped kitchens, laundry facilities, wide-screen televisions, and VCRs. Rates vary with the season.

Amenities — Coffeemaker, microwave, refrigerator (unstocked), voice mail, VCR, in-room safe, video rentals, pizza delivery, hair dryer upon request.

Recreation — White sand beach, four pools, tennis, volleyball, shuffleboard, boating, bicycling, jogging path, fitness center, sauna, whirlpool, massage, video arcade.

HOTEL TIPS

● A rental car is a must for guests who want to see it all or visit other resorts.

● Room locations that are close to the recreation area and lobby are in buildings 12, 13, and 14. Buildings 11 and 15 are secluded, but still close to the common areas. Buildings 20, 34, 37, and 45 are near bus stops. Building 55 has a romantic water view and is farthest from the lobby.

● Disney's Old Key West Resort is a Disney Vacation Club timeshare and a member of several timeshare exchange programs. Units not used by timeshare owners are available to guests as full-service hotel accommodations.

Attractions
Hotels
Restaurants
Special Events
Recreation
Resources

Hotels Inside Walt Disney World • Hotels Outside Walt Disney World

Essentials

Attractions

Hotels

Restaurants

Special Events

Recreation

Resources

Hotels Outside Walt Disney World • Hotels Inside Walt Disney World

DISNEY'S POLYNESIAN RESORT

See the "Essentials" section for
Hotel Selection Guides and updates.

Rates — Standard rooms 👑 👑. Royal Polynesian concierge-service rooms 👑 👑 👑 (which include Continental breakfast, mid-afternoon snacks, evening wine and appetizers, no-host cocktails, and other amenities). Rates vary with the season.

Amenities — In-room safe, voice mail, room service (limited), daily newspaper, valet parking, hair dryer, iron and ironing board.

Recreation — Themed pool, quiet pool, white sand beach, boating, waterskiing, jogging path, volleyball, video arcade, parasailing.

HOTEL TIPS

● Lagoon view rooms are very popular. For a secluded setting, request a room in Tuvalu, which is farthest from the lobby at the edge of the lagoon. Upper-floor rooms offer the most privacy. For the best value, reserve a garden view room, which can be upgraded after you arrive.

● The Transportation and Ticket Center is just a pleasant stroll away from Rapa Nui or Tahiti. Tahiti is also close to a particularly nice stretch of beach.

● Concierge rooms are a good value for guests who spend considerable time at the hotel. The fireworks display from the lounge is wonderful.

● Neverland Club, Walt Disney World's most popular child care program, is located here and provides dinner and entertainment for little ones.

A Disney-Owned Hotel
1600 South Seas Drive, Lake Buena Vista, Florida 32830
Telephone (407) 824-2000 • Fax (407) 824-3174

A Magic Kingdom Resort: Disney's Polynesian Resort is one of seven hotels in the Magic Kingdom Resorts Area. It is conveniently located on the monorail line that serves the Magic Kingdom and Epcot, and it has a long white sand beach that fronts Seven Seas Lagoon.

Ambience: This island-themed resort is situated in a fabulous tropical garden. Guest rooms are patterned after South Pacific lodges, long two- and three-story buildings spanned by heavy wooden beams. The hotel buildings spaced across the expertly landscaped grounds all have pleasant garden or water views. The atrium lobby wraps around a lush tropical garden with blooming orchids. Guest rooms have ceiling fans and batik bed canopies. Most upper-floor rooms have balconies. Some rooms sleep five.

Restaurants: *Kona Cafe* — Traditional breakfasts including Tonga Toast; lunch and dinner with an Asian flair and upscale presentation.

'Ohana — Daily Character Breakfast and Hawaiian-themed dinner served family style, featuring open-hearth grilled meats.

Polynesian Luau — Polynesian cuisine served family style at this very popular Disney dinner show.

Features: Beautiful landscaped gardens with tropical plant specimens and flaming torches create an enchanting island atmosphere at night. There are great views of the Electrical Water Pageant and the Magic Kingdom fireworks from the beach in front of the hotel.

Hammocks scattered on the beach offer a great place to unwind.

Guests interested in golfing are within walking distance of the Magnolia and Palm golf courses.

Hotel Transportation: Monorail or water launch to the Magic Kingdom. Bus to Disney-MGM Studios, Animal Kingdom, and Blizzard Beach. Walk or monorail to the Transportation and Ticket Center (TTC) and change trains for Epcot or transfer to buses for all other attractions or distant resorts. Monorail or water launch to the Magic Kingdom and transfer to the water launch to Fort Wilderness and River Country. Taxi service is available.

Making Reservations: Contact the Disney Central Reservations Office (407 934-7639). Ask about special rates and seasonal vacation packages.

Essentials
Attractions
Hotels
Restaurants
Special Events
Recreation
Resources

Hotels Inside Walt Disney World • Hotels Outside Walt Disney World

DISNEY'S PORT ORLEANS RESORT – French Quarter

See the "Essentials" section for Hotel Selection Guides and updates.

A Disney-Owned Hotel
2201 Orleans Drive, Lake Buena Vista, Florida 32830
Telephone (407) 934-5000 • Fax (407) 934-5353

A Downtown Disney Resort: Disney's Port Orleans Resort – is one of four Disney hotels in this area. It is connected by carriage path and waterway to its partner hotel, Port Orleans – Riverside, and by waterway to Downtown Disney.

Ambience: Port Orleans – French Quarter is designed to capture the atmosphere of the New Orleans preparing for Mardi Gras festivities. Beyond the large steel-and-glass atrium lobby is a courtyard where a Dixieland band often entertains guests. The resort is arranged in a complex grid of cobblestone streets with names like Rue D'Baga and Reveler's Row. The three-story row house–style buildings, some in red brick and others painted in shades of peach, aqua, and French blue, mimic the diverse architectural styles of New Orleans. Ornate wrought-iron railings, varying rooflines, louvered shutters, French doors, and small front-yard gardens all heighten the atmosphere. At night, old-fashioned street lamps form soft pools of light among the magnolia and willow trees. The moderate-sized guest rooms have ceiling fans and are decorated simply in soft neutral colors. The small vanity area features two old-fashioned pedestal sinks.

Restaurants: *Sassagoula Floatworks and Food Factory* — Mardi Gras–themed food court; open for breakfast, lunch, and dinner.

Features: Guests looking for a quiet pool will have many choices at nearby Port Orleans – Riverside, which also has a marina where guests can rent boats and bicycles.

This resort is compact and very well laid out, making all guest rooms convenient to the theme pool, main building, and bus stop.

Hotel Transportation: Bus or water taxi to Downtown Disney. Bus to theme parks, including the Magic Kingdom, Epcot, Disney-MGM Studios, Animal Kingdom, Blizzard Beach, and Typhoon Lagoon. To reach other destinations or resorts, connect to destination buses at Downtown Disney. Taxi service is available.

Making Reservations: Contact the Disney Central Reservations Office (407 934-7639). Ask about special rates and seasonal vacation packages.

Rates — Standard rooms **$$$**. Rates vary with the season.

Amenities — Voice mail, pizza delivery, in-room safe, hair dryer on request, coffeemaker on request, refrigerator on request for a fee.

Recreation — Theme pool, whirlpool, fishing, jogging path, video arcade.

HOTEL TIPS

● This limited-amenity resort offers great value for the price. Upgrade to a top-floor river-view room and you'll have a luxury view for a fraction of the cost of a premier resort.

● Port Orleans will reserve rooms with king-sized beds.

● For a quiet river view, the best bets are buildings 1 and 6.

● This budget resort is geared to families, and the fantasy-themed pool scene is designed primarily for the young at heart.

● A rental car can save a lot of commuting time from this location, especially when visiting restaurants at other resorts.

● Walt Disney World resorts offer discounts to members of the Disney Club and AAA, as well as to Annual Passholders and Florida residents. Be sure to inquire.

DISNEY'S PORT ORLEANS RESORT – Riverside

See the "Essentials" section for
Hotel Selection Guides and updates.

Rates — Standard rooms **$$$**. Rates vary with the season.

Amenities — Voice mail, pizza delivery, refrigerator on request for a fee, trundle beds available on request in the Bayou lodge rooms.

Recreation — Five pools, boating, bicycling, jogging path, whirlpool.

HOTEL TIPS

● This limited-amenity resort offers an excellent value for the price. Upgrade to a river-view room and you'll have a luxury setting for significantly less than the cost of Walt Disney World's premier resorts. Most rooms sleep five. Bayou lodge rooms have trundle beds, making these rooms a great choice for a family of five.

● Boatwright's, the hotel's only full-service restaurant, is now shared by Port Orleans – French Quarter. Reservations are a must for both breakfast and dinner.

● The most popular locations are those close to the common areas and lobby. If you prefer a plantation home, request a room in Oak Manor; for a more rustic setting, request Alligator Bayou, lodges 14, 18, or 27.

● A rental car can save commuting time from this location, especially when visiting other resorts.

● This budget-priced hotel is very popular with young families, especially during peak seasons. If you're seeking a quiet, romantic setting, request Alligator Bayou, lodge 38.

A Disney-Owned Hotel
1251 Dixie Drive, Lake Buena Vista, Florida 32830
Telephone (407) 934-6000 • Fax (407) 934-5777

A Downtown Disney Resort: Disney's Port Orleans Resort – Riverside is one of four Disney hotels in this area. It is connected by waterway and carriage path to its partner hotel, Port Orleans – French Quarter, and by waterway to Downtown Disney.

Ambience: This resort, formerly named Dixie Landings, is styled after the rustic bayous and antebellum mansions of the Old South. The large, sprawling resort has two sections. On one side is Alligator Bayou, set in a dense moss-hung pine forest. It has two-story Cajun-style brick or stucco lodges and sports wide front porches and rough-hewn railings. On the other side is Magnolia Bend, with elegant three-story plantation manors set apart by fountains, sweeping lawns, and weeping willows. The Sassagoula River loops through the resort, and in the center is the reception area, designed as a riverboat depot, circa 1880. The rooms in this limited-amenity resort are decorated simply in soft neutral colors; furnishings in the Bayou rooms are more rustic than in the Magnolia rooms. Guest rooms have a vanity-dressing area with two pedestal sinks.

Restaurants: *Boatwright's Dining Hall* — Breakfast and dinner featuring Cajun specialties.

Colonel's Cotton Mill — Food court with five service counters for breakfast, lunch, and dinner, housed in an old cotton mill.

Cotton Co-Op — Casual lounge with a full-service bar, serving appetizers and light snacks. Live entertainment five nights a week.

Features: The resort is conveniently located for guests interested in golfing at Walt Disney World. The Bonnet Creek Golf Club is just a short distance away.

Guests may rent their own boats at the marina and commute by water to Downtown Disney and to other Downtown Disney resorts.

Hotel Transportation: Bus or water taxi to Downtown Disney. Bus to theme parks, including the Magic Kingdom, Epcot, Disney-MGM Studios, Animal Kingdom, Blizzard Beach, and Typhoon Lagoon. To reach other destinations or resorts, connect to destination buses at Downtown Disney. Taxi service is available.

Making Reservations: Contact the Disney Central Reservations Office (407 934-7639). Ask about special rates and seasonal vacation packages.

DISNEY'S WILDERNESS LODGE

See the "Essentials" section for
Hotel Selection Guides and updates.

A Disney-Owned Hotel
901 Timberline Drive, Lake Buena Vista, Florida 32830
Telephone (407) 824-3200 • Fax (407) 824-3232

A Magic Kingdom Resort: Disney's Wilderness Lodge is one of seven hotels in the Magic Kingdom Resorts Area. The resort is located deep in the forested area on the southwest shore of Bay Lake, halfway between Disney's Contemporary Resort and Fort Wilderness.

Ambience: Disney's Wilderness Lodge was inspired by the U.S. National Park lodges built in the early 1900s. The seven-story quarry-stone pine-beamed building is surrounded by forest on three sides and filled with natural light. Dark wood furnishings and Native American design motifs give the hotel its rustic lodge-retreat atmosphere. The atrium lobby features unusual chandeliers of striking design, a massive rock fireplace, and two gigantic totem poles from the Pacific Northwest. A "warm" spring bubbling in the lobby appears to flow to the outdoor courtyard, where it is transformed into a waterfall that cascades into the resort's rock-carved swimming pools and spas. Nearby, a geyser modeled on Yellowstone's Old Faithful erupts frequently and dramatically. There are rooms overlooking the atrium lobby, but most accommodations are in the two long wings on either side of the resort's pool area.

Restaurants: *Whispering Canyon Cafe* — Hearty family-style breakfast and all-you-care-to-eat lunch and dinner served with a rustic flair; meats are roasted, grilled, and barbecued.

Artist Point — Character Breakfast daily; dinner featuring Pacific Northwest cuisine and smoked-on-premises meats.

Features: The resort is adjacent to Fort Wilderness, which provides nature trails, bike paths, fishing, tennis, volleyball, horseback riding, and a particularly good jogging trail that meanders through a beautiful forested area with exercise stations along the way.

Each day, the resort chooses one family to help raise the flag, situated atop the hotel, and another to lower the flag. Inquire at Guest Services.

Hotel Transportation: Water launch to the Magic Kingdom. Walk or bus to Fort Wilderness and River Country. Bus to all other theme parks. For other destinations or resorts, bus to the Transportation and Ticket Center (TTC) and connect to destination buses or transfer to monorails for Epcot and the Magic Kingdom. Taxi service is available.

Making Reservations: Contact the Disney Central Reservations Office (407 934-7639). Ask about special rates and seasonal vacation packages.

Rates — Standard rooms 👑. Rates vary with the season.

Amenities — Room service (limited), valet parking, voice mail, in-room safe, iron and ironing board upon request, refrigerator on request for a fee.

Recreation — One pool, whirlpool, white sand beach, boating, waterskiing, bicycling, jogging path, parasailing, video arcade, fishing.

HOTEL TIPS

● Upper rooms in the main lodge area offer the most privacy. Rooms on the top floor have balconies with solid walls that will ensure privacy, although they can block some views. The lake-view rooms offer an unparalleled vista of Bay Lake. The woods-view rooms provide peaceful seclusion. Although the forest-view rooms face the Magic Kingdom, tall trees in front of some rooms can block views of the fireworks show.

● While the hotel common areas are huge, the guest rooms are only moderately sized and thin walls allow noise to enter from hallways and other rooms.

● Guests may use the sports and fitness center as well as the pool at The Villas at Wilderness Lodge, next door.

● Walt Disney World resorts offer discounts to members of Magic Kingdom Club and AAA, as well as to Annual Passholders and Florida residents. Be sure to inquire.

Essentials

Attractions

Hotels

Hotels Inside Walt Disney World • Hotels Outside Walt Disney World

Restaurants

Special Events

Recreation

Resources

DISNEY'S YACHT CLUB RESORT

See the "Essentials" section for
Hotel Selection Guides and updates.

Essentials
Attractions
Hotels
Restaurants
Special Events
Recreation
Resources

Hotels Outside Walt Disney World • Hotels Inside Walt Disney World

Rates — Standard rooms ♕ ♕. Concierge-service rooms ♕ ♕ ♕ (including Continental breakfast, afternoon snacks, evening wine, cordials, appetizers, and special room amenities). Rates vary with the season.

Amenities — Room service (24 hour), coffeemaker, refrigerator (stocked), in-room safe, turndown service, hair dryer, voice mail, valet parking, beauty/barber shop, small refrigerator available upon request.

Recreation — One pool, white sand beach, mini water park, boating, bicycling, tennis, jogging path, lawn bowling, croquet, volleyball, fitness center, sauna, steam room, whirlpool, fitness training, massage.

HOTEL TIPS

● Rooms surrounding the "quiet pool" are popular and secluded. Upper-floor garden-view or standard rooms facing the entrance are a very good value.

● Reserve the lowest-priced room here; you can always upgrade after you arrive.

● During peak seasons, buses to the Magic Kingdom can be slow; a rental car or taxi can be especially convenient for guests who would like to visit distant resorts during their stay.

● Walt Disney World resorts offer discounts to members of Magic Kingdom Club and AAA, as well as to Annual Passholders and Florida residents. Be sure to inquire.

A Disney-Owned Hotel
1700 Epcot Resorts Boulevard, Lake Buena Vista, Florida 32830
Telephone (407) 934-7000 • Fax (407) 934-3450

An Epcot Resort: Disney's Yacht Club Resort is one of seven hotels in the Epcot Resorts Area. It is located within walking distance of the International Gateway to the World Showcase at Epcot. It faces Crescent Lake and shares a white sand beach and harbor waterfront with Disney's Beach Club Resort.

Ambience: The rambling, New England-style gray and white Yacht Club, designed by architect Robert Stern, has rope-slung boardwalks and a picturesque lighthouse along its waterfront. Its motif is decidedly nautical and it shares resort amenities with the more casually appointed Beach Club next door. The sophisticated yet comfortable lobby has dark wood floors with tufted leather couches and bright brass fixtures. The guest rooms impart a home-away-from-home feeling, with white furniture, ceiling fans, and roomy balconies.

Restaurants: *Yacht Club Galley* — Breakfast buffet or a la carte; lunch and dinner with emphasis on New England specialties.

Yachtsman Steakhouse — Dinner featuring prime-cut steaks and a small selection of seafood and poultry dishes.

Features: This full-amenity resort is in a great location for guests who plan to focus on nearby Epcot and Disney-MGM Studios.

The Yacht Club's location between the Beach Club and the Dolphin hotel makes the amenities at either resort easily accessible.

Guests interested in nightlife will appreciate the easy access to Disney's BoardWalk with its restaurants, shops, and entertainment.

Stormalong Bay, the resort's mini water park, is one of the best and most popular recreation facilities at any resort in Walt Disney World.

Hotel Transportation: Walk or water launch to the World Showcase at Epcot and Disney's BoardWalk. Water launch to Disney-MGM Studios. Bus to the Magic Kingdom, Animal Kingdom, Blizzard Beach, Typhoon Lagoon, and Downtown Disney. For other destinations or distant resorts, bus to Downtown Disney and connect to destination buses. Taxi service is available.

Making Reservations: Contact the Disney Central Reservations Office (407 934-7639). Ask about special rates and seasonal vacation packages.

DOUBLETREE GUEST SUITES RESORT

See the "Essentials" section for
Hotel Selection Guides and updates.

DoubleTree Hotels Corporation
2305 Hotel Plaza Boulevard, Lake Buena Vista, Florida 32830
Telephone (407) 934-1000 • Fax (407) 934-1015

A Hotel Plaza Resort: DoubleTree Guest Suites Resort is one of seven independently owned Hotel Plaza Resorts located on Walt Disney World property near Downtown Disney. The hotel provides shuttle bus service to the major Walt Disney World attractions.

Ambience: This contemporary mirror-glassed hotel is a quasi-pyramidal seven-story building. Its modern, comfortable lobby is decorated with large murals and bright color accents. DoubleTree is the only all-suites hotel inside Walt Disney World. The guest suites are generous in size and have been handsomely refurbished in soft pastel shades. Each suite has a kitchenette and separate bedroom.

Restaurants: *Streamers* — Large restaurant for a la carte and buffet breakfast. American-style dishes are offered at lunch and dinner.

Features: DoubleTree Guest Suites is an excellent value for a suite at Walt Disney World. Each suite has a large living room that includes a dining area and limited kitchen facilities. For grocery shopping, Gooding's Supermarket is within walking distance. The resort also has a small convenience store that stays open late.

DoubleTree Guest Suites Resort participates in the American Express Membership Miles program.

The resort has a pleasant free-form pool that is large enough for swimming laps. The Tropical Pool Bar serves lunch and cocktails.

Budget car rental agency is conveniently located here for visitors who might like to rent a car during their stay.

Hotel Transportation: Walk to Crossroads Shopping Center. Bus to the Magic Kingdom, Epcot, Disney-MGM Studios, and Animal Kingdom. Bus service to the water parks varies seasonally. After 6 PM, shuttle to Pleasure Island every 20 minutes. Taxi service is available.

Making Reservations: First, call for rates through DoubleTree Central Reservations (800 222-8733), then call the hotel directly and compare rates (407 934-1000). Reservations can also be made through the Disney Central Reservations Office (407 934-7639). Ask about special promotional rates, such as the SuiteSaver, which may have discounts of up to 40 percent.

Rates — One-bedroom suites **$$$**. Rates vary with season.

Amenities — Room service (limited), in-room safe, microwave, coffeemaker, refrigerator (unstocked), hair dryer, pay-per-view movies, video rentals.

Recreation — One pool, whirlpool, tennis, fitness center, jogging path, video arcade.

HOTEL TIPS

● Rooms with a pool view are very pleasant. Ground-floor rooms have sliding glass doors that open onto small patios. Rooms with a view of Walt Disney World are popular room locations and the most frequently requested.

● The hotel offers vacation packages that include accommodations, breakfast, and other amenities. For a brochure, call the hotel (407 934-1000).

● DoubleTree Guest Suites offers discounts to members of several travel clubs, including the American Association of Retired Persons (AARP). AAA members can receive a 20 percent discount on accommodations; be sure to ask.

● A rental car can save considerable commuting time from this location.

Essentials
Attractions
Hotels
Restaurants
Special Events
Recreation
Resources

Hotels Outside Walt Disney World • Hotels Inside Walt Disney World

GROSVENOR RESORT

See the "Essentials" section for Hotel Selection Guides and updates.

Rates — Standard rooms **$$**. Rates vary with the season.

Amenities — Room service (limited), coffeemaker, daily newspaper, in-room safe, hair dryer, refrigerator (stocked), pay-per-view movies, valet parking.

Recreation — Two pools, tennis, volley-ball, basketball, handball, fitness center, jogging path, whirlpool, massage, video arcade, shuffleboard.

HOTEL TIPS

● The garden-wing rooms facing the pool are popular. Tower rooms lack balconies but they offer good views of Walt Disney World.

● The Grosvenor offers discounts to members of travel clubs, including the American Association of Retired Persons (AARP), AAA, Orlando Magicard, and Entertainment Publications.

● The Grosvenor offers vacation packages that include accommodations, meals, and theme park admission. For a brochure, call the Grosvenor Resort's toll-free number (800 624-4109).

A Grosvenor Properties Hotel
1850 Hotel Plaza Boulevard, Lake Buena Vista, Florida 32830
Telephone (407) 828-4444 • Fax (407) 827-8230

A Hotel Plaza Resort: Grosvenor Resort is one of seven independently owned Hotel Plaza Resorts located on Walt Disney World property near Downtown Disney. Guests are provided with bus service to the major Walt Disney World attractions and can walk to Downtown Disney.

Ambience: The stately, solid exterior of this nineteen-story high-rise hotel belies its warm, comfortable interior. The lobby decor is British Colonial, with dark green carpets, rattan furnishings, and understated chandeliers. Rooms in the Grosvenor's central tower have Walt Disney World views. The tower is flanked by garden wings with exterior corridors facing the landscaped recreation area and gardens and Lake Buena Vista beyond.

Restaurants: *Crumpet's Cafe* — Lobby deli market for light snacks; open 24 hours.

Baskervilles — British-themed dining room serving buffet and a la carte breakfast, lunch, and dinner featuring prime rib. Disney Characters are on hand three times a week.

Features: On weekends, the very popular MurderWatch Mystery Dinner Theatre is held at Baskervilles, where guests are involved in solving a murder staged by professional actors (see *Special Events* → "Dinner Shows").

Thrifty car rental agency is conveniently located here for visitors who might like to rent a car during their vacation. Buses to some attractions and other resorts are inconvenient from this location.

Although newly remodeled, the low ceilings in some guest rooms can make them seem smaller than they are; the bathrooms are compact.

Hotel Transportation: Walk or shuttle bus to Downtown Disney. Bus to the Magic Kingdom, Epcot, Disney-MGM Studios, and Animal Kingdom. To reach all other destinations or resorts, connect to destination buses at Downtown Disney. Taxi service is available.

Making Reservations: Contact the Grosvenor Resort through their toll-free number (800 624-4109). Be sure to ask about special promotional rates. Reservations can also be made through the Disney Central Reservations Office (407 934-7639).

THE HILTON RESORT

See the "Essentials" section for Hotel Selection Guides and updates.

A Hilton Hotel
1751 Hotel Plaza Boulevard, Lake Buena Vista, Florida 32830
Telephone (407) 827-4000 • Fax (407) 827-3890

A Hotel Plaza Resort: The Hilton Resort is one of seven independently owned Hotel Plaza Resorts located on Walt Disney World property near Downtown Disney. The hotel provides bus service to the major Walt Disney World attractions.

Ambience: This hotel, one of the largest in the Hotel Plaza area, is a sprawling medium high-rise with wings that angle off to each side of the central structure. The hotel is situated on several acres of open land and has a duck pond and fountains in front. The angular lobby has a muted tropical decor with brass-railed staircases, pink conch-shell wall sconces, and a fountain with long-legged birds made of sculptured metal. Saltwater fish swim in the large aquarium behind the long rose-colored marble reception desk. The recently renovated guest rooms are pleasantly decorated with peach and light yellow accents and sand-colored bedspreads. The hotel caters to business travelers and seminar attendees.

Restaurants: *Finn's Grill* — Dinner featuring creatively prepared seafood, steaks, and live entertainment.

Benihana — Japanese steak and seafood dinners grilled and served at communal tables by teppan chefs.

Covington Mill — All-day dining featuring a large variety of salads, pastas, pizzas, and sandwiches. Disney Character Breakfast on Sunday.

Features: Hilton Honors members can earn points and upgrade rooms.

Avis car rental agency is conveniently located here for guests who might like to rent a car during their vacation.

The Hilton Vacation Station offers supervised activities from 5 PM until midnight for kids age four through twelve, so that parents can get away for the evening.

Hotel Transportation: Walk to Downtown Disney. Bus to the Magic Kingdom, Epcot, Disney-MGM Studios, and Animal Kingdom, as well as to the water parks. For all other attractions and resorts, transfer to destination buses at Downtown Disney. Taxi service is available.

Making Reservations: Call Hilton Central Reservations (800 221-2424), then call the hotel's toll-free number and compare rates (800 782-4414). Be sure to ask about special promotions, such as the Bounce-Back Weekend, which can save up to 40 percent on the room rate. Reservations can also be made through the Disney Central Reservations Office (407 934-7639).

Rates — Standard rooms ♛. Tower Concierge rooms ♛ (which includes Continental breakfast, all-day snacks, evening tea and petits fours, no-host cocktails, and special room amenities). Rates vary with the season.

Amenities — Room service (24 hour), refrigerator (stocked), voice mail, pay-per-view movies, valet parking.

Recreation — Two pools, jogging path, fitness center, sauna.

HOTEL TIPS

● Most rooms have nice views, but be sure to put in a request for an upper floor room with a view of Walt Disney World and evening fireworks shows when making reservations.

● The Hilton Resort offers vacation packages that include accommodations, daily breakfast, and theme park admission. Call the hotel's toll-free number for a brochure (800 782-4414).

● The Hilton offers AAA members significant discounts on rooms, often over 30 percent.

● The Hilton is a convention hotel and does not orient its hotel services to the vacation traveler. It may not be a good choice for first-time visitors.

● Last minute travel deals can sometimes be found on the hotel's web site (www.hilton.com).

Essentials

Attractions

Hotels

Restaurants

Special Events

Recreation

Resources

Hotels Outside Walt Disney World • Hotels Inside Walt Disney World

HOTEL ROYAL PLAZA

See the "Essentials" section for Hotel Selection Guides and updates.

Rates — Standard rooms **$$$**. Rates vary with the season.

Amenities — Room service (limited), refrigerator (stocked), in-room safe, hair dryer, coffeemaker, VCR, video rentals, video camera rentals.

Recreation — One pool, jogging path, tennis, shuffleboard, fitness center, sauna, whirlpool, putting green.

HOTEL TIPS

● The most popular rooms are the higher-floor tower rooms with a view of Walt Disney World and the evening fireworks show at Pleasure Island. Also popular are the ground-floor poolside garden rooms.

● For the best room value, request a premier room. Premier rooms cost about $30 more than standard rooms, but offer large, deep corner-style whirlpool tubs, great for relaxing after a hard day of touring.

● Hotel Royal Plaza offers discounts to a number of travel clubs, including Entertainment Publications. Members of AAA can receive discounts of up to 40 percent on rooms. Military guests can save 15 percent on standard rates, depending on availability.

● The Royal Plaza offers vacation packages that include accommodations, daily breakfast, theme park admission, and other amenities. Call the hotel for a brochure (800 248-7890).

● A rental car can save considerable commuting time from this location.

A Davidson Hotel
1905 Hotel Plaza Boulevard, Lake Buena Vista, Florida 32830
Telephone (407) 828-2828 • Fax (407) 827-3977

A Hotel Plaza Resort: Hotel Royal Plaza is one of seven independently owned Hotel Plaza Resorts located on Walt Disney World property near Downtown Disney. The hotel provides bus service to the major Walt Disney World attractions.

Ambience: The high-rise hotel, with its pagoda-style roof and garden wing, is detailed in shades of rose and pure white. The lobby is modeled with a Caribbean theme, and guest rooms are tastefully furnished in pale pastels. All tower rooms and suites have small half-moon-shaped balconies; the higher floors offer sweeping views of Walt Disney World. The ground-level garden-wing rooms have private patios.

Restaurants: *Bermuda Onion* — Open all day until midnight for breakfast, lunch, and dinner, featuring American cuisine.
　　Giraffe Lounge — Casual lounge. Open until 2 AM.

Features: The hotel's Giraffe Lounge offers a happy hour buffet and televised sporting events for guests who would like to unwind after a day in the theme parks.

　　The hotel is often overlooked as an affordable and pleasant place to stay for visitors on a budget. Room rates vary seasonally.

Hotel Transportation: Walk (or bus after 6 PM) to Downtown Disney. Bus to the Magic Kingdom, Epcot, Disney-MGM Studios, and Animal Kingdom. Bus service to the water parks varies with the seasons. For transportation to other attractions or distant resorts, connect to destination buses at Downtown Disney. Taxi service is available.

Making Reservations: Contact the Hotel Royal Plaza through their toll-free number (800 248-7890) and ask about promotional rates. Room reservations can also be made through the Disney Central Reservations Office (407 934-7639).

Essentials

Attractions

Hotels

Restaurants

Special Events

Recreation

Resources

LAKE BUENA VISTA RESORT

See the "Essentials" section for
Hotel Selection Guides and updates.

A Best Western Hotel
2000 Hotel Plaza Boulevard, Lake Buena Vista, Florida 32830
Telephone (407) 828-2424 • Fax (407) 828-8933

A Hotel Plaza Resort: Lake Buena Vista Resort is one of seven independently owned Hotel Plaza Resorts located on Walt Disney World property near Downtown Disney. The hotel provides bus service to the major Walt Disney World attractions.

Ambience: The wide entrance portico of the hotel's eighteen-story tower leads to its tropically themed interior, done in the style of a Barbados plantation manor. The comfortable lobby is filled with plants, rattan furniture, and green faux-marble pillars. In the center, a circular staircase leads up to the meeting rooms on the mezzanine level. Inside the staircase is a revolving display of scenes from classic Disney movies. The hotel grounds and the large pool area are landscaped with lush tropical foliage. The nicely sized guest rooms are serene and pleasantly decorated in soft neutral colors. All rooms have balconies, and most, especially on the higher floors, have impressive views of Walt Disney World.

Restaurants: *Parakeet Cafe* — Lobby deli serving light meals and snacks all day.

Traders Int'l Restaurant & Terrace — Breakfast and dinner, a la carte or buffet, indoors or outside on the patio. Early Bird specials are offered.

Features: Toppers Nite Club, located on the eighteenth floor, offers large-screen video entertainment until 2 AM and has sweeping views of Walt Disney World and the fireworks shows. Hotel guests receive discounts on drinks.

Room service provides a "Family Movie Fun Pack" for about $30. This package includes delivery of an appetizer platter, two large pizzas, a pitcher of soda, and a pay-per-view movie.

Hotel Transportation: Walk or bus to Downtown Disney. Bus to Epcot, Disney-MGM Studios, Magic Kingdom, and Animal Kingdom. Bus service to the water parks varies with the seasons. For transportation to other attractions or distant resorts, connect to destination buses at Downtown Disney. Taxi service is available.

Making Reservations: First call the Best Western Central Reservations Office (800 528-1234); ask for "Best Rates." Then call the hotel's toll-free number (800 348-3765) and compare rates. Reservations can also be made through the Disney Central Reservations Office (407 934-7639).

Rates — Standard rooms **$$**. Rates vary with the season.

Amenities — Room service (limited), refrigerator (stocked), coffeemaker, hair dryer, in-room safe, pay-per-view movies, daily newspaper, iron and ironing board.

Recreation — One pool, jogging path.

HOTEL TIPS

● For the best room location, request a room with a view of Walt Disney World. The fireworks at Pleasure Island can be seen from the upper-floor guest rooms.

● Lake Buena Vista Resort offers discounts to members of several organizations, including American Association of Retired Persons (AARP), AAA, military, American Airlines, and Gold Crown Club International. Seniors save 10 percent.

● Buses to some smaller attractions and other resorts are very inconvenient from this location.

Hotels Inside Walt Disney World • Hotels Outside Walt Disney World

SHADES OF GREEN

*See the "Essentials" section for
Hotel Selection Guides and updates.*

Rates — Standard rooms **$** to **$$**. Rates increase based on military rank.

Amenities — Room service (limited), valet parking, voice mail.

Recreation — Two pools, tennis, nature walk, fitness center, two PGA golf courses, pro shop, putting green, driving range.

HOTEL TIPS

● Buses to distant attractions and other resorts for dining events can be inconvenient during peak seasons. A rental car can save considerable commuting time. Shades of Green's shuttles to and from the Transportation and Ticket Center (TTC) depart every 20 minutes until 2 AM.

● Rooms 101 to 113 surround the "quiet pool," and rooms 301 to 313 on the top floor have sweeping fairway views.

● If the hotel is fully booked, ask about overflow rooms. Military personnel are often able to stay at other Disney-owned hotels at a considerable discount if rooms are available.

*A U.S. Armed Forces Recreation Center
1950 West Magnolia/Palm, Lake Buena Vista, Florida 32830
Telephone (407) 824-3400 • Fax (407) 824-3460*

A Magic Kingdom Resort: Shades of Green is one of seven hotels in the Magic Kingdom Resorts Area. As a U.S. Armed Forces Recreational Center, its accommodations are available only to Department of Defense, National Guard, active and retired military personnel, and their families; however, the restaurants and golf courses are open to all visitors. The resort is located adjacent to the Magnolia and Palm golf courses in a quiet area that is a short drive from the Magic Kingdom.

Ambience: This wood-shingled low-rise hotel seems set apart from the rest of Walt Disney World. The long entrance road winds through the two golf courses that surround the hotel. Guest rooms are spacious mini-suites with a country-inn atmosphere enhanced by pine furnishings and are comfortable for larger families. All rooms feature balconies or patios with views of the pools, the golf courses, or the resort's lush landscaping. The resort is very low-key and could be located anywhere — although the unmistakable whistle of the Walt Disney World Railroad trains at the Magic Kingdom can be heard from the grounds.

Restaurants: *The Garden Gallery* — A la carte breakfast and a dinner buffet with a different culinary theme every night.

Evergreens Sports Bar & Grill — Poolside restaurant serving snacks and light meals all day.

Back Porch Lounge — Lunch only; popular with the golf crowd.

Features: All military personnel and their dependents, regardless of whether they are staying at the resort, can purchase theme park and area attraction tickets here at a 10 percent discount. Call Shades of Green Guest Services (407 824-1403).

During value seasons, guests staying at Shades of Green can enjoy a 50 percent discount on golf through Shades of Green Guest Services.

Hotel Transportation: Bus to Disney-MGM Studios, Animal Kingdom, and Blizzard Beach. Bus to the Transportation and Ticket Center (TTC) to catch monorails to the Magic Kingdom and Epcot or to transfer to Disney buses to reach other destinations. From the Magic Kingdom, water launch to Fort Wilderness and River Country. Taxi service is available.

Making Reservations: Military personnel and their families can book rooms by calling Shades of Green Reservations (407 824-3600).

THE VILLAS AT THE DISNEY INSTITUTE

Available to all visitors as well as those attending the Disney Institute
1901 Buena Vista Drive, Lake Buena Vista, Florida 32830
Telephone (407) 827-1100 • Fax (407) 934-2741

A Downtown Disney Resort: The Villas at the Disney Institute is one of four Disney hotels in this area. Spread out across 250 acres of woodlands, waterways, and golf greens, the resort fronts Buena Vista Lagoon along with Downtown Disney. The campus of the Disney Institute, a learning center that offers a seminar retreat for corporations, is also located here. (See *Special Events* → "The Disney Institute.")

Ambience: This resort resembles a large country club and encompasses the fairways of Lake Buena Vista Golf Course. The facility is very spread out, with four distinct resort areas and interconnecting roadways. The dark brown Fairway Villas and Grand Vista Suites are scattered along tree-lined lanes or situated at the edge of the golf course. The tall Treehouses are isolated in a forested area, and some overlook waterways resembling bayous. The cozy Bungalow suites and some of the Townhouses are within walking distance of Downtown Disney. Other Bungalows are at the edge of the Disney Institute's small lake and closer to the hotel lobby.

Restaurants: *The Gathering Place* — Small eatery and piano bar serving continental breakfast and a varied selection of appetizers, sandwiches, and desserts. Open all day.

Reflections — Gourmet coffee and pastry bar.

Features: Electric carts can be rented for use both within the resort and at nearby Downtown Disney.

The Gathering Room is a handsome lounge with comfortable plush chairs and live piano. It's an ideal spot to relax after golf or a hectic day at the theme parks.

Hotel Transportation: Walk, bus, water taxi, or rent an electric cart to travel to The Marketplace at Downtown Disney. Bus to the Magic Kingdom, Epcot, Disney-MGM Studios, Animal Kingdom, Blizzard Beach, and Typhoon Lagoon. To reach other destinations, connect with destination buses at Downtown Disney. Taxi service is available.

Making Reservations: For hotel reservations, call the Disney Central Reservations Office (407 934-7639).

Rates — Bungalow suites 👑, one-bedroom Townhouses 👑👑 and two-bedroom Townhouses 👑👑👑 (both with refrigerator, microwave, and coffee maker), three-bedroom Treehouse Villas 👑👑👑, two-bedroom Fairway Villas 👑👑👑, and large two- and three-bedroom Grand Vista Suites 👑 (all with fully equipped kitchens). Rates vary with the season.

Amenities — Room service (limited), voice mail, refrigerator (unstocked), coffeemaker, microwave, grocery delivery service, valet parking.

Recreation — Six pools, bicycling, volleyball, tennis, jogging path, fitness center, full service spa, PGA golf course, driving range, putting green, pro shop.

HOTEL TIPS

● The circular Treehouse Villas are ideal for secluded romantic getaways. Request a water view. Grand Vista Suites, designed like spacious suburban homes, are ideal for small groups or large families.

● Although Walt Disney World buses operate within the resort, a rental car is quite helpful from this location if your focus is on the theme parks.

● Because the resort is spread out across many acres, visitors without a car may wish to request accommodations closest to Downtown Disney, the shopping and transportation hub for all of Walt Disney World.

Essentials

Attractions

Hotels

Hotels Inside Walt Disney World • Hotels Outside Walt Disney World

Restaurants

Special Events

Recreation

Resources

THE VILLAS AT WILDERNESS LODGE

*See the "Essentials" section for
Hotel Selection Guides and updates.*

Attractions

Hotels

Hotels Inside Walt Disney World • **Hotels Outside Walt Disney World**

Restaurants

Special Events

Recreation

Resources

Rates — Studios 👑👑 (including wet bar, refrigerator, microwave, and coffeemaker), one-bedroom vacation homes 👑👑👑, two-bedroom vacation homes 👑. All vacation homes except studios have fully equipped kitchens, laundry facilities, wide-screen televisions, and VCRs. Rates vary with the season.

Amenities — Room service (24 hour), coffeemaker, daily newspaper, in-room safe, hair dryer, valet parking, voice mail, microwave, refrigerator (unstocked), turn-down service, VCR, iron and ironing board.

Recreation — One pool, whirlpool, white sand beach, boating, waterskiing, bicycling, jogging path, parasailing, video arcade, fishing.

HOTEL TIPS

● A rental car will save a lot of commuting time from this location, especially when visiting other resorts for restaurants or dining events.

● The Villas at Wilderness Lodge is a Disney Vacation Club timeshare and a member of several timeshare exchange programs. Units not used by timeshare owners are available to guests as full-service hotel accommodations. Guests at The Villas will use the check-in counter at the Wilderness Lodge.

*A Disney Vacation Timeshare
901 Timberline Drive, Lake Buena Vista, Florida 32830
Telephone (407) 824-3200 • Fax (407) 824-3232*

A Magic Kingdom Resort: The Villas at Wilderness Lodge is the newest of the resorts in the Magic Kingdom Resorts Area. The resort is located next door to the Wilderness Lodge, in a deep forested area on the southwest shore of Bay Lake, halfway between the Contemporary resort and Fort Wilderness.

Ambience: This Disney timeshare resort is inspired by the rustic grandeur and timbers of the Rocky Mountain national park geyser country. Fashioned after hotels built by railroad workers during the late 1800s, the theming behind this resort predates the adjacent Wilderness Lodge (modeled after Yellowstone, circa 1904). The studios and one- and two-bedroom units feature either woods, lake, or pool views.

Restaurants: Counter-service eatery for light meals; open all day. It also shares dining facilities with the Wilderness Lodge next door, including:
Whispering Canyon Cafe — Hearty family-style breakfast and all-you-care-to-eat lunch and dinner served with a rustic flair; meats are roasted, grilled, and barbecued.
Artist Point — Character Breakfast daily; dinner featuring Pacific Northwest cuisine and smoked-on-premises meats.

Features: The hotel's sports and fitness center offers the very latest in exercise and fitness equipment.
Surrounded by dense woods and beautiful Bay Lake, guests will feel far removed from the hustle and bustle of everyday life; however, every modern convenience and luxury of a deluxe resort is at hand.

Hotel Transportation: Water launch to the Magic Kingdom. Walk or bus to Fort Wilderness and River Country. Bus to all other theme parks. For other destinations or resorts, bus to the Transportation and Ticket Center (TTC) and connect to destination buses or transfer to monorails for Epcot and the Magic Kingdom. Taxi service is available.

Making Reservations: Contact the Disney Central Reservations Office (407 934-7639). Ask about special rates and seasonal vacation packages.

WALT DISNEY WORLD DOLPHIN

See the "Essentials" section for Hotel Selection Guides and updates.

A Sheraton Hotel
1500 Epcot Resorts Boulevard, Lake Buena Vista, Florida 32830
Telephone (407) 934-4000 • Fax (407) 934-4099

An Epcot Resort: The Dolphin is one of seven hotels in the Epcot Resorts Area. It is located a short distance from the International Gateway to the World Showcase at Epcot. It faces Crescent Lake and shares a waterfront plaza, white sand beach, and recreational facilities with the Swan hotel.

Ambience: The plaza entrance of this pyramid-shaped high-rise hotel features a multistory fountain that cascades down tiers of giant clam shells. The lobby is in a huge striped tent with a dolphin-motif fountain, and the spacious guest rooms have a fantasy tropical beach decor.

Restaurants: *Cabana Bar & Grill* — Light meals, snacks, and specialty drinks served poolside.

Coral Cafe — Pleasant coffee shop with all-day dining; full-buffet breakfast and dinner.

Dolphin Fountain — Light dining, hamburgers, sandwiches, and ice cream and soda fountain treats.

Shula's Steakhouse — Award-winning restaurant featuring steaks; open for dinner.

Juan & Only's — Dinner featuring southwest cuisine.

Tubbi's Buffeteria — Cafeteria, snack bar, and convenience market; open 24 hours.

Features: Members of the ITT Sheraton Club earn points and may upgrade rooms. It's a short walk to Disney's BoardWalk for shopping, dining, dancing, and entertainment.

Guests staying at the Dolphin can participate in Early Entry Mornings at the theme parks and E-Ride Nights at the Magic Kingdom.

Hotel Transportation: Walk or water launch to Disney's BoardWalk. Water launch to the World Showcase at Epcot and Disney-MGM Studios. Bus to the Magic Kingdom, Animal Kingdom, Blizzard Beach, Typhoon Lagoon, and Downtown Disney. To reach other attractions or distant resorts, bus to Downtown Disney and connect to destination buses. Taxi service is available.

Making Reservations: First call the Sheraton Central Reservations Office (800 325-3535), then call the hotel and compare rates (800 227-1500). Ask about special promotional rates. Reservations can also be made through the Disney Central Reservations Office (407 934-7639).

Rates — Standard rooms ♔ ♔. Concierge rooms ♔ ♔ ♔ (including Continental breakfast, no-host cocktails, appetizers, and special room amenities). Rates vary with the season.

Amenities — Room service (24 hour), refrigerator (stocked), in-room safe, daily newspaper, pay-per-view movies, voice mail, valet parking, coffeemaker, hair dryer, turndown service, iron and ironing board, Nintendo.

Recreation — Lap pool, grotto pool, small beach, tennis, fitness center, sauna, whirlpool, massage, boating, volleyball, jogging path.

HOTEL TIPS

● The most popular room locations are those with views of IllumiNations or the pool area.

● Members of AAA are offered discounts of up to 25 percent on rooms.

● The Dolphin offers vacation packages that offer accommodations, some meals, theme park admissions, and other amenities. Call the hotel's toll-free number for a brochure (800 227-1500).

● Windows open only in rooms that have a balcony; request a balcony room during the cooler seasons.

Essentials

Attractions

Hotels

Restaurants

Special Events

Recreation

Resources

Hotels Outside Walt Disney World • Hotels Inside Walt Disney World

WALT DISNEY WORLD SWAN

See the "Essentials" section for Hotel Selection Guides and updates.

Rates — Standard rooms 👑 👑. Royal Beach Club concierge rooms 👑 👑 👑 (which includes Continental breakfast, snacks and appetizers, no-host cocktails, and special room amenities). Rates vary with the season.

Amenities — Room service (24 hour), refrigerator (stocked), in-room safe, daily newspaper, pay-per-view movies, valet parking, voice mail, coffeemaker, hair dryer, iron and ironing board, Nintendo, beauty salon, turndown service.

Recreation — Lap pool, grotto pool, small beach, tennis, jogging path, fitness center, sauna, whirlpool, massage, boating, volleyball.

HOTEL TIPS

● The Swan offers resort packages that include accommodations, some meals, and theme park admission. For a vacation package brochure, call the hotel's toll-free number (800 248-7926).

● AAA members can get discounts of up to 25 percent on accommodations. Be sure to ask.

● Guests staying at the Swan may participate in Early Entry Mornings at the theme parks and E-Ride Nights at the Magic Kingdom.

A Westin Hotel
1200 Epcot Resorts Boulevard, Lake Buena Vista, Florida 32830
Telephone (407) 934-3000 • Fax (407) 934-4499

An Epcot Resort: The Swan is one of seven hotels in the Epcot Resorts Area. It is just a short distance from Disney-MGM Studios and the International Gateway to the World Showcase at Epcot. It faces Crescent Lake and shares a waterfront plaza, white sand beach, and recreational facilities with the Dolphin hotel.

Ambience: This contemporary high-rise hotel, designed by noted architect Michael Graves, is a standout example of entertainment architecture. The Swan's water-fantasy theme is expressed in soft splashes of turquoise and coral, which extend to the guest rooms. The large lobby is divided into smaller alcoves, giving an overall impression of quiet sophistication.

Restaurants: *Palio* — Dinner featuring homemade pasta, brick-oven pizza, and light entertainment in an Italian trattoria.
    Garden Grove Cafe — Family-style dining for breakfast and lunch.
    Gulliver's Grill — Dining with Disney Characters five nights a week.
    Splash Grill & Terrace — Breakfast a la carte and buffet and all-day light meals.
    Kimonos — Evening cocktails, Asian hors d'oeuvres, and sushi.

Features: The resort is conveniently located for guests who are primarily interested in Disney-MGM Studios and Epcot, and it is right next door to the nightlife at Disney's BoardWalk.
    Fantasia Gardens, one of Walt Disney World's miniature golf complexes, is located right across the street.

Hotel Transportation: Walk or water launch to Disney-MGM Studios and Disney's BoardWalk. Water launch to the World Showcase at Epcot. Bus to the Magic Kingdom, Animal Kingdom, Blizzard Beach, Typhoon Lagoon, and Pleasure Island and Disney Village Marketplace at Downtown Disney. To reach other destinations or resorts, bus to Downtown Disney and connect to destination buses. Taxi service available.

Making Reservations: First call the Westin Central Reservations Office (800 228-3000), then call the hotel's toll-free number and compare rates (800 248-7926). Ask about special promotional rates. Room reservations can also be made through the Disney Central Reservations Office (407 934-7639).

Essentials

Attractions

Hotels

Hotels Inside Walt Disney World • Hotels Outside Walt Disney World

Restaurants

Special Events

Recreation

Resources

WYNDHAM PALACE RESORT & SPA

See the "Essentials" section for
Hotel Selection Guides and updates.

A Privately Owned Hotel
1900 Buena Vista Drive, Lake Buena Vista, Florida 32830
Telephone (407) 827-2727 • Fax (407) 827-6034

A Hotel Plaza Resort: The Wyndham Palace Resort & Spa is one of seven independently owned Hotel Plaza Resorts located on Walt Disney World property within walking distance to Downtown Disney. The hotel provides bus service to the major Walt Disney World attractions.

Ambience: Large fountains mark the entrance to this imposing and majestic mirror-paneled high-rise hotel. The Wyndham Palace is situated on twenty-seven acres of open land and pine forest and boasts its own private lagoon. The elegant multilevel lobby encircles a twenty-seven story atrium. The guest rooms have private balconies and have recently been refurbished. The Palace Suites, in an adjacent low-rise building, offer spacious suites with separate bedrooms and kitchenettes.

Restaurants: *The Outback* — Steak and seafood dinners, Australian-style cuisine.

Arthur's 27 — Elegant Continental dining in an award-winning rooftop restaurant.

Watercress Cafe & Bake Shop — Breakfast, lunch, and dinner, with soup and salad bar. A Disney Character Breakfast is held on Sunday.

Features: The full-service Spa at the Wyndham Palace offers visitors a complete range of treatments and massage therapy in an elegant setting. (See *Recreation* → "Spas and Fitness Centers.")

Alamo rental agency is conveniently located here for visitors who might like to rent a car during their stay.

The Wyndy Harbour Kid's Klub offers supervised day and evening programs for children age four through twelve.

Hotel Transportation: Walk (or bus after 6 PM) to Downtown Disney. Bus to Epcot, Magic Kingdom, Disney-MGM Studios, and Animal Kingdom. Limited bus service to Typhoon Lagoon and Blizzard Beach; schedules vary by season. For transportation to other destinations or resorts, connect to destination buses at Downtown Disney. Taxi service available.

Making Reservations: Call the hotel's toll-free number (800 327-2990) and ask about special promotional rates. Reservations can also be made through the Disney Central Reservations Office (407 934-7639).

Rates — Standard rooms 👑. Crown-Level concierge rooms 👑👑 (including Continental breakfast, appetizers, no-host cocktails, and special room amenities). Palace Suites 👑👑 (including separate bedroom, refrigerator, wet bar, two baths, and in-room coffeemaker). Rates vary with the season.

Amenities — Room service (24 hour), refrigerator (stocked), in-room safe, hair dryer, turndown service, pay-per-view movies, valet parking, voice mail, coffeemaker, daily newspaper.

Recreation — Two pools, lap pool, boating, tennis, volleyball, jogging path, full service spa, fitness center, beauty salon, fitness training, steam room, sauna, whirlpool, massage, video arcade.

HOTEL TIPS

● The resort offers vacation packages that include hotel accommodations, some meals, theme park admission, and other amenities. Call the hotel directly (800 327-2990) for a brochure.

● The hotel offers discounts to members of the American Association of Retired Persons (AARP) and the military.

● Buses to minor attractions and other resorts can be inconvenient from here, but the Downtown Disney transportation hub is located right across the street.

OFF-SITE HOTELS

Hotels, Suites, and Inns Surrounding Walt Disney World:
The Best Picks for Location, Value, and Uniqueness

The numerous hotels surrounding Walt Disney World range from no-frills budget motels to deluxe resorts to vacation homes suitable for large families or groups. The hotels listed on the pages that follow were selected for location and value; their rooms are tasteful and the hotel atmosphere is pleasant. Many are all-suites hotels, which offer spacious accommodations and the welcome convenience of an in-room kitchen for about the cost of a moderate hotel room on Walt Disney World property. Suites offer exceptional value to larger families and small groups: They have separate bedrooms, the sitting rooms have foldout beds, and they sleep about six persons.

Some of the hotels reviewed here offer standard rooms at budget prices. A few are premier resorts that feature luxurious vacation experiences. Most hotels provide a complimentary breakfast each morning and free shuttles to and from the major theme parks, although renting a car is generally a good idea when staying off Disney property. Most are within a 5-minute drive of Walt Disney World.

HOTEL ROOM PRICING KEY

$ – $60 to $100

$$ – $80 to $150

$$$ – $130 to $200

👑 – $170 to $280

👑 👑 – $260 to $380

👑 👑 👑 – $350 to $550

👑 – over $500

The rates shown in the reviews are the starting price of a typical (non-view) room or suite averaged across peak and value seasons, without taxes (which are about 11 percent).

Savings on Off-Property Accommodations

As with all hotels at Walt Disney World, it is a good idea to make reservations as far in advance as possible. However, the off-site hotels are usually willing to make last-minute deals just to fill up rooms. Travelers can often find special rates by calling around shortly before they leave.

Be sure to ask whether the hotel offers discounts to members of any travel clubs you may belong to, such as AARP (The American Association of Retired Persons), Entertainment Publications, or AAA (the American Automobile Association). These club discounts can amount to as much as 50 percent at participating off-site hotels during value seasons. Hotel discounts are also available through the Orlando and the Kissimmee-St. Cloud convention and visitors bureaus. (See *Essentials* → "Discount Strategies.")

Some off-site hotels, such as Embassy Suites and Summerfield Suites, offer discount vacation packages throughout the year. To find out about these special offers you must ask! Most of the off-property hotels offer their best seasonal discounts during September and January.

Vacation homes and condos are an excellent value and have become very popular with visitors. For links to these, see "Online Resources," page 10. ◆

*See the "Essentials" section for
Hotel Selection Guides and updates.*

Buena Vista Suites

The suites in this seven-story hotel are spacious, handsomely decorated, and feature a separate living room with VCR, pullout bed, and dataport. The full kitchen has a coffeemaker, microwave, and refrigerator. Deluxe suites have a king-size bed and whirlpool bath. Hotel amenities include a complimentary daily breakfast buffet, evening room service, pool, exercise room, whirlpool spa, arcade, tennis courts, and complimentary transportation to Walt Disney World. Transportation to Universal Studios Escape and Sea World is provided for a fee.

Location: Buena Vista Suites is located about three miles from the Epcot entrance to Walt Disney World.

Average Rates: Standard suites **$$**, deluxe suites **$$$**. Rates vary with the season.

Telephone: Hotel 407 239-8588. Hotel toll free 800 537-7737.

8203 World Center Drive, Lake Buena Vista, FL 32830

Caribe Royale Resort Suites

Caribe Royale has over twelve hundred pleasantly decorated suites housed in ten-story V-shaped towers. Each suite has a coffeemaker, microwave, and refrigerator, as well as a separate living room with wet bar. Resort amenities include a restaurant, room service, pool with slide, whirlpool spa, two fitness centers, child care center, tennis courts, valet parking, daily complimentary buffet or Continental breakfast, and complimentary transportation to Walt Disney World. Transportation to Universal Studios Escape and Sea World is provided for a fee.

Location: Caribe Royale Resort Suites is located three miles from the Epcot entrance to Walt Disney World.

Average Rates: Standard rooms 👑. Two-bedroom villas 👑 👑. Rates vary with the season.

Telephone: Hotel 407 238-8000. Hotel toll free 800 823-8300.

8101 World Center Drive, Orlando, FL 32821

Clarion Suites

Clarion Suites features one- and two-bedroom villas decorated with rich colors and contemporary furnishings. Guest rooms have a fully-equipped kitchen with refrigerator, oven, microwave, dishwasher, coffeemaker, dishes, and utensils as well as a washer and dryer. Resort amenities include two tennis courts (one lighted), a swimming pool, basketball court, billiards room, fitness room, laundry service, and a playground. The resort does not provide transportation to Walt Disney World.

Location: Clarion Suites is located one mile from the Downtown Disney entrance to Walt Disney World.

Average Rates: One-bedroom villas **$$$**, two-bedroom villas 👑. Rates vary with the season.

Telephone: Hotel 407 238-1700. Hotel toll free 800 423-8604. Central reservations 800 252-7466.

8451 Palm Parkway, Lake Buena Vista, FL 32836

Courtyard by Marriott

Courtyard by Marriott features both moderately-sized suites and standard rooms. Each standard room has a hair dryer, coffeemaker, iron, and ironing board. Suites feature a separate sitting area, microwave, refrigerator, and wet bar. Hotel amenities include two pools, kiddie pool, whirlpool, game room, playground, shuffleboard area, a full-service restaurant, deli, and complimentary transportation to Walt Disney World.

Location: Courtyard by Marriott Lake Buena Vista is less than one mile from the Downtown Disney entrance to Walt Disney World.

Average Rates: Standard rooms **$$** to **$$$**, suites **$$$** to 👑. Rates vary with the season.

Telephone: Hotel 407 239-6900. Hotel toll free 800 635-8684.

8501 Palm Parkway, Lake Buena Vista, FL 32836

Cypress Glen

This gorgeous Art Deco–styled carriage house offers a change of pace from a regular hotel stay. The premier suite has a king-size bed, a whirlpool bath for two, a walk-in shower, and a large study. Guests have full access to all areas of the exquisitely decorated house: the cigar room, lounge, library, wine cellar, gourmet kitchen, grotto pool, and spa. An upscale Continental breakfast, served daily, is complimentary. Innkeeper Sandy Sarillo provides complete concierge service with a friendly touch. Cypress Glen does not provide transportation to Walt Disney World.

Location: Cypress Glen is located three miles from the Downtown Disney entrance to Walt Disney World.

Average Rates: Premier suite 👑 👑 👑, deluxe room 👑.

Telephone: Hotel 407 909-0338. Hotel toll-free 888 909-0338.

10336 Centurion Court, Lake Buena Vista, FL 32830

Embassy Grand Beach

Embassy Vacation Resort Grand Beach at Lake Bryan offers the largest accommodations in the Walt Disney World area. The low-rise buildings of this all-suites resort are clustered beside a lake, creating a beach resort atmosphere. Suites feature three bedrooms, three baths, a kitchen and dining area, a large screened porch, and VCR. Resort amenities include a pool, exercise room, tennis courts, volleyball, and jet-skiing and waterskiing. The hotel does not provide transportation to Walt Disney World.

Location: Embassy Vacation Resort Grand Beach at Lake Bryan is located two miles from the Downtown Disney entrance to Walt Disney World.

Average Rates: Three-bedroom suites 👑 to 👑 👑. Rates vary with the season.

Telephone: Hotel 407 238-2500. Reservations toll free 800 350-3382.

8317 Lake Bryan Beach Boulevard, Orlando, FL 32821

Embassy Suites Resort

This six-story hotel features comfortable two-room suites, each with a microwave, refrigerator, wet bar, coffeemaker, and VCR. Resort amenities include a complimentary breakfast buffet, room service, cocktails and beverages in the evenings, an indoor-outdoor pool, exercise room, sauna, tennis courts, volleyball, shuffleboard, and transportation to Walt Disney World. A child care center is on the premises, and the hotel was designed to provide exceptional accessibility for visitors with disabilities.

Location: Embassy Suites Resort, Lake Buena Vista is located one mile from the Downtown Disney entrance to Walt Disney World.

Average Rates: Standard suites **$$$** to 👑. Rates vary with the season.

Telephone: Hotel 407 239-1144. Hotel toll free 800 257-8483. Central reservations 800 362-2779.

8100 Lake Avenue, Orlando, FL 32836

Hampton Inn

This five story, 147-room hotel features spacious, comfortable guest rooms. Most rooms have two queen beds; however, handicap-accessible rooms have one king bed. Each guest room has a coffeemaker, iron, and ironing board. Hotel amenities include a pool, spa, exercise room, jogging trail, and complimentary Continental breakfast buffet. Complimentary transportation is provided to Walt Disney World, as well as to Universal Studios Escape and Sea World.

Location: Hampton Inn — Lake Buena Vista is located one mile from the Downtown Disney entrance to Walt Disney World.

Average Rates: Standard rooms **$$**. Rates vary with the season.

Telephone: Hotel 407 465-8150. Central reservations 800 370-9259.

8150 Palm Parkway, Orlando, FL 32836

Essentials

Attractions

Hotels

Hotels Inside Walt Disney World • Hotels Outside Walt Disney World

Restaurants

Special Events

Recreation

Resources

*See the "Essentials" section for
Hotel Selection Guides and updates.*

Holiday Inn Family Suites Resort

The east courtyard of this large hotel houses Kidsuites, with a small room housed inside the parents' suite. Suites have a separate living area with pullout sofa, VCR, refrigerator, coffeemaker, and wet bar with microwave. Kids' rooms have bunk beds and a junior pullout bed. The master bedroom has a king bed, hair dryer, iron, and ironing board. The west courtyard houses traditional suites. Resort amenities include daily complimentary breakfast buffet, fitness center, and complimentary transportation to Walt Disney World.

Location: Holiday Inn Family Suites Resort is located one mile from the Epcot entrance to Walt Disney World.

Average Rates: Suites **$$$**. Rates vary with the season.

Telephone: Hotel 407 387-5437. Hotel toll free 877 387-5437. Central reservations 800 465-4329.

18000 International Drive South, Orlando, FL 32821

Holiday Inn SunSpree Resort

Three vivid pink, low-rise hotel buildings surround a tropically landscaped pool area. Rooms are spacious and have convenient kitchenettes. Kidsuites, featuring a small room housed inside the parents' suite, have bunk beds, a TV, VCR, and video games. Hotel amenities include a fitness center, arcade, pool, whirlpools, room service, full-service restaurant, and complimentary transportation to Walt Disney World. There is a child care and activity center on the premises.

Location: Holiday Inn SunSpree Resort, Lake Buena Vista is located less than one mile from the Downtown Disney entrance to Walt Disney World.

Average Rates: Standard rooms **$$**, Kidsuites **$$$**. Rates vary with the season.

Telephone: Hotel toll free 800 366-6299. Central reservations 800 465-4329.

13351 State Road 535, Lake Buena Vista, FL 32830

Homewood Suites

This four-story hotel houses spacious, two-room suites. The living area has a pullout sofa and recliner, plus a full kitchen with refrigerator, freezer, microwave, stove top, and dishwasher. Bedrooms come with either two queen beds or one king. All suites come with iron, ironing board, and hair dryer. Hotel amenities include complimentary breakfast buffet, weeknight evening social hour, pool, whirlpool spa, exercise room and complimentary transportation to Walt Disney World, Universal Studios Escape, and Sea World.

Location: Homewood Suites Lake Buena Vista is located approximately one mile from the Downtown Disney entrance to Walt Disney World.

Average Rates: Suites **$$** to **$$$**. Rates vary with the season.

Telephone: Hotel 407 465-8200. Hotel toll free 800 370-9894.

8200 Palm Parkway, Orlando, FL 32836

Hyatt Regency Grand Cypress

This dramatic eighteen-story atrium building is situated on fifteen hundred acres of forest and landscaped recreation areas. Standard guest rooms are compact yet pleasant and each has a balcony, mini bar, and pay-per-view movies. This self-contained resort has five full-service restaurants and 24 hour room service. Recreational facilities include a free-form grotto pool, full-service spa, health club, and day care center. Tennis and racquetball courts, a PGA golf course, stables and trails for horseback riding, and a lake with canoes, sailboats, and paddle boats are available for guest use.

Location: Hyatt Regency is located one mile from the Downtown Disney entrance to Walt Disney World.

Average Rates: Standard view rooms 👑 to 👑 👑, Regency Club concierge rooms 👑 👑 👑.

Telephone: Hotel 407 239-1234. Central reservations 800 233-1234.

One Grand Cypress Boulevard, Orlando, FL 32836

For hotel photos, visit www.AmazingGuide.to/disneylinks

Marriott's Orlando World Center

Elegant rooms and suites are housed in a twenty-seven-story central tower flanked by tiered wings. An additional wing has 500 guest rooms with a pool and health club. Each guest room has a balcony, mini bar, coffeemaker, in-room safe, and pay-per-view movies. Resort amenities include five full-service restaurants, 24 hour room service, health club, child care center, tennis courts, and an eighteen-hole golf course. Transportation to Walt Disney World is available for a small fee.

Location: Marriott's Orlando World Center is located less than two miles from the Epcot entrance to Walt Disney World.

Average Rates: Standard rooms $$$ to 👑. Rates vary with the season.

Telephone: Hotel 407 239-4200. Hotel toll free 800 621-0638. Central reservations 800 228-9290.

8701 World Center Drive, Orlando, FL 32821

Perri House, Bed & Breakfast Inn

Hosts Nick and Angi Perri built and decorated this tranquil country inn, which is surrounded by sixteen acres of natural preserve for many species of native birds. The inn has eight unique non-smoking guest rooms with private baths and entrances, a pool and spa, and a library on area attractions. A complimentary Continental breakfast is served daily. Luxury "Birdhouse Cottages" are scattered across the property and are ideal for honeymoons and independent getaways for two. Transportation to Walt Disney World is not provided.

Location: Perri House is located three miles from the Downtown Disney entrance to Walt Disney World.

Average Rates: Guest rooms $$ to $$$. Birdhouse Cottages 👑.

Telephone: Hotel 407 876-4830. Hotel toll-free 800 780-4830.

10417 Vista Oaks, Lake Buena Vista, FL 32836

Premier Vacation Homes

Premier Vacation Homes are private, furnished homes that are rented daily, weekly, or monthly to vacationers. These luxury- and executive-style homes are all at least 1,300 square feet in size. Each contains a full kitchen, washer and dryer, and two to six bedrooms. Many homes also have a king-size bed, pool, and barbecue. Rentals are located in subdivisions throughout Kissimmee, off State Route 192, and are no more than 10 minutes from Walt Disney World. A rental car is a must when staying in a Premier Vacation Home, which can be arranged through the front office. A cleaning fee applies to stays of less than four nights.

Location: All houses are less than 10 minutes from the main entrance to Walt Disney World.

Average Rates: Two-bedroom luxury house (sleeps six) $$$. Four-bedroom luxury house (sleeps ten) 👑.

Telephone: Hotel toll free 800 396-2401.

3160 Vineland Road, Suite 1, Kissimmee, FL 34746

Radisson Inn Lake Buena Vista

This six-story hotel is situated on 120 acres of waterfront property and features two hundred spacious guest rooms with balconies. Rooms have double beds and include a coffeemaker, iron, ironing board, and hair dryer. Hotel amenities include a full-service restaurant, room service, pool with waterfall and slide, whirlpool spa, playground, sandbox, arcade, and complimentary transportation to Walt Disney World (transportation to Universal Studios Escape is available for a fee). Several restaurants and specialty shops, including Crossroads Shopping Center, are within walking distance.

Location: Radisson Inn is located one mile from the Downtown Disney entrance to Walt Disney World.

Average Rates: Standard rooms $$ to $$$. Rates vary with the season.

Telephone: Hotel 407 239-8400. Central reservations 800 333-3333.

8686 Palm Parkway, Orlando, FL 32836

Essentials

Attractions

Hotels

Hotels Inside Walt Disney World • Hotels Outside Walt Disney World

Restaurants

Special Events

Recreation

Resources

See the "Essentials" section for Hotel Selection Guides and updates.

Attractions

Hotels

Sheraton Safari

This African-themed family hotel has a tropically landscaped courtyard pool surrounded by a quartet of six-story buildings. Accommodations include both standard guest rooms and moderately sized suites. The suites include a kitchenette and a separate bedroom. Each standard guest room is equipped with a coffee-maker, in-room safe, iron, ironing board, and hair dryer. Most rooms have a balcony. Resort amenities include a pool with a seventy-nine-foot water slide, full-service restaurant, room service, and complimentary transportation to Walt Disney World.

Location: Sheraton Safari is located one block from the Downtown Disney entrance to Walt Disney World.

Average Rates: Standard rooms **$$**, suites **$$$**. Rates vary with the season.

Telephone: Hotel 407 239-0444. Reservations toll free 800 423-3297. Central reservations 800 325-3535.

12205 Apopka-Vineland Road, Orlando, FL 32836

Sierra Suites

The studio suites at this hotel feature either a king bed or two queen beds, as well as a pullout sofa. Bathrooms have a separate vanity area with a hair dryer. Each studio suite has a kitchenette with stove top, microwave, dishwasher, refrigerator, coffeemaker, toaster, plates, utensils, and small dining table. Two roomy closets, an iron, and ironing board are also included. Hotel amenities include a juice and coffee bar, exercise room, and a courtyard swimming pool. The hotel does not provide transportation to Walt Disney World.

Location: Sierra Suites Lake Buena Vista is located approximately one mile from the Downtown Disney entrance to Walt Disney World.

Average Rates: Studio suites **$$**. Rates vary with the season.

Telephone: Hotel 407 239-4300. Hotel toll free 800 830-4964. Central reservations 800 474-3772.

8100 Palm Parkway, Orlando, FL 32836

Summerfield Suites Hotel

Set in a tropical garden, this 150 unit all-suites hotel offers one- and two-bedroom suites that sleep between four and eight people. All have a fully equipped kitchen, dining area, and living room with VCR. The two-bedroom suites have two bathrooms. Hotel amenities include a daily complimentary Continental breakfast buffet, exercise room, game room, whirlpool spa, swimming pool, kiddie pool, and complimentary transportation to Walt Disney World.

Location: Summerfield Suites Hotel is located approximately one-half mile from the Downtown Disney entrance to Walt Disney World.

Average Rates: One-bedroom suites **$$$**, two-bedroom suites 👑. Rates vary with the season.

Telephone: Hotel 407 238-0777. Central reservations 800 833-4353.

8751 Suiteside Drive, Orlando, FL 32836

Other Off-Site Hotels

Our readers have also recommended the hotels listed below. They were cited for their convenience and value.

Celebration Hotel: 700 Bloom Street, Celebration, FL, 34747. Fifteen minutes from the main entrance to Walt Disney World. (407 566-6000) Standard rooms 👑.

DoubleTree Orlando Resort and Conference Center: 3011 Maingate Lane, Orlando, FL 34747. Five minutes from the main entrance to Walt Disney World. (800 239 6478) Standard rooms 👑.

Holiday Inn Nikki Bird: 7300 Irlo Bronson Highway, Kissimmee, FL 34747. Five minutes the main entrance to Walt Disney World. (800 206 2747) Standard rooms **$$** to **$$$**.

Vistana Resort: 8800 Vistana Center Drive, Orlando, FL 32821. Ten minutes from the Epcot entrance to Walt Disney World. (800 877-8787) One-bedroom vacation apartments **$$$**.

Restaurants

Special Events

Recreation

Resources

RESTAURANTS

Dining at the Walt Disney World Attractions:
Planning Entertaining Meals During Your Disney Vacation

T*he full-service restaurants located at the theme parks and attractions areas provide unique dining atmospheres and are designed to be an extension of the Walt Disney World experience. In the theme parks, the food may not always be up to epicurean standards and the prices tend to be high, but most visitors enjoy memorable dining experiences. Alcohol is served in all full-service restaurants except those in the Magic Kingdom, and smoking is prohibited at all Disney-owned restaurants. Most restaurants offer low-fat entrees, and most do a good job accommodating vegetarians with special entrees. Kosher, sugar-free, and other special meals can be requested in advance.*

RESERVATIONS

Experienced visitors plan where they will be each day and then make reservations at nearby restaurants well in advance of their trip. Restaurant seating usually fills early, especially during peak seasons. All Walt Disney World visitors can make reservations between 60 to 120 days in advance by calling Disney Dining Reservations (407 939-3463). If the restaurant you want is already booked, make a backup reservation at another restaurant then call back often to check for openings.

Visitors can make restaurant reservations after 10 AM on the day they are touring by calling Disney Dining (939-3463). Same-day reservations can also be made in person at the following theme park locations:

Epcot: At the Disney Dining telephone kiosk near Guest Relations at Innoventions East in Future World, and at the Disney Dining telephone kiosk in the Germany pavilion.

Disney-MGM Studios: At the Hollywood Junction restaurant desk, where Hollywood and Sunset boulevards meet.

Magic Kingdom: At City Hall, located near the park entrance on Main Street, U.S.A. ◆

Key to Restaurant Pricing

Most of the restaurant reviews show the **average price range** for a single entree only, and not necessarily for a meal. In the case of buffets or Character Meals, which are generally all-you-care-to-eat affairs that include beverages, the prices shown are for a complete adult meal (children's meals cost about half). The key to pricing is as follows:

$ – under $10

$$ – $8 to $20

$$$ – $15 to $25

$$$$ – $20 to $30

$$$$$ – Over $25

Saving Money on Meals

You can save time and money if you eat your main meal in the afternoon while lunch prices are still in effect, then have a light dinner at a counter-service restaurant. You can also save up to 30 percent at selected restaurants in the World Showcase and elsewhere. Throughout the year, from 4:30 until 6 PM, Early Evening Value Meals are offered, which include an appetizer, entree, and beverage. You must ask which restaurants offer these when making reservations. ◆

Essentials

Attractions

Hotels

Restaurants • Restaurants at the Attractions

Restaurants at the Resorts

Special Events

Recreation

Resources

BIERGARTEN

See the "Essentials" section for Dining Selection Guides.

The World Showcase at Epcot

German Buffet

Location — The entrance to the restaurant is tucked in the back of the Germany pavilion in the World Showcase at Epcot. Guests can reach it by strolling through the platz, past St. George's statue and fountain.

Dining Hours — Lunch from 11:30 AM, dinner from 4 PM until park closing.

Average Price Range — Lunch buffet **$$**, dinner buffet **$$$**.

Features & Tips — This restaurant is a favorite of many visitors, who rave about the food. Biergarten has recently added more options for vegetarians.

At various times throughout the day, diners can enjoy a lively stage show of German music and dance. Check the entertainment schedule for show times.

For those traveling solo, Biergarten can be a great place to meet fellow Disney vacationers.

The large dining hall can be noisy and crowded during peak dining hours.

Reservations — All visitors to Walt Disney World can make reservations between 60 and 120 days in advance by calling Disney Dining Reservations (407 939-3463). Same-day reservations can be made by calling Disney Dining after 10 AM (939-3463). They can also be made at the Disney Dining telephone kiosks located in the Germany Pavilion and at Guest Relations in Future World.

Food: Biergarten features a traditional buffet of hearty German cuisine, including roasted meats and chicken, sauerbraten (a marinated beef dish), a variety of German sausages (weisswurst, bratwurst, and knockwurst), along with red cabbage and potato salad.

Atmosphere: Biergarten is a spacious dining room fashioned after the famous beer halls of Munich. Ornate street lamps, balconies overflowing with geraniums, and water cascading from an old mill create an instant vacation to Germany and lend an outdoor air to the restaurant. Communal seating and Bavarian-costumed servers carrying giant steins of beer add to the festivities. On the stage at the front of the hall, performances of German music, folk dancing, singing, and yodeling are featured throughout the day. The robust atmosphere of the Biergarten captures the essence of Oktoberfest, a traditional harvest celebration in Germany.

Sample Dinner Entrees: *Selections from the Hot Buffet* — Sauerbraten (marinated beef), Bratwurst (steamed pork sausage), Knockwurst and Weisswurst (sausages), Wein Kraut (sauerkraut), Chicken Schnitzel, Rotisserie Chicken, Spätzle (noodles).

Selections from the Cold Buffet — Rotkohl (red cabbage), Heringsalat (herring and apple salad), Kartoffelsalat (potato salad), and an array of salads and breads.

Healthy-Choice Entrees: *Selections from the Hot Buffet* — Huhn (rotisserie chicken), Kartoffel (roasted potatoes).

Selections from the Cold Buffet — Apfelmus (applesauce), Gurkensalat (marinated cucumbers and onion), Heringsalat (herring salad).

Lunch: Lunch and dinner menus are similar, although the buffet price is lower at lunch.

Beverages: A selection of fine German wines is offered, along with Beck's beer on tap, served in thirty-three ounce steins. Spirits, including German liqueurs such as Jägermeister and Kirschwasser, are available, as are soft drinks, coffee, and tea.

BIG RIVER GRILLE & BREWING WORKS

See the "Essentials" section for Dining Selection Guides.

New American Cuisine

Food: Big River Grille & Brewing Works offers traditional pub fare as well as familiar entrees updated with a new twist. Salads, sandwiches, burgers, and heartier dishes such as chicken, char-grilled meatloaf, and pork ribs are designed to pair with the brews, and many entrees incorporate beer in their preparation.

Atmosphere: The smell of malt greets guests as they pass under bright green awnings to enter this sleek, modern restaurant with a fully operating microbrewery. The huge stainless-steel vats and other brewing equipment are visible behind glass walls, and guests walking through or sitting in the bar area can watch the brewmasters at work. An explanation of the brewing process is printed on the back of the menu.

Sample Dinner Entrees: Rocket Red Ale Chicken (chicken sautéed in Shiitake mushroom sauce, served with rice and fresh vegetables); Char-grilled Meatloaf (meatloaf grilled and served with white Cheddar mashed potatoes, gravy, and vegetable); Drunken Ribeye (12 ounces of ribeye marinated in beer, served with white Cheddar mashed potatoes and sautéed vegetables); Grilled Chicken and Cashew Salad (sliced chicken breast served over greens with tomatoes, cashews, artichoke hearts, feta, and balsamic vinaigrette dressing; served cold).

Healthy-Choice Entrees: Sesame Tuna (tuna covered with sesame seeds, pan sautéed and topped with ginger rémoulade sauce, served with rice and vegetables); Jamaican Jerk Chicken (marinated chicken breast coated in a special herb-spice blend and grilled, served with pineapple salsa).

Lunch: The menu remains the same throughout the day.

Beverages: Big River Grille offers six microbrewed specialties on tap: Tilt Pale Ale, Gadzook's Pilsner, Rocket Red Ale, Southern Flyer Light, and two seasonal brews which are made on the premises. Soft drinks, mineral water, tea, coffee, espresso, and cappuccino are also available, as are wine and spirits, including a selection of fine Scotches and cognacs.

Disney's BoardWalk

Location — Big River Grille & Brewing Works is located on Disney's BoardWalk Promenade, near the Atlantic Dance and Jellyrolls nightclubs.

Dining Hours — Open all day from 11 AM until 2 AM.

Average Price Range — Entrees **$$**.

Features & Tips — For one set price, guests can sample all house microbrews, each served in a four-ounce glass.

The Spinach Con Queso appetizer is a popular dish among guests who like spicy foods.

Big River Grille is one of the few Walt Disney World eateries that stays open late, and it is an ideal spot for a bite to eat after an evening touring the theme parks or visiting the clubs.

Vegetarians may find the variety of hot selections somewhat limited, but can request the Chicken Marinara dish without the chicken.

Some guests may find the smell of the malt used in the brewing process unpleasant. To avoid it, request outdoor seating.

Reservations — No reservations are accepted; diners are seated on a first-come, first-served basis. Smoking is permitted in the bar and cocktail area.

BISTRO DE PARIS

See the "Essentials" section for Dining Selection Guides.

The World Showcase at Epcot

Location — Bistro de Paris is located on the second floor at the France pavilion in the World Showcase at Epcot. Guests can find the restaurant by walking down the pavilion's cobblestone street.

Dining Hours — Dinner from 4:30 until 9:30 PM.

Average Price Range — Dinner entrees $$$$$.

Features & Tips — Three of France's premier cuisiniers, Gaston Lenôtre, Paul Bocuse, and Roger Vergé, designed the menu for Bistro de Paris.

With its low lighting, intimate decor, and its secluded location overlooking the Parisian street scene below, the award-winning Bistro de Paris is an especially romantic setting.

Because the entrees can be quite expensive, Bistro de Paris is not a good choice for the budget-minded.

Reservations at Bistro de Paris are difficult to secure since it is very popular and is open for just one meal.

Reservations — All visitors to Walt Disney World can make reservations between 60 and 120 days in advance by calling Disney Dining Reservations (407 939-3463). Same-day reservations can be made by calling Disney Dining after 10 AM (939-3463). They can also be made at the Disney Dining telephone kiosks located in the Germany Pavilion and at Guest Relations in Future World.

French Cuisine

Food: Bistro de Paris features classic French haute cuisine, including such appetizers as pâté de foie gras and smoked salmon. Entrees include seafood, meats, and vegetables served with a variety of unique light sauces. Despite its name, suggesting casual food, Bistro de Paris is the more upscale of the restaurants in the France pavilion.

Atmosphere: Guests ascend a dramatic spiraling stairway to this lovely restaurant. Hanging brass and milk glass chandeliers fill the dining room with soft, romantic light. The bistro motif is reflected in the seating arrangements, which features long banquettes and red upholstered chairs. Mirrors and paintings in ornate gold frames adorn the walls, evoking a Parisian turn-of-the-century atmosphere.

Sample Dinner Entrees: Gratinee de Homard Feuillete de legumes au basilic (lobster gratinee served with a vegetable Napoleon flavored with basil); Cailles farcies au foie gras et aux champignons sur un lit de choux braise (roasted quails stuffed with foie gras and mushrooms, served with braised cabbage); Tournedos grille aux cepes et sa pomme Darphin (grilled filet mignon and wild mushroom sauce, served with potato galette and French green beans).

Healthy-Choice Entrees: Poisson du Jour (fish of the day). A vegetable plate is available on request.

Beverages: French wine and beer, as well as spirits, are served. Soft drinks, mineral water, tea, coffee, and café express are also available. The restaurant's most popular after-dinner drink, Café Grand Marnier, is made with café express (similar to espresso), Grand Marnier liqueur, and whipped cream.

BONGOS CUBAN CAFE

See the "Essentials" section for Dining Selection Guides.

Cuban Cuisine

Food: Bongos Cuban Cafe serves authentic Cuban cuisine, derived from both tropical and European influences. The menu features beef, chicken, and seafood prepared with traditional Cuban spices and techniques.

Atmosphere: Housed in an elegantly tropical two-story, sand-white building, Bongos harkens back to the Cuba of the 1940s. The walls are inlaid with mosaic tilework and portray scenes of Cuban life, and bongo drums serve as seats at three separate bars. Colored glass crowns the tall windows overlooking Buena Vista Lagoon and serves as tabletops on the upper level booths, where they are lit from underneath. The restaurant's ceiling resembles a giant banana leaf, and the columns supporting it are fashioned after tall palm tree trunks. To reach the top floor, guests wind their way up a large spiral staircase with wrought-iron banana leaves scattered throughout the railing. A Latin jazz band plays during the week.

Sample Dinner Entrees: Ropa Vieja (shredded beef in a light tomato sauce with onions and peppers); Zarzuela de Mariscos (lobster, shrimp, scallops, calamari, fish, baby clams, and mussels in a homemade Creole sauce); Chicharrones de Pollo (lightly floured chicken chunks marinated in Cuban Mojo); Masitas de Puerco (Cuban Mojo marinated pork chunks served with grilled onions).

Healthy-Choice Entrees: Filete de Pescado Grille (grilled filet of fish); Pechuga de Pollo a la Plancha (grilled chicken breast topped with grilled onions); Vegetarian Dish (mixed vegetables with white rice and choice of sweet plaintains or green plantains).

Lunch: Although visitors may order off the dinner menu at lunch, there are Cuban-style sandwiches and hamburgers available only from 11 AM to 5 PM. One such sandwich is Pan con Bistec, thin Cuban steak with grilled onions, lettuce, and tomato on Cuban bread, served with plantain chips.

Beverages: Domestic and imported beer and wine are featured at Bongos, as are champagne and sparkling wine. Bongos Cuban Cafe offers a number of specialty drinks such as The Babaloo, a mixture of Bacardi Anejo rum, citrus juices, cream of coconut, and a touch of blue curaçao. Juice, soft drinks, mineral water, tea, and coffee are also available.

West Side at Downtown Disney

Location — Bongos Cuban Cafe is located at Downtown Disney's West Side, across from the AMC Theatres.

Dining Hours — Open all day from 11 AM until 2 AM.

Average Price Range — Lunch entrees **$**, dinner entrees **$$$**.

Features & Tips — A Cuban band, fronted by a Desi Arnaz look-a-like, plays Wednesday through Sunday, from 10:30 PM until 2 AM. Guests are encouraged to dance to the rousing tunes right in front of the band.

Cafe Cubano, a Bongos Cuban Cafe express window, serves limited menu items from 10 AM until 1 AM. It is located outside to the left of the restaurant entrance. This is a great place to pick up fresh, hot food while waiting for a performance.

A favorite entree among frequent visitors is the beef dish Ropa Vieja.

Reservations — No reservations are accepted; guests are seated on a first-come, first-served basis.

Essentials

Attractions

Hotels

Restaurants

Special Events

Recreation

Resources

Restaurants at the Resorts • Restaurants at the Attractions

CAP'N JACK'S RESTAURANT

See the "Essentials" section for Dining Selection Guides.

The Marketplace at Downtown Disney

Location — The restaurant is located at the end of a pier in the center of The Marketplace. It sits on Buena Vista Lagoon, and guests can reach it by walking along the waterfront.

Dining Hours — Open all day from 11:30 AM until 10:30 PM.

Average Price Range — Entrees $$$$.

Features & Tips — Cap'n Jack's is a casual restaurant with a relaxed atmosphere. The hexagonal bar is a great place to meet fellow vacationers while waiting for a table. Guests can order seafood appetizers at the bar.

Although the entrees provide a variety of choices, the Steamed Oysters, Steamed Clams, and Peel & Eat Shrimp are skillfully prepared and are the real draw here.

If they are in season and on the menu, try the stone crab from the Florida coast, which is wonderful and very hard to find.

During peak dining times, there can be long waits and signs at the entrance do not make it clear how guests are seated. Guests who would like a table must wait in line at the podium. If you just want to sit at the bar for a beverage or snack, simply bypass the line.

Reservations — No reservations are accepted; diners are seated on a first-come, first-served basis.

Seafood and Traditional American Cuisine

Food: Cap'n Jack's features an array of fresh seafood, including shrimp, oysters, crab, clams, and scallops. The seafood is served in salads, cooked into crab cakes, steamed, baked, or prepared in other entrees. Chicken, beef, and pot roast are also served.

Atmosphere: The galley-style entrance at Cap'n Jack's has a glass-fronted display of the day's fresh seafood. The restaurant has two dining areas, one to the left of the galley and another surrounding the large hexagonal copper-topped bar in the middle of the restaurant. Both dining areas are small, but offer great views of Buena Vista Lagoon and the picturesque riverboat with Fulton's Crab House aboard. A boathouse atmosphere has been achieved at Cap'n Jack's with plank-wood flooring, thickly varnished wooden tables, and leather-slung chairs.

Sample Dinner Entrees: Alaskan King Crab Legs (steamed to order and served with coleslaw, a garlic bread stick, and melted butter); Oysters (baked with garlic butter or steamed; available by the half or full dozen); Grilled Chicken (marinated breast of chicken served with pesto smashed potatoes, fresh vegetables, and a garlic breadstick); Seafood Pasta (pasta with Alfredo sauce, topped with a combination of shrimp and scallops, served with a garlic breadstick); Cap'n Jack's Pot Roast (served with pesto smashed potatoes, fresh vegetables, gravy, and a garlic breadstick).

Healthy-Choice Entrees: Cap'n's Catch (broiled fresh fish served with rice and a garlic bread stick).

Lunch: A limited lunch menu is available, although guests can also choose from the dinner selections.

Beverages: Cold beer is served in Mason jars with handles. Wine and spirits are also offered, as are coffee, tea, and soft drinks. Cap'n Jack's is known for its Frozen Strawberry Margarita, served in a large frosted glass.

CHEFS DE FRANCE

See the "Essentials" section for
Dining Selection Guides.

French Cuisine

Food: Chefs de France features French nouvelle cuisine: seafood, meat, poultry, and vegetable dishes accompanied with distinctive sauces created by three of France's premier chefs. One or two of the beautifully prepared appetizers and a salad, ordered together, can serve as a meal.

Atmosphere: Chefs de France has a very French look with delicate, classical touches to the decor. The walls in the main dining area are a creamy eggshell color, and natural light streams in through the large windows. Tables are dressed with crisp white linen and set with fresh flowers. Guests may dine in the main dining room, or in the large light-filled veranda area, where potted flowers hang and tall windows overlook the World Showcase Promenade.

Sample Dinner Entrees: Pot-au-Feu aux deux viandes et ses legumes (assortment of beef and chicken simmered in a seasoned broth, served with fresh vegetables and horseradish sauce); Navarin d'agneau aux legumes printaniers (lamb braised in its own juices, served with spring vegetables); Le Filet de Boeuf grille, sauce Bordelaise et son gratin Dauphinois (grilled tenderloin of beef with a cabernet sauvignon wine sauce, served with Savoy potato gratin).

Healthy-Choice Entrees: Saumon grille aux Agrumes (grilled salmon served on grilled fennel and artichoke hearts, served with mixed greens and a citrus vinaigrette); Loup de Mer plaqué, pommes a l'anglaise sauce au Champagne et champignons (seared sea bass with red potato, served with champagne and mushroom sauce); Gratin de Legumes du soleil a l'huile d'olive au thym (vegetable gratin of zucchini, eggplant, and tomato with olive oil and thyme).

Lunch: Entree selections differ only slightly. Lunch prices are lower than dinner prices.

Beverages: French wine and beer are served, as are spirits, soft drinks, and mineral water. Thick and strong café express, very similar to espresso, is also offered. The comprehensive wine list includes vintages specially selected by the chefs who created the menu.

The World Showcase at Epcot

Location — Chefs de France restaurant is located in the mansard-roofed building that stands on the corner at the entrance to the France pavilion in the World Showcase at Epcot.

Dining Hours — Lunch from 12 noon; dinner from 4:30 PM until park closing.

Average Price Range — Lunch entrees **$$**, dinner entrees **$$$$$**.

Features & Tips — Chefs de France received the Ivy Award for restaurant excellence. The dishes on the menu were created by three of France's premier chefs, Paul Bocuse, Roger Vergé, and Gaston Lenôtre.

A magnificent and tempting array of not-to-be-missed and reasonably priced desserts is offered here.

The escargots with garlic and herb butter is the favorite appetizer among frequent diners here.

It can be very difficult to get same-day reservations at this popular restaurant.

Reservations — Visitors to Walt Disney World can make reservations between 60 and 120 days in advance by calling Disney Dining Reservations (407 939-3463). Same-day reservations can be made by calling Disney Dining after 10 AM (939-3463). They can also be made at the Disney Dining telephone kiosks located in the Germany Pavilion and at Guest Relations in Future World.

Essentials

Attractions

Hotels

Restaurants   •   Restaurants at the Attractions

Restaurants at the Resorts

Special Events

Recreation

Resources

CINDERELLA'S ROYAL TABLE

See the "Essentials" section for Dining Selection Guides.

The Magic Kingdom

Location — The restaurant is tucked inside Cinderella Castle at the Magic Kingdom. The entrance can be found at the rear of the castle, facing Fantasyland.

Dining Hours — Character Breakfast from 7:30 AM, lunch from 11:30 AM, dinner from 4 PM until park closing.

Average Price Range — Character Breakfast **$$$**, lunch entrees **$$**, dinner entrees **$$$$**.

Features & Tips — Cinderella's Royal Table is the only elevated restaurant with a view in the Magic Kingdom.

It can be difficult to secure same-day reservations here; the Character Breakfast is often booked to capacity as soon as visitors are allowed to make them.

Reservations — All visitors to Walt Disney World can make reservations between 60 and 120 days in advance by calling Disney Dining Reservations (407 939-3463). Same-day reservations can be made at City Hall on Main Street or by calling Disney Dining after 10 AM (939-3463).

New American Cuisine and Character Breakfast

Food: Cinderella's Royal Table serves chicken, fish, and beef dishes creatively prepared in a style influenced by New American cuisine.

Atmosphere: Cinderella's Royal Table recalls the fairy-tale splendor of once upon a time. Wall torches light the stone archways, and shields, swords, and suits of armor glint near the fireplace. Burgundy-carpeted stairs lead up to the large two-tiered dining room where the tall cathedral ceiling, carved beams, patterned carpeting, and tapestry-covered chairs exude a royal atmosphere. Tall, narrow arched windows inset with stained glass give guests an overview of Fantasyland. For twenty-five years, the restaurant inside Cinderella Castle was named King Stefan's Banquet Hall after Sleeping Beauty's father (it is a small world, after all).

Sample Dinner Entrees: Grand Duke (New York strip steak with Stilton and potato quiche, topped with horseradish bearnaise); Kingdom Feast (beef tenderloin steak with root smash and oven-roasted shallot mayonnaise); The Loyal Knight (spice-crusted salmon served with red pepper coulis and topped with aioli sauce). Dinner entrees include a choice of soup or salad.

Healthy-Choice Entrees: Earl's Poulet (herbed chicken and sautéed vegetables, served over polenta); Mariner (Thai barbecued tuna steak served with Asian-style vegetable slaw and jasmine fried rice).

Lunch: Lunch and dinner menus are similar; however, the lunch menu also features large salads and smaller entrees, including The Coachman (smoked turkey breast, ham, and Muenster cheese with beefsteak tomatoes on foccacia). Lunch entrees include soup or salad, and prices are considerably lower at lunch.

Character Breakfast: Breakfast in the castle is a plated, all-you-care-to-eat affair. Menu items include fruit, scrambled eggs, breakfast meats, potato casserole, muesli with fruit and yogurt, and banana French toast.

Beverages: Coffee, tea, orange juice, mineral water, and soft drinks are served.

CORAL REEF RESTAURANT

See the "Essentials" section for
Dining Selection Guides.

Fresh Seafood and New American Cuisine

Food: Coral Reef Restaurant serves a wide variety of fresh seafood that is prepared smoked, sautéed, or grilled. A small selection of chicken and beef dishes is also available.

Atmosphere: One wall of this softly lit multitiered restaurant is formed by one of the largest saltwater aquariums in the world, holding more than 5.7 million gallons of seawater and nearly eight thousand underwater inhabitants. Diners can watch the colorful coral reef sea life swim by behind eight-foot-high acrylic windows and use the brochure provided on arrival to help identify the fish. The undersea dining atmosphere is augmented by the room's dark blue walls and carpeting, its dim lighting, and its endlessly fascinating view.

Sample Dinner Entrees: Tuna Two Ways (chili dusted loin, southwestern cake, black beans with vegetable slaw); Cast Iron Seared Filet Mignon (with bacon and herb mashed potatoes and autumn vegetables); Pan Seared Chicken Breast (with buttered red skin potatoes and creamed leeks); Sauteed Shrimp (with penne pasta, smoked pork, and Chardonnay herb sauce). All entrees are served with soup or salad.

Healthy-Choice Entrees: Market Fresh Vegetables (fresh vegetables with spinach Boursin cheese wrapped in filo, served with lentil salad); Alaskan Halibut (with Chinese long bean and noodle stir fry).

Lunch: The lunch menu differs slightly from dinner and features such items as Southwestern Marinated Shrimp and Spinach Salad. Neither soup nor salad is included with lunch, and prices are a bit lower.

Beverages: Soft drinks, mineral water, tea, coffee, and espresso are served. International beers are offered, along with domestic and imported wines, spirits, and specialty drinks such as the Sea Star, a blend of Chablis wine, strawberries, lime juice, banana, and club soda.

Future World at Epcot

Location — Coral Reef Restaurant is located in the Living Seas pavilion in Future World at Epcot. The restaurant has its own entrance at the side of the pavilion, where blue waves painted on the wall lead guests inside.

Dining Hours — Lunch from 11:30 AM, dinner from 4:30 PM until park closing.

Average Price Range — Lunch entrees $$$, dinner entrees $$$$.

Features & Tips — Diners sit at eye-to-eye level with an array of Caribbean reef fish, including sharks and barracuda. Keep an eye out for the grouper, weighing in at more than five hundred pounds. The best views are from tables in the middle of the third and fourth tiers.

The entrees can be quite expensive — some visitors say "too expensive." Coral Reef may not the best choice for budget-minded visitors.

The Coral Reef's atmosphere and the fact that there are only two full-service restaurants in Future World make reservations here hard to get. Lunch is often easier than dinner.

Reservations — Visitors to Walt Disney World can make reservations between 60 and 120 days in advance by calling Disney Dining Reservations (407 939-3463). Same-day reservations can be made at the Disney Dining telephone kiosk near Guest Relations at Future World or by calling Disney Dining after 10 AM (939-3463).

Essentials
Attractions
Hotels
Restaurants • Restaurants at the Attractions
Restaurants at the Resorts
Special Events
Recreation
Resources

THE CRYSTAL PALACE

See the "Essentials" section for Dining Selection Guides.

The Magic Kingdom

Location — The Crystal Palace is a Magic Kingdom landmark and is located at the end of Main Street on the left, facing Cinderella Castle. It can also be approached from the bridge that leads into Adventureland.

Dining Hours — Breakfast from 8 AM, lunch from 11:30 AM, dinner from 4 PM until park closing.

Average Price Range — Character Breakfast $$$, Character Lunch $$$, Character Dinner $$$$.

Features & Tips — This restaurant has a wide selection of salad and dessert items. The Sundae Bar will appeal to ice-cream lovers.

Health-conscious diners may order breakfast dishes made with EggBeaters.

The Crystal Palace is very popular with families, so there can be a long wait for tables during peak dining hours.

Visits by Disney Characters make meals here noisy, lively, and crowded. Pooh, Tigger, Piglet, and Eeyore often drop in for socializing.

Reservations — Visitors to Walt Disney World can make reservations between 60 and 120 days in advance by calling Disney Dining Reservations (407 939-3463). Same-day reservations can be made at City Hall or by calling Disney Dining after 10 AM (939-3463).

American Buffet Character Meals

Food: The Crystal Palace features all-you-care-to-eat buffet-style Character Meals for breakfast, lunch, and dinner. Hot entrees include beef, chicken, turkey, fish, and pasta.

Atmosphere: This pretty, light-filled restaurant resembles the Victorian-era glass conservatory in San Francisco's Golden Gate Park, and gives guests the feeling that they're dining inside a giant greenhouse. A glass dome in the ceiling enhances the gazebo effect, as do the latticework ceilings and wrought-iron tables and chairs. Hot entrees are served cafeteria style at a long food counter in the center of the restaurant, and guests serve themselves from the nearby soup, salad, bread, and dessert bars. The tables along the window walls offer diners a view of beautifully landscaped gardens outside and the Cinderella Castle beyond. Disney Characters make frequent appearances to greet guests.

Character Dinner Entrees: The all-you-care-to-eat menu includes spit-roasted carved meats; chicken, beef, and fish creations; and the chef's selection of freshly prepared pastas. Rice, potatoes au gratin, vegetables, salads, freshly baked breads, and desserts are included.

Healthy-Choice Entrees: The long buffet includes a salad bar with a large variety of greens and vegetables, as well as fresh fruit.

Character Lunch: The lunch buffet offers a creative array of salads, chef's choice of soup, a variety of freshly prepared pastas, and the Executive-Style Deli. Freshly baked breads and muffins, as well as a variety of desserts such as cookies, brownies, and ice cream sundaes, are also available.

Character Breakfast: The all-you-care-to-eat breakfast menu includes seasonal fresh fruit, freshly baked pastries, spit-roasted ham, scrambled eggs and omelettes, Crystal Palace French Toast, oven-roasted potatoes, and breakfast lasagna. Hotcakes and a variety of cereals are also available.

Beverages: Coffee, tea, and soft drinks are served with unlimited refills. All beverages are included with the meal.

ESPN CLUB

See the "Essentials" section for Dining Selection Guides.

Casual American Cuisine

Food: ESPN Club offers American fare such as sandwiches, hamburgers, hot dogs, pasta, and salads. Guests who come to watch the ongoing sports events can order appetizers.

Atmosphere: ESPN Club immerses guests in the atmosphere of a raucous sports bar and sports broadcast studio. Seventy-one television monitors showing sports events are scattered throughout the club: mounted overhead, inset in walls, and even in the rest rooms. The restaurant has hardwood floors, sports murals on the walls, and an eight-by-twelve-foot viewing screen at one end of the room. Tables are arranged around the large square central bar. Guests can also eat in Sports Central, which is actually an ESPN broadcast studio, complete with scaffolding for the studio lights and a glassed-in control booth. Tiers of small tables surround the stage floor, which is patterned on a miniature basketball court.

Sample Dinner Entrees: Grand Slam Blackened Prime Rib (blackened prime rib topped with onion rings and served on a roll, accompanied by horseradish blue cheese sauce and fries); Championship Chicken Sandwich (marinated grilled chicken breast with choice of Cheddar or Swiss cheese on a roll, served with fries); Tailgate BBQ Pork (slow-roasted pulled pork simmered in house barbecue sauce, on a freshly baked roll, served with fries and coleslaw).

Healthy-Choice Entrees: In The Pocket Pita (pita bread loaded with chilled, marinated, grilled vegetables, cucumbers, and spouts, served with fruit or chips); Bull Penne Pasta (grilled sautéed vegetables, pureed tomatoes, garlic, and basil tossed with penne pasta).

Lunch: The menu is the same for lunch and dinner.

Beverages: Coffee, tea, and soft drinks are served, as well as a wide selection of beer and wine. A full bar is available in The Sidelines bar area, and features such specialty drinks as the Postgame Interview, a blend of Southern Comfort, Midori liqueur, sour mix, and cranberry juice.

Disney's BoardWalk

Location — ESPN Club is located at the far end of Disney's BoardWalk, near the International Gateway to the World Showcase at Epcot and below Disney's BoardWalk Inn.

Dining Hours — Open all day from 11:30 AM; closes at 1 AM, 2 AM on weekends.

Average Price Range — Entrees **$$**.

Features & Tips — ESPN Club has a good selection of domestic and imported beers, including Bass Ale and Red Stripe.

To one side of ESPN Club is Sports Central, with a working radio and television studio, where guests can dine while watching ESPN sports reviews and interview shows take place.

Guests who are more interested in sports than a large entree can order Bloody Mary Chili and other light appetizers to snack on as they watch the game. Or they can try the restaurant's most popular dessert, Mile-High Apple Pie.

TV monitors broadcast multiple sports events at the same time and at full volume throughout the dining area, so meals can be quite noisy.

Local residents recently voted ESPN Club the home of the Best Burger in Central Florida.

Reservations — No reservations are accepted; diners are seated on a first-come, first-served basis. Smoking is permitted in the bar area.

Hotels

Restaurants at the Attractions • Restaurants at the Resorts

Restaurants

Special Events

Recreation

Resources

Essentials

Attractions

Hotels

Restaurants • Restaurants at the Attractions

Restaurants at the Resorts • Restaurants at the Attractions

Special Events

Recreation

Resources

50'S PRIME TIME CAFE

See the "Essentials" section for
Dining Selection Guides.

Disney-MGM Studios

Location — The restaurant is located on Vine Street across from Echo Lake at Disney-MGM Studios. Guests can find the restaurant by looking for the sign in the shape of a giant television.

Dining Hours — Lunch from 11 AM, dinner from 4 PM until park closing.

Average Price Range — Lunch entrees **$$**, dinner entrees **$$**.

Features & Tips — Talented servers stay in character and provide memorable entertainment.

The Tune-In Lounge, decorated with black and white TVs, offers comfortable seats and a unique setting for before-meals cocktails.

Reservations — Visitors to Walt Disney World can make reservations between 60 and 120 days in advance by calling Disney Dining Reservations (407 939-3463). Same-day reservations can be made at Hollywood Junction (at the intersection of Hollywood and Sunset Boulevards) inside Disney-MGM Studios, or by calling Disney Dining after 10 AM (939-3463).

American Home Cooking

Food: The 50's Prime Time Cafe serves cuisine popular in that era, such as pot roast, meat loaf, chicken, and steak, prepared from family-style recipes and topped with lots of gravy. Seafood, hamburgers, and sandwiches are also available.

Atmosphere: Unique kitchenettes are the setting for the home-style meals at the 50's Prime Time Cafe. There are ruffled curtains, linoleum flooring, vintage wallpaper, and plenty of vinyl and chrome. Servers known as "Brother" or "Auntie" act as though they are bossy family members, watching diners' manners and making sure they've cleaned their plates. During meals, clips from the opening day at Disneyland, "The Mickey Mouse Club," and vintage sitcoms are broadcast on old-fashioned black and white TVs scattered throughout the restaurant's kitchenettes.

Sample Dinner Entrees: Granny's Pot Roast (country-style pot roast served with mashed potatoes and gravy, and a carrot, celery, and onion medley); Dad's Barbecue Chicken (barbecue spice-rubbed chicken breast grilled and topped with creamy peppercorn sauce, served over mashed potatoes and house vegetables); Magnificent Meatloaf (traditional-style meat loaf, served with mashed potatoes and tomato glaze); Charbroiled Ribeye Steak (ribeye steak grilled to order).

Healthy-Choice Entrees: Uncle Giovanni's Pasta (penne pasta sautéed with garlic, olive oil, crimini mushrooms, roasted tomatoes, and baby spinach; garnished with Parmesan cheese); Grandpa's Fishin' Trip (spice-crusted salmon fillet, seared, served over green beans, red onions, and julienne carrots sautéed in a mustard seed vinaigrette; topped with shoestring potatoes).

Lunch: Lunch features more sandwiches and salads than dinner and prices are slightly lower.

Beverages: Coffee, tea, and soft drinks are served with complimentary refills. The soda fountain features such specialties as root beer floats, ice cream sodas, and milk shakes, including the unique peanut-butter-and-jelly flavor. Beer, wine, and spirits are also available. Specialty drinks include The Diner, a blend of vodka, rum, cranberry, pineapple, and orange juice with a dash of grenadine and a squeeze of lime; and The Poodle Skirt, a frozen concoction of rum, banana mix, and fruit juices.

FLYING FISH CAFÉ

See the "Essentials" section for Dining Selection Guides.

Fresh Seafood and New American Cuisine

Food: The Flying Fish Café serves distinctive cuisine with innovative flavor combinations. Entrees change frequently to reflect seasonal ingredients. Fresh seafood is featured, as well as steaks and homemade pastas.

Atmosphere: The large murals and whimsical flying-fish motif at this relaxed, yet sophisticated restaurant pay tribute to the roller coaster and flying fish carousel of an earlier era at Atlantic City's Boardwalk. The main dining area is studded with large pillars surrounded by sleek tables inlaid with brushed steel. The look is both trendy and elegant. Copper tiles cover the restaurant's striking bar and the counter fronting the kitchen's open grill. In a small, secluded dining area at the rear of the restaurant, comfortable booths surround a small fountain.

Sample Dinner Entrees: Char-Crusted New York Strip Steak (with roasted German Butterball potatoes, sugar snap peas, and sauce Foyot); Ginger Crusted Yellowfin Tuna (with Chino yard-long bean stir fry, double garlic, and crispy lotus root); Housemade Kabocha Squash Ravioli (with wilted spinach, manchego cheese, and brown butter balsamic drizzle); Oak Grilled Double Cut Pork Chop (with braised red cabbage, Tillamook Cheddar potato gratin, and apple butter).

Healthy-Choice Entrees: Oak Grilled Alaskan King Salmon (with Savoy spinach, golden beets, polenta croutons, and pancetta vinaigrette); Potato-Wrapped Florida Red Snapper (with leek fondue and a Cabernet Sauvignon reduction).

Beverages: Flying Fish Café offers a large selection of domestic and imported wines that includes over a dozen types of champagne and a variety of sparkling wines. The restaurant also features microbrewed beer, including the Flying Fish, made specially for the restaurant. Champagne-based cocktails are also available, as are soft drinks, mineral water, tea, coffee, cappuccino, and espresso.

Disney's BoardWalk

Location — Flying Fish Café is located near the center of Disney's BoardWalk, overlooking the BoardWalk Green.

Dining Hours — Dinner only, Sunday through Thursday from 5:30 until 10 PM; Friday and Saturday from 5:30 until 10:30 PM.

Average Price Range — Dinner entrees **$$$$**.

Features & Tips — Guests who enjoy watching the chefs at work can request seating at the counter along the front of the show kitchen. If you find the area too smoky from the grills, request a nearby table.

Chocolate-lovers will want to try the Chocolate Lava Cake (with a warm liquid chocolate center and tarragon ice cream). The dessert takes some time to prepare; if you know it's what you will want, order it ahead of time.

Visitors should plan ahead if wishing to dine here; same-day reservations can be difficult to secure in busy seasons.

Reservations — Visitors to Walt Disney World can make reservations between 60 and 120 days in advance by calling Disney Dining Reservations (407 939-3463). Same-day reservations can be made by calling the restaurant (939-2359) or by calling Disney Dining after 10 AM (939-3463).

Restaurants at the Attractions • Restaurants at the Resorts

Essentials

Attractions

Hotels

Restaurants • Restaurants at the Attractions

Restaurants at the Resorts • Restaurants at the Attractions

Special Events

Recreation

Resources

FULTON'S CRAB HOUSE

See the "Essentials" section for Dining Selection Guides.

Pleasure Island at Downtown Disney

Location — This restaurant is inside a replica nineteenth-century riverboat docked at Buena Vista Lagoon, between The Marketplace and Pleasure Island at Downtown Disney. It is across from Portobello Yacht Club and the Wildhorse Saloon.

Dining Hours — Lunch from 11:30 AM, dinner from 5 PM until midnight.

Average Price Range — Lunch entrees **$$$**, dinner entrees **$$$$$**.

Features & Tips — Guests waiting for a table can enjoy the view in the Stone Crab Lounge, which is located on the first deck.

Without reservations, the wait can be up to an hour at this popular restaurant.

Reservations — Visitors to Walt Disney World can make reservations up to thirty days in advance for dinner by calling the restaurant directly (407 934-2628). Fulton's Crab House has a smoking area.

Fresh Seafood

Food: The focus at Fulton's is primarily on seafood, including lobster, crab, and fresh fish. Steak, chicken, and pasta are also served. The menu changes frequently to take advantage of seasonal fish from around the world.

Atmosphere: With its dark mahogany paneling, Oriental rugs, and soft lighting, Fulton's Crab House has a warm, comfortable, clubby atmosphere. The walls are hung with handsome prints depicting fish and a few mounted specimens, including a seven-hundred-pound marlin that hangs above the stairwell. The dining rooms on board the three-story riverboat include the Industry Room, which also features outdoor dining on the deck, and the Constellation Room, with its celestial-painted ceiling and lovely views of the sunset over Buena Vista Lagoon.

Sample Dinner Entrees: Rock Shrimp Pasta (Florida rock shrimp with fettuccine, roasted peppers, scallions, and spinach, tossed in a lobster butter sauce); Whole Maine Lobster (steamed, served with red-skinned potatoes and drawn butter); Fulton's Cioppino (crab, shrimp, scallops, fresh fish, clams, and mussels in a tomato-herb broth); Tuna Filet Mignon (center cut yellowfin tuna steak, marinated and charcoal grilled rare, served with a side of lemon grass dipping sauce, jasmine rice cake, and steamed bok choy).

Healthy-Choice Entrees: Marathon Key Mahi Mahi (charcoal grilled, served with spicy pineapple salsa, mixed seasonal vegetables, and Fulton's rice); Roasted Chicken (oven-roasted half chicken with garlic, lemon, and oregano, served with seasonal vegetables and Fulton's rice).

Lunch: Fulton's lunch menu has sandwiches and salads, as well as several crab options and a few seafood entrees. Lunch prices are lower than at dinner.

Beverages: The restaurant's wine list features an excellent selection of Pacific Coast wines. Beers from around the world are served, as are spirits and specialty drinks such as The Sailor's Knot, a blend of rum, orange and pineapple juices, and coconut milk. Soft drinks, coffee, espresso, and cappuccino are also served.

THE GARDEN GRILL RESTAURANT

See the "Essentials" section for
Dining Selection Guides.

American Cuisine Character Meals

Food: The Garden Grill Restaurant serves all-you-care-to-eat traditional American cuisine, including meat, chicken, and seafood that may be smoked, grilled, or rotisserie-grilled. Some of the fish and vegetables served are actually grown in The Land pavilion's gardens.

Atmosphere: The Garden Grill Restaurant overlooks the Living with The Land attraction and revolves, giving guests an excellent view of its environmental exhibits. Diners pass through dioramas depicting a rainforest, a desert, and a prairie complete with buffalo. Roomy booths on two tiers make the excursion quite comfortable. Farmer Mickey and a cast of Disney Characters drop by from time to time to greet diners.

Character Lunch and Dinner: Pork Roast Slices, Catfish Sticks, and BBQ Grilled Flank Steak are served family style in sizzling skillets. The trio of all-you-care-to-eat entrees is accompanied with farm fresh garden salad, mashed potatoes, mashed sweet potatoes, garden vegetables, and sunflower seed grain bread with honey butter. Dessert is included. The same menu is served at lunch and dinner.

Healthy-Choice Entrees: Garden Pasta Primavera (pasta tossed with fresh grilled vegetables and savory herbs) is available as a special order for guests who want a vegetarian meal.

Character Breakfast: The family-style, all-you-care-to-eat Character Breakfast dishes include scrambled eggs, breakfast casserole, sausage, ham steak, fresh fruit, biscuits and gravy, French toast sticks, and cheese grits.

Beverages: Coffee, tea, and soft drinks are included in the price of the Character Meal. Also available but not included are regional American beers and California wines. The restaurant's full bar features such specialty drinks as the popular Garden Grill Bloody Mary, a house concoction that is garnished with celery from The Land's own greenhouses.

Future World at Epcot

Location — The restaurant is located inside The Land pavilion in Future World at Epcot. To reach it, guests walk to the back of the pavilion, along the balcony overlooking the attractions and the Sunshine Season Food Fair below.

Dining Hours — Breakfast from before park opening, lunch from 11:30 AM, dinner from 4 PM until park closing.

Average Price Range — Character Breakfast, Lunch, or Dinner **$$$**.

Features & Tips — The slowly revolving restaurant provides an entertaining atmosphere at meals. For the best view, request a table on the lower tier. It takes about 35 minutes to make a complete revolution.

Guests with 7:30 AM reservations can enter Epcot early by showing their admission ticket and reservation number at the entrance gate.

During periods of peak-attendance, it is very difficult to get same-day reservations for lunch. Dinner reservations are sometimes easier to secure.

Reservations — Visitors to Walt Disney World can make reservations 60 to 120 days in advance by calling Disney Dining Reservations (407 939-3463). Same-day reservations can be made at the Disney Dining telephone kiosk near Guest Relations at Future World or by calling Disney Dining after 10 AM (939-3463).

HOLLYWOOD & VINE

See the "Essentials" section for Dining Selection Guides.

Attractions
Hotels
Restaurants at the Resorts • Restaurants at the Attractions
Restaurants
Special Events
Recreation
Resources

Disney-MGM Studios

Location — The restaurant is located on Vine Street across from Echo Lake at Disney-MGM Studios, next door to the 50's Prime Time Cafe.

Dining Hours — Open all day. Breakfast from 8 AM, lunch from 11:30 AM until 4 PM. The restaurant is open seasonally for dinner until park closing.

Average Price Range — Character Breakfast, Lunch, or Dinner **$$$**.

Features & Tips — This is a great place to meet Mickey and the gang dressed in their Hollywood best, in keeping with the theme of the park.

The Tune-In Lounge is an entertaining and relaxing stop for a before- or after-dinner drink. It can be entered from inside the Hollywood & Vine.

Although reservations are important at Character Meals, visitors are likely to find seating if they drop in mid-afternoon, when the lunch crowd thins out.

Reservations — Visitors to Walt Disney World can make reservations for Character Meals between 60 and 120 days in advance by calling Disney Dining Reservations (407 939-3463). Same-day reservations can be made by calling Disney Dining after 10 AM (939-3463).

American Buffet Character Meals

Food: Hollywood & Vine serves an all-you-care-to-eat buffet, featuring beef, chicken, veal, seafood, and pasta dishes, along with sandwiches and a variety of large salads.

Atmosphere: Hollywood & Vine is a replica of a Tinseltown diner from the late 1940s. In one room, a sprawling forty-foot mural features famous landmarks from Hollywood and the San Fernando Valley. Another very vivid mural features a detailed nighttime view of Hollywood Boulevard. Black and white photographs with scenes of early Hollywood hang on the walls. The large dining room, decorated with pink geometric carpeting and black Venetian blinds, is divided in half, with a long chrome cafeteria counter taking center stage. Guests dine at a Formica-topped dinette table or in one of the restaurant's pale-pink Naugahyde booths.

Character Lunch and Dinner Entrees: Rotisserie Turkey, Marinated Grilled Flank Steak, Roasted Pork Loin, Catch of the Day, Penne Pasta with Tomato and Garlic, Pesto Pasta, Roasted Vegetable Fried Rice, Skillet Potatoes, and Smoked Seafood.

Healthy-Choice Entrees: Catch of the Day, Penne Pasta with Tomato and Garlic, Yukon Gold Potatoes, Green Salad, and Cucumber and Onion Salad.

Character Breakfast: The menu includes traditional American egg dishes, pancakes, French toast, and breakfast meats.

Beverages: Coffee, tea, and soft drinks are included in the price of the Character Meal. Also available but not included are wine and beer.

Essentials

Attractions

Hotels

Restaurants

Special Events

Recreation

Resources

THE HOLLYWOOD BROWN DERBY

See the "Essentials" section for
Dining Selection Guides.

Classic American Cuisine

Food: The Hollywood Brown Derby serves charbroiled beef, grilled lamb and pork, sautéed veal, roasted chicken, seafood, and pasta. Many of the menu items change weekly.

Atmosphere: Red carpet paves the way through the two-tiered Hollywood Brown Derby. The main dining area has white linen–covered tables favored by visiting celebrities. Booths line the walls of the surrounding upper tier, and there are shaded tables on the outdoor patio. The restaurant's mahogany wainscoting, chandeliers, airy lace curtains, and heavy velvet drapes impart the atmosphere of vintage Hollywood power dining. The restaurant's signature collection of caricatures adorns the walls, and Streetmosphere performers, impersonating such Hollywood figures as Hedda Hopper, mingle with diners to search out good gossip or provide musical interludes on the piano in the main dining area.

Sample Dinner Entrees: Seared Salmon (served over saffron risotto, with julienne carrots, asparagus, and crispy leeks); Grilled Tournedos of Beef Tenderloin (with seared mushrooms, asparagus, creamy maytag blue cheese, and crushed fingerling potato mash); Brown Derby Cobb Salad (with chopped greens, turkey breast, bacon, egg, tomatoes, crumbled blue cheese, avocado, chives, and Cobb dressing).

Healthy-Choice Entrees: Pan Seared Tofu (with a spicy tomato glaze, quinoa, roasted vegetables, and fried spinach); Half Roasted Chicken (rubbed with garlic and black peppercorn spice, served with crushed fingerling potato mash, pencil asparagus, and black truffle rosemary jus).

Lunch: The lunch menu features more salads and sandwiches than the dinner menu. Prices are slightly lower at lunch.

Beverages: The wine list offers a selection of vintage California wines. Beer and spirits are also available, as are mineral water, soft drinks, tea, coffee, espresso, and cappuccino. Several after-dinner drinks are featured, including vintage ports and the specialty drink Cafe Henry III, a blend of Kahlúa, brandy, Galliano, Grand Marnier, and coffee.

Disney-MGM Studios

Location — The Hollywood Brown Derby is housed in a Mediterranean-style building on the plaza at the end of Hollywood Boulevard in Disney-MGM Studios. It is across the plaza from the Chinese Theater.

Dining Hours — Lunch from 11 AM, dinner from 4:30 PM until park closing.

Average Price Range — Lunch entrees **$$**, dinner entrees **$$$$**.

Features & Tips — The Hollywood Brown Derby is quite popular and usually fully booked, especially during peak vacation seasons. It can be difficult to secure same-day reservations.

Hollywood Brown Derby is one of the Disney-MGM Studios restaurants that offers a "Fantasmic!" seating package. While eating lunch or dinner, guests can reserve seats to the "Fantasmic!" show. Be sure to ask your server.

Reservations — Visitors to Walt Disney World can make reservations between 60 and 120 days in advance by calling Disney Dining Reservations (407 939-3463). Same-day reservations can be made at Hollywood Junction (at the intersection of Hollywood and Sunset Boulevards) inside Disney-MGM Studios or by calling Disney Dining after 10 AM (939-3463).

Restaurants at the Attractions • Restaurants at the Resorts

Essentials

Attractions

Hotels

Restaurants • Restaurants at the Resorts • Restaurants at the Attractions

Special Events

Recreation

Resources

HOUSE OF BLUES

*See the "Essentials" section for
Dining Selection Guides.*

West Side at Downtown Disney

Mississippi Delta Cuisine

Location — House of Blues is located on the waterfront at Disney's West Side, near Cirque du Soleil's performance hall.

Dining Hours — Open all day from 11 AM until 2 AM.

Average Price Range — Entrees **$$**. Gospel Brunch **$$$$**.

Features & Tips — A jazz band plays nightly in the restaurant, starting about 11 PM.

A Gospel Brunch is served Sundays in the concert hall. After eating from the all-you-care-to-eat buffet, a lively gospel spiritual is performed by some of the most talented gospel singers in the area.

Concerts are held in the concert hall almost nightly. Tickets to these shows can be bought at the ticket booth located near the entrance. Buying tickets here eliminates a surcharge that is charged at other ticket brokers.

Reservations — No reservations are accepted; diners are seated on a first-come, first-served basis. To make reservations for the Gospel Brunch, call the House of Blues (407 934-2583).

Food: The House of Blues serves updated Mississippi Delta dishes that incorporate fresh seasonal ingredients. Pastas, barbecued meats, hamburgers, and wood-fired pizzas are prepared with a New Orleans point of view. The restaurant is known for its Jambalaya.

Atmosphere: The House of Blues resembles a dilapidated old southern home. Folk art, scattered musical instruments, a medley of bold colors and textures, and dim lighting create a warm, funky dining environment. The Bluesmobile, an icon from the movie *The Blues Brothers,* is parked outside. Video and audio monitors situated throughout the restaurant play tribute to blues greats. A jazz trio entertains while guests dine.

Sample Dinner Entrees: Smoked Double Cut Pork Chop (with bourbon-cider sauce, mashed sweet potatoes, and sautèed vegetables); Classic New Orleans Shrimp Po-Boy (served with French fries and coleslaw); Creole Jambalaya (with shrimp, chicken, tasso ham, and Andouille sausage); Sauteed North Atlantic Salmon (with shrimp and eggplant stuffing, crab claws, and lemon butter).

Healthy-Choice Entrees: Grilled Rosemary Marinated Breast of Chicken (served with mashed potatoes and sauteed vegetables); Roasted Portobello Mushroom Sandwich (on toasted whole grain bread with Roma tomatoes, smoked Gouda cheese, and radish sprouts, served with a watercress jicama salad).

Lunch: The menu is the same for lunch and dinner.

Gospel Brunch: Every Sunday, House of Blues puts on an all-you-care-to-eat southern style buffet followed by a gospel celebration. There are two seatings at 10:30 AM and 1 PM. The menu includes a Gourmet Omelette Station, Barbecued Chicken, Sausage and Bacon, Chicken Jambalaya, Garlic Roasted Potatoes, Jalapeno Cornbread, Mini-muffins, Prime Rib Carving Station, Peel and Eat Shrimp, Caesar and Pasta salads, and Bread Pudding with Whisky Sauce.

Beverages: Soft drinks, juices, coffee, cappuccino, and espresso are available. The full bar serves domestic and imported beers, vintage wines, spirits, and specialty drinks.

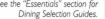
Canadian–American Cuisine

Food: Le Cellier is a full-service Canadian steakhouse, the only theme park restaurant that offers steaks, prime rib, and seafood as the featured cuisine. Traditional dishes are prepared with an updated twist and gourmet ingredients. Midwestern cornfed beef is prominent on the menu.

Atmosphere: The warmth of Canadian hospitality along with the cool, comfortable feeling of dining inside a giant wine cellar welcomes guests at Le Cellier Steakhouse. Thick stone walls are adorned with wrought-iron lanterns, and dramatic archways divide the dining room into several smaller, more intimate areas. The dark wood panels that line the walls are topped here and there with ironwork fashioned into Canadian maple leaf patterns. Guests are seated at tables surrounded by tapestry-upholstered high-back chairs.

Sample Dinner Entrees: Midwestern Cornfed Steak (prepared to order, served with roasted potatoes gratin); Grilled Pork T-Bone (served over smashed potatoes with an apple rhubarb chutney); Venison Osso Buco (tender Cabernet braised venison shank garnished with Parmesan smashed potatoes and braised root vegetables); Roasted Mushroom Chevre Ravioli (served with pan seared rock shrimp tossed with fresh autumn vegetables).

Healthy-Choice Entrees: Maple Glazed Canadian Salmon (served over a wild rice and barley blend with market-inspired vegetables); Grilled Vegetarian Napoleon (portobello mushroom layered with yellow squash, roasted peppers, oven dried tomato, and black bean spread).

Lunch: Lunch and dinner menus are similar, and most entrees are available at both meals. However, lunch prices are somewhat lower and the menu also features hamburgers and meal-sized salads, such as a Moullard Duck Confit Salad.

Beverages: In keeping with the wine-cellar atmosphere, Le Cellier Steakhouse features an exclusive selection of Inniskillin Wines from the Niagara Peninsula. La Batt's and Molson's beer are served, along with a variety of Canadian wines. Coffee, tea, mineral water, and soft drinks are also offered.

The World Showcase at Epcot

Location — The entrance to Le Cellier Steakhouse is at the side of the Canada pavilion in the World Showcase at Epcot. Guests can reach it by walking down the ramp along the river flowing through the flowering Victoria Gardens.

Dining Hours — Lunch from 11:30 AM, dinner from 4:30 PM until park closing.

Average Price Range — Lunch entrees **$$$**, dinner entrees **$$$$**.

Features & Tips — Le Cellier may have one of the best entrances in the World Showcase. To reach the restaurant, guests meander through gorgeous flowering gardens, with a view of a rugged, tree-topped mountain and gently flowing stream.

On hot afternoons, this dimly lit restaurant is a great place to relax and cool off. The best time to go is about 2 PM, when the lunch crowd is gone.

The restaurant's location at the center of Epcot makes it an excellent rendezvous spot for visitors who have been touring separately.

Reservations — Visitors to Walt Disney World can make reservations between 60 and 120 days in advance by calling Disney Dining Reservations (407 939-3463). Same-day reservations can be made by calling Disney Dining after 10 AM (939-3463). They can also be made at the Disney Dining telephone kiosks located in the Germany Pavilion and at Guest Relations in Future World.

Essentials

Attractions

Hotels

Restaurants • Restaurants at the Attractions

Restaurants at the Resorts

Special Events

Recreation

Resources

LIBERTY TREE TAVERN

See the "Essentials" section for Dining Selection Guides.

The Magic Kingdom

Location — The restaurant is located at Liberty Square in the Magic Kingdom. It is housed in a colonial-style building across from the Liberty Square Riverboat Landing.

Dining Hours — Lunch from 11:30 AM, dinner from 4 PM until park closing.

Average Price Range — Lunch entrees **$$**, Character Dinner **$$$$**.

Features & Tips — On hot days, Liberty Tree Tavern is a great place to relax and cool off. At about 2 PM, the lunch crowds have gone and seating is often available without a reservation.

    The familiar American dishes at this restaurant make it a Magic Kingdom favorite for guests of all ages. The New England Clam Chowder is a lunch favorite among frequent guests.

    Same-day reservations can be very difficult to get during peak seasons, and noise levels can be quite high.

Reservations — Visitors to Walt Disney World can make reservations between 60 and 120 days in advance by calling Disney Dining Reservations (407 939-3463). Same-day reservations can be made at City Hall on Main Street or by calling Disney Dining after 10 AM (939-3463).

Traditional American Cuisine & Character Dinner

Food: Liberty Tree Tavern features a Character Dinner with an Early American menu including turkey, steak, and ham. Traditional roast turkey accompanied with all the trimmings is available on the lunch menu every day, as are several New England–style dishes.

Atmosphere: The Liberty Tree Tavern immerses guests in the atmosphere of an eighteenth-century American dining hall, with pegged wood flooring and paned-glass windows. The restaurant is divided into six themed dining areas, each decorated with reproductions of items associated with a famous historical figure, such as Ben Franklin's printing press and Betsy Ross' eyeglasses. One wall is fashioned from rough-cut stone and features a massive fireplace with an oak mantel. Iron candelabra hang from the beamed ceilings, and pewter and copper artifacts decorate the walls and moldings.

Character Dinner: The all-you-care-to-eat menu includes Salad, Honey-Mustard Ham, Roasted Turkey Breast, Marinated Flank Steak, Mashed Potatoes, Garden Vegetables, Macaroni and Cheese, and Herb Bread Stuffing. Beverages are included with the meal; dessert, however, is not.

Healthy-Choice Entrees: Fresh from the Harbor (fresh catch of the day); Independence Salad (sautéed shrimp and scallops blended with fresh greens, tossed with strawberry vinaigrette dressing); Capitol Idea (a medley of vegetables and red beans tossed in herb oil, served with vegetable rice).

Lunch: The lunch menu offers special salads and sandwiches, as well as hot entrees such as New England Pot Roast (braised beef in a Burgundy wine sauce, served with mashed potatoes and sautéed garden vegetables); Chesapeake Cheddar (an array of seafood in white wine sauce served in a pastry shell and topped with Cheddar cheese, accompanied with sautéed garden vegetables).

Beverages: Coffee, tea, soft drinks, juice, espresso, and cappuccino are served. The Star-Spangled Sherbet Punch, a special nonalcoholic thirst quencher, is served in a Liberty Tree Tavern souvenir glass.

L'ORIGINALE ALFREDO DI ROMA RISTORANTE

See the "Essentials" section for Dining Selection Guides.

Italian Cuisine

Food: L'Originale Alfredo di Roma Ristorante serves Italian cuisine and freshly made pasta with a selection of sauces. The featured pasta is Le Originali Fettuccine Alfredo, a creation of the namesake restaurant in Rome. Also on the menu are chicken, veal, and seafood dishes prepared in regional styles.

Atmosphere: Photographs of international celebrities cover the walls of the restaurant's spacious entry area, where waiting guests are seated beneath an elaborate crystal chandelier. The elegant dining area, with mauve velvet chairs and pink tablecloths, has large windows looking out onto the piazza. The walls are covered with masterful trompe l'oeil murals depicting scenes from Italian country estates. Strolling musicians create a festive dining experience as they wander the room singing and playing Italian ballads and operatic arias.

Sample Dinner Entrees: Costoletta di Vitello Salsa al Chianti e Tartufo Nero (grilled veal chop with Chianti and black truffle sauce, sautéed mushrooms, and fresh asparagus, served with roasted potatoes); Ziti alla Mediterranea (ziti pasta with a cold sauce of fresh mozzarella, Sicilian olives, fresh tomatoes, and basil); Le Originali Fettuccine Alfredo (house-made wide-noodle pasta tossed with butter and Parmesan cheese); Trenette con Coda di Aragosta Fradiavola (linguine with lobster tail in a slightly spicy sauce made with lobster bisque, tomato, and a touch of cognac).

Healthy-Choice Entrees: Salmone Fresco al Limone e Capperi (North Atlantic salmon sautéed in a lemon, white wine, and caper sauce, served with roasted potatoes and spinach); Polletto Ruspante di Campagna (roasted free-range chicken with rosemary and sage served with roasted potatoes and vegetables).

Lunch: Lunch and dinner menus are similar, although there are more veal dishes at dinner. Prices are slightly lower at lunch than at dinner.

Beverages: Wine, beer, soft drinks, tea, and coffee are served, along with espresso and cappuccino. The wine list includes selections from various regions of Italy.

The World Showcase at Epcot

Location — The restaurant is located across from the cascading Fontana di Nettuno, at the back of the Italy pavilion in the World Showcase at Epcot. Guests pass under a white-pillared portico, softly lit at night by hanging lanterns, to enter the palatial pink-stuccoed building.

Dining Hours — Lunch from 12 noon, dinner from 4 PM until park closing.

Average Price Range — Lunch entrees **$$**, dinner entrees **$$$$**.

Features & Tips — The restaurant's pasta is made fresh daily on the premises. Guests can watch the pasta-making process through the large kitchen windows.

Since this is one of the most popular restaurants in the World Showcase, it can be extremely difficult to book same-day reservations for dinner.

The tables are set very close together, and this busy restaurant can be quite noisy at mealtimes.

Reservations — Visitors to Walt Disney World can make reservations between 60 and 120 days in advance by calling Disney Dining Reservations (407 939-3463). Same-day reservations can be made by calling Disney Dining after 10 AM (939-3463). They can also be made at the Disney Dining telephone kiosks located in the Germany Pavilion and at Guest Relations in Future World.

MAMA MELROSE'S RISTORANTE ITALIANO

See the "Essentials" section for Dining Selection Guides.

Disney-MGM Studios

Location — The restaurant is tucked away in the New York Street Backlot, "behind" New York Street and just around the corner from Muppet*Vision 3D at Disney-MGM Studios.

Dining Hours — Lunch from 11 AM, dinner from 4 PM until park closing.

Average Price Range — Lunch entrees **$$**, dinner entrees **$$**.

Features & Tips — The oak wood–burning brick ovens and a hardwood charbroiler enable chefs to produce top-quality grilled pizzas and meats. The individual-sized pizzas are popular appetizers.

Mama Melrose's is a pleasant place to drop in for a beverage in the afternoon, once the mealtime crowds have gone. Guests are seated at dinner tables and given fresh-baked bread with seasoned olive oil to snack on.

Visitors can enjoy a quiet and unhurried meal by avoiding the peak dining hours.

Reservations — Visitors to Walt Disney World can make reservations between 60 and 120 days in advance by calling Disney Dining Reservations (407 939-3463). Same-day reservations can be made at Hollywood Junction (at the intersection of Hollywood and Sunset Boulevards) inside Disney-MGM Studios or by calling Disney Dining after 10 AM (939-3463).

Italian Cuisine

Food: Mama Melrose's serves Italian cuisine with a California flair and thin-crust pizzas baked in an oak wood–burning oven. Beef, veal, fresh fish, and chicken are prepared with a variety of Italian sauces. An all-you-care-to-eat pasta special is featured, topped with a choice of traditional Italian sauces.

Atmosphere: Mama Melrose's is permeated with delicious smells from the wood-burning ovens and open kitchen where guests can catch a view of the chefs preparing meals. The rafters and walls are festooned with grapevines, hanging wine bottles, tiny lights, and other paraphernalia. The dim lighting evokes the feeling of twilight. Hardwood floors, red-and green-checked tablecloths, and loud good humor create an offbeat trattoria atmosphere.

Sample Dinner Entrees: Grilled Chicken Pizza (with pesto, spinach, bacon, and Asiago cheese); Grilled Prime Rib Steak (with pappardella pasta, charred sweet peppers, onions, tomatoes, and Gorgonzola); Orecchiette Pasta (with chicken, broccoli, and bacon tossed in Parmesan cream sauce). Dinner entrees include soup or salad.

Healthy-Choice Entrees: Sophia's Wood-Fired California Vegetables (fresh vegetables marinated in a pesto dressing and cooked over a wood-fired grill); Grilled Atlantic Salmon (fresh salmon with portobello mushrooms, spinach, and a carmelized garlic red wine sauce); Linguine Fra Diabolo (with clams, shrimp, mussels, and calamari tossed in a spicy marinara sauce).

Lunch: Lunch and dinner menus are similar, although prices are slightly lower at lunch and entrees do not include soup or salad.

Beverages: Californian and Italian wines are featured at Mama Melrose's. Coffee, tea, soft drinks, espresso, and cappuccino are offered, as are beer and spirits. The Sicilian Margarita, a house favorite, is made with Jose Cuervo tequila, Cointreau, lime juice, sweet and sour, and fresh orange juice.

NINE DRAGONS

See the "Essentials" section for Dining Selection Guides.

Chinese Cuisine

Food: Nine Dragons Restaurant serves several different styles of Chinese cuisine: light and mild Mandarin, hot and spicy Szechuan and Hunan, subtly flavored Cantonese, and internationally inspired Kiangche from Shanghai. Meats, poultry, seafood, and vegetables are prepared with a variety of seasonings and sauces. The menu was created by the chefs at the Beijing Hotel in China.

Atmosphere: An elaborately carved rosewood partition dominates the entry to the large open dining room of the Nine Dragons Restaurant. Plush, dark cranberry-colored carpeting, black-lacquered chairs, intricately painted ceilings, and white linen tablecloths give the dining room a formal atmosphere. Ornate paper lanterns add to the light that pours in from octagonal windows. The tables in the front of the restaurant offer a good view of the World Showcase promenade.

Sample Dinner Entrees: Beef in Spicy Sha Cha Sauce (sliced beef stir-fried with baby corn, snow peas, zucchini, and carrots); Rainbow Kang Bao Chicken (stir-fried chicken with peanuts, vegetables, dried hot peppers, and spicy Kang Bao sauce); Treasure Duck (boneless duckling braised and deep-fried, served with sweet and sour sauce); Imperial Cone Fish (Beijing-style, crispy whole deboned fish glazed with a sweet and sour sauce); Stir Fried Shrimp with Garden Vegetables (stir-fried in spicy black bean sauce with green pepper). All entrees are served with rice and tea.

Healthy-Choice Entrees: Saucy Chicken (stir-fried chicken, onions, carrots, and green peas); Eggplant Sautéed in Garlic Sauce (Chinese eggplants, sautéed in a savory garlic sauce); Ma Po Tofu (diced tofu stir-fried in Szechuan spicy sauce).

Lunch: Lunch and dinner menus are similar, although prices of some dishes are quite a bit lower at lunch.

Beverages: Wine, Tsing Tao beer, and spirits are served. Fresh melon juice is available, as are soft drinks, mineral water, coffee, and tea. The restaurant features several specialty drinks, including the Shanghai Surprise, made with ginseng, brandy, rum, grapefruit, lemon, and orange juice; and the Xian Quencher, a mixture of fresh melon juice and rum or vodka.

The World Showcase at Epcot

Location — The restaurant, a reproduction of the Summer Palace in Beijing, is located just past the Gate of the Golden Sun at the China pavilion in the World Showcase at Epcot. It is entered through an elaborately carved arched doorway.

Dining Hours — Lunch from 12 noon, dinner from 4:30 PM until park closing.

Average Price Range — Lunch entrees **$$**, dinner entrees **$$$$**.

Features & Tips — It is fairly easy to secure same-day or last-minute reservations for lunch and dinner at Nine Dragons.

Popular dishes among frequent diners are the Kang Bao Chicken and Beef in Spicy Sha Cha Sauce.

Dishes are served as individual meals with rice (with the exception of one family sampler) rather than family style as in most Chinese restaurants in the United States. Many visitors consider the restaurant overpriced.

Reservations — Visitors to Walt Disney World can make reservations between 60 and 120 days in advance by calling Disney Dining Reservations (407 939-3463). Same-day reservations can be made by calling Disney Dining after 10 AM (939-3463). They can also be made at the Disney Dining telephone kiosks located in the Germany Pavilion and at Guest Relations in Future World.

OFFICIAL ALL STAR CAFE

See the "Essentials" section for Dining Selection Guides.

Attractions

Hotels

Restaurants • Restaurants at the Attractions

Restaurants at the Resorts

Special Events

Recreation

Resources

Disney's Wide World of Sports

Location — The Official All Star Cafe is located at Disney's Wide World of Sports, near the main entrance to Walt Disney World off Highway 192.

Dining Hours — Open all day from 11 AM, closes at 1 AM.

Average Price Range — Entrees **$$**.

Features & Tips — The Official All Star Cafe features dreamy milk shakes and spectacular desserts. The two most popular desserts among regulars are the Banana Split Cheesecake (guaranteed to satisfy any sweet tooth) and the Chocolate Chip Cookie Supreme (a must for chocolate lovers).

This is the closest full-service restaurant for guests staying at Disney's All-Star Resorts and is a great place for late-night dining after a long day in the theme parks.

During peak dining times, there can be a long wait for seating.

The restaurant's loud music levels can make conversation very difficult. This is a place to soak up the atmosphere and goings-on.

From time to time, bright lights play across the room. If strobe lights bother you, request a table in an unaffected area.

Reservations — No reservations are accepted; diners are seated on a first-come, first-served basis.

Casual American Cuisine

Food: The Official All Star Cafe serves chicken, steaks, seafood, pasta, pizza, huge salads, and hamburgers with a beef, turkey, or veggie patty.

Atmosphere: Giant photos of athletes and signs that spin with flashing lights mark the entrance to this restaurant. Inside, the walls are lined with an amazing array of sports memorabilia, and racing cars and other sports vehicles hang from the ceiling. A huge scoreboard sits above the central bar, and projection screens and video monitors are scattered throughout the dining room. While dining, guests can watch televised sports events and sports-themed videos selected by a live VJ, who provides updates on breaking scores and other happenings. The Official All Star Cafe is part of the Planet Hollywood restaurant group.

Sample Dinner Entrees: All American Chicken Fried Chicken; Wayne's Cracked Ribs; Bull Penne Smoked Chicken and Broccoli; Gameday Grilled Tuna Sandwich (served with fries); Tomahawk Turkey Steak.

Healthy-Choice Entrees: Griffey's Grilled Chicken Sandwich (served with fries, onion rings, or baked potato); Andre's Ace Pomodoro.

Lunch: The menu is the same for both lunch and dinner.

Beverages: The Official All Star Cafe serves beer, wine, and spirits, including specialty drinks such as The All Star (Absolut vodka, Bacardi rum, Chambord, and Triple Sec with a splash of sour mix and cranberry juice, served in a take-home sports bottle) and The Super Bowl (Cuervo Gold, Cointreau, shaken with sweet and sour mix, served with a ring of salt). Milk shakes, malts, lemonade, soft drinks, tea, and coffee are also served, as are cappuccino, latte, mocha, and espresso.

American & International Cuisine

Food: Most of the dishes at Planet Hollywood were developed by the restaurant chain's creative owners and highly skilled chefs. Entrees include salads, hamburgers, pasta, pizza, ribs, chicken, steak, and the chef's special seasonal entrees, all served in generous portions.

Atmosphere: A long canopied stairway (perfect for that "Hollywood" entrance) leads up to the intricately designed tri-level restaurant. Each level reflects a different movie genre, such as science fiction or action-adventure, and props and memorabilia from famous films hang from the walls and ceilings. There are two bars, and enormous monitors show music videos, film clips, and scenes from Planet Hollywood grand openings around the world. A new outdoor dining plaza encircling part of the bright blue globe provides bird's-eye views of the busy entrance to West Side. There's an air of excitement here — the sense that a celebrity could show up at any moment. Planet Hollywood is always busy, its staff is upbeat, and its razzle-dazzle ambience is memorable.

Sample Dinner Entrees: Chicken Penne and Broccoli (grilled chicken, fresh broccoli, and penne pasta blended with roasted garlic cream sauce); Eggplant Parmesan Sandwich (breaded fresh eggplant slices, tomato sauce, mozzarella, and Parmesan on herb foccacia, served with penne pasta); Fajitas (choice of chicken, beef, or a combination, with a traditional presentation of whole-wheat tortillas, guacamole, pico de gallo, sour cream, and mixed cheeses, served with black beans and Mexican rice).

Healthy-Choice Entrees: Gardenburger (a meatless patty made from fresh mushrooms, onions, low-fat cheese, seasonings, and spices, served on a Hollywood roll with lettuce, tomato, red onions, and dill pickle); Yaki Soba (stir fry bell peppers, cabbage, ginger, onion, and Japanese noodles in teriyaki rice wine sauce with Chinese lemon grass, with chicken or portobello mushroom).

Lunch: The menu is the same for lunch and dinner.

Beverages: Along with beer, champagne, and wine, Planet Hollywood features a large selection of specialty drinks in souvenir glasses, including Alize in Wonderland (a mixture of Finlandia vodka, Alize Red, and orange juice). Coffee, tea, and soft drinks are also served, as are espresso and cappuccino.

Pleasure Island at Downtown Disney

Location — Planet Hollywood is located at Pleasure Island, across from the AMC Theatres and Disney's West Side. Hovering dramatically over the lagoon inside a gigantic blue celestial sphere, the restaurant is impossible to miss.

Dining Hours — Open all day from 11 AM, closes at 2 AM.

Average Price Range — Entrees **$$**.

Features & Tips — Parties of six can reserve a "VIP room" (one of two semi private rooms with an adjustable sound system) 24 hours in advance. When the reservation time comes up, parties are taken to their seats immediately.

A popular dish with frequent guests is the Chicken Crunch appetizer, chicken strips breaded with a crunchy sweet coating, served with Creole mustard sauce.

Arrive before 11 AM for lunch and before 5 PM or after 9 PM for dinner to ensure a short wait time.

Reservations — No reservations are accepted; diners are seated on a first-come, first-served basis. To reserve a VIP room only, call 407 827-7827.

Essentials

Attractions

Hotels

Restaurants at the Resorts • Restaurants at the Attractions   Restaurants

Special Events

Recreation

Resources

THE PLAZA RESTAURANT

See the "Essentials" section for
Dining Selection Guides.

The Magic Kingdom

Location — The Plaza is located at the end of Main Street to the right, facing Cinderella Castle in the Magic Kingdom. It can also be reached from the walkway leading into Tomorrowland.

Dining Hours — Open all day from 11 AM until park closing.

Average Price Range — Entrees **$$**.

Features & Tips — Ice cream lovers will feel right at home in The Plaza Restaurant. In addition to the listed specialties, there is the Bicycle Built for Two, a create-your-own-fantasy ice cream treat.

The Plaza Restaurant is a great place to come in and cool off on hot afternoons after the lunch crowd has thinned out. Ask to be seated at a table on the veranda.

For health-conscious diners, fountain specialties can be prepared with nonfat and sugar-free ice cream.

The Plaza is very popular. Since no advance reservations are taken, there are sometimes long lines during peak dining times. Waits can be up to an hour.

Reservations — No reservations are accepted; diners are seated on a first-come, first-served basis.

American Deli Cuisine

Food: The Plaza Restaurant offers a typical American lunchroom menu of grilled and cold sandwiches and hamburgers. Its biggest draw, however, is a whimsical selection of soda fountain treats, including the Magic Kingdom's best and largest ice cream sundae.

Atmosphere: The Plaza Restaurant is housed in an ornate Victorian building with a light-filled atrium veranda off to the side. The interior has splendid Art Nouveau touches, with carved white wall panels and an array of gold-etched mirrors. Marble-topped tables are scattered throughout the cheerful dining room, which has an abundance of windows topped with gauzy white valances. The view from the round veranda takes in both Cinderella Castle and the sci-fi archway to Tomorrowland. As a tribute to the restaurant's turn-of-the-century atmosphere, waitresses wear long Victorian-style dresses.

Sample Dinner Entrees: Cheesesteak Sandwich (beef grilled with onions, provolone and mozzarella cheeses, served on a freshly baked roll); Grilled Turkey Sandwich (smoked turkey, melted mozzarella cheese, bacon, tomato, and onion on wheat bread); Reuben Sandwich (corned beef, Swiss cheese, sauerkraut, and Thousand Island dressing grilled on marble rye bread); Grilled Onion and Mushroom Burger (ground hamburger served with lettuce, tomato, onion, and provolone cheese, served with fries,). All sandwiches are served with German-style potato salad.

Healthy-Choice Entrees: Chef's Salad (garden greens and tomatoes tossed with ham, turkey, Swiss cheese, and choice of dressing); Fresh Vegetable Sandwich (sliced cucumber, squash, alfalfa sprouts, tomato, and Swiss cheese on multi-grain bread with dill spread). On request, sandwiches can be prepared on reduced-calorie bread.

Lunch: The same menu is offered throughout the day.

Beverages: Coffee, tea, soft drinks, and juice are served, and espresso, cappuccino, and cafe mocha are also featured. Creamy Hand-Dipped Milk Shakes, the Plaza's signature specialty, come in vanilla, chocolate, and strawberry. Ice cream floats and sodas are also available.

PORTOBELLO YACHT CLUB

See the "Essentials" section for
Dining Selection Guides.

Italian Cuisine

Food: Portobello Yacht Club has an extensive menu of regional Italian cuisine, including individual thin-crust pizzas, original pasta creations, and seafood flown in fresh daily. Also served are charcoal-grilled steaks, chicken, and veal flavored with fresh herbs and roasted in the restaurant's wood-burning oven.

Atmosphere: Despite its Italian name, Portobello Yacht Club seems to capture the casual, breezy atmosphere of a New England yacht club. High-beamed ceilings shelter an array of nautical paraphernalia and an entire wall of yachting photos. The tables are covered in white and mint-green tablecloths, with a decorative Italian plate at each setting. The long, comfortable mahogany bar is accented with brass and surrounded with black leather stools. Portobello's has several nooks and crannies for more intimate dining.

Sample Dinner Entrees: Grigliata di Vitello con Capellini (veal flank marinated with garlic and parsley, charcoal grilled, sliced over capellini pasta with crimini mushrooms and tomato basil cream sauce); Spaghettini alla Portobello (Alaskan crab legs, scallops, clams, and shrimp with tomatoes, garlic, olive oil, wine, and herbs, lightly tossed with spaghettini pasta); Bistecca alla Griglia (grilled ribeye steak topped with a Parmigiano cheese crust, served with roasted garlic whipped potatoes and seasonal vegetables); Gamberi con Fettuccine (fettuccine pasta with charcoal grilled gulf shrimp, asparagus, and roasted garlic white wine cream sauce).

Healthy-Choice Entrees: Linguine con Vongole (linguine pasta with fresh Manila clams, garlic, white wine, plum tomatoes, and parsley); Pollo alla Griglia (grilled semi-boneless half chicken with roasted garlic whipped potatoes, rosemary sauce, and seasonal vegetables).

Lunch: Lunch and dinner menus are similar; prices are somewhat lower at lunch.

Beverages: Coffee, cappuccino, and espresso are offered. Caffè Portobello, a specialty of the house, is concocted with Grand Marnier and Frangelico. Wine, beer, and spirits are served. The impressive wine list features several exceptional California and Italian wines.

Pleasure Island at Downtown Disney

Location — Portobello Yacht Club is located at Pleasure Island at Downtown Disney and faces The Marketplace. The restaurant's entrance is located outside of Pleasure Island.

Dining Hours — Open all day, lunch from 11:30 AM, dinner from 4 PM until midnight.

Average Price Range — Lunch entrees **$$**, dinner entrees **$$$$**.

Features & Tips — The restaurant features one of Walt Disney World's most extensive selections of grappa, single-malt Scotch, and cognac.

Portobello Yacht Club is popular among frequent visitors and, along with Fulton's Crab House and the Wildhorse Saloon, is one of the few late-night full-service restaurants at Walt Disney World.

Tables for two are very hard to get when the restaurant is crowded, and there can be long waits.

Reservations — Visitors to Walt Disney World can make reservations up to 60 days in advance by calling the Portobello Yacht Club (407 934-8888). The restaurant has a smoking area.

Essentials

Attractions

Hotels

Restaurants • Restaurants at the Resorts • Restaurants at the Attractions

Special Events

Recreation

Resources

RAINFOREST CAFE

*See the "Essentials" section for
Dining Selection Guides.*

Animal Kingdom & The Marketplace

Location — Rainforest Cafe has two locations at Walt Disney World. One, at The Marketplace, is distinguished by the sixty-five-foot "active" volcano situated above it. A second Rainforest Cafe is located at the entrance of Animal Kingdom.

Dining Hours — The Animal Kingdom location serves breakfast from 7:30 until 9:30 AM, and lunch and dinner from 10:30 AM until 8 PM. The Marketplace location is open all day from 10:30 AM until 11 PM; midnight on weekends.

Average Price Range — Breakfast entrees **$$**, lunch and dinner entrees **$$$**.

Features & Tips — While waiting for a table, the Rainforest Cafe's gift shop is a fun place to browse. It sells nature-themed items from all over the globe, many highlighting endangered animals.

For a small fee, guests can join the Safari Club, which entitles members to guaranteed reservations for larger parties, "awards" towards restaurant and retail purchases, a newsletter, and special offers.

Reservations — Visitors to Walt Disney World can make reservations at the Animal Kingdom location between 60 and 120 days in advance by calling Disney Dining Reservations (407 939-3463).

Reservations for the Downtown Disney location can be made between 60 and 120 days in advance by calling the Rainforest Cafe at The Marketplace (407 827-8309).

World Cuisine

Food: The Rainforest Cafe serves up familiar ingredients prepared with a multicultural influence. Steak, chicken, seafood, pasta, pizza, and salads are presented in unique flavor combinations.

Atmosphere: The Rainforest Cafe has created a tropical jungle within its spacious dining rooms. Large trees and vines form a leafy canopy overhead. Among the cascading waterfalls and on overhanging cliffs, Audio-Animatronics animals inhabit the dining areas. Impressive aquariums filled with coral and tropical fish provide great views and soft glowing light. The environmental sounds of thunder, lightning, and rain are continuous, and visitors can always spot a wild animal or two monkeying around.

Sample Dinner Entrees: Rasta Pasta (bow tie pasta, grilled chicken, walnut pesto, broccoli, red peppers, spinach, and fresh herbs tossed in a garlic cream sauce); Rumble in the Jungle (roasted turkey tossed with Caesar salad and stuffed into a warm grilled pita bread, served with tomatoes and cranberry relish, and topped with crispy fried onions); Jamaica, Me Crazy! (grilled pork chops, dusted with Jamaican and Cajun seasonings, nestled on a bed of red beans and rice); China Island Chicken Salad (shredded lettuce, grilled chicken breast, rice noodles, shredded carrots, and chopped scallions, tossed with sesame seed dressing).

Healthy-Choice Entrees: The Southern Cross (vegetable lasagna layered with spinach, mushrooms, zucchini, Bermuda onions, eggplant, and fresh peppers, topped with salsa marinara and Parmesan); Pelican's Catch (catch of the day).

Breakfast: Breakfast fare, including omelets, steak and eggs, French toast, and breakfast pizza, is offered from 7:30 until 9:30 AM at the Animal Kingdom location only.

Lunch: The menu is the same for lunch and dinner.

Beverages: Soft drinks, fruit smoothies, and organic fruit and vegetable juices are served, as are coffee, espresso, cappuccino, and specialty coffee drinks. Wine, beer, and spirits are also available. The Rainforest Cafe features a variety of signature cocktails, including the Margarilla, a Margarita made with orange sherbet; and the Rainbow Colada, a combination of spiced rum, strawberries, banana, and pineapple.

RESTAURANT AKERSHUS

See the "Essentials" section for
Dining Selection Guides.

Norwegian Cuisine

Food: Restaurant Akershus features an all-you-care-to-eat Norwegian buffet known as a koldtbord. The cold selections include an array of Norwegian salads and smoked fish, and the hot dishes incorporate meat, poultry, seafood, and vegetables. Diners are encouraged to return to the buffet for separate courses, beginning with the appetizers, continuing with the cold buffet, and ending with hot entrees and cheeses.

Atmosphere: Restaurant Akershus is fashioned after the medieval castle fortress that spans most of Oslo, Norway's harbor. Its four dining areas feature such period touches as beamed cathedral ceilings hung with iron chandeliers, tall clerestory-style leaded-glass windows with lace curtains, and walls of massive whitewashed bricks broken by dramatic stone archways. Tables are set with crisp white tablecloths, and diners serve themselves at the long buffet. Servers bring beverages and take orders for dessert.

Sample Dinner Entrees: *Selections from the Cold Buffet* — Chicken Salad, Meat Salad, Potato Salad, Egg and Ham Salad, Assorted Herring, Chilled Shrimp, Smoked Salmon Scrambled Eggs, Roast Beef, Cheese Platter, and Stuffed Pork Loin. A variety of traditional breads is also available.

Selections from the Hot Buffet — Smoked Pork, Venison Strips, Meatballs in Gravy, Fresh Fish, Macaroni and Cheese. Side dishes include mashed rutabagas, fresh vegetables, and boiled red potatoes.

Vegetarian Selections — Mixed Green Salad, Pasta Salad, Cucumber Salad, Cabbage Salad, Vegetable Salad, and Tomato Salad.

Healthy-Choice Entrees: Fresh Fish, Smoked Mackerel, Chilled Shrimp, Vegetable Salad, Tomato Salad, Cucumber Salad, and Cabbage Salad.

Lunch: The food selection available at lunch and dinner varies slightly, although the price is quite a bit lower at lunch.

Beverages: Soft drinks, mineral water, tea, and coffee are available, as is Ringnes beer on tap. The wine list features a good selection from California vineyards, along with a more limited selection from France, Italy, and Portugal. Spirits are served, featuring Norway's Linie aquavit.

The World Showcase at Epcot

Location — The restaurant is located inside the Norway pavilion in the World Showcase at Epcot. The entrance is across the traditional town square from Kringla Bakeri og Kafé.

Dining Hours — Lunch from 11:30 AM, dinner from 4:30 PM until park closing.

Average Price Range — Lunch buffet **$$**, dinner buffet **$$$**.

Features & Tips — Since Norwegian cuisine is not well known, guests may find it easy to get same-day reservations or walk in and be seated.

The lower lunch price makes this buffet ideal for visitors eating their main meal at midday.

The restaurant is a favorite among many visitors, although some find the unfamiliar tastes unappealing. Before dining, walk in and look over the choices.

Vegetarian diners may find the variety of hot selections somewhat limited.

Reservations — Visitors to Walt Disney World can make reservations between 60 and 120 days in advance by calling Disney Dining Reservations (407 939-3463). Same-day reservations can be made by calling Disney Dining after 10 AM (939-3463). They can also be made at the Disney Dining telephone kiosks located in the Germany Pavilion and at Guest Relations in Future World.

RESTAURANT MARRAKESH

See the "Essentials" section for Dining Selection Guides.

The World Showcase at Epcot

Location — The restaurant is tucked away in the back of the Morocco pavilion in the World Showcase at Epcot. Guests can reach it by wandering past the courtyard fountain and following the passages through Morocco's exotic shopping bazaar.

Dining Hours — Lunch from 11:30 AM, dinner from 4 PM until park closing.

Average Price Range — Lunch entrees **$$$**, dinner entrees **$$$$**.

Features & Tips — Moroccan musicians and belly dancers entertain at both lunch and dinner. The unusual entertainment and the rich decor create an exotically romantic setting. Shows begin about 25 minutes after the hour.

Since many visitors are unfamiliar with Moroccan cuisine, it is often possible to dine without a reservation.

If planning a leisurely meal, let your server know. Service can sometimes be fast to a fault.

Reservations — Visitors to Walt Disney World can make reservations between 60 and 120 days in advance by calling Disney Dining Reservations (407 939-3463). Same-day reservations can be made by calling Disney Dining after 10 AM (939-3463). They can also be made at the Disney Dining telephone kiosks located in the Germany Pavilion and at Guest Relations in Future World.

Moroccan Cuisine

Food: Restaurant Marrakesh serves the cuisine of North Africa, featuring meats and fish cooked with aromatic spices, as well as couscous, a light and flavorful steamed-grain dish that is generally regarded as the national dish of Morocco.

Atmosphere: The opulent, multitiered Restaurant Marrakesh has slim carved pillars reaching up to a high ceiling that is hung with chandeliers and painted in the colorful geometric patterns of North Africa. The banquettes along the tiled walls provide seating in the upper-tier dining area, while the tables on the main floor below surround a small stage and dance floor where belly dancers and musicians perform. All the servers wear djellabas, the traditional long robes of Morocco.

Sample Dinner Entrees: Shish Kebab (grilled brochettes of beef marinated in Moroccan herbs and spices, served with vegetable couscous); Couscous (rolled semolina steamed and served with seasonal vegetables and a choice of chicken, lamb, or vegetables); Lemon Chicken (braised half chicken seasoned with garlic, green olives, and preserved lemon); Roast Lamb Meshoui (lamb roasted in natural juices, served with vegetable couscous); Sultan's Sampler (brochette of chicken, beef kefta, and beef shish kebab, served with yellow rice and vegetable couscous).

Healthy-Choice Entrees: Vegetable Couscous (rolled semolina steamed and served with seasonal vegetables); Brochette of Chicken (grilled brochettes of chicken breast marinated in Moroccan herbs and spices).

Lunch: Lunch and dinner menus are similar, and prices are slightly lower at lunch.

Beverages: Wine, beer, spirits, soft drinks, and mineral water are served. Along with coffee and espresso, atai benna'na', or fresh-brewed mint tea, is also offered. Restaurant Marrakesh features a special cocktail called Marrakesh Express, a mix of apricot brandy, orange juice, and cranberry juice, topped with peach schnapps. The wine list offers an interesting selection of French and Moroccan wines.

RESTAURANTOSAURUS

See the "Essentials" section for Dining Selection Guides.

Character Breakfast Buffet

Food: Restaurantosaurus hosts Donald's Prehistoric Breakfastosaurus, a Character Breakfast. The all-you-care-to-eat buffet features traditional American breakfast fare including pancakes, egg dishes, and breakfast meats. Starting at 11 AM, the building is open for counter service dining only and offers hot dogs, salads, and McDonald's menu items.

Atmosphere: Restaurantosaurus resembles a roadside diner founded in the midst of a dig site. The rustic wood and stone interior provides the backdrop for numerous dig artifacts. Each dining room has a theme, such as the recreation room, the garage, or the plaster room, a work area set aside to restore excavated fossils. Excavating tools, maps, dinosaur bones, and depictions of dinosaurs all pay homage to the life of a paleontologist. Friendly servers help set the tone of the dining experience. (Diners should be careful when asking for water — they most likely will become the target of a water pistol.) Explorers Mickey, Goofy, Donald, and Pluto visit during the meal.

Character Breakfast: The all-you-care-to-eat breakfast buffet includes Western Eggs, Hash Browns, Pancakes, French Toast, Sausage, Bacon, Scrambled Eggs, Oatmeal, Grits, Dino Eggs (tiny doughnuts), Dino Hash, Assorted Breads and Pastries, Fruit, and Assorted Cold Cereals.

Healthy-Choice Entrees: Oatmeal, Pancakes, Cold Cereals, and Fruit. Eggbeaters are available on request.

Lunch: During the day, from 11 AM until 5 PM, Restaurantosaurus becomes a counter-service restaurant. Cheeseburgers, hot dogs, and popular McDonald's menu items are offered.

Beverages: Juice, coffee, milk, hot chocolate, beer, and soft drinks are available.

Animal Kingdom

Location — Restaurantosaurus is located in Dinoland U.S.A., at Disney's Animal Kingdom. It is directly across the path from The Boneyard playground.

Dining Hours — Breakfast from 7 until 10:30 AM. Open all day for light counter-service meals.

Average Price Range — Character Breakfast **$$$**.

Features & Tips — Guests and families can have their pictures taken against a Dinoland U.S.A. backdrop while waiting to be seated for breakfast. The set-up is on the front porch near the podium. Developed pictures are brought to the table during the meal and diners have the option of purchasing them.

During lunch and dinner hours, when Restaurantosaurus offers counter-service dining only, Safari Amber beer is available. It is brewed especially for Disney's Animal Kingdom by Budweiser.

Reservations — Visitors to Walt Disney World can make Character Breakfast reservations 60 to 120 days in advance by calling Disney Dining Reservations (407 939-3463). Same-day seating can be arranged in person at the restaurant.

Essentials

Attractions

Hotels

Restaurants

Restaurants at the Resorts • Restaurants at the Attractions

Special Events

Recreation

Resources

ROSE & CROWN DINING ROOM

See the "Essentials" section for Dining Selection Guides.

The World Showcase at Epcot

British Cuisine

Location — The Rose & Crown Dining Room, housed in a charming old English countryside-style building, is the only full-service restaurant that sits on the edge of the World Showcase Lagoon. It is located directly across the promenade from the main pavilion at the United Kingdom.

Dining Hours — Lunch from 11:30 AM, dinner from 4:30 PM until park closing.

Average Price Range — Lunch entrees **$**, dinner entrees **$$$**.

Features & Tips — The lively Rose & Crown Pub is a favorite spot among frequent visitors from around the world. It's a great place for cocktails and conversation in a convivial setting.

The Rose & Crown's unique location on the World Showcase Lagoon and its wide outdoor terrace provide excellent views. Diners who have reserved a late dinner and are seated at a terrace table can watch IllumiNations from here.

The Rose & Crown fills its reservations quickly during peak seasons, so it can be difficult to secure same-day reservations.

Reservations — Visitors to Walt Disney World can make reservations between 60 and 120 days in advance by calling Disney Dining Reservations (407 939-3463). Same-day reservations can be made by calling Disney Dining after 10 AM (939-3463). They can also be made at the Disney Dining telephone kiosks located in the Germany Pavilion and at Guest Relations in Future World.

Food: The Rose & Crown Dining Room serves traditional British fare, including cottage pie, prime rib, and London-style fish and chips wrapped in newspaper.

Atmosphere: The Rose & Crown Dining Room features cozy pub-style architecture, with wood-plank flooring, mahogany wainscoting, and shiny hardwood tables. Milk glass chandeliers, white pressed-tin ceilings, and stained-glass room dividers provide atmospheric highlights. At the entrance to the Rose & Crown Pub is a stand-up wraparound mahogany bar with etched-glass paneling. The restaurant and its adjoining terrace overlook the World Showcase Lagoon.

Sample Dinner Entrees: London-style Fish & Chips (cod fried in beer batter, served with fried potatoes); Bangers and Mash (traditional English sausages accompanied with mashed potatoes and Yorkshire pudding); Prime Rib (served with oven-roasted potatoes, Yorkshire pudding, and seasonal vegetables); English Pie Sampler (miniature steak and mushroom, chicken and leek, and cottage pies, served with seasonal vegetables).

Healthy-Choice Entrees: Vegetable Curry (a mixture of seasonal vegetables sautéed with a spicy curry sauce, served over rice).

Lunch: The lunch menu differs slightly from dinner and includes a traditional Ploughman's Lunch (sliced turkey and ham served with English cheeses, a Branson pickle, and fresh baked potato bread). Lunch prices are lower than at dinner.

Beverages: Bass ale, Guinness stout, and lager are served chilled or at room temperature. Wine and spirits are offered, including specialty drinks such as the English Rose, a blend of gin, apricot brandy, sweet vermouth, pineapple juice, and orange and cranberry juice; and the Nutty Irishman, a mixture of Frangelico, Baileys Irish Cream, and half and half. Soft drinks, coffee, and tea are also available.

Essentials

Attractions

Hotels

Restaurants   Restaurants at the Attractions • Restaurants at the Resorts

Special Events

Recreation

Resources

SAN ANGEL INN RESTAURANTE

See the "Essentials" section for
Dining Selection Guides.

Mexican Cuisine

Food: San Angel Inn Restaurante features regional Mexican dishes and Tex-Mex favorites. Seafood, beef, and chicken are prepared in savory sauces enhanced with chilies and a wealth of Mexican spices.

Atmosphere: After entering Mexico, the only enclosed pavilion at the World Showcase, guests walk through a festive village setting at twilight to reach the restaurant at the edge of the river. A distant view of a smoking volcano and an exotic Mayan pyramid lend an aura of mystery to this romantic dining room. Red-sashed servers attend guests seated in rustic colonial-style tables and chairs. The restaurant is very dark, and tables are lit with lanterns.

Sample Dinner Entrees: Chiles en Nogada (chiles poblanos stuffed with pork picadillo, made with assorted fresh fruits, covered with a walnut sauce and garnished with pomegranate seeds and parsley, served with Mexican rice); Ensalada Mexicana (mixed greens with grilled chicken, tomatoes, avocado, sweet Mexican turnip, cheese and cactus strips, tossed in house dressing and served in a fried tortilla shell); Tacos de Pescado (grilled swordfish served in flour tortillas, served with coleslaw and pico de gallo).

Healthy-Choice Entrees: Filete de Mero en Achiote (grouper filet marinated in achiote and guajillo chilies, baked in a banana leaf and served with corn, chayote, and red bell pepper slaw); Pollo Con Fideos (grilled chicken breast served over angel hair pasta with tomatoes and chipotle pepper sauce).

Lunch: Lunch and dinner menus are similar, although lunch does not include soup or salad, and prices are much lower than at dinner.

Beverages: Mexican beers such as Bohemia, Dos Equis, and Tecate are served, as are wine and spirits. After-dinner drinks include Mexican Coffee (a mix of Kahlúa, tequila, and cream) and Café de Olla (coffee with cinnamon and brown sugar). Juice, soft drinks, mineral water, coffee, and tea are also available.

The World Showcase at Epcot

Location — San Angel Inn Restaurante can be found at the very back of the Mexico pavilion in the World Showcase at Epcot. The dining room overlooks a charming indoor river.

Dining Hours — Lunch from 11:30 AM, dinner from 4:30 PM until park closing.

Average Price Range — Lunch entrees **$$**, dinner entrees **$$$**.

Features & Tips — San Angel Inn Restaurante has a small adjacent lounge where diners can unwind and enjoy a Margarita with chips and salsa as they wait for a table.

San Angel Inn Restaurante is regarded by many visitors as one of the most romantic dining spots at Walt Disney World.

Reservations — Visitors to Walt Disney World can make reservations between 60 and 120 days in advance by calling Disney Dining Reservations (407 939-3463). Same-day reservations can be made by calling Disney Dining after 10 AM (939-3463). They can also be made at the Disney Dining telephone kiosks located in the Germany Pavilion and at Guest Relations in Future World.

Essentials

Attractions

Hotels

Restaurants • Restaurants at the Attractions

Restaurants at the Resorts

Special Events

Recreation

Resources

SCI-FI DINE-IN THEATER RESTAURANT

See the "Essentials" section for Dining Selection Guides.

Disney-MGM Studios

American Cuisine

Location — The restaurant is adjacent to the Chinese Theater at Disney-MGM Studios. Guests can find it by looking for the restaurant's sign, which resembles a movie theater marquee.

Dining Hours — Lunch from 11 AM, dinner from 4 PM until park closing.

Average Price Range — Lunch **$$**, dinner entrees **$$$**.

Features & Tips — Dining here can be a memorable experience for those who enjoy unique dining environments.

Watching science fiction and horror films while eating is literally out of this world, and the dining room is somewhat eerie and quiet because of the attention paid to the on-screen flicks. Not the place for conversation; except in a few cars, most guests face forward.

Reservations — Visitors to Walt Disney World can make reservations between 60 and 120 days in advance by calling Disney Dining Reservations (407 939-3463). Same-day reservations can be made at Hollywood Junction (at the intersection of Hollywood and Sunset Boulevards) inside Disney-MGM Studios, or by calling Disney Dining after 10 AM (939-3463).

Food: The Sci-Fi Dine-In Theater Restaurant features hot entrees such as prime rib, oven-roasted turkey, barbecued chicken, broiled fresh fish, and pasta, along with a selection of hot and cold sandwiches and large salads.

Atmosphere: The waiting area for guests at the Sci-Fi Dine-In Theater Restaurant resembles the back of a typical movie set, with exposed wall studs and bolts. Guests enter the large dining area through what looks like a movie ticket booth and are seated at tables resembling miniature 1950s-style convertibles. It's always evening at the Sci-Fi Dine-In Theater Restaurant, with make-believe stars glistening in the sky against a moonlit Hollywood Hills mural. Cartoons and clips from campy science fiction films play continuously on the giant movie screen; sound is piped through drive-in speakers mounted on each car. All of the cars and most of the seats face forward. The restaurant's drive-in snack bar–style kitchen is located in the back of the fenced-in theater, where servers dressed as carhops pick up the food and deliver it to the cars.

Sample Dinner Entrees: Out of the Inferno (smoked pork loin in a citrus marinade, served with peach brandy glaze, red skin au gratin potatoes, and Bavarian style cabbage); Creature From the Pasta Lagoon (cavatappi pasta with a sundried tomato, roasted garlic, and basil sauce with choice of chicken or shrimp); Plucked From Deep Space (fried breaded chicken breast topped with mozzarella cheese, tomatoes, and marinara sauce on tomato basil bread, served with pasta salad). All dinner entrees come with choice of salad or soup.

Healthy-Choice Entrees: King of the Winged Things (flame broiled chicken breast marinated in Wild Turkey bourbon and honey, served with roasted potatoes, onions, and red peppers). Hamburgers made with vegetable patties are available on request.

Lunch: The lunch menu has lower-priced sandwiches and salads and fewer entrees.

Beverages: Coffee, tea, juice, soft drinks, and milk shakes are served, as are beer, wine, and spirits. Cosmic Coffee, a popular house drink, is spiked with white crème de cacao and Malibu rum. The wine list includes California vintages.

SPOODLES

See the "Essentials" section for Dining Selection Guides.

Mediterranean Cuisine

Disney's BoardWalk

Food: Spoodles serves Mediterranean dishes based on the Spanish tradition of tapas, an assortment of small mix-and-match dishes that arrive individually, and are shared at the table. The menu draws from the foods of Greece, Spain, Italy, Turkey, and France, and includes salads, pasta, pizza, chicken, beef, lamb, and seafood. At lunch and dinner, guests can choose a full-sized entree accompanied with side dishes or design their own epicurean feast by ordering an array of tapas (Mediterranean appetizers).

Atmosphere: A large olive press, walls scattered with tapestries and mirrors, Moorish light fixtures, and unmatched furniture and tableware combine to create a hodgepodge decor at this casual high-energy restaurant. The main dining area has an open kitchen and wood-fired brick ovens. Tapas are served family style for sharing, and each table has a stack of small colorful plates and a ceramic pot filled with utensils for diners to use.

Sample Dinner Entrees: Penne with Eggplant (accompanied with peppers, portobello mushrooms, roasted tomato sauce, goat cheese, and basil pesto); Pan Roasted Red Snapper (served with fingerling potatoes and frissee with smoky bacon vinaigrette); Grilled Lamb Loin (with olive basil mashed potatoes, Chianti sauce, tomato jam, and crispy onions).

Healthy-Choice Entrees: Grape Leaf Wrapped Salmon (with roasted vegetables and sauce Catalan); Seafood Linguine (with clams, mussels, rock shrimp, salmon, tuna, and spicy tomato-chili broth).

Lunch: Lunch entrees are similar to those at dinner, although the lunch menu also features a selection of Mediterranean-style hot and cold sandwiches, such as the Grilled Portobello Mushroom Sandwich (with roasted red peppers and goat cheese on herb foccacia).

Breakfast: The all-you-care-to-eat breakfast buffet includes scrambled eggs, bacon, sausage, ham, assorted baked goods, frittatas, and house specials such as Pizza del Sol (pizza topped with fire-blasted egg, fresh asparagus, Italian sausage, and mozzarella) and Oven-Roasted Vegetarian Rotolo (fresh Moroccan flat bread wrap with roasted vegetables).

Beverages: Spoodles wine list features a large selection of Mediterranean wines. Coffee, tea, soft drinks, espresso, and cappuccino are offered, as are beer and spirits.

Location — The restaurant is located on the Promenade at Disney's BoardWalk and looks out over the midway and Crescent Lake.

Dining Hours — Breakfast buffet from 7:30 AM, lunch from 12 noon, dinner from 5 until 10 PM.

Average Price Range — Breakfast buffet **$$**, lunch entrees **$$**, dinner entrees **$$$$**.

Features & Tips — At the BoardWalk Pizza Window, visitors strolling on the Promenade can sample Spoodles' pizza-by-the-slice, or get a whole pie to go.

Plan ahead if wishing to dine at peak hours; Spoodles can become crowded and noisy at these times. Late diners (those eating after 8:30 PM) should not have trouble getting a table.

Reservations — Visitors to Walt Disney World can make reservations between 60 and 120 days in advance by calling Disney Dining Reservations (407 939-3463). Same-day reservations can be made in person at the restaurant, by calling the restaurant (939-2380) or by calling Disney Dining after 10 AM (939-3463).

TEMPURA KIKU

*See the "Essentials" section for
Dining Selection Guides.*

The World Showcase at Epcot

Japanese Cuisine

Location — Tempura Kiku is located in the Japan pavilion in the World Showcase at Epcot. The restaurant is on the second floor, above the Mitsukoshi Department Store.

Dining Hours — Lunch from 12 noon, dinner from 4:30 PM until park closing.

Average Price Range — Lunch entrees **$$**, dinner entrees **$$$**.

Features & Tips — Since no reservations are taken, Tempura Kiku is a good choice for visitors who do not have dining reservations, especially at off-peak hours. Guests waiting for seats can enjoy the view of the World Showcase Lagoon from the adjacent Matsu No Ma Lounge.

The counter service is fast and efficient, making Tempura Kiku an excellent choice for lunch. It's a particularly nice place for solo travelers. The chefs are entertaining, and the tradition of seating diners next to other parties creates a wonderful opportunity to meet other visitors.

Reservations — No reservations are accepted at this restaurant. The counter seats twenty-five.

Food: Tempura Kiku features seafood, chicken, beef, and vegetables dipped in a light batter, deep-fried, and served with a dipping sauce. While tempura is considered by many to be a traditional Japanese dish, it actually originated with Portuguese sailors, who opened Western trade with Japan. Sushi and sashimi are also available.

Atmosphere: This small dining room is just off the waiting room for Teppanyaki Dining, the larger restaurant next door. Warm gold-toned walls and traditional Japanese wood detailing contrast pleasantly with high-tech cookware in the center of this sushi bar–style restaurant. Guests are seated at the counter surrounding the cooking area, where they can enjoy the personal attention of their own white-hatted chef. Questions regarding ingredients and cooking styles are welcomed, and the chefs will gladly suggest meals for newcomers to Japanese cuisine.

Sample Dinner Entrees: Tori (deep-fried chicken strips with fresh vegetables); Matsu (deep-fried shrimp, scallop, lobster, and fish with fresh vegetables); Ume (deep-fried shrimp and chicken strips with fresh vegetables); Take (deep-fried shrimp, skewered beef, and chicken strips with fresh vegetables); Ebi (deep-fried shrimp with fresh vegetables). Soup, salad, and steamed rice are included with the meal.

Healthy-Choice Entrees: Several of the side dishes are excellent choices for light eaters. Hiyayakko (chilled tofu served with green onions and fresh ginger); Sashimi (assorted raw fish); Sushi Appetizer (assorted raw fish on seasoned rice; tuna rolled in rice and seaweed); California-rolled Sushi (crabmeat, avocado, cucumber, and smelt roe rolled in seasoned rice with sesame seeds and seaweed).

Lunch: Lunch and dinner menus are similar, although lunch does not include a salad, and prices are much lower than at dinner.

Beverages: Wine, plum wine, sake, and Kirin beer are available, as are soft drinks, coffee, and traditional Japanese green tea. The wine list offers a small but interesting selection of California wines. Specialty drinks offered from the full bar in the adjacent Matsu No Ma Lounge include the Momonoki, made with light rum, peach schnapps, and peaches; and the Sakura, made from light rum, white curaçao, strawberries, and lemon juice.

TEPPANYAKI DINING ROOM

See the "Essentials" section for Dining Selection Guides.

Japanese Cuisine

Food: Teppanyaki Dining Room offers an array of meat, seafood, poultry, and vegetable dishes deftly prepared at the table by a stir-fry chef. All the entrees are fresh, crisp, and sizzling.

Atmosphere: Guests are seated in one of the five tatami-floored rooms that are separated by hand-painted shoji screens. Each dining room has four black-lacquered tables under gleaming copper venting hoods, and the sounds of traditional koto music can be heard in the background. The tables each accommodate eight guests around the teppan grill, where the stir-fry chef prepares the meals. Once the orders are placed, the entertainment begins. The chef dons a large white hat, pulls knives from a holster, and artfully slices, dices, seasons, and stir-fries each order. Those familiar with the Benihana of Tokyo restaurant chain will notice some similarity in the style of presentation.

Sample Dinner Entrees: Ebi (grilled shrimp); Fujiyama (grilled sirloin and shrimp); Nihon-kai (grilled shrimp, scallops, and lobster); Beef Tenderloin (grilled steak). All entrees are accompanied with a salad with ginger dressing, grilled fresh vegetables with udon noodles, and steamed rice.

Healthy-Choice Entrees: Tori (grilled chicken), Kaibashira (grilled scallops), and Yasai (grilled vegetables), served with salad, vegetables, noodles, and rice.

Lunch: Lunch and dinner menus are similar and prices are lower — almost by half — than they are at dinner.

Beverages: A fair selection of American wines is offered, as is plum wine from Japan. Kirin beer and hot sake are also available, as are cocktails from the full bar. A popular specialty drink, Tachibana, is concocted from light rum, orange curaçao, mandarin orange, and orange juice. Nonalcoholic blended drinks are also available, such as the Momo, which contains peaches, orange juice, and light cream. Soft drinks, green tea, and coffee are also served.

The World Showcase at Epcot

Location — Teppanyaki Dining Room is located in the Japan pavilion in the World Showcase at Epcot. Guests enter this second-floor restaurant from the wide staircase at the side of the Mitsukoshi Department Store.

Dining Hours — Lunch from 12 noon, dinner from 4:30 PM until park closing.

Average Price Range — Lunch entrees **$$**, dinner entrees **$$$$**.

Features & Tips — With their speedy chopping and clever preparation and cooking techniques, the stir-fry chefs at Teppanyaki Dining Room provide memorable mealtime entertainment.

The nearby Matsu No Ma Lounge, overlooking the World Showcase Lagoon, makes waiting for tables a relaxing experience. After dinner, guests can watch IllumiNations from the upper terrace in front of the lounge.

Solo travelers and parties of two can sometimes find available seating here without reservations.

Reservations — Visitors to Walt Disney World can make reservations between 60 and 120 days in advance by calling Disney Dining Reservations (407 939-3463). Same-day reservations can be made by calling Disney Dining after 10 AM (939-3463). They can also be made at the Disney Dining telephone kiosks located in the Germany Pavilion and at Guest Relations in Future World.

Essentials

Attractions

Hotels

Restaurants at the Resorts • Restaurants at the Attractions

Restaurants

Special Events

Recreation

Resources

TONY'S TOWN SQUARE RESTAURANT

*See the "Essentials" section for
Dining Selection Guides.*

The Magic Kingdom

Italian Cuisine

Location — Visitors will find Tony's Town Square Restaurant at the beginning of Main Street, U.S.A., on the right, across Town Square from City Hall, in the Magic Kingdom.

Dining Hours — Open all day. Breakfast from before park opening, lunch from 11:30 AM, dinner from 4 PM until park closing.

Average Price Range — Breakfast entrees **$**, lunch entrees **$$**, dinner entrees **$$$**.

Features & Tips — On hot afternoons, Tony's is a great place to relax and cool off. After 2:30 PM, there are many empty tables, and guests may order beverages or appetizers as a light meal (a great way to save money and still experience the atmosphere).

Tony's Fried Calamari, served with marinara and aioli sauces, is the most popular appetizer among frequent diners.

Patio diners facing Town Square can catch glimpses of afternoon parades from their table.

The restaurant is located in a very busy part of the Magic Kingdom and attracts many families, which can distract from a quiet lunch or dinner during busy hours.

Reservations — Visitors to Walt Disney World can make reservations between 60 and 120 days in advance by calling Disney Dining Reservations (407 939-3463). Same-day reservations can be made at City Hall on Main Street or by calling Disney Dining after 10 AM (939-3463).

Food: Tony's Town Square Restaurant offers Italian-style hot entrees and pastas, as well as lighter dishes such as pizza, calzone, frittatas, pasta, and Italian sandwiches.

Atmosphere: The centerpiece at Tony's Town Square Restaurant is a large statue of the leading canine characters in *Lady and the Tramp*. Other reminders of the delightful Walt Disney film are placed throughout the restaurant. Guests may choose to dine in the main dining room, with its stained-glass windows, mahogany-beamed ceilings, and banquette seating or in the sunny glassed-in patio, with its ceiling fans, terrazzo floors, and pleasant view of busy, bustling Town Square. Lively Italian music playing in the background enhances the setting.

Sample Dinner Entrees: Penne di Campagna (penne pasta, Italian sausage, artichokes, broccoli, and cannellini beans tossed with Asiago tomato pesto sauce); Spaghetti della Casa (traditional tomato sauce with meatballs served on a bed of spaghetti); Petto di Pollo alla Fiorentina (grilled chicken breast served with spinach cream sauce and house-made polenta); Gamberetti Saute (shrimp sautéed with garlic, tomatoes, and seasonal vegetables in cream sauce over fettuccine with a blend of cheese).

Healthy-Choice Entrees: Pesce del Giorno (fresh catch of the day).

Lunch: The lunch and dinner menus are similar. The lunch menu also offers pizza, salads, and Italian sandwiches. The lunch menu items are less expensive and somewhat healthier.

Breakfast: The breakfast picks at Tony's include Lady and the Tramp Waffles and Tony's Italian Toast, as well as a selection of traditional egg dishes.

Beverages: Coffee, tea, and soft drinks are served, along with espresso and cappuccino.

WILDHORSE SALOON

See the "Essentials" section for
Dining Selection Guides.

Western-American Cuisine

Food: The Wildhorse Saloon is known for its "unbridled barbecue," a tasty variety of smoked and grilled beef, chicken, and baby back pork ribs. Hamburgers, salads, and seafood entrees round out the menu.

Atmosphere: The Wildhorse Saloon's intriguing decor combines the country-western heritage of the Grand Ole Opry with modern highlights. Low lighting, neon accents, and a thirty-foot oil painting of stampeding horses set the tone. Cutouts of galloping horses circle the ceiling, and guests can dine looking down on the line dancers. While waiting for tables, guests can browse the Wildhorse Saloon's western store for that Stetson they've been looking for. The latest country tunes and live performances can be heard from the Wildhorse Saloon's dance hall, which boasts "It's as much fun as you can have with your boots on." The dance hall can be accessed from Pleasure Island with separate admission.

Sample Dinner Entrees: Stampede Platter (one half barbecue chicken and Memphis ribs served with beans and slaw); Bourbon Mustard Pork Chops (marinated in Kentucky bourbon and maple syrup, grilled and served with mashed potatoes and vegetables); Pan Fried Pecan Trout (brook trout dusted with pecan breading, sautéed, topped with pecan salsa butter, served over spicy bean mash, with vegetable); Sawtooth Chicken Salad (tidbits of Southern fried chicken, cucumbers, tomatoes, peppers, mixed cheeses, fried sweet potato shoestrings, and chopped eggs on a bed of mixed greens, accompanied with cornbread and pecan butter).

Healthy-Choice Entrees: Oak Plank Salmon (Pacific Northwest salmon dusted with barbecue spices and oak plank–roasted, served with white bean mash and vegetable of the day). A vegetarian platter is available upon request.

Lunch: The lunch menu features sandwiches and salads, such as the Smoky Brisket Sandwich (hickory-smoked brisket on a toasted roll, topped with smoked Cheddar cheese, lettuce, and barbecue sauce, served with fries).

Beverages: Coffee, tea, and soft drinks are served, as well as domestic and imported beers and wine. The Wildhorse Saloon bar offers a number of unique specialty drinks such as the Boot Scoot, a mixture of Amaretto, Southern Comfort, and cranberry and pineapple juices.

Pleasure Island at Downtown Disney

Location — The Wildhorse Saloon is located at Pleasure Island, across from the Fulton's Crab House riverboat. It faces The Marketplace and is entered from outside Pleasure Island.

Dining Hours — Lunch from 11:30 AM (Friday and Saturday only), dinner from 5 PM until 2 AM.

Average Price Range — Lunch entrees **$$**, dinner entrees **$$$**.

Features & Tips — Along with neighboring Fulton's Crab House and Portobello Yacht Club, Wildhorse Saloon is one of the few late-night eating spots at Walt Disney World.

Desserts are home cooking at its best. Don't miss the Wrangler's Revenge, two brownies layered with chocolate ganache and vanilla ice cream.

The dance club setting makes for a festive, if not noisy, evening meal. Even if country music isn't your favorite, you can't help but have an enjoyable time here.

Dance classes and competitions are held during the week. For times, call the Wildhorse Saloon (407 827-4947).

Reservations — No reservations are accepted; diners are seated on a first-come, first-served basis.

Essentials
Attractions
Hotels
Restaurants
Restaurants at the Resorts • Restaurants at the Attractions
Special Events
Recreation
Resources

WOLFGANG PUCK CAFE

*See the "Essentials" section for
Dining Selection Guides.*

The West Side at Downtown Disney

New American Cuisine

Location — Wolfgang Puck Cafe is located in the heart of Disney's West Side, overlooking the Buena Vista Lagoon waterfront.

Dining Hours — Open all day from 11:30 AM until midnight.

Average Price Range — Lunch entrees **$$**, dinner entrees **$$$**.

Features & Tips — For a romantic afternoon setting, ask for a window table or outdoor dining, which offers lovely views of Buena Vista Lagoon.

Between peak mealtimes, Wolfgang Puck Cafe is a good choice for a walk-in meal. There is also a take-out counter, Wolfgang Puck Express, serving sandwiches, rotisserie chicken, pizzas, and salads. It's great for an impromptu bite on the waterfront or for a flavorful meal to take back to your hotel room.

Upstairs from the Cafe is a small formal dining room that overlooks the lagoon. The menu offers a more upscale dining experience, and reservations are accepted by calling the restaurant directly (407 938-9653). A chef's table can be set for parties of up to six.

The fanciful tiling can make for a noisier-than-ideal environment. If you are seeking a quiet, conversational setting, come back another time when you can better enjoy the Cafe's pizzazz!

During peak dining hours, waits for a table can be lengthy.

Reservations — No reservations are accepted in the Cafe; diners are seated on a first-come, first-served basis.

Food: Wolfgang Puck, known for his uniquely innovative cuisine, brings a California flair to Disney's West Side with his eclectic and colorful cafe. Specialty pizzas, pastas, salads, chicken, beef, seafood, and sandwiches showcase his "no-boundaries" approach to cooking. Puck's daring cross-cultural style has strongly influenced many talented young chefs.

Atmosphere: The high-energy atmosphere was created by acclaimed designer/restaurateur (and Puck's wife and partner) Barbara Lazaroff. The Cafe's distinctive postmodern design features boldly colored mosaic tiles, dramatic custom lighting and furniture, handcrafted ceramics, and vintage serigraphs by Puck himself. The feeling is casual, bright, and fun — a whimsical setting in which to enjoy some truly creative cuisine.

Sample Dinner Entrees: Chinois Chicken Salad (with spicy honey mustard dressing and crispy wontons); Rotisserie Rosemary Chicken (with garlic mashed potatoes, French fries, or Caesar salad); Papardelle with Goat Cheese (with sun-dried tomatoes, goat cheese, double-blanched garlic, arugula, and basil); Peppered Tuna Steak (charred rare, with horseradish potato puree, baby carrots, and brandy-mustard sauce); Signature Wood-fired Pizzas, such as Vegetable Pizza (prepared with basil pesto, mozzarella and fontina cheese, and organic tomatoes, topped with roasted red peppers, mushrooms, fennel, eggplant, and caramelized onion); Wolf's Meat Loaf (in port wine sauce, wrapped with bacon, with garlic mashed potatoes).

Healthy-Choice Entrees: Grilled Salmon (with warm spinach salad, rosemary scented potatoes, and marinated tomato vinaigrette); Wood-fired Cheeseless Pizza (with marinated grilled vegetables, herbs, and garlic tomato sauce).

Lunch: Although visitors may order from the dinner menu at lunch, there are designated lunch-only sandwiches and light entrees available from 11:30 AM until 4 PM.

Beverages: Coffee, peach ice tea, soft drinks, fresh-squeezed lemonade, espresso, and cappuccino are served. There is an extensive wine list; beer and spirits are also available.

Essentials

Attractions

Hotels

Restaurants at the Attractions • Restaurants at the Resorts

Restaurants

Special Events

Recreation

Resources

RESORT RESTAURANTS

Hotel Dining at Walt Disney World:
Entertaining Meals Outside the Theme Parks

*I*n recent years, the restaurants located at the hotels and resorts have been offering some of the finest chefs and best dining experiences at Walt Disney World. Many are now favorites among Walt Disney World regulars, and visitors frequently plan many of their meals at resorts other than where they are staying. The resort food courts can also be quite good, and the prices are relatively reasonable. For the most recent restaurant ratings and comparisons, see Essentials → "Restaurant Charts."

RESERVATIONS & PRICING

The resort restaurants are open every day and most serve beer, wine, and spirits. Some resort restaurants have smoking sections, which are noted in the reviews. Disney-owned restaurants do not permit smoking. The resort restaurants are popular and reservations should be made well in advance, especially for busy holidays such as Thanksgiving and Easter. Kosher, vegetarian, sugar-free, and other special meals can be requested at least 24 hours in advance or at the time reservations are made.

Most of the restaurant reviews show the average price range for a *single entree* only and not necessarily for a meal. In the case of buffets, prix-fixe menus, or Character Meals, which are generally all-you-care-to-eat affairs that include beverages, the prices shown are for a complete adult meal (meals for children cost about half). The key to the pricing is as follows:

$ — under $10

$$ — $8 to $20

$$$ — $15 to $25

$$$$ — $20 to $30

$$$$$ — $25 to $40

♛ — Over $40

E.A.R.S.
Expert Advisor Rating System
AWARDS

TOP 5 FAVORITE RESORT DINING EXPERIENCES

California Grill at Disney's Contemporary Resort

Artist Point at Disney's Wilderness Lodge

Narcoossee's at Disney's Grand Floridian Resort & Spa

Flying Fish Café at Disney's BoardWalk

Kona Cafe at Disney's Polynesian Resort

Palio at Walt Disney World Swan

On the California Grill...

"The architects who built the Contemporary once stormed Imagineer John Hench's office complaining about his plan to run the monorail right through the lobby. They thought it would make the place seem like Grand Central Station. What did they know? Monorail sightings add charm to the superb nouveau cuisine."

Margaret King, Ph.D., E.A.R.S. Panelist

Arthur's 27
Wyndham Palace Resort & Spa

Food: Arthur's 27 offers a prix-fixe menu showcasing its award-winning international cuisine. Diners choose either a four- or five-course menu with wine pairings. Entrees are prepared with flair and highlight fresh and seasonal seafood, lamb, steak, or chicken. Special diets or requests are welcome.

Atmosphere: Guests dine in cozy booths with breathtaking views of Walt Disney World. The dramatic dining room, along with the five-star food and service, makes this the place to celebrate a special occasion.

Dining Hours: Dinner only from 6 PM.

Price Range: Prix-fixe dinner ♛ .

Reservations: Required (407 827-3450). Business casual or evening dress is appropriate here. There is a smoking area.

Artist Point
Disney's Wilderness Lodge

Food: Artist Point serves Pacific Northwest specialties, including smoked meats and seafood. Varietals from Oregon and Washington highlight the extensive wine list. A pre-plated all-you-care-to-eat Character Breakfast is served daily, and Pooh and friends are on hand to mingle with guests.

Atmosphere: Enormous cast iron chandeliers, heavy wood chairs and tables, and artwork from the Northwest add to the rustic ambience of Artist Point. Large windows afford terrific views of Bay Lake.

Dining Hours: Character Breakfast is served from 7:30 until 11:30 AM, dinner from 5:30 until 10 PM.

Price Range: Character Breakfast plate **$$$**, dinner entrees **$$$$**.

Reservations: Disney Dining (407 939-3463).

Baskervilles
Grosvenor Resort

Food: A popular all-you-care-to-eat prime rib dinner buffet is the draw for visitors. A traditional buffet-style breakfast is offered daily; lunch is a la carte and features salads, sandwiches, and light entrees.

Atmosphere: Sherlock Holmes memorabilia is showcased in Baskervilles. The MurderWatch Mystery Dinner Theatre appears here on weekends (see *Special Events* → "Dinner Shows").

Dining Hours: Breakfast is served from 7 AM, lunch from 11:30 AM, dinner from 5 until 10 PM.

Price Range: Breakfast buffet **$$**, lunch entrees **$$**, dinner buffet **$$$**.

Reservations: Dinner reservations are accepted (407 827-6534). There is a smoking area.

Beaches & Cream
Disney's Beach Club Resort

Food: Decadent ice cream desserts, such as ice cream sodas and shakes, are the main attraction here. Hot dogs, steak sandwiches, and juicy hamburgers make this a great spot for lunch or a casual dinner. Traditional diner breakfast fare is also served.

Atmosphere: Modeled after an old-fashioned soda shop, this casual restaurant has limited seating options; there is, however, a long bar with comfortable stools where guests can watch the cook fry up hamburgers.

Dining Hours: Breakfast 6:30 until 10:30 AM, all-day dining from 11 AM until 11 PM.

Price Range: Breakfast entrees **$**, lunch and dinner entrees **$**.

Reservations: None. Diners are seated on a first-come, first-served basis.

Essentials · Attractions · Hotels · Restaurants · Special Events · Recreation · Resources

Restaurants at the Resorts • Restaurants at the Attractions

Boatwright's Dining Hall
Disney's Port Orleans Resort – Riverside

Food: Southern home cooking inspires the entrees here, which include seafood jambalaya, steaks, prime rib, and Cajun dishes. A popular breakfast buffet is served daily, or diners can order from a menu featuring tin pan breakfasts.

Atmosphere: Authentic tools adorn the walls of this boatwright's workshop, and the ribs of an uncompleted sailing vessel hang overhead. Rustic details extend to the tabletops where mason jars hold dining utensils and condiments.

Dining Hours: Breakfast served from 7 until 11:30 AM, dinner from 5 until 10 PM.

Price Range: Breakfast entrees **$**, breakfast buffet **$$**, dinner entrees **$$$$**.

Reservations: Disney Dining (407 939-3463).

Boma – Flavors of Africa
Disney's Animal Kingdom Resort

Food: The cuisines of many African nations are the main influence of this family oriented buffet. Dinner entrees include grilled seafood, roasted meats, and vegetarian selections. Salads, fresh breads, and dessert are also included.

Atmosphere: Traditional African marketplace is the theme of this restaurant where guests are greeted by hosts representing Africa's great heritage. The on-stage kitchen and wood-burning rotisserie grill are the showcase of the thatched roofed dining room.

Dining Hours: Breakfast from 7 until 11 AM, dinner from 5:30 until 10 PM.

Price Range: Breakfast buffet **$$**, dinner buffet **$$$**.

Reservations: Strongly recommended. Disney Dining (407 939-3463).

California Grill
Disney's Contemporary Resort

Food: The culinary focus here is on fresh, seasonal ingredients in inventive combinations with an emphasis on presentation. The menu features entrees of seafood, poultry, steaks, and pastas as well as flatbreads, sushi, and sashimi. California Grill boasts an extensive wine list including many from premier California vineyards.

Atmosphere: Located on the resort's 15th floor, the California Grill is a beautiful, modern dining room with an open kitchen. Magic Kingdom Resorts Area views are breathtaking; when the Magic Kingdom fireworks begin, the dining room lights are dimmed.

Dining Hours: Dinner only from 5:30 until 10 PM.

Price Range: Dinner entrees **$$$$**.

Reservations: Disney Dining (407 939-3463).

Cape May Cafe
Disney's Beach Club Resort

Food: Cape May Cafe hosts a popular New England–style clambake every evening. The dinner buffet features fresh fish, mussels, oysters, shrimp, baby back ribs, chicken, soups, salads, and desserts. Lobster can be ordered separately. Goofy, Mickey, and Chip 'N Dale hobnob with guests at a daily Character Breakfast.

Atmosphere: Beach scenes and striped umbrellas create a casual seaside resort atmosphere in the spacious dining room. Croquet mallets and old fashioned cabana chairs adorn the walls.

Dining Hours: Character Breakfast is served from 7:30 until 11 AM, dinner from 5:30 until 10 PM.

Price Range: Character Breakfast buffet **$$$**, dinner buffet **$$$$**.

Reservations: Disney Dining (407 939-3463).

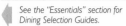
*See the "Essentials" section for
Dining Selection Guides.*

Essentials

Attractions

Hotels

Restaurants

Restaurants at the Resorts • Restaurants at the Attractions

Special Events

Recreation

Resources

Captain's Tavern
Disney's Caribbean Beach Resort

Food: Island-inspired dishes make up the menu at Captain's Tavern. Entrees include Paradise Pasta, Calypso Chicken, and Goombay Shrimp. Steak, prime rib, and pork dishes round out the menu. The full-bar features special tropical drinks.

Atmosphere: Dark wood walls adorned with seaside decor, nautical patterned carpeting, and subtle lighting give Captain's Tavern a cozy feel. Several tables provide guests with a view of Barefoot Bay and the resort's pool at Old Port Royale.

Dining Hours: Dinner only from 5 until 10 PM.

Price Range: Dinner entrees $$$.

Reservations: Disney Dining (407 939-3463).

Chef Mickey's
Disney's Contemporary Resort

Food: The breakfast buffet at this popular Character Meal restaurant includes corn beef hash, frittatas, and breakfast pizzas. The dinner buffet includes soup and salad, carved roasts, roasted chicken, seafood, and all the accompaniments. Children and the young-at-heart will enjoy making cupcakes with Goofy.

Atmosphere: This noisy but fun restaurant features Mickey, Minnie, Goofy, Donald, and Chip 'N Dale. Bright colors in geometric shapes, clean lines, and lots of chrome set a light-hearted and lively tone.

Dining Hours: Character Breakfast is served from 7 until 11:30 AM, Character Dinner from 5 until 9:30 PM.

Price Range: Character Breakfast buffet $$$, Character Dinner buffet $$$$.

Reservations: Disney Dining (407 939-3463).

Citricos
Disney's Grand Floridian Resort & Spa

Food: The menu highlights Mediterranean cuisine, with dishes such as Six Hour Braised Veal Shank, Roast Duckling, and Open Faced Ravioli. Citricos also offers three wine pairings with select courses. There is a large variety of scrumptious desserts, including the Chef's Sampler Platter for those who simply cannot decide.

Atmosphere: Citricos subdued lighting, mosaic tilework, exhibition kitchen, and on-stage dessert counter create a decidedly upscale air. From its second floor location, diners are afforded a view of the resort's pool and courtyard area, with the Seven Seas Lagoon in the background.

Dining Hours: Dinner only from 5:30 until 10 PM.

Price Range: Dinner entrees $$$$.

Reservations: Disney Dining (407 939-3463).

Concourse Steakhouse
Disney's Contemporary Resort

Food: Steaks are the draw for dinner at this sleek eatery, although chicken dishes and seafood are also available. At lunch, lighter fare includes hamburgers, salads, and pizzas. Breakfast highlights include omelets, Mickey waffles and Mickey Stickeys.

Atmosphere: The monorail whizzes by overhead at this atrium restaurant. It's a wonderful lunch spot, but since it is separated from Chef Mickey's by only a partition, breakfast and dinner can be a noisy experience.

Dining Hours: Breakfast is served from 7:30 until 11 AM, lunch from noon until 2 PM, dinner from 5:30 until 10 PM.

Price Range: Breakfast entrees $, lunch entrees $$$, dinner entrees $$$.

Reservations: Disney Dining (407 939-3463).

Coral Cafe
Walt Disney World Dolphin

Food: Guests may choose either the extensive buffet or traditional American and Japanese breakfast dishes. On Sundays, Goofy, Pluto, and Chip 'N Dale host a Character Breakfast buffet. The lunch menu offers a wide variety of salads and sandwiches, whereas dinner is a la carte or from the buffet.

Atmosphere: Sea-inspired hues color this friendly restaurant, while whimsical fish "float" from the ceiling.

Dining Hours: Breakfast from 6 until 11 AM, lunch from 11:30 until 3 PM, dinner from 5 until 11 PM.

Price Range: Breakfast buffet **$$**, lunch entrees **$$**, dinner entrees **$$**, dinner buffet **$$**.

Reservations: Highly recommended for the Character Breakfast buffet; call Disney Dining (407 939-3463) or the hotel (407 934-4000).

Finn's Grill
The Hilton Resort

Food: Finn's Grill offers several fresh fish entrees each night, along with lobster, pasta dishes, steaks, and its own version of bouillabaisse. Fish can be prepared broiled, grilled, or sautéed. An extensive wine selection complements the many varieties of seafood served.

Atmosphere: A brightly colored fin and fish motif adorns the walls in this Key West–style eatery. Nautical decorations scattered throughout the restaurant create a decidedly whimsical and relaxed atmosphere.

Dining Hours: Dinner from 5:30 until 11 PM.

Price Range: Dinner entrees **$$$**.

Reservations: Recommended (407 827-3838). There is a smoking area.

Garden Grove Cafe
Walt Disney World Swan

Food: During the week, a traditional breakfast menu is available. On Saturdays, a Character Breakfast buffet features salmon, eggs Benedict, and other standard fare. The lunch menu offers salads and sandwiches.

Atmosphere: Potted plants and fanciful greenery create a lush garden setting in this inviting dining room. Colorful bird sculptures perch in the branches overhead, and large windows provide lagoon views.

Dining Hours: Breakfast is served from 6:30 until 11:30 AM, lunch from 11:30 AM until 2 PM.

Price Range: Breakfast entrees **$**, Character Breakfast buffet **$$$**, lunch entrees **$$**.

Reservations: Reservations can be made through the hotel (407 934-3000) or through Disney Dining (407 939-3463).

Grand Floridian Cafe
Disney's Grand Floridian Resort & Spa

Food: The Grand Floridian Cafe serves classic breakfast dishes in the morning. Specialty sandwiches and flatbreads highlight the lunch menu. The dinner menu is comprised of pork, chicken, fish, and steak as well as a few sandwich selections.

Atmosphere: This casual family restaurant looks out on the hotel's courtyard and pool area. It has a peaches and cream color scheme; the ceilings are very high and, combined with the tall arched windows, provide for a very light and spacious dining atmosphere.

Dining Hours: Breakfast is served from 7 AM, lunch from 11 AM, dinner from 5 until 11 PM.

Price Range: Breakfast entrees **$$**, lunch entrees **$$**, dinner entrees **$$$**.

Reservations: Disney Dining (407 939-3463).

Essentials · Attractions · Hotels · Restaurants · Special Events · Recreation · Resources

Restaurants at the Attractions • Restaurants at the Resorts

Essentials

Attractions

Hotels

Restaurants • Restaurants at the Attractions

Restaurants at the Resorts

Special Events

Recreation

Resources

Gulliver's Grill
Walt Disney World Swan

Food: Gulliver's Grill offers hearty and creatively prepared dinner entrees such as prime rib, filet mignon, lamb, seafood, steak, and chicken. Healthy choices and vegetarian options are available upon request.

Atmosphere: Gulliver's interior is inspired by the well-known tale, *Gulliver's Travels*. The dining room is a replica of the bird cage where Queen Caribbean kept her giant pet swan. A popular Character Dinner is held here five nights a week (see *Special Events* → "Character Meals").

Dining Hours: Dinner from 5:30 until 10 PM.

Price Range: Dinner entrees **$$$$**.

Reservations: Reservations can be made through the hotel (407 934-3000)

Juan & Only's
Walt Disney World Dolphin

Food: Juan & Only's southwest menu features creative entrees, such as Texas Black Skillet Ribeye, Lobster Tacos al Carbon, Honey Pecan Chicken, and Jicama Crusted Red Snapper. A wine list is available.

Atmosphere: The old southwest is alive and well at Juan & Only's; cacti are fashioned out of metalwork and a "jail cell" encloses the restaurant's bar area. The tables and chairs are fashioned from hard wood and the color scheme is tones of rust and beige.

Dining Hours: Dinner only from 6 until 11 PM.

Price Range: Dinner entrees **$$$$**.

Reservations: Reservations can be made through the hotel (407 934-4000) or through Disney Dining (407 939-3463). There is a smoking area.

Jiko – The Cooking Place
Disney's Animal Kingdom Resort

Food: Fresh ingredients are emphasized in this African-themed restaurant. Creatively augmented by Asian and Indian flavors, the entrees include seafood, steak, chicken, and vegetarian dishes. Unique dishes such as Roasted Peanut Soup promise a flavorful meal. The wine list includes African vintages.

Atmosphere: Twin wood-burning ovens are the centerpiece to this stylishly designed restaurant. A banquet room for parties up to forty may also be reserved. The adjacent Cape Town Lounge and Wine Bar provides an authentic sampling of South African wines.

Dining Hours: Dinner from 5:30 until 10 PM.

Price Range: Dinner Entrees **$$$$**.

Reservations: Strongly recommended; deposit required. Disney Dining (407 939-3463).

Kona Cafe
Disney's Polynesian Resort

Food: The South Seas–inspired dinner menu features skillfully prepared seafood, meats, vegetables, and pasta. Traditional breakfast fare as well as Tonga Toast are available each morning. A variety of salads, sandwiches, and hot entrees is served for lunch. The fine ingredients and presentation of the dishes have made Kona Cafe a favorite among frequent visitors.

Atmosphere: This sleek dining room has low-backed booths with colorful patterns and hammered ironwork fixtures creating a sophisticated, modern ambience.

Dining Hours: Breakfast is served from 7 AM, lunch from 11:30 AM, dinner from 5 until 11 PM.

Price Range: Breakfast entrees **$**, lunch entrees **$$**, dinner entrees **$$$**.

Reservations: Disney Dining (407 939-3463).

Maya Grill
Disney's Coronado Springs Resort

Food: Fresh seafood and steaks prepared with a Nuevo Latino flair highlight the dinner menu at the Maya Grill. The dinner menu changes weekly. In the morning, a breakfast buffet offers tasty breakfast burritos in addition to more traditional fare.

Atmosphere: The elegantly lighted dining room is designed as an ancient temple; the elements of fire, sun, and water are depicted throughout. Tiki torches, along with Native and Central American baskets and pottery, accentuate the restaurant decor.

Dining Hours: Breakfast is served from 7 until 11 AM, dinner from 5 until 10 PM.

Price Range: Breakfast buffet **$$**, dinner entrees **$$$$**.

Reservations: Disney Dining (407 939-3463).

Narcoossee's
Disney's Grand Floridian Resort & Spa

Food: Narcoossee's uses only the freshest ingredients to make their fish entrees and innovative seafood selections. Surf and turf, lamb chops, and risotto round out the menu. The skilled chefs are always receptive to dietary requests.

Atmosphere: The windows in this octagonal shaped building afford diners an unobstructed view of the Magic Kingdom and the Seven Seas Lagoon, making this an ideal spot for watching the fireworks and Electrical Water Pageant. Hardwood floors, linen table-cloths, dim lighting, and a show kitchen make for a modern and pretty dining room.

Dining Hours: Dinner only from 5 until 10 PM.

Price Range: Dinner entrees **$$$$**.

Reservations: Disney Dining (407 939-3463).

1900 Park Fare
Disney's Grand Floridian Resort & Spa

Food: In the morning, an extensive buffet features standard breakfast items. At dinner the buffet offers prime rib, chicken, fish, ham, pork, side dishes, and salads. There is a separate children's buffet.

Atmosphere: The subtle Victorian theming is carried throughout this dining room, which features a turn-of-the-century pipe organ. In the morning, Characters from *Alice in Wonderland* and *Pinocchio* make the rounds. In the evening, Disney Villains host the dinner buffet, including Cruella De Vil and Captain Hook.

Dining Hours: Character Breakfast buffet from 7 until 11:30 AM, Character Dinner from 5:30 until 10 PM.

Price Range: Character Breakfast buffet **$$$**, Character Dinner buffet **$$$$**.

Reservations: Disney Dining (407 939-3463).

'Ohana
Disney's Polynesian Resort

Food: Much of the all-you-care-to-eat Polynesian dinner is served family style. Lazy susans are filled with salads, Oriental dumplings, seasoned flatbread, and grilled meats, including chicken, jumbo shrimp, turkey, beef, and fish. In the morning, Minnie's Menehune Character Breakfast buffet is served here.

Atmosphere: Giant tikis, wood and stone floors, and a thatched ceiling set the South Seas ambience in this friendly restaurant. The Magic Kingdom fireworks are visible from window tables.

Dining Hours: Character Breakfast is served from 7:30 until 11 AM, dinner from 5 until 10 PM.

Price Range: Character Breakfast buffet **$$$**, prix-fixe dinner **$$$$**.

Reservations: Disney Dining (407 939-3463).

Restaurants at the Attractions • Restaurants at the Resorts

*See the "Essentials" section for
Dining Selection Guides.*

Essentials

Attractions

Hotels

Restaurants at the Resorts • Restaurants at the Attractions

Restaurants

Special Events

Recreation

Resources

Olivia's Cafe
Disney's Old Key West Resort

Food: The dinner menu features uniquely prepared entrees as well as steaks, chicken, and fish selections. At lunch, diners can choose from a variety of interesting sandwiches. On Sunday, Monday, and Wednesday, Pooh and Tigger show up for breakfast.

Atmosphere: This bright, airy restaurant has tiled floors, potted plants, and large paddle fans which evoke the laid back ambience of Key West. Extra seating is available on the veranda overlooking the water.

Dining Hours: Breakfast is served from 7:30 until 10:30 AM, lunch from 11:30 AM until 5 PM, dinner from 5 until 10 PM.

Price Range: Breakfast entrees **$**, Character Breakfast plate **$$**, lunch entrees **$**, dinner entrees **$$$**.

Reservations: Disney Dining (407 939-3463).

The Outback
Wyndham Palace Resort & Spa

Food: The Outback features the open pit, flame grilled cooking style of Australia's bush country. Entrees include steaks, barbecued baby back ribs, poultry, seafood, and fresh fish. Many dishes are specially created by the hotel's spa chef and nutritionist.

Atmosphere: Diners are transported to the Australian bush country; servers are decked out in their outback garb. Guests are seated at the base of a waterfall that cascades down three stories of rough-hewn rock into a sparkling pond. Low lighting adds to the relaxed, casual atmosphere.

Dining Hours: Dinner only from 5:30 until 11 PM.

Price Range: Dinner entrees **$$$**.

Reservations: Recommended (407 827-3430). There is a smoking area.

Palio
Walt Disney World Swan

Food: Palio serves traditional Northern Italian cuisine with a wide variety of entree choices, including veal, fish, pasta, and steak. There is an extensive Italian wine list and a wide selection of desserts.

Atmosphere: This casually-elegant dining room is decorated with colorful flags and patterns designed to evoke the spirit of "il Palio," the prized banner Italian jockeys competed for in horse races long ago. The open kitchen and strolling musicians make for a truly fine Italian bistro.

Dining Hours: Dinner only from 6 until 11 PM.

Price Range: Dinner entrees **$$$$**.

Reservations: Reservations can be made through the hotel (407 934-3000) or through Disney Dining (407 939-3463). There is a smoking area.

Shula's Steakhouse
Walt Disney World Dolphin

Food: Shula's offers an assortment of steaks, prime rib, and beef dishes. All entrees are prepared to order. Grilled and baked chicken and seafood entrees add variety to the menu. All items are a la carte.

Atmosphere: Shula's Steakhouse, owned by the NFL's winningest coach, Don Shula, presents the quintessential steakhouse experience in a clubby, polished environment. Tables are set with heavy linen, silver, and wood-handled steak knives. Photos of the 1972 Miami Dolphins adorn the walls.

Dining Hours: Dinner only from 5 until 11 PM.

Price Range: Dinner entrees **$$$$**.

Reservations: Reservations can be made through the hotel (407 934-4000) or through Disney Dining (407 939-3463). There is a smoking area.

Victoria & Albert's
Disney's Grand Floridian Resort & Spa

Food: Diners select from a seven-course, prix-fixe menu with optional wine pairings. Entrees might include Muscovy Duck Breast with a Savory Bread Pudding and Blood Orange Sauce or Veal Tenderloins and Petit Colorado Lamb Chops with Crispy Sweetbreads over Truffle Gnocchi and Sauce Perigordiene.

Atmosphere: Guests are seated at elegant tables beneath an impressive domed ceiling. A harpist or violinist plays during dinner. Diners can request to sit at the chef's table, which provides the unique experience of dining in the kitchen and sampling all the dishes that are prepared that evening.

Dining Hours: Dinner only from 6 until 9 PM.

Price Range: Prix-fixe menu ♔ . Wine pairings are additional.

Reservations: Disney Dining (407 939-3463).

Whispering Canyon Cafe
Disney's Wilderness Lodge

Food: All-you-care-to-eat barbecue favorites are placed on a lazy susan in the center of the table and refilled as requested. Diners can also order from the menu which offers a variety of fish and chicken dishes. At lunch, sandwiches and lighter fare are offered. Breakfast features many hearty skillet selections.

Atmosphere: The rustic decor of the resort extends to this boisterous family restaurant. The servers tend to be a lively, fun-spirited group and enjoy joking with diners.

Dining Hours: Breakfast from 7:30 until 11 AM, lunch from noon until 3 PM, dinner from 5 until 10 PM.

Price Range: Breakfast entrees $, lunch entrees $$, dinner entrees $$$$, dinner plate $$$.

Reservations: Disney Dining (407 939-3463).

Yacht Club Galley
Disney's Yacht Club Resort

Food: Breakfast diners may choose the buffet with its traditional offerings, or they may order separately from the regular menu. Lunch and dinner selections include a variety of interesting sandwiches, with dinner featuring steak and seafood dishes as well.

Atmosphere: This large, casual, family restaurant is accented with sailor's knots and models of yesteryear's racing boats. The pleasant dining room is done in subdued tones of pink and blue, with patterned nautical carpeting.

Dining Hours: Breakfast is served from 7 until 11 AM, lunch from 11:30 AM until 3 PM, dinner from 5 until 10:30 PM.

Price Range: Breakfast entrees $, breakfast buffet $$, lunch entrees $$, dinner entrees $$$$.

Reservations: Disney Dining (407 939-3463).

Yachtsman Steakhouse
Disney's Yacht Club Resort

Food: Steak is the specialty of the house in this popular, upscale restaurant. Yachtsman Steakhouse also boasts a broad menu with plenty of fresh fish and chicken selections. Roasted garlic with warm bread is served at the table. An extensive wine list is available.

Atmosphere: Upon entering the steakhouse, diners have a view of the open display kitchen. Several tables have a view of Stormalong Bay, and some tables are tucked away into nooks for intimate dining. The yachting theme of the resort is carried throughout the restaurant.

Dining Hours: Dinner only from 5:30 until 10 PM.

Price Range: Dinner entrees $$$$.

Reservations: Disney Dining (407 939-3463).

Restaurants at the Attractions • Restaurants at the Resorts

Essentials

Attractions

Hotels

Restaurants

Special Events

Recreation

Resources

Celebrations & Gatherings • Party Boats • Character Meals • Dinner Shows • Holiday Events • Weddings & Honeymoons • Guided Tours • Disney Institute • Disney Cruises

SPECIAL EVENTS

Extraordinary Adventures for Families and Friends, Small Groups, and Solo Voyagers

*T*here is an amazing variety of activities, attractions, and accommodations at Walt Disney World that make it an ideal destination for family vacations, group getaways, holiday gatherings, reunions, birthdays, and weddings. Organizing and planning special events presents unique challenges, but returns great fun and lasting memories.

CELEBRATIONS & GATHERINGS

Walt Disney World is a great spot for gatherings and special celebrations. Private parties can be held at such unlikely places as the stage of the Indiana Jones Epic Stunt Spectacular and the American Adventure Rotunda. Event catering for large groups can be arranged by calling Resort and Cruise Group Sales (407 828-3074).

Group Dining at Full-Service Restaurants: Most restaurants in the resorts and theme parks can accommodate large and small groups. To reserve seating for groups of up to twenty or to make special requests for a birthday cake or special menu, call Disney Dining (407 939-3463).

Holiday Travel: Fall is the best time of year for group vacations. During Thanksgiving week and the following three weeks, the parks have very light crowds, yet offer festive holiday entertainment. Easter week is ideal for touring since the weather is mild and visitors are scarce. The most difficult holidays for groups to visit are Memorial Day, Labor Day, the week between Christmas and New Year's, and the Fourth of July (see *Special Events* → "Holiday Festivities").

Romantic Settings and Celebrations for Two: There are so many romantic dinner spots at Walt Disney World that entire vacations can be planned around them. Among the most acclaimed dining experiences and romantic settings are Bistro de Paris and San Angel Inn Restaurante in the World Showcase at Epcot, Victoria and Albert's at Disney's Grand Floridian Resort & Spa, and Arthur's 27 at the Wyndham Palace Resort & Spa. ◆

Organizing Tips for Groups

Arrivals: Groups that are meeting at the Orlando International Airport should plan carefully to avoid confusion. If members are arriving at many different times or late in the day, it may be smart and economical to spend that first night at the airport's Hyatt Regency. (See *Resources* → "Orlando International Airport.")

Staying in Touch: There are Message Centers in the Magic Kingdom, Epcot, Animal Kingdom, and Disney-MGM Studios where visitors touring separately can leave and retrieve messages on a network that connects the four parks. Messages can also be phoned into the Message Center (407 824-4321). Personal pagers can be rented through Guest Services at any Walt Disney World resort. Cellular phone communication can be unreliable in the theme parks.

Two-Way Radios: These devices are becoming an increasingly popular means of communication for groups and families who are touring separately within the theme parks. They can be purchased beforehand or rented. Several companies in the Orlando area provide rentals and have even set up regional antennae to ensure good connections. One large provider in the area is In Touch Family Communications (407 812-4220). ◆

Essentials · Attractions · Hotels · Restaurants · Special Events · Recreation · Resources

Disney Cruises • Disney Institute • Guided Tour • Weddings & Honeymoons • Holiday Events • Dinner Shows • Character Meals • **Party Boats** • Celebrations & Gatherings

PARTY BOAT EXCURSIONS

Cruising in Style

The Breathless — This beautiful mahogany Chris-Craft speedboat leaves from the Bayside Marina at the Yacht and Beach Club. It skims across Crescent Lake, touring the bright lights of the BoardWalk before anchoring in the World Showcase Lagoon for a spectacular view of Epcot's nightly IllumiNations fireworks show. *The Breathless* holds up to seven people and costs about $180 to rent for the 45 minute cruise. Night cruises can be booked through Disney's Sports and Recreation Line (407 939-7529). Day cruises, including the Breathless Burst, a 15 to 45 minute high-speed whirl around Crescent Lake, can be arranged through the Bayside Marina at the Beach Club resort (407 934-8000).

The *Grand I* — This forty-five-foot yacht can be charted for tours of Bay Lake and Seven Seas Lagoon, affording unique views of the Magic Kingdom fireworks and Electrical Water Pageant. The *Grand I* holds up to twelve people and can be rented for about $350 an hour, driver included. Beverages, snacks, birthday cakes, and even full meals can be served on board. The *Grand I* is booked directly through the Captain's Shipyard marina at the Grand Floridian (407 824-2439). All catering must be arranged through Grand Floridian Dining (407 824-2474). ◆

Excursion cruises take visitors onto Bay Lake, Seven Seas Lagoon, Crescent Lake, or through the Downtown Disney Waterways. In the evenings, excursion cruises provide great views of the dramatic lighting at the resorts and theme parks, including the fireworks shows. Guests can arrange private dining cruises as a unique way to celebrate a special occasion. Evening cruise times vary according to the fireworks show schedules. Any Walt Disney World visitor can reserve an excursion cruise up to 60 days in advance through Disney's Sports and Recreation Line (407 939-7529).

IllumiNations Cruises: Visitors take a scenic evening tour of Crescent Lake before anchoring at the World Showcase Lagoon for an up-close view of IllumiNations, the nighttime fireworks extravaganza at Epcot. Pontoon boats depart from the BoardWalk Marina or from the Bayside Marina at the Yacht Club. The boats carry up to twelve people and rent for about $120, driver included.

Moonlight Cruises: At night, special pontoon boats depart from the Grand Floridian, Polynesian, Contemporary, or Wilderness Lodge. They cruise Bay Lake and Seven Seas Lagoon, providing spectacular views of the Electrical Water Pageant and the Magic Kingdom fireworks. Cruise boats carry up to twelve people and rent for about $120, driver included.

Birthday or Anniversary Cruises: Pontoon boats decorated with balloons, streamers, and party favors are available to groups for special occasions. These evening cruise packages include a decorated cake and beverages. Boats depart from the Yacht Club, the BoardWalk Inn, the Contemporary, or Wilderness Lodge. The cost for the boat and driver is about $175 for one to seven people and about $230 for eight to twelve people.

Picnic Cruises: These afternoon cruises cast off from the Wilderness Lodge and the Contemporary resort for a leisurely tour of Bay Lake and Seven Seas Lagoon. A picnic lunch of salad, sandwiches, chips, sodas, and cookies is included. There are two sailings, one at about 12:45 PM and one at about 2 PM. The cost, including a driver, is around $175 for one to four people, about $200 for five to six people, and approximately $230 for seven to eight people.

Special Group Cruises: Larger pontoons that can carry up to twenty people are available on a walk-up basis at Cap'n Jack's Marina in Downtown Disney and at most resort marinas. Cruises can be booked throughout the day until dusk when the marinas close. Pontoon boat rentals cost about $70 per half hour, including a driver. ◆

DINING WITH DISNEY CHARACTERS

Over the past few years, meals hosted by Disney Characters have become increasingly popular. Character Meals are scheduled daily in the theme parks and at the resorts and are frequented by young families and a large number of young-at-heart adults. During the meals, Disney Characters drop by tables to greet diners, sign autographs, and take pictures with guests. Character Meals are usually all-you-care-to-eat events, and prices range between $15 and $30 for adults, and $10 and $20 for children, including beverages. Except where otherwise noted, reservations can be made between 60 and 120 days in advance through Disney Dining (407 939-3463). From time to time, new Character Meals are added and others disappear, so check ahead. See the "Restaurants" section for complete reviews and reservation details.

Artist Point, Disney's Wilderness Lodge: *Breakfast Plate* — Winnie the Pooh, Tigger, and Eeyore join guests in the rustic dining room at Artist Point. Guests are served all-grain pancakes, breakfast meats, eggs, breakfast potatoes, and other restaurant specialties. Character Breakfasts are served daily from 7:30 until 11:30 AM.

Cape May Cafe, Disney's Beach Club Resort: *Breakfast Buffet* — Admiral Goofy, Pluto, and Chip 'N Dale visit as guests serve themselves from the large buffet. Biscuits with sausage gravy, cheese blintzes, meats, fruit, and bread pudding are among the beach-party-inspired dishes offered. Character Breakfasts are served daily from 7:30 until 11 AM.

Chef Mickey's, Disney's Contemporary Resort: *Breakfast and Dinner Buffet* — The large selection of dishes at this buffet, along with the appearance of Mickey and friends, make this one of the most popular Character Meals at Walt Disney World. Mickey Waffles are the signature dish among familiar breakfast items; dinner dishes include carved meats, peel-and-eat shrimp, and a make-your-own-sundae bar. A Character Breakfast buffet is served daily from 7:30 until 11:30 AM; a Character Dinner buffet is served daily from 5 until 9:30 PM.

Coral Cafe, Walt Disney World Dolphin: *Breakfast Buffet* — Goofy, Pluto, and Chip 'N Dale are on hand at the Dolphin on Sunday mornings. The all-you-care-to-eat buffet features pastries, made-to-order omelettes, eggs Benedict, fruit, breakfast meats, hash browns, and Japanese breakfast specialities. Character Breakfasts are served Sundays from 7 until 10 AM. Reservations are not accepted for this breakfast; seating is on a walk-up basis only.

Character Meals at the Magic Kingdom

Cinderella's Royal Table

Breakfast — By far the most popular theme park Character Meal, the *Once Upon a Time Breakfast* is highlighted with appearances from Cinderella, Aurora, Fairy Godmother, Snow White, Belle, and Peter Pan. Guests feast on platters of eggs, potato casserole, fruit, breakfast meats, and banana French toast. Character Breakfasts are served daily from 7:30 until 10 AM.

The Crystal Palace

All Day Dining — An extensive buffet accompanied by Winnie the Pooh, Tigger, and Eeyore have made this restaurant the most popular in the Magic Kingdom. Breakfast items include eggs, waffles, fruit, breakfast meats, and cereal. Lunch and dinner guests choose from a variety of salads, spit roasts, fish, pasta, cakes, pies, and a make-your-own sundae bar. Breakfast is served from 8 AM, lunch is served from 11:30 AM, dinner is served from about 4 PM until the park closes.

Liberty Tree Tavern

Dinner — Minnie, Pluto, Goofy, and friends host a colonial-style buffet dinner housed within an eighteenth-century dining hall at Liberty Square. The Early American menu includes flank steak, honey-mustard ham, vegetables, salads, and roast turkey with all the trimmings. A special children's menu is available. Character Dinners are served daily from 4 PM until park closing. ➤

Essentials   Attractions   Hotels   Restaurants   Special Events   Recreation   Resources

Disney Cruises • Disney Institute • Guided Tour • Weddings & Honeymoons • Holiday Events • Dinner Shows • Character Meals • Party Boats • Celebrations & Gatherings

SPECIAL EVENTS
Character Dining

Theme Park Dining

Future World at Epcot

The Garden Grill Restaurant — *All Day Dining* — Every meal is a Character experience at this rotating restaurant. Farmer Mickey, Minnie, and Chip 'N Dale play host all day. The familiar dishes are influenced by home cooking and include smoked ham, eggs, and grits at breakfast and steak, chicken, seafood, and mashed potatoes and gravy at dinner. Character Meals are served all day from before park opening until park closing.

Disney-MGM Studios

Hollywood & Vine — *All Day Buffet* — Minnie, Pluto, Chip 'N Dale, and Goofy mingle with visitors at this Art Deco diner. Diners choose from a breakfast buffet of eggs, breakfast meats, waffles, fruit, and skillet-fried potatoes. Luncheon items include rotisserie turkey, seafood, pasta, citrus chicken, salads, and breads. A full bar is available in the afternoon. Character Breakfasts are served daily from 8 AM. Character Lunch and Dinner are served from 11:30 AM until 3:30 PM. Hours are often extended in the summer months.

Animal Kingdom

Donald's Prehistoric Breakfastosaurus *Breakfast Buffet* — Donald, Mickey, Goofy, and Pluto welcome guests to this nostalgic roadhouse-style dining room. The buffet includes sausage, bacon, hash browns, pancakes, western omelettes, biscuits with gravy, pastries, fruit, cereals, scrambled eggs, and French toast. Character Breakfasts are available from 7:30 until 10:30 AM. ◆

Garden Grove, Walt Disney World Swan: *Breakfast Buffet* — Goofy and Pluto visit with guests in a colorful and imaginative dining room. The extensive breakfast buffet includes eggs, waffles, breakfast meats, potatoes, salmon, fruit, and Japanese breakfast specialties. Cooked to order breakfast dishes are also available. Character Breakfasts are served Saturdays 8:30 until 11 AM. Reservations are not accepted for this breakfast; seating is on a walk-up basis only.

Gulliver's Grill, Walt Disney World Swan: *Dinner a la Carte* — Gulliver's Grill offers an upscale version of the typical Character Meal. On Sunday, Monday, Wednesday, Thursday, and Friday, Rafiki, Goofy, Timon, and Pluto mingle with guests, signing autographs and posing for pictures. The entertainment turns to balloon art on Tuesday and Saturday. Menu items include steak, seafood, lamb, chicken, and pasta. Character Dinner or balloon artist hours are from 5:30 until 10 PM. Reservations can be made 60 to 120 days in advance by calling the Swan (407 934-3000), or through Disney Dining (407 939-3463).

Minnie's Menehune Breakfast, Disney's Polynesian Resort: *Breakfast Buffet* — Minnie and her friends in tropical dress and leis welcome guests to this island-themed breakfast at 'Ohana. Buffet items include eggs, potatoes, pork, biscuits with sausage gravy, fruit, and cherry jello. Character Breakfasts are served from 7:30 until 11:00 AM.

1900 Park Fare, Disney's Grand Floridian Resort & Spa: *Breakfast and Dinner Buffet* — Mary Poppins, Alice in Wonderland, and other favorites greet guests at this popular Character Breakfast. The Character Dinner features a rotating cast of Disney Villains. Both meals feature a hearty, ample buffet, including French toast and omelettes at breakfast and roasted meats, seafood, and vegetable dishes in the evening. Children can serve themselves from their own buffet. Character Breakfasts are served daily from 7 until 11:30 AM; Character Dinners are served from 5:30 until 10 PM.

Olivia's, Disney's Old Key West Resort: *Breakfast Plate* — Winnie the Pooh, Eeyore, and Tigger do the honors at this bright and airy restaurant. Guests are served platters of muffins, fruit, waffles, eggs, bacon, and potatoes. Healthy menu items are also available. Character Breakfasts are served Mondays, Wednesdays, and Sundays from 7:30 until 10:30 AM.

Wonderland Tea Party, Disney's Grand Floridian Resort & Spa: *High Tea* — Alice and the Mad Hatter host this children-only tea at the 1900 Park Fare restaurant. Kids nibble on peanut butter and jelly sandwiches, rice crispy treats, ham, cheese, and crackers while they drink apple tea, bake their own cupcakes, and listen to a story. This fun one-hour tea is served Mondays and Wednesdays at 1:30 PM. ◆

DINNER SHOWS & ENTERTAINING MEALS

Walt Disney's classic dinner shows are popular with both first-time visitors and regulars alike. Guests enjoy top-notch performers while dining in a variety of settings. All Walt Disney World visitors can book most Disney dinner shows up to two years in advance by calling Disney Dining (407 939-3463). The Hoop-Dee-Doo, in particular, is extremely popular, and reservations should be made as far in advance as possible.

THE ALL-AMERICAN BARBECUE

Disney's Fort Wilderness Resort and Campground

The All-American Barbecue is in the River Country Pavilion in Fort Wilderness (see *Attractions* → "Fort Wilderness & River Country"). Guests sit at long communal picnic benches in an open-air pavilion decorated with red, white, and blue bunting (bring bug spray as mosquitoes can be a problem). The seating and food are plentiful and the atmosphere is relaxed, making it a great event for families and groups.

The evening's entertainment begins with a visit from cowboy Mickey and cowgirl Minnie, wrangler Goofy, and Indian braves Chip 'N Dale. A country & western band plays popular songs while guests dine. The all-you-care-to-eat buffet includes hot dogs, barbecued chicken and ribs with spicy barbecue sauce, cole slaw, salad, potato salad, corn bread, corn-on-the-cob, watermelon slices, and yellow and fudge Swirl Cake. Beer, wine, soft drinks in a can, coffee, and tea are included.

Tickets are about $45 for adults and $30 for children. All taxes and gratuities are included. The All-American Barbecue is held on Tuesdays and Thursdays from March to November at 6:30 PM. During the winter months, it is held only on selected evenings. The barbecue is relatively uncrowded and tickets are usually available on short notice.

Transportation to Fort Wilderness can be complicated. There are direct ferries to River Country from the Magic Kingdom and the Contemporary resort. If you choose to drive, you must leave your car in the visitor parking lot and then catch an internal Fort Wilderness bus to River Country. You can also park at nearby Wilderness Lodge and catch the Fort Wilderness bus. If you are relying on the Disney bus system, ask Guest Services at your resort for the best way to get to River Country; allow at least 60 minutes travel time. Taxis offer door-to-door service.

MurderWatch Mystery Dinner Theatre

MurderWatch Mystery Dinner Theatre is staged in Baskervilles restaurant at the Grosvenor Resort, located on Hotel Plaza next to Downtown Disney. The restaurant has a Sherlock Holmes theme and the walls are hung with framed illustrations of scenes from the detective stories. While dining, guests are engaged in a mystery by a troupe of talented actors. Sleuths who guess the identity of the murderer receive awards. Show plots and endings vary, so there's always a new "whodunit" to enjoy.

The all-you-care-to-eat buffet includes roast prime rib, fresh red snapper, coq au vin, baked stuffed pasta shells, fresh mixed vegetables, wild-blend rice with raisins and almonds, Duchess potatoes, and a complete salad bar. Guests select from an array of desserts at the dessert bar. Coffee and tea are available at the buffet. Soft drinks, wine, and beer, as well as cocktails from Moriarty's Pub next door, are brought to the table by servers.

Tickets are about $35 (about $20 for children), including tax and gratuity. Guests pay as they enter. There are shows at 6 PM and 8:45 PM on Saturday nights. Shows may also be scheduled on additional nights during peak seasons. Reservations for MurderWatch Mystery Dinner Theatre can be made up to 90 days in advance by calling the MurderWatch Reservations line (407 827-6534) or the Grosvenor Resort (800 624-4109). Same-day reservations are available as space permits. ◆

Attractions · Hotels · Restaurants · Special Events · Recreation · Resources

Celebrations & Gatherings • Party Boats • Character Meals • **Dinner Shows** • Holiday Events • Weddings & Honeymoons • Guided Tours • Disney Institute • Disney Cruises

Essentials

Attractions

Hotels

Restaurants

Special Events

Recreation

Resources

Disney Cruises • Disney Institute • Guided Tour • Weddings & Honeymoons • Holiday Events • **Dinner Shows** • Character Meals • Party Boats • Celebrations & Gatherings

Dinner Shows

Entertainment Dining

Many restaurants throughout the resort offer free entertainment during dinner hours. Some of the more intriguing offerings are listed below:

Belly Dancing — Traditional Arabian belly dancers and Middle Eastern musicians perform for diners at Restaurant Marrakesh in Morocco at Epcot's World Showcase. Shows usually begin about 25 minutes after the hour.

Italian Tenors — L'Originale Alfredo di Roma Ristorante in Italy at Epcot's World Showcase features strolling singers and musicians who serenade dinner guests with Italian ballads and operatic arias.

Oktoberfest — Musicians, yodelers, and folk dancers perform throughout the day at the Biergarten restaurant in Germany at Epcot's World Showcase.

Cuban Mambo — A Cuban band fronted by a Desi Arnaz look-alike performs hot Latin mambo and salsa, not to mention a mean "Babaloo" at Bongos Cuban Cafe in Downtown Disney. The band plays Wednesday through Sunday, from 10:30 PM until 2 AM.

Country Western — At the Wildhorse Saloon at Downtown Disney, country & western bands and line-dancers are showcased on the stage and gigantic 1,500 square foot dance floor. ◆

HOOP-DEE-DOO MUSICAL REVUE

Disney's Fort Wilderness Resort & Campground

The Hoop-Dee-Doo Musical Revue is held nightly at Pioneer Hall in the heart of Fort Wilderness. (See *Attractions* → "Fort Wilderness & River Country.") This Wild West hoedown is performed by the enthusiastic Pioneer Hall Players. The show starts with a banjo and piano serenade followed by a song-and-dance vaudeville that relies heavily on broad humor, sight gags, pratfalls, and audience participation.

The family-style all-you-care-to-eat dinner includes salad, country fried chicken, barbecued ribs, spicy corn or corn-on-the-cob, beans, and homemade strawberry shortcake. Kosher, vegetarian, or other special meals may be ordered at least 24 hours in advance through the Hoop-Dee-Doo Musical Revue Office (407 824-2803). Soft drinks, milk, coffee, iced tea, beer, and wine are included with the meal.

The ticket price is about $55 including tax and gratuity ($30 for children). The revue is held nightly at 5, 7:15, and 9:30 PM. Families with young children generally frequent the first show. Reservations should be made as far in advance as possible. Tickets can be picked up at Guest Services in any Walt Disney World resort or at Pioneer Hall at least one hour before show time (see *"The All-American Barbecue"* on the previous page for information about transportation to Fort Wilderness). Visitors should arrive at least one half hour before show time or their reservation may be canceled.

POLYNESIAN LUAU

Disney's Polynesian Resort

The Polynesian Luau dinner show is staged nightly in Luau Cove, an open-air dinner theater near the beach at Seven Seas Lagoon, behind Disney's Polynesian Resort. A partial roof covers the large fan-shaped outdoor dining area, protecting guests from the occasional rains, but leaving the stage open to the sky.

The show begins after dinner with a musical interlude from a Hawaiian band; customs and costumes are explained. Talented performers appear on stage showcasing traditional songs and dances from Hawaii, Tonga, Tahiti, and Samoa. The performance is most dramatic when it is dark, so try to book the late show during the summer.

The family-style, all-you-care-to-eat dinner includes fresh tropical fruit with banana rolls, barbecued roast chicken with Polynesian fried rice, oven-roasted pork, fresh sautéed vegetables in garlic butter, and pineapple cake. The menu changes occasionally. Restricted diet meals must be ordered at least 24 hours in advance through the Polynesian Luau Office (407 824-1593). Soft drinks, coffee, iced tea, hot chocolate, milk, beer, and wine are included with the meal.

The ticket price is about $55, including tax and gratuity (about $30 for juniors). The luau is held Tuesdays through Saturdays at 5:15 and 8 PM. Tickets can be purchased at Guest Services at any Walt Disney World resort or at the Guest Relations Desk in the Magic Kingdom, Epcot, Disney-MGM Studios, and Animal Kingdom. Arrive about one half hour before show time. Shows are rarely canceled, even in the rain, but if the weather is very cold, call the Luau Cove Podium (824-2189) to confirm.

Disney's Polynesian Resort, home of the luau, is located on the Magic Kingdom monorail line. Buses to the Polynesian are available from the theme parks and from Downtown Disney. Guests with Polynesian Luau reservations may drive their cars to the Polynesian resort and park there.

SUNDAY GOSPEL BRUNCH

House of Blues

The Sunday Gospel Brunch is held weekly in the Music Hall adjoining the House of Blues Restaurant. Diners sit at picnic tables or small cocktail tables and listen to rousing spirituals and hymns performed by touring gospel groups. Audiences are encouraged to sing along, clap their hands, and stomp their feet along with the singers.

The all-you-care-to-eat brunch buffet includes gourmet omelettes, barbecued chicken, sausage, bacon, chicken jambalaya, garlic roasted potatoes, jalapeño cornbread, peel-and-eat shrimp, Caesar and pasta salads, and bread pudding with whisky sauce. Soft drinks, milk, coffee, fruit juices, lemonade, and iced tea are included in the price. Guests may also purchase cocktails, beer, and wine from the bar.

The ticket price is about $30 including tax and gratuity ($16 for children). The Gospel Brunch is held every Sunday at 10:30 AM and 1 PM. Reservations can be made up to thirty days in advance by calling the House of Blues Box Office (407 934-2583). The House of Blues is located at Downtown Disney's West Side. There are buses to Downtown Disney from all Disney resorts and theme parks. A large, free parking lot is also available for visitors traveling by car. ◆

Essentials · Attractions · Hotels · Restaurants · Special Events · Recreation · Resources

Celebrations & Gatherings • Party Boats • Character Meals • **Dinner Shows** • Holiday Events • Weddings & Honeymoons • Guided Tours • Disney Institute • Disney Cruises

SPECIAL EVENTS
Dinner Shows

E.A.R.S.
Expert Advisor Rating System
AWARDS

TOP 5 DISNEY BREAKFAST EXPERIENCES

Once Upon a Time Character Breakfast in Cinderella's Royal Table at the Magic Kingdom

1900 Park Fare Character Breakfast at Disney's Grand Floridian Resort

The Crystal Palace Character Breakfast at the Magic Kingdom

The Breakfast Buffet in Spoodles at Disney's BoardWalk

The Character Stampede at The Enchanted Forest in Artist Point at Disney's Wilderness Lodge

TOP 5 DINING EVENTS

The Polynesian Luau Dinner Show (the second show)

The Hoop-Dee-Doo Musical Revue at Fort Wilderness

Whispering Canyon Cafe at Disney's Wilderness Lodge (for the humorous servers)

Chef Mickey's at Disney's Contemporary Resort (encounters with favorite Disney Characters)

'Ohana at Disney's Polynesian Resort (Hawaiian Dinner Feast)

HOLIDAY FESTIVITIES

Mickey's Not-So-Scary Halloween Party

The Magic Kingdom

On selected dates in late October, the Magic Kingdom closes early and reopens one hour later for those holding tickets to Mickey's Not-So-Scary Halloween Party.

This 5 hour event is filled with trick-or-treating throughout the park, specially themed parades, and opportunities to meet Disney Characters in their not-so-scary Halloween costumes. The spooky theme music from The Haunted Mansion attraction is broadcast throughout the park, and even in the monorail station at the Transportation and Ticket Center. Witches, ghosts, and jack o'lantern silhouettes are projected along Main Street, U.S.A., and the entire park glows darkly with specially designed lighting.

All visitors, especially children, are encouraged to come in costume. Kids have their own special parade to march in and many are selected to ride on Mickey's Hay Wagon during the main parade. The parade has a spectacular beginning — The Headless Horseman, holding his own glowing pumpkin face, gallops through the park on an inky black stallion.

Special admission tickets for Mickey's Not-So-Scary Halloween Party cost about $35 for adults and about $20 for children. Advance ticket purchases can be made through Disney's Central Reservations Office (407 934-7639). ◆

Any holiday is fair game for the imaginative entertainment staff at Walt Disney World, where just about every holiday from around the world is celebrated somewhere, including Chinese New Year, Mardi Gras, and St. Patrick's Day. If you are visiting during a major holiday, you may encounter some of the following:

Easter: The Magic Kingdom celebrates Easter with its nationally televised Happy Easter Parade. The parade features Disney Characters, singers and dancers, the Easter Bunny, remarkable Easter bonnets, and giant Easter-themed floats. Epcot is specially decorated with Fantasia topiary. Downtown Disney's The Marketplace and many of the resorts host Easter egg hunts and other special events, and selected restaurants throughout Walt Disney World offer traditional Easter dinners.

Mother's Day and Father's Day: Special Mother's Day festivities are featured in the major theme parks, while restaurants throughout Walt Disney World offer Mother's Day meals. On Father's Day, past events have included a classic and hot rod car show, look-alike contests, monster truck exhibitions, and the Father's Day Parade at Disney-MGM Studios.

July Fourth: Flags are raised and bunting draped for Independence Day celebrations at Walt Disney World. Pleasure Island starts the festivities on July 3rd with an expanded midnight fireworks show. Marching bands parade through the Magic Kingdom and Epcot, and on the night of the Fourth, the fireworks shows at the Magic Kingdom and Disney-MGM Studios are the longest and most spectacular of the summer. A special patriotic IllumiNations presentation in the World Showcase at Epcot lights up the sky in traditional red, white, and blue.

Halloween: The Magic Kingdom puts on the big event of the season at Mickey's Not-So-Scary Halloween Party (see sidebar). Stores at Downtown Disney's Marketplace get in the spirit by handing out treats to little ones in costume. The BoardWalk hosts Halloween games and is embellished with haystacks and scarecrows.

Thanksgiving: For Thanksgiving, Walt Disney World actually offers two holidays in one. On Thanksgiving day, selected full-service restaurants in the theme parks and resorts serve guests traditional Thanksgiving dinners. (Make your reservations early.) Meanwhile, during Thanksgiving week, Disney Cast Members work overtime to transform all of Walt Disney World into a Christmas wonderland with special holiday entertainment and events.

CHRISTMAS

It's Christmas from Thanksgiving week on at Walt Disney World and it's one of the most enchanting times of the year for a visit. The theme parks sport over-hanging garlands and towering Christmas fir trees that come alive in nightly tree-lighting ceremonies. Opportunities for Christmas shopping are abundant and festive food can be had everywhere. The following is a sample of some of the best of the holiday events.

The Theme Parks: The Magic Kingdom celebrates with Mickey's Very Merry Christmas Parade, complete with colorful floats and holiday music and Characters. The parade travels down Main Street on the weekends.

It's Christmas in New York at Disney-MGM Studios, with carolers and roasted chestnut vendors. On The Backlot along Residential Street, the Osborne Family's "Spectacle of Light" features more than three million twinkling lights that adorn two blocks of homes in a display that includes angels, Christmas trees, snowmen, and reindeer.

The World Showcase at Epcot presents Holidays Around the World. Each pavilion's version of Santa Claus describes Christmas and the holiday traditions unique to that nation. The Christmas Candlelight Processional, with a 450-member chorus, 50-piece orchestra, and bell choir, parades from Germany to the America Gardens Theatre. There, *The Story of Christmas* show is narrated by a celebrity guest. (Special Candlelight Dinner admission tickets are available and include dinner at selected Epcot restaurants, complimentary preferred parking, VIP seating at the Candlelight Processional, and merchandise discounts.) Restaurants in the World Showcase feature holiday menus from each nation.

Downtown Disney: The Marketplace presents an old-fashioned Christmas shopping atmosphere, complete with strolling carollers. Each night a charming ceremony is held to light the fifty-foot fir tree. At West Side, visitors can rent ice skates for a spin on the frozen pond. Next door, Pleasure Island puts a fun twist on the traditional with its Longest Holiday Office Party, complete with food, prizes, and a chance to win tickets to the "REAL New Year's Eve" party on December 31.

The Resorts: Every Disney resort is decked out for Christmas and hosts daily events and entertainment. At the Disney Institute, a talented cast performs Charles Dickens' *A Christmas Carol* in the style of an old-time live radio drama. Disney's Magical Holidays vacation package, which includes accommodations, tickets to Mickey's Very Merry Christmas Party and dinner, is offered at selected Walt Disney World resorts and is a good value for an unforgettable holiday vacation with family and loved ones (see also *Essentials* → "Vacation Packages").

Holiday Festivities

Mickey's Very Merry Christmas Party

The Magic Kingdom

For a little extra holiday spirit, visitors can purchase special tickets to Mickey's Very Merry Christmas Party. On selected evenings, the theme park closes to the general public and reopens for the Christmas Party, which lasts 5 hours. There are live holiday shows, two performances of Mickey's Very Merry Christmas Parade, a special fireworks show, and opportunities to meet Disney Characters throughout the park, including Santa Goofy.

The holiday magic starts on Main Street as visitors walk through a beautiful "snow" shower serenaded by carolers and other performers. Each land has its own holiday theme and most attractions are open for the party. The fireworks show is choreographed to holiday music and features a unique 360-degree panoramic display. Family photos, souvenir buttons, and hot chocolate and cookies are included in the price.

Admission tickets for Mickey's Very Merry Christmas Party cost about $40 for adults and $25 for children if purchased in advance (add $5 if purchased at the door). Party tickets, along with dinner and accommodations at a Disney resort, are also available as part of Disney's Magical Holidays vacation package (see *Essentials* → "Vacation Packages"). Tickets to the party can be purchased in advance through Disney's Central Resort Reservations (407 934-7639). ◆

Essentials · Attractions · Hotels · Restaurants · Special Events · Recreation · Resources

Disney Cruises • Disney Institute • Guided Tour • Weddings & Honeymoons • **Holiday Events** • Dinner Shows • Character Meals • Party Boats • Celebrations & Gatherings

SPECIAL EVENTS

Holiday Festivities

E.A.R.S.

Expert Advisor Rating System

A W A R D S

TOP 6 FAVORITE SEASONAL EVENTS AT WALT DISNEY WORLD

International Food & Wine Festival at Epcot's World Showcase
(held in late fall)

International Flower and Garden Festival at Epcot's World Showcase
(held in the spring)

Christmas Decorations Around the World
(in the resorts and the theme parks)

Candlelight Processional at Epcot's World Showcase
(held during the Christmas season)

Mickey's Very Merry Christmas Party at the Magic Kingdom

On Seasonal Events ...

"Tea at the Grand Floridian for the jolliest holiday ever. Sumptuous baked goods, mounds of strawberries, and airy Victorian ambience."

"The Puffin's Roost in Norway is a favorite shopping spot; you can't beat Scandinavian Christmas items."

Paul Anderson, E.A.R.S. Panelist

On Favorite Seasonal Events...

E.A.R.S. Panelist Stephen Fjellman, Ph.D., shares his top five favorite seasonal events:

1. All the Christmas Events
2. The Food & Wine Festival
3. Epcot Flower & Garden Show
4. Atlanta Braves Spring Training
5. Did I mention the Food & Wine Festival?

NEW YEAR'S EVE

The holiday season ends with the magic and excitement people have come to expect from Disney. On New Year's Eve, the theme parks stay open into the wee hours with park-wide celebrations and midnight fireworks shows. The Magic Kingdom presents a fireworks extravaganza and live musical events. World Showcase at Epcot puts on a spectacular presentation of IllumiNations and has a party in each pavilion. Disney-MGM Studios hosts dance parties, live music, and a special fireworks show.

Pleasure Island stages a special-admission "REAL New Year's Eve" street party, with buffets, complimentary champagne, favors, celebrity performers, fortune tellers, and a ticker-tape frenzy at midnight. Disney's BoardWalk has a special-admission New Year's Eve party along the Promenade, featuring live music, hors d'oeuvres, complimentary champagne, and an after-hours Continental breakfast, and ESPN Club hosts an end-of-the-year bash with complimentary champagne and appetizers. At the Hoop-Dee-Doo Musical Revue dinner show, a country music band creates a down-home New Year's celebration.

Several Walt Disney World resorts, including the Yacht Club, Beach Club, and Wilderness Lodge, offer cocktails in their lobby areas. The Grand Floridian, Contemporary, and Grosvenor resorts, among others, stage themed festivities that range from 1950s dance parties to elegant balls. Guests at Arthur's 27, at the Wyndham Palace Resort & Spa, bring in the new year with an elegant meal, champagne, and great views of all the Walt Disney World fireworks shows from the hotel's top floor.

So that parents can celebrate New Year's Eve, many Walt Disney World child care centers have parties of their own and will keep children until about 2 AM (see *Resources* → "Babysitting & Day Camps").

HOLIDAY TIPS

The holiday season is a great time to visit Walt Disney World, and if you choose the right weeks, you can save money on accommodations and enjoy light crowds during all the festivities and celebrations. Thanksgiving week can be pretty crowded, and the week between Christmas and New Years Day is the busiest week of the year at Walt Disney World. Hotel rates are at their highest during these weeks. However, from the week after Thanksgiving until the week before Christmas, visitors will find lower rates on hotels and shorter lines at the attractions. ◆

WEDDINGS & HONEYMOONS

World-class entertainment, recreation, and exquisitely themed resorts make Walt Disney World ideal for destination weddings and romantic honeymoon adventures. Disney's Fairy Tale Weddings arranges over 2,300 weddings each year in the resorts and theme parks, and for years Walt Disney World has remained the number one honeymoon destination in the nation.

WEDDINGS

Disney's Fairy Tale Weddings: Fairy Tale Weddings can be tailored to fit each couple's budget and taste, whether simple or elaborate, traditional or entirely original. Ceremonies can be held at any resort or in Disney's Wedding Pavilion. The wedding pavilion is a beautiful Victorian structure on a private island in the Seven Seas Lagoon. The ceremony is held in a glass-enclosed enclave with views of Cinderella Castle in the background.

There are two wedding categories, Customized and Intimate. With a Customized Wedding, the couple's wedding day fantasy is meticulously designed by a wedding consultant and the ceremony locations also include the theme parks (see sidebar). All details of the ceremony and reception, accommodating any number of guests, are included in a Customized Wedding (total costs start at about $15,000 and average about $25,000 for one hundred people).

Disney's Fairy Tale Weddings coordinators will also help arrange room reservations for wedding participants and their guests. All attendees are offered specially priced resort rates and Multiday Passes.

The simplest Fairy Tale Wedding, which doubles as a vacation package for couples, is the Intimate Wedding Package. Intimate Weddings include a cozy ceremony for two, honeymoon accommodations, and theme park admissions (total costs start at about $4,000). Contact Disney's Fairy Tale Weddings (407 828-3400) to request a brochure.

Resort Weddings: The large Wyndham Palace Resort & Spa has two wedding gazebos situated on either side of Lake Buena Vista, each with a cascading fountain nearby. The Wyndham hosts hundreds of weddings and receptions each year. Contact Wyndham Palace Convention Services (407 827-3360). The majestic Hyatt Regency Grand Cypress also boasts a charming wedding pavilion in a garden setting on Lake Windsong. Contact Hyatt Regency Grand Cypress Catering (407 239-3933) for wedding planning information.

Magical Ceremonies

Any wedding fantasy can become reality at Walt Disney World. Does the bride want to ride to her vows in Cinderella's Glass Coach with liveried footmen? Invite Mickey, Minnie, or other favorite Characters to the reception? Have the Main Street Barbershop Quartet serenade the guests? It is all possible. Couples can even have their ceremony in Cinderella Castle, followed by a banquet upstairs in the dining hall overlooking Fantasyland.

Disney themes are not the only way couples celebrate their vows. In fact, they only comprise about a third of the weddings at Disney.

Traditionalists can find exquisite and tasteful surroundings at many of the deluxe resorts. Movie buffs can plan a reception at the Chinese Theatre or The Hollywood Brown Derby at Disney-MGM Studios. International themes are easily accommodated at any of the pavilions in World Showcase, including the Rotunda in the American Adventure. The Voices of Liberty singers are even available to entertain guests.

Some other unique wedding locations include the Adventurers Club on Pleasure Island, the aquarium in The Living Seas pavilion at Future World, The Backlot at Disney-MGM Studios, and The Haunted Mansion at the Magic Kingdom.

Walt Disney World fantasy wedding events are priced at a premium, but for many couples, the magical surroundings make it all worthwhile. ◆

Essentials • Attractions • Hotels • Restaurants • Special Events • Recreation • Resources

Celebrations & Gatherings • Party Boats • Character Meals • Dinner Shows • Holiday Events • Weddings & Honeymoons • Guided Tours • Disney Institute • Disney Cruises

Essentials

Attractions

Hotels

Restaurants

Special Events

Recreation

Resources

Disney Cruises • Disney Institute • Guided Tour • **Weddings & Honeymoons** • Holiday Events • Dinner Shows • Character Meals • Party Boats • Celebrations & Gatherings

HONEYMOONS

Walt Disney World is a one-stop shop for fantasy vacations, which explains its honeymoon popularity. Here, newlyweds can pursue a different romantic adventure every day — or many each day. They can ride horses through the forest at dawn, tour the world that afternoon with a stop for lunch in Paris, and fly across the waters on a speedboat that night in pursuit of spectacular fireworks. It's hard to put that kind of day together anywhere else, or to create such unique and magical memories.

Disney's Fairy Tale Honeymoons: Fairy Tale Honeymoon packages include accommodations, theme park admissions, and a selection of details that bring magic to the moment: chilled champagne, a private in-room breakfast, and romantic floral arrangements. These packages have a minimum four-night stay and start at about $1,200 per couple. Couples who would like to spend time by the ocean can add one or two nights at Disney's Vero Beach Resort, two hours away on Florida's eastern coast. Contact Disney's Central Resort Reservations (407 828-7200) for information about Fairy Tale Honeymoons.

Disney's Honeymoons at Sea: A land and sea honeymoon package is available in conjunction with Disney Cruise Line. This seven-night package is similar to Disney's general cruise packages. Couples can spend either three or four days at Walt Disney World and the remaining time aboard the *Disney Magic* or *Disney Wonder*. The ship cruises the Bahamas and docks for the day at Disney's private island, Castaway Cay. Some of the amenities for newlyweds include champagne, truffles, cheese, and fruit delivered to guests' stateroom, and priority seating at Palo, the adult-only restaurant on board. (See *Special Events* → "Disney Cruises.") Packages start at about $2,100 per couple.

Resort Honeymoons: A range of honeymoon packages from the informal to the luxurious is offered by the following resorts at Walt Disney World: Wyndham Palace Resort & Spa, The Hilton Resort, Hotel Royal Plaza, Shades of Green, Walt Disney World Dolphin, Walt Disney World Swan, and the Grosvenor Resort. Contact the resort directly for vacation package details. ◆

GUIDED TOURS

Walt Disney World offers visitors a variety of behind-the-scenes, special-interest, and private theme park tours. Some tours are especially useful for orienting first-time visitors, and many delight experienced visitors who want to make new discoveries. The guided tours below are designed for visitors age sixteen and over. Reservations are recommended and can be made up to one year in advance through Walt Disney World Tours (407 939-8687).

MAGIC KINGDOM

Keys to the Kingdom: This 4 to 5 hour walking tour offers visitors an informative overview of the Magic Kingdom, lets them experience several attractions, and takes them into backstage areas and the famous "utilidors" located under the park. Two tours depart daily from City Hall at about 10 AM. Advance reservations are recommended. If space is available, visitors without reservations may join the tour that same day by signing up early at City Hall. Cost: About $50; theme park admission is required.

Magical Storytelling: This 6 hour tour presents the Magic Kingdom as Walt Disney envisioned it. Visitors explore the lands of the Magic Kingdom in an interactive fashion, listening to the stories behind Main Street, U.S.A., Fantasyland, Liberty Square, and Frontierland. This tour is given on Fridays and leaves at about 8 AM from the Transportation and Ticket Center. Cost: About $150; theme park admission is not required.

EPCOT

Hidden Treasures: This 3 hour tour examines the art and architecture of the international pavilions in the World Showcase. The cultures and traditions of these nations are also discussed. The tour is given on Tuesdays, Thursdays, and Saturdays at 9 AM and leaves from Guest Relations located inside the park. Cost: About $50; theme park admission is required. On Wednesdays, in addition to the regular tour, visitors also explore the Epcot wardrobe department and have lunch at Marrakesh Restaurant in the Morocco pavilion. This 5 hour extended tour begins at about 9 AM from Guest Services located directly outside the entrance gate. Cost: About $90; theme park admission is not required.

Gardens of the World: This 3 hour tour allows visitors to survey the beautiful gardens of the World Showcase. A horticulturist leads the tour and provides expert background on the design and maintenance of Walt Disney World's renowned landscaping. This daily tour leaves at about 9:30 AM from Guest Relations in Future World. Cost: About $50; theme park admission is required.

Family Tours

The tours listed here can accommodate adults and children under the age of sixteen. Theme park admission is required.

Magic Kingdom

Family Magic Tour — This 2 hour tour takes families on a scavenger hunt for clues to the whereabouts of a Disney Character, usually Peter Pan. The interactive adventure leads visitors through the entire theme park. The Family Magic Tour is given twice daily at 9:30 AM and 11:30 AM and departs from City Hall on Main Street. Cost: About $25 for adults ($15 for children).

The Magic Behind Our Steam Trains — This 2 hour tour lets visitors join the crew on one of the Magic Kingdom's steam trains. Participants learn about the operation of Disney's four steam locomotives and Walt Disney's life-long passion for trains. The tour includes a visit to the Round House where the steam locomotives are housed. This tour is given on Thursdays and meets at about 7:30 AM at Guest Relations outside the Magic Kingdom. Cost: About $25.

Epcot

Behind the Seeds — This walking tour takes visitors through The Land pavilion's greenhouses. Participants learn about hydroponics, fish farming, plant biotechnology, and integrated pest management. Tours are booked on a same-day basis at the Green Thumb Emporium in The Land pavilion. Cost: About $6 for adults ($4 for children). Tours last about an hour. ◆

SPECIAL EVENTS

Guided Tours

Resort-Wide Tours

These special-interest resort-wide tours visit many locations throughout Walt Disney World. They can be booked through Walt Disney World Tours (407 939-8687).

Backstage Magic — This 7 hour excursion takes participants behind the scenes at the Magic Kingdom, Disney-MGM Studios, Epcot, and other sites at the resort to examine how the Walt Disney World experience is created and maintained. The tour visits a working animation studio where Disney feature films are in production. Participants stop to have lunch in a memorable setting. Tours depart at 9 AM on weekdays and should be booked well in advance. Cost: About $200 (including lunch); theme park admission is not required.

Disney's Architecture — Disney's commitment to design and architecture is on display during this 3¹/₂ hour tour. Visitors view several examples of postmodern construction outside the theme parks. This tour leaves in the afternoon on Mondays, Wednesdays, and Fridays from the Disney Institute. Cost: About $55.

Yuletide Fantasy — This 3 hour tour explores holiday traditions at Walt Disney World. Participants discover how decorations are created and used to transform the Magic Kingdom, Disney-MGM Studios, Epcot, and selected resorts into Christmas wonderlands. This tour is offered only in December. Reservations are required. Cost: About $50; theme park admission is required. ◆

DiveQuest: Visitors with open water SCUBA certification can dive in The Living Seas pavilion's six-million-gallon aquarium for close-up views of sharks, sea turtles, manta-rays, and hundreds of species of tropical fish. This 3 hour tour includes an introduction to the various forms of marine life and a 30 to 45 minute dive in the aquarium. SCUBA equipment, wetsuits, towels, and lockers are provided. The dive is offered twice daily in the late afternoon. Divers meet at Guest Services outside Epcot's main entrance gate. Cost: About $150; theme park admission is not required.

Dolphins in Depth: During this 3¹/₂ hour tour, participants interact with the dolphins in The Living Seas pavilion's aquarium. A marine biologist provides background information on dolphins and the research being conducted at The Living Seas pavilion. Visitors then enter waist-high water to interact with the dolphins. Showers, lockers, wet suits, and towels are provided. This tour begins at about 9 AM at the Guest Services window outside Epcot's main entrance gate. Cost: About $150; theme park admission is not required. The tour price includes a tee-shirt and videotape.

DISNEY-MGM STUDIOS

Inside Animation: This 2¹/₂ hour walking tour details how animated films are created. Visitors get a behind-the-scenes look inside a Disney animation studio where feature films are produced and learn how to create a Mickey Mouse animation cel of their own. The tour departs at about 9:30 AM on Tuesdays and Thursdays; tour days may change. Cost: About $55; theme park admission is required.

ANIMAL KINGDOM

Backstage Safari: This 3 hour jaunt takes visitors on a tour of Disney's wildest theme park. Animal care and behavioral studies, conservation, diet, and nutrition are featured as well as background on the design and landscaping of Animal Kingdom. This tour is given on Mondays, Wednesdays, and Fridays and leaves at about 8:45 AM from Conservation Station inside Animal Kingdom. Cost: About $60; theme park admission is required.

◆

VIP Tours: These private, custom-tailored tours let visitors explore Walt Disney World in any way they wish: from the theme parks and resorts to backstage and production areas, and even maintenance and greenhouse facilities. Knowledgeable guides lead the tours, which can span from 3 to 8 hours (a meal in a full-service restaurant is required for tours longer than 4 hours). VIP Tours are booked through Disney Special Activities (407 560-6233) and must be reserved at least 3 days in advance. Cost: About $70 per hour per guide (meals and theme park admissions are not included). ◆

DISNEY INSTITUTE CORPORATE RETREAT

PROFESSIONAL DEVELOPMENT AND BUSINESS SEMINAR PROGRAM

At the Disney Institute, corporations and professional organizations can attend Disney seminars that focus on innovative management and leadership strategies and explore Disney's philosophy for gaining customer loyalty. The Disney Institute campus at one time offered unique learning programs to vacationers, but now its focus is providing distinctive business programs for professionals.

Disney's Professional Program seminars are typically three days in length and focus on management, leadership, quality service, creativity, customer relationships, and operational excellence. Customized seminar programs can accommodate small teams of five, up to groups in the hundreds. Field trips to the theme parks and backstage areas give participants an opportunity to observe the Disney management machine in action. Instructors also have access to the Disney Institute's legacy resources, such as the rock climbing structure, which are sometimes used for team building and related workshops.

Seminar participants are granted complimentary access to the Disney Institute's impressive 38,000 square-foot Sports and Fitness Center, where guests will find the very latest exercise equipment, as well as a full service spa for the ultimate pampering after a hard day of note-taking. Recreation facilities also include an NBA regulation gym, a PGA championship golf course, and clay tennis courts overlooking Buena Vista Lagoon.

Seminar program fees vary by factors such as size of group, seminar focus, length of stay, and food and lodging selections. Typically, the nominal cost is about one-thousand dollars per day per person. Contact Disney Institute Professional Programs for more information (407 566-2629).

Location — The Disney Institute is located on the Buena Vista Lagoon across from Downtown Disney. It has pathways leading to The Marketplace and Disney's West Side.

Campus — The seminar facilities are clustered in a setting that combines the laid-back bustle of a college campus with the ambience of a small town. At the same time, the presentation technologies are cutting edge.

Accommodations — Disney Institute accommodations are scattered across 250 acres of woodlands, waterways, and golf greens. Guests have a choice of accommodations, including Bungalow suites with wet bars and one- or two-bedroom Townhouses with kitchenettes. (See *Hotels* → "The Villas at the Disney Institute.")

Shopping and Dining — A coffee shop, snack bar, and lounge are located near the hotel lobby. During seminars, the dining room is used for catered buffets and banquets. Downtown Disney, with its many restaurants and shops, is within walking distance. Walt Disney World buses provide transportation for Disney Institute seminar participants. ◆

Essentials

Attractions Hotels Restaurants Special Events Recreation Resources

Disney Cruises • Disney Institute • Guided Tour • Weddings & Honeymoons • Holiday Events • Dinner Shows • Character Meals • Party Boats • Celebrations & Gatherings

EXCELLENT ADVENTURES & OUTINGS

Discovery Cove

SeaWorld's Discovery Cove embraces a dramatically unconventional water park concept. Limited admission gives visitors access to an uncrowded tropical paradise for an all day adventure and exploration. Lush foliage, inviting lagoons, waterways filled with colorful fish, exotic birds, and secluded white sand coves all enhance a sense of discovery. Snorkeling reveals the beautiful sea life, nonstinging rays, colorful reefs, and bottom bound treasures and adornments, such as shipwrecks. The highlight of the experience is a long and memorable swim with the dolphins, which is video taped for guests to keep. An admission is also available that includes everything except the Dolphin Swim. On the other end of the scale is the Trainer for a Day admission, which provides a tour guide to teach and manage experience, including exclusive interaction with the park's wildlife. All admissions include a meal, plus a seven-day pass to SeaWorld Orlando. Reservations are recommended. Call 877 434-7268.

All-Inclusive Package, about $200.
Non-Dophin Swim Package, about $90.
Trainer for a Day Package, about $370.

SeaWorld Orlando

SeaWorld attracts visitors of all ages to its amazing sea life shows, demonstrations, encounters, and attractions. It is also a sanctuary where distressed sea mammals are restored to health. Both SeaWorld and Discovery Cove are located between Universal Studios and Walt Disney World, off Interstate 4. For park information and hours call 800 327-2424.

Adult admission about $50; child about $40.

Kennedy Space Center

Sixty-five miles east of Walt Disney World, America's space program works around the clock to ready shuttles for launch into high orbit. Cape Canaveral, on the Atlantic coast, is home to Kennedy Space Center, headquarters for NASA's space program. Kennedy Space Center Visitors Complex (KSCVC) bridges the gap between the ever curious public and NASA's top secret operations. It's a magnificent and fascinating attraction.

Simply driving into Kennedy Space Center's parking lot inspires awe. Arriving visitors are greeted by the majestic Explorer space shuttle, and the stunning enormity of its fuel tank and rocket boosters. Inside the Main Visitor Complex, an astronaut clad in full attire welcomes visitors and poses for photographs. The Main Complex, has many shows, exhibits, and attractions suitable for visitors of all ages. Including two IMAX theaters, featuring dazzling space footage on screens over fifty feet tall. Other attractions include Astronaut Encounter, Rocket Garden, Space Shuttle Plaza, Astronaut Memorial, Robot Scouts, Universe Theater, and the Launch Status Center. Allow about four hours to see these attractions.

The hallmark attraction is beyond the Main Visitor Complex, on the Kennedy Space Center tour, which begins shortly after opening and runs continuously until about 3 PM. Visitors embark on a breathtaking tour aboard climate controlled, multimedia-equipped buses. Each bus features a video presentation that mesmerizes passengers with dramatic music, historical sounds, facts, trivia, and detailed narration synchronized to the points of interest visible from the bus windows. The tour is actually a constant stream of buses dropping off and picking up passengers at each of three distant attraction areas, where visitors may disembark and spend as much time as they wish enjoying an array of fascinating exhibits and activities. The first stop is the *LC 39 Observatory Gantry,* where a sixty-foot observation tower provides a fine view of NASA's two working shuttle launch pads. The next stop is the *Apollo/Saturn V Center,* which features an exciting immersion into American moon missions, including an actual 363-foot Saturn V moon rocket. The final stop is the *International Space Station Center,* where visitors can walk through a working space station project and watch, behind glass, the real station in progress. The KSCVC tour alone could easily occupy a full day.

The Essentials: Kennedy Space Center Visitors Complex is open from about 9 AM to 7 PM. Arrive early and expect to stay the day. Admission is about $25 for adults; $15 for children. There is a full-service restaurant, Mila's Roadhouse, which is patterned after the favorite eatery of the early astronauts. There are also a number of snack bars. For additional information and park hours, call 321 452-2121. ◆

DISNEY CRUISES

The Disney Cruise Line offers families and adults yet another memorable vacation option aboard its two luxurious cruise ships. Three and four-day cruises on the Disney Wonder leave from Port Canaveral and sail the Bahamas with stops in Nassau, Freeport, and at Disney's private island, Castaway Cay. The Disney Magic tours the eastern Caribbean for a seven-day cruise, docking at St. Maarten, St. Thomas, and Castaway Cay. A glorious throwback to the golden age of luxury ocean liners, both the Disney Magic and the Disney Wonder are designed to appeal to all ages. One-third of the cruise ship passengers are multi-generational families — grandparents, parents, and kids traveling together. Couples, including honeymooners, also make up a substantial part of the passenger list. The magic of Disney design is evident in every detail of the ships; even in the horn, which sounds the first seven notes of "When You Wish Upon a Star" upon leaving port. Cruises can be purchased as three-, four-, or seven-day sea-only excursions, or as part of a vacation package which includes three or four nights at a Walt Disney World resort along with passes to the Disney theme parks. Prices start at about $899 per adult, $499 per child.

ACCOMMODATIONS

The staterooms aboard the *Disney Magic* and the *Disney Wonder* are cleverly designed and feature many shipboard innovations. There are twelve categories of rooms, ranging from a standard inside stateroom to the Royal Suite with veranda. There are no gimmicks here; the nicer the stateroom, the higher the category and price.

All staterooms have either a queen size bed or two twin beds. There is also a seating area with a convertible sofa and a privacy divider. Most rooms have a bath and a half, a Disney innovation that allows the bathrooms to be used by more than one person at a time. Storage is cleverly designed and ample. Televisions with satellite programming, telephones (watch out, ship-to-shore calls are expensive), personal safes, and hair dryers are also provided in all rooms.

Every room (and most of the ship) is designated as non-smoking. Smoking is only permitted on private verandas, in some public lounges, and on outside decks.

Comparing the Cruise Ships

The *Disney Magic* and *Disney Wonder* are virtually identical in layout, yet they each have their own distinct look and feel. The *Disney Magic's* design is pure Art Deco: linear, classic, and sophisticated. The *Disney Wonder* pays homage to Art Nouveau with whimsy, color, and grace.

A bronze of Captain Mickey at the helm stands in the lobby atrium of the *Disney Magic*, while Ariel is showcased on the *Disney Wonder*. The artwork throughout each ship also reflects its individual motif.

Each ship has an elegant restaurant with a different theme. Triton's, on the *Disney Wonder*, evokes an undersea palace, while Lumiere's, on the *Disney Magic*, recalls classic French elegance. In addition, the *Disney Wonder's* Beach Blanket Buffet is accented with bright kites and beach balls, while Topsider's, on the *Disney Magic*, is strictly nautical.

The adults' entertainment districts also differ in their atmosphere. Beat Street on the *Disney Magic* is home to Rockin' Bar D, Off-Beat, and Sessions. The *Disney Wonder* captures the nostalgia of the open road with Route 66. Wavebands, Barrel of Laughs, and the Cadillac Lounge are housed here.

While in port, be sure to take a look at the stern. The *Disney Magic's* passengers will see Goofy putting the finishing touches on the paint job. Passengers on the *Disney Wonder* spy Donald trying to complete the job in spite of his nephew Huey's pranks. Sorcerer Mickey adorns the *Disney Magic's* bow, while Helmsman Mickey oversees the *Disney Wonder*. ◆

Attractions • Hotels • Restaurants • Special Events • Recreation • Resources

Celebrations & Gatherings • Party Boats • Character Meals • Dinner Shows • Holiday Events • Weddings & Honeymoons • Guided Tours • Disney Institute • Disney Cruises

Essentials

Attractions

Hotels

Restaurants

Special Events

Recreation

Resources

Disney Cruises • Disney Institute • Guided Tour • Weddings & Honeymoons • Holiday Events • Dinner Shows • Character Meals • Party Boats • Celebrations & Gatherings

Disney Cruises

Additional Dining Spots

Buffets and Snacks

Buffets — Topsider's on the *Disney Magic* and Beach Blanket Buffet on the *Disney Wonder* provide buffet dining in a casual setting with knockout views of the ocean. Eggs, potatoes, breakfast meats, fruit, pastries, cereals, and oatmeal are served from 7:30 until 10:30 AM. A luncheon buffet of salads, pastas, roasted meats, breads, and desserts is served from 12 noon until 2 PM.

Snacking — Passengers in the mood for a snack can visit Pinocchio's pizzeria for pizza or Pluto's Dog House for hamburgers, hot dogs, tacos, and fries. Soft-serve ice cream and sundaes are available at Scoops and fresh fruit is served in the afternoons on Deck 9.

Substantial snacks and hors d'oeuvres are served in the Promenade Lounge, Studio Sea, and Beat Street/Route 66 venues from 11:30 PM until 12:30 AM.

A 24 hour coffee station is located on Deck 9, and 24 hour room service is available to all staterooms.

Master Chef's Series

On longer cruises, passengers enjoy a special menu created and prepared by the best chefs from the Walt Disney World resorts in Orlando. A cooking demonstration and wine tastings are also offered during the day. ◆

SHIPBOARD DINING

Rotation dining is one of the hallmarks of the Disney Cruise Line. Passengers are given dinner reservations in a different restaurant each night during the course of the cruise; servers rotate along with the passengers. Passengers may dine wherever they wish for breakfast and lunch. These full-service restaurants serve cocktails and wine by the glass or bottle. The wine list has a nicely varied selection of vintages that are reasonably priced. Bottles that are not consumed in one night can be re-corked and served with the next evening's dinner.

Lumiere's on the Disney Magic & Triton's on the Disney Wonder: These elegant restaurants are situated just off the lobby atrium. At Lumiere's, guests dine under chandeliers accented with Belle's rose from the animated movie *Beauty and the Beast.* A hand-painted mural depicting the famous waltzing scene from the movie adorns the back wall. At Triton's, guests are treated to an exquisite Italian tile mosaic of the underwater kingdom from *The Little Mermaid* movie and dine under glowing blue, green, and aqua lights. Both restaurants feature fine cuisine such as salmon in puff pastry and lamb shank with grilled vegetables. Breakfast, lunch, and dinner are served here.

Animator's Palate: This is perhaps the most technologically advanced dining room ever dreamed up by Disney Imagineers. Diners begin the evening in a black and white hall with pillars shaped like gigantic paint brushes. During dinner, various black and white cartoon sketches on the wall are slowly transformed into color scenes from Disney animated features. Menu items include pan-seared salmon, chicken filled with crabmeat, and Parmesan-crusted veal chops. Open for dinner only.

Parrot Cay: This Caribbean-themed buffet restaurant welcomes guests with the sounds of parrots and other tropical birds. Island inspired specialties such as jerk-seasoned chilled calamari, roasted pork loin, and angel hair pasta Martinique are complemented by a colorful, casual setting. Tropical drinks, specialty coffees, and island desserts are also featured. Open for dinner; a brunch buffet is also served from 9:30 AM.

Palo: The fourth restaurant on board is reserved for adults age sixteen and older. This exquisitely designed dining room boasts a 280-degree view of the ocean and an intimate, candlelit setting. The Northern Italian menu is inspired and the service very professional. Some of the most popular dishes include wood-fired pizzas, beef carpaccio, and tiramisu. Reservations for Palo are required and should be made as soon as possible after embarkation. Passengers without reservations can visit the restaurant's small lounge for cocktails or dessert. Open for dinner only; there is an additional service charge of about $5 per person.

ENTERTAINMENT

The Disney Cruise Line prides itself on its state-of-the-art entertainment venues and top quality performers. Stage shows, vocalists, comedy troupes, and jazz combos are some of options available on every cruise. Consistent with Disney's mission to provide something for everyone, families, kids, and adults have dedicated entertainment offerings in separate areas of the ship.

The Walt Disney Theatre: This venue is the home of three original Disney musicals and other shows that alternate each night at sea. The formal, Art Deco–inspired, 1,040 seat theater is equipped with advanced theatrical technology and is one of the largest of its kind on any cruise ship. Cocktails, wine, and specialty coffees are available before and after performances at Preludes Bar, located just outside the entrance to the theater.

The Buena Vista Theatre: First-run movies and Disney cartoons are shown in this large, plush theater. Four movies, including the latest Disney animated feature, are shown daily. *Island Magic,* a musical for children, is performed twice here on the day before the ship docks at Castaway Cay.

Studio Sea: This family club is staged like a giant sound set. Disney trivia and nautical knowledge are tested in the afternoons as families and kids compete in game show style contests. Later in the evening, Studio Sea becomes a nightclub where families can dance together to popular tunes.

Promenade Lounge: This lovely lounge features live music nightly. Featured combos and vocalists perform jazz and standards suitable for listening and dancing on the small dance floor.

ESPN SkyBox: Disney bills this as the "world's only floating sports bar." Situated high atop the ship, the SkyBox features several televisions mounted on the walls that broadcast major sporting events by satellite. The full bar is open every evening as well as during some afternoons and on weekends. Sandwiches and chips are set out during major sporting events such as "Monday Night Football."

Deck Parties: Deck parties are given during the cruise on Deck 9, the Midship. The most extravagant deck party is usually held on the second evening of the cruise. A special floor rolls over Goofy's Family Pool, creating a great spot for passengers to dance to live bands. A dessert buffet, complete with ice sculptures, is set out for dancers to refuel. The party is highlighted by a fireworks show launched from the ship's smoke stacks.

Disney Cruises

Floating Night Clubs

Disney's cruise ships have extensive entertainment decks that are reserved for adults. Each entertainment area features a comedy club, dance club, and intimate piano bar.

Beat Street — This lively club district on the *Disney Magic* is designed to resemble a city nightscape, complete with manhole covers placed in the hallways. Improvisational comedy is offered at Off-Beat, with decor to match the name. The Rockin' Bar D (despite its western theme) features dance hits and Top 40 tunes. Passengers enjoy champagne, classic martinis, and even caviar while a pianist/singer performs popular tunes at Sessions. In between sets, passengers can select and listen to their favorite songs through headphones placed near the tables.

Route 66 — This nightclub district on the *Disney Wonder* features billboards of old-time roadside attractions along with a custom-made carpet depicting a map of the famous road from Chicago to Los Angeles. Route 66's venues include the comedy club Barrel of Laughs, presenting improvisational comedy in an elaborate brewery setting. At Wavebands, dance hits are played over a sophisticated sound system. Those seeking a quieter setting can walk over to the Cadillac Lounge for cocktails and live vocals with piano accompaniment. The Cadillac Lounge also features listening stations near the booths complete with headphones. ◆

Essentials • Attractions • Hotels • Restaurants • Special Events • Recreation • Resources

Celebrations & Gatherings • Party Boats • Character Meals • Dinner Shows • Holiday Events • Weddings & Honeymoons • Guided Tours • Disney Institute • Disney Cruises

Disney Cruises

Vista Spa & Fitness Center

This elegant nine thousand square foot full-service spa, salon, and fitness center is one of the largest on any cruise ship. The Spa features eleven treatment rooms and a variety of services such as body wraps, massage therapy, and facials. Two hydrotherapy rooms and a treatment room equipped for mud treatments are also available.

One of the best bargains aboard ship is the Spa's Tropical Rain Forest. For about $15 a day, guests can relax in this exquisite, Italian-tiled thermal treatment area. The various treatments include two tropical rain showers with essence of passion fruit and peppermint, a gentle sauna, a mild steam room, an aromatic steam room with extracts of chamomile, and a mint-scented fog shower.

Hair and nail care are provided by the Vista Salon. Cutting, styling, and coloring services are offered, as are permanents, waxing, manicures, and pedicures.

The fully equipped Fitness Center is free of charge for all passengers. It is uniquely positioned over the ship's bridge, affording guests a panoramic view of the bridge's computerized workings and the ocean beyond. Cardio machines have their own video monitors. Resistance equipment and free weights are also available. For an extra charge, there are daily aerobics classes and personal trainers. Body composition and fitness analysis programs are also available. ◆

RECREATION

An array of special on board activities are available for passengers of all ages. Both ships offer traditional sports such as shuffleboard and swimming.

Pools: There are three guest pools aboard each ship on Deck 9. Mickey's Children's Pool resembles Mickey's head with a water slide held up by his white gloved hand. At Goofy's Family Pool, adults and kids can splash in the pool or lounge in one of the two whirlpools. The Quiet Cove pool and its two whirlpools are reserved for adults.

Deck Activities: Shuffleboard courts and table tennis can be found on Deck 9. The Promenade Deck (Deck 4) offers an uninterrupted track around the ship for both runners and walkers.

Wide World of Sports: This mini-sports complex on Deck 10 features a basketball and volleyball court. It can also accommodate badminton.

Quarter Masters: Tucked away on Deck 9, Quarter Masters offers a variety of video and arcade games. No quarters are needed here — players can use their room key and have the games charged to their account, or they can purchase debit cards.

Shopping: Mickey's Mates, Treasure Ketch, and ESPN Locker Room all offer tax- and duty-free goods, including Disney Cruise Line merchandise.

KIDS' PROGRAMS

It should be no surprise that the children's programming on the Disney Cruise Line is excellent. Fully supervised activities are available for all age groups. Parents can leave their children for a few hours or the day.

Oceaneer's Club: Children age three to eight can climb on a replica of Captain Hook's pirate ship, dress up in clothes from an enormous costume collection, or play with computers. Activities include dancing, animation lessons, story telling, and science experiments.

Oceaneer's Lab: Children age nine to twelve become "scientists" in this mini-laboratory. Experiments, computers, and music entertain kids inside the Lab; sports and tours of the ship keep them active outside.

Common Grounds: This New York–style coffeehouse is for teens only. Disney has wisely decided not to organize this age group too much, rather, it lets them hang out with other teens in a relaxing environment.

Flounder's Nursery: Babies from twelve weeks to three years of age are welcome at this nursery. Reservations are recommended.

PORTS OF CALL

Depending on the cruise, passengers can visit the Eastern Caribbean or the Bahamas. All stops are the length of a day, docking early in the morning and departing in the late afternoon or evening. Every Disney Cruise makes a day-long stop at its private Bahamian island, Castaway Cay.

Eastern Caribbean: The *Disney Magic's* seven-day cruise takes passengers to the islands of St. Maarten and St. Thomas. Duty-free shopping, beaches, and tours emphasizing the culture and history of these islands are offered as shore excursions. Trips to St. John are available from St. Thomas.

The Bahamas: Three- and four-day cruises aboard the *Disney Wonder* travel through the Bahamas, stopping in Nassau, the Bahamian capitol. Some cruises also dock in Freeport. Shore excursions include a harbor cruise, a stroll through an aquarium, duty-free shopping, or a swim with dolphins.

Castaway Cay: Disney's private island in the Bahamas seeks to provide passengers with a day in a tropical paradise. It was first "discovered" by four intrepid adventurers in the 1930s; Disney Imagineers would like visitors to believe that the remnants of their exploration are still visible today. The result is a charming set of buildings and recreation areas that provide a day's worth of activity.

Like the ships, Castaway Cay is designed to appeal to all ages. The island is divided into separate areas for adults, families, kids, and teens. In the largest area, the Family Beach, guests can lie in the sun, swim, or rent snorkeling equipment to explore the man-made reef. Small sail boats, canoes, and sea kayaks can also be rented. Scuttle's Cove provides comprehensive programs for kids age three to twelve. Teens can explore their own beach turf, as well as take part in a supervised adventure program, The Wild Side. Adults can relax in a quiet setting and arrange for open-air massages at Serenity Bay, a beach reserved for guests eighteen and older.

For lunch, families dine at Cookie's Bar-B-Q buffet, which serves roast chicken and ribs, hamburgers, salads, and fruit. At Serenity Bay, grilled salmon, steaks, and fruit are offered. There are several open-air bars on Castaway Cay: Conched Out Bar by the family beach, Heads Up Bar on the pier, and Castaway Air Bar at Serenity Bay.

For Castaway Cay souvenirs, She Sells Sea Shells and Everything Else is located near the entrance to the Family Beach. Farther down the beach is Cultural Illusions where traditional Bahamian arts and crafts are sold. ◆

Disney Cruising Tips

Dining at Palo (the ship's adults-only restaurant), shipboard spa treatments, and the open-air massages on Castaway Cay are extremely popular diversions and should be reserved immediately upon embarkation. Massage therapy and spa treatments can be booked at the Vista Spa. Seatings for Palo are reserved at different locations, depending on the cruise and ship. Any member of the welcoming crew can provide information on where reservations can be made.

Don't feel compelled to go ashore when in port. The ship has a roster full of activities and dining events for those who stay aboard. This is the perfect time to explore the vessel or simply enjoy the peace and quiet of a relatively empty cruise ship.

The main dinner seating at 6 PM is most popular with families with smaller children. For a quieter dining experience, the late seating at 8:30 PM is the best choice.

Serenity Bay on Castaway Cay is lovely but limited in size and facilities. The good spots go quickly and adults should stake their claim to chairs and umbrellas early in the morning if they plan to spend the day at the beach. ◆

Essentials • Attractions • Hotels • Restaurants • Special Events • Recreation • Resources

Celebrations & Gatherings • Party Boats • Character Meals • Dinner Shows • Holiday Events • Weddings & Honeymoons • Guided Tours • Disney Institute • **Disney Cruises**

RECREATION

**Playful Adventures and Sporting Challenges:
Discoveries Outside the Theme Parks**

Walt Disney World prides itself on the quality and diversity of its recreational facilities and programs, designed to appeal to visitors who would like to enhance their vacation with sporting events, outdoor activities, golfing, spa treatments, or one of the many other options.

ANNUAL SPORTING EVENTS

Throughout the year, Walt Disney World hosts sporting events that attract participants and spectators from around the world. To find out about sporting events vacation packages, call Walt Disney Travel Company Sports Reservations (407 939-7810). The most popular annual events at Walt Disney World are:

The Indy 200 at Walt Disney World: Indy 200 drivers compete each January in this high-speed auto race held at the Walt Disney World Speedway, a 1.1 mile tri-oval track located near the Magic Kingdom. Advance tickets can be purchased through the Indianapolis Motor Speedway Ticket Office (800 822-4639). Race day tickets can be purchased at the Speedway.

U.S. Men's Clay Court Championships: In late April, the United States Tennis Association (USTA) launches the men's clay-court season with the men's singles and doubles competition. The event, held at Disney's Wide World of Sports, features some of the world's top-ranked tennis competitors. For more information, Call Disney's Wide World of Sports Information Line (407 363-6600); to order tickets call the Disney Professional Sports Ticket Line (407 939-4263).

Oldsmobile Scramble Championship: This golf competition is held in early October. Tournament teams are made up of one professional and four amateur golfers. The teams compete for a grand prize of over $15,000 awarded to the winning pro. For information, call the Oldsmobile Scramble Headquarters (800 582-1908).

Walt Disney World Golf Classic: Walt Disney World has hosted this major PGA Tour event every October since 1971. About 200,000 spectators attend the tournament to watch the top names in golf compete on Disney's Magnolia, Palm, and Lake Buena Vista courses for a $1.5 million prize. Call the Golf Classic Office (407 824-2250) for information. ◆

Walt Disney World Marathon

In early January, over 15,000 runners from all over the world gather to compete in one of the country's most popular marathons. The 26.2 mile course travels through four major theme parks and several Disney resort hotels.

Runners can participate in the full marathon or a half marathon. Disney Characters and Disney Cast Members are on hand to cheer on the runners. Live bands and entertainment performed throughout the day help keep the energy up. The day before the race, a 5K fun run and other family activities are held. At Disney's Wide World of Sports, a Sports and Fitness Expo is held during the two days prior to the marathon and is open to all visitors.

Participation in the marathon is open to anyone who signs up in advance. Spaces in this marathon fill up very quickly and runners should register early. For information and registration forms, call Disney's Wide World of Sports Information Line (407 363-6600). There are Walt Disney World Marathon vacation packages available through Walt Disney Travel Company Sports Reservations (407 939-7810). The packages include marathon entry fees, resort accommodations, and a spaghetti dinner the night before the race. ◆

Essentials
Attractions
Hotels
Restaurants
Special Events
Recreation
Resources

Wide World of Sports • Watersports • Tennis Clubs • Spas & Fitness Centers • Miniature Golf • Golf Courses • Fishing • Boating • Bicycling • Auto Racing • Sports Events

AUTO RACING

E.A.R.S.
Expert Advisor Rating System
AWARDS

TOP 5 FAVORITE RECREATION ACTIVITIES AT WALT DISNEY WORLD

Water Mice
(on Bay Lake and Seven Seas Lagoon, waving at the Ferries)

Miniature Golf
(Fantasia Fairways)

Water Parks
(especially Typhoon Lagoon)

Golf
(Palm and Eagle Pines golf courses)

Boating
(Caribbean Beach and Dixie Landings resorts)

On Fort Wilderness Campfire Program...

"My research into some of Walt's original, early 1960s concepts for a destination resort found the idea for the campfire program that exists today, complete with Disney cartoons and movies, a sing-along, and a visit with Chip and Dale."

Paul Anderson, E.A.R.S. Panelist

TOP 3 FAVORITE POOLS FOR KIDS AT THE DISNEY RESORTS

Stormalong Bay
(Disney's Yacht & Beach Club Resort)

The Dig Site
(Disney's Coronado Springs Resort)

Port Orleans Pool
(Disney's Port Orleans Resort)

If the thrill rides in the theme parks aren't realistic enough, visitors can strap themselves in an authentic Winston Cup stock car and take a spin around the Walt Disney World Speedway at speeds of 145 miles per hour. The Richard Petty Driving Experience offers visitors the chance to be a race car driver or passenger for a few exhilarating hours. Drivers must be at least eighteen years old, have a valid driver's license, and be able to drive a manual transmission. Passengers must be at least sixteen years old. While there are no height or weight restrictions, it should be noted that there are no doors on the racing cars and the window opening measures 15 inches high by 30 inches wide. For more information or to make reservations, call the Richard Petty Driving Experience (800 237-3889).

THE DRIVING EXPERIENCE

The Richard Petty Driving Experience at the Walt Disney World Speedway offers three different levels of experiences. At the conclusion of the Rookie Experience course and the Experience of a Lifetime, drivers are honored at a closing ceremony and are presented certificates of achievement.

The Ride-Along Program: Visitors ride shotgun with a professional driver for three heart-pounding laps around the one mile tri-oval track. Speeds can exceed 145 miles per hour. The Ride-Along Program costs about $100. Reservations are not required, and rides begin at 9 AM daily.

Rookie Experience: Visitors who like to be in the driver's seat can sign up for the 3 hour Rookie Experience. After suiting up and attending a short introduction in the "mobile classroom" (a passenger van that takes drivers around the track), drivers enter their cars and follow a lead car for eight laps. Rookies can drive at the speed at which they feel most comfortable, often reaching speeds of 125 miles per hour. This program costs about $350 and is usually given three times daily. Reservations and advance deposits are required.

Experience of a Lifetime: If eight laps aren't enough, drivers can go for the ultimate — three sessions of ten laps each for 5 hours of NASCAR excitement. Drivers work on building speed and establishing a comfortable driving line. After each session, pit road instructors meet with each driver and discuss ways to improve driving skills. This program costs about $1,200. Reservations and advance deposits are required. ◆

Essentials

Attractions

Hotels

Restaurants

Special Events

Recreation

Resources

BICYCLING & BIKE PATHS

Bicycling is one of the more pleasant exercise diversions at Walt Disney World. Rental fees start at about $6 per hour or $12 per day, depending on the resort and type of bike. Surrey bikes that hold from two to eight peddlers range from $15 to $20 per half hour. Bicycle rentals end at dusk. Bikes can be rented year-round at the following resorts:

The Disney Institute: Single and tandem bicycles and surreys can be rented at the Recreation Center. Only guests staying at a Walt Disney World resort may rent bicycles here.

Disney's BoardWalk: Singles and tandems can be rented at Community Hall, and surreys can be rented at Surrey Rentals, located across from the BoardWalk dock. Bicycles and surreys are available to both Walt Disney World resort guests and day visitors. Bicycles can be rented at night here.

Disney's Caribbean Beach Resort: Bicycles and surreys can be rented at the Barefoot Bay Boat Yard, located at Old Port Royale. Walt Disney World resort guests and day visitors may rent bicycles here.

Disney's Coronado Springs Resort: Single and tandem bicycles and surreys can be rented at the marina. Walt Disney World resort guests may rent bicycles here.

Disney's Dixie Landings Resort: Single and tandem bicycles can be rented at Dixie Levee, near the marina. Bicycles may be rented only by registered guests of the resort.

Disney's Fort Wilderness Resort: Single and tandem bicycles and surreys can be rented at the Bike Barn in the Meadow Recreation Area. Bicycles are available to both Walt Disney World resort guests and day visitors.

Disney's Old Key West Resort: Hank's Rent 'N Return rents single and tandem bicycles and surreys. Only guests staying at a Walt Disney World resort may rent bicycles at this resort.

Disney's Port Orleans Resort: Singles and tandem bicycles can be rented at Port Orleans Landing, near the marina. Bicycles may only be rented by registered guests of the resort.

Disney's Polynesian Resort: Any Disney resort guest can rent surrey bikes seating either two or six at the Catamaran Corner marina.

Disney's Wilderness Lodge: Single and tandem bicycles and surreys can be rented at the Teton Boat and Bike Rental. Both Walt Disney World resort guests and day visitors may rent bicycles here. ◆

Bike Paths

Disney's Port Orleans and Dixie Landings Resorts

Single or tandem bicyclists can follow the paved Carriage Path connecting these two picturesque resorts on a countryside tour through the Old South. The bicycle path is about 2.5 miles.

Disney's Wilderness Lodge and Fort Wilderness Campground

Approximately 9 miles of meandering roads and trails in Fort Wilderness serve as bike paths for visitors riding either single or tandem bicycles. This is considered one of the best bicycle paths in Walt Disney World. Active families or groups should consider this as an alternative afternoon event.

Disney's Caribbean Beach Resort

The paved promenade encircling Barefoot Bay Lake lets bikers spin casually past white sand beaches and sample a range of exotic tropical landscaping and colorful Caribbean-style lodges. The path, about 1.5 miles long, travels past aviaries filled with vibrant birds before continuing across Barefoot Bay to the main promenade.

Disney's Old Key West Resort and the Disney Institute

Combining the features of two adjoining resorts, this 3-mile path curves through the winding streets of Old Key West, lined with charming vacation cottages, past the green fairways of the Buena Vista Golf Course and the Treehouses at the Disney Institute. It continues on to The Marketplace at Downtown Disney. ◆

Essentials

Attractions

Hotels

Restaurants

Special Events

Recreation

Resources

Wide World of Sports • Watersports • Tennis Clubs • Spas & Fitness Centers • Miniature Golf • Golf Courses • Fishing • **Boating** • Bicycling • Auto Racing • Sports Events

BOATING & MARINAS

Resort Lagoons and Creeks

Barefoot Bay Lake at Disney's Caribbean Beach Resort

This forty-acre lake is actually three interconnected lakes, one of which has Parrot Cay island in its center, spanned on both sides by wooden footbridges. There are white sand beaches along the shoreline, and the lake is encircled by a promenade used by pedestrians and bicyclists. Boaters can rent their craft at Barefoot Bay Boat Yard.

Lago Dorado at Disney's Coronado Springs Resort

This shimmering fifteen-acre lake is surrounded by the rustic cabanas of the sprawling Coronado Springs resort. The mile-long Esplanade encircles the lake and is used by bicyclists and pedestrians. Boaters can rent watercraft at La Marina.

The Fort Wilderness Waterways

Friendly ducks and not-so-friendly swans share these shady waterways with native waterfowl and boaters. The canals resemble bayous, closed in by pine forests and overhanging gray-green Spanish moss. Here and there, boaters will find picnic-perfect inlets or coves filled with water reeds and an occasional blue heron standing guard. Watercraft can be rented at the Bike Barn. ◆

Walt Disney World is home to the largest privately owned fleet of watercraft in the world — and much of it is available to visitors who would like to explore the extensive waterways and interconnected lakes that span the Walt Disney World Resort. Most marinas rent boats every day from about 10 AM until dusk.

LAKES AND WATERWAYS

Seven Seas Lagoon and Bay Lake: Together, these two busy lakes total 650 acres, forming the largest body of water at Walt Disney World. They are connected by a unique water bridge and are used for boating, waterskiing, and fishing excursions. Forests and wetlands surround the lakes, which are accented by miles of white sand beaches. The wetlands are home to a large population of native waterfowl, including egrets, herons, and pelicans. Watercraft can be rented at the following marinas:

Marina Pavilion at Disney's Contemporary Resort
Teton Bike & Boat at Disney's Wilderness Lodge
The Marina at Disney's Fort Wilderness Resort and Campground
Catamaran Corner at Disney's Polynesian Resort
Captain's Shipyard at Disney's Grand Floridian Resort & Spa.

Buena Vista Lagoon and Downtown Disney Waterways: Buena Vista Lagoon, thirty-five acres of man-made lake, is the showcase lake of the Downtown Disney Resorts Area. Along its shores is the sprawling architecture of Downtown Disney. The narrow waterways angle off from the lagoon and wind through pine forests and shady, vine-covered bayous. They lead past Willow Lake at the Disney Institute, branch off into the Trumbo Canal at Old Key West, and become the Sassagoula River at Dixie Landings and Port Orleans. Boaters can rent their craft at the following marinas:

Cap'n Jack's Marina at The Marketplace at Downtown Disney
Hank's Rent 'N Return at Disney's Old Key West Resort
The Landing at Disney's Port Orleans Resort
Dixie Levee at Disney's Dixie Landings Resort
The Sports and Fitness Center at the Disney Institute.

Crescent Lake: This lake is surrounded by some of the most intriguing architecture at Walt Disney World, including the fanciful Dolphin and Swan resorts, the New England seaside architecture of the Yacht Club and Beach Club resorts, and the lively Atlantic City–style waterfront at Disney's BoardWalk. Watercraft can be rented at the Bayside Marina at Disney's Yacht Club and Beach Club Resorts.

WATERCRAFT

Visitors can select from a wide variety of watercraft at the Walt Disney World marinas, including speedboats, sailboats, canopy boats, pontoon boats, pedal boats, kayaks, canoes, and rowboats. Boats can be rented by the hour or half hour and are available to both Walt Disney World resort guests and day visitors with a valid driver's license (a few exceptions are noted below). Self-operated boats are rented on a first-come, first-served basis and cannot be reserved.

Water Mice: These tiny one- to two-passenger mini speedboats sit low in the water and zip along at about ten miles per hour. Water Mice are used exclusively on the lakes and are not allowed in the canals or narrow waterways. Rentals start at about $30 per hour. Water mice are available to both Walt Disney World resort guests and day visitors and can be rented at the following marinas and resorts: Contemporary, Grand Floridian, Wilderness Lodge, Coronado Springs, Polynesian, Yacht Club, Beach Club, Caribbean Beach, and Cap'n Jack's Marina at Downtown Disney.

Sailboats: Experienced sailors may charter sailboats and catamarans in a variety of sizes and styles. Sailboat rentals start at about $12 per hour. Sailboats are available at the following resort marinas: Contemporary, Wilderness Lodge, Grand Floridian, Polynesian, Yacht Club, Beach Club, and Caribbean Beach.

Pontoon Boats: These motor-powered watercraft are canopied and sit high in the water atop gleaming stainless-steel pontoons. Pontoon boat rentals start at about $46 per hour for twenty-foot boats. They are available at the following marinas and resorts: Contemporary, Grand Floridian, Polynesian, Yacht Club, Beach Club, Old Key West, Port Orleans, Dixie Landings, Caribbean Beach, Fort Wilderness Marina, Wilderness Lodge, and Cap'n Jack's Marina at Downtown Disney. For larger pontoon boats, which require a driver, see *Special Events* → "Party Boat Excursions."

Canopy Boats: Motorized canopy boats may be used on both the lakes and waterways. Their striped canvas canopies provide shade, and they are ideal sightseeing craft for up to eight passengers. Rental fees for canopy boats run about $22 per half hour. Canopy boats can be rented at the following marinas and resorts: Contemporary, Grand Floridian, Polynesian, Yacht Club, Beach Club, Old Key West, Port Orleans, Dixie Landings, Caribbean Beach, Fort Wilderness Marina, Wilderness Lodge, and Cap'n Jack's Marina at Downtown Disney. ◆

People-Powered Vessels

Pedal Boats: These people-powered watercraft, also called paddle boats, will cruise along as fast as you can pedal. Pedal boat rentals start at about $12 per hour and are available at the following marinas and resorts: Polynesian, Yacht Club, Beach Club, Port Orleans, Disney Institute, Dixie Landings, Old Key West, Caribbean Beach, Coronado Springs, and the Bike Barn at Fort Wilderness. The Dolphin and Swan resorts have swan-shaped pedal boats.

Canoes & Kayaks: Three-passenger canoes and single or double kayak rentals start at about $12 per hour. Canoes are available at these resorts: Caribbean Beach, Dixie Landings, Grand Floridian, Polynesian, Port Orleans, and the Disney Institute. Kayaks are available at Coronado Springs, Dixie Landings, Grand Floridian, and Port Orleans.

Outrigger Canoes: These large sturdy canoes were fashioned by the Polynesians for steady travel through the pounding surf. Outrigger canoes are restricted to Seven Seas Lagoon and are only available at the Polynesian resort. Outriggers hold up to eight passengers and require a minimum of five persons of substantial weight to row. Outrigger canoes are free and there is no time limit. ◆

Essentials

Attractions

Hotels

Restaurants

Special Events

Recreation

Resources

Wide World of Sports • Watersports • Tennis Clubs • Spas & Fitness Centers • Miniature Golf • Golf Courses • Fishing • Boating • Bicycling • Auto Racing • Sports Events

FISHING EXCURSIONS

Pole Fishing

The Fort Wilderness Waterways

Fishing is permitted in the miles of picturesque waterways that traverse Fort Wilderness. Fish may be caught from the grassy banks of the canals, or visitors can rent pedal boats, kayaks, or canoes. Poles can be rented at the Bike Barn in the Meadow Recreation Area at Fort Wilderness. Cane poles rent for about $2 per hour or $4 per day; rod-and-reel combinations rent for about $4 per hour or $8 per day. Bait is sold at the Meadow Trading Post nearby. The Bike Barn is open from 8 AM until dusk.

Cap'n Jack's Marina at Downtown Disney

Walt Disney World visitors can rent old-fashioned cane poles to fish for bluegill in the Buena Vista Lagoon from the dock at Cap'n Jack's Marina at The Marketplace. Cane poles can be rented for about $4 at Cap'n Jack's Marina. Cap'n Jack's Marina is open from 10 AM until sundown.

The Fishing Hole at Disney's Dixie Landings Resort

Visitors fish from an old-fashioned roped-off dock at The Fishing Hole, which is stocked with bass, bluegill, and catfish. So far, the biggest catfish pulled from this fishing hole weighed in at seven pounds. Cane poles can be rented for about $4 per hour at The Fishing Hole on Ol' Man Island. Bait is provided and worm-hooking instructions are offered, a rare treat for the squeamish. The Fishing Hole is open from 8 AM until 3 PM (varies seasonally). ◆

Fishing at Walt Disney World is extremely popular and seats on fishing excursions fill quickly. Professional anglers lead the tours, and they are knowledgeable about the waterways and the most propitious fishing spots. The two main fishing areas are Bay Lake and Buena Vista Lagoon. At the time that Disney began development at Walt Disney World, Bay Lake supported a number of native fish such as largemouth bass, bluegill, Seminole killfish, lake chubsuckers, and spotted gar. The fish continue to propagate well and provide a balanced ecosystem that supports a large population of native waterfowl. To reserve a spot on a guided fishing tour, call the Walt Disney World Sports and Recreation Line (407 939-7529).

GUIDED EXCURSIONS

Private fishing excursions are available at most marinas. Visitors can and should reserve their spot up to sixty days in advance. No fishing license is required at Walt Disney World. Visitors may use their own equipment, although tackle is provided and bait is readily available. All fishing is done on a catch-and-release basis, with the exception of fish weighing over eight pounds.

Bay Lake Excursions: Bay Lake, the largest natural lake at Walt Disney World, is the fishing ground for these excursions. The lake is surrounded by wetlands that are home to a large population of native waterfowl, including great white egrets, herons, and pelicans. Largemouth bass that have been caught here have weighed as much as thirteen pounds. Fishers take pontoon boats, which depart from the Fort Wilderness Marina. Bay Lake excursions cost about $150 for 2 hours and $50 for an additional hour and include boat, guide, all tackle, bait, and refreshments. Shiners are about $10 a dozen. Fishing boats usually leave at 8 and 11:30 AM, and 3 PM; there is a limit of five participants each. Times vary throughout the year. Tip: Boats will also pick up guests at the Polynesian, Wilderness Lodge, Grand Floridian, and Contemporary.

Buena Vista Lagoon Fishing Excursion: This excursion travels the waterways of both Buena Vista Lagoon and Downtown Disney. Buena Vista Lagoon and the picturesque bayous that feed it were excavated from swamp land. A mounting service is available for visitors who catch fish weighing over eight pounds. Pontoon boats generally depart at 6:30 and 9 AM from Cap'n Jack's Marina at Downtown Disney. Times vary throughout the year. The excursions cost about $150 for 2 hours for two to five people or $75 for one person, including boat, guide, bait, and all tackle. Tip: Excursion boats will also pick up guests at Dixie Landings, Port Orleans, Old Key West, and Disney Institute.

Yacht Club Fishing Excursion: Fishing the waters of Crescent Lake makes visitors feel they are in the midst of a New England coastal resort. The 2 hour fishing excursion is limited to a maximum of five participants on each trip. Cruises generally cast off at 7 and 10 AM from the Bayside Marina at Disney's Yacht Club Resort. Times vary throughout the year. The cost is about $150 for 2 hours, which includes boat, guide, all tackle, bait, and snacks. Tip: The first fishing trip of the day enters the World Showcase Lagoon and is the most enjoyable for both atmosphere and catch ratio.

BoardWalk Fishing Excursion: This 2 hour fishing adventure begins on the waters of Crescent Lake and continues to the World Showcase Lagoon at Epcot to fish along the waterfront of the international pavilions. Each trip is limited to a maximum of five participants and usually leaves three times daily at 7 and 9 AM and 1 PM. Times vary throughout the year. Excursions leave from the boat dock at Disney's BoardWalk and cost about $150 for 2 hours, which includes boat, guide, all tackle, bait, and refreshments. Tip: Usually the first trip of the day will enter the World Showcase Lagoon, where the atmosphere is peaceful and the catch ratio is higher than at Crescent Lake.

Sassagoula River Fishing Excursion: This 2 hour fishing excursion begins along the tree-lined Sassagoula River, which feeds into Buena Vista Lagoon, a primary fishing site. The early-morning fishing trip departs once daily at 6:30 AM from the Dixie Levee at Disney's Dixie Landings Resort. The cost is about $60 per person, which includes boat, guide, all tackle, bait, and beverage. Space is booked on a party-boat basis, where anyone can join the group. It carries up to five participants at a time and is a great way for solo travelers to meet others in a relaxed setting. Tip: One of the best features is that the fishing excursion will take place even if only one participant is aboard, making this a real treat during the occasional times when bookings are slow. ◆

Seafood Restaurants

The catch-and-release policy throughout Walt Disney World may prevent anglers from enjoying the fruits of their labor, but it doesn't mean good fish and seafood can't be found. Listed below is a selection of some of Walt Disney World's best seafood restaurants. See the "Restaurants" section for full descriptions.

Coral Reef Restaurant

The Coral Reef Restaurant inside The Living Seas pavilion in Future World at Epcot serves a variety of fresh seafood. One wall of this restaurant is formed by one of the largest saltwater aquariums in the world. Open for lunch from 11:30 AM, dinner from 4:30 PM until park closing.

The Flying Fish Café

The popular Flying Fish Café near the center of Disney's BoardWalk serves distinctive cuisine with innovative flavor combinations. Fresh seafood is featured, as well as steaks and homemade pastas. This relaxed, yet sophisticated restaurant serves dinner Sunday through Thursday from 5:30 until 10 PM; Friday and Saturday from 5:30 until 10:30 PM.

Fulton's Crab House

The food focus at Fulton's is primarily on lobster, crab, and fresh fish. The menu changes frequently to take advantage of seasonal fish from around the world. The three-story riverboat serves lunch from 11:30 AM and dinner from 5:30 PM until midnight. ◆

Essentials • Attractions • Hotels • Restaurants • Special Events • Recreation • Resources

Sports Events • Auto Racing • Bicycling • Boating • **Fishing** • Golf Courses • Miniature Golf • Spas & Fitness Centers • Tennis Clubs • Watersports • Wide World of Sports

Essentials • Attractions • Hotels • Restaurants • Special Events • Recreation • Resources

Wide World of Sports • Watersports • Tennis Clubs • Spas & Fitness Centers • Miniature Golf • Golf Courses • Fishing • Boating • Bicycling • Auto Racing • Sports Events

GOLF COURSES

Golf Course Facilities

All 18-hole courses have driving ranges, putting greens, locker rooms, and a pro shop that sells golf apparel, equipment, and accessories.

Food and Beverages

The Garden Gallery — Golfers playing the Magnolia, Palm, and Oak Trail courses can walk over to the Shades of Green resort for a bite to eat. Breakfast, lunch, and dinner are served, and the adjoining Back Porch Lounge is open all day.

The Sand Trap Bar and Grill — This eatery at the Bonnet Creek Golf Club serves breakfast and lunch for those playing Eagle Pines and Osprey Ridge golf courses. An adjoining lounge is open all day.

Seasons — This award-winning restaurant, located at the Disney Institute, is adjacent to the Lake Buena Vista Golf Course. Breakfast, lunch, and dinner are served.

Transportation

Complimentary taxi service to and from golf courses is available to guests staying at any Walt Disney World resort. The Magnolia, Palm, and Oak Trail courses are located in the Magic Kingdom Area. Eagle Pines and Osprey Ridge golf courses are part of the Bonnet Creek Golf Club, which lies between Fort Wilderness and Downtown Disney. The Lake Buena Vista Golf Course is located at the Disney Institute and is within walking distance of most Hotel Plaza resorts. ◆

Walt Disney World sometimes calls itself "The Magic Linkdom" and with good reason: It boasts five outstanding championship golf courses (three are on the PGA Tour) and a par-36 practice course. With ninety-nine holes of golf and nearly twenty-five thousand guest rooms, Walt Disney World is the largest golf resort on the planet. Each year, more than 250,000 rounds of golf are played on the Walt Disney World golf courses and nearly four hundred golf tournaments are held here, including the biggest on the PGA Tour, the Walt Disney World/National Car Rental Golf Classic (see Recreation → "Annual Sporting Events").

Advance reservations are necessary for the Walt Disney World golf courses, especially during peak seasons and holidays; greens fees average about $125. Clubs, shoes, and range balls can be rented at all golf courses. All visitors to Walt Disney World can secure time on the greens. Guests staying at a Walt Disney World resort can reserve tee times up to ninety days in advance, and day visitors may reserve up to thirty days in advance. To make reservations, call Disney Golf (407 939-4653).

THE GOLF COURSES AT WALT DISNEY WORLD

Magnolia Golf Course   Rating 73.9   Slope 133

Designed by Joe Lee, the Magnolia Golf Course is long and tight and requires a great deal of accuracy. More than fifteen hundred magnolia trees dot the course. A unique "mousetrap" on the sixth hole is a sand trap with the shape of a particular mouse's profile. The course has a preponderance of sand and water, with large greens on a rolling terrain. The layout covers 6,642 yards from the middle tees. The final round of the PGA Tour's Walt Disney World/National Car Rental Golf Classic is played on this course, and the Disney pros rate the Magnolia the third toughest of the five courses at Walt Disney World. Nearby resorts are Shades of Green, Grand Floridian, Polynesian, Contemporary, and Wilderness Lodge.

Greens Fees: Peak-season fees are about $110 for Walt Disney World resort guests and about $120 for day visitors; fees include an electric cart.

Palm Golf Course

Rating 73   Slope 133

Like the nearby Magnolia Golf Course, the graceful Palm Golf Course is lined with beautiful trees and mature greens. On this picturesque course, it is not unusual to see deer and other wildlife in the early mornings, as well as a certain alligator with a habit of strolling along the outlying fairways. This Joe Lee–designed course is a challenging one, with narrow greens, plenty of water hazards and sand traps, and some difficult doglegs. The layout covers 6,461 yards from the middle tees. The eighteenth hole has been rated the fourth toughest on the PGA Tour, and the Disney pros rate the Palm the second toughest of the five courses at Walt Disney World. Nearby resorts are Shades of Green, Grand Floridian, Polynesian, Contemporary, and Wilderness Lodge.

Greens Fees: Peak-season fees are about $110 for Walt Disney World resort guests and about $120 for day visitors; fees include an electric cart.

Lake Buena Vista Golf Course

Rating 72.7   Slope 128

The play on the Lake Buena Vista Golf Course is short and tight, but the views and fairways are wide and open. The greens are fully mature on this course, although they can be bumpy at times since many beginning golfers play here. The island green at the sixteenth hole is considered particularly challenging. This beautiful country club–like PGA course, which was designed by Joe Lee, is blanketed with pine trees, oaks, and magnolias. The layout covers 6,655 yards from the middle tees, and the Disney pros rate Lake Buena Vista the fifth toughest of the five courses at Walt Disney World. Nearby resorts include the Disney Institute, Wyndham Palace, Hilton, Grosvenor, Hotel Royal Plaza, Courtyard by Marriott, Old Key West, Port Orleans, Dixie Landings, Lake Buena Vista Best Western, and DoubleTree.

Greens Fees: Peak-season fees are about $110 for Walt Disney World resort guests and about $120 for day visitors; fees include an electric cart.

Osprey Ridge Golf Course

Rating 73.9   Slope 135

This extra-long links-style course was designed by Tom Fazio with plenty of berms and mounds as well as some excellent par-3s. Lakes and creeks were excavated to create the elevated ridge that is the course's central feature. Nesting platforms have attracted ospreys to the course, and red-tailed hawks can be seen perched in the tall pine trees or flying overhead as they patrol the area. The course features large greens interspersed

---

RECREATION
Golf Courses

Improving Your Game

Golf Lessons

Walt Disney World Golf offers a variety of lessons for novice and experienced golfers who wish to improve their game. All lessons are taught by PGA professionals. Private lessons can be arranged through Disney Golf (407 939-4653).

Private Lessons — Thirty-minute private lessons are available for about $50. Players can also have their swings taped and analyzed in a private video lesson for about $75. The tapes are theirs to keep for repeated viewing at home.

The Playing Lesson — Advanced golfers can have a pro walk the course with them and observe their game. The Playing Lesson costs about $150.

Golf Clinics

Two-hour golf clinics are available to all visitors through the Disney Institute. In groups of twelve to sixteen, players can work on their swing under the tutelage of PGA professionals. Offered daily in the morning, the clinics are usually held at the driving range at the Lake Buena Vista Golf Course.

Golf Clinics cost about $75. Guests who have purchased a Disney Institute package can reserve clinics up to six months in advance. Guests at other Walt Disney World resorts and day visitors can reserve a clinic up to thirty days in advance. To make reservations, call the Disney Institute (800 282-9282). ◆

Essentials

Attractions

Hotels

Restaurants

Special Events

Recreation

Resources

Wide World of Sports • Watersports • Tennis Clubs • Spas & Fitness Centers • Miniature Golf • **Golf Courses** • Fishing • Boating • Bicycling • Auto Racing • Sports Events

RECREATION
Golf Courses

Golf Tips & Specials

Golf for half price at Walt Disney World by playing at the right times! During peak golf season (September through mid-May), play after 2 or 3 PM and get a 50 percent discount on greens fees. Be sure to ask for the Twilight Golf rate when making reservations. Call Disney Golf (407 939-4653).

During the summer months (from mid-May through August), you can book a game any time after 9 AM at any course for about $50, more than 50 percent off the cost of a preferred tee time.

Guests staying at a Walt Disney World resort receive a discount of about 10 percent on golf during peak seasons.

Walt Disney Travel Company offers an all-inclusive Golf Getaway vacation package for visitors who would like to play often during their stay. Call the Walt Disney World Travel Company (800 828-0228) for more information.

with wilderness areas and has become a favorite with experienced golfers. The layout covers 6,705 yards from the middle tees, and the Disney pros rate Osprey Ridge the toughest of the five courses at Walt Disney World. Nearby resorts include Fort Wilderness, Wilderness Lodge, Dixie Landings, Port Orleans, Old Key West, and Disney Institute.

Greens Fees: Peak-season fees are about $130 for Walt Disney World resort guests and about $135 for day visitors; fees include an electric cart.

Eagle Pines Golf Course   *Rating 73.9   Slope 135*

This challenging course designed by Pete Dye requires strategic play. Golfers must think their way from tee to green through the stark, low-profile terrain. It's a tricky course, and its inwardly sloping fairways and unusual landscaping can be visually intimidating. Water offers a challenge at sixteen holes, and instead of rough, the fairways are lined with pine needles and sand, giving the course a distinctive look and allowing for fast play. The layout covers 6,224 yards from the middle tees, and the Disney pros rate Eagle Pines the fourth toughest of the five courses at Walt Disney World. Nearby resorts are Fort Wilderness, Wilderness Lodge, Dixie Landings, Port Orleans, Old Key West, and Disney Institute.

Greens Fees: Peak-season fees are about $130 for Walt Disney World resort guests and about $135 for day visitors; fees include an electric cart.

Oak Trail Golf Course

The Oak Trail Golf Course, also called the Executive or Family Course, has some of the most challenging holes at Walt Disney World. The nine-hole, par-36 course features two par-5s, two par-3s, and five par-4s. Local pros often play here to work on their game. The layout covers 2,913 yards from the men's tees. Nearby resorts are Shades of Green, Grand Floridian, Polynesian, Contemporary, and Wilderness Lodge.

Greens Fees: About $25 for one round and about $35 for two rounds; fees include a pull-cart. No electric cart; this course is walking only. ◆

MINIATURE GOLF

Walt Disney World offers two themed miniature golf parks that provide a fun couple of hours. The Fantasia park, composed of Fantasia Gardens and Fantasia Fairways, is located in the Epcot Resorts Area, across the street from the Walt Disney World Swan. Winter Summerland is adjacent to Blizzard Beach water park. A round of miniature golf costs about $10 for adults, $8 for children. Visitors can play consecutive rounds at any of the three courses for half price. A discounted combination ticket for Blizzard Beach and Winter Summerland is also offered.

Fantasia Gardens

Fantasia Gardens, or "The Hippo-est Golf in Town," is whimsically designed around musical pieces from the Disney animated classic *Fantasia*. Dancing ostriches, twirling hippos, and other characters from the film appear at each of the course's holes. At the final hole, Mickey presides as the sorcerer's apprentice, surrounded by brooms and water pails that tip and "spill" their contents, surprising and occasionally splashing players and other passersby. Experienced mini golfers rate Fantasia Gardens as so-so by mini golf standards and disappointing as a Disney attraction.

Fantasia Fairways

Fantasia Fairways is a scaled-down version of an actual golf course. Artful landscaping, small hills, and manicured greens create a pleasant outdoor environment where visitors can practice and hone their putting skills. Water hazards, sand traps, and some tricky doglegs enhance the "golf course" ambience. Experienced mini golfers rate Fantasia Fairways as an interesting change from typical mini golf themes. Golfers may find Fantasia a charming and easy putting exercise.

Winter Summerland

This mini golf park located next to Blizzard Beach shares the water park's "snowstorm in Florida" theme with Snow and Sand, each one an eighteen-hole course. The Snow course features various winter scenes with Santa and his elves playing hockey, skiing, and building toys. Squirting snowmen, surprise gift boxes, and Christmas carols over the sound system add to the festive air. On the Sand course, music from The Beach Boys takes center stage. Surfboards, sandcastles, and Santa's summer house are featured. Both courses are amusing and easy to play, but like Fantasia Gardens, the theming may seem disappointing by Disney standards. ◆

Sporting Gear

Athletes and sports enthusiasts can find a variety of sports merchandise throughout Walt Disney World. In addition to various golf and tennis pro shops, stores throughout Walt Disney World also stock athletic wear and equipment.

Disney's Wide World of Sports

D-Sports — Located just outside the main gates to Wide World of Sports, this shop offers a large selection of athletic wear, including performance swimsuits for men and women, and game balls for just about every sport. A small collection of sports memorabilia can be found here.

Downtown Disney

Team Mickey — This store has a large selection of athletic wear for men and women, including ABC Sports logo merchandise. It is the only location in Walt Disney World where athletic shoes can be purchased.

The Magic Kingdom

Main Street Athletic Club — Better sportswear, such as golf and tennis sweaters, can be purchased here. Golf accessories and sports-related toys for children are also available. In the Hall of Champions room, a fine collection of sports memorabilia is on display.

Disney's All-Star Sports Resort

Sport Goofy — This small store carries footballs, soccer balls, and sports-related toys for children. ◆

SPAS & FITNESS CENTERS

Fitness Centers at the Resorts

Among the best-staffed fitness centers are Body By Jake Health Studio, Ship Shape Health Club, and Muscles and Bustles. Fitness centers at the Contemporary, Dolphin, and BoardWalk are open to guests staying at other Walt Disney World resorts. The following resorts have fitness centers that feature up-to-date fitness equipment.

Disney's Old Key West Resort

This small facility is open from 6 AM until midnight and is stocked with basic fitness equipment. Massage is available by appointment. Admission is complimentary and available to registered guests only.

Disney's Yacht Club and Beach Club Resorts

Ship Shape Health Club — Open from 6 AM until 9 PM. Guests are charged about $12 per person for the first day, about $20 for a length-of-stay pass, and about $40 for a family length-of-stay pass for up to five people. Services include massage therapy and aromatherapy.

Disney's BoardWalk Inn and Villas

Muscles and Bustles — Open from 6 AM until 9 PM. Guests are charged about $12 per person for the first day, about $20 for length-of-stay pass, and about $40 for a family length-of-stay pass for up to five people. A tanning booth is available. Services include massage therapy and aromatherapy. ➤

In recent years, several upscale full-service spas have opened in the resorts at Walt Disney World. The spas are available to all visitors for massage or other spa treatments, which sounds pretty good after a hard day in the theme parks. Hotels with full-service spas are ideal destination resorts for visitors who would like to include a spa experience as part of their Walt Disney World vacation. For visitors who want to continue their exercise program while on vacation or even start a new one, many of the better Walt Disney World resorts have well-appointed fitness centers, some staffed with professional fitness trainers.

FULL-SERVICE SPAS

The Spa at the Disney Institute: As part of Disney's expanding focus on wellness, this facility offers cutting-edge exercise equipment along with a full-service spa with ten private rooms for body and skin care treatments. The Sports and Fitness Center offers weight circuit training and computer analysis of strength and agility. The Spa specialists use holistic products and techniques, including aromatherapy massage, seaweed therapy, and hydration treatments. French body polish, facials, manicures, pedicures, after-workout body therapy, and personal training are also available.

The spa also has a fully equipped fitness club with a jogging track, up-to-the-minute Cybex cardiovascular and strength training equipment, free weights, an indoor current pool, sauna, steam room, and whirlpool. Spa guests can make appointments with fitness experts for personal training and nutrition consultation.

Guests staying at The Villas are charged about $15 per day or about $35 per length of stay for the use of spa and fitness center facilities. Family rates cost $30 a day or $50 for a length-of-stay pass. Spa services are sold a la carte, and spa facilities are included in full- or half-day spa packages. Half-day packages at The Spa start at about $190 and include four treatments. A three-day spa package, which includes selected spa services, Disney Institute programs, accommodations, meals, and events, starts at about $650 per person. The Spa at the Disney Institute is open from 8 AM until 8 PM. Advance reservations are required; for appointments call the Disney Institute Spa (407 827-4455). For information on spa vacation packages, call Disney Institute Day Visitor Programs (407 827-4800).

Disney's Grand Floridian Resort & Spa: The Grand Floridian extends its first-rate service and attention to detail to include its luxurious Spa and Health Club. The paned glass windows of the turn-of-the-century-era building fill the elegant interior with cheery brightness. The pleasant nine-thousand-square-foot spa has sixteen private treatment rooms — including a couples room — for massage, body wraps, hydrotherapy, manicures, and pedicures. Therapies include a jet-lag treatment for weary travelers and a pampering leg and foot massage for weary park hoppers. A "Spa to Go" consultation includes a series of treatments and instructions on how to adapt them to individual lifestyles.

The Health Club is fully equipped with Cybex cardiovascular and strength training equipment. Professional trainers are on hand for personal training consultations and fitness evaluations that analyze current levels of flexibility and strength.

Walt Disney World resort guests are charged about $12 per day for the use of the spa and fitness center facilities. Spa services may be purchased a la carte, or in full- or half-day spa packages. A half-day spa package starts at about $190 and includes three treatments. Complete spa vacation packages are also available. All spa packages include use of the health club facilities. The Spa and Health Club is open from 9 AM until 7 PM. Advance reservations are recommended; for appointments, call the Grand Floridian Spa and Health Club (407 824-2332).

The Spa at the Wyndham Palace: The Spa at the Wyndham Palace is a ten-thousand-square-foot spa offering luxurious beauty treatments and wellness therapies. The spa features a private lap pool, outdoor whirlpools, men's and women's locker rooms, steam rooms, saunas, and showers as well as a first-rate fitness center.

Massages, hydrotherapy, reflexology, body wraps, scrubs and polishes, and facials can be administered in one of fourteen treatment rooms. A beauty salon provides hair styling, manicures, pedicures, and waxing.

The fitness club is fully equipped with LifeFitness cardiovascular machines, strength training implements, and free weights. A nutritionist and fitness specialist is on staff for consultation and personal training.

Hotel guests at the Wyndham Palace are charged $10 for use of the fitness center, and day visitors pay $20. Spa treatments can be purchased individually or in packages starting at $200. A spa lunch can be included as part of a package or ordered a la carte. Fees for all individual spa treatments and spa packages include use of the fitness center. The Spa at Wyndham Palace is open from 6 AM until 9 PM. Reservations are recommended about two weeks prior to arrival; for appointments, call the Wyndham Palace Resort & Spa's toll-free number (800 327-2990). ◆

RECREATION
Spas & Fitness Centers

Disney's Contemporary Resort

Contemporary Health and Fitness Club — Open from 6 AM until 9 PM. Guests are charged about $12 per visit, about $20 for their entire stay, and about $20 per family stay for up to five people. Staff services include massage therapy and aromatherapy. A tanning booth is available.

Disney's Coronado Springs Resort

The Fitness Center — This small, modern facility is open from 6 AM until 9 PM. Guests are charged about $12 per visit, about $20 for their entire stay, and about $20 per family stay for up to five people. Services include massage therapy and aromatherapy.

Walt Disney World Dolphin

Body By Jake Health Studio — Open from 6 AM until 9 PM. Club admission is complimentary to hotel guests. Guests staying at other Walt Disney World resorts pay $10 a day. Services include massage therapy and aromatherapy.

Walt Disney World Swan

Swan Health Club — Open from 6 AM until 11 PM. The club is complimentary and open to hotel guests only. Services include massage therapy, Swedish massage, and deep tissue massage. ◆

Essentials • Attractions • Hotels • Restaurants • Special Events • Recreation • Resources

Sports Events • Auto Racing • Bicycling • Boating • Fishing • Golf Courses • Miniature Golf • Spas & Fitness Centers • Tennis Clubs • Watersports • Wide World of Sports

Essentials · Attractions · Hotels · Restaurants · Special Events · Recreation · Resources

Wide World of Sports • Watersports • **Tennis Clubs** • Spas & Fitness Centers • Miniature Golf • Golf Courses • Fishing • Boating • Bicycling • Auto Racing • Sports Events

TENNIS CLUBS

Tennis Courts at the Resorts

The following resorts have lighted tennis courts on their grounds. Use of these courts is complimentary and reservations are not required. Tennis equipment is often available to registered guests at no charge or for a nominal fee.

Disney's BoardWalk Inn and BoardWalk Villas
Disney's Fort Wilderness Resort and Campground
Disney's Old Key West Resort
Disney's Yacht Club and Beach Club Resorts
DoubleTree Guest Suites Resort
Grosvenor Resort
Hotel Royal Plaza
Shades of Green
Walt Disney World Dolphin and Swan
Wyndham Palace Resort & Spa

Disney's Grand Floridian Resort & Spa has two clay-surfaced courts. Reservations are recommended and court time costs about $15 a hour. Instructors from the Contemporary's Racquet Club will conduct lessons at the Grand Floridian. Reservations for both courts and lessons can be made through Disney's Sports and Recreation Line (407 939-7529). ◆

Most Walt Disney World resorts have well-designed tennis courts hidden inside forests or overlooking beaches, lakes, golf courses, and pools. Serious tennis players may want to take advantage of the tennis programs available at Walt Disney World, where certified tennis pros offer private lessons and challenging tennis clinics.

Disney's Racquet Club at the Contemporary Resort: The tennis courts at Disney's Racquet Club are located next to the Contemporary resort's north garden wing along the shore of Bay Lake. All six courts are surfaced in top-of-the-line Hydro-Grid clay. Several of the courts are set up for competition play, complete with bleachers. Courts are open from 7 AM until 7 PM. Rental equipment is available at the Racquet Club pro shop, which also has two practice courts. The pro shop offers restringing services and a "Tennis Anyone?" program that matches tennis players with game partners. Call the Racquet Pro Shop for matching (407 824-3578). Court time costs about $15 per hour (about $40 per family for an entire stay). Play-by-play video analysis can be arranged for about $60 per hour. Private lessons cost about $50 per hour and a ball machine may be rented for about $25 per hour. Reservations for courts and lessons are recommended and can be arranged through Disney's Sports and Recreation Line (407 939-7529). Courts can be reserved by both Walt Disney World resort guests and day visitors.

Tennis Programs at Disney Institute: The Disney Institute's four clay tennis courts were specifically constructed to ensure an even moisture content year round. Visiting tennis players can sign up for one or more of the instructional courses offered in the Tennis Program at the Disney Institute. The 2 hour courses were designed in conjunction with Peter Burwash International, a world-renowned professional tennis organization. The courses in the Tennis Program offer play-by-play video analysis and focus on fine-tuning fundamentals, developing playing strategies, and combining weight resistance training with game techniques. Customized private and group lessons with a tennis pro are also available. The Tennis Program costs about $50 per course. Private tennis instruction is about $50 per hour. All visitors enrolled in Tennis Program courses may use the Sports and Fitness Center facilities. All Walt Disney World visitors can reserve Tennis Program courses up to thirty days in advance by calling Disney Institute Day Visitor Programs (407 827-4800). To arrange for private tennis instruction, call Disney Sports and Recreation (407 939-7529). ◆

WATER SPORTS

Waterskiers skim across the surface of Bay Lake all year long, and if you look up, you may see someone parasailing in the sky, tethered by a rope to a speedboat below. Everyone from novices to experts can make use of Walt Disney World's fleet of speedboats and waterskiing and parasailing equipment. All technical water sports are run by Sammy Duvall's WaterSports Center and leave from the Contemporary's Marina Pavilion. Speedboat drivers are professional instructors and certified by the American Waterski Association. Tney offer instruction and helpful tips to both beginning and advanced skiers. Waterskiing and parasailing excursions are available to all visitors. Reservations are required at least one day in advance and can be made up to ninety days in advance by calling Disney Sports and Recreation (407 939-7529).

Waterskiing: Ski boats reaching speeds of up to fifty miles per hour tow waterskiers close behind as they glide across the water. Groups of up to five people can waterski together, with a two-person minimum. The fee for waterskiing excursions is per hour rather than per person, so teaming up with other waterskiers can be economical. Along with standard water-skis, excursion boats carry Scurfers (mini surfboards), Hydraslides (knee boards), slalom skis, inner tubes, and wakeboards.

Excursions cost about $125 per hour and include ski boat, driver-instructor, and waterskiing equipment. Participants may bring their own waterskis if they wish. There is a maximum of five persons per boat.

At least two waterskiing boats are in operation at all times on Bay Lake, where all waterskiing is done at Walt Disney World. Times vary with the season, and excursions can sometimes be delayed or canceled due to poor weather conditions. Waterskiing is extremely popular during peak-attendance seasons, on warm weekends, and during holidays, so make reservations well in advance if you will be traveling to Walt Disney World at any of these times.

Parasailing: Parasailing may look very daring, but it requires no prior experience. Paired or solo parasailers only need to settle into the parasail seat, put on the harness, and away they go, soaring up to 600 feet in the air as they are towed around Bay Lake by a speedboat. The views are spectacular (there is no higher vantage point in the entire resort) and the ride is unforgettable!

Excursions cost about $70 per person for 4 to 6 minutes of soaring, $110 for a tandem ride, and about $30 per person to ride along on the boat without going aloft. Parasailers who weigh less than 200 pounds must ride double, and will be paired with another visitor in order to ride. ◆

Swimming Pools and White Sand Beaches

Every Walt Disney World resort has at least one swimming pool for registered guests to cool off from the hot Florida sun. There are numerous beaches at the Walt Disney World resorts, and anyone bringing along a towel can stake a place in the sand. Generally, swimming in the lakes is not allowed.

Lap Pools — Lap pools or Olympic-sized pools suitable for swimming laps can be found at the following resorts:

> The Disney Institute
> Disney's Beach Club Resort
> Disney's Contemporary Resort
> Disney's Fort Wilderness Resort
> Disney's Yacht Club Resort
> Walt Disney World Swan and Dolphin
> Wyndham Palace Resort & Spa.

White Sand Beaches — Most Walt Disney World resorts offer stretches of white sand beach with comfortable lounge chairs and cabanas to relax in. Beaches can be found at the following resorts:

> Disney's Beach Club Resort
> Disney's Caribbean Beach Resort
> Disney's Contemporary Resort
> Disney's Coronado Springs Resort
> Disney's Fort Wilderness Resort
> Disney's Grand Floridian Resort
> Disney's Old Key West Resort
> Disney's Polynesian Resort
> Disney's Wilderness Lodge
> Walt Disney World Swan and Dolphin.

Attractions • Hotels • Restaurants • Special Events • Recreation • Resources

Sports Events • Auto Racing • Bicycling • Boating • Fishing • Golf Courses • Miniature Golf • Spas & Fitness Centers • Tennis Clubs • Watersports • Wide World of Sports

DISNEY'S WIDE WORLD OF SPORTS

To Do or Dine

The NFL Experience — In this interactive exhibit, football fans can spend an hour or two at a simulated NFL training camp. Visitors can throw and receive passes, punt for distance, field tacklers, receive punts, and run for the touchdown. There is also an obstacle course and photo opportunities with static NFL players and crowds. One of the most popular activities is Go For Distance! where visitors attempt to kick field goals through real goal posts. Football-themed arcade games are available for the less physically inclined. Children can kick and pass mini-footballs in the NFL Kid's Zone and play in a helmet-shaped moon bounce. Entrance is included in the general admission ticket to Disney's Wide World of Sports.

Official All Star Cafe — This sports-themed restaurant has an extensive collection of authentic sports memorabilia and a sleek, contemporary look. Video monitors placed throughout the dining and bar areas show a dazzling array of live and taped sports events. The menu offers all-American fare including steaks, chicken, seafood, pasta, hot dogs, and specialty hamburgers with beef, turkey, or veggie patties. Beer, wine, and spirits are served, as are espresso and cappuccino. Open all day from 11 AM until 1 AM. (For a complete description, see *Restaurants*→ "*Official All Star Cafe*.") ◆

Walt Disney World visitors who are also sports fans will find a number of activities to interest them at Disney's Wide World of Sports. The athletic complex offers visitors the opportunity to be spectators at top-caliber amateur and professional sports competitions and even to participate in selected competitive events scheduled at various times of the year. Disney's Wide World of Sports hosts events and programs that are ideal for families and groups who would like to share in an athletic experience.

Disney's Wide World of Sports is located in the southwestern quadrant of Walt Disney World, near Blizzard Beach water park and Disney's Animal Kingdom. It covers more than 175 acres and features professional-level training and playing facilities for over thirty types of sports activities. There is a fieldhouse for basketball and other indoor competitions, a ball park, quadraplexes for baseball and softball, youth baseball fields, a tennis complex, track and field complex, multi-purpose fields, and a Velodrome, billed as "the fastest bicycle track on earth."

The Atlanta Braves call Disney's Wide World of Sports their home during spring training season, as do the Orlando O-Rays and the Tampa Bay Devil Rays' AA farm club. The complex is also the activity headquarters for the Gulf Coast Rookie League and Instructional League. The Harlem Globetrotters use Disney's Wide World of Sports as their training and development base and schedule games here each year. The United States Tennis Association's Men's Clay Court Championships are held here each spring. The Amateur Athletic Union (AAU) also schedules numerous regional and national championship events at Disney's Wide World of Sports each year.

Radio and television broadcast facilities, a full-service restaurant, and a large "town commons" area for outdoor gatherings and awards ceremonies are housed at this extensive sports complex. D-Sports, one the better equipped stores for athletic wear and sporting gear in Walt Disney World, can be found here.

Sporting events at Disney's Wide World of Sports are very popular, and tickets sell out quickly. Purchasing advance tickets through any local Ticketmaster outlet is recommended. To participate in events or to inquire about upcoming games, call Disney's Wide World of Sports Information Line (407 363-6600). For information on sports events vacation packages, call Walt Disney Travel Company Sports Reservations (407 939-7810). ◆

Essentials

Attractions

Hotels

Restaurants

Special Events

Recreation

Resources

Packing • Orlando Airport • Airport Hotels • Local Transportation • Babysitting & Day Camps • Visitors with Special Needs • Shops & Services • Crossroads Shopping Center • Guidebook Index

RESOURCES

Important Travel Tips and Planning Logistics
For Smarter, Smoother, Carefree Vacations

PACKING FOR A DISNEY VACATION

Casual clothes are the norm throughout Walt Disney World. A few of the more elegant restaurants require evening dress, and some visitors bring along fancy clothing for the nightclubs at Pleasure Island or Disney's BoardWalk. The items listed on this page are "musts" for touring Walt Disney World in comfort.

Clothing: Pack comfortable, well broken-in walking shoes — not only will you be spending much of your time on your feet, but good-quality shoes will protect your feet and toes from being trampled. Sandals can cause problems when boarding and disembarking rides and should be used poolside only. In winter, bring a sweater for layering, and pack a jacket that is lined. Don't forget gloves to keep off the chill when standing in line outdoors. Most hotels have coin-operated washers and dryers.

Sun & Weather Protection: Pack a lightweight hat or visor that shades your eyes. Bring a pair of sunglasses that provide full protection from UV rays. Choose a sun block rated SPF 15 or higher; the Florida sun will burn you even in the winter. Reapply it every hour or so (sunburn is the most frequently treated problem at first-aid stations and nearby clinics). It rains daily in the summer, so pack a rain hat and collapsible umbrella that fit in your tote bag (rain ponchos can be uncomfortably hot if worn too long).

Upon Arrival: Fill your pockets with quarters for the toll roads and dollar bills for tipping. On your drive to Walt Disney World, you may want to stop and pick up supplies for your room. The most convenient grocery store is Gooding's Supermarket at Crossroads Shopping Center (See *Resources* → "Crossroads Shopping Center"). Purchase bottled water, including some small bottles of water you can refill and carry with you as you tour. Don't forget juice, soft drinks, coffee (if your room has a coffeemaker), and any alcohol, such as beer or wine. You may also want to pick up light snacks and fresh fruit or breakfast items, which can save lots of time and money on those early-morning tours. Many resorts have small refrigerators in the rooms, or you can request one for about $10 per day. You'll save money by buying snacks and beverages outside the resorts, and you will be thankful that you have refreshments in your room after a long day of touring or as a wake-up treat first thing in the morning. ◆

Touring Essentials

Bring a fanny pack, backpack, or roomy, lightweight tote bag with a comfortable shoulder strap — you will find it invaluable for carrying around brochures, entertainment schedules, sun block, small purchases, and bottled water.

Self-sealing plastic bags are good for stashing wet bathing suits or food in your tote bag while you're touring.

All resorts provide soap and shampoo, at the very least, and the better resorts also supply hair dryers. Hair dryers can also be requested from housekeeping at most resorts.

Pack a lightweight flashlight such as a penlight, which is useful for reading maps and entertainment schedules after dark, consulting guidebooks while waiting in line at dark attractions, and reading menus in dimly lit restaurants.

Consider bringing a book to read while waiting in lines or a cassette player with headphones for audio books or music tapes. You might want to carry a bottle of soap bubbles — they provide instant soothing entertainment if you (or any young-at-heart companions) begin to get restless.

In the winter, Orlando can experience cold snaps, so before leaving, check with Disney Weather (407 824-4104). ◆

Essentials | Attractions | Hotels | Restaurants | Special Events | Recreation | Resources

Guidebook Index • Crossroads Shopping Center • Shops & Services • Visitors with Special Needs • Babysitting & Day Camps • Local Transportation • Airport Hotels • **Orlando Airport** • Packing

ORLANDO INTERNATIONAL AIRPORT

Meeting Spots at the Airport

Travelers arriving on different airlines who want to rendezvous at the airport should plan carefully. To avoid mix-ups, it is always best to meet on Level Three of the Main Terminal, since Levels One and Two have duplicate services on both sides, and you must return to Level Three to cross over. For example, there are three Dollar Rental Car counters, so if you decide to meet at Dollar on Level One, you must specify the Dollar location nearest the airline of the passenger holding the car rental reservation (reservations are held at specific counters). If there is time between arrivals, you may want to meet on Level Three after retrieving your luggage. Among the most pleasant and reliable meeting spots on Level Three are:

Orlando Marketplace (West Hall) — The food court counters close between 8 and 11 PM. Nathan's Hot Dogs is open twenty-four hours. The tables can be used at anytime.

Chili's Too — Southwest cuisine; open until 11 PM. (West Hall, mezzanine level)

Stinger Ray's — Restaurant and bar; open until 11 PM. (West Hall)

The Atrium Rotunda — A pleasant waiting area with fountain. (East Hall)

Shipyard Brewery Pub — Cafe and microbrewery; open until 11 PM. (East Hall)

Hyatt Regency — Meeting spots include the comfortable lobby area and McCoy's bistro-style restaurant, which is open until 11 PM. (East Hall, mezzanine level) ◆

This large futuristic airport is the fastest growing in the world and the first stop for most Walt Disney World visitors. The main terminal has a variety of restaurants and retail shops, including large gift shops for the area's major theme parks. The elegant Hyatt Regency hotel is inside the main terminal and is particularly convenient for visitors who are arriving late or leaving early (See Resources → *"Airport Hotels"). Automated trains transport passengers from three distant gateways to the huge main terminal where ticketing areas, baggage claim, and ground transportation are located.*

After landing in Orlando, all passengers board automated trains at their satellite terminals to reach the main terminal. The trains arrive at both ends of the long main terminal, either in the light-filled East Hall, where the atrium is surrounded by the Hyatt hotel on the upper floors, or in the West Hall, where most restaurants and the Disney Store and travel center are located. Moving walkways connect the two large halls. Passengers arrive on Level Three, where all ticket counters, shops, restaurants, and the hotel are located.

The long main terminal is also divided north and south into two very long mirror-image areas: Landside A (North) and Landside B (South). Baggage claim and ground transportation services are on both sides of Level Two. Car rental counters are on both sides of Level One. Each Landside is used by specific airlines, and each has its own ticket counters, baggage claim areas, car rental agency counters, ground transportation services, and parking lots. The main terminal can be confusing when you have several things to accomplish, such as renting cars, storing baggage, or meeting others, so listen to the recorded announcement on your train and keep an eye on the airport signs.

Airport Phone Numbers

Information about airline gate locations, general airport information, and help with departure and arrival times (24 hour recorded message and live operators from 8 AM until 5 PM):
407 825-2353

Paging number for callers outside the airport:
407 825-2000

AIRPORT HOTELS

If you're arriving at the Orlando International Airport at night, you might consider spending the night near the airport instead of driving twenty miles in the dark to find Walt Disney World and your hotel. This travel strategy can also help save money on one day of car rental and on the cost of more expensive resort accommodations on that first night. The strategy works for early morning departures as well. The hotels listed below are clustered within two miles from the airport and provide regular shuttle service to and from the airport. Most have complimentary breakfast.

AmeriSuites: The rooms in this efficiency-suites hotel have a refrigerator, microwave, coffeemaker, cable TV, hair dryer, and ironing board. An outdoor pool and fitness club are also on-site. Rates range from $90 to $150. To make reservations, call AmeriSuites Central Reservations (800 833-1516) or call the hotel directly (407 240-3939).

DoubleTree Guest Suites: This handsome hotel features two-room suites. Amenities include coffeemaker, refrigerator, hair dryer, ironing board, dataport, and voice mail. There is a full service restaurant and bar, indoor/outdoor pool, exercise room, and guest laundry. Suite rates range from $100 to $160. For reservations, call the national DoubleTree Reservation Center (800 222-8733) or call the hotel directly (407 240-5555).

Embassy Suites: Suites in this pleasant atrium building offer spacious two-room accommodations with coffeemaker, microwave, refrigerator, dataport, and weekday newspaper delivery. The hotel has a full-service restaurant, outdoor pool, fitness room, and business center. Rates range from $100 to $160. To make reservations, call Embassy Suites Central Reservations (800 362-2779) or call the hotel directly (888 729-8880).

Fairfield Inn: Clean, well-sized rooms are offered at this nice, moderately priced hotel. Local telephone calls are free, and the hotel has a fitness center. Rates range from $90 to $200. For reservations, call Fairfield Inn Central Reservations (800 228-2800) or call the hotel directly (407 888-2666).

Hilton Garden Inn: This casual offspring of the Hilton hotel chain offers spacious rooms equipped with refrigerators, microwaves, coffeemakers, hair dryers, ironing boards, and dataports. There is also a full-service restaurant and lounge, fitness center, outdoor pool, guest laundry, and business center. Rates range from $90 to $170. Ask about weekend rates and other promotional discounts. For reservations, call Hilton Central Reservations (800 445-8667) or call the hotel directly (407 240-3725). ◆

The Hyatt Regency at the Orlando International Airport

This elegant hotel occupies the upper floors of the East Hall in the main terminal of the Orlando International Airport. It overlooks the airport's beautiful atrium and fountain. Amenities include 24 hour room service, coffeemaker, in-room safe, hair dryer, newspaper delivery, turndown service, voice mail, outdoor pool, and fitness club.

For the ultimate in convenience, the Hyatt Regency can't be beat. Forget all about going to baggage claim. While guests check in, bellhops will retrieve luggage from the baggage claim area and deliver it to guest rooms. Bags are also transported from rooms to the ticket counter for departing guests. The hotel is accessible from within the airport and has its own entrance court outside.

Travelers can choose from two restaurants that are conveniently open for late arriving guests. Hemispheres Restaurant, offering Italian cuisine, is open for breakfast, lunch, and dinner until 10 PM. Great steaks and seafood are the specialty at McCoy's Bar and Grill, open daily for lunch and dinner until 11 PM.

Standard rooms are about $200 during the week and about $130 on weekends. For reservations, first call the Hyatt Central Reservations Office (800 233-1234), then call the hotel directly (407 825-1234) to compare rates. Be sure to ask about AAA discounts and the Hyatt's promotional or corporate rates. ◆

Packing • Orlando Airport • **Airport Hotels** • Local Transportation • Babysitting & Day Camps • Visitors with Special Needs • Shops & Services • Crossroads Shopping Center • Guidebook Index

Attractions   Hotels   Restaurants   Special Events   Recreation   Resources

BABYSITTING & DAY CAMPS

Guidebook Index • Crossroads Shopping Center • Shops & Services • Visitors with Special Needs • **Babysitting & Day Camps** • Local Transportation • Airport Hotels • Orlando Airport • Packing

Attractions   Hotels   Restaurants   Special Events   Recreation   Resources

Hotel Room Babysitting

ABC Mothers, Teachers, and Grannies

This service provides both in-room and within-park child care. Many guests have been very impressed with ABC's services. All caregivers have undergone extensive background checks. They are bonded and licensed and also completely knowledgeable about Walt Disney World. Cost: About $9 an hour for one child and one dollar for each additional child. There is a 4 hour minimum and a $5 transportation charge. Admission and lunch are additional if the sitter is to accompany children into the parks. Reservations required; call ABC (407 857-7447).

KinderCare

For seventeen years, KinderCare-trained sitters have provided both in-room and in-park child care at Walt Disney World, as well as other area hotels. Caregivers, who are bonded and licensed, bring along age-appropriate activities. A meal must be provided for the caregiver if the sit time runs 8 hours. KinderCare's office is open every day from 7 AM to 9 PM. Cost: About $10 per hour for one child and about $12 for two children, with a 4 hour minimum (which includes 30 minutes travel time). The cost of the caregiver's admission is added for in-park child care. Reserve at least one day in advance and up to thirty days ahead (407 827-5444; outside of Orlando, call 407 846-2027).

Guests have also recommended Fairy Godmothers (407 277-3724) and All About Kids (407 812-9300). ◆

Visitors traveling with children have a wealth of child care options at Walt Disney World, which can free them to explore the many adult-oriented entertainment and attractions that are offered. At the same time, Walt Disney World's child care centers are unique environments where kids feel entertained, not "sat." The programs are designed for children age four through twelve. Drop-off programs require that children be toilet trained; no diapers, including pull-ups, are allowed. In-room sitting and in-park child care are also available and are widely used at Walt Disney World.

BoardWalk Harbor Club: *(Disney's BoardWalk Resort)* — This clubhouse offers guests a place to keep their children amused while the adults head to the BoardWalk for some grown-up entertainment. Facilities include a large-screen TV, free video games, arts and crafts, and an assortment of Disney plush toys. Open to guests staying at any Disney-owned resort. The Harbor Club is open from 4 PM until 11:45 PM daily. Cost: About $6 per hour; children's meals are available for about $8 extra. Reservations are suggested at least 24 hours in advance (407 939-3463).

Camp Dolphin: *(Walt Disney World Dolphin)* — This busy child care and activity center provides a dinner, crafts and games, and movies in the evening. Daytime camps run seasonally. Although Camp Dolphin is available to all Walt Disney World visitors, priority is given to guests staying at the Dolphin and Swan hotels. Occupancy is limited to fifteen children. Camp Dolphin is open from 6 until 11 PM. A full night of entertainment, including dinner, costs about $50. To reserve space, call Camp Dolphin (407 934-4241).

Cub's Den: *(Disney's Wilderness Lodge)* — The Cub's Den is a fully supervised Western-themed dining and entertainment club. As children get tired, they can cuddle up with a pillow and blanket in front of a wide-screen TV to watch Disney movies. Cub's Den services are available to guests staying at any Disney-owned resort. Space is limited to twenty children. The Cub's Den is open from 5 PM until midnight. Cost: About $6 per hour with a one hour minimum. A picnic dinner can be purchased for an additional $8. Reservations should be made at least 24 hours in advance through Disney Dining (407 939-3463).

Hilton Youth Hotel: *(The Hilton Resort)* — In addition to the usual array of games, movies, and activities, this child care facility offers small beds set off in a quiet area for children who wish to take a nap or go to sleep before their parents return. Services are available to children staying at any resort on Walt Disney World property. The Hilton Youth Hotel is open from 5 PM until midnight. Cost: About $6 per hour. Children's meals can be purchased through room service. Reserve at least one day in advance by calling the hotel (407 827-4000).

Wyndy Harbor Kid's Klub: *(Wyndham Palace Resort & Spa)* — This fun and educational camp is available to Wyndham Palace Resort & Spa guests and those using the conference facilities. Enrollment is on a first-come, first-served basis, and day camps run from 9 AM until 4 PM. Cost: About $7 per hour. Evening camps are available on selected nights from 6 until 11 PM for about $7 per hour. Meals can be purchased through room service. To make reservations, call Wyndy Harbor (407 827-3374).

Mouseketeer Club: *(Disney's Grand Floridian Resort & Spa)* — This small, pleasantly decorated club accepts a maximum of twelve children at one time. An assortment of toys, board games, computer games, books, and Disney movies is provided. A children's meal is served between 7:30 and 8 PM. The Mouseketeer Club is open from 4:30 PM until midnight. Cost: About $9 per hour with a 4 hour maximum. Dinner is included. Reservations are recommended through Disney Dining (407 939-3463).

Mouseketeer Clubhouse: *(Disney's Contemporary Resort)* — The small Mouseketeer Clubhouse is a short-term care center with limited facilities and amusements. The Clubhouse accepts guests from any Disney-owned resort and is limited to ten children. The Mouseketeer Clubhouse is open from 4:30 PM until midnight. Cost: About $6 per hour with a 4 hour maximum; children's meals are about $7. Reserve at least two days in advance by calling the hotel (407 824-1000).

Sandcastle Club: *(Disney's Beach Club Resort)* — This pleasant child care and activity center is open to children age four through twelve and features computer games, arts and crafts projects, and a library of children's books and movies. Available to guests at the Yacht and Beach Club resorts; guests staying at other Disney-owned resorts can use the facility on a drop-in basis after 4 PM if space is available. The Sandcastle Club is open from 4:30 PM until midnight. Cost: About $6 per hour. Meals cost about $8. Reserve at least one day ahead through Disney Dining (407 939-3463). ◆

RESOURCES
Babysitting & Day Camps

Popular Programs for Kids

Neverland Club — Located at Disney's Polynesian Resort, this popular kids' club is based on the story of Peter Pan. Guests enter the building and find themselves in Wendy's bedroom, where they watch as their child is sprinkled with pixie dust and climbs through the window into the wonderful world of Never-Never Land. The fun includes unlimited arcade games and a wealth of Disney toys. The children are supervised in both group and individual activities, and a kid-pleasing buffet dinner is included. This service is available to all Walt Disney World visitors. Neverland Club is open from 4 PM until midnight. A buffet is served from 6 until 8 PM. Cost: About $9 per hour for one child, about $6 for each additional child with a 3 hour minimum. Reservations are recommended and can be made up to sixty days in advance through Disney Dining (407 939-3463).

Camp Disney at the Disney Institute — A wide variety of programs and field trips are offered to younger visitors staying anywhere at Walt Disney World. Youngsters age seven to ten can enjoy nature treks and theme park expeditions with peeks into backstage areas. Visitors age eleven to fifteen can sign up for fun and informative activities, including a unique scavenger hunt at one of the major theme parks. Half- or full-day programs are available. Prices start at about $75 per child. Reservations can be made up to thirty days in advance through Walt Disney World Tours (407 939-8687). ◆

Essentials

Attractions

Hotels

Restaurants

Special Events

Recreation

Resources

Guidebook Index • Crossroads Shopping Center • Shops & Services • **Visitors with Special Needs** • Babysitting & Day Camps • Local Transportation • Airport Hotels • Orlando Airport • Packing

VISITORS WITH SPECIAL NEEDS

Vision Enhancements

Visitors who travel with a guide dog should inform the hotel when making reservations. They may keep their animal with them, or they can arrange to board their dog at a Walt Disney World kennel. Walt Disney World's *Guidebook for Guests with Disabilities* lists attractions that accommodate guide dogs.

Most Walt Disney World resorts have Braille-marked elevators. The high-rise hotels are the easiest to get around in, with the exception of the Walt Disney World Dolphin, where the floor plan is very confusing. The following resorts have sprawling layouts that may present a challenge to guests with sight impairments: Polynesian, Port Orleans, Dixie Landings, Caribbean Beach, Coronado Springs, and the All-Star Resort complex. The Grand Floridian resort also has rambling grounds, but offers trolley escort service from its outbuildings to the main lobby.

All of the major theme parks have Braille maps at their entrances. Braille guidebooks and complimentary tape players with touring cassettes are available at Guest Relations in the Magic Kingdom, Epcot, and Disney-MGM Studios (deposit required). Visitors with a guide dog may want to bring a companion to take charge of the dog while they enjoy attractions that restrict guide animals. Cast Members are not permitted to take charge of guide animals. Special passes that allow visitors with limited sight impairments to ride an attraction twice in a row are sometimes issued. Check at the Guest Relations window before entering the parks. ◆

In keeping with the cutting-edge technologies used throughout Walt Disney World, the services and facilities for visitors with disabilities, although mostly invisible to the general traveler, are unparalleled in the travel industry. To accommodate visitors with hearing impairments, many attractions are in the process of being equipped with innovative captioning systems. Visitors with sight impairments are given Braille guidebooks or cassette players to help them tour the parks. For visitors with mobility restrictions, Walt Disney World has assembled the largest wheelchair fleet in the world, including both standard wheelchairs and Electric Convenience Vehicles (ECVs). First-aid offices in all the parks will let guests take a break from their wheelchair to rest on a cot. (They will also refrigerate insulin for visitors with diabetes.) And, of course, all hotels and public transportation are outfitted with devices for the convenience of visitors with disabilities. Visitors with special needs should specify their requirements when making hotel reservations and request that Walt Disney World's Guidebook for Guests with Disabilities be mailed to them or be waiting for them at check-in; to order, call Walt Disney World Central Reservations (407 934-7639).

MOBILITY SOLUTIONS

All theme parks and resorts have ample handicapped parking areas near their entrances. Valet parking is complimentary at the following resorts: Polynesian, Grand Floridian, Contemporary, Yacht Club, Beach Club, BoardWalk, Wilderness Lodge, and Hotel Royal Plaza. Resorts that charge valet parking fees ranging from $5 to $10 are: Swan, Dolphin, Hilton, Grosvenor, and Wyndham Palace. Downtown Disney offers valet parking after 5:30 PM for about $6.

Many, but not all, Walt Disney World buses are wheelchair accessible. Visitors may have to wait for a specially equipped van. All monorail stations are wheelchair accessible. Most water launches are wheelchair accessible; however, for Fort Wilderness and Wilderness Lodge trips, visitors may have to wait for a specially equipped ferry.

Walt Disney World's *Guidebook for Guests with Disabilities* specifies which attractions are wheelchair accessible and which require that visitors leave their chair in order to ride. Cast Members are not trained in transferring guests to and from wheelchairs, so visitors should bring companions to assist them. Special passes that allow visitors with specific problems to use auxiliary entrances to attractions are sometimes issued. Check at the Guest Relations window before entering the parks.

All Walt Disney World resorts have rooms equipped for guests with limited mobility. Some of the better facilities include Old Key West (lower beds, roll-in showers, handicapped parking near rooms), Dixie Landings and Caribbean Beach (handicapped parking near rooms), Grand Floridian (door peepholes at wheelchair level, hand-held showers, elevator access to monorail), and Polynesian (automatic entrance doors, elevator access to monorail). The best off-site hotels include Embassy Suites Resort and Caribe Royale Resort Suites. Both have roll-in showers, push-handle doorknobs, low-height counters, and control switches.

All Walt Disney World resorts have complimentary wheelchairs (with refundable deposit) for guests to use throughout their stay. Wheelchairs and ECVs can be rented on a first-come, first-served basis at the major theme parks. A limited number of complimentary wheelchairs (deposit required) are also available through Guest Services at Downtown Disney, Typhoon Lagoon, Blizzard Beach, and Fort Wilderness.

HELPING RESOURCES

Visitors with disabilities have a number of resources available locally to help them make the most of their Walt Disney World vacation. Those most often cited by frequent visitors are:

Guided Tours: VIP Tours are private guided tours that let visitors explore Walt Disney World in any way that meets their special interests. Tours can be designed to meet special communication or interpretive needs as well, which makes them especially well suited to visitors with disabilities. To make reservations, call Disney Special Activities (407 560-6233: voice; 407 827-5141: TDD) at least three days in advance.

Medical Supplies and ECV Rentals: While Walt Disney World rents ECVs at the major theme parks, there are a limited number available and they rent quickly. Visitors who need the support and assurance of an ECV for touring the theme parks and for touring recreation areas such as BoardWalk and Downtown Disney, might want to consider an outside provider such as CARE Med. This medical supply and referral service helps visitors secure resources such as wheelchair rentals, ECV rentals, portable oxygen machines, insulin, and dialysis assistance. Visitors can rent ECVs for 24 hours for about $30; weekly rentals cost $200. CARE Med includes free delivery to guests' hotel. Reserve in advance by calling CARE Med (800 741-2282). Other companies that rent ECVs include Walker Mobility (888 726-6837) and Randy's Mobility (407 855-6562). Randy's Mobility provides weekly rentals only but offers good rates. ◆

RESOURCES

Special Needs

Hearing Enhancements

Walt Disney World recently began installing innovative new systems and devices at attractions to make them even more accessible to hearing-impaired guests.

All Walt Disney World resorts can supply guest rooms with strobe lights and a telecommunications device for the deaf (TDD). To make hotel reservations and special requests, call Walt Disney World Resorts Special Reservations (407 939-7807: voice; 407 939-7670: TDD). Closed-caption television is available in all guest rooms throughout Walt Disney World; check ahead at the Hotel Plaza and off-site resorts.

All theme parks have amplified and hearing aid–compatible pay phones. TDDs for visitors with hearing impairments are available at City Hall in the Magic Kingdom, at The Global Neighborhood in Epcot, and at Guest Relations inside Disney-MGM Studios.

A written text of the narration for attractions and a special device that triggers captions to appear on preshow videos at attractions are available at Guest Relations in the Magic Kingdom, Epcot, and Disney-MGM Studios. Sign-language interpretation for the live shows in the theme parks should be arranged at least one week in advance through Walt Disney World Resorts Special Reservations (407 939-7807: voice; 407 939-7670: TDD). A new system called reflective captioning has been implemented at many of the attractions in the major theme parks. A list of attractions and their available technologies can be obtained through Guest Relations at the parks. An Assistive-Listening device is also available at Guest Relations. ◆

Essentials

Attractions

Hotels

Restaurants

Special Events

Recreation

Resources

Guidebook Index • Crossroads Shopping Center • **Shops & Services** • Visitors with Special Needs • Babysitting & Day Camps • Airport Hotels • Orlando Airport • Packing

SHOPS & SERVICES

See the "Essentials" section for area map and shopping locations.

Banks and ATMs

Walt Disney World resorts will cash checks for guests (up to $50). Many resorts have automatic teller machines (ATMs) that are on the PLUS, Cirrus, and Honor networks. There are ATMs at all major theme parks as well as at some smaller parks such as Blizzard Beach. Epcot also has American Express Travel Services and Cash Machines. All ATMs are provided by SunTrust Bank and charge a transaction fee for non-SunTrust customers.

Epcot — There is one ATM outside the park across from the kennel and two ATMs inside the park: one on the East side of the walkway to the World Showcase near the Odyssey bridge, and one across from Germany in the World Showcase.

Magic Kingdom — There is one ATM outside the Main Entrance and two inside the park. One is in the walk-through between Frontierland and Adventureland, the other is near the Tomorrowland Arcade.

Disney-MGM Studios — There is one ATM outside the Main Entrance.

Animal Kingdom — An ATM is located outside the Main Entrance.

Downtown Disney — There is an ATM located outside of Guest Services in The Marketplace, one outside the Rock & Roll Beach Club in Pleasure Island, and one on the side of Forty-Thirst Street. A full-service branch of SunTrust Bank is located across Buena Vista Drive.

Crossroads — Gooding's Supermarket has an ATM and also provides foreign currency exchange. ◆

If you forgot it, Walt Disney World probably has it. Some of the most sought-after items and services are listed here.

Eyeglasses & Sunglasses: All Walt Disney World resorts carry sunglasses, and many carry reading glasses. At Crossroads Shopping Center, Sunglass Hut International sells and repairs sunglasses. Gooding's Pharmacy also carries both sunglasses and reading glasses.

Florist: Floral arrangements and fruit baskets can be ordered from Walt Disney World Florist (407 827-3505). At Crossroads, Gooding's Florist delivers to all area resorts (407 827-1206).

Groceries: Most budget resorts and the "Home Away from Home" resorts (Old Key West, BoardWalk Villas, The Villas at Wilderness Lodge, Fort Wilderness Resort, and The Villas at Disney Institute) offer a limited selection of groceries; all resorts carry beverages and snacks. In The Marketplace at Downtown Disney, Gourmet Pantry has limited groceries, a bakery, and a deli. Gooding's Supermarket is open 24 hours a day.

Medical Care & Medications: Main Street Physicians provides 24 hour physician house calls and dental referrals to all Walt Disney World area resorts (396-1195). The clinic is open daily from 8 AM until 8 PM and is one-quarter mile east of Walt Disney World, off Highway 192 at Parkway Boulevard. Transportation is available.

Centra Care Walk-in Medical Care is open from 8 AM until midnight during the week, and from 8 AM until 8 PM on weekends (934-2273). It provides free shuttle service for resort guests.

Doctors On Call service (399-3627) provides 24 hour physician house calls in the resorts.

Emergency services are provided by Sand Lake Hospital, just north of Walt Disney World on Interstate 4 at Exit 27A (351-8500) or Celebration Health off Route 192 (303-4000).

Prescriptions can be filled at Eckerd Drug, nearby (238-9333). Turner Drugs (828-8124) will deliver prescriptions to the resorts.

Shipping: Most retail shops at Walt Disney World will ship purchases for visitors. The resorts will also ship from their front desks. A U.S. Post Office is located at the Shoppes at Buena Vista, along with Mail Boxes, etc. which provides shipping materials and uses all major carriers. Nearby, Kinkos offers 24 hour copy services.

Tobacco: Cigarettes are available at resort gift shops and selected merchandise shops in the theme parks. They are not on display, and must be requested. Cigars are sold at premier resorts and specialty shops. ◆

CROSSROADS SHOPPING CENTER

See the "Essentials" section for area map and shopping locations.

Crossroads Shopping Center was built on a section of Walt Disney World property that is located on State Road 535, just across from the entrance to Hotel Plaza Boulevard. A large 24 hour supermarket, several restaurants, and more than twenty-five different merchants are located here. While technically on Disney property, Crossroads is not serviced by Disney transportation. It is within walking distance to many of the resorts on Hotel Plaza Boulevard and a short taxi ride from Downtown Disney (about $7). Taxis from other Disney resort areas will run from $10 to $15.

Shops: A step above the usual strip mall fare, Crossroads hosts nationally known franchises and smaller boutiques. Shops include Sunglass Hut International; Chico's (women's sportswear); Brightwater Boutique (women's and girl's apparel from Fresh Produce); Marble Slab Creamery (ice cream and candies); Disney's Character Connection; Swim & Sport (women's sportswear and bathing suits); Wyland Gallery (art work); Gold Crown Hallmark; Foot Locker; Electronics Plus; and Bath & Body Works.

Restaurants: Visitors will find many reasonably priced, nationally known restaurants to choose from at Crossroads, including Jungle Jim's (featuring barbecued ribs and more than one hundred hamburger combinations); Chevy's (fresh Mexican cuisine); Pebbles (American cuisine); Perkins Family Restaurant (above-average coffee-shop fare; breakfast served all day); Red Lobster (seafood and steak); TGI Friday's (American cuisine); Pizzeria Uno (pizza and pasta); McDonald's; and Taco Bell. Paesano's Ristorante and Liquors is a combination restaurant and liquor store featuring regional Italian dishes. Paesano's Liquors, next door, is a fully stocked liquor store that also offers a wide array of miniature liquors and a large selection of wine.

Gooding's Supermarket: Gooding's Supermarket, which is open 24 hours a day, is by far the largest store at Crossroads, and while some area supermarkets may be less expensive, you can't beat Gooding's for convenience and selection. It has a full-service florist, and a large deli with prepared meals. Gooding's is an easy-to-find, no-hassle first stop on your way into Walt Disney World. It's the perfect place to pick up snacks and beverages for your hotel room, and can be much less expensive than room service or sampling from the mini bar. ◆

Discount Souvenirs

Visitors looking for bargains will find plenty of them at Disney's outlet stores, located in Belz Outlet Mall, just north of Walt Disney World. Here, Character Warehouse and its sister store, Character Premiere, sell over-stocked and discontinued Disney merchandise. Shoppers will find Disney Character apparel, Mickey-themed housewares, plush toys, jewelry, totebags, and souvenirs at significant discounts.

Belz Outlet Mall is located about 20 minutes north of Walt Disney World on International Drive, off of Highway I-4. Character Warehouse is located in Mall 1 and Character Premiere is located in Mall 2 next door. Character Premier is the newer of the two stores and has what appears to be a wider selection of merchandise; Character Warehouse has greater markdowns on discontinued or irregular merchandise. For driving directions, check with Guest Services at any Disney resort; most have printed maps to Belz Mall. ◆

INDEX

Essentials

Attractions · Packing · Orlando Airport · Airport Hotels · Airport Hotels · Babysitting & Day Camps · Visitors with Special Needs · Shops & Services · Crossroads Shopping Center · Guidebook Index

Hotels

Restaurants

Special Events

Recreation

Resources

Essentials
Attractions
Hotels
Restaurants
Special Events
Recreation
Resources

Packing • Orlando Airport • Airport Hotels • Babysitting & Day Camps • Visitors with Special Needs • Shops & Services • Crossroads Shopping Center • **Guidebook Index**

Essentials
Attractions
Hotels
Restaurants
Special Events
Recreation
Resources

Guidebook Index • Crossroads Shopping Center • Shops & Services • Visitors with Special Needs • Babysitting & Day Camps • Airport Hotels • Orlando Airport • Packing

INDEX

E — H

Essentials

Attractions

Hotels

Restaurants

Special Events

Recreation

Resources

INDEX
H — M

Packing • Orlando Airport • Airport Hotels • Babysitting & Day Camps • Visitors with Special Needs • Shops & Services • Crossroads Shopping Center • Guidebook Index

Essentials
Attractions
Hotels
Restaurants
Special Events
Recreation
Resources

Guidebook Index • Crossroads Shopping Center • Shops & Services • Visitors with Special Needs • Babysitting & Day Camps • Airport Hotels • Orlando Airport • Packing

Essentials
Attractions
Hotels
Restaurants
Special Events
Recreation
Resources

Essentials

Attractions

Hotels

Restaurants

Special Events

Recreation

Resources

Guidebook Index • Crossroads Shopping Center • Shops & Services • Visitors with Special Needs • Babysitting & Day Camps • Airport Hotels • Orlando Airport • Parking

INDEX

T — Y

UNIVERSAL STUDIOS ORLANDO

An Exciting and Entertaining Vacation Destination:
Universal's Theme Parks, Restaurants, Night Clubs, and Resorts

Universal Studios has been a favorite Orlando attraction for many years. It has now transformed into an important and fascinating vacation destination — Universal Studios Orlando. There is now an imaginative new theme park, Islands of Adventure; CityWalk, a collection of shops, restaurants, and nightclubs; and Universal's own on-property resorts and transportation system. Visitors who resist the urge to compare it to Walt Disney World and surrender to the Universal experience will enjoy a memorable and exciting trip. Plan to spend at least two days to explore everything it has to offer.

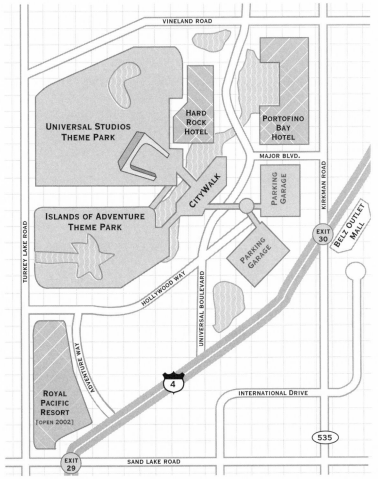

When to Go

Like other Orlando attractions, crowds are largest during summers and school holidays. Universal Studios Orlando is close to the heart of Orlando, so crowds are also heavily influenced by the local populace. The most crowded times are weekends, when the park is open late. CityWalk is most crowded on Fridays and Saturdays. Monday and Tuesday are the least crowded days.

How to Get There

Universal Studios Orlando is about 20 minutes north of Walt Disney World. Taxis, shuttle buses, town-cars, and limousines provide service to Universal from the airport, Walt Disney World, and most hotels.

Universal's Movie Star Shuttle is a combination ticket/transportation package, which includes one, two, or three days' admission to the parks and vouchers for Mears Shuttle service from any hotel in the

Orlando area, including Walt Disney World Resorts. The cost of the package is the price of the park pass (see "Admission" below) plus about $17 a day per adult and $15 for each child for shuttle fees.

Visitors with cars can take I-4 eastbound (from Walt Disney World or Tampa) to Exit 30A, or I-4 westbound (from Orlando or the Florida Turnpike) to Exit 29B, and follow the signs to Universal Studios.

One-day self-parking in the parking decks at Universal Studios Orlando costs around $7 (free after 6 PM). Valet parking costs about $14. The restaurants at CityWalk will validate valet parking for up to two hours.

Admission

Passes can be purchased at the gate, online, or over the telephone (888 837-2273). Prices shown include tax. Discounted tickets are often available on the Universal web site and at AAA.

One-day One-Park Passes: These passes are good for one day's admission to either Universal Studios or Islands of Adventure.

A One-Day One-Park Pass costs about $55 for adults; $45 for children.

Multi-Day Multi-Park Passes: Multi-Day Passes allow visitors to hop between the two theme parks at substantial savings. Both two-day and three-day passes also include admission to CityWalk clubs on the same days that they are used to enter the theme parks. Days do not have to be used consecutively and never expire. The Universal Studios web site frequently offers a modest discount for admission tickets purchased online.

A Two-Day Multi-Park Pass costs about $100 for adults; $85 for children.

A Three-Day Multi-Park Pass costs about $115 for adults; $100 for children.

Annual Passes: Annual Passes offer one year of unlimited admission to both parks, free self-parking, and other discounts on food and merchandise.

An Annual Pass costs about $180 for all ages.

CityWalk Party Pass: Visitors who would like to experience the nightlife at Universal can purchase a CityWalk Party Pass for one night of admission to all clubs.

A CityWalk Party Pass costs about $10; about $14 with admission to a movie at the Universal Cineplex.

Four-Park FlexTicket: This ticket is good for fourteen consecutive days of unlimited admission and park hopping privileges at Universal Studios, Islands of Adventure, Sea World, and Wet 'n Wild.

A Four-Park FlexTicket costs about $175 for adults; $140 for children.

Five-Park FlexTicket: This ticket is the same as the Four-Park, above, but also includes Busch Gardens in Tampa. FlexTickets must be used on consecutive days. These tickets are a great value for the active visitor.

A Five-Park FlexTicket costs about $200 for adults; $160 for children.

Touring Tip

Universal Express: Universal's most popular attractions now have pass dispensers. Like Disney's FastPass system, it lets visitors bypass lines at a later time.

VIP Tours

Visitors who hate lines or want to learn more about the parks can take advantage of Universal's VIP Tours. Starting at about $125 per person, visitors get a guided tour of either Universal Studios or Islands of Adventure and receive priority entrance at popular attractions. For more information or reservations, call 407 363-8295.

Special Events

In addition to a year-round schedule of concerts, parades, and shows, Universal Studios hosts Mardi Gras, a six-week festival featuring parades, New Orleans cuisine, and live music. On October weekends, Universal Studios is open all night for Halloween Horror, with parades and haunted mazes. For more information, call 888 837-2273. ◆

UNIVERSAL STUDIOS THEME PARK

Universal Studios is a theme park, with attractions that recreate some of the most popular movies of all time, and it is also a working studio that produces feature films and television programs — at times before your very eyes. The attractions are merged with street scenes that mirror famous landscapes, from the skyline of San Francisco to a small New England village named Amity with a very large shark problem. A children's area, Woody Woodpecker's Kidzone, is designed for the young at heart, while the Hollywood section gives older movie buffs the chance to walk along Rodeo Drive, or visit Sunset and Hollywood boulevards as they appeared in the 1950s. If you are interested in seeing a production in progress, be sure to check at the Studio Audience Center near the entrance.

Attractions

Back to the Future... The Ride — Visitors climb onboard motion simulators — time-traveling DeLoreans — for a wild chase into the past, and back into the future again. Height requirement is 40 inches.

Earthquake — The Big One — Immediately after an audience-participation preshow demonstrating special effects with cutaway sets and miniatures, visitors board a BART train and are "trapped" beneath San Francisco in a realistic simulation of an 8.3 earthquake.

The Funtastic World of Hanna-Barbera — Yogi Bear and Boo Boo, along with a host of other Hanna-Barbera cartoon favorites, invite visitors to take a wild ride inside their cartoon universe. Animation and 3-D, combined with seats that respond to the on-screen action, make this a family favorite. Children under 40 inches must use available non-moving seats.

Jaws — Visitors embark on an idyllic waterfront tour of quaint Amity Village in New England. The peace is interrupted by a 3-ton, 32-foot long great white shark.

Kongfrontation — In this attraction set in New York City, visitors board the Roosevelt Island tramway and come face to face with the four-story high King Kong.

Men In Black Alien Attack — On this interactive ride, visitors fire space age weapons at alien targets. Aliens fire back at visitors and can even cause the visitor's ride vehicles to spin out of control. Visitors who hit enough targets make Men In Black status. *TIP:* Men in Black Alien Attack has very long lines, however, there is usually a single-rider line at this and many other popular attractions. While visitors will have to split up their party to take advantage of this option, they will be rewarded by skipping past almost all of the lines.

Terminator 2: 3D — This action-packed theater attraction employs impressive 3-D cinematography effects and stunt actors to portray a dark vision of the future.

Twister... Ride It Out — This walk-through attraction and demonstration showcases the sets and special effects used in *Twister*. The creation of a five-story tornado is the highlight of this performance. The tornado's devastating force includes fierce winds, rain, and even a life-like cow hurled through the air.

Live Shows

Live shows are performed throughout the day. Check the park guides for durations, locations, and times.

Alfred Hitchcock: The Art of Making Movies — The cinematic genius of Alfred Hitchcock and his films is explored here. Visitors can participate in a demonstration of the making of famous scenes from the classic thriller *Psycho*.

Beetlejuice's Rock 'n' Roll Graveyard Revue — Set in a graveyard of an amphitheater, this tongue-in-cheek show has an ensemble cast of classic movie monsters, including Dracula, the Phantom of the Opera, and the Bride of Frankenstein. The other-worldly creatures have a frightfully good time performing classic rock favorites.

The Blues Brothers — Several times throughout the day on Delancy Street, the Blues Brothers perform their greatest hits.

The Gory, Gruesome & Grotesque Horror Make-up Show — Especially for the not-so-squeamish, this show uses humor and audience participation to demonstrate make-up tricks used in modern horror films. Shows run continuously. Some of the show's humor hits on an adult level.

The Wild, Wild, Wild West Stunt Show — Stunts, fist fights, explosions, special effects, and lots of bad jokes make up the bulk of this show. Cowboy actors put on a high-energy performance that lasts about 15 minutes.

Tours & Exhibits

AT&T At the Movies — At this attraction, visitors take an informative tour exploring aspects of television and sound recording. This small, interactive museum uses sound booths, video screens, and hands-on exhibits to enhance visitors' experience.

The Boneyard — This outdoor walk-through exhibit features recognizable props and vehicles used in Universal movie productions.

Stage 54: Production Central — Visitors walk through this production house featuring props, trivia, and behind the scenes vignettes from the making of recent Universal films, such as *The Grinch*.

Lucy: A Tribute — A museum focusing on the life and career of Lucille Ball, this walk-through attraction houses set models, costumes, and videos of her work. A wide variety of memorabilia, including awards, snapshots, and home movies, is also housed here.

Nickelodeon Studios — Visitors go behind the scenes on a tour of Universal's working studios where Nickelodeon programming originates. The tour includes a look at the wardrobe and makeup departments, and winds up in the Game Lab, a simulation of a Nickelodeon game show.

Woody Woodpecker's Kidzone

A Day In The Park With Barney — Children love this musical sing-along with the famous purple dinosaur in Barney's Backyard Theater. Shows run continuously throughout the day.

Animal Actors Stage — This live animal show features those famous four-footed movie stars Lassie, Babe, and Beethoven. Check the park guide for show times.

Curious George Goes to Town — Visitors follow the familiar footsteps of Curious George through this interactive playground. A ball factory and *a lot* of water provide endless entertainment for small children — and quite a few parents, too.

E.T. Adventure — After a walk through the forest, visitors fly through the air on bicycles with E.T., the lovable extraterrestrial. Visitors help E.T. escape from government agents and then travel over the moon and into the stars.

Fievel's Playland — Filled with tunnels, nets, places to climb, and a waterslide, Fievel's playground puts a colorful, mouse-sized perspective on kids' favorite things.

Woody Woodpecker's Nuthouse Coaster — For kids, this pint-sized coaster provides wacky but mild thrills on a tour through Woody's Nut Factory. Children under the age of three may not ride. ◆

ISLANDS OF ADVENTURE THEME PARK

Islands of Adventure theme park breathes new life into famous stories, ancient myths, exotic lands, and comic book superheroes. Visitors approach the park through the Port of Entry, a festive, bustling bazaar featuring a mosaic of cultures, eras, and distant lands. Just beyond is the tall arch that leads to the five islands. Inscribed with runes, it declares "The Adventure Begins."

Marvel Superhero Island

Everything in this island is big, bold, and fantastically colorful; with its design, architecture, and cast of characters, visitors may feel they have entered into the pages of a Marvel Comic book. Action-packed thrill rides, tributes to revered childhood heroes, and attention to detail create an exciting land.

The Amazing Adventures of Spider-Man — This adventure combines realistic 3-D effects with a simulator vehicle that moves up and down, forward, and even spins as it travels through a giant indoor cityscape in a battle between Spider-Man and a group of nefarious villains.

Doctor Doom's Fearfall — Doctor Doom has created a device designed to "suck the fear right out of you." On each of its 200 foot high twin towers, visitors are catapulted to a height of 150 feet and then whisked back down faster than gravity.

Incredible Hulk Coaster — Dr. Bruce Banner's gamma ray experiment lab is the setting for the entrance to this high-speed coaster. After a catapult launch from 0 to 40 miles per hour in just two seconds, thrill seekers go directly into a barrel roll and then a series of loops and twists that may leave them as green as the Hulk.

Storm Force Accelatron — The young at heart will whirl and twirl in this "tea-cup" style ride located just past the Incredible Hulk Coaster.

Toon Lagoon

Cartoon characters come to life in this whimsical island. Much of the island is designed for photo opportunities with clever background props and characters.

Dudley Do-Right's Ripsaw Falls — In this cartoon version of a classic flume ride, visitors wind their way through the slapstick adventures of Dudley Do-Right as he tries to save Nell from the villainous Snidely Whiplash. The final plummet takes visitors 15 feet below the level of the lagoon. Expect to get wet.

Me Ship, The Olive — Adjacent to the Bilge-Rat Barges and on the edge of Toon Lagoon is Popeye's ship, a playground for youngsters. It has three levels of climbing and interactive activities. On the top level at the Cargo Crane, young-at-heart visitors can try their hand at soaking passing Bilge-Rat riders.

Cartoon Theater — Check the park guide for current shows and performance times at this amphitheater.

Popeye and Bluto's Bilge-Rat Barges — Whitewater rapids carry visitors, along with Popeye, to save Olive Oyl from the nasty Bluto. Twisting and turning, the ride raft drops into the home of a giant octopus. Everyone aboard is splashed during this river trip.

Toon Trolley — Several times a day, a trolley filled with cartoon characters makes a stop on Comic Strip Lane and unloads for an amusing musical comedy revue. Check park guides for show times.

Jurassic Park

Designed after the park depicted in the popular movie Jurassic Park, *this island is guarded at both entrances by the gigantic torch-lit gates of its namesake. The dense jungle atmosphere is set with pathways full of fossils and sweeping — yet slightly unnerving — music.*

Camp Jurassic — At this playground, kids can climb in a rainforest, explore dark caves and lava pits, slide, and have a great time in a prehistoric jungle setting.

Jurassic Park Discovery Center — This museum is filled with interactive exhibits, including life-sized dinosaurs, a dinosaur egg incubator with a view of a raptor egg hatching, and the chance to create a new creature by combining human and dinosaur DNA.

Jurassic Park River Adventure — Visitors take a river journey through the habitats of Jurassic Park's gentle, plant-eating dinosaurs. But wait … could something be about to go terribly wrong? A detour through the Raptor Containment Area sets up a thrilling ride that culminates in an 85-foot splashdown.

Pteranodon Flyers — Kids soar through the air in these amusing two-seater pteranodon-shaped vehicles on an overhead track through Jurassic Park. Adults can only ride if accompanied by a child. The line moves slowly; if there is a long line, consider flying at another time.

Triceratops Encounter — This walk-through attraction features a stable with a "living, breathing" triceratops. Its keeper explains the reptile's history and answers visitors' questions.

The Lost Continent

Guarded at both entrances by fierce griffins, this area is home to myths and legends from several parts of the world. A stroll down the pathway takes visitors through an enchanted medieval village, a noisy and colorful Middle Eastern bazaar, and ancient Greek ruins.

Dueling Dragons — Representing a fire dragon and an ice dragon, these twin suspended multiple-loop coasters duel each other in the sky with their ride vehicles passing as close as 12 inches from each other at several points in the journey. After riding either coaster, visitors may take a shortcut to the loading area to experience the other coaster.

The Eighth Voyage of Sindbad — This spectacular stunt show features acrobatics, pyrotechnics, and water explosions on Sindbad's eighth exciting quest for adventure and wealth.

Flying Unicorn — Kids will enjoy this short (25 second) roller coaster ride through an enchanted forest.

Poseidon's Fury: Escape from the Lost City — A clever combination of walk-through and theater attraction, this unique extravaganza combines screen projection, surging water, and pyrotechnic effects as Zeus and Poseidon match up for an epic battle in Atlantis.

Seuss Landing

Taken directly from the pages of the beloved Dr. Seuss books, this island has barely any straight lines or right angles. The odd characters of the books are all brought magically to life in this land.

Caro-Seuss-el — On this magnificent, brightly colored carousel, visitors ride on their choice of fantastical Seuss creatures. The detailed figures are "interactive"; they blink, nod, and wag their tails.

The Cat in the Hat — Inspired by the original Cat in the Hat storyline, this ride's moving couch transports visitors throughout the house. The Cat in the Hat, along with Thing 1 and Thing 2, pay a visit to the children and liven things up while their mother is out.

Dr. Seuss Presents: "A Something for Everyone" — This musical revue features headliners from Dr. Seuss books, including Horton the elephant, Sam I Am, the Grinch, and other characters. Street performances happen throughout the day.

If I Ran the Zoo — Kids and the young at heart will have a great (and wet) time in this interactive playground featuring strange and curious beasts from its namesake Seuss book.

One Fish, Two Fish, Red Fish, Blue Fish — Visitors guide their fishy ride vehicle up and down, as well as round and round while trying to duck periodic streams of water shot into their path. A rhyme broadcast throughout the ride warns visitors whether to swim up or down to avoid getting soaked. ◆

Full-Service Dining at Universal's Theme Parks

Universal Studios Restaurants

FINNEGAN'S BAR & GRILL

Food: This is a place to enjoy a yard or pint of your favorite ale. The menu at Finnegan's is mostly pub grub with traditional Irish favorites such as Scotch Eggs, Corned Beef and Cabbage, and Shepherd's Pie. Soup and sandwich selections round out the menu.

Atmosphere: Finnegan's Bar & Grill will remind visitors of a comfortable neighborhood pub, with dark, heavy wood, and a long, mirrored bar. There is ample seating in the main bar and in the separate dining room area. Finnegan's features live entertainment and a happy hour every afternoon.

Hours: Lunch and dinner are served from 11:30 AM until park closing.

Reservations: No reservations are taken. Seating is on a first-come, first-served basis.

LOMBARD'S LANDING

Food: Lombard's Landing has something for everyone, from hamburgers to soups, sandwiches, and health conscious cuisine. Entrees include Aged Prime Rib of Beef, Fried Shrimp, Chinatown Chicken, Lombard's version of the Cobb salad, and Cape Cod Fish and Chips. Lombard's Landing has a full-service bar.

Atmosphere: This pleasant restaurant has a large fountain in the lobby, colorful tilework on the floors, and exposed brick throughout the dining area. Large windows afford views of the park's lagoon.

Hours: Lunch and dinner are served from 11:30 AM until park closing.

Reservations: Reservations are accepted 24 to 48 hours in advance; call 407 224-6400.

Islands of Adventure Restaurants

CONFISCO GRILLE

Food: Unique appetizers, such as a Crab and Cheese Spread or a Mediterranean Sampler with hummus, baba ghanoush, tabbouleh, feta cheese, greek olives, and flatbread chips start the meal with a worldly flair. A variety of burgers and pastas are available, as well as grilled entrees. Confisco Grille features the same menu at lunch and dinner.

Atmosphere: This eclectic, casual dining room features paper covered tables perfect for doodling upon. From noon until 2 PM, diners can mingle with the likes of Dudley Do-Right, Popeye, Olive Oyl, Spider-Man, and Woody Woodpecker. The adjacent lounge, Backwater Bar, is host to a daily Happy Hour from 3 until 5 PM.

Hours: Lunch and dinner are served from 11 AM until park closing.

Reservations: Advance reservations are accepted; call 407 224-4406.

MYTHOS

Food: The menu at Mythos has many creative selections, including a Lobster Stuffed Potato and Balsamic Chicken with baked potato tart and roasted garlic. Salad selections include Chinese Chicken Salad with wasabi vinaigrette and California Sushi Salad. Mythos also has more standard fare for the less adventurous, such as hamburgers and New York Strip Steak. There is an extensive wine list and specialty drink menu.

Atmosphere: The carved stone walls create a cavern-like setting in the dining room, yet numerous windows provide great views of the lagoon and park. Guests can watch the chefs at work in the display kitchen. There is plenty of seating outside along the water, which is a relaxing spot to take a break while touring the park.

Hours: Open for lunch from 11:30 AM; dinner is served seasonally, until 7 PM.

Reservations: Advance reservations are accepted; call 407 224-4533. ◆

CityWalk

Dining and Entertainment Center
At Universal Studios Orlando

CityWalk is a 30-acre waterfront entertainment complex that serves as the center gateway for Universal's theme parks. Visitors are surrounded by both upscale and casual restaurants, nightclubs, stores and boutiques, and a twenty-screen theater complex with stadium seating and digital sound. The Palm and Plaza outdoor stages feature dancers, bands, and other live entertainment. Shows often encourage guest participation, adding to the festive atmosphere of CityWalk.

CityWalk visitors can park in the Universal Studios Orlando parking garage, which costs about $7, or they can valet park for about $14. Parking is free of charge after 6 PM. There is no cost to visit CityWalk itself, but many individual venues do have a cover charge in the evenings.

Guests who have Multi-Day Passes can show their park tickets to gain complimentary admission to the nightclubs. Those without passes can purchase one of two CityWalk Party Passes: Unlimited access to all nightclubs for one evening costs about $10 and unlimited access to all nightclubs plus a movie costs about $14. CityWalk Party Passes can be purchased at Guest Services or at the ticket window located beside the groove nightclub. Several of the restaurants offer AAA members a 10 percent dining discount.

Visitors interested in shopping will find many specialty shops, including a Fossil Store, which sells watches, sunglasses, and other trendy accessories. Fresh Produce features resort wear for men, women, and girls. Other shops include All Star Collectibles, which has an array of sports memorabilia; Captain Crackers; Cigarz, with an assortment of fine cigars; Dapy, for unique gifts; Elegant Illusions, featuring famous copy jewelry; Endangered Species, presenting environmental gifts; Glow!, with a collection of illuminating gifts; Quiet Flight surf shop, featuring beach wear and custom surfboards; Silver, a fine jewelry store; and of course, a large Universal Studios Store. For more information on CityWalk dining, shopping, or ticket information, call 407 363-8000.

Bob Marley, A Tribute To Freedom — This replica of the late Bob Marley's charming cottage home in Kingston, Jamaica, features live entertainment nightly. The walls are covered with photos of the Marley family and the Wailers, the band that took reggae into the mainstream. Caribbean inspired appetizers, including Jerk Marinated Chicken and Jamaican Beef Patties in a flaky pasty crust served with spicy yucca fries, are served.

After 8 PM, a cover charge of about $5 goes into effect, and a live band plays from the courtyard gazebo stage. After 10 PM, all visitors must be age 21 and older. Open from 4 PM (2 PM on weekends) until 2 AM. No reservations. Phone: 407 224-2262.

CityJazz — This sophisticated club features live music in a cozy setting with rich woods, upholstered chairs, and plush booths. The large stage plays host to both rising stars as well as legendary greats. Memorabilia from Jazz luminaries such as Ella Fitzgerald and Miles Davies adorn the walls. Instruments, including Glen Miller's first trombone, are showcased behind the bar. CityJazz features a menu of specialty drinks, including their signature martinis.

Open from 8:30 PM until 1 AM and until 2 AM most weekends. There is a cover charge of about $4. Live entertainment usually starts about 9 PM. For more information, including a schedule of current acts, call 407 224-2189.

🍴 *Emeril's Restaurant Orlando* — Emeril Lagasse, star of the popular television show "Emeril Live," brings his penchant for spice and creativity to Orlando with this Creole-inspired restaurant. Entrees include New Orleans Barbecue Shrimp, Andouille Crusted Texas Redfish, grilled meats, roasted rack of lamb, seafood, duck, poultry, and vegetarian specialties.

Open for lunch from 11:30 AM until 2:30 PM. Dinner is served from 5:30 until 10 PM (11 PM on the weekends). Guests are encouraged to make reservations several weeks in advance. A jacket is recommended for dinner. There is a wine room and a cigar room on the second floor. Phone: 407 224-2424.

🎵 *the groove* — This state-of-the-art nightclub is the place to dance the night away. A video wall broadcasts music video clips. Throughout the club are different bars and gathering areas, three with a 'color theme' and their own unique drink menus. The Green Room features a carved bar and stone sculptures. The Red Room has bright red velvet chairs and flames depicted on the walls; and the Blue Room is furnished with neon lights and retro furniture.

The groove is open nightly from 9 PM until 2 AM (3 AM on the weekends). Visitors must be 21 or older. On Wednesdays, visitors 18 or older are invited. There is a cover charge of about $6.

🍴 *Hard Rock Cafe Orlando* — This 650 seat eatery is the largest Hard Rock Cafe in the world. This multi-level restaurant dedicates its rooms to popular or innovative music bands. A "Florida room" pays tribute to the Backstreet Boys and Tom Petty, while the Beatles and Elvis are featured in other areas. Classic rock artifacts fill practically every inch of space. The menu has something for everyone, from salads, burgers, smokehouse entrees, and sandwiches, to their own signature pot roast and pasta dishes.

Open from 11 AM until midnight. Seating is on a first-come, first-served basis. Phone: 407 351-7625.

🎵🍴 *Jimmy Buffet's Margaritaville* — Here is the place to sink your teeth into the famous "Cheeseburger in Paradise." Margaritaville is a 15,000 square foot restaurant which features three themed bars, patio and balcony seating, and nightly live entertainment. The restaurant's volcano bar, in the back of the restaurant, has a 18-foot-high volcano that erupts a river of Margaritas. Menu choices include a variety of sandwiches, salads, munchies, and American entrees.

Open from 11:30 AM until 2 AM. Live entertainment begins nightly at 10 PM. There is a cover charge of $3.25 after 10 PM. Seating here is on a first-come, first-served basis. Phone: 407 224-2155.

🎵🍴 *Latin Quarter* — This bi-level establishment features a restaurant, a nightclub, and dance and art studios that celebrate creative and culinary arts from all twenty-one Latin American nations. Nuevo Latino cuisine is served, featuring beef, chicken, and seafood, as well as salads and sandwiches. An expansive stage, flanked by Aztec-inspired stone carvings and fountains, plays host to live bands and performers.

Open from 11 AM until 2 AM. There is a cover charge of about $5 after 10 PM. Reservations are accepted. The Latin Express walk-up window outside serves Cuban sandwiches, pizza, and octopus specialties all day. Phone: 407 363-5922.

🎵🍴 *Motown Cafe* — This bi-level restaurant and nightclub is decorated in deep reds and black with gold records highlighting the walls. The cafe also displays Motown memorabilia such as Michael Jackson's costume from the video "Billie Jean" and one of Stevie Wonder's harmonicas. The menu features a variety of down-home cooking items, including specialties of the cafe such as "It Takes Two" Chicken and Waffles and "Mercy Mercy" Meatloaf.

Motown Cafe Moments, the house band, plays every evening. Dining reservations are accepted. A cover charge of about $3 goes into effect after 9 PM ($5 on Saturday). Open from 11 AM until midnight (until 2 AM on weekends). Phone: 407 224-2500.

Get Ready to Go • Universal Studios • Islands of Adventure • Theme Park Restaurants • CityWalk • Universal Hotels

UNIVERSAL STUDIOS ORLANDO

NBA City — This two-tiered restaurant is designed to look like a basketball court, complete with hardwood floors and nets. Two side-by-side screens show continuous player bios and 'classic moments' from the history of the National Basketball Association. Games, including NBA trivia and shooting hoops, provide entertainment. Pastas, pizzas, salads, and sandwiches comprise most of the menu. Other entrees include grilled salmon, stuffed chicken breast, and pork chops.

Open from 11 AM until midnight (sometimes until 1 AM on the weekends). Seating is on a first-come, first-serve basis. Phone: 407 363-5919.

NASCAR Cafe — The race car of the reigning Winston Cup champion is on display outside this bi-level restaurant. A bar, merchandise shop, and small arcade make up the lower level; a patio outside serves a limited menu. The main dining room can be found at the top of the black-and-white checkered staircase. NASCAR racing memorabilia abounds. The menu features salads, sandwiches, seafood, and steaks. Comfort food selections include Chicken Fried Chicken, SuperClash Catfish, and Smoky Mountain Barbecue Ribs. Happy Hour daily from 4 PM until closing.

Open at 11 AM; closing hours vary from 9 PM until midnight, depending on the season. Reservations are accepted. Phone: 407 224-9255.

Pastamore — This is both a full-service restaurant and a carry-out market. In the morning, pastries are available; at lunch and dinner there are antipasti dishes, salads, and sandwiches. Gelato, espresso, coffees, sodas, wines by the glass, and beer are available to take to a nearby table or enjoy outside on the patio. The dinner menu features Italian fare that can be ordered family style or a la carte. Entrees include lasagna, veal Marsala, sirloin, and an array of pasta dishes. The contemporary, Italian, and Mediterranean inspired dining room is busy and boisterous.

Market hours are 8 AM until 2 AM. Pastamore Restaurant serves dinner from 5 PM until midnight. Reservations are accepted. Phone: 407 224-9255.

Pat O'Brien's Orlando — This club is a replica of the famous bar in New Orleans. Dueling pianos provide a raucous good time in the Piano Bar. The dark and cozy Main Bar features a big-screen television showing continuous sporting events, while the Patio Bar on the outdoor courtyard has a flaming fountain. A limited menu is available after 4 PM and includes crawfish nachos, jambalaya, and hot wings.

The Main Bar opens at 4 PM and the piano bar at 6 PM. Pat O'Brien's closes at 2 AM. After 8 PM, only age 21 and older are admitted. There is a $3 cover charge after 9 PM. At the walk-up window outside, guests can purchase drinks. Phone: 407 224-2100.

Universal Cineplex

This two-story, state-of-the-art, twenty-screen theater shows first-run movies and features stadium seating and digital sound. Each auditorium has the capacity to hold up to 500 guests. In addition to the standard concessions, beer, wine, and TCBY yogurt are available on both floors. Universal Studios holds many of its premieres and other film events here, complete with spotlights and movie stars. To purchase tickets or for the current film schedule, call 407 354-5998.

Casual Eateries

For a quick and inexpensive bite to eat, there are several counter-service spots throughout CityWalk.

South Beach Deli serves sandwiches, ice cream, sodas, and beer.

Big Kahuna Pizza window is a good spot to grab a slice of fresh, hot pizza.

St. Augustine's serves hamburgers, hot dogs, and sandwiches.

The Galaxy Ice Cream window dishes out Carvel premium ice cream. ◆

The Hotels at Universal Studios Orlando

The hotels at Universal Studios Orlando offer guests special privileges that include transportation, front-of-the-line access to selected attractions before 10 AM, early admission on select days, priority seating for restaurants and shows, and resort-wide charging privileges. For hotel reservations, call 888 837-2273. Ask about special promotions or discounts for AAA members, Florida residents, or Universal Passholders.

Portofino Bay Hotel

5601 Universal Boulevard, Orlando, Florida 32819
Telephone: 407 503-1000   Fax: 407 224-7118

Portofino Bay Hotel is located inside Universal Studios Orlando Resort. The 750-room hotel was designed to resemble the seaside village of Portofino, Italy. The theme is carried out in numerous details, such as boats docked in the harbor, the piazza seating of the restaurants, and the cobblestone and brick walkways. The luxurious and spacious guest rooms are tastefully decorated in neutral colors and spare elegance. They have either two queen-sized beds or one king-sized bed with a pull-out sofa.

Guest Transportation: Water taxi is the quickest and most pleasant way to reach CityWalk or the theme parks. Guests can also walk along a mile-long garden pathway leading from the hotel to the entrance of Universal Studios. Bus transportation is also available. The resort provides complimentary scheduled transportation to Sea World and Wet 'n Wild, as well.

Restaurants: *Trattoria del Porto* — Family-oriented restaurant for breakfast, lunch, and dinner. Universal Characters visit on select evenings.

Mama Della's Ristorante — Open for dinner, the restaurant features traditional Italian entrees that may also be ordered as family-style dinners.

Delfino Riviera — Upscale dining room overlooking the harbor piazza, serving specialties of the Portofino region. Dinner only.

Hot Tips: Guest rooms can accommodate five. Rooms on the harbor level have French doors which open to the piazza and a few have a small patio area outside.

Amenities: Bathrobes, coffeemaker, newspaper delivery, in-room safe, hair dryer, iron and ironing board, pay-per-view movies, stocked mini-bar, 24 hour room service, turndown service, Playstation video console, and umbrella.

Room Rates: Rates vary with the seasons. Standard rooms range from $250 to $350; spacious Villa suites start at $800 to $1,400 (including VCR, fax machine, compact disc player, complimentary Continental breakfast, afternoon hors d'oeuvres, and evening cocktails in the concierge lounge); Kidsuites cost $400 to $460.

Hard Rock Hotel

5600 Universal Blvd., Orlando, FL 32819
Telephone: 407 503-7625   Fax: 407 503-2020

Hard Rock Hotel is located adjacent to Universal Studios theme park. Guests are just a few minutes' stroll from their rooms to the attractions, making it a popular resort location. Water taxi service to CityWalk is also available.

The design of this 650 room resort was inspired by the early California missions. A rock 'n' roll museum in the common area houses rare and funky rock memorabilia. Resort amenities include two full-service restaurants, two bars, numerous shops, pool, fitness center, and a supervised children's activity center.

Guest rooms are spacious. The hotel's in-room amenities include hair dryer, in-room safe, coffeemaker, daily newspaper, iron and ironing board, stocked mini-bar, and room service.

Rates: Standard rooms range from $200 to $240; spacious Concierge rooms start at $275 to $450 (including special room amenities and Continental breakfast, snacks, and cocktails in the concierge lounge); Kidsuites range from $350 to $450. Rates vary with the seasons.

Royal Pacific Resort

This 1,000 room hotel (open in 2002) is the closest resort to Islands of Adventure theme park. Guests are able to walk or take a bus to the parks and CityWalk.

This moderately-priced hotel has lush South Pacific theming throughout and features full-service restaurants, a grotto pool, fitness center, supervised children's activity center, and business center.

TELEPHONE DIRECTORY

The area code at Walt Disney World is 407.

General Disney Information

Walt Disney World Information	407 824-4321
Switchboard to All Walt Disney World Hotels	407 824-2222
Hearing-Impaired Guests (TDD)	407 827-5141

General Reservations

Disney Hotel Reservations (WDISNEY)	407 934-7639
Disney Dining Reservations (WDW-DINE)	407 939-3463
Disney Travel Co. (Hotels & Packages)	800 828-0228
Universal Hotel Reservations	888 837-2273
CityWalk Dining Reservations	407 224-9255

(Also see "Dinner Shows," "Hotels," "Off-Site Hotels," "Restaurants," and "Resort Restaurants" for specific telephone numbers.)

Attractions Information

Blizzard Beach	407 560-3400
Cirque du Soleil Box Office	407 934-6110
CityWalk General Information	407 224-9255
Disney-MGM Studios Production Information	407 560-4651
Disney's Wide World of Sports	407 363-6600
House of Blues Box Office	407 934-2583
Pleasure Island	407 934-7781
Pleasure Island AMC Theatres, Show Times	407 827-1308
River Country	407 824-2760
Typhoon Lagoon	407 560-4141
Universal Cineplex, Show Times	407 354-5998
Universal Studios Tickets	407 363-8000
Walt Disney World Information	407 824-4321
Weather, Disney	407 824-4104

Services

Celebration Health (Medical Care)	407 303-4000
Centra Care Walk-In Medical Care	407 239-6463
Doctor's On Call Service	407 399-3627
Eckerd Drug	407 238-9333
Florist, Gooding's Supermarket	407 827-1206
Florist, Walt Disney World	407 827-3505
Lost and Found at Walt Disney World	407 824-4245
Message Center at WDW	407 824-4321
Sand Lake Hospital	407 351-8500
Turner's Drugs	407 828-8125

Recreation Reservations

Boating Excursions	407 939-7529
Disney Institute Tennis Programs	407 939-7529
Disney Recreation Reservations (WDW-PLAY)	407 939-7529
Disney's Wide World of Sports (hotline)	407 363-6600
Fishing Excursions	407 939-7529
Golf Reservations (WDW-GOLF)	407 939-4653
The Grand Floridian Spa & Health Club	407 824-2332
Grand Floridian Tennis	407 939-7529
Parasailing, Contemporary	407 939-7529
Racquet Club, Contemporary	407 939-7529
The Spa at the Wyndham Palace Resort	407 827-2727
The Spa at the Disney Institute	407 827-4455
Waterskiing Excursions	407 939-7529

Guided Tours

Walt Disney World Tours (WDW-TOUR)	407 939-8687
VIP Tours (Walt Disney World)	407 560-6233
VIP Tours (Universal Studios Orlando)	407 363-8295

Transportation Services

AAA Emergency Road Service	800 222-4357
Atlantis Limousine & Towncar	407 592-7433
Advantage Limousine	800 438-4114
Ann's Towncar Service	888 657-0936
Car Care Center, Walt Disney World	407 824-0976
Disney Travel Center, Ocala, FL	352 854-0770
Happy Limousine & Towncar	888 394-4277
Mears Transportation Service (Taxi & Shuttle)	407 423-5566
Orlando Airport, Paging	407 825-2000
Tiffany Towncar & Limousine	888 838-2161

Rental Car Agencies

Rental Cars Are Located Inside the Airport:

Avis	800 831-2847	At WDW	407 827-2847
Budget	800 527-0700	At WDW	407 850-6700
Dollar	800 800-4000	At WDW	407 827-3038
National	800 227-7368	At WDW	407 934-4930

Customers Are Shuttled to a Remote Location:

Alamo	800 327-9633	At WDW	407 827-6363
Hertz	800 654-3131		
Thrifty	800 367-2277	At WDW	407 370-0444